An Historical Geography
of England and Wales

AN HISTORICAL GEOGRAPHY OF ENGLAND AND WALES

SECOND EDITION

Edited by

R. A. DODGSHON

Institute of Earth Studies, The University College of Wales, Aberystwyth

R. A. BUTLIN

Department of Geography, Loughborough University of Technology

ACADEMIC PRESS
Harcourt Brace Jovanovich, Publishers
London   San Diego   New York   Boston
Sydney   Tokyo   Toronto

This book is printed on acid-free paper.

ACADEMIC PRESS LIMITED
24–28 Oval Road
London NW1 7DX

United States Edition published by
ACADEMIC PRESS, INC.
San Diego, CA 92101

First edition published 1978

British Library Cataloguing in Publication Data
An historical geography of England and Wales.–2nd. ed.
1. England. Historical geography
I. Dodgshon, R. A.   II. Butlin, R. A.
911.42

ISBN 0–12–219253–2
ISBN 0–12–219254–0 (pbk)

Typeset by Paston Press, Loddon, Norfolk
Printed in Great Britain by the University Press, Cambridge

Contributors

R. A. BUTLIN, *Department of Geography, Loughborough University of Technology, Loughborough, Leicestershire, LE11 3TU, England.*

B. M. S. CAMPBELL, *Department of Economic History, Queen's University, Belfast, BT7 1NN.*

H. C. CARTER, *Department of Geography, Institute of Earth Studies, University College of Wales, Aberystwyth, Dyfed, SY23 3DB, Wales.*

S. DANIELS, *Department of Geography, University of Nottingham, University Park, Nottingham, NG7 2RD, England.*

R. DENNIS, *Department of Geography, University College, 26 Bedford Way, London, WC1H 0AP, England.*

R. A. DODGSHON, *Department of Geography, Institute of Earth Studies, University College of Wales, Aberystwyth, Dyfed, SY23 3DB, Wales.*

P. GLENNIE, *Department of Geography, University of Bristol, University Road, Bristol, BS8 1SS, England.*

D. GREGORY, *Department of Geography, University of British Columbia, 217–1984 West Mall, Vancouver, British Columbia, Y6T 1W5, Canada.*

I. HODDER, *Department of Archaeology, University of Cambridge, Downing Street, Cambridge, CB2 3DZ, England.*

G. R. J. JONES, *School of Geography, University of Leeds, Leeds, LS2 9JT, England.*

R. LAWTON, *formerly Department of Geography, University of Liverpool, presently Department of Geography, Loughborough University of Technology, Loughborough, Leicestershire, LE11 3TU, England.*

M. MILLETT, *Department of Archaeology, University of Durham, 46 Saddler Street, Durham City, Durham, DH1 3NV, England.*

E. PAWSON, *Department of Geography, University of Canterbury, Christchurch 1, New Zealand.*

B. K. ROBERTS, *Department of Geography, University of Durham, South Road, Durham City, Durham, DH1 3LE, England.*

B. T. ROBSON, *School of Geography, University of Manchester, Manchester, M13 9PL, England.*

S. SEYMOUR, *Department of Geography, University of Nottingham, University Park, Nottingham, NG7 2RD, England.*

R. M. SMITH, *All Souls College, Oxford, OX1 4AL, England.*

N. THRIFT, *Department of Geography, University of Bristol, University Road, Bristol, BS8 1SS.*

P. T. H. UNWIN, *Department of Geography, Royal Holloway and Bedford College, Egham Hill, Egham, Surrey, TW20 0EX.*

J. R. WALTON, *Department of Geography, Institute of Earth Studies, University College of Wales, Aberystwyth, Dyfed, SY23 3DB, Wales.*

J. YELLING, *Department of Geography, Birkbeck College, University of London, 7–15 Gresse Street, London W1P 1PA, England.*

Preface

If the vigour of a subject can be measured by the speed at which debate over its central themes moves forward and by the extent to which it pushes out its bounds into wholly new perspectives and themes, then British historical geography is in good heart. Since the first edition of *An Historical Geography of England and Wales* was published in 1978, the amount of published work has increased substantially. With this expansion have come significant shifts in the way British historical geographers are tackling their research problems. Four particular developments can be mentioned. First, there has been a dramatic broadening of theme. Alongside staples like the historical geography of settlement and population, there now exist very active debates on a whole range of socio-cultural and political topics from the impact of industrialization on the constitutive character of cultural regions to nineteenth-century trade unions. Second, with this broadening of theme has come a greater range of methodologies. Whilst the subject has further strengthened its empirical traditions, notably via the computer-handling of vast data sets and the detailed specification of time–space paths, it can also boast studies whose concern is with more elusive themes, like the symbolism and meaning of landscape, whose articulation calls for a more refined use of language. Thirdly, prompted by these changes in theme and methodology, historical geographers are now working on a wider variety of sources. In addition to the use of aggregated data sets like Domesday Book or the population censuses, they can now be found building up regional and national patterns through the improvised and collated use of fragmented sources like *inquisitiones post mortem*, probate inventories, banking records, literary texts and paintings. Fourthly and finally, historical geographers have become more ideologically aware. Not only has this new sense of relativism enriched their debate over historical themes, but significantly, it has established fresh channels through which they have contributed to geographical thought at large. Indeed, historical geographers have been at the leading edge of recent philosophical and methodological debate in human geography. Given the pace at which these changes have taken place since the first edition of *An Historical Geography*, both editors and publisher felt that a new edition was now needed.

Our intention has been to produce a fully revised and enlarged edition, one mindful of the changes that are currently helping to both broaden and deepen the subject. Amongst the fourteen authors who contributed to the first edition, two felt unable to take part in the second edition due to changes in their interests and perspectives. Together with changes in the layout of chapters and the addition of extra themes, this has enabled us to bring in nine new authors. The sum effect has been to produce a radically new book, one that provides an up-to-date survey of standard themes and perspectives but which has been successfully expanded so as to embrace some of the newer themes and approaches.

R. A. DODGSHON   R. A. BUTLIN

Preface to the First Edition

The historical geography of England and Wales has never boasted a wide range of textbooks. To some extent, this reflected justified satisfaction with those available. However, the last decade has witnessed important changes in the content of historical geography. Stated simply, there has been a shift towards a more interpretative approach to the past. No longer concerned solely with the reconstruction of past spatial patterns, or historical map-making, more and more geographers are showing an equal if not greater concern for the processes which helped structure such patterns. Assisting this transition has been the marked increase in the number of practising historical geographers since the early 1960s, an increase now manifest in the growing volume of published work and organized conference activity. With these developments has come a changing evaluation of past problems. Previously neglected issues have suddenly been cast into sharp focus, sometimes via energetic, multi-sided debates which have injected a new vitality into the subject.

As the impact of these changes has grown, there has emerged an urgent need for a textbook which takes stock of what has been achieved so far in respect of the historical geography of England and Wales. This volume of edited essays seeks to fulfil this need. A series of broad syntheses dealing with the periods before 1500 is followed by a series of detailed discussions of systematic themes within the early modern (1500–1730) and modern (1730–1900) periods. The greater space devoted to the periods after 1500 matches the balance of current work and interest. Their organization on a systematic basis is consistent with the growing tendency amongst historical geographers to identify themselves more by theme (i.e. urban, population) than by period. The editors have not tried to impose a formal structure or format on the discussion. In deference to the fact that once the weight is shifted from description to interpretation, a variety of differing or even conflicting viewpoints is admitted, contributors have therefore been allowed, within limits, to be the architects of their own houses. The editors feel the result is a text that should stimulate the student's mind rather than just fill it, and that will convey many of the ideas and conclusions embodied in much recent literature. Indeed, most contributions would have been substantially different had they been written ten years ago. In short, they demonstrate the progress which has been made in recent years. Above all, they highlight the areas of the subject which have responded most to the challenge of 'new' geography by articulating their ideas or interpretations through concepts, theories or models. However, they also show that this response has not been a slavish application of modern spatial theory to historical data. Whether we talk in terms of historicism or in terms of what E. P. Thompson called 'the discipline of context' whereby each fact or event is given meaning only within 'an ensemble of other meanings', so that we can never totally abstract them from the context of the past, historical geography will always have claim to problems and processes that are distinctly its own. Herein will always lie the originality of its contribution to the wider subject of geography.

Inevitably, a book of this nature cannot be compiled without the editors building up a network of debt. Needless to say, we have a special debt to all the contributors for making the book possible and for working to very strict and tight deadlines. We are also indebted to Anthony Watkinson of Academic Press for his constant help and guidance in the production of the book. Finally, we would like to express our thanks to the technicians in the Departments of Geography at both the University College of Wales, Aberystwyth and Queen Mary College, University of London, who have helped re-draw and re-photograph maps and diagrams, especially D. D. Griffiths and D. Williams of Aberystwyth and D. Shewan of Queen Mary College.

R. A. DODGSHON   R. A. BUTLIN

Contents

4

People and Land in the Middle Ages, 1066–1500
B. M. S. CAMPBELL 69

5

Towns and Trade 1066–1500
P. T. H. UNWIN 123

6

Geographical Aspects of Population Change in England 1500–1730
R. M. SMITH

7

Agriculture 1500–1730
J. YELLING

8

Industry and Towns 1500–1730
P. D. GLENNIE

12
Agriculture and Rural Society 1730–1914
J. R. WALTON 323

13
'A New and Differing Face in Many Places':
Three Geographies of Industrialization
D. GREGORY 351

14
Towns and Urban Systems 1730–1914
H. CARTER 401

List of Illustrations

List of Tables

1

Perspectives on Prehistory

B. K. Roberts

Introduction: a Time Perspective

In an old country like Britain the beginnings of settlement are deeply rooted in the past and this is a sufficient justification for starting this text with a review of the millennia before the Roman conquest. The thousands of years represented by the word 'prehistory' saw the exploration and exploitation of all environments and the occupation and significant alteration of most, either by relatively temporary activity or by permanent settlement. All this is qualitatively demonstrable even if not quantitatively assessed. Given the large literature and multiplicity of themes a single chapter is a limited framework within which to attempt a summary of the historical geography of this very long period. Any treatment must be rigorously selective.

When the first farmers arrived on British shores in about 4500 B.C., Britain was already an island. The six and a half thousand years between then and now represents some 260 generations, reckoning 25 years for each generation to be born, mature and reproduce again. Faced with creating order in the measureless distances of time when written records did not exist, the nineteenth-century Danish scholar Thomsen recognized three ages, of Stone, Bronze and Iron, implying a universal technological progression and creating a fundamental temporal and conceptual outline still in use. The first agricultural communities establishing themselves in Britain, like the hunter-gatherers who preceded them, were stone users, and the dull thump of their polished stone axes striking timber reverberates through all succeeding landscapes. With axe and fire they cleared woodlands, amplifying those processes of soil impoverishment which have resulted in the landscapes of dereliction which now dominate much of northern and western Britain.[1] In such contexts, where it is difficult to obtain absolute dates, the recognition of stages allows the mind to comprehend what at first sight can seem to be only a thin layer of the past. Excavation frequently establishes a relative chronology by using the principles of stratigraphy; layer x is older than y, y is older than z, z is younger than x and the surgical techniques involved in dissecting archaeological sites are becoming increasingly sophisticated.[2] In 1951 a revolutionary scientific breakthrough brought a radical change in providing dates. This is illustrated in Table 1.1 by the discontinuity between the 1951 column and that for 1974. During the lifetime of all living organisms a small part of the carbon in their tissues is converted, by means of cosmic radiation, into radioactive carbon. On death this radioactivity is gradually lost, and

Table 1.1: A basic chronology of British prehistory.[4]

(a) 1951 (H.M.S.O.)	(b) 1974 (Renfrew et al.)		(c) 1979 (Megaw and Simpson et al.)
	(Begin)	(End)	
Palaeolithic ('Old Stone Age') ?–10,000 B.C.			Final Palaeolithic and Mesolithic 10,000–3700 B.C.
Mesolithic ('Middle Stone Age') 10,000–2500 B.C.	8415 ± 170	2670 ± 140 b.c.	
Neolithic ('New Stone Age') 2500–1850 B.C.	3795 ± 90 b.c. **4580 B.C.**	1430 ± 120 b.c. **1670 B.C.**	Earlier Neolithic c. 3500–2500 B.C.
			Later Neolithic c. 2500–1700 B.C.
Bronze Age 1850–450 B.C.	2100 ± 50 b.c. **2760–2540 B.C.**	420 ± 95 b.c. **480 B.C.**	Early Bronze Age c. 2000–1300 B.C.
			Later Bronze Age c. 1400–500 B.C.
Iron Age 450 B.C.–A.D. 43	1560 ± 180 b.c. **2050–1750 B.C.**	A.D. **43**	Iron Age c. 600 B.C.–A.D. 200
Beginning of Roman invasion			A.D. 43

b.c. = radiocarbon date; B.C. = calibrated date

after about 5730 years (the current view is 5730 ± 40 years) the original proportion of radiocarbon is reduced by one half—the half-life. This constant can be used as the basis for calculating the absolute age of stratified organic remains from archaeological sites and these radiocarbon dates are conventionally indicated by using b.c. instead of the historical B.C. Further research has shown that they can diverge substantially from true calendar years, and correlations between radiocarbon dating systems and the wood of the incredibly long-lived bristlecone pine of California (up to 4000 years), whose age can be counted using the annual growth rings of both living and dead trees, suggests that in about 2000 B.C. the dates should be of the order of 350 years older than radiocarbon dating was indicating and by 5000 B.C. about 800 years older. The details of these calibrations are complex, thus all non-corrected dates are initially given as 'before present' (b.p.), the 'present' being 1950, while the nature of the material, size of sample, the degree of contamination and even barometric pressure when the laboratory processing occurs can affect the result. All dates are qualified by the statement of one standard deviation ± so many years, i.e. there is a 66 per cent chance of the date falling within the given time period.[3] Nevertheless, in spite of all the problems, these dates have given prehistoric archaeology a framework within which to construct more precise relative and absolute chronologies. It is now clear, as was expected, that there is a considerable overlap between the temporal span of each technological age, while the dates are precise enough, even with their known limits of uncertainty, for their exact geographical context to become significant. The generalized picture seen in Table 1.1, particularly that in column (c), represents a key framework around which all facts, models and discussions concerning prehistory are organized.[5]

The Environmental Foundations

No words or printed pages can give a real impression of the varied character of the British scene (for in this chapter we *must* consider the British scene), from the rearing cliffs of Hoy and the flat profile of Sanday in the Orkneys, through mountain, fen and bog, upland and lowland, wood and plain, field and pasture, river and stream, to the white chalk cliffs of the south-east and the sea-fretted headlands and coves of the south-west. Differences of climate, vegetation and soil abound; they may be generalized to identify Highland and Lowland Zones, the former lying to the west and north, warmer, wetter and developed on the rocks of Carboniferous age or older; the latter, lying to the south and east is, in contrast, generally lower, drier, essentially a landscape of scarp and vale developed on newer softer post-Carboniferous rocks. In detail, the local variety is bewildering, from squelchy fens and bird-haunted salt-marshes, where the rise of a metre or so creates an island, to savage frost-riven mountains. The importance of these physical contrasts should never be underestimated: even today winter crossings of the Pennine uplands must be undertaken with care, while the great rivers and broad estuaries we now cross on fine bridges once presented substantial problems and dangers. And yet there is more, for this is a landsman's view; the sea is another country, from the vicious tide rips of the northern and western coasts, to flat shorelands where the tides flow in 'like galloping horses' and trap the unwary; from deep, safe havens and open passages to treacherous estuaries; from iron-sharp skerries to shallow fish-rich banks. The colour, the surface texture, the presence or absence of mud or sand, of two tides or one, all create diverse seascapes which must also be seen as part of early human environment. To those with boats the sea is no barrier but an open dangerous highway, binding lands together long before woodland, wold or fen were netted by trackways. To appreciate this diversity there is no substitute for direct on-ground or on-water experience, but an afternoon with a good atlas is a well-spent preliminary to any study of historical geography. There is, however, another fundamental lesson in all this variety: generalization is difficult, and while there is a universal tendency to over-generalize from limited evidence, the rich mosaic of land and water environments, with their great floral and faunal diversities, are always present as a matrix within which things happened. In particular, *developments at one location need not be replicated at another*, and we must have the imagination to look beyond the flint chips and hill-forts to the varied life-styles in prehistory.[6] Furthermore, the particular fascination of the period lies in the fact that not only have these environments changed naturally, as frost, flood and storm alter the land and as sea levels adjust and storm-belts shift, *they have changed because of human presence*, with axe, fire, crops, grazing animals and insatiable demands for sustenance and comfort, pleasure, ceremony and conflict, the exotic, the decorative and the strange.

The Nature of the Evidence

The special problems of archaeology within the prehistoric period derive from the fact that the evidence for reconstructing the cultural scene is, in the absence of documentary evidence, 'mute'. Men do not always write the truth, but only through documents do we get direct insights into the workings of the mind. Only in the later part of the Iron Age in one part of the British Isles, Ireland, do the tales of the Ulster cycle, of the Cattle Raid of Cooley, of MacDatho's Pig and their like, tell of society's perception of itself, a precious 'window on the Iron Age'.[7] However, one cannot dig up the tenurial obligations (surely including building services?) linked to an Iron-Age hill-fort or Bronze-Age farmstead. Undoubtedly some of the problems of archaeology derive from the circumstance that the more thoroughly a site is studied and the more completely it is excavated, the more completely is that particular body of evidence totally destroyed. For all archaeologists this is a challenging and uncomfortable situation; on some sites, Stonehenge, for example, excavation is an awesome responsibility. This total destruction is probably the basis of these elements of acerbity which notoriously colour many archaeological debates. Nevertheless, debate is essential, for it leads to re-evaluation. To these problems must be added those inevitable tensions caused by period bias: 'found nothing yet, still ploughing through medieval layers' is the apocryphal note on a postcard—from a Roman period archaeologist of course—but the geographical world should perhaps remember those soil scientists who have reputedly dug through Roman tessellated pavements, oblivious to their existence! There is a serious point here: all observation is selective, we see what we are trained to see and what we expect to see, and the advent of a 'flint-person' upon a local scene, adept at seeing these, can dramatically increase the incidence of such sites.[8] This is an old problem, in a new guise, of an 'active archaeological society' distorting distribution maps.

Archaeology evolved from the systematic study of surviving, visible structures, Stonehenge, hill-forts, megalithic tombs and round barrows, together with chance finds of objects, stone and metal implements, ornaments and ritual items. The development of excavation, to search for objects buried in significant locations upon undisturbed sites, went hand in hand with the application of systematic field-work to find and identify, but not necessarily excavate, new sites. Contemporary archaeology rests upon these two foundations, which provide most of the hard data. To these, however, must be added a third vital element, the laboratory work and publishing, which support field-work and follow up excavations and are now an important part of making the results available, encouraging excavators to wet-sieve soil samples and recover the most delicate floral and faunal remains and integrate their own discoveries within wider patterns. These techniques produce a body of material, evidence, which it is necessary to organize within spatial, temporal and conceptual frameworks. However, the non-archaeologist should be under no doubt concerning the importance of those critical boundaries between fact, reasonable inference, preconceptions based upon *a priori* reasoning, and hypotheses attempting social explanations by analogy.

The identification of stratigraphically associated assemblages of artifacts, some of which can be used as type-fossils, provided the means of identifying cultures. Gordon Childe argued in 1940 that each assemblage of excavated material was ultimately related to the life-style of a social group or community, going on to point out:

> Did we know the homes, working places and graves of a prehistoric community, together with a large selection of its tools, weapons, ornaments and cult objects, we should be able to form a fair idea of its social structure, religious and artistic ideals. By plotting on maps the distribution of its distinctive products we could trace the peoples' territorial expansion. By comparing these products with those of precursors, neighbours and successors we could evaluate the group's role in local and British history.[9]

These were bold claims, a vision of the past which ultimately touches upon all of the questions and perspectives to be considered below. Renfrew has argued that such cultures do indeed represent highly artificial and imposed categories,[10] but to the student faced with ordering both the factual substance of the past as well as the interpretational images currently in use, such classifications do serve a vital mnemonic purpose.[11] Childe reminded us, however, that his conditions are never satisfied, for time, that capricious filter, wreaks appalling havoc with all human handiwork. The last two or three decades have seen the discovery of hitherto unimagined qualities of new sites and an increasing appreciation of the complex ways in which all later developments have acted as a filter.

Undoubtedly the single most important factor revealing the presence of new archaeological sites is the air photograph, and these have become increasingly available as a result of work by both professional and amateur scholars. Broadly three categories of evidence can be culled from these:

(i) Where earthworks remain as upstanding features, subject to correct lighting and vegetational conditions, they can be detected as shadow or shine marks. When linked with fieldwork and excavation this reveals new details of known sites or the presence of new ones, and in particular allows the relocation of relict landscapes, involving settlements, arable fields, pasture areas, roads and burial grounds.[12]

(ii) Where sites have been ploughed out they are often visible as soil marks, where changes in colour and texture reveal the presence of buried structures. These can, after autumn ploughing, often be seen at ground level, but the perspective of the air view is necessary to reveal the patterns they create.

(iii) Where such ploughed-out sites are under a standing crop, depending upon the nature of the crop, the state of growth, the lighting, and the groundwater conditions, then the buried structures are often revealed, sometimes with startling clarity by differential growth (over a buried ditch) or parching (over a buried bank or stonework). One simple point must be stressed: all sites are not always visible and even a known site can appear, disappear and reappear quite unpredictably. The visible details of a site can also vary enormously from time to time, from photograph to photograph, so that what seems to be a single enclosure when first detected, can, following careful study, be seen to lie at the centre of a complex of ploughed-out earthworks. In short, a known, unexcavated site is always worth re-photographing.[13] A steady succession of discoveries have appeared and their numbers are revealing. There are few areas of lowland Britain, under crop, which in the six weeks before harvest, will not reveal at least some signs of earlier occupations. Published work reveals great numbers of sites in diverse environments, the river gravels of the Thames, the Severn–Avon, the upper Nene, the Welland and the Trent, in uplands such as the Cheviots, the Pennines, Dartmoor, Bodmin Moor, the Mendips, in lowlands, of north-eastern and north-western England and throughout the Midlands, demonstrating the presence of hitherto unsuspected amounts of landscape survival.

There is an allied problem which concerns not so much the way in which evidence can be discovered as the context in which it survives to be discovered. Lands which have been subject to continuous ploughing (with attendant soil drift), erosion, stone-picking and (presumably) casual artifact recovery will show fewer archaeological features than those marginal pastoral areas, be these chalklands, heathlands, or uplands, where upstanding earthworks still remain clearly in evidence, even if degraded by eighteenth- and nineteenth-century improvements. Fowler and Bowen demonstrated that surviving Romano-British field systems in Dorset and Wiltshire lie above the limits of local medieval open-field cultivation, and in a very different environment a similar relationship can be clearly seen at Grassington in Wharfedale. Below the medieval head-dyke the earlier systems were destroyed or, as is more probable, subtly integrated with new arrangements.[14] The last two decades have, however, seen the recovery of extensive traces of prehistoric fields from diverse environments.[15] A concentration of archaeological discoveries may occur within intensively cultivated field lands where these lie upon river gravels, as these soils are particularly suitable for cropmark sites. Even here, the use of air photographs together with sophisticated techniques of field-walking, to gather scattered artifacts, is producing more sites.[16] Of particular value in preserving ancient landscapes are the parklands, created throughout the lowlands since Norman times. Recent work is also producing evidence for extensive Romano-British, if not prehistoric settlement, beneath those areas set aside as forests or chases.[17] Such fossil landscapes are important in that they show what formerly could have existed in areas subjected to intense agricultural exploitation in post-prehistoric times. Ford, writing of the claylands of south Warwickshire, suggests that the layout of medieval open-field landscapes of strips and furlongs often reflect older lines, such as the presence of farmsteads, field boundaries and tracks. How many of these are Romano-British and how many are prehistoric has yet to be resolved, but this does introduce a rather daunting problem: the extent to which many of the details of medieval and later landscapes are subtly related to more ancient sub-structural landscape features. A classic case is seen at the deserted medieval village of Wharram Percy on the chalk of the Yorkshire Wolds; excavation of this site has shown that the medieval, Anglo-Saxon and Roman developments were framed by even older field and ranch foundaries.[18] A distribution map then, seen as record of hard archaeological evidence, contains many problems. Two in particular are significant when developing hypotheses and arguments: first, within any map there will always be two zones, what Taylor has termed a 'Zone of Survival' and a 'Zone of Destruction', affecting the reliability of the primary observations concerning the presence or absence of data. Furthermore our

> inability to recover the total pattern is made worse by the fact that we have no idea of how complete our evidence is. If we knew that any given pattern was 75 per cent or even 50 per cent complete it would help, but we never do. The recoverable number of settlements may be only 1 per cent of the original total, or it may be as much as 90 per cent. It is very difficult to draw valid conclusions from such evidence.[19]

Atkinson emphasizes a second point,

> all archaeological maps . . . represent the projection onto a single plane of sites which will not in general have co-existed. The effect . . . is . . . to exaggerate the level and density of human activity, or for that matter population size in the area concerned.[20]

The difficult questions raised by overlapping temporal sequences, successive occupations and continuity may be better tackled in terms of very detailed local studies, where a small region forms a laboratory for the accumulation of multiperiod data and the testing of hypotheses, the technique of 'landscape' or 'total' archaeology.[21] To give but one example, Powlesland's West Heslerton project in north-east Yorkshire is examining a 10 × 10 km square extending from the chalk uplands of the Wolds, across the scarp and scarp-foot zone, with chalk downwash, clays and superficial blown sand, to the lacustrine deposits of the floor of the Vale of Pickering. Sites are known on the chalk, in some quantity, but these are largely destroyed because ploughing, much of it comparatively recent, has denuded the landscape. This is witnessed in the landscape by the large areas of white chalk visible after modern cultivation. However, at the foot of the escarpment is a zone where spring action, hill-wash from the chalk and successive sand blows have resulted in a 'zone of survival'. Here large-scale excavations (over several hectares, stripping off the ploughsoil with motorway earth-movers) show that this was a 'preferred settlement zone'. Mesolithic occupation is present and a mixture of air photographs and excavation have revealed a band of continuous superimposed settlement remains, a hundred or so metres wide, but extending across the whole of a ten kilometre sample strip at the foot of the escarpment! What is exceptional here is that the blown sand, the result of human clearance of the former glacial lake shore, has resulted in stratification. Nevertheless, there are no grounds for assuming that the density of sites in this part of Yorkshire is in any way atypical of scarp-foot zones elsewhere, nor indeed need be uncharacteristic of occupation anywhere upon medium soils. In this case the well-known 'spring line villages', sited on the varied soils at the foot of the scarp face, represent only the latest, visible, stage of occupation, taking root in later Anglo-Saxon or Norman times. However, as at Wharram Percy, the Wolds proper, prehistoric features will surely appear *beneath* this later occupation. Such superimposition is hardly surprising, but raises fundamental questions about the quantity of prehistoric occupation which lies concealed and serves to reinforce Taylor's point.

Changing Interpretational Contexts

While the West Heslerton evidence shows that geomorphological change is a necessary part of understanding the interaction between prehistoric societies and the land, for within the excavated sample an entire stream course has been buried, it is vegetation change that is most obviously and closely related to human activities. The millennia between the Mesolithic period and the Iron Age saw a gradual transition from ephemeral settlements of a few days or temporary settlements of a few weeks' duration through to seasonal and permanent settlements taking advantage of the possibilities for rational exploitation of localized economic resources over long periods of time, although we should perhaps always hesitate to use the term permanent in any settlement context. Surviving sites and artifacts suggest a transition from an economy based entirely upon collecting, hunting and fishing to one based upon the exploitation of arable and grazing lands whose productivity was maintained by means of careful plough tillage and schemes of manuring and management. It can be argued that one critical break was occasioned by the advent of a new food-producing economy with the arrival, during the second half of the fourth millennium B.C., of ecologically potent Neolithic farming groups, and there is agreement that the ancestors of cultivated wheat and barley and domesticated sheep and goats originate in the Middle East and that both the idea and the domesticates were diffused throughout Europe. Nevertheless, there is an increasing awareness of the degree to which the economy of the Mesolithic period was securely based upon a full exploitation of both the animal and the vegetational worlds, and the Mesolithic flints, notably the tiny worked blades—microliths—were suitable for hafting in multibladed gathering implements as well as hunting weapons. The degree to which the environment was managed may have been very much greater than previously thought, involving burning and deer herd manipulation.[22] Spratt and Simmons have detected temporary clearances created by these folk in North Yorkshire, and have postulated complex group territories encompassing seashore, lowlands, foothills and uplands.[23] Summer hunting grounds in the hills were exploited by small groups, which met in larger concentrations in the fat autumn (when hazelnuts may have been a key dietary item) only to disperse again for the lean months, with winter and spring being spent in the lowlands and gathering and fishing along the coasts. This hypothesis, supported by the evidence of pollen diagrams and flint-working sites, hints at well-established patterns of territoriality by the Mesolithic period and a standard of life probably, because of the variety of plants and animals available within the primeval woodlands and water-bodies, at times more stable than the precarious farming economy which was to follow.

Cultivation within fields, however, no matter how temporary, represents a more complex and potentially more potent form of land use which eventually had a permanent impact upon vegetation, initiating the processes leading to the almost wholly cleared landscapes of today. The vegetational history of Britain has been reconstructed by counting the almost indestructible pollen grains preserved at various levels in peat deposits (which have been accumulating over thousands of years). Absolute dates for critical phases of woodland clearance or regeneration are obtained by radiocarbon methods. The interpretation of the resulting diagrams remains an art rather than an exact science: the supply of pollen to a bog or lake surface involves three components, the local component from the vegetation immediately adjacent to the deposit, a regional component from the general environs, and finally pollen which has been transported long distances and is washed in by rainfall. Pollen in lake deposits also includes material transported by water from the area of the drainage basin. Obviously the proportions of these components can show entirely natural temporal variations, reflecting post-glacial vegetation successions, but clearance, local, regional or general, can cause variations in the pollen spectrum, most basically in the proportions of tree, shrub and grass pollen present, as well as in the amounts associated with each species of plant. This work stimulates questions concerning the precise character of early woodland clearances, their location, their extent, their duration and the land use within them, while increasing numbers of diagrams, from varied environments, lead towards a broader quasi-national picture.[24] In regions where pollen is not available, for example on the chalklands of the south and east and along the coastlands of western Britain, detailed counts of fossilized molluscan faunas, snail shells, provide the basis for an assessment of environment change, for they can be grouped into shade-loving species, open-country species and intermediate species.

No brief summary can do justice to the volume of palaeo-botanical material now available, but two broad trends may be distinguished: first, the prehistoric period sees the penetration of wooded areas by what have been termed 'landnam' clearances (from the Danish, literally 'land taking'): these occur from areas as far apart as Ayrshire, the Cumberland lowlands, Wales, Yorkshire and the Somerset Levels, and appear in Neolithic and Bronze-Age contexts. They are generally interpreted as small temporary clearances associated with shifting agriculture and are associated with the phenomenon of the 'elm decline', a sharp reduction in the proportion of elm pollen found throughout Britain, indeed northern Europe, and generally explained in terms of human activity, taking leaves and twigs for fodder or even human consumption. This view has been questioned, but the presence of cereal pollens is a vital pointer to cultural activity. Second, in regions as far apart as the chalklands, and on other areas of well-drained rather light soils, for example the Brecklands, the coastal plain of Cumberland and probably in parts of the middle and upper Thames, large permanent clearances occurred, with the possibility of permanent fields. Many of the henges of Wiltshire, circular ritual enclosures of Neolithic provenance, have produced buried soils indicating that after clearance and cultivation grassland developed, grassland which may have been maintained by grazing animals for a period as long as 500 years! During the Bronze Age, from 2000 B.C. onwards, more and more forest was being cleared, a situation which can be interpreted in terms of an increasing population. There is evidence for upland clearances, leading to soil degeneration and the establishment of moorland, from the Pennines, Dartmoor, the North Yorkshire Moors and the Cheviots, i.e. regions with bogs, and many of these uplands are also producing evidence for very large areas of Bronze-Age fields. Significantly, however, the West Hesleton excavations reveal much lowland activity: the palaeo-botanical evidence is regionally biased. During the Iron Age, in contrast, extensive disforestation frequently occurred, a process surely linked with the widespread availability of iron for tools, higher populations and more developed permanent agriculture, and it appears that the relative importance of cereal production and pastoral activities can be detected in the changing proportions of certain indicator herbs.[25]

As Simmons concludes, forest disappearance on a large scale is characteristic of this final phase of prehistory, and, it is generally assumed that there were concentrations of tillage on the lower ground and pastoralism in the uplands.[26] Evans makes the point that the real contrasts between the Highland and Lowland Zones began to appear with clarity only during the first millennium B.C. Before this the contrasts between the two were more muted; indeed the differences between them in terms of the quality of their present environment may well reflect man's impact, changes in soil type being initiated by the prehistoric clearances.[27] This is an important process. As early as the Neolithic period marked regional differences in cultural activity were beginning to emerge, detectable in pottery types, tomb styles and in the extent of clearances, and these represent the beginnings of the process of regional differentiation still continuing today.

The succession of changes generated by human activity resulted in the spread of settlement and fields; yet they were in many ways more fundamental. To select only one aspect: the woodlands forming the home of Mesolithic people, generally composed of warmth-loving trees, oak, elm, alder, lime, with hazel, birch and some pine in less clement areas, were never without some 'clearings'. Along rivers, where trees had fallen in storms, where landslips had occurred, and where lightning fires had struck: these were maintained and perhaps even extended by herbivores such as deer and wild cattle, and were thus attractive to hunters, who may have extended them further by fire. In uplands areas this initiated a process of podzolization, eventually resulting in the moorlands of today. On lighter lowland soils, however, some of the woodlands near such 'lawns' eventually attracted farmers and were cleared by axe and fire to create new fields, while the adjacent forest openings were maintained and extended by taking timber, fodder and fuel and grazing cattle, sheep, goats and pigs. From such beginnings clearance and cultivation spread to medium and heavy soils, and there is increasing evidence that this was an organized activity, based upon very long rather broad strips.[28] One may postulate that by the Iron Age such uncleared woods as did survive were carefully managed and Rackham guesses that 'half of England' already ceased to be wildwood as early as 500 B.C. There is indeed clear evidence from the Somerset Levels for the production of coppiced and pollarded trees by about 4000 B.C. showing that woodland management began at a very early stage.[29] This must have repercussions upon our perception of the prehistoric past. The transition from slash and burn clearances to permanent manured fields—manuring is proven by pottery scatters, representing the rubbish carted out with the dung—reveals a developing ability to sustain food production, and this was done by integrating diverse environmental possibilities within varied farming systems, involving diverse balances between the proportions of arable, pasture, woodland and marsh exploited. This brings the discussion to the troubled question of the population levels which were supported.

Prehistoric Populations

Population levels form a vital link between the physical evidence of artifacts, from pottery and metalwork to field sites such as tombs and fortifications, and environmental change and the less tangible aspects of economy and society. Sometimes the evidence can be startling specific; to cite a case from Orkney, the undisturbed Neolithic chambered tomb at Isbister, South Ronaldsay, contained some 16,000 fragments of human bone. These represent the remains of a minumum of 342 individuals. The structure was begun in about 3150 ± 80 B.C. and finally sealed in about 2650 ± 80, possibly as late as 2400 B.C., giving of the order of 800 ± 180 years of use, although it is likely that the main deposits, consisting of bodies which had been excarnated, i.e. exposed to the elements before burial and generally dismembered, took place during the first two or three hundred years of use. None of these people had lived beyond 50, most were dead by 30, with high mortality during the first ten years of life. On average women died earlier than men, most deaths being between the ages of 15 and 24. General life expectancy at birth was only 20 years, compared with over 70 in Britain today. This reveals, as nothing else can, the hard lives of these first farmers, particularly their womenfolk, who frequently suffered from osteoarthritis, the result of carrying heavy burdens. While admitting that this was an environmentally marginal community this demographic picture is in accord with those found elsewhere, and we have here a glimpse of the restraints upon cultural advance; the 'old' of the community were in their thirties and the 'very old' in their forties. The essential concerns of such a group must have been preserving their lifestyle and cultural traditions.[30]

Nevertheless, this splendid sample is far from a national estimate. 'How many people are there?' is a question which constantly reverberates down the well of the past, particularly in the light of the thousands of sites now known from aerial photography. Fowler has been bold enough to publish a tentative graph of trends between 3000 B.C. and A.D. 2000, suggesting that just before the Roman conquest, population levels in Britain falling between 0.5 and 2.5 million are possible.[31] All estimates of prehistoric populations must ultimately derive from structured estimates balanced against intensely localized studies; tombs and cemeteries, known settlement densities, known site densities, excavated samples (here the 10 × 10 km square of the Heslerton project is useful), together with the use of material from ethnographic and anthropological sources. None are wholly reliable, but the present author would strongly support Fowler's conclusion that 'late prehistoric population of two million is certainly conceivable'. This overall total would produce the local densities of the order of 11 per square kilometre (29 per square mile) that Stanford suggests for late Iron-Age Hereford and Shropshire. In these two counties alone he argues for an increase from 24,000 to 58,000 between *c.* 1400 B.C. and A.D. 50. His view is by no means universally accepted, but for England and Wales a figure in excess of two million may be realistic and the picture of a well-populated prehistoric country-side is one we can project with growing certainty. It is reasonable to argue that such populations were subject to cyclic change, with population increases resulting from good harvests and malnutrition, disease and increased mortality following a suc-cession of poor harvests.[32]

It is helpful to try to summarize how the late prehistoric population was distrib-uted; Cunliffe recognizes four broadly defined later Iron-Age settlement zones: (a) the open village settlements of eastern England; (b) a landscape dominated by large hill-forts found in southern England, the Severn valley and along the Welsh Borders, and in south-eastern Scotland (c) dispersed fortified settlements of the western coastlands and peninsulas, from Devon and Cornwall, via Wales to the west coasts of Scotland; (d) dispersed settlements, perhaps of more pastoral communities, found in north-eastern and northern England.[33] The broad contrast, between a western zone of many fortifications and an eastern zone of open settlements, surely defended by chariot-using field armies, is noteworthy. This generalization is helpful. A line drawn from the Wash to the Severn, and from the Quantocks to Portland Bill delimits a south-eastern regional complex which in the latest phases of the Iron Age saw the appearance of the most advanced tribes, engaged in vigorous trade with the classical world and partly documented by classical writers. In terms of population and economic activity this was clearly the most developed economic zone. A glance at the distribution of population in 1086 (generally considered to range between 1.1 and 2.0 million—see below p.70) and more specifically at annual values in shillings per square mile, one measure of economic development, shows that the *same* zone was involved. This is interesting, for it shows that the economic primacy of south-east England was already a fact of regional geography. Today the great ramparts of the hill-forts survive only as chaotic rock-tumbles or smoothed earthen contours perched upon what, to us, are seen as unattractive hill-tops: to their builders and owner they represented security, pride and power, often set between productive lowland fields and cattle-rich upland pastures. In the minds' eye bind and box the earth and stone with timber, have them four, five or even more metres of height and with stoutly defended entrances, often cunningly maze-like to encourage the attacker to turn his shield-protected left-side away from the defenders, add sentry-walks and gates, surely topped with human head trophies, and a living picture emerges. Through the gates of these distinctive 'central places' (to apply a wholly anachronistic term) flowed people; on foot, horseback, in chariots, waggons and leading pack-trains; warriors to be feasted, farmers to pay tribute and seek justice, traders and itinerant craftsmen to supplement the skills of the indigenous smiths, carpenters and wheelwrights. Remote to us in time, remote to us in habit, values and beliefs, these people were nevertheless as real as the London commuter, the stock-exchange speculator, the motor mechanic and the Pennine hill-farmer. They were present in sufficient numbers to have moulded the foundations of even modern landscapes.

Developing Interpretational Frameworks

Gordon Childe's 1940 study of Britain envisaged successive waves of colonization, by Neolithic farmers, who took over from hunter-gatherers, bringing causewayed camps and various types of communal collective tombs, by Beaker folk and other warriors and traders in bronze, by land-seeking peasants of the late Bronze-Age Deverel-Rimbury culture, and finally by three main waves of Iron-Age peoples. There was indeed a place for fusion, between Mesolithic hunters and the Neolithic agriculturalists, between stone-using farmers and bronze-using immigrants, but essential innovations came from without, and even the splendid Bronze-Age Wessex culture was not seen as an entirely indigenous flowering for there were, following Piggott, hints of invaders from Britanny.[34] In a closely reasoned paper in 1966 Clark challenged this 'invasion hypothesis': while not ignoring folk movements he was able to demonstrate the extent to which cultural traits which developed most fully in the Iron Age were already present during the Bronze Age. Thus the great round houses of the early Iron Age of England and Wales, classically seen at Little Woodbury, are now seen to have Bronze-Age antecedents, while the complex roots of hill-forts, pastoral, military, social and religious, have their origins in patterns of territoriality extending back, in certain areas at least, to the farmers of the Neolithic Age.[35]

There is an important lesson here; the preceding paragraph outlines one interpretational model. This drew ultimately upon the details of artifacts and sites, upon their classification and possible chronology, and built upon the reasonable inference that developments such as agriculture, stock breeding or metalworking are likely to have occurred in one or more particularly favoured locations and the idea that people and the domesticates were spread to successively more peripheral zones as innovation waves. However, radiocarbon dates, particularly those of the third millennium B.C., are confirming that prehistoric European cultures are all earlier than once thought. In practical terms this means that the great communal chambered megalithic tombs and monuments of Western Europe, generally used in the later Neolithic and the earlier Bronze Age, are earlier than structures in the Mediterranean once supposed to be their antecedents, a conclusion which demands a re-assessment of the nature of western Neolithic communities and their achievements and destroys the essential premise that culture change in Britain was necessarily brought about by a series of folk migrations bringing higher levels of culture derived ultimately from European and Mediterranean contacts. This must raise questions about the forces leading to indigenous developments. However, one dilemma of archaeology is illustrated by Fig. 1.1. A key interpretational problem is to break out from the upper portion of the diagram to the lower; to concentrate only upon the interactions within the upper, 'man and the land', 'man's role in changing the face of the earth', is to pursue description and environmental determinism, and perhaps sexism, but it is by crossing the 'bridge of inference' that explanations of how change took place must be sought. Paradoxically, it is in making this switch that the limitations of mute archaeological evidence are felt most strongly.

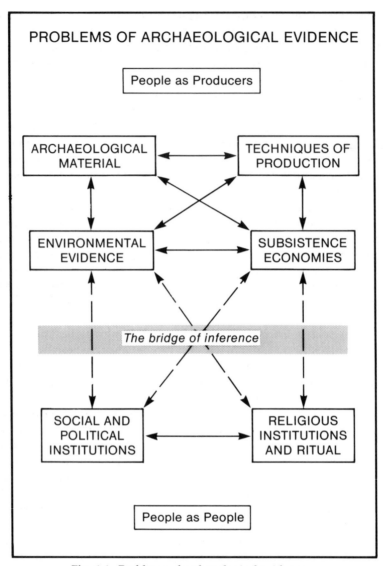

Fig. 1.1. Problems of archaeological evidence.

Social and Political Organization

Renfrew puts the key question squarely: 'How can the archaeologist reconstruct the social organization of prehistoric communities?'[36] Social anthropology has created the ideas of identifying distinctive typologies of society. Service defined four categories, band, tribe, chiefdom and state. *Band* societies comprise local groups only tenuously linked to one another at a larger scale and with economies based upon hunting and gathering. Generally groups range between 25 and 100 people, with 500 being a maximum. *Tribes,* in contrast, are linked to agricultural economies and are characterized by greater cohesiveness because of the existence of varied means of linking the members of different local social groups, for example by exchanging women in marriage and prestige goods and perhaps above all by the pressures of external contacts and warfare.

Both bands and tribes conduct their social relationships on the basis of reciprocity and do not have any centralized institutions. However, within the structure of tribes, if power becomes centralized in the hands of an individual or a family, who co-ordinates social activity and has special privileges, then a *chiefdom* emerges. This is a hierarchically organized, ranked society, with centres, 'central places', at which some aspects of religious, social and economic activity are co-ordinated. Here the characteristic mode of exchange is redistribution, with some at least of the tribute to the chief being passed on as gifts or more generally through feasts. Finally, *early state systems* are more centralized than chiefdoms, with more institutional differentiation at their centres, larger numbers of people and often a codified system of legal rights and obligations. These ideas can indeed be applied to the materials of prehistory, although it is terribly easy to elevate them to the status of an evolutionary sequence, through which human societies must inevitably pass. Reality is more complex than this, and it is important to grasp that the categories can co-exist. Fried, in contrast, has emphasized not the means of social integration but the nature of social differentiation which appears and identified egalitarian societies, ranked societies, stratified societies and the state, categories which in fact overlap Service's groupings rather discordantly. These ideas have stimulated much debate amongst some archaeologists; the rather uniform material remains of the Neolithic and early Bronze Ages can be interpreted as the remains of essentially egalitarian societies, while by the middle Bronze Ages the richer 'elite' burials in certain barrows of Wiltshire and Dorset, containing rich jewellery, symbols of rank such as decorated maces and even products as exotic as Mediterranean faience—a form of glass bead— suggest the emergence of chiefdoms. Nevertheless, Renfrew, in a re-evaluation of the Neolithic and early-Bronze-Age evidence for the same area has concluded that the region saw 'emerging chiefdoms in the early neolithic', developing full-scale chiefdoms at the time of the henges (elaborate late-Neolithic/early-Bronze-Age ritual enclosures, some clearly possessing some astronomical/calendrical significance), and possibly a single unified chiefdom with four or five sub-regions at the time of the construction of Silbury Hill and Stonehenge III, representing respectively labour inputs of the order of 18 million and 30 million man-hours. This is a convincing hypothesis. By the later Iron Age the stratified societies of southern Britain pos-sessed some at least of the categories of early state systems. Such social categoriza-tions applied to the mute archaeological testimony have undoubtedly led to new questions and new debates and do form a way of creating models, and perhaps glimpses of the true complexities, of emerging prehistoric societies and policies. Dodgshon has argued that each socio-economic category is associated with differing ways of organizing space. Each represents a change of scale, that at each level there are different levels of energy capture from the environment, moves from relative social homogeneity to heterogeneity, and from uniformity to hierarchy, but again it must be stressed that there is no inevitable progression; the groupings suggest not only temporal stages but also interactive categories within early societies, much as today's societies differ. It is the interaction within and between varied possibilities which creates the dynamism of human culture. To understand the categories noted above all the concepts they represent must be questioned: How many people are represented by each? How are these arranged within geographical space and how permanent or ephemeral are their settlements? Do the groups have an identifiable duration in time? What social organizations are present—involving language, kinship, resource allocation arrangements, governance in peace and war, forms of exchange—in all of which the essential features of individual and group obligations of society must be considered. What are the external relationships of each? One fact is inescapable; few, if any of the answers can be excavated but the ideas represent models, filters, through which the archaeological data can be passed and more sophisticated questions asked. This is as it should be. This is a model which encompasses the spatial organization of the hunter-gatherer bands of the Mesolithic and the warrior states of the later Iron Age, from seasonal base camps to exploit ephemeral resources, salmon runs and the hazel-nut crop, to proto-urbanism within hill-forts and defended lowland *oppida* and the import of Mediterranean wines and craft products.[37]

Archaeological material does, however, have one great advantage, denied any scholar focusing upon contemporary or near contemporary societies; the lengthy sequences of evidence afford a temporal 'bird's eye view' and, as Bradley points out, within this accumulated material archaeologists may be able to recognize patterns which they had not expected to see. He illustrates this by arguing that between the advent of the Neolithic and the end of the Iron Age 'settlement plans show the greatest variation during phases in which burial rites are fairly uniform', and conversely when settlements are rather less complex, cemeteries, and it may be said, large ritual monuments, show a more elaborate structure. The corollary is that access to a limited number of prestige goods was associated with periods when the elaboration of ritual took place, contexts in which communal ritual sites and rich single graves (elite burials) represented respectively expressions of the coherence of the social group or an emphasis upon the role of the individual. In contrast, social differences were expressed through settlements mainly in periods when status was linked directly to control over food production rather than prestige objects. All this may be no more than an expression of changing property rights but the method of analysis is at the moment perhaps rather more convincing than the specific conclusions achieved, for it opens the important idea of open and closed social systems.[38]

Perspectives on Continuity

This carries the argument to a key problem, the nature of culture change, implying the adoption of new skills, of metallurgy, of organization and of agriculture, new customs, of decoration, of personal adornment, of burial, of settlement and of warfare, and new social patterns, modes of organization to focus wealth and energy for private and public purposes. Any model of causation must balance elements of change against elements of inertia and continuity. Continuity, however, is a difficult concept to define: it is a word which begs definition. Continuity of what? Settlement sites, institutions, population, territorial organization, burial customs, agricultural practices or inheritance customs? A practical illustration is provided by the great communal tombs of the Neolithic period, some constructed of timber and earth, others of massive stones and rubble, and which show marked regional differentiation. They are clearly a product of much effort and if the regional variations and the small locality distributions are a guide they were constructed by local population groups within larger regional groupings, as may have been the case with the ritual sites known as 'henges'.

These tombs, as the case of Isbister showed, were clearly used throughout a long period of time, often with successive additions to their structures, and invariably with successive internments. Piggott is of the opinion that the great long-barrow at West Kennet, Wiltshire, a member of the Severn–Cotswold tomb group, was built in the middle of the third millennium B.C. but the chambers were not fully sealed until the seventeenth century B.C. and produced pottery ranging from primary Neolithic to early-Bronze-Age types.[39] Such discoveries must be set in the context of plough marks found beneath the barrow at South Street, Avebury, Wiltshire, where the barrow could be at least 30, possibly 100 or 200 years later than the agricultural activity. The recognition that many barrows are indeed composite structures, incorporating several earlier and distinct monuments into a final overall conception, opens many perspectives. Here we are at one and the same time faced with several distinct types of continuity, of use, of belief, of sacredness of site, of territorial occupation, and, perhaps, of population. Atkinson believed that at Lanhill in the Cotswolds nine out of the 19 burials, because of distinctive bone deformations, could all belong to one family, but in this southern region, in marked contrast to the case of Isbister noted above, the small number of remains suggests the internment of a privileged group, or perhaps even that the barrow was more important as a focus for ritual and ceremonial than as a burial site.[40]

The people who built long-barrows presumably lived within the adjacent landscapes and even though Neolithic settlements are singularly elusive, Renfrew has pointed out how in Arran and Rousay, conveniently bounded islands, the megalithic tombs have a logical relationship to the available arable resources, while Ashbee was able to divide the earthen long-barrows of Dorset and Wiltshire into five distinctive regional groups reflecting strongly localized traditions.[41]

Territorial Identification

The identification of territories involves a classic problem of inferring the areas and possible boundaries from a known distribution of points. It must be recognized that at least three scales of enquiry are possible, the national, the regional and the local, and in practical terms these merely represent three points on a continuum. The recognition at a local scale that the economy of a given site depended directly upon the character and possibilities inherent within the terrains to which access was possible has roots in the concepts of economic prehistory enunciated by Clark in his 1952 volume *Prehistoric Europe: The Economic Basis*. When this is allied to the recognition that the archaeological site is a repository of matter imported from this site-catchment zone, then the possibilities for environmental archaeology become enormously enhanced and we face, once again, the problems and limitations of excavation techniques.[42] Information painstakingly and imaginatively collected at a single point in space must be interpreted logically in the context of the surrounding area, eventually permitting the identification of territories and possibly of boundaries. Of one thing alone can we be certain, reality will prove to be infinitely more complex than our models, and the territories of Iron-Age hill-forts, so often emphatically demarcated by Thiessen polygons, will surely be proved to have had unexpected patterns of configuration.

An example of territory identification has already been noted: Simmons and Spratt in their study of the Mesolithic of North Yorkshire have concentrated upon the interconnections between individual sites rather than upon their particular artifact assemblages. They make the assumption that the variations in artifacts and areal extent of sites reflect differing types of economic activity rather than distinct cultures, and that we are seeing the remains of spatially and seasonally distributed contrasts in the life-style of a single group or community.[43] A fascinating example from later prehistory is to be found in Clarke's re-analysis of the finds from the Iron-Age lake-village of Glastonbury, where he demonstrates vividly the possibilities inherent in a rigorous application of this spatial thinking. A key section in the argument, which follows a lengthy examination of the possible relationships between the modular units which make up the village and Celtic social structures, concerns the link between the lake-village and Maesbury, a hill-fort, over eight miles away. The ridge upon which this fort sits apparently produced the clays which are the most likely source of the fine 'Glastonbury Group 2' pottery, and the sandstone used as querns by the fen-dwellers. He concludes, 'we may hypothesize and subsequently test by excavation that it was from this centre that Glastonbury imported much of its raw materials and to which it exported its own products . . . it was to this centre that Glastonbury owed its political allegiance and thus its customary tribute', a logical leap which is challenging, if unprovable. He continues his argument to construct a schematic model of the fully developed Celtic settlement hierachy—essentially hut-groups, small enclosures, large enclosures (hill-forts) and very large enclosed sites (*oppida*)—suggesting the nature of its possible integration with the social hierarchy and grades on one hand and the economic hierarchy on the other. This model, emphasizing the degree to which individual settlements would 'inexorably tend to become reciprocially specialized and mutually supporting . . . provides a basis for prediction and thus for testing the degree of its reality or unreality'. It is grounded in known archaeological facts, draws upon the 'literary' evidence of Irish laws and Caesar, and incorporates concepts, questions and attitudes derived from anthropology.[44] It is an exciting and stimulating synthesis, even for those who may challenge certain of the interpretations. Explicit within Clarke's argument is the difficult question of hypothesis testing. It can hardly be doubted that the excavation of any site should occur within a wider context of scholarly questions, but as Barker has recently pointed out an excavation designed to answer one specific question will almost certainly run into completely unexpected evidence, quite unconnected with the original problem and hypothesis it may have generated. Many new excavators are now wholly committed to the problems of complex multiperiod sites and Barker is quite explicit: 'I am becoming more and more convinced that the only valid questions to ask of a site are "What is here?" and

"What is the whole sequence of events on this site from the beginnings of human activity to the present day?" Any other question must only be part of this all-embracing one.[45]

Before leaving this question of territories reference must be made to a corpus of work concerning the historical period: G. R. Jones in a long series of papers has argued that certain estates, comprising groups of hamlets and villages answering to a chief place, a lord's court, with collective rents, renders and services, and documented in twelfth- and thirteenth-century sources, may be of pre-Saxon origin, and his general conclusion is that they could be very old indeed (see Chapter 3). He repeatedly draws attention to the fact that refuges are an integral part of their structure and that hill-forts often appear in significant association with such territories—an example being the presence of the great hill-fort of Almondbury within the multiple estate of Wakefield. In short, the presence of the antecedents of such territories during the Iron Age could, in part, account for the construction of hill-forts, whose rulers drew upon the labour services of their territories. Jones goes as far as pointing out that Stonehenge lies within the great royal estate of Amesbury and suggest that this could echo important earlier territorial situations. The case for the antiquity of these estates and their pre-Saxon origin is, subject to some qualifications concerning the processes of change which could affect them, a strong one. Projection to earlier periods is, however, a stimulating hypothesis upon which, at the moment, a verdict of 'not-proven' must be returned. Nevertheless, there is an important point here: the attraction of theoretical notions of territories must not detract from an awareness that actual territories may sometimes be detectable and that such evidence is worth seeking and considering.[46] The fact Roman roads appear to cut across parish boundaries, suggesting that these are older than the road, and that in some areas Bronze-Age burials and settlements appear to possess logical relationships to parish and township boundaries raises fundamental questions concerning the antiquity of some of these familiar territorial units. Burgess notes that certain styles of Bronze weapons and axes have distributions which broadly coincide with the territories of known late-Iron-Age tribal groups, commenting further that 'it is interesting . . . to note how many early Medieval political divisions resemble "Iron Age" tribal territories'.[47]

Exchange and Trade

Throughout the prehistoric period exchange and trade were undoubtedly present, ranging from the dispersal of Neolithic axes made from a tough volcanic rock found only in Upper Langdale in the Lake District, to the importing of Roman goods into southern Britain before the formal conquest begun in A.D. 43.[48] In general terms there is an important transition from almost entirely self-sufficient societies to communities where coinage was available even if not in everyday use, but it would be wrong to see this as a rigid or formal progression, for even to this day reciprocal giving between equals is found, sometimes without even an exchange of money— generally termed the Black Economy! Different systems can operate side by side. Before looking at some of the models which have been proposed as frames for interpreting the known archaeological facts, it is helpful to begin with two questions:

what was traded and how was it carried? Scattered find-spots demonstrate the movement of distinctive stone and flint for practical toolmaking and creating 'objects of power'—such as axes or maces of great beauty and workmanship or jet for buttons—in the Neolithic. Eventually metals, copper, tin, their alloy bronze, some gold, and eventually iron, had to be redistributed from their points of origin, often in upland Britain, to consuming societies, all of which had to be moved either as ingots, semi-finished or finished products, while furs and some animals, hunting dogs, horses and cattle (as tribute or tax), women (for marriage), could all be part of indigenous patterns of exchange and trade as well as raid and pillage. Looking further afield, northern Europe undoubtedly sought Mediterranean products, metalwork and wine, fine textiles and pottery (which may be containers for other luxury items, perfume and spices), coral and dyes, while exporting animals and leather, woollen fabrics and a range of foodstuffs, and above all people, as mercenaries, auxiliary troops and slaves.[49] Two problems arise when creating models to interpret trade: first, there is a world of difference between a virtually indestructible stone axe and a woman given in marriage: if the former is discovered its exotic origin can be traced through petrological sectioning, but a skeleton, if it survives, may reveal pathological evidence but it can tell nothing of the presence or absence of the agreement or contract. Second, the active terms used above are all value-loaded; 'gift', 'exchange', 'trade', 'pillage' and 'tribute' can all move goods which then appear as 'find-spots' in the archaeological record.

There are three ways of transporting goods on land: by manpower, carried on the backs of animals (generally oxen or horses), or in vehicles. The history of wheeled vehicles in Europe is one of increasing sophistication; in Britain nave bands are known from the later Bronze Age and by the Iron Age Cunliffe suggests that 'skilled wheelwrights were present in most communities', an interesting indirect comment on the presence of roads.[50] Vehicles could be drawn by oxen or the more prestigous horse. However, manpower should never be underrated, particularly if goods were moved gradually from exchange centre to exchange centre, be this for religous or ceremonial purposes, as tribute or for perceived gain. The great stone monuments attest the ability of communities and rulers to harness great amounts of energy for public works, energies that were usually directed towards making a living. Boats present a similar problem; in the raft, the skin boat, the bark boat and the dugout lie innumerable technological possibilities—how did the first farmers transport cattle over stretches of water too wide to swim? The three late Bronze-Age plank-built boats—surely ferries for the Humber crossing—found at North Ferriby, Yorkshire, while Caesar's description of the boats of the Venetii of Brittany, whatever the problems of detail, suggest substantial late-Iron-Age sea-going vessels in a tribe capable of mustering 220 ships. Although difficult to quantify, both goods and people could be and were moved by indigenous techniques, while as part of a zone of procurement, attractive to those outside involved in exchange and trade, the British seaways were clearly visited by vessels from Europe and the Mediterranean.[51]

The processes involved in the movement of commodities between one cultural group or one region and another involves several ideas: *reciprocity* links equal partners in exchanges, thus catching, quarrying, felling, gathering and robbing are one-sided, undertaken via the hunt, the expedition and the raid; *gift trade*, a system in which the ceremonial element of trading dominates, involving political dealings between rulers and chiefs, mutual presentations, in which goods are prestige items, treasures, gold, horses, ivory, fine clothing and slaves, often passed on by the chief amongst the elite of the receiving group; *redistribution* describes movements towards the centre and out again, classically seen in the flows of metal ingots, while *exchange* refers to movements taking place between 'hands' under a market system. All of these elemental patterns may appear within the framework of trade built upon treaties or *administrative trade*, subject to agreements between rulers, often involving control and standardization, and *market trade*, involving the integration of market mechanisms in the hands of diverse individuals—traders and merchants, mechanisms adaptable to the handling of not only the goods, but in addition all elements of a developed trading system—'storage, transportation, risk, credit, payments and the like'.[52] When translating these ideas to the realities of prehistoric cultural groups, economic zones, landscapes and seascapes, three further ideas are useful: (i) that of *boundaries, frontiers*, and *interfaces*, the former being a peaceful limit to influence or control, or a line of geographical discontinuity, the second to be seen looking outwards in an aggressive sense, and the third being a more general concept; such a boundary will usually have social and political as well as economic implications but will often reflect underlying terrain contrasts, upland and lowland, wood and plain, emerging as a fundamental antecedent structure in the landscapes of later periods; (ii) a *port-of-trade* or *emporium*, a 'neutrality device', a place set aside for commercial transactions, where foreign traders were given protection by the local ruler and usually situated at a route node such as a good harbour, meeting of roads or transhipment point; (iii) the concept of the *gateway community*, developed along natural corridors of communication where these impinge upon boundaries between differing economic regions, using the chance of location to their own advantage. Gift trade, the exchange of luxuries ('items of power'), women and food gifts between equals have very ancient roots in the Mesolithic and Neolithic periods—what more precious gift could any small band give another than a daughter, a gift of valuable labour and potential fertility—and by the later Bronze Age ports-of-call were undoubtedly found in southern England at Mount Batten, near Plymouth, the Portland–Weymouth Bay region and at Hengistbury Head.

In conclusion, at the advent of the Roman conquest Cunliffe defines three broad economic zones in Britain, a core, a periphery and beyond. The core lay in the south-east, well-populated, with trading centres, coinage and links to the Roman consumer market in Gaul (essentially France).[53] Luxury imports were disseminated through this zone by gift trade. Around this core lay four peripheral tribal groupings, also coin using, with urban or proto-urban foci where commodities could be exchanged and whose elites benefited from the inflow of luxury goods and acted as middlemen for their transfer, often by gift, within their local society and further afield. These correspond essentially to the south-eastern settlement region noted above. Beyond, in the rest of Britain, lay a procurement zone, providing raw materials. Here, added to endemic warfare and cattle-raiding, slave raiding provided a new and disruptive element, a precursor to political interference by a colonial power and the formal Roman invasion beginning in A.D. 43 yet not wholly complete in any sense until A.D. 84 when Agricola defeated the Caledonians at the battle of Mons Graupius. Forty years of hard warfare against four legions is a tribute to the levels of political and economic organization achieved by the Britons.

References

1. J. G. Evans, S. Limbrey and H. Cleere (eds.), *The Effect of Man on the Landscape: The Highland Zone*, Council for British Archaeology, Research Report No. 11 (1975); S. Jørgensen, *Tree-Felling in Draved*, (National Museum of Denmark, 1985).

2. P. Barker, *Techniques of Archaeological Excavation*, (London, 1977); E. C. Harris, *Principles of Archaeological Stratigraphy*, (London and New York, 1979).

3. T. Watkins (ed.), *Radio-carbon: Calibration and Prehistory*, (Edinburgh, 1975); C. Renfrew *British Prehistory* (London 1974), pp. 1–40; I. G. Simmons and M. J. Tooley (eds), *The Environment in British Prehistory* (London, 1981), pp. 44–7.

4. Table 1.1 is derived from H.M.S.O. *Field Archaeology*, Ordnance Survey Professional Papers, New Series, No. 3 (London, 1951), p. ii, pp. 67–8; Renfrew, *British Prehistory*; J. V. S. Megaw and D. D. A. Simpson, *Introduction to British Prehistory* (Leicester, 1979).

5. Megaw and Simpson, *Introduction to British Prehistory*.

6. D. Clarke, 'Mesolithic Europe: The economic basis', in G. de Sieveking, I. H. Longworth and K. E. Wilson (eds.), *Problems of Prehistoric and Social Archaeology*, (London, 1976), pp. 449–81; P. Fowler, 'Wildscape to Landscape; "enclosure" in prehistoric Britain', in R. Mercer (ed.), *Farming Practice in British Prehistory*, (Edinburgh, 1981), pp. 9–54.

7. K. H. Jackson, *The Oldest Irish Tradition: A Window on the Iron Age*, (Cambridge, 1964).

8. R. M. Jacobi, 'Population and landscape in Mesolithic lowland Britain', in S. Limbrey and G. Evans (eds.), *The Effect of Man upon the Landscape: the Lowland Zone*, Council for British Archaeology Research Report, No. 21, p. 75.

9. V. G. Childe, *The Prehistoric Communities of the British Isles*, (Edinburgh, 1940, reprint 1952).

10. C. Renfrew, *Approaches to Social Archaeology*, (Edinburgh, 1984), p. 35.

11. A similar discord between arguments at the research frontier; what appears in standard texts and that a student actually needs has been visible in geography for many years. A solution was offered by the editors in R. J. Chorley and P. Haggett (eds.), *Frontiers in Geographical Teaching*, (London 1964), pp. 360–4.

12. H. C. Bowen, 'Celtic Fields and 'ranch' boundaries in Wessex', in Limbrey and Evans, *The Effect of Man on the Landscape: the Lowland Zone*, pp. 115–23.

13. D. Benson and D. Miles, *The Upper Thames Valley: an Archaeological Survey of the River Gravels*, Oxfordshire Archaeological Unit, Survey No. 2 (1974); D. R. Wilson, *Air Photo Interpretation for Archaeologists*, (London, 1982).

14. P. J. Fowler (ed.), *Field Survey in British Archaeology*, Council for British Archaeology, (1972); C. Thomas (ed.), *Rural Settlement in Roman Britain*, Council for British Archaeology, Research Report No. 7 (1966), pp. 43–67, especially pp. 54–5; C. P. Hall and J. R. Ravensdale, *The West Fields of Cambridge*, (Cambridge, 1976), pp. 121–35; H. C. Bowen and P. J. Fowler, *Early Land Allotment*, (British Archaeological Reports 48, 1978), pp. 159–62.

15. H. C. Bowen, and P. J. Fowler, *Early Land Allotment*, British Archaeological Report 40, 1978; P. J. Fowler, *The Farming of Prehistoric Britain*, (Cambridge 1983), pp. 94–158.

16. C. Hayfield (ed.), *Fieldwalking as a Method of Archaeological Research*, Department of the Environment, Occasional Paper No. 2 (1980); J. Hinchcliffe and R. T. Schadla-Hall (eds.), *The Past Under the Plough*, Department of the Environment, Occasional Papers No. 3 (1980).

17. Fowler, *Rural Archaeology*, pp. 121–35.

18. W. J. Ford, 'Some settlement patterns in the central region of the Warwickshire Avon', in P. H. Sawyer (ed.), *Medieval Settlement*, (London, 1976), pp. 292–4; P. J. Fowler (ed.), *Rural Archaeology*, (Moonraker Press, Bradford-on-Avon, 1975), pp. 105–19; J. Hurst, 'The Wharram Research Project: Results to 1983', *Medieval Archaeology*, **28** (1984), pp. 77–111.

19. C. Taylor, 'The study of settlement patterns in pre-saxon Britain', in P. J. Ucko, R. Tringham and G. W. Dimbleby (eds.), *Man, Settlement and Urbanism*, (London, 1972), pp. 52–4.

20. R. J. C. Atkinson, in E. Fowler (ed.), *Field Survey in British Archaeology*, pp. 60, 62.

21. Fowler, *Rural Archaeology*, pp. 121–3, 136; D. A. Spratt and I. G. Simmons, 'Prehistoric activity and environment on the North York Moors', *Jnl. of Archaeological Science*, 3 (1976), pp. 193–210; R. Miket, in C. Burgess and R. Miket (eds.), *Settlement and Economy in the Third and Second Millennia B.C.*, British Archaeological Reports, 33 (1976), pp. 113–42.

22. J. G. Evans, *The Environment of Early Man in the British Isles*, (London, 1975), p. 110.

23. Spratt and Simmons, 'Prehistoric activity and environment on the North York Moors', p. 116.

24. Evans, *The Environment of Early Man*; Simmons and Tooley, *The Environment in British Prehistory*.

25. W. Pennington, *The History of British Vegetation*, (London, 1969), pp. 62–77.

26. Simmons and Tooley, *The Environment in British Prehistory*, pp. 287–8.

27. Evans, *The Environment of Early Man*, pp. 113–57.

28. Fowler, *The Farming of Prehistoric Britain*, pp. 104–7.

29. J. Coles and B. J. Orme, *Prehistory of the Somerset Levels*, (Somerset Levels Project, 1980), p. 21; O. Rackham, *The History of the British Countryside*, (London, 1986), p. 72.

30. J. W. Hedges, *Tomb of the Eagles*, (London, 1984), pp. 174–90; C. Burgess, *The Age of Stonehenge*, (London, 1980), pp. 160–80.

31. P. J. Fowler, *The Farming of Prehistoric Britain*, (Cambridge, 1983), pp. 32–6.

32. Fowler, *The Farming of Prehistoric Britain*, p. 35.

33. B. Cunliffe, *Iron Age Cummunities in Britain*, (2nd edn.), (London, 1978), pp. 334–5.

34. V. G. Child, *The Dawn of European Civilisation*, (1st edn.), (Edinburgh, 1925); *idem*, *Prehistoric Communities*, pp. 1–15 *et seq.*, p. 141; Renfrew, *Before Civilisation*, (London, 1976; Harmondsworth, 1976), Chapter 2.

35. C. Renfrew, *Before Civilisation*, pp. 93–132; G. Clark, 'The invasion hypothesis in British archaeology', *Antiquity*, 40 (1966), pp. 172–89; C. Musson, 'House-plans and prehistory', *Current Archaeology*, 21 (1970), pp. 267–74.

36. C. Renfrew, *Approaches to Social Archaeology*, (Edinburgh, 1984), p. 30.

37. R. A. Dodgshon, *The European Past; Social Evolution and Spatial Order* (London, 1987); T. Champion, C. Gamble, S. Shennan and A. Whittle, *Prehistoric Europe* (London and New York, 1984), p. 170; E. R. Service, *Primitive Social Organisation*, (New York, 1962); M. H. Fried, *The Evolution of Political Society*, (New York, 1967).

38. R. Bradley, *The Social Foundations of Prehistoric Britain: Themes and Variations in the Archaeology of Power*, (London, 1984), pp. 157–67, 164–5.

39. S. Piggott, *The West Kennet Long Barrow Excavations 1955–6*, Ministry of Works Archaeological Report, No. 14 (H.M.S.O., 1962).

40. D. D. A. Simpson, *Economy and Settlement in Neolithic and early Bronze Age Britain and Europe*, (Leicester, 1971), pp. 40–52; Smith, in Renfrew, *British Prehistory*, p. 132; J. X. W. P. Corcoran: a report on his work in *Current Archaeology*, 34 (1972), pp. 381–7, *idem*, 'The Cotswold-Severn Group', in T. G. E. Powell (ed.), *Megalithic Enquiries in the West of Britain*, (Liverpool, 1969), pp. 13–104; *idem*, 'Multiperiod construction and the origins of the chambered long cairn in Western Britain and Ireland', in F. Lynch and C. Burgess (eds.), *Prehistoric Man in Wales and the West*, (Bath, 1972), pp. 31–63; R. J. C. Atkinson, 'Old Mortality: some aspects of burial and population in Neolithic England', in J. M. Coles and D. D. A. Simpson (eds.), *Studies in Ancient Europe*, (London, 1968), pp. 83–93.

41. Renfrew, *Approaches to Social Archaeology*, pp. 165–99, 225–45.

42. J. G. D. Clark, *Prehistoric Europe: the Economic Foundations* (London 1952); E. S. Higgs (ed.), *Papers in Economic Prehistory*, (Cambridge, 1972), pp. 27–36.

43. Simmons and Spratt, 'Prehistoric activity and environment on the North York Moors'; E. Higgs, 'Prehistoric economies; a territorial approach' in E. S. Higgs (ed.), *Papers in Economic Prehistory*, (Cambridge, 1967), pp. 27–36.

44. D. L. Clarke (ed.), *Models in Archaeology*, (London, 1972), pp. 801–69.

45. Barker, *Techniques of Archaeological Excavation*, pp. 37–67.

46. The papers by G. R. J. Jones are listed in the References, Chapter 3, of this volume.
47. D. Bonney, 'Early boundaries in Wessex', in P. J. Fowler (ed.), *Archaeology and the Landscape*, (London, 1972), pp. 168–86; D. A. Spratt, *Prehistoric and Roman Archaeology of North-East Yorkshire*, British Archaeological Reports, British Series 104, (Oxford, 1982), pp. 158–66; Burgess, *The Age of Stonehenge*, p. 176.
48. Megaw and Simpson, *Introduction to British Prehistory*, pp. 109–12.
49. B. Cunliffe, *Greeks, Romans and Barbarians: Spheres of Interaction*, (London, 1988); Dodgshon, *The European Past*.
50. S. Piggott, *The Earliest Wheeled Transport*, (London, 1983); Cunliffe, *Iron Age Communities in Britain*, p. 290; Burgess, *The Age of Stonehenge*, pp. 280–94.
51. B. Greenhill, *The Archaeology of the Boar*, (London, 1976); G. Bass, *A History of Seafaring*, (London, 1972), pp. 113–32.
52. Cunliffe, *Greeks, Romans and Barbarians*, pp. 4–5; K. Polanyi, *The Livelihood of Man*, (London, 1977); G. Dalton, (ed.), *Primitive, Archaic and Modern Economies: Essays of Karl Polanyi*, (Boston, 1968), pp. 238–60.
53. Cunliffe, *Greeks, Romans and Barbarians*, pp. 193–201

2

The Human Geography of Roman Britain

I. Hodder and M. Millett

Until recently study of the human geography of Roman Britain has made little use of modern geographical approaches. Even quantitative analysis is often shunned 'since it cloaks the information that we have with a spurious authenticity'.[1] This is claimed despite the increasingly large amounts of quantitative data (for example, on regional pottery distributions, or town size) available in Romano-British studies, and is in direct contrast to the objective and explicit qualities usually claimed for quantitative work. As to geographical model-building Professor Frere has rejected any such approach while wondering 'whether there is not . . . a close connection between the present-day ungovernability of our society—the modern rejection of authority—and the comfortable geographical approach to early settlement'.[2] It is not surprising, therefore, that two recent major syntheses make little use of either artifact distribution studies or geographical models concerning analogous societies.[3]

Rigorous analytical methods and more explicit hypothesis formation have begun to be used in Romano-British archaeology. This is especially the case in the sphere of pottery studies, analyses of the distribution of coins, examination of rural economies and urban development.[4] There will necessarily be a strong emphasis on these studies in this chapter, the basic themes of which comprise the spatial structure of late-Iron-Age society and its influence on Romano-British society, the pattern and nature of rural settlement, the growth of towns and their character, and the route network of England and Wales during the Roman period.

The Late Pre-Roman Iron Age

The latest Iron Age in England and Wales saw a series of changes in patterning which provide the background against which we must understand the structure of Roman Britain, for it was characteristic Roman practice to incorporate and adapt existing societies rather than altering them wholesale. The fundamentals of late-Iron-Age organization lie in the development of a complex regional pattern of agriculturally based societies which originates in the late Bronze Age. These societies were largely based on settlements in small farmsteads, which were often bounded within enclosures. In many areas more substantial defended settlements (hill-forts) acted as foci for some activities of the societies. The regional patterns of settlement type and material culture style, based in part on varying adaptations to different ecological circumstances and in part on differences in social and cultural organization, become more evident in the period after *c.* 100 B.C. as external contacts with the Roman world served to accelerate existing trends and exaggerate differences. This increasing differentiation is most clear in the areas of the south and east which were in closest contact with Gaul.[5]

We can isolate three major phases of change leading up to the Roman conquest of the south-east in A.D. 43. The first phase is defined by the arrival of Roman Republican imports in Britain, and follows the invasion of south Gaul in the 120s B.C., and lasts until Caesar's annexation of Gaul in the 50s B.C. Caesar's intervention in Britain during the Gallic Wars is followed by the Civil Wars at Rome, and this prevents any consolidation in Gaul so the phase to the 20s B.C., although marked by some changes in Britain, does not witness any radical development. However, from Augustus' reorganization of Gaul and his campaigns in Germany, there is an intensification of diplomatic and economic contacts between Britain and the continent which results in a series of major changes in both social organization and settlement pattern. This contact, and the stresses it created in Britain, provide the context for Claudius' annexation in A.D. 43.

In the period from *c.* 120 to 55 B.C. contact with the Roman world is witnessed through the arrival of amphorae which contained wine produced in Italy. These amphorae (in particular the form Dressel 1A) arrived via the Gallic trade networks, and are particularly concentrated on the site at Hengistbury Head near Christchurch on the south coast where a trading community seems to have been located. The finds from this site also include material from Armorica and thus indicate a variety of cross-channel connections, although it is notable that the imports do not achieve a wide distribution within Britain.[6] At about the same date as the establishment of the trade the first Gallo-Belgic coinage also became common over the whole of south-east England, and there is some evidence for a dislocation of the existing pattern of centralized settlements, with the destruction of some hill-forts like Danebury. Whilst some would see these processes as being connected[7], the small quantities of imported goods and their very limited distribution lends little weight to this hypothesis.

From around the period of Caesar's annexation of Gaul, the quantity of Roman material found in Britain increases, with a widespread, if thin, distribution of wine amphorae and other pottery. These goods now occur in a number of rural settlement sites as well as graves and nucleated sites. The evidence from the major aristocratic burials which characterize this phase of the Iron Age (known as the Welwyn type burials) show that the imported goods (which were now entering Britain through the south-east and Thames estuary rather than Hengistbury) were fulfilling a status-defining role for the tribal elites. This evidence suggests that the goods may have been the result of diplomatic gift-exchange rather than extensive trade, and were directed towards an elite who resided in rural farmsteads rather than in emergent nucleated centres.

During the 30s B.C. Roman control of northern Gaul was reinforced with the development of a road network and the establishment of a formal administrative system which preceded Augustus' military campaigns across the Rhine into Germany. This increased activity led to an enhancement of cross-channel contact, both through trading and as a result of Roman attempts to control their neighbours through diplomacy. In this phase of contact the quantities and varieties of goods moving across the Channel seem to have increased greatly, although the objects rarely moved beyond the south-east of England. The arrival of these goods coincides with changes in the settlement pattern in the south-east, which are usually inter- preted as a result of an increasing social differentiation and organization into more centralized political units stimulated by the inter-group conflicts which were exploited by Roman foreign policy. Throughout the south-east, we see the emerg- ence of a series of lowland nucleated centres known as *oppida*. These were extensive sites often enclosed by discontinuous dykes and occupied at comparatively low intensity, but containing areas suggestive of specialized functions of exchange, production, religion and administration.[8] Most notable amongst these are the centres at Verulamium (St Albans), Calleva (Silchester) and Camulodunum (Col- chester), which are known from inscribed coinages to have been the centres of tribal territories.[9] In addition, there were a number of smaller centres (like Braughing, Herts.) which were probably the foci for subsidiary social groups. The nature and permanence of the larger territorial units is uncertain although it is clear that a series of processes of inter-group conflict led to their differential success. By the eve of the Roman conquest of A.D. 43, the site at Camulodunum was the centre of a major

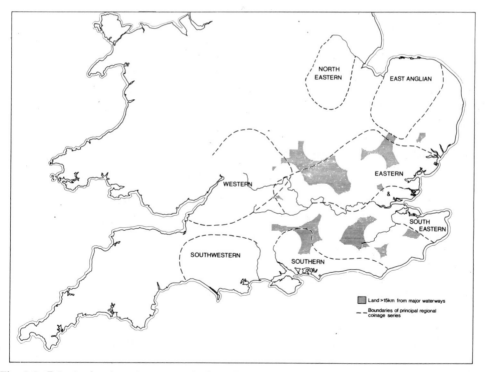

Fig. 2.1. Principal coin-using zones in later-Iron-Age Britain. These distributions correlate broadly with the main tribal groups of the late Iron Age, and form the foundation upon which the administrative units of the Roman Province were based (after Haselgrove).

regional unit and was able to control much of the south-east. Beyond this territory were a number of less developed *oppida* with more circumscribed functions, together with a series of territories (like Dorset or Devon/Cornwall) which seem comparatively unaffected by continental contact.

In all these areas the recent assessments of agricultural production suggest a highly productive social system, which may account for the reference to Britain being a grain exporter.[10] This evidence has been taken to support an hypothesis of large-scale economic exploitation of the areas from Roman Gaul, but the limited quantities of imports known and their generally thin distribution up to the Claudian period do not support this hypothesis, but rather suggest an intensification of distribution through existing social systems.

The territories of the latest Iron-Age tribes can be tentatively identified from the distributions of coinages and some ceramic styles (see Fig. 2.1). Whilst we cannot be certain that these distributions relate to social groupings, their patterning seems sufficiently consistent to allow us to present a tentative political geography of south-east Britain at the time of the Roman conquest.[11]

The Incorporation of Britain into the Empire

The discussion provided above is important for our understanding of many aspects of the period after the Claudian invasion of Britain in A.D. 43. In particular, the establishment of Roman control was considerably easier amongst the more centralized political groups to the south-east. Here, ultimate control passed from one authority to another under local leaders such as Cogidubnus. The Catuvellauni, Trinovantes and Cantiaci formed early cantons or *civitates*, with Atrebates and Iceni added as client kingdoms.[12] 'Within little more than a month of landing, the south-east was firmly in Roman hands.'[13] In addition, it is precisely these areas which had previously had greatest contact with the romanized world in the late Iron Age so that the establishment of the new regime may have been somewhat easier.

The conquest and control of the more northerly and western areas of Britain where there were less developed centralized systems was more difficult. This was seen most clearly in the subjugation of the Durotrigian area, where the Second Legion under Vespasian found it necessary to destroy more than twenty separate fortified settlements.[14] Archaeological evidence such as the finds from Hod Hill provide ample evidence of these attacks. Throughout the newly conquered territories it was necessary for the invaders to place forts at strategic points within the tribal territories (e.g. Camulodunum and Hod Hill) but those forts in the less centralized territories needed to remain longer before control could pass to native civil authority. The Roman system of government worked through the native tribal elites in Britain, with the convenient pre-Roman tribes incorporated as *civitates*. Each such unit comprised a territory which was governed from a town, usually its pre-Roman focus, although away from the south-east new centres were established on the sites of military camps (e.g. Exeter, Wroxeter). The date of the establishment of these administrative divisions varies with the periods of conquest, beginning before A.D. 50 and continuing to the early second century. The frontier areas of Wales and the far north

Fig. 2.2. The administrative divisions, the *civitates*, of Roman Britain. These divisions are broadly based on the Iron-Age tribal groups after which they are named. The chief town of each *civitas* also bore the tribal name; thus Canterbury was *Durnovernum Cantiacorum*.

remained under military occupation beyond this date as the military conquest became bogged-down, and a frontier was formed.

The Roman use of administrative areas or *civitates* encourages the archaeologist to draw up political maps of Roman Britain (see Fig. 2.2) indicating the territories of each civitas.[15] But as Rivet points out, there is limited evidence for the construction of such maps.[16] The attribution of most towns to their *civitates* is now possible on the basis of literary, epigraphic and numismatic evidence,[17] although the evidence for their territories is far more scanty. Some can be defined with care from the Iron-Age coin distributions, but away from the coin using areas their territories are far from certain.

Some of the *civitates* away from the south-east, and in particular their precise territories, may have been much more artificial creations than is often supposed. The *civitas* of the Belgae at least 'appears to have been an artificial creation of the Roman government'.[18] A possibly analogous situation concerns the colonial approach to government in Africa and the problem of the concept of 'tribe'. Groups and areas without centralized political control were often artificially classified into tribes by the British authorities in order to facilitate administration. Fried has in fact suggested that tribes often did not exist prior to colonial rule.[19] In many areas in Africa the tribal concept was imposed on a less structured social pattern. Much the same may have been true of some areas in Britain in the Roman period.

The Growth of Towns

At the hub of each Roman administrative district or *civitas*, was a *civitas* capital generally located on or near a major pre-Roman site (see Fig. 2.3). This development is especially clear in the more centralized areas in the south-east. Outside this administrative organization there were also four major Roman towns called *coloniae*. These colonies were established as settlements of Roman citizens—often veterans from the Roman legions—(as at Colchester, Lincoln, Gloucester), whilst the *colonia* at York lay outside a major military camp.

These two categories of town (together with Verulamium which although like a *civitas* capital was technically a *municipium* and so had a higher status) were typical of Roman urban centres. They were laid out on rectangular street grids, and focused on a major suite of public buildings (fora, basilicas, baths and temples) which provided facilities for the administration of their territories as well as acting as major social,

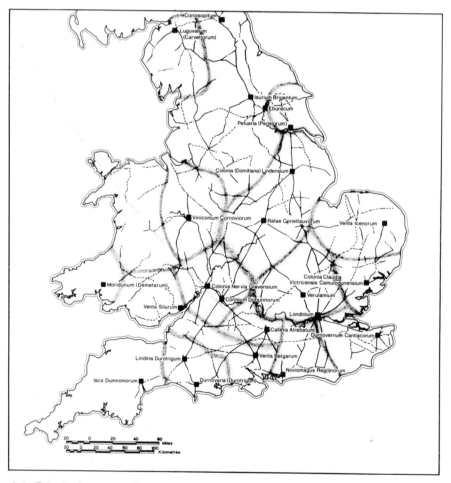

Fig. 2.3. Principal towns and roads of Roman Britain. The towns shown are those which had self-governing status, either as Roman colonies or as centres of cantons.

political and religious foci. These towns came to be occupied by a range of larger houses by the second century, but never developed as the centres of a large urban productive workforce, although craft and trading activities were present. Their principal function was the integration of the native elites into the Roman system through their active participation in the administrative system. In contrast to these major towns, London, which began to develop soon after the conquest, was not located at an Iron-Age social focus but rather at a social boundary. It was a thriving trading centre by A.D. 60, probably as a result of its neutral boundary location, and became the provincial capital soon afterwards, although we have no certain information about its administrative status. All we can be certain about is that it did not administer its own *civitas*. London's development seems to owe its success to overseas traders taking advantage of its boundary location where the new route-ways had also focused on a fording point of the Thames.[20] The city became highly Romanized and developed to thrive very quickly as an *entrepôt* for the new province and subsequently as a convenient location for the governor and procurator's staff. All these major Romanized towns were focal to the development of the province in the first to third centuries A.D. but gradually became less dynamic and were overtaken as economic centres by the small towns.[21]

These smaller centres include a variety of lesser nucleated centres sometimes capable of being called towns, or villages. Some of these *vici* were walled and while there is no literary or epigraphical clue as to which sites had an administrative role, archaeological research has identified a large number of walled centres.[22] These seem to have been densely packed nodes, although in contrast to the major towns they are characteristically less organized, almost never having street grids and often comprising ribbon development along a major road, with additional minor roads infilling behind the street frontage. Unlike the major towns they have few if any public buildings because they lacked their key administrative roles, although they were instead occupied by numerous artisan houses and minor industrial premises indicative of a function as thriving economic centres.[23] Although many originate in the Iron Age or the period soon after the conquest,[24] they rose to their maximum scale in the third to fourth centuries at the time that the major towns were becoming less dynamic. The overall impression is that whilst these centres may have acted as secondary administrative nuclei, especially in connection with the imperial messenger/postal service, they were primarily economic centres.

Their distribution is predominantly at or near the peripheries of the *civitates*. This suggests that they developed as a result of a combination of administrative and economic factors in the areas least well served by the major towns. An influential factor in their development may have been their neutral boundary locations which enabled inter-tribal exchange to take place.[25] The development of these sites should be distinguished from the provision of some with defences around the end of the second century. This probably resulted from the strategic and administrative importance of some of these existing centres to the administration and follows from, rather than causing, their development. The administrative importance of these centres, which may not have been related to their economic success, probably accounts for the apparently arbitrary array of sites which receive walls, some of which are far smaller than those which remained undefended.[26] The resultant pattern does, however, mean that lowland Britain was more or less evenly provided with defended towns during the later Roman period, and this does seem to have been the administrative requirement.

Town–Country Relationships: Regional Artifact Studies

The Roman system of municipal government encouraged centralization around the major towns in the early empire as these were actively involved in the territorial administration and in particular the collection of taxes.[27] This focal function accounts for the importance of the towns in the early empire, which also had a major impact on the countryside in that Romanized settlements tended to cluster around them.[28] In the later empire, the change towards taxation in kind,[29] which was less focused on the principal administrative towns, led to some decentralization of the system, and may account for the rise in importance of the minor towns. Nonetheless the Romanized settlements continued to focus on the traditional power centres, although there is substantial evidence that the elites were now less involved in municipal administration (which was perceived as burdensome) and were thus retreating to live more in their increasingly elaborate country residences, whilst no longer embellishing the towns with public buildings, statues and inscriptions. These processes must have had an impact on town–country relationships, but little attempt has been made to study systematically the territories served by major or minor towns.

The exception to this is the increasing number of artefact studies. The relatively large number of sites from which Romano-British pottery has been collected, and the ability to identify several classes as to origin (either by style, makers' stamps or petrological analysis) mean that detailed studies of Romano-British pottery distributions are feasible. Most effort in pottery studies has, however, been concerned with establishing chronologies and allocating types to kilns without the use of any explicit theoretical framework.[30]

The production and distribution of coarse wares was carried out at different scales, larger concerns being especially common in the later Roman period. At the most localized level, a few coarse ware kiln centres are known which are not located near any major centre. For example, Hamstead Marshall is placed between Silchester and Mildenhall, while the Woodrows Farm (Compton), Bradfield and Maidenhatch Farm kilns are between Silchester and Dorchester-on-Thames. Although certain of these kilns have distinctive products, their distribution areas are very scanty and restricted or without any evidence at all. Although the overall evidence is slight, it seems possible that there were quite a number of small-scale production concerns providing small overlapping areas of rural markets with many of the coarser wares. The distribution of pottery tiles at this localized rural level is indicated in Sussex at Itchingfield.[31]

In the first and second centuries A.D. much coarse ware pottery seems to have been channelled through the towns. In many cases coarse ware kilns are located within easy reach of a town and the main area of distribution of the products appears to relate to that town's area of influence.[32] For example, Fig. 2.4 shows the distribution of Savernake ware. This pottery was made in the first and second centuries A.D. at a number of kilns in an area two miles south of Mildenhall (a town

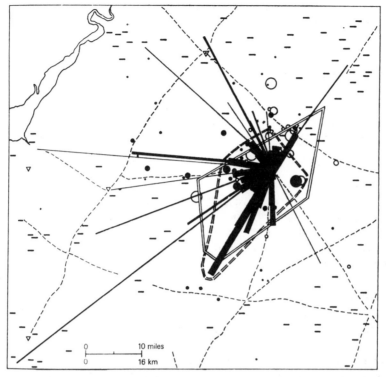

Fig. 2.4. The distribution of early Romano-British Savernake pottery. Radiating bars connect sites to the main marketing centre at Mildenhall. Their width and the size of the circles indicate the percentages of pottery found at the sites. Radiating bars: sites with more than 30 coarse ware sherds and only first and second centuries A.D. pottery. Filled circles: sites with more than 30 coarse ware sherds and more than first and second centuries A.D. pottery. Open circles: sites with less than 30 coarse ware sherds. Triangles: walled towns. Double dashed line encloses the area covered by Savernake ware lids. Continuous double line: the market area of Mildenhall predicted by the gravity model. Dashed lines: roads. Horizontal bars: contemporary sites without Savernake pottery.

walled in the fourth century). The main distribution of the products is the localized area around Mildenhall, and this area appears to correspond with Mildenhall's probable market or service area as predicted by Reilly's breaking point formula derived from the gravity model.[33]

A further example is provided by the distribution of Malvernian pottery.[34] In the second century A.D. a centre in Malvern area, but whose exact location is as yet unknown, was producing a number of types distinctive in shape and fabric. The area in which sites with the highest percentages of these products are found includes both the presumed kiln centre and the town of Worcester, while high percentages are also found in and near the town at Kenchester. It is also of interest that the overall distribution of the pottery covers a very similar area to that covered by late-Iron-Age pottery manufactured in the same Malvern district.

There is thus evidence that Romano-British coarse ware kiln centres were often

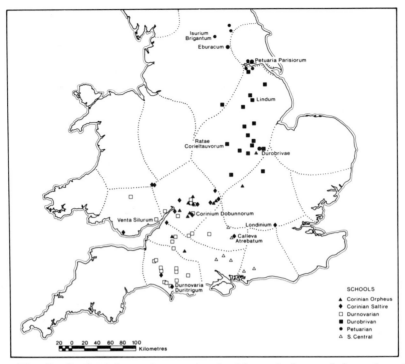

Fig. 2.5. The distribution of mosaics associated with particular workshops (or schools) in fourth-century Britain. Note the broad association between their distributions and the *civitates* (after D. J. Smith).

located in such a way that their products could be channelled through the existing marketing mechanisms centred on a nearby town. This may solely have involved sale in the town market, or in addition, sale in the surrounding minor markets connected to the main town market by traders or pedlars moving according to some periodic cycle of market days. But coarse pottery is only one of a number of goods supplied at the local level which could probably be obtained in both large and small towns. Other distributions in which walled towns appear central include that of the types of stamped tiles found around Cirencester and Gloucester.[35] The distribution of stone tiles made of Purbeck Limestone quarried in either the Portland or Swanage area[36] is not evenly distributed around the source but is found in the *civitas* capital at Dorchester and in the area around Winchester whither the stone may have been taken much of the way by boat.

Rather more specialist services, with less local demand, were only provided in the more important towns. An example is the expensive installation of mosiacs. Smith's examination of fourth-century mosaics in rich villas led to the conclusion that there is a 'tendency for certain subjects and themes to appear more or less localized' so that groups of related mosaics can be identified (see Fig. 2.5).[37] Each group is characterized by features which are not found, or are found significantly less often or in a significantly different form, elsewhere.[38] Smith suggests that this indicates 'schools' of mosaicists with their workshops at, for example, the cantonal capitals of Cirences-

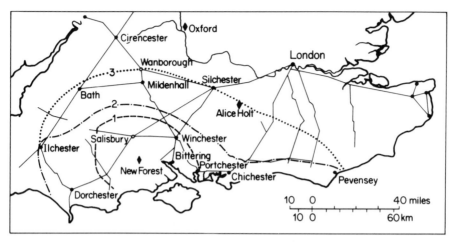

Fig. 2.6. The distribution of pottery from the New Forest kilns. *Source*: Fulford.

ter and Dorchester (Dorset). The mosaics produced by each 'school' are, in general, confined to the service areas around these towns as predicted by the gravity model and Thiessen polygons.[39] These two mosaic distributions correspond to the pre-Roman Durotrigian area and what can be ascertained as to the Dobunnic *civitas*. Although servicing factors are adequate to explain the distributions, and although discrete distributions only occur when the two schools are contemporary, an additional factor which may be relevant is the desire for the expression of a common group identity. This will be further discussed below.

The evidence discussed above demonstrates the importance of the towns as foci for the surrounding areas. In the later empire many large-scale concerns, producing both coarse pottery, and more valuable fine wares, were located away from the towns. The goods were probably channelled through the towns, but the production was not necessarily dependent on them and the distribution was on a wide scale, well beyond the area of influence of one town. Thus the large-scale fine pottery production centre at Oxford is located midway between the towns of Alchester and Dorchester-on-Thames and the pottery made there is found widely in southern England.[40] The fine ware products from the Nene Valley and the dispersal of coarse wares from Alice Holt (Farnham, Surrey), at least in the late third and fourth centuries A.D.,[41] reached far beyond the areas served by Water Newton and the centre at Neatham, near Farnham.

A good example of this type of large-scale production is provided by the detailed studies carried out on New Forest pottery.[42] The New Forest kilns produced a wide range of pottery types in the late third and fourth centuries A.D. and Fulford has shown that the distribution of each type varied considerably. In Fig. 2.6, contour 1 shows the limit of the coarse wares made at the kilns. Contour 2 shows the area reached by colour-coated and painted wares and *mortaria*. Particular types of colour-coated wares (bottles, jugs and beakers) reach contour 3, while beyond this line occasional finds of these types occur, but probably not as regularly traded items. These differences in distributions relate to the level of demand for the different products. Coarse wares, of lower value and high demand, were produced by neighbouring centres (for example, Alice Holt) within the total area covered by the New Forest fine wares. The latter, with less local demand, were produced by more widely spaced centres, such as at Oxford. The greater distribution of New Forest beakers occurs because the nearest competitor producing this form in quantity was not Oxford, but the Nene Valley centre.

The marketing patterns so far considered have been concerned with the civilian market in lowland Britain. Another class of distributions consists of those distorted by supply to the army. Most notable amongst these distributions is that of Black Burnished ware. This low technology coarse pottery was produced in two centres in Dorset and around the Thames estuary.[43] Because of its poor quality it would not normally be expected to achieve a large distribution but it seems to have captured the northern military market during the second century and is thence the principal product on Hadrian's Wall into the fourth century. This success is most likely to result from it being carried as a return cargo, or together with necessary supplies like grain. The distribution of *Classis Britannica* tiles shows the influence of non-civilian forces in the dispersal of another commodity.[44]

In most of the above discussion it has been assumed that straightforward market forces were the main determinants of the structure of the Romano-British economy. But the existence of identity-conscious tribes in some areas of Britain has been suggested in the immediately pre-Roman period, while the Roman *civitates* formalized less distinct groupings in other areas. It is possible that 'tribal' feelings had an effect on the distribution of goods and ideas in the Roman period. In many parts of Africa the pre-colonial groupings still affect the present-day dispersal of cultural items, while the identities imposed by outside administrations often came to take on an overtly expressed reality.[45] In this context it is of interest to examine the diffusion of religious cults in Roman Britain. 'It is possible to isolate a few local cults—a horse-cult among the Cornovii, a Mars-horse-man cult among the Catuvellauni, . . . the "Matres" and Genii Cucullati among the Dobunni.'[46] Other deities such as Mercury, Mars and Jupiter are more widespread, but in general there are major distinctions between the Dobunnic and Catuvellaunian *civitates* in religious evidence. For example, 'the Catuvellauni may have favoured the more Roman-influenced "sky-cults" whereas the Dobunni inclined more to local nature-gods and deities connected with fertility and prosperity'.[47] The greater familiarity with and acceptance of continental traditions seen in the south-east in the late Iron Age continues in the Roman period, and differences between 'tribal' groups are perhaps detected.

Similar non-market constraints seem to be isolated in many of the pottery distributions. Thus, the location of the Oxfordshire kilns on the boundary of three tribal areas allowed them to distribute their products into several different social networks,[48] whilst, for instance, the late Roman pottery of East Yorkshire is regionally distinctive and seems limited to the territory of the *Civitas Parisiorum*.[49] These examples lend support to the hypothesis that Roman Britain remained a society largely dominated by traditional regional social/political groupings and was not a free-market economy despite the widespread existence of coinage, which functioned to enable the state to pay its debts and collect taxation.[50]

Rural Settlement

Whilst the towns are the most obvious feature of Roman Britain, it seems unlikely that the urban population represented more than 10 per cent at most of the population of the province. In the countryside villas ('Romanized' rural habitations) are found widely in lowland Britain and to a limited extent in South Wales (see the distribution map provided by Rivet).[51] But throughout England and Wales the majority of farmsteads and hamlets followed the form common in the pre-Roman phase, as is only now being discovered through detailed survey and the expanding cover of aerial photography. The density of rural settlement sites suggests a densely occupied rural landscape, with an estimated 92,000 or so rural settlement sites on the basis of recent surveys, only about 700 of which are known villas.[52] These rural settlements exploited a patchwork of small field systems which, like the farmsteads, largely continued the Iron-Age pattern.

The villa sites seem to represent an elite element in the society of the province. Analyses of the villa distributions show that they are spatially closely related to the major towns.[53] This supports the hypothesis, based on classical sources, that these villas represent the rural seats of the landowning aristocracy that made up the ruling aristocracy of the *civitates*. In this respect the commonly observed pattern of villa sites being located on top of Iron-Age farmsteads reinforces the view that the ruling elite of the province were Romanized natives. The villas become more obvious and opulent in the later Roman period, probably as a result of the decline in the importance of the towns as centres for elite display. The elaboration of the villas with mosaics, hypocausts etc., suggests that they had become an alternative venue for status display after the third century.

Despite the un-Romanized character of many of the other settlements, which continue many of the characteristics of the later pre-Roman Iron Age, they should not be considered to have been poverty-stricken or solely based on subsistence agriculture. A variety of sources now suggest that Iron-Age and Romano-British agriculture was sophisticated and highly productive, with grain exports known from the later pre-Roman Iron Age to the fourth century A.D. It is significant in this respect that agricultural innovation seen through crop and equipment changes does not follow the Roman invasion of A.D. 43, but rather the existing systems of agriculture continued until a major period of change in the late third century.[54] These rural settlement sites also received a variety of Roman goods implying a function within the Roman economy, so we cannot simply dismiss them as irrelevant. We should rather see them as representing the agricultural backbone of the Romano-British economy. According to this hypothesis the absence of a high level of *Romanitas* seems to result from the social status and the lack of Roman aspirations of their inhabitants rather than from any absolute poverty. Two detailed regional surveys illustrate the character of the Romano-British countryside.

The distribution of sites in the Fenlands has been established from air photographs and field survey by Phillips *et al.*[55] As a result of the fieldwork, an individual site was defined as a 'scatter of ploughed domestic debris, often over an area of dark occupation soil'.[56] The sizes of these sites ranged from about 50 ft (15.2 m) long to 300 ft × 400 ft (91 × 122 m). Such surface spreads in the ploughsoil may represent farms

Fig. 2.7. Homesteads in north-west Wales. Morphological classes 1a, 1b, 1c and 1d. *Source:* C. A. Smith.

which sometimes clustered into settlements. The investigators confronted the problem common to many archaeologists of how groupings of sites can be distinguished. 'Although it is very convenient to regard the world's population as distributed in a series of discrete and isolated clusters . . . this is a somewhat artificial concept. Our definition of a cluster depends largely upon how we draw our boundaries, and how we define the term isolated'.[57] Sites were grouped into the same 'settlement' when separated by less than an arbitrary 500 ft (152 m), although support for this figure was obtained from other studies. An attempt was made at a more objective clustering of 'settlements' into 'complexes'. Histograms of the frequencies of distances between 'settlements' were examined. These frequency distributions appeared bimodal, suggesting that 'neighbouring settlements lie between 500 and 1500 ft of each other, more frequently than one would expect if they showed random scatter, giving a unimodal curve of spacing'.[58]

As a result of the analysis, the changing settlement pattern in the Fens could be demonstrated. In the first century A.D. there was a pattern of single farms and small hamlets. In the second century all the existing settlements grew bigger and 'new ones are added, often near an existing bunch'.[59] In the third and fourth centuries A.D. the percentage of people living in agglomerations increased. This trend towards larger and more agglomerations was seen as being possibly related to the changing drainage patterns and wetter conditions, although the pattern is now widely recognized in a variety of different landscape zones.

In a very different, 'un-Romanized' and upland area in north-west Wales, Smith has examined the enclosed hut groups which he terms homesteads of the Iron-Age and Romano-British periods.[60] Few of these have been excavated but many are well preserved and their stone walls can be planned by surface survey. Twenty-one attributes were used to describe these sites—for example, the area enclosed, thickness of enclosing wall, shape index (site area/area of smallest enclosing circle × 100), number of round huts. A Simple Matching Coefficient was employed in assessing the similarities between all pairs of sites and average link cluster analysis was used to group the homesteads. The Class I subdivisions resulting from this cluster analysis are shown in Fig. 2.7. But what do the differences between types mean? The houses or compartments within the homesteads appear, from what exavation has been carried out, to have been roofed. The high proportion of open to covered space in Class 1b is taken as possibly suggesting that these homesteads were mainly engaged in stock rearing. Rectangular and subrectangular buildings have been suggested by excavation to have been stalls for plough oxen or milch cattle. Therefore, 'Class Id could be interpreted as representing wealthy members of the community having small amounts of residential accommodation in relation to the other installations provided.'[61]

Routes and Networks

It is commonplace that the network of metalled roads in Roman Britain had a profound impact on the economic landscape. Settlements were attracted to the roads and goods reached further along these corridors of easier communication. We should not, however, over-estimate their economic importance in comparison with other modes of transport. Evidence from elsewhere in the Empire, and from Britain itself, demonstrates that many goods like pottery utilized the rivers and coasts for transport in preference to overland routes. The same pattern seems to dominate military supply, since legionary bases were generally located close to estuaries. Nonetheless, the road system represents a major innovation in the infrastructure. Dicks has used a graph-theoretic approach to examine the relationship between the road system and the provincial capital of London.[62] Dicks ordered the main roads on the basis of accessibility to London. Initially 'indifference points' were identified on the network that were equidistant from London. A hierarchy of roads was then established using the path ordering method shown in Fig. 2.8, and the ordered network is shown in Fig. 2.9. This pattern supports what is already known about the

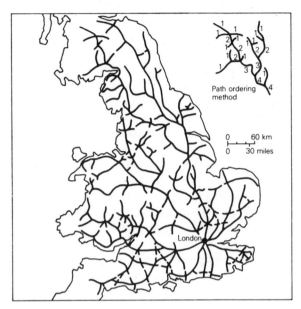

Fig. 2.8. The Roman road network centred on London. Roads are broken where alternative routes to London are estimated to be of equal length.

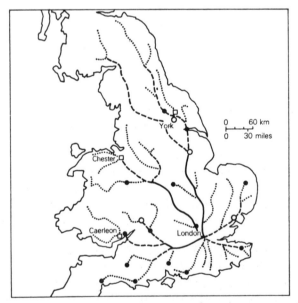

Fig. 2.9. The Roman road network ordered with reference to London, showing *coloniae* (open circles), cantonal capitals (filled circles) and fortresses (squares). Dotted lines: second order routes; dashed lines: third order routes; solid lines: fourth order routes.

road system. The three main arterial routes are identified, leading to the legionary fortresses at York, Chester and Caerleon reflecting the primacy of military needs in the original provision of roads. The *coloniae* are also linked to London by major routes. 'Of the cantonal capitals, eight are . . . on fourth or third order routes and eight on second order routes. The majority of the smaller settlements, together with the forts of the highland zone are related to the first order routes which have been omitted from figure [2.9] for the sake of clarity.'[63] Problems affecting this analysis include the incomplete evidence of the road network, while there has been adequate further discussion by Hindle, Hutchinson and Langton.[64] There is clearly scope here for comparisons with the literary sources which list the principal routes used by the Roman administration.[65]

In some areas, the growth of the road network can be compared with that proposed by Taaffe, Morrill and Gould for developing countries,[66] with a basic skeleton network penetrating the interior and thereby allowing the establishment of political control and the exploitation of primary products, followed later by a more intricate network of feeder roads extending outwards from nodes on the main lines of penetration. A similar sequence might be read into the pattern of road and villa development in the area to the west of the cantonal capital at Verulamium during the first and second centuries A.D. The first-century villas stand close to the arterial routes connecting the major nodes. 'All the known first-century villa sites were therefore able to transport surplus produce quickly to Verulamium'.[67] In the second century a new crop of villas emerged in the Chiltern valleys, possibly connected with the filling in of the road network although there is little reliable independent dating evidence for the roads. The end result was a pattern of villas spaced every $1\frac{1}{2}$ to 2 miles along the valleys.

Conclusion

As we understand the province at present, it remained a comparatively under-developed system, where the movement of goods and the development of urban and rural patterns was dominated by social relations which remained embedded within a fundamentally Iron-Age structure. This structure remained central to the development of Roman Britain through to the fourth century A.D. There was a major refocusing of the system during the third century during which we see an increase in the relative importance of small towns, villas and rurally based industry at the expense of the major towns. This seems to relate to the declining importance of the *civitas* centres, and throws the focus back on to the rural areas which had also been central in the late Iron Age.

A fuller assessment of the influence of tribal groupings on Romano-British marketing patterns, the growth of towns and the development of the road network would benefit from the application of more sophisticated techniques of spatial analysis and the use of a wider range of explanatory models. It is clear from the above account that large amounts of data could be collected which would allow detailed analysis of the shifting patterns. Such work is underway and is helping Romano-British studies break out of a narrow historical approach so that they can contribute more to our understanding of wider problems of development, town growth, early economies and human relationships.

References

1. J. S. Wacher, *The Towns of Roman Britain*, (London, 1974), p. 13.
2. S. S. Frere, 'The origins of small towns', in W. Rodwell and T. Rowley (eds.), *Small Towns of Roman Britain*, British Archaeological Reports, **15** (1975), p. 4.
3. S. S. Frere, *Britannia: a History of Roman Britain*, (3rd edn.) (London, 1987), P. Salway, *Roman Britain*, (Oxford, 1981).
4. D. P. S. Peacock, *Pottery in the Roman World*, (London, 1982); R. Reece, *Coinage in Roman Britain*, (London, 1987); M. Millett, 'Town and Country: a review of some material evidence', in D. Miles (ed.), *The Romano-British Countryside*, British Archaeological Reports, **103** (1982); M. Millett, *The Romanization of Britain*, (Cambridge, 1990).
5. C. C. Haselgrove, 'Wealth, prestige and power; the dynamics of late Iron Age political centralization in South East England', in C. Renfrew and S. Shennan (eds.), *Ranking, Resource and Exchange*, (Cambridge, 1982); S. Macready and F. H. Thompson (eds.), *Channel Trade between Gaul and Britain in the Pre-Roman Iron Age*, (London, 1984).
6. B. W. Cunliffe, *Hengistbury Head, Dorset, Vol. 1*, (Oxford, 1987); A. Fitzpatrick, 'The distribution of Dressel 1 amphorae in NW Europe, *Oxford Jnl. Archaeology*, **4**(3), (1985), 305–40.
7. B. W. Cunliffe, 'Relations between Britain and Gaul in the First Century B.C. and the Early First Century A.D.' in S. Macready and F. H. Thompson, *Channel Trade between Gaul and Britain*.
8. J. R. Collis, *Oppida: Earliest Towns North of the Alps*, (Sheffield, 1984).
9. C. C. Haselgrove, *Iron Age Coinage in South East England: the Archaeological Context*, British Archaeological Reports, **174** (1987).
10. P. J. Reynolds, *Iron Age Farm, the Butser Experiment*, (London, 1979).
11. B. W. Cunliffe, *Iron Age Communities in Britain*, (2nd edn.) (London, 1978).
12. J. S. Wacher, *The Towns of Roman Britain*, (London, 1974), p. 25; M. Millett, 'Forts and the origins of towns', in A. King and T. F. C. Blagg (eds.), *Military and Civilian in Roman Britain*, British Archaeological Reports, **136** (1984).
13. B. W. Cunliffe, *The Regni*, (London, 1973), p. 20.
14. Suetonius, *Lives of the Twelve Caesars, Vespasian*.
15. A. L. F. Rivet, *Town and Country in Roman Britain*, (2nd edn.) (London, 1964), Fig. 9.
16. *Ibid.*, pp. 131–4.
17. A. L. F. Rivet and C. Smith, *The Place-names of Roman Britain*, (London, 1979); C. C. Haselgrove, *Iron Age Coinage in South East England: the Archaeological Context*, British Archaeological Reports, **174** 52–4.
18. Rivet, *Town and Country in Roman Britain*, p. 140.
19. M. H. Fried, 'On the concept of "tribe"', in *Essays on the Problem of Tribe*, American Ethnological Society (1968), pp. 3–22.
20. P. Marsden, *Roman London*, (London, 1980).
21. M. Millett, *The Romanization of Britain*, (Cambridge, 1990), Chapter 6.
22. W. Rodwell and T. Rowley (eds.), *The Small Towns of Roman Britain*, British Archaeological Reports, **15** (1975).
23. B. Burnham, 'The morphology of Romano-British Small Towns', *Archaeological Jnl.*, **144** (1987), pp. 156–90.
24. B. Burnham, 'The origins of Romano-British Small Towns', *Oxford Jnl. Archaeology*, **5**(2) (1986), 185–203
25. I. Hodder, 'The spatial distribution of Romano-British small towns', in Rodwell and Rowley, *Small Towns of Roman Britain*, pp. 67–74.
26. J. Maloney and B. Hobley (eds.), *Roman Urban Defences in the West*, (London, 1983).

27. A. H. M. Jones, 'Taxation in antiquity', in P. A. Brunt (ed.), *The Roman Economy*, (Oxford, 1974).

28. I. Hodder and M. Millett, 'Romano-British Villas and Towns; a systematic analysis', *World Archaeology*, **12**(1), (1980), pp. 69–76.

29. Jones, 'Taxation in antiquity'.

30. A. P. Detsicas (ed.), *Current Research in Romano-British Coarse Pottery*, (London, 1973), J. Dore and K. Green (eds.), *Roman Pottery Studies in Britain and Beyond*, British Archaeological Reports, **s30** (1977); P. Arthur and G. Marsh (eds.), *Early Fine Ware in Roman Britain*, British Archaeological Reports, **57** (1978); A. C. and A. S. Anderson (eds.), *Roman Pottery Research in Britain and North-West Europe*, British Archaeological Reports, **s123** (1981).

31. T. K. Green, 'Roman tileworks at Itchingfield, *Sussex Archaeological Collections*, **108**, (1970), pp. 23–8.

32. I. Hodder, 'Some marketing models for Romano-British coarse pottery', *Britannia*, **5** (1974), pp. 340–59.

33. W. J. Reilly, *The Law of Retail Gravitation*, (New York, 1931); I. Hodder, 'The distribution of Savernake Ware', *Wiltshire Archaeological and Natural History Magazine*, **69** (1974), pp. 67–84.

34. D. P. S. Peacock, 'Romano-British pottery production in the Malvern district of Worcestershire', *Transactions of the Worcestershire Archaeological Society*, **1** (1967), pp. 15–28.

35. A. D. McWhirr and D. Vyner, 'The production and distribution of tiles in Roman Britain', *Britannia*, **9** (1978), pp. 359–77.

36. J. H. Williams, 'Roman building materials in south-east England', *Britannia*, **2** (1971), p. 178.

37. D. J. Smith, 'The mosaic pavements', in A. L. F. Rivet (ed.), *The Roman Villa in Britain*, (London, 1969), pp. 71–126; D. J. Smith 'Roman mosaics in Britain: a synthesis', in F. Campanati (ed.), *Atti del III Colloquia Internazionale sul Mosaico Antico, Ravenna, 1980*, (Ravenna, 1984).

38. Smith, 'The mosaic pavements', p. 95.

39. Hodder, 'The spatial distribution of Romano-British Small Towns', p. 68.

40. C. J. Young, *The Roman Pottery of the Oxford Region*, British Archaeological Reports, **43** (1977).

41. M. Lyne and R. Jefferies, *The Alice Holt/Farnham Roman Pottery Industry*, (London, 1979).

42. M. G. Fulford, *New Forest Roman Pottery*, British Archaeological Reports, **17** (1975).

43. D. F. Williams, 'The Romano-British Black Burnished Industry', in D. P. S. Peacock (eds), *Pottery and Early Commerce*, (London, 1977), pp. 163–220.

44. G. Brodribb, 'Stamped tiles of the "Classis Britannica"', *Sussex Archaeological Collections*, **107** (1969), pp. 102–5.

45. Fried, 'On the concept of "tribe"'.

46. M. J. Green, *A Corpus of Religious Material from the Civilian Areas of Roman Britain*, British Archaeological Reports, **24** (1978), p. 78.

47. *Ibid.*

48. Millett, *The Romanization of Britain*, Chapter 7.

49. J. Evans, *Aspects of Later Roman Pottery, Assemblages in Northern England*, (unpublished Bradford University Ph.D. thesis (1985).

50. R. Reece, *Coinage in Roman Britain*, (London, 1987).

51. Rivet, *The Roman Villa in Britain*, Fig. 5. 6.

52. Millett, *The Romanization of Britain*, Chapter 8.

53. I. Hodder and M. Millett, 'Romano-British villas and towns: a systematic study', *World Archaeology*, **12**(1) (1980), pp. 69–76.

54. M. K. Jones, 'The development of crop husbandry', in G. Dimbleby and M. K. Jones (eds.), *The Environment of Man; the Iron Age to the Anglo-Saxon Period*, British Archaeological Reports, **87,** (1981).

55. C. W. Phillips (ed.), *The Fenland in Roman Times*, (London, 1970).

56. *Ibid.*, p. 49.

57. P. Haggett, *Locational Analysis in Human Geography*, (London, 1965), p. 100.

58. Phillips, *The Fenland in Roman Times*, p. 57.
59. *Ibid.*
60. C. A. Smith 'A morphological analysis of late prehistoric and Romano-British settlements in north-west Wales', *Proceedings of the Prehistoric Society,* **40** (1974), pp. 157–69.
61. *Ibid.*
62. T. R. B. Dicks, 'Network analysis and historical geography', *Area,* **4** (1972), pp. 4–9.
63. *Ibid*, pp. 7–8.
64. B. P. Hindle, P. Hutchinson and J. Langton, 'Network and Roman roads, Comments', *Area* **4** (1972), pp. 137–8, 138–9, 279–80.
65. A. L. F. Rivet and C. Smith, *The Place-names of Roman Britain,* (London, 1979).
66. E. J. Taaffe, R. L. Morrill and P. R. Gould, 'Transport expansion in underdeveloped countries: a comparative analysis', *Geographical Review,* **103** (1963), pp. 503–29.
67. K. Branigan, 'Romano-British rural settlement in the western Chilterns', *Archaeological Jnl.,* **124** (1967), p. 136.

3

Celts, Saxons and Scandinavians

G. R. J. Jones

According to the British monk Gildas writing in the early sixth century, Britain was already an old and well-settled country where even the 'agreeably set hills' were 'excellent for vigorous agriculture'.[1] Moreover it contained no less than 28 cantons with central places, or 'cities (*civitates*)', and was well equipped with fortifications. Nevertheless, the period between the departure of the Roman legions and the coming of the Normans was one of the most formative in our history. It witnessed the subjugation of the Britons at the hands of the incoming Saxons and later, in the north, the settlement of the Scandinavians. In the same period the territorial foundations of the economy were strengthened. All these were momentous developments but their elucidation is fraught with difficulty, depending as it must on the integration of archaeological evidence and the testimony of place-names with the sparse record of written sources.

The Phase of Transition and the Coming of the Saxons

Between Roman Britain and Saxon England there was neither a sudden nor a complete break. Such at least is the implication of some of the events recorded, albeit in a confused fashion, in the fullest narrative about the coming of the Saxons, that presented by Gildas.

In the face of continued onslaughts by 'the Scots from the north-west and the Picts from the north', together with the final withdrawal of the army of the usurper Constantine III, the rulers of the *civitates* were told by the rightful Emperor Honorius in the famous rescript of 410 to look to their own defences. Yet, other sources indicate that in Britain between 410 and mid-century, Britain appears to have been divided between those who wished to see the restoration of imperial power and those who preferred independence; hence, the missions of Germanus to south-eastern Britain in 429 and *c.* 435 to counter widespread heresy among a large wealthy Christian humanist faction,[2] and the unsuccessful appeal for aid against barbarian assaults made by some Britons to the General Aetius, probably in 446.

Meanwhile the Scots and Picts seized 'the whole of the extreme north of the island from its inhabitants, right up to the wall'. Thus 'our citizens abandoned the "cities" and the high wall'; irretrievably scattered, they resorted to looting each other, for 'the whole region (*regio*)' came to be deprived of food save that provided by the art of the huntsman. A 'dreadful and notorious famine' forced many Britons to give in to the plunderers but others 'kept fighting back, basing themselves in the mountains, caves, heaths and thorny thickets'. After many years they achieved victory and the enemy withdrew. In the respite from devastation the island was 'flooded with abundance of goods that no previous age had known' but the kings then anointed became tyrants. Subsequently, towards mid-century it would appear, there were rumours of further invasions by the peoples of the north bent on 'settlement from one end of the region to the other'; and a deadly plague killed so many that the living could not bury all the dead. Thus 'all the councillors together with the proud tryant', probably the over-king Vortigern, stupidly decided to invite Saxon troops into the island in order to repel the northern invaders. To this end, Gildas claims, three boat-loads of troops were settled on the east side of the island. These defenders prospered and a second larger troop followed.[3] The defenders, however, complained that their monthly allowances of provisions were inadequate and became plunderers. They spread devastation 'from sea to sea', laid low all the major towns (*coloniae*) by the repeated battering of rams, and killed 'all the inhabitants—church leaders, priests and people alike'. The area thus devastated although not named by Gildas appar-ently lay in the north but to the west of the Saxon lands. Besides its fortified settlements it contained an important ecclesiastical centre with stone-built towers. The plunderers may then have turned south and pillaged the Midlands. Yet there were survivors; of these some, as the price of food, surrendered to the enemy to be slaves forever; some emigrated beyond the sea; but others remained 'in their own land', trusting their lives to dense forests and *fortified hills*.[4]

After a time when the cruel plunderers had gone home, apparently to the north-east of the island, the Britons led by Ambrosius Aurelianus won a victory. There ensued a period of indecisive warfare until a great victory was won by the Britons at the *siege* of Mount Badon *c.* 595. The scene of the encounter has been variously identified but is most probably the hill-fort of Liddington Castle in hill country near an important junction of Roman roads some 20 miles south-east of Cirencester.[5] Nevertheless, wherever it took place, this British victory served to stem further Saxon advances for 44 years, until the time when Gildas was writing. Unfortunately, however, civil wars continued between contending kings and thus 'the "cities (*civitates*)" of our land are not populated even now as they once were; right to the present they are deserted, in ruins and unkempt'.[6]

Yet the presence of kings, however tyrannical, denotes the survival of more than the rudiments of administrative and fiscal organization. To the west, British kings, claiming to be the legitimate heirs of Roman authority, but governing their subjects by ancestral Celtic custom, put armies into the field and even made gifts to the Church. Of five such kings castigated as sinners by Gildas, three are clearly recognizable as the rulers of Dumnonia, Dyfed, and Gwynedd (Fig. 3.1). A fourth king can perhaps be identified, from his 'Bear's Stronghold' at Dinarth, as the ruler of Ceredigion; and the fifth king can be identified probably as a descendant of Ambrosius Aurelianus ruling either in Wroxeter or in Cirencester. In the event there were also other unnamed smaller kingdoms, like Ergyng whose name harked back to the Roman town of Ariconium, and gave rise to that of the district of Archenfield.[7]

In the north there was at least one major kingdom, probably not named by Gildas so as to prevent identification of the tyrant in whose kingdom he was writing;[8] and

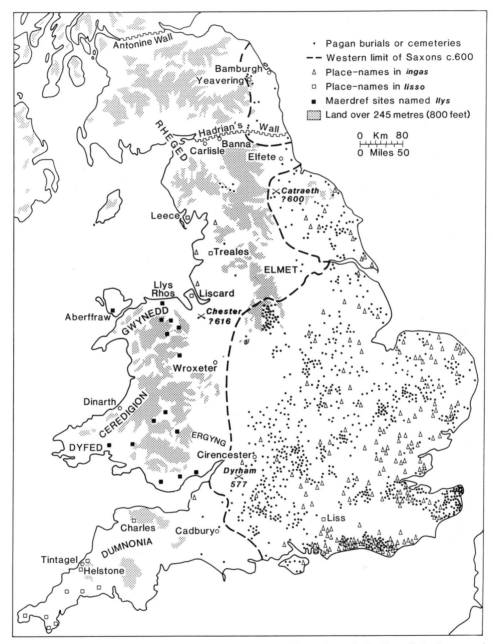

Fig. 3.1. The Saxons in southern Britain *c.* 600. (Based on Campbell, Ekwall, Jackson and Smith.)

since he records that 'our citizens' could not gain access to the martyrs' graves at St Albans and Caerleon, because of 'the unhappy partition with the barbarians', his 'region (*regio*)' was probably in the north.

Like the late Roman province of Valentia, a single unit extending from sea to sea but with its capital at York, this northern 'region' came to form one kingdom, probably ruled by Coel Hen during the first half of the fifth century.[9] Coel was possibly 'the proud tyrant' who, after the council seemingly held at York, invited three boat-loads of Saxons to settle on the eastern side of the island, probably on the Yorkshire Wolds. This single northern kingdom was later subdivided among Coel's many descendants into lesser kingdoms which included among others York, Elmet and Rheged. Of these the largest was Elmet which originally appears to have extended from the Don in the south to Elfete in Durham (Fig. 3.1).

Bede, writing much later *c.* 731, used the narrative of Gildas but added further details such as the approximate dates 449–455 for the coming of 'the Angles or Saxons' and one 'about forty-four years later' for the siege of Mount Badon.[10] Bede implied that the three boat-loads of troops invited by 'the proud tyrant' came to Kent, a suggestion possibly intended to justify the later Kentish royal line's rights of overlordship of the southern kingdoms of England.[11] He also recorded that hordes of other newcomers from 'three very powerful Germanic tribes, the Saxons, Angles and Jutes' settled in different parts of southern and eastern Britain. Even before their arrival, however, these tribal groupings were already to some degree mixed, but the claim that they came in large numbers is justified by the archaeological evidence of pagan burials from the early fifth century onwards, unless that is, substantial sections of the surviving British population were very rapidly converted to Anglo-Saxon burial customs.[12]

The Emergence of the English Kingdoms

The Saxons, as all the newcomers were known to the Britons, had resumed their advance before the middle of the sixth century, possibly by taking advantage of the ravages caused by the plague of 549.[13] Meanwhile the many kingdoms of England had already begun to take shape. The earliest to emerge were those of the south and east: Kent, Sussex, Essex, East Anglia and Lindsey. These kingdoms were hemmed in behind interior forest or fen. For the future, however, the more significant powers were those of Wessex, Mercia and Northumbria, all kingdoms with a frontier against the Britons of the west and north, because these had more to offer, in loot and land, to the noble warriors of heroic society. These major English kingdoms battled long against each other and the Britons for supremacy, a struggle which carried Saxon colonists to the foothills of the Highland Zone by the middle years of the seventh century. Such events, and notably the expansion of Wessex, are fitfully outlined by the Anglo-Saxon Chronicle (written *c.* 892);[14] but for a more detailed impression of the spread of the Saxons as a whole we must turn to the testimony of pagan burials accompanied by grave goods (Fig. 3.1).[15] These belong to the age before the conversion of the Saxons to Christianity, a process initiated by Augustine's mission to Kent in 597, and which led to the conversion of every English king by 670.

The extension of English rule appears to have been achieved by an incorporative process whereby pre-existing British kingdoms were absorbed *en bloc* into the expanding English kingdoms. Even in the east the absence of pagan cemeteries around St Albans until the seventh century probably means that the surrounding area remained under British rule until the 570s.[16] Further west, as the Anglo-Saxon Chronicle records, when three British kings lost their lives at the battle of Dyrham in 577 the Wessex victors captured the three cities (*ceastra; civitates*) of Bath, Cirencester and Gloucester,[17] with their dependent territories, apparently three petty kingdoms. Again both Deira and Bernicia in the north had been British kingdoms before they were taken over by the Anglians. Following the defeat of the Britons of the north at Catraeth (Catterick or more probably the site of Richmond) *c.* 600 the two kingdoms were united in a powerful Northumbria whose forces inflicted another major defeat on the Britons at Chester *c.* 616; and shortly afterwards the once powerful British kingdom of Elmet, already confined to the area south of the Wharfe (Fig. 3.2), was occupied by Edwin, king of the Northumbrians, and its British ruler, Ceredig son of Gwallog, expelled.[18] According to Bede, Edwin brought under English rule even Anglesey, then part of Gwynedd, as well as the Isle of Man, 'and ruled over all the inhabitants of Britain, English and Britons alike, except for Kent only'.[19] Cadwallon of Gwynedd, however, rebelled and with the assistance of Penda of Mercia campaigned in the area around Elmet until Edwin was defeated at Hatfield in 633. Like Gwallog of Elmet before him Cadwallon claimed the *imperium* of Britain,[20] but with his defeat by Oswald of Northumbria at Heavenfield near Hadrian's Wall in 634, the last attempt by a British king to dispute the supremacy of English rule in Britain came to an end.

Thereafter the Britons of the north were severed from their fellows in Wales, at least by overland links, in the same way that the Britons of Dumnonia had earlier been isolated by the expansion of Wessex. The Britons of Wales were marked off as a separate people in their western strongholds and in the late eighth century were confined behind the defensive dyke ascribed to the Mercian Offa (Figs. 3.1 and 3.3).

Early Social Organization

The social structure of the Welsh kingdoms which peristed behind Offa's Dyke is perhaps our surest guide to the social order which had once existed within the British petty kingdoms incorporated into the expanding English kingdoms. Within the typical early Welsh petty kingdom, embracing some 300 square miles, the old social order was essentially hierarchical with the king at the apex followed in descending order by his officers, including the reeve, then the nobles and freemen and, at the lowest levels, the bondmen and slaves who supported the higher echelons. Already by Gildas' day the larger kingdoms like Gwynedd had absorbed most of the old petty kingdoms but the latter retained their identity as coherent entities and emerged in later centuries as administrative hundreds. Within the typical hundred there would be two or three administrative neighbourhoods (commotes) and in each, reflecting the social order, was a hierarchy of landed estates. The most important was that of the king, a multiple estate comprising his court (*llys*) with its hall or palace, arable demesne lands for the sustenance of this court in an adjoining reeve's vill or township (*maerdref*), distant royal pastures and hunting grounds, as well as a network of satellite hamlets spread over wide areas of countryside. The hamlets were occupied in the main by bondmen who practised mixed farming on the lands they held from their lord, the king. In return they paid the king food rents and performed various services including the tasks of cultivating the king's demesnes, constructing his court with its complex of buildings, creating encampments for his warriors, and helping with the hunt. Nobles in return for rents and services, principally military, held lesser estates but even these merit the designation multiple estate for they contained a multiplicity of satellite hamlets, occupied by bond undertenants, and scattered farms inhabited by dependent freemen. It was the king's court, however, which served as the main local focus of early Welsh society. Administered by a reeve it was visited periodically by the king and his retinue of warriors. Here the scattered inhabitants of the neighbourhood looked for government and here too they paid their dues in accordance with a complex system of assessment, based on sharelands, each notionally the area needed to support a freeman and his family.[21] Gildas implied that extensive lordship in such neighbourhoods, organized not only for production but also for the economic exploitation of integrated upland and lowland resources, already existed in the sixth century by his reference to 'mountains especially suited to varying the pasture for animals'.[22] Of these Welsh courts one of the earliest to be recorded appears to have been named Llys Rhos, in the Hundred of Rhos in Gwynedd. It was at this court, probably midway between the local *maerdref* and the Iron-Age hill-fort of Dinorben, that Maelgwn of Gwynedd, one of the five kings castigated by Gildas, died of the plague in 549.[23] Even more celebrated was the court, adjoining the *maerdref* at Aberffraw proper in the Hundred of Aberffraw, which had probably become the *llys* of Maelgwn's forebears when they expelled the Irish from Anglesey in the early sixth century. Located some two miles from Llangadwaladr, the monastic church endowed by Cadwaladr son of Cadwallon which served as the burial place of the dynasty in the seventh century, Llys Aberffraw was the traditional capital of Gwynedd to which, according to early Welsh verse, the dismembered head of Edwin of Northumbria was brought after the battle of Hatfield in 633.[24]

The *llys* (court) with its *maerdref* (reeve's vill) and satellite hamlets was a characteristic feature of other early Welsh kingdoms (Fig. 3.1). That similar estates existed within the early British kingdoms in territories which became English is implied by settlements bearing names in *lisso*, the British word from which *llys* was derived.[25] Among them in Dumnonia was Helstone, the settlement of the *hen-lys* (old court), whose name indicates that it was the focus of a multiple estate for which Tintagel, periodically occupied from at least 450 to 600, was probably the stronghold of the ruler and his retinue.[26] Towards the eastern limits of Dumnonia the Iron-Age hill-fort of Cadbury, re-fortified between 470 and 530, and repaired in the late sixth century, contained a hall, which although not recorded as part of a *llys* was probably the royal British focus of a multiple estate exploiting a variety of surrounding environments.[27] Still further east, Liss (Hampshire) refers to a court and indicates the late survival on the western fringe of the Weald of an organized British estate; this subsequently formed part of the Out-Hundred of Odiham, a component of a large English royal estate whose focus was at Odiham proper some 15 miles to the north.

Multiple estates closely resembling those of Wales, alike in terms of their structure and their dues, were to be found in many parts of early England. Such were the districts known at a later date as lathes in Kent, sokes in the midlands, and as 'shires' in Northumbria. As in Wales the basis of assessment was normally the holding of one free family but in England such a unit was known usually as a hide.[28] Among estates of this kind was that of Selsey in Sussex where, according to Eddi, the biographer of Bishop Wilfrid, writing *c.* 720, King Æthelwealh in the 680s granted his own vill where he resided to be the seat of a bishopric, adding to it afterwards 87 hides. As Bede recorded in 731 the king had given the land together with the men, among whom were no less than 250 male and female slaves. These men, as a later corrupt charter revealed, appear to have dwelt in at least 15 settlements, some near Selsey, some east of Chichester, and still others over 15 miles from Selsey on the flanks of the South Downs.[29]

At the north-eastern extremity of England, near Bamburgh, the capital of Bernicia, was the royal estate of Islandshire which extended from the mainland to the tidal island of Lindisfarne; but its headquarters (*urbs regis*), with a resident reeve, was still known to Eddi *c.* 720, by the British name of Broninis, literally 'Breast-island', with *bron* meaning the island's source of nourishment.[30] Some 15 miles to the south-west was Yeavering the royal vill (*villa regia*) recorded by Bede after its abandonment, but where earlier in the reign of Edwin crowds had flocked from the surrounding settlements to be converted to Christianity. Here, as excavation has revealed, was a centre of authority, with a succession of great halls and forts as well as other structures including a place of assembly capable, when at its maximum *c.* 627, of accommodating about 320 people. As is implied by its British name of Gefrin (Hill of the goats), applied to the adjoining hill which was surmounted by an Iron-Age hill-fort, Yeavering had earlier been a British focus.[31]

The dues imposed on such royal estates occasionally bore names indicative of a British origin, as for example with *metreth*, the render paid for moving cattle on the estates of Durham.[32] Again, Welsh ale, among other products of mixed farming, was a normal component of the food rents paid to the king from estates of ten hides in Wessex during the late seventh century. Welsh ale, indicative of British skill in arable farming as well as brewing, was recorded as far east as Lympne on the edge of Romney Marsh (Kent) in 806, and at Sempringham (Lincolnshire) near the Fens in 852.[33] These identities of terminology and usage as between England and Wales can hardly be ascribed either to parallel evolution or to diffusion. Instead they must be attributed to a common origin for the socio-economic system of the multiple estate in the period before the coming of the Saxons. Among these common usages no doubt was the duty of building encampments, and constructing or re-furbishing fortifications, for a striking feature of multiple estates in northern, southern and western England, as in Wales, is the frequency with which their focal settlements are located near hill-forts. The chief sufferers from the Saxon conquest, as the Chronicle makes evident, were British kings and nobles. On the other hand, more lowly Britons are likely to have survived, for without their labour the conquerors could not have exploited the estates seized from the displaced British nobles. The decline and fall of the Roman villa was linked to a general economic and social collapse, accompanied by the elimination of the villa proprietors, or their flight to the west; hence, in Britain the loss of all specific villa names, save four.[34] Nevertheless, in parts of Britain like the Cotswolds some kind of rural life based on the villas could well have continued for at least two centuries after 400. There is also the possibility that newcomers either took over villa estates after a very brief abandonment or were deliberately planted on such estates, perhaps under British direction in the fifth century and by Anglo-Saxon leaders in the sixth.[35] Moreover, abandonment of a Roman villa probably did not entail the abandonment of its arable land; instead this is likely to have remained in continued use, albeit from another centre and under new direction. Yet, attached to the former villas were dependants in outlying settlements, part of a complex of socio-economic relationships increasingly seigneurial in character.

Some Saxon immigrants no doubt secured for themselves substantial rural holdings. If these or their heirs prospered they would have formed an upper crust supported by their own dependants; but if these did not prosper they would lose their freedom and become the dependants of more powerful men. Indeed, it is possible that, as in the Celtic west so in England, whole kindred groups could descend to servile status if all kinsmen could not be provided with a standard holding;[36] for the evidence of early laws makes it clear that the English countryside in the seventh century was largely dominated by nobles or thegns holding their own lands, demesnes cultivated for them partly by slaves and partly by tenants with servile antecedents. Nobles like these held inherited lands, but in addition would have acquired lands as a result of royal favour. Their male heirs would have succeeded to the inalienable heritable lands, but even if sons succeeded to the acquired lands these would have been held only precariously in return for service to the king, and royal grants could be revoked.[37] At first only the church could gain by charter permanent endowments carrying full possessionary rights, and not until the late eighth century did kings grant lands to laymen in hereditary possession.[38] With the proliferation of such permanent endowments, initially to the Church, and later directly to laymen, royal multiple estates could be so reduced that only a few satellite settlements would have remained as dependencies of the estate focus, the king's vill or settlement (*cyninges tūn*). The latter, managed by royal reeve, would normally have retained its function as the administrative centre for the encompassing hundred.

The survival on some estates of British dependants would help to explain the persistence not only of names in *lisso*, but also of other British names like Andover later the focus of a multiple estate. Other names indicative of early organized and settled communities are those in *ecles*, meaning church. In most cases *ecles* should be regarded as a loan from Welsh, but the three examples of Eccles noted in south-east England, one in Kent and two in East Anglia, probably represent a very early borrowing direct from Latin into Old English before 500. The majority of these names, however, are found in north-western England where they represent a borrowing after 600 through the intermediary of surviving Welsh speech.[39] There are, moreover, some settlements, often satellites of multiple estates, which bear names indicating that they had once been inhabited by Britons, among them Bretton (*Bretta-tūn*, settlement of the Britons) in Derbyshire, and Walton (*Weala-tūn*, settlement of the Welsh) in Essex. A Walton of the same meaning together with Tidover (Tuda's bank), a neighbouring settlement recorded by Eddi as the abode of Britons in late-seventh-century Yorkshire, formed part of a small multiple estate severed from a larger royal estate so that it could be granted to Bishop Tuda *c.* 663–4.[40] Within the limits of the former kingdom of Elmet as it was *c.* 600 there were several large estates embracing numerous dependencies, some with names indicative of British occupation. Thus among the numerous satellites of Sherburn-in-Elmet was Bretton-in-Elmet. Again, among the widely scattered dependencies of Wakefield were no less than four such settlements, West Bretton, Walton, Walshaw (copse of the Welsh) and Upper Cumberworth (Welshman's homestead), as well as Eccleshill whose name betokens the presence of a British church somewhere within the confines of this estate (Fig. 3.2).[41]

The claim that the settlement of England was organized by large estates at an early date accords well with recent interpretations of English place-names. At first it was argued that the oldest identifiable English place-names were those in *ingas*. When suffixed to a personal name the Old English *ingas* denotes the followers or dependants of the person named so that Reading, for example, means 'the followers or dependants of Reada'. It was claimed that there was a close relationship between these place-names and Anglo-Saxon pagan burial sites. There are, it is true, occasional coincidences between the two, as at Reading, later the focus of a royal estate, but given that both occur in substantial numbers in the same southern and eastern areas of England, these coincidences are comparatively rare. Thus it was later argued that *ingas* names do not go back to the earliest immigration phase of the Anglo-Saxon settlements. Instead it was claimed that, in general, they belong to a phase of internal colonization when the Anglo-Saxons were settling lands avoided by their immigrant forebears and their burial places were no longer pagan cemeteries but Christian churchyards.[42] No consideration was given to the possibility that names in *ingas* could represent the early take-over of wide pre-existing estates and that subsequent fragmentation of these estates had obscured the spatial relationship between estate centres and pagan cemeteries.[43]

The gap left by the revised dating of *ingas* names was filled, in part, by the demonstration that the Old English *wīchām* was used by the earliest Germanic immigrants. This compound of *wīc*, derived from the Latin *vicus* (vill), and the Old English *hām* (homestead), denoted a small settlement bearing a special relationship to a Romano-British settlement.[44] Its presence was deemed to indicate not only some direct connection between the Britons and the Saxons, but also the early date of *hām*, whereas *ingahām*, in which the genitive plural of *inga* is compounded with *hām*, was deemed to be later. A recent detailed investigation of the relationship between place-names and every fifth-century archaeological site in the areas of Saxon and Jutish settlement in southern England has, however, cast serious doubt on the theory that *hām* names indicate primary settlement and *ingas* secondary settlement. This investigation has also revealed that, if any correlation is to be found between types of place-names and the earliest Saxon settlements in southern England it is to be found in the broad category of place-names with a pre-English element, including *wīc*, other Latin loan-words, British river names and some of those in Old English *weala* indicative of Welshmen.[45] Nevertheless in Anglian areas place-names in *ingahām* and *hām*, frequently occur close to, or in association with, Roman villas,[46] and with forts. Among numerous examples are Hovingham (Yorkshire) where the villa was some 500 yards from a church which has recently revealed evidence of a late-fifth-century structure; Bramham, in the part of Elmet which was most closely settled in Roman times, where the church in its huge oval churchyard was possibly the *llan* (church enclosure) of Llan Lleynnog, the church endowed by Lleynnog, father of Gwallog, in the late sixth century; and Kirkham (Lancashire) near a Roman fort and the

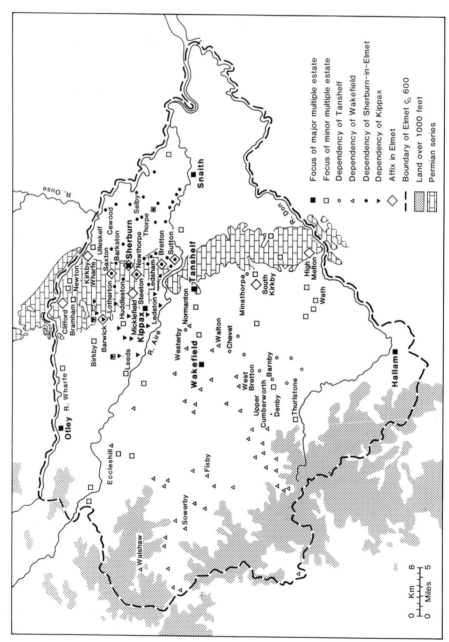

Fig. 3.2. Multiple estates, as recorded during the eleventh century, within the early-seventh-century limits of the British kingdom of Elmet.

significantly named Treales (*tref* or vill of the *llys* or court).[47] Such diagnostic place-names often occur in meaningful association in multiple estates, as in the Hundred of Weighton on the flank of the Yorkshire Wolds, the one part of Deira where pagan burials have been found in substantial numbers. Here at Goodmanham (*Godmundd-ingahām*) was the pagan temple where, according to Bede, the high priest Coifi abjured heathenism *c.* 626. Along with other satellites including Sancton, the site of a major pagan cremation cemetery, Goodmanham was a dependency of the multiple-estate focus of Weighton (*Wīctūn*); yet Goodmanham, together with other satellites including Londesborough, the site of a major pagan inhumation cemetery, was also a dependency of the multiple-estate focus of Everingham, an *ingahām* designated after an Eofor. An Eofor figures too in *Eoforwīc*, the old English name for York, where in 627 following Coifi's abjuration King Edwin was baptized a Christian.[48] Clearly therefore habitative place-name elements like *wīc*, *hām*, and *ingahām* could indicate ancient units of extensive lordship.

The existence of Roman villas, as of hill-forts, presupposes a number of dependent settlements within their catchment areas. As the recent explosion in archaeological evidence has shown, Britain outside the Highland Zone was characterized by a close network of Romano-British settlements,[49] many of which were probably dependencies of Roman villas. With the decline of Roman administration in the fifth century and a considerable reduction of the population much land must have gone out of cultivation and reverted to scrub or to woodland. Yet, despite the abandonment of most villas and, save in the favoured areas, the recession of their arable lands, parts of the villa estates and their once-dependent settlements could have survived. Thus, for example, when Garth Benni in southern Ergyng was donated by King Peibio, probably in the early seventh century, to be 'a house of prayer and an episcopal place for ever',[50] its small *maenor* (multiple estate) extended westwards over some 2800 acres to include a series of ridges and the very fertile lands of the former Roman villa at Huntsham.

Given the likely persistence of some villa estates it is possible that during the turmoil of the barbarian invasions some villas began to turn into hamlets by the concentration around them of the dwellings earlier located in outlying dependencies; hence the frequent occurrence of Roman remains under, or in the immediate proximity of churches.[51] At Rivenhall (Essex) the stone villa buildings remained in use for domestic and agricultural purposes until they passed beyond economic repair, so that there appears to be no evidence for discontinuity of settlement at the villa–church site. In the absence of testimony for the displacement of the Romano-British population, there must be a strong presumption in favour of the continuation of the Romano-British farming economy but with small numbers of Germanic folk settling in an orderly fashion on a fully functioning Romano-British estate, which appears to have remained as a functioning unit through the Saxon period and ultimately emerged in 1066 as a royal vill.[52] In other instances the villa buildings were demolished or abandoned. Such was the case at Barton Court Farm (Oxfordshire) where there appears to have occurred a reduction of agricultural activity and the villa buildings were systematically demolished. Nevertheless, there were Germanic settlers among the occupants of the villa site from at least the early fifth century until the sixth when a neighbouring site was occupied.[53] In other words into the interstices enlarged between surviving Romano-British settlements the newer settlements of Saxon settlers appear to have been intruded; hence the establishment on an unoccupied site in the early fifth century of a Saxon settlement at West Stow (Suffolk) whose economy was based on the mixed farming of land already under cultivation. This settlement consisted of three substantial juxtaposed halls each with a cluster of attendant sunken buildings so that the community probably consisted of three extended families with a larger number of slaves.[54]

A persistence of pre-existing patterns of settlement is likewise evident in the vicinity of some Roman forts. Thus near the *vicus* Banna, a dependent settlement of the fort of Birdoswald, the father of St Patrick had a small estate staffed with slaves at the beginning of the fifth century (Fig. 3.1).[55] Moreover a striking feature of early donations to the Church is the frequency with which these were made by kings and yet involved Roman forts. Among a number of examples was Reculver (Kent), which, according to the Anglo-Saxon Chronicle, was given by King Egbert in 669 to Bass the priest to build a minster, then sited within the Roman fort.[56] Such siting appears to be due less to the availability for re-use of the stones of a ruin whose ramparts provided a ready-made church enclosure than to the survival, adjoining these fort sites, of centres of royal authority. The largest rural settlements were those located at such centres of authority but, as in the east so in the west, these were usually little more than hamlets, or small villages.

At many small scattered Romano-British farmsteads occupation likewise continued in simple huts. This later occupation has been ascribed to the post-Roman period because of finds of friable herb-tempered pottery called 'Saxon' but probably used alike by true Saxons and the descendants of Romano-Britons. These finds indicate that over much of England there was a dispersed pattern of hamlets and farmsteads akin to that found at a later date in the Celtic west. Thus, for example, within the area of the later parish of Brixworth (Northamptonshire), where Anglo-Saxon structures were erected on the villa site, and where there were three Saxon cemeteries, nine small 'Saxon' settlements of the fifth and sixth centuries have been located by the recovery of this kind of pottery.[57] Similarly in north Essex where even on heavy clayland there were large numbers of Roman sites, careful search for this friable pottery has revealed that occupation continued into the fifth, sixth and seventh centuries. The overall pattern of 'Saxon' settlement thus appears to have resembled that of Roman times but with the addition of small new settlements. Under such circumstances small rectilinear Roman fields continued to be used, or came to be re-used. Substantial areas of such fields arranged on a co-axial system over wide stretches of countryside remained in use, as at Rivenhall and in parts of East Anglia.[58] With population growth many such fields came to be subdivided, presumably through the continued effects of partible inheritance and the need to convert areas formerly exploited for grazing into arable land; hence the division of many rectangular fields into bundles of open narrow strips in sharelands. Exactly how the cultivation of these sharelands was organized we do not know, although a passage in the early laws of Wessex indicates that a simple form of open-field agriculture was practised in the late seventh century; thus, when crops or grass were growing on the shareland each individual shareholder was responsible for fencing that part of his land which lay on the outer limit of the shareland.[59] In the far west too, as on the small multiple estate of Meddyfnych in Llandybïe c. 800, there appear to have been similar sharelands, both centrally placed and outlying, in association with scattered farmsteads, and a hint as well of the seasonal exploitation of the uplands.[60]

Urban Decline and Rebirth

After 410 when the *civitates* had to look to their own defences they probably continued as centres of government controlled at first by urban oligarchs and later by native kings or Germanic princes. Thus there was continued activity in many 'cities' well into the fifth century. At Verulamium, adjoining St Albans, the provision of a water supply provides evidence of an ordered civic life perhaps even in the late fifth century.[61] Likewise at Wroxeter there was a sequence of ambitious timber buildings which must have been of fifth century date and could well have lasted longer.[62] Even at Carlisle a town house may well have lasted into the fifth century and when, much later in 685, King Ecgfrith was taken on a conducted tour by the reeve he was shown not only the city wall but also the still operating Roman fountain.[63] Yet, with the decline in trade, intensified by the ravages of warfare, most Romano-British cities came to be effectively non-urban for, by the middle of the sixth century, all signs of corporate civic existence had disappeared.

In these settlements royal residence was probably the operative factor in maintaining a thread of continued occupation. Thus in Winchester it has been plausibly suggested that a West Saxon royal palace was established near the *forum* and occupied for part of year as a focal point in a new pattern of settlement and administration.[64]

London was perhaps an exception. According to the Anglo-Saxon Chronicle, the Britons of Kent, presumably nobles, had fled there after their defeat in 457 but thereafter the record is silent until 604 when King Æthelberht of Kent constructed the cathedral of St Pauls not far from the Roman fort at Cripplegate. Given this development, and the continuity of Roman streets in this vicinity at Cheapside and Eastcheap, it is possible that organized urban life had continued in London. By the 630s London almost certainly had the first substantial mint in England. With the revival of overseas trade London by the end of the seventh century had become a major 'port of trade' which was centred, however, not within the Roman city walls but to the west along the Strand foreshore at *Lundenwīc*, where it was controlled apparently by the king's reeve.[65]

Similar in some respects was the history of York, where the *principia* of the legionary fortress was, at least in part, used (and repaired) into the late Saxon period. York appears to have been subject to the authority of Britons, among them Efrawc Iarll (literally York Earl) and his son Peredur, descendants of Coel Hen until, in the late sixth century, it came under the control of Deira.[66] In 627 King Edwin was baptized in York at a church built for the occasion in or near the *principia*, whose imposing standing remains may well have been incorporated into a prestigious Northumbrian royal palace. Northumbrian royal authority was probably responsible also for the refurbishment of the Roman defences west of the *principia*, an act which amply testifies to the continuing importance of York. The revival of overseas trading functions, however, apparently came later than in London, but in York too this development took place outside the centre of administration, in the Fishergate area near the confluence of the Ouse and the Foss where coins dating from 700 onwards, and other finds, attest the importance of trade at what must have been at least one focus of *Eoforwīc*.[67]

Around the beginning of the eighth century new settlements for trade and industry were established at coastal or riparian sites in southern and eastern England. Thus a regularly laid-out town was built *c.* 700 at Hamwic on the river Itchen to serve as a port of entry and focus of industrial production for the newly expanded and increasingly prosperous kingdom of Wessex. Functionally very different from Winchester, which remained essentially an administrative and cere-monial centre, Hamwic developed a symbiotic relationship with Winchester.[68] So too Ipswich on the Orwell estuary, engaged in pottery production by *c.* 650, and well established by the eighth century, developed into an international trading centre with a similar role in relation to the kingom of East Anglia. Indeed, each of the early Anglo-Saxon kingdoms of the south-east came to be served by one or more new coastal or riparian 'ports-of-trade'.[69]

Apart from these major peripheral towns, royal vills, the centres of authority of units of government of lathe, soke or 'shire' type for multiple estates, even before 800 had probably become the nuclei of communities which had some urban features. When royal courts ceased to move from royal vill to royal vill it is likely that the disposal of food renders gathered there became a strong inducement for the establishment of an occasional market. Sometimes this would be located near the royal palace but often it was at the minster already established within a mile or two of the palace. Since the minster would have served the same territory as that governed from the royal vill, the crowds attracted to it on major church festivals would have provided a more regular basis for the organic growth of trading activity and would lead ultimately, as at Aylesbury, to the development of a town.[70] Soon, however, these developments alike in coastal and interior locations were to be interrupted by the advent of newcomers from beyond the North Sea.

The Impact of the Scandinavians

Sporadic raids on England and Wales by Vikings began in the closing years of the eighth century with Norwegians and gradually increased in intensity until the early 850s when a Danish army wintered in the Isle of Thanet and later in Sheppey. Then in 866 the nature of the Scandinavian impact changed when, after wintering in East Anglia, a great army captured York and one of the leaders, Halfdan, placed a Saxon puppet on the Northumbrian throne. Ten years later, as the Anglo-Saxon Chronicle records, 'Halfdan shared out the lands of the Northumbrians and they proceeded to plough and to support themselves' or, as a later chronicler reports, 'Halfdan occupied Northumbria and divided it among himself and his thegns (*ministris*) and had it cultivated by his army'.[71] Other groups from the great army settled soon after in Mercia and East Anglia. But, despite their settlement, the invaders continued to make plundering raids in the south and west. There then ensued a period of confused warfare until Alfred of Wessex placed by treaty a limit on the Danish held area. This gave formal recognition to the Danelaw where a predominantly Danish aristocracy administered Danish laws. The heart of this Danelaw lay in the East

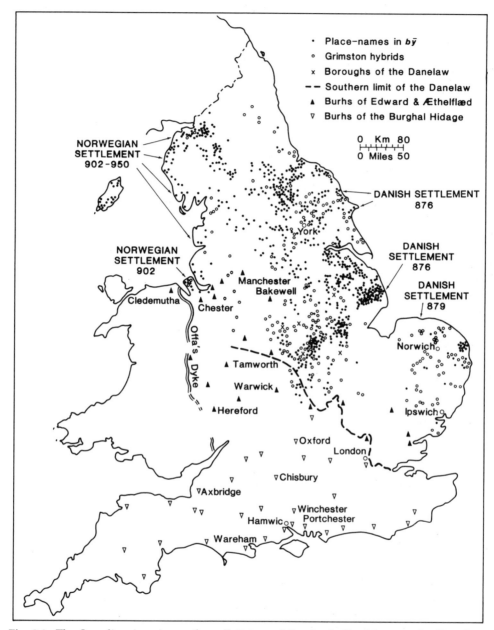

Fig. 3.3. The Scandinavians in southern Britain and the Anglo-Danish struggle. (Based on Cameron, Ekwall, Fellows Jensen, Hill and Smith.)

Midlands where the Danes grouped themselves in and around the probably pre-existing towns of Lincoln, Stamford, Nottingham, Leicester and Derby, later known collectively as the Five Boroughs (Fig. 3.3). In the north, Yorkshire, particularly to the north-west and north-east of the capital at York, was also well settled.

Norwegians, largely drawn from the Norse kingdom of Dublin, colonized large areas of north-west England in the early tenth century, and c. 911 Ragnald of Dublin established himself at York as king. Thereafter, the kingdom of York continued, not without some interruptions, until 954 when it was re-absorbed into Northumbria, which in turn was incorporated into the new pan-English state.

The struggle to re-establish English control had been mounted from Wessex, but the process was interrupted after 980 by the renewal of Danish raids which ravaged parts of southern England. These raids, after much internal strife, culminated in 1016 with the succession of Cnut, son of Swein, to a united kingdom, the whole of England apart from the extreme north-west.[72]

The nature of Scandinavian rural settlement has long been the subject of debate. Apart from numerous pieces of churchyard sculpture it has left few archaeological traces; and only exceptionally, as with the late-ninth-century farm site at Ribblehead (Yorkshire), have Scandinavian rural settlements been positively identified, probably because the Scandinavians adopted the settlements of the indigenous people.[73] Accordingly, recourse has been made to the evidence of Scandinavian place-names of which there are large numbers in northern and eastern England (Fig. 3.3). Originally these were seen as a direct result of the settlements made by the Danish armies from 876 onwards. Stenton tentatively assumed that these armies were large and suggested that a newly founded settlement was likely where the Danish $b\bar{y}$, broadly the equivalent of 'village', or *thorp*, broadly the equivalent of 'hamlet', was united in a strict grammatical compound with a Danish personal name; and that the Dane who left his name to a $b\bar{y}$ or *thorp* has normally been the leader of the rank and file who had brought the village or hamlet into being. Where, however, a Danish personal name was compounded with the Old English *tūn*, as in Grimston, a Dane was likely to have replaced an Englishman as the lord of an existing village.[74]

Sawyer subsequently argued that the largest Danish army in the ninth century was to be counted in hundreds rather than in thousands.[75] Other scholars, while in the main accepting the case for small armies, argued for large numbers of settlers to account for the numerous Scandinavian place-names and general Scandinavian linguistic influence. Cameron suggested that these came as secondary migrants, colonists who settled in the north-east Midlands under the protection of the armies of the Five Boroughs.[76] Of these boroughs only Derby was given a Scandinavian name. Similarly the names of other important centres like Cambridge and Northampton were left unchanged and the same must have been true of many existing villages. Cameron further argued that since places bearing hybrid names of the Grimston type were sited on excellent agricultural land they probably represented English villages taken over by the Danes at a very early date and partially re-named. A slightly later stage of settlement, on sites less satisfactory for agriculture, was represented by place-names in $b\bar{y}$, meaning 'a farmstead, village', and on the basis of the personal names with which they were compounded these were taken in the main to refer to the earliest new settlements on land not colonized on a large scale by the English. Appropriately, such names were most numerous in Lincolnshire behind the protective screen of the Five Boroughs. A still later stage in the colonization, characterized it was claimed by the exploitation of land immediately less favourable for agriculture, was equated with place-names in *thorp* meaning 'a secondary settlement, an outlying farmstead, a hamlet dependent on a larger place'.

This new interpretation was presented with many qualifications. Thus Cameron conceded that place-names in *thorp* were not necessarily evidence of Danish settlement, but merely of Danish influence, and that places with names in *bȳ* were not necessarily on virgin land but rather were sites not at that time occupied.[77] Meanwhile it had been demonstrated that some settlements bearing names in *bȳ*, notably appellatives like Kirkby, meaning 'a village with a church', occupied sites resembling those of English villages, thus suggesting that these at least represented earlier English settlements re-named by the Scandinavians.[78] In due course Gillian Fellows Jensen, like Sawyer, came to accept the view, advanced at an earlier date, that the Scandinavian settlement should be viewed not as an occupation of virgin land but rather as an adaptation of a pre-existing, and in large measure surviving, organization of the multiple estate.[79] Thus it was the fragmentation of large estates, sokes or 'shires', by grant or purchase into smaller territorial units of private ownership more independent of the estate centre to which tribute and service were due, which led to the adoption of personal names plus *bȳ* or, particularly on the Yorkshire Wolds, names in *thorp*. This fragmentation did not begin until some time after the ninth-century conquests. Thus Scandinavian names are rare in areas recovered fairly soon by the English, as, for example, a large estate of 60 hides encompassing Bakewell which was re-purchased before 916.[80] On the other hand, for pioneering settlements in areas first fully exploited by the Scandinavians, the best indicator is the word *thwaite* meaning 'a clearing in a woodland'. Such names in *thwaite* are common in north-west England on steep slopes, or in narrow valleys, and it was here rather than in the *bȳs* and *thorps* of the more hospitable lowlands that the true Viking pioneers settled.[81]

In the more hospitable lowlands Scandinavian name giving was associated with the process whereby large pre-existing multiple estates were fissioned into smaller multiple estates or even unitary manors. Thus within the limits of the former kingdom of Elmet as it was *c.* 600 the names of the foci of two out of three multiple estates, as recorded in the late eleventh century, were English rather than Scandinavian, although all these estates had probably been subject to Scandinavian control (Fig. 3.2). The remainder bore names in whole or in part Scandinavian but, as with Thurlstone and Ulleskelf, they were usually the foci of small multiple estates. Approximately half the names in *bȳ* were borne by estate dependencies and half by separate manors. Among the latter was Denby (the *bȳ* of the Danes), but this was hardly a new creation for its location amidst estate dependencies suggests that earlier it had also been a dependency, and even the particular form of the genitive-plural of *Denebi* implies that the name was coined by neighbouring Englishmen in an area then inhabited predominantly by the English.[82] Again Birkby, the one name in *bȳ* borne by the focus of a multiple estate, albeit a very small one, was probably an old-established settlement as is suggested by the earlier form of its name, *Bretebi* (the *bȳ* of the Britons).[83] Moreover the names in *thorp* in the Elmet area were also divided almost equally between estate dependencies and separate manors. Of these only Newthorpe-in-Elmet, one of the many dependencies of Sherburn, but with soils less favourable than its immediate neighbours, is likely to have been a new creation; yet this too was dovetailed into the framework of an ancient multiple estate.

Rural Development

Scandinavian settlement, by speeding the process which brought about the fragmentation of multiple estates, exerted a profound influence on the patterns of
settlement and land management in those parts of northern and eastern England
where the old socio-economic order had persisted. On the typical lesser estate, often
a vill severed from a larger entity, the presence of a lord less remote than his
aristocratic predecessor and more dependent on local resources no doubt led to a
more intensive agrarian effort; hence the expansion of arable land at the expense of
common pastures and woods. Frequently this appears to have been accompanied by
a re-organization of the countryside, with the hamlets and scattered farms of a vill
now being grouped in a nucleated village, usually sited next to the largest hamlet;
and the arable holdings within permanently cultivated infield sharelands being
replaced by long parallel lands laid out in two or three large fields.[84] With access to
distant upland pastures no longer possible following the fragmentation of larger
multiple estates, and pasture within a vill confined to small areas, it was necessary to
introduce regular cereal–fallow rotations so as to ensure the sustenance of livestock,
including the all important work animals; hence the adoption of two or three field
systems.[85]

Such appears to have been the course of development at the vill of Wharram Percy
where the settlement pattern into the middle Saxon period was a continuation of the
pattern of the Roman period, but perhaps slightly reduced, and with some concentration, if not nucleation, on the site of the later village. This was later followed by
Scandinavian re-organization which resulted in the laying out of large open fields in
long parallel lands.[86]

In parts of the West Midlands, where a more precocious development of the
economy had promoted the fragmentation of multiple estates and enhanced the role
of local lordship, there was probably even earlier a similar growth of villages at the
expense of outlying hamlets. In the northern and western parts of this region
references in charters to settlements on the boundaries of some estates suggest that
scattered hamlets were characteristic. In the southern and eastern part of the region,
however, where arable farming was dominant and seignorial control appears to
have been most firmly maintained, nucleation of settlement probably took place
after the mid eighth century and certainly by the later Anglo-Saxon period. Thus, for
the estate of Daylesford (Gloucestershire) the boundary was defined in relation to
the *tūn* on the present village site to the south-west of 'the open field of Daylesford'.[87]

Alike in northern and in southern England, estates which prospered became
unitary manors severed from the multiple estates of which they had once formed
part. In keeping with these changes the unitary manor would come to be less
dependent on the religious provision hitherto made for the whole multiple estate by
the minster. With growing prosperity manorial lords were able to endow local
churches; hence the appearance of the village church serving a parish coterminous
with the manor, or in some cases, with prospering thegns in the Danelaw, two
churches serving two manors within one vill.

In western Britain, on the other hand, given the more limited amount of arable
farming even in fertile areas like the Vale of Clwyd, multiple estates survived so that

scattered farms and hamlets persisted alongside spring-sown infield s
at Llanynys where appropriately the minster continued to serve a hug

Urban Growth

With the coming of the Scandinavians urban life received a new stimulus. Their principal settlements, like the Five Boroughs, well-fortified and under military control for at least the first generation, developed into thriving trading towns. York, as a capital, grew quickly to become one of the main urban centres of England with wide-ranging internal and overseas trading contracts. Moreover at Coppergate, between the *Eoforwic* at Fishergate and the legionary fortress, recent excavation has shown that planned tenements regularly laid out *c.* 910 formed part of a densely occupied manufacturing-artisan quarter which may also have extended to much of the fortress area.[89] Lincoln thrived similarly and there are indications that its street plan was at least partly laid out while it was under Scandinavian sway.

Already in the eighth century the rulers of Mercia had begun the fortification of major settlements, as at Hereford on the Welsh border, but it was the need for an integrated system of defence versus the Danes which promoted the most rapid growth of defended centres in southern England. Thus in Wessex no less than 30 defended places were established and so spaced out that no part of the kingdom was more than 20 miles from a fortified centre of refuge and resistance. According to the Burghal Hidage, a text from the early tenth century but which probably recapitulates the practice of Alfred the Great, responsibility for fortifying and garrisoning these *burhs*, as they were known, was placed on the surrounding countryside.[90] In the main the *burhs* were fortified towns devised for permanent settlement so that military effectiveness was based on economic viability and a growing population. Some were new creations like Axbridge in Somerset, yet this was within the framework of a large multiple estate recorded in the 880s and some two miles west-north-west of the royal residence at Cheddar. Thus placed, Axbridge was provided with a ready-made market catchment to favour its trade, for traditionally the occupants of such an estate would have repaired to the estate focus for the discharge of their customary obligations.[91]

Some of the *burhs* were re-used Roman walled towns like Winchester. Among these was London, which was only brought into Alfred's comprehensive system of town strongholds in 886. After some two centuries of existence as the trading-port of *Lundenwic* the town was refounded inside the walls of the Roman town. It took up to a century, however, for the population of the walled town of *Lundenburh* to equal in size that of *Lundenwic* and for London to surpass Winchester in wealth and population, thus becoming the pre-eminent town in England.[92]

The re-conquest of England and the eventual unification of the state was based on the gradual extension of *burh* foundation. Thus Æthelflæd adopted the burghal system for the protection of Mercia by the fortification of towns like Warwick. Subsequently, between 911 and 919, the system was extended over the remainder of England south of the Humber by her brother Edward the Elder of Wessex, except in East Anglia where Danish conquest and English re-conquest were too rapid for a burghal system to have been organized; hence the pre-eminence in East Anglia of ıNorwich which appears to have become a major centre while under Scandinavian control.[93]

By contrast the towns which came into being during the last century of the Anglo-Saxon state appear to have been the result of a general expansion of economic life and to have emerged more gradually. Yet, like the majority of *burhs* these towns, except when they were ecclesiastical foundations, stood in most cases on land which was royal property. By reserving their rights over the *burhs* the rulers of an increasingly unified England began a close association with their boroughs which was to be beneficial to them both. It was no accident that the towns and the power of the ruler grew together. The grafting of new on to old, evident with the towns, epitomizes much of the process whereby southern Britain came to be more closely settled between the departure of the Romans and the coming of the Normans.

References

1. M. Winterbottom (ed.), *Gildas: The Ruin of Britain and Other Works*, (London, 1978) p. 17.
2. I. Wood, 'The fall of the Western Empire and the end of Roman Britain', *Britannia*, **XVIII** (1987), pp. 260–2.
3. *Gildas*, p. 26.
4. *Ibid.*, p. 28.
5. J. N. L. Myres, *The English Settlements*, (Oxford, 1986), pp. 158–61.
6. *Gildas*, p. 28.
7. C. Thomas, *Christianity in Roman Britain to AD 500*, (London, 1981), pp. 251–2.
8. D. M. Dumville, 'The chronology of the *De Excidio Britanniae, Book I*', in M. Lapidge and D. N. Dumville (eds.), *Gildas: New Approaches*, (Woodbridge, 1984), pp. 79–84.
9. N. K. Chadwick, 'The British or Celtic part in the population of England', in *Angles and Britons, O'Donnell Lectures*, (Cardiff, 1963), pp. 113–47.
10. B. Colgrave and R. A. B. Mynors (eds.), *Bede's Ecclesiastical History of the English People*, (Oxford, 1969), pp. 48–63.
11. *Ibid.*, pp. 148–51; J. M. Wallace-Hadrill, *Bede's Ecclesiastical History of the English People, A Historical Commentary*, (Oxford, 1988), p. 214.
12. C. Hills, 'The archaeology of Anglo-Saxon England in the pagan period', *Anglo-Saxon England*, **8** (1979), pp. 312–19.
13. P. H. Sawyer, *From Roman Britian to Norman England*, (London, 1978), pp. 84–6.
14. D. Whitelock (ed.), *The Anglo-Saxon Chronicle*, (London, 1961).
15. A. L. Meaney, *A Gazetteer of Early Anglo-Saxon Burial Sites*, (London, 1964).
16. J. Campbell (ed.), *The Anglo-Saxons*, (London, 1982), pp. 34, 36.
17. *The Anglo-Saxon Chronicle*, p. 14.
18. A. O. H. Jarman (ed.), *Aneirin: Y Gododdin, Britain's Oldest Heroic Poem*, (Llandysul, 1988); J. E. C. Williams (ed.), *The Poems of Taliesin*, (Dublin, 1968), pp. 1v-lix, 12–5; G. R. J. Jones, 'Early territorial organization in Gwynedd and Elmet' *Northern History*, **X**, (1975), pp. 3–27; J Morris (ed.), *Nennius, British History and The Welsh Annals*, (London, 1980), p. 38.
19. *Bede's Ecclesiastical History*, pp. 148–9.
20. J. G. Gruffydd, 'Canu Cadwallon ap Cadfan', in R. Bromwich and R. B. Jones (eds.), *Astudiaethau ar yr Hengerdd, Studies in Old Welsh Poetry*, (Cardiff, 1978), pp. 25–41.
21. J. E. A. Jolliffe, 'Northumbrian institutions', *English Historical Review*, 41 (1926), pp. 1–42; G. R. J. Jones, 'Early territorial organization in England and Wales', *Geografiska Annaler*, **43** (Stockholm, 1961), pp. 174–81; *idem*, 'Post-Roman Wales', in H. P. R. Finberg (ed.), *The Agrarian History of England and Wales*, **1-ii** (Cambridge, 1972), pp. 281–382; *idem*, 'Multiple estates and early settlement', in P. H. Sawyer (ed.), *Medieval Settlement; Continuity and Change*, (London, 1976), pp. 15–40; *idem*, 'Early historic settlement in border territory. A

case study of Archenfield and its environs in Herefordshire', in C. Christians and J. Claude (eds.), *Recherches de Géographie rurale*, (Liège, 1979), pp. 126–9; *idem*, 'Multiple estates perceived', *Jnl. of Historical Geography*, **11** (1985), pp. 352–63; G. W. S. Barrow, *The Kingdom of the Scots; Government, Church and Society from the Eleventh to the Fourteenth Century*, (London, 1973), pp. 8–68.

22. *Gildas*, p. 17.
23. *Nennius*, p. 45.
24. Gruffydd, *Canu Cadwallon*, pp. 41–3.
25. K. Jackson, *Language and History in Early Britain*, (Edinburgh 1953), pp. 285, 343.
26. O. J. Padel, *Cornish Place-Name Elements*, (Cambridge, 1985), pp. 150, 271; C. Thomas, 'Tintagel Castle, *Antiquity*, **LXIII** (1988), pp. 421–34; *idem*, 'The 1988 C.A.U. excavations at Tintagel Island: discoveries and their implications', *Cornish Studies*, **16**, (1988), pp. 49–57.
27. L. Alcock, 'Cadbury-Camelot: a fifteen-year perspective', *Proceedings of the British Academy*, **LXVIII** (1982), pp. 355–88.
28. Campbell, *The Anglo-Saxons*, pp. 58–61.
29. B. Colgrave (ed.), *The Life of Bishop Wilfrid by Eddius Stephanus*, (Cambridge, 1927), pp. 72–5, 173; *Bede's Ecclesiastical History*, pp. 374–7; W. de G. Birch (ed.), *Cartularium Saxonicum*, I (London, 1885), p. 99; E. E. Barker, 'Sussex Anglo-Saxon charters', *Sussex Archaeological Collections*, **86** (1947), pp. 59–65; **88** (1949), pp. 82–8; M. G. Welch, *Early Anglo-Saxon Sussex*, British Archaeological Reports, British Series, **112**, (1983), pp. 262–9.
30. *Eddius Stephanus*, pp. 72–5; 173; *Geiriadur Prifysgol Cymru*, (Cardiff, 1950–67), p. 333.
31. B. Hope-Taylor, *Yeavering, An Anglo-British centre of early Northumbria*, (London, 1977); R. Miket, 'A re-statement of evidence for Bernician Anglo-Saxon burials' in P. A,. Rahtz, T. Dickinson and L. Watts (eds.), *Anglo-Saxon Cemeteries*, British Archaeological Reports, British Series, **82**, (1980), pp. 289–305.
32. W. Greenwell (ed.), *Boldon Buke*, Surtees Society, **25** (1852).
33. F. L. Attenborough (ed.), *The Laws of the Earliest English Kings*, (Cambridge, 1922), pp. 58–9; F. E. Harmer (ed.), *Select Historical Documents of the Ninth and Tenth Centuries*, (Cambridge, 1914), pp. 1–2, 39–40, 73–4; A. Robertson (ed.), *Anglo-Saxon Charters*, (Cambridge, 1939), pp. 12–13, 271–4.
34. C. C. Smith, 'The survival of Romano-British toponymy', *Nomina*, **4** (1980), pp. 27–40.
35. K. Branigan, *Latimer*, (Bristol, 1971), pp. 173, 186–9; P. J. Fowler, 'Agriculture and rural settlement', in D. M. Wilson (ed.), *The Archaeology of Anglo-Saxon England*, (London, 1976), pp. 23–48; J. Percival, *The Roman Villa*, (London, 1976), pp. 166–82.
36. T. M. Charles-Edwards, 'Kinship, status and the origins of the hide', *Past and Present*, **56**, (1972), pp. 3–33.
37. P. Wormald, *Bede and the Conversion of England; The Charter Evidence*, Jarrow Lecture 1984, pp. 22–4.
38. E. John, *Land Tenure in Early England*, (Leicester, 1960), pp. 24–63;*idem, Orbis Britanniae and Other Studies*, (Leicester, 1966), pp. 64–127.
39. M. Gelling, 'Latin loan-words in Old English place-names', *Anglo-Saxon England*, **6** (1977), pp. 11–13.
40. *Eddius Stephanus*, pp. 38–41, 165; G. R. J. Jones, 'Historical geography and our landed heritage', *University of Leeds Review*, **19** (1976), pp. 66–74; K. Cameron, 'The meaning and significance of Old English *walh* in English place-names', *Jnl. of the English Place-Name Society*, **12**, (1979–80), pp. 1–53.
41. Jones, 'Early territorial organization in Gwynedd and Elmet', pp. 12–23.
42. J. M. Dodgson, 'The significance of the distribution of the English place-names in -*ingas*, -*inga*—in south-east England', *Medieval Archaeology*, **10** (1966), pp. 1–29.
43. Myres, *The English Settlements*, pp. 31–45.
44. M. Gelling, 'English place-names derived from the compound *wīchām*', *Medieval Archaeology*, **11** (1967), pp. 87–104; *idem, Signposts to the Past, Place-Names and the History of England* (2nd edn.) (Chichester, 1988), pp. 245–50; J. Campbell 'Bede's words for places', in J. Campbell, *Essays in Anglo-Saxon History*, (London, 1986), pp. 99–119.
45. G. Copley, *Archaeology and Place-Names in the Sixth Century*, British Archaeological Reports, British Series, **147** (1986), pp. 3–4, 74.

46. B. Cox, 'The significance of the distribution of English place-names in *hām* in the Midlands and East Anglia', *Jnl. of the English Place-Name Society*, **5** (1973), pp. 15–73.

47. E. Ekwall, *The Oxford Dictionary of English Place-Names*, (4th edn.) (Oxford, 1960), pp. 253, 479; A. H. Smith, *The Place-Names of the West Riding of Yorkshire*, **IV** (Cambridge, 1961), pp. 84, 108; Williams, *The Poems of Taliesin*, pp. lv-lvii, 13, 15.

48. *Bede's Ecclesiastical History*, pp. 182–7; G. R. J. Jones, 'Nucleal settlement and its tenurial relationships: some morphological implications', in B. K. Roberts and R. E. Glasscock (eds.), *Villages, Fields and Frontiers*, British Archaeological Reports, International Series, **185** (1983), pp. 164–7.

49. C. C. Taylor, *Village and Farmstead*, (London, 1983), pp. 83–106.

50. J. G. Evans and J. Rhys (eds.), *The Text of the Book of Llan Dav*, (Oxford, 1893), p. 72; W. Davies, *An Early Welsh Microcosm*, (London, 1978). pp. 123–4, 152, 165.

51. W. Rodwell with K. Rodwell, *Historic Churches: A Wasting Asset*, Council for British Archaeology, Research Report No. 19, (1977), pp. 90–2; P. Wade Martins, *Fieldwork and Excavation on Village Sites in Launditch Hundred, Norfolk*, East Anglian Archaeology Report No. 10, (1980), pp. 82–4.

52. W. I. Rodwell and K. A. Rodwell, *Rivenhall: Investigations of a Villa, Church and Village, 1950–1977*, Chelmsford Archaeological Trust Report 4, Council for British Archaeology Research Report No. 55, (1985), pp. 56–7, 75, 178–80.

53. C. J. Arnold, *Roman Britain to Saxon England*, (London, 1984), pp. 64–6.

54. G. West, *West Stow: the Anglo-Saxon Village*, East Anglian Archaeology Report **24,** (1985), **1,** pp. 6, 151, 167–8, 171–86.

55. R. P. C. Hanson and C. Blane (eds.), *St. Patrick, Confession et Lettre à Coroticus*, (Paris, 1978), pp. 70–1, 142–3; Thomas, *Christianity in Roman Britain*, pp. 307–22.

56. *The Anglo-Saxon chronicle*, p. 22.

57. D. Hall and P. Martin, 'Brixworth, Northamptonshire—an intensive field survey', *Jnl. of the British Archaeological Association*, **CXXXII** (1979), pp. 1–6; Taylor; *Village and Farmstead*, pp. 113, 116.

58. Rodwell and Rodwell, *Rivenhall*, pp. 67–8; T. Williamson, 'Parish boundaries and early fields: continuity and discontinuity' *Jnl. of Historical Geography*, **12** (1986), pp. 241–7; idem, 'Early co-axial field systems on the East Anglian boulder clays', *Proceedings of the Prehistoric Society*, **53** (1987), pp. 419–31; idem, 'Settlement chronology and regional landscapes: the evidence from the claylands of East Anglia and Essex', in D. Hooke, (ed.), *Anglo-Saxon Settlements*, (Oxford, 1988), pp. 153–75.

59. H. P. R. Finberg 'Anglo-Saxon England to 1042', in H. P. R. Finberg (ed.), *The Agrarian History of England and Wales*, **I-ii** (Cambridge, 1972), pp. 416–20; R. A. Dodgshon, *The Origin of British Field Systems; An Interpretation*, (London, 1980), pp. 75–6.

60. Jones, 'Post-Roman Wales', pp. 308–11.

61. S. S. Frere, *Britannia*, (3rd edn.) (London, 1987), pp. 368–9.

62. P. A. Barker, 'The latest occupation of the site of the baths basilica at Wroxeter', in P. J. Casey (ed.), *The End of Roman Britain*, British Archaeological Reports, British Series, **71** (1979), pp. 175–81.

63. B. Colgrave (ed.), *Two Lives of Saint Cuthbert*, (Cambridge, 1940), pp. 122–3, 242–5, 334–6.

64. M. Biddle, 'Winchester: the development of an early capital', in H. Jankuhn, W. Schlesinger and H. Steuer (eds), *Vor-und Fruhformen der europaischen Stadt im Mittelalter*, (Gottingen, 1973), pp. 234–42; idem, 'The study of Winchester. Archaeology and history in a British town, 1961–1983', *Proceedings of the British Academy*, **LXIX** (1983), pp. 116–26.

65. B. Hobley, 'Lundenwic and Lundenburh: two cities rediscovered', in R. Hodges and B. Hobley (eds.), *The Rebirth of Towns in the West AD 700–1050*, Council for British Archaeology, Research Report No. 68, (1988), pp. 69–73; A. Vince, 'The economic basis of Anglo-Saxon London', in Hodges and Hobley, *The Rebirth of Towns*, pp. 83–90.

66. R. Bromwich (ed.), *Trioedd Ynys Prydein, The Welsh Triads*, (Cardiff, 1978), pp. 488–92.

67. R. A. Hall, 'York 700–1050', in Hodges and Hobley, *The Rebirth of Towns*, pp. 125–32.

68. M. Brisbane, 'Hamwic (Saxon Southampton): an 8th-century port and production centre' in Hodges and Hobley, *The Rebirth of Towns*, pp. 101–8.

69. K. Wade, 'Ipswich', in Hodges and Hobley, *The Rebirth of Towns'*, pp. 93–100; T. Tatton-Brown, 'The Topography of Anglo-Saxon London', *Antiquity*, **LX** (1986), pp. 24–5.

70. C. Phythian Adams, 'Jolly cities: goodly towns', *Urban History Yearbook 1977*, (1977), pp. 33–7; P. H. Sawyer, 'Kings and merchants', in P. H. Sawyer and I. N. Wood (eds.), *Early Medieval Kingship*, (Leeds 1977), pp. 143–58; R. A. Dodgshon, *The European Past: Social Evolution and Spatial Order*, (London, 1987), pp. 202–12; J. Blair, 'Minster churches in the landscape', in Hooke, *Anglo-Saxon Settlements*, pp. 40–50.

71. P. H. Sawyer, *Kings and Vikings. Scandinavia and Europe AD 700–1100*, (London, 1982), pp. 99–108.

72. *idem, From Roman Britain to Norman England*, (London, 1978), pp. 114–31.

73. D. M. Wilson, 'The Scandinavians in England' in D. M. Wilson (ed.), *The Archaeology of Anglo-Saxon England*, (London, 1976), pp. 392–403; A. King, 'Gauber high pasture, Ribblehead—an interim report', in R. A. Hall (ed.), *Viking Age York and the North*, Council for British Archaeology, Research Report No. 27, (1978), pp. 21–5.

74. F. M. Stenton, *Anglo-Saxon England*, (3rd edn.) (Oxford, 1986), pp. 520–5.

75. P. H. Sawyer, 'The density of Danish settlement in England', *University of Birmingham Historical Journal*, **VI** (1958), pp. 1–17; *idem, The Age of the Vikings*, (2nd edn.) (London, 1971), pp. 159–69.

76. K. Cameron, *Scandinavian Settlement in the Territory of the Five Boroughs: the Place-Name Evidence*, (Nottingham, 1965), pp. 1–24; *idem*, (ed.), *Place-name evidence for the Anglo-Saxon Invasion and Scandinavian Settlements*, (Nottingham, 1975); H. Loyn, *Anglo-Saxon England and the Norman Conquest*, (London, 1962), p. 52.

77. K. Cameron, 'The significance of English place-names', *Proceedings of the British Academy*, **LXII** (1976), pp. 17–21.

78. Gillian Fellows Jensen, *Scandinavian Settlement Names in Yorkshire*, (Copenhagen, 1972), pp. 5–41, 209–10, 221–8; *idem*, 'The Vikings in England: a review', *Anglo-Saxon England*, **4** (1975), pp. 181–206.

79. G. R. J. Jones, 'Early territorial organization in Northern England and its bearing on the Scandinavian settlement', in A. Small (ed.), *The Fourth Viking Congress (1961)*, (Edinburgh, 1965), pp. 67–84; C. D,. Morris, 'Aspects of Scandinavian settlement in northern England: a review', *Northern History*, **XX** (1984), pp. 1–22.

80. Gillian Fellows Jensen, *Scandinavian Settlement Names in the East Midlands*, (Copenhagen, 1978), pp. 368–72; *idem*, 'Scandinavian settlement in England: the place-name evidence', in H. Bekker-Nielsen and H. Frede-Nielsen (eds.), *Vikingesymposium, Odense Universitet 1982*, (Odense, 1985), pp. 9–32; *idem*, 'Place-names and settlements: some problems of dating as exemplified by place-names in *By'*, *Nomina*, **8** (1984), pp. 29–39; Sawyer, *Kings and Vikings*, pp. 102–8.

81. Gillian Fellows Jensen, *Scandinavian Settlement Names in the North-West*, (Copenhagen, 1985), pp. 415–17.

82. *idem, Scandinavian Settlement Names in Yorkshire*, p. 25.

83. *Ibid.*, p. 21; G. R. J. Jones, 'To the building of Kirkstall Abbey', in M. W. Beresford and G. R. J. Jones (eds), *Leeds and Its Region*, (Leeds, 1967), pp. 121–4.

84. M. Harvey, 'The origin of planned field systems in Holderness, Yorkshire', in T. Rowley (ed.), *The Origins of Open-Field Agriculture*, (London, 1981), pp. 184–201; D. N. Hall, 'The late Saxon countryside: villages and their fields', in Hooke, *Anglo-Saxon Settlements*, pp. 99–122; B. K. Roberts, *The Making of the English Village*, (Burnt Mill, 1987), pp. 60–1.

85. Finberg, 'Anglo-Saxon England to 1042', pp. 489–96; H. S. A. Fox, 'Approaches to the adoption of the Midland System', in Rowley, *The Origins of Open-Field Agriculture*, pp. 64–111.

86. J. G. Hurst, 'The Wharram research project: results to 1983', *Medieval Archaeology*, **XXVII** (1983), pp. 80–90; *idem*, 'Introductory note', in P. Stamper (ed.), *Wharram Research Project Interim Report on the 39th Season*, (1988), p. 1.

87. D. Hooke, *The Anglo-Saxon Landscape: The Kingdom of the Hwicce*, (Manchester, 1985), pp. 137–44, 210–11.

88. G. R. J. Jones, 'Hereditary land and its effects on the evolution of field systems and

settlement patterns in the Vale of Clwyd', in R. C. Eidt, K. N. Singh and R. P. B. Singh (eds.), *Man, Culture and Settlement,* (New Delhi, 1977), pp. 82–96; *idem,* 'The Dark Ages', in D. H. Owen (ed.), *Settlement and Society in Wales,* (Cardiff, 1989), pp. 185–7.

89. R. A. Hall, 'The topography of Anglo-Scandinavian York', in Hall, *Viking Age York,* pp. 31–6; *idem,* 'The making of Domesday York', in Hooke, *Anglo-Saxon Settlements,* pp. 233–47.

90. M. Biddle and D. Hill, 'Late Saxon planned towns', *The Antiquaries Journal,* **LI** (1971), pp. 70–85; D. Hill, 'Towns as structures and functioning communities through time: the development of central places from 600 to 1066', in Hooke, *Anglo-Saxon Settlements,* pp. 197–212; N. P. Brooks, 'England in the ninth century: the crucible of defeat', *Transactions, Royal Historical Society,* 5th ser., **29** (1978), pp. 1–20.

91. P. Rahtz, *The Saxon and Medieval Palaces at Cheddar; Excavations 1960–62,* British Archaeological Reports, British Series, **65** (1979), pp. 1–17, 371–7, 379–97.

92. Hobley, 'Lundenwic and Lundenburh', in Hodges and Hobley, *The Rebirth of Towns,* pp. 73–82; Vince, 'The economic basis of Anglo-Saxon London', in Hodges and Hobley, *The Rebirth of Towns,* pp. 83–92.

93. J. Campbell, 'Norwich', in M. D. Lobel (ed.), *The Atlas of Historic Towns,* **2** (London, 1975), pp. 2–6; *idem, The Anglo-Saxons,* pp. 174–5.

4

People and Land in the Middle Ages, 1066–1500

Bruce M. S. Campbell

Introduction

The four centuries which followed the Norman Conquest of 1066 saw far-reaching changes in the rural economy and society of both England and Wales. For much of the early Middle Ages expansion was the keynote of change: population grew, the tools and techniques of husbandry improved, the economy expanded, and there was a growth in the power and institutions of central government. The buoyancy and self-confidence of the twelfth and thirteenth centuries are particularly striking and are associated with the flowering of the rich and sophisticated material culture of high medieval Europe.[1] The seeds of many of these developments had been sown in the pre-Conquest period, so in that respect there was continuity rather than change, but it was only now that their full harvest was reaped. Never before had productive forces been combined in quite the same kind of way, nor, except perhaps in the Romano-British period, had growth been pushed to such limits.[2] This great demographic and economic upswing was a Europe-wide phenomenon and it lasted for the better part of a quarter of a millennium. There were, of course, short-term setbacks but its impetus was not finally broken until the first half of the fourteenth century, when expansion was first halted and then reversed.

The processes responsible for this fundamental shift in direction were complex and arose from the coincidence of several separate strands of development at roughly the same point in time. Ecological, demographic, socio-economic, and political factors all contributed to the crisis of the fourteenth century and although there is much debate as to their respective roles there is no mistaking the outcome of their combined impact. The change in demographic trends is especially striking and no subsequent period has experienced crises of subsistence and of public health on a par with those of the famine of 1315–18 and the plague outbreak of 1348–49. Thereafter, the late fourteenth and fifteenth centuries stand out as a period of prolonged demographic recession associated with a corresponding scaling-down of prevailing levels of economic activity. In certain superficial respects the experience of the later Middle Ages was thus the opposite of that of the early. Nevertheless, it was also a time of rationalization and realignment during which the established institutional framework of society was progressively transformed, thus unleashing the potential for the emergence of a wholly new socio-economic and spatial order in the ensuing early modern period.

  The complex dynamic which underlay this tripartite chronology of expansion, crisis, and contraction/reorientation possessed both temporal and spatial dimensions. The nature of the former has been hotly debated but much less attention has been lavished on the way in which the processes of change mapped themselves on to the landscape, let alone the possibility that change itself may in part have been geographically driven. Yet economy and society in the Middle Ages were both intensely local and regional in character and, as such, spatially highly differentiated. More so than in many other periods, national trends were the net product of many separate local and regional threads of development whose contributions to the whole have yet to be disentangled. Hence the danger of extrapolating to the country as a whole from the experience of a single estate or region, or vice versa. Moreover, as Dodgshon has recently argued, the spatial tensions arising from interaction between these different regions may have provided part of the dynamic which drove change on.[3] In his view changes in societal organization are usually underpinned by changes in spatial order. Much careful empirical work remains to be done before these ideas can be properly evaluated but there is every reason to suppose that a closer consideration of the spatial component will provide considerable new insights into the nature and processes of medieval social and economic development. Historical geographers thus have much to contribute to an understanding of the period; the documentary sources are rich and the scope for further research is considerable.

Expansion

Population

Throughout the twelfth and thirteenth centuries it is plain that the prevailing demographic trend all over western Europe was upwards. In England, Domesday Book of 1086 and the Poll Tax of 1377 can both be used to derive gross estimates of total population. In neither case is the exercise straightforward due to ambiguities in the data and problems of non-enumeration: different assumptions produce different results and there is a wide margin of error. Estimates of Domesday population range from a minimum of 1.1 million (Russell) to a maximum of 2.25 million (Hallam).[4] Darby cautiously placed the population midway in this range at about 1.5 million but in Harvey's more recent assessment 'a reasonable estimate would approach 2 million, and should not exclude a somewhat higher figure'.[5] Comparable estimates based on the 1377 Poll Tax place the country's population in the range of 2.14 to 3.08 million, depending upon assumptions about the age-structure of the population, the number of those ineligible to pay, and the level of evasion.[6] Extrapolation backwards from this figure, making due allowance for a cumulative mortality of 40–50 per cent in the plague outbreaks of 1348–49, 1360–62, 1369, and 1375, as well as for the possibility that the population may have been declining for at least a generation before the Black Death, gives a medieval population at peak, c. 1300, variously estimated at between 3.75 million (Russell) and 8.0 million (Hallam), but with the weight of historical opinion increasingly coming to favour a figure of 5–6 million.[7] Such a total may only have been approached once before, in the late third century A.D., and was not again exceeded until the late eighteenth century. It implies an approximately three-fold increase in numbers since Domesday. For Wales the evidence is even flimsier but a late-thirteenth-century population of approximately 300,000 has been suggested by Williams-Jones.[8]

The impression of vigorous population growth implied by these aggregate estimates is confirmed by various more localized sources of evidence, many of which permit a more direct comparison between late-thirteenth-century and Domesday conditions. For instance, on the Prior of Norwich's manor of Martham in east Norfolk, situated in a locality which was already densely populated at the time of Domesday, the tenant population rose from 74 in 1086 to 107 at some unspecified date in the middle of the twelfth century, and then to no less than 376 in 1292.[9] A similarly dramatic increase has been identified by McIntosh on the royal manor of Havering in Essex, from 87 in 1086, to 368 in 1251, and 493 in 1352–53.[10] Nor are Martham and Havering isolated examples as a comparison between Domesday Book and the surviving Hundred Roll Returns of 1279 makes plain. Harley has compared tenant numbers in the two Warwickshire Hundreds of Stoneleigh and Kineton in 1086 and 1279 and found that although tenant numbers rose almost everywhere, the increase was much more pronounced in the Hundred of Stoneleigh on account of its weaker manorial structure, freer land tenure, and greater opportunities for colonization.[11] These also demonstrate, as one might expect, that the rate of increase was geographically uneven and that for environmental and institutional reasons some localities possessed a much greater capacity for growth than others. As detailed studies of individual communities are making clear, local rules governing the inheritance and acquisition of land could exercise an important influence upon both fertility (via nuptiality) and migration and result in contrasting demographic trajectories between individual townships and regions.[12]

The cumulative effect of these developments was to transform England from the relatively underpopulated country which it had been at the time of the Norman invasion to the crowded agrarian society which it had undoubtedly become by the close of the thirteenth century. A parallel trend can be detected in Wales. Domesday Book shows just how sparsely populated most of late-eleventh-century England was.[13] As will be seen from Fig. 4.1A, densities of less than 10 recorded persons per square mile prevailed over the greater part of the country, and north of the Trent, in the Fens, the Weald, and much of the far south-west these fell to less than 5, and often less than 2.5, recorded persons per square mile. Elsewhere higher population densities occurred in pockets, usually on the richer lowland soils, as in north Berkshire and south Cambridgeshire, but only in coastal Sussex, part of eastern Kent, central Suffolk, south-eastern Norfolk, and parts of Lincolnshire did densities exceed 15 recorded persons per square mile and, in Sussex, Suffolk and Norfolk alone, 20 persons per square mile (over twice the national average). Three hundred and sixty years later the 1377 Poll Tax shows that population densities were highest in a solid wedge of countries stretching diagonally across England from the East Riding of Yorkshire, Lincolnshire, Norfolk, and Suffolk in the east to Somerset and

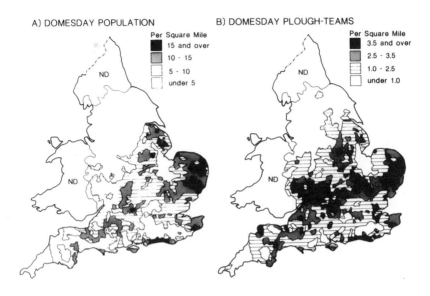

A) DOMESDAY POPULATION

Per Square Mile
- 15 and over
- 10 - 15
- 5 - 10
- under 5

B) DOMESDAY PLOUGH-TEAMS

Per Square Mile
- 3.5 and over
- 2.5 - 3.5
- 1.0 - 2.5
- under 1.0

CHANGING PROSPERITY 1086–1334 and 1334–1524/5
(after Darby, Glasscock and Sheail)

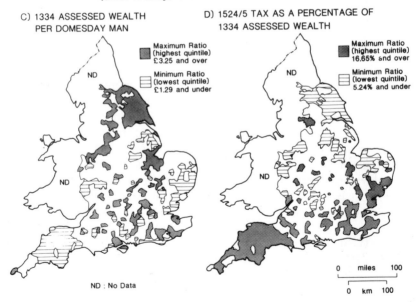

C) 1334 ASSESSED WEALTH
PER DOMESDAY MAN

Maximum Ratio
(highest quintile)
£3.25 and over

Minimum Ratio
(lowest quintile)
£1.29 and under

D) 1524/5 TAX AS A PERCENTAGE OF
1334 ASSESSED WEALTH

Maximum Ratio
(highest quintile)
16.65% and over

Minimum Ratio
(lowest quintile)
5.24% and under

ND : No Data

Fig. 4.1. Domesday population (A) and plough-teams (B) (after Darby); changing prosperity 1086–1334 (C) and 1334–1524/25 (D) (after Darby, Glasscock, Sheail and Versey).

Dorset in the south-west, and were highest of all in Norfolk, south Lincolnshire, Rutland, Northamptonshire, and Bedfordshire.[14] Before the dreadful culling of the plague their landscapes had been literally teeming with people.

Colonization and the Extension of Settlement

The powerful demographic imperative of the early Middle Ages found its most immediate expression in a widespread movement of colonization. The distribution of Domesday plough-teams (Fig. 4.1B) reveals the progress made by colonization up to 1086 and shows that there were few parts of the country without at least some potential for the extension of cultivation.[15] Most of England north of the Trent, the Weald, the New Forest, the Fenland, the Breckland, and the heathlands of the south had less than one plough-team per square mile, and over much of the rest of the country there were less than 3.5 plough-teams per square mile. Only in the Exe valley, coastal Sussex, parts of the West Midlands (north Oxfordshire, south Warwickshire), and the eastern part of East Anglia, and in scattered patches elsewhere, was the density of teams higher, exceeding 4.5 teams per square mile in the most fully developed districts. Yet even these districts possessed some colonizable reserves. For instance, in the densely populated Deanery of Waxham in eastern Norfolk the number of tenants' teams quadrupled during the 150 years after Domesday.[16] In this case an area of established settlement was pushing cultivation to its physical limits so that by the close of the thirteenth century a veritable sea of arable stretched from village to village interrupted only by scattered islands of meadow, pasture, heath, and marsh. Domesday Book shows that by 1086 the area had already been stripped of much of its natural tree cover and by that date the natural peat resources of Broadland were probably already being exploited as an alternative source of fuel: 250 years later most of the residual woodland had succumbed to the plough and approximately 900 million cubic feet of peat had been removed to create what are now the Norfolk Broads.[17]

This filling-out of the interstices of the established settlement pattern, of which eastern Norfolk provides an extreme example, was going on all over England and Wales. Some measure of the change that was accomplished, as Darby and Glasscock have shown, can be obtained by comparing the distributions of men and ploughteams recorded in Domesday Book with the distribution of lay wealth as recorded by the Lay Subsidy of 1334 (Fig. 4.1C).[18] Throughout the country the greatest increases were consistently concentrated in areas of settlement expansion in former pockets of wood, fen, and waste. Population was spilling out from the older settled lands, where opportunities for expansion were nearing exhaustion and powerful centrifugal pressures were forcing it into the gaps within the established settlement network as well as outwards into the under-occupied lands of the periphery. This process has been described by Brandon in the wooded Weald of Kent and Sussex, by Vollans in the Chiltern Hills, by Harley and Roberts in the Forest of Arden in Warwickshire, and by Tupling in the Forest of Rossendale in Lancashire.[19] Known as assarting, the piecemeal creation of farmland from woodland and waste can be traced from early charters and, as case-studies of Laughton and Stockingham in south-eastern

England and Wheldrake in south Yorkshire have demonstrated, its progress may be read from the resultant pattern of fields.[20]

As the farmed area expanded so existing settlements got larger, although sometimes secondary settlements were also brought into being in the form of isolated farms, farm clusters, and hamlets. These daughter settlements frequently remained dependent upon their parent settlements for certain essential services, such as religion and law, and never became separate self-governing settlements in their own right. In hilly areas the initial stage in the establishment of a daughter settlement often entailed the establishment of a seasonal settlement on upland pastures and only with population growth and continued reclamation did such settlements subsequently become permanent. Hodgson has provided a vivid description of this in Upper Ryedale on the edge of the North Yorkshire Moors.[21] Here he has traced a progressive altitudinal shift in settlement during the course of the twelfth and thirteenth centuries. Whereas at the time of Domesday Book there were few inhabitants in northern Ryedale, and little economic activity, by 1300 there is clear evidence of a scatter of single homesteads within the dale. Some of these settlements probably began as summer shielings and were later converted to permanent occupation and held in severalty by small freeholders. Many of them were late established and early abandoned and as such represent the high-water mark of medieval colonization. McDonnell has documented a very similar process in the adjoining valley of Bilsdale and there must have been many another upland dale in which the same basic sequence of development was followed.[22] As a movement it can be traced in Wales, where many secondary settlements were created during the twelfth and thirteenth centuries, and is particularly well-documented on Anglesey.[23] Here settlement gradually expanded out of the richer, sheltered, well-drained soils along the coast on to the more exposed and impoverished soils of the interior, creating secondary settlements which were sometimes as much as seven or eight miles distant from the original base.

This process of *internal colonization,* as it is often termed, derived its momentum from the natural increase of population and gradually changed the face of the countryside as wood, heath, and fen were reclaimed and converted to productive farmland. It was matched by a corresponding movement known as *external colonization* in which new lands were opened up through the recruitment of settlers by migration. These lands were of three sorts: virgin land never previously settled, land which had been wasted and which lay abandoned, and land which had been won by conquest from the Welsh and the Irish.

Virgin land was already extremely scarce at the time of Domesday Book, which shows that the vast majority of medieval settlements were already in existence. Only the estuarine marshes fringing the south and east coasts remained largely unoccupied and awaiting settlement. These were potentially rich lands but their reclamation required labour and organization and it was only in the twelfth and thirteenth centuries that these came to be applied on a sufficient scale, as they were across the North Sea in Flanders. It was during these two centuries that much of Romney Marsh in Kent, the Essex marshes, and the Somerset Levels were drained and brought into agricultural use.[24] But the most spectacular change of all was wrought in the East Anglian Fens, particularly the silt fens of south Lincolnshire and west Norfolk.[25] Here many entirely new settlements came into being and subsequently grew to great size, often spawning daughter settlements in the process. In south Lincolnshire the large townships of Emneth and Tilney appear for the first time in the late twelfth century where previously there had been nothing, whilst across the country boundary in Norfolk the four separate townships of Wiggenhall St Germans, Wiggenhall St Mary the Virgin, Wiggenhall St Peter, and Wiggenhall St Mary Magdalen grew out of what had been one. Immigration from the increasingly congested countryside of the surrounding 'uplands', coupled with naturally high rates of increase, produced quite remarkable rates of population growth in many of these new fenland settlements.[26] Here, as elsewhere, the attraction to colonists lay as much in the area's freer land tenure and weak manorial structure as in the physical opportunities which it presented. Hallam has documented in detail the process by which reclamation proceeded on both the seaward and landward sides of the silt ridge upon which the major settlements were sited, one of the most remarkable features of which was the maintenance of an efficient dyke-reeve organization through voluntary co-operation between villages.[27] Sometimes this was facilitated through the organizing initiative of the various local monasteries, such as Crowland Abbey, Thorney Abbey, and Spalding Priory, which had received large land grants in the Fens which they were anxious to develop. The net result was that by the early fourteenth century the silt fens had been transformed into one of the most intensively exploited and prosperous districts in England.[28]

On a par with this movement of population into these low-lying marshlands was the resettlement of abandoned lands in the north of England. Much of Yorkshire, along with portions of Nottinghamshire, Derbyshire, Staffordshire, Shropshire, Cheshire, and Lancashire were still waste in 1086.[29] In Yorkshire the initial response to the devastation which William and his army had meted out was the resettlement of as many demesne manors as possible by regrouping local survivors into manorial type communities on the site of pre-existing villages. The remaining settlements which had thus been stripped of their populations were then resettled through the recruitment of free colonists from outside the region. This was an altogether slower process and required the offering of inducements in the form of generous land holdings, low rents, and favourable terms of tenure. The villages thus created often lacked a manorial demesne and contained a predominantly freeholding population which was little burdened with feudal obligations. Most striking of all, the village and associated fields often possessed a planned layout. According to Sheppard, villages with plans typically comprising regular toft rows facing a street or green with service lanes to the rear, are common in much of lowland Yorkshire, with no less than 18 out of 29 villages in the Vale of Pickering meriting the term 'planned'. Moreover, these planned villages tend to be associated with particular estates, which indicates the crucial role of lordship in the whole resettlement process.[30]

Several of the new monastic orders of the age—the Cistercians, Praemonstratensians, and Augustinians—also obtained large land grants in the region and subsequently proved active in the task of reconstruction. The work of the Cistercians is especially notable since they were attracted to remote locations and worked their estates themselves using the labour of lay brothers or conversi.[31.] The Cistercian order grew immensely in popularity and importance during the twelfth century: there were many new foundations, with the peak in the 1140s, and large numbers of monks were recruited into the lay brotherhood. With the aid of this manpower substantial arable granges were laid out by the monks in the Vale of York on the site of devastated villages, additional land was assarted, and strenuous efforts were made to consolidate the many miscellaneous land grants which this new and austere order attracted.[32] Along the upland fringes there was further reclamation from forest and moor and substantial vaccaries and bercaries were established where the monks reared cattle and sheep. The monastic grange with its staff of white-robed conversi thus became an established feature throughout the region and made an important and distinctive contribution to its economic recovery.

Parallel with these colonization movements in the east and the north was a substantial exodus of settlers to the Celtic lands of the north and west. While English social and economic historians often overlook it, their Scottish, Welsh and Irish counterparts are in no doubt of the scale and significance of this migration flow, which must rank as one of the most substantial population movements of the time.[33] In Scotland settlement assumed the form of a peaceful infiltration and was mainly urban in character, as English townsmen and traders were attracted during the course of the twelfth century to the new royal burghs.[34] In Wales and Ireland, on the other hand, conquest preceded colonization. Thus, in South Wales colonization began in the immediate aftermath of the Norman occupation of the late eleventh and early twelfth centuries and was in part sponsored by the new military lords. At first, as in Scotland, it was the newly founded boroughs which attracted settlers but before long the movement expanded to include extensive peasant colonization of the countryside.[35] The latter sometimes involved the settlement of virgin land but more usually entailed the displacement of the native population. Many of the settlers probably came from the West Midlands, some certainly came from the south-western counties of Devon and Cornwall, and there was a small but significant injection of Flemings. Collectively, they transformed the racial composition and social character of lowland Pembroke, Gower, Glamorgan, and Gwent, the lower valleys of the Wye and Usk, and some other districts along the English border.

Towards the end of the twelfth century, as opportunities for further settlement in South Wales began to dwindle, so new opportunities opened up further west in Ireland. The Anglo-Normans had invaded Ireland in 1169 and for the next hundred years they extended and consolidated their hold until almost two-thirds of the island was under their control. As in Wales, conquest was followed up by colonization and in much of eastern and south-eastern Ireland it is plain that the latter was on a substantial scale.[36] The movement was probably at a peak during the first half of the thirteenth century and it successfully attracted settlers from south-western and north-western England, as well as South Wales. The Anglo-Normans were anxious to secure a settled population upon whose loyalty they could rely and towards that end they offered prospective settlers substantial holdings, privileged social status, and low rents, although there is little evidence outside the towns of the settlement planning which is such a feature of the contemporary colonizing movement in Germany east of the Elbe. During the final quarter of the thirteenth century the security situation began to deteriorate in Ireland and the flow of settlers probably began to abate but then, following the Edwardian Conquest of 1277–84, new opportunities opened up in North Wales.

Whereas evidence for the earlier migration flows into Scotland, South Wales, and Ireland is poor and takes the form of place-names, field names, personal names, and

so forth, the Edwardian settlement of North Wales is much more firmly documented. Following extensive land confiscation a colonization movement was
effected with considerable speed and under firm royal and seignorial control. The
key to this process, as earlier in South Wales and Ireland, was the establishment of a
series of strategically placed fortified towns or 'bastides' with a privileged and
almost exclusively English civilian population. The most successful of these towns—
Beaumaris, Conway, Ruthin, and Denbigh—prospered and eventually outgrew the
limits of their original walls. East of the River Conwy they were reinforced by the
plantation of English settlers in the countryside. According to Davies, sustained and
effective attempts were made to introduce English colonists in numbers to the new
seignorial lordships of Bromfield and Yale, Dyffryn Clwyd, and Denbigh in north-
east Wales. In Denbigh at least 10,000 acres were transferred—either through
forfeiture or compulsory exchange—from native Welshmen to these new settlers,
especially in the fertile lowlands of the Vale of Clwyd and near the new castle-
borough of Denbigh. Those who took up these land grants were typical of many
another plantation movement: there were adventurers in search of a fortune,
craftsmen and soldiers who had been involved in the military subjugation of Wales,
land-hungry peasants, and the social flotsam and jetsam which all such ventures
inevitably attracted. They came from the border counties and more generally from
the north-west of England, as well as from the English estates of the new lords of
Wales.[37] They were the last wave in a rising tide of colonization which had lasted
more than two centuries and carried English settlers and some others deep into the
outlying portions of the British Isles.

These external migration flows syphoned off some of England's population
growth. This would undoubtedly have been the greater without it, especially if, as in
later colonization movements, marriage rates were depressed by a disproportionate
exodus of young adult males.[38] In Scotland and, more particularly, Wales and
Ireland, colonization strongly reinforced the indigenous trend towards population
increase. There was a gain both in absolute numbers and in potential fertility. The
populations of all three countries became racially much more diverse and the social,
economic, cultural, and political impact of settlement was tremendous. Alien
communities were created which furthered English military and political domination of the greater part of the British Isles and which in Wales and Ireland long
remained defiantly separate. Without this colonization the emergent human geographies of Scotland, Wales, and Ireland would have been very different.

Changes in Social Status

Population growth and colonization operating in conjunction with other contemporary developments—the growth of central government, evolution of customary
law, growth of towns and of marketing, and increasing sophistication of material
life—brought about significant changes in the established fabric of society. Medieval
society was feudal.[39] That is to say, the majority of the population was legally
subordinated to a dominant lordly class made up of laymen and clerics. Lords
ensured their superior social and economic position through their control of land
and thus the means of production. In that respect this was a highly territorialized
society. Notionally all land was ultimately held from the king in a clearly defined

social ladder of superordination and subordination, according to a principle which had been introduced from France by the Normans and grafted on to the nascent feudalism of late Anglo-Saxon England. It is embodied in the final format of Domesday Book which is organized on a tenurial rather than a topographical basis to record who held what of whom. This shows that the greater barons and ecclesiastical magnates held major fiefs of the king which sometimes, as in the Welsh Marches, formed consolidated territories but more usually comprised a geographical scatter of properties. These fiefs were further subdivided or subinfeudated to produce a number of much smaller military tenancies or fees. Each fee was held in return for homage and service (usually military service) and it gave its owner the right to live on the labour of the tenants settled upon it. The latter were exploited through the institution of serfdom.

Serfs were legally unfree and subject to the will of their lords in a wide range of social and economic activities. Although they owned their own labour and provided their own subsistence on holdings held from their lord, they were denied personal and occupational mobility and were restricted in their freedom of contract and in the disposal of property. Those who worked on the soil were tied to the soil and they worked for their lord's benefit as well as their own. Much of the surplus which they produced over the immediate needs of subsistence was thus syphoned off in various forms of feudal rent. Typically these comprised direct labour services on the lord's demesne, seignorial taxation (tallage), fines levied in the manor court to which they owed suit, and the obligation to submit to seignorial monopolies of milling and baking.[40] Additionally, all peasants, whether free or unfree, owed tithes to the church, paid taxes to the crown, and were subject to the purveyancing prerogative of the royal household. Hatcher has argued that serfdom is best interpreted as a response to relative labour shortage within a predominantly self-sufficient economy, both of which conditions pertained in eleventh-century England.[41] Morever, there can be little doubt that serfdom became more onerous following the Conquest as the new Norman lords actively asserted their authority and extended their powers. In due course English villeins thus became subject to the continental obligations of merchet (payment for permission to marry off a son or daughter), heriot (death duty), and toll (payment for permission to sell livestock). There was also a drive to attach freemen to manors and to erode the status of the semi-free. At Bergholt in Suffolk the number of sokemen was reduced from 210 to 119 between 1066 and 1086 and in neighbouring Cambridgeshire their numbers were reduced from over 900 to little more than 200 over the same period.[42] With no source of legal redress at this stage peasants plainly found it difficult to resist the coercive pressures of a powerful lord and Hatcher believes that many no doubt ended up owing rents and services in excess of the value of the lands which they held.[43]

During the course of the twelfth and thirteenth centuries this relationship between land, labour, and feudal authority became substantially modified. One reason was that some of the wealthier tenants succeeded in freeing themselves and converting their customary holdings to freehold. Another, and more important, as Hilton and Dodgshon have both noted, is that colonization promoted a disproportionate growth of free tenures.[44] This was partly because free tenants possessed the mobility to move to new areas, and partly, too, because landowners used free tenure to attract new tenants. It has been estimated that the unfree amounted to not more than 60 per cent of the English tenantry by the late thirteenth century.[45] In the areas of old settlement subdivision had reduced many of these freeholdings to a very small size and their tenants to poverty, although in the areas of new settlement, particularly in the north and west, some substantial holdings were created. At the same time a situation of labour shortage had been changed into one of labour surplus so that landlords were less dependent upon forced labour to work their demesnes. Accordingly, many of them chose to commute labour service for cash and to employ a permanent labour force of hired servants.[46] The result was that by the close of the thirteenth century weekworks were regularly being performed by substantially less than a third of all villein households and hence no more than one in six of all peasant households. The unfree, of course, remained in a weak bargaining position, the more so on account of the relative surplus of labour; but against this must be set the growth of custom, which gave them a measure of protection from arbitrary actions on the lord's part, and the enhanced value of their land. Population pressure had driven up land values everywhere so that, according to Hatcher, the unfree were now often paying less for their lands than they would have had to pay if their rents had been freely negotiated. Customary conditions of tenure thus made the unfree an increasingly protected, even privileged, tenurial group. Rather than further exploit their villeins, the most enterprising landlords came to realize that the best and most acceptable opportunities for profit lay in the exploitation of favourable market forces. Moreover, they increasingly demanded rents in cash rather than in kind thus forcing their tenants also to participate in the market. The self-sufficiency of the late eleventh century had become very much a thing of the past.

These developments varied geographically as, indeed, the legal status of the population always had done, and further emphasized the contrast between core areas of old settlement and peripheral areas of new. At the time of Domesday freemen and sokemen had been most strongly represented in the old Danelaw counties of the East Midlands and East Anglia: Lincolnshire possessed the highest proportion of all (50.7 per cent), followed by Suffolk (44.9 per cent), Norfolk (40.4 per cent), Nottinghamshire (30.6 per cent), and Leicestershire (30.4 per cent).[47] Over much of the rest of the country villeins, bordars, and cottars made up over 80 per cent of the rural population, these groups differing from one another less in status than in the size of their land holdings and the terms on which they held them, for all were unfree. It was, however, in the counties of the extreme south-west and the Welsh borderland that the servility of the population was most complete, for it was here that servi or slaves were recorded in large numbers and that freemen were barely represented at all. Slavery had been an important aspect of Anglo-Saxon class structure, and it still was of Welsh: significantly, slaves still accounted for approximately 21.4 per cent of the population of Cornwall and 25.5 per cent of the population of Gloucestershire. At a regional level there was thus a strong east–west gradient, from freedom to unfreedom, although superimposed upon this were important local variations.[48] The latter derived in part from the nature of the prevailing manorial structure.

The manor was the minimal unit of local administration and feudal property ownership. It typically comprised the lord's residence, a demesne or home farm belonging to the lord and intended to provision him and his household, a number of holdings for the lord's tenants over which the lord enjoyed a superior real property right which entitled him to charge rents and entry fines, a dependent tenantry of various classes, and a manor court (the records of which provide the single most important source for the study of medieval rural society). Large manors coterminous with vills and containing few free tenants naturally tended to endow their holders with considerable power and authority, whereas the tenants of small manors tended to be in a much more independent position. The relative proportions of large and small manors can be gauged from Kosminsky's classic analysis of the surviving portions of the 1279 Hundred Rolls which provide information on the characteristics of approximately 1000 manors for a cross-section of the country from Suffolk in the east to Warwickshire in the west.[49] This shows that large manors comprising in excess of 1000 acres of arable accounted for 13 per cent of all manors and 41 per cent of the total area, in contrast to small manors of less than 500 acres arable which accounted for 65 per cent of the total number and 29 per cent of the total area. Large manors were therefore far from typical and yet it was they which were most likely to be coterminous with a vill and which contained the greatest proportions of villein land. They tended to be associated with the larger estates and especially those belonging to the church, with the result that the church, which held 26 per cent of all manors, held 31 per cent of all arable and 37 per cent of all villein land. Since these estates are disproportionately well served by extant records there is a tendency for the large and highly feudalized manor to loom too large in historical perceptions of the period. The small manor, by contrast, was rarely coterminous with a vill and was generally less well furnished with villein land so that its demesne, when it existed (which was not always), occupied a more independent position within the manorial economy. A high proportion of these manors were in lay hands and, apart from their appearance in documents such as the Hundred Roll Returns and *Inquisitiones Post Mortem*, are frequently unrepresented by surviving records.[50]

In most parts of the country the co-existence of these different types of manor gives rise to much localized variation in the detailed pattern of socio-economic change. But there were also certain broader trends. The Hundred Rolls show that arrangements were most complex in East Anglia. In Cambridgeshire, for example, manor and vill were coterminous in only 11 per cent of cases and the evidence of Feudal Aids shows that a situation of even greater complexity prevailed in much of Norfolk.[51] In many vills within these counties manors were intertwined and merged with one another with such complexity that even the jurors making the returns were confused. Not infrequently large holdings of complicated structure occurred among the freeholdings of a manor, with a demesne and dependent holdings of their own, which fully merit the title of manor. Sometimes on such a sub-manor a further sub-manor apeared in its turn, and so on. As Kosminsky observes, 'the ladder of holdings intervening between the "chief lord" and the last tenant might be very involved'.[52] According to Stenton analogous arrangements prevailed in the Danelaw counties, notably in Rutland, Leicestershire, Lincolnshire, Nottinghamshire, Derbyshire, and Yorkshire.[53] Elsewhere in northern England 'manors' were territorially extremely extensive and typically encompassed several vills. Demesnes were either non-existent or of limited scale, labour dues were of little significance, and individual vills enjoyed considerable independence from seignorial administration. In contrast, it was in central and southern England that the manorial system attained its fullest development and that manor and vill were most frequently coterminous. The

Hundred Rolls cover only part of this area but in the portions of Huntingdonshire, north Buckinghamshire, and Oxfordshire for which there are returns manor and vill were coterminous in over 50 per cent of all cases. Moreover, in Huntingdonshire and Oxfordshire, as well as southern Warwickshire, villein land accounted for over half of the recorded total, a sure indication of the importance of labour services and thus of the lord's demesne within the manorial economy.

These twin maps of freedom and manorialization in turn acted as a filter upon the processes of population growth and colonization. Notwithstanding Duby's belief that seignorial demands were one of the major stimuli to agricultural and demographic expansion, it was in the areas of weak manorialization and among the free rather than the unfree that population growth and colonization were most vigorous.[54] The institutional framework of society channelled the forces of change and imposed upon developments a distinctive spatial stamp. Economically, too, the more weakly manorialized districts acted as the pace-setters of change and it was within them that the forces and processes first manifested themselves which ultimately dissolved the established feudal fabric of society. New social and economic developments diffused from the free to the unfree, and from the weakly manorialized to the strongly manorialized, thus subtly transforming the social and economic geography of the country.

Growth

During the twelfth and more particularly the thirteenth centuries the English economy underwent growth as well as expansion with the result that its overall productivity grew.[55] The essential catalyst was the growth of marketing, which underwent what Lopez has described as a commercial revolution.[56] Marketing, of course, had always been present in some form or other but hitherto it had been too weakly developed to structure space in any comprehensive or systematic way. During the thirteenth century, however, production for exchange came more and more to rival production for use and regional economies at last began to become integrated into a spatially coherent whole.

The transformation of economic life is nowhere more apparent than in the case of agriculture—the largest and most important sector within the economy—which came increasingly under the influence of expanding urban and industrial markets both at home and overseas. Foremost among these was London. By 1300, it was the second largest city north of the Alps and had a population approaching 100,000.[57] Its growth, along with that of the major provincial capitals, was only possible because of a commensurate rise in agricultural productivity, which was in turn a response to the greater opportunities presented by the market place, as marketing became more sharply focused as well as more widespread. As the metropolis grew and its tentacles and those of the other leading towns reached out, so old patterns of self-sufficiency began to break down and a more specialized and spatially differentiated agrarian economy began to emerge. The extent to which individual regions were drawn into this trading nexus varied a great deal, and they were drawn into it in different ways, but there were few parts of the country which remained wholly untouched.

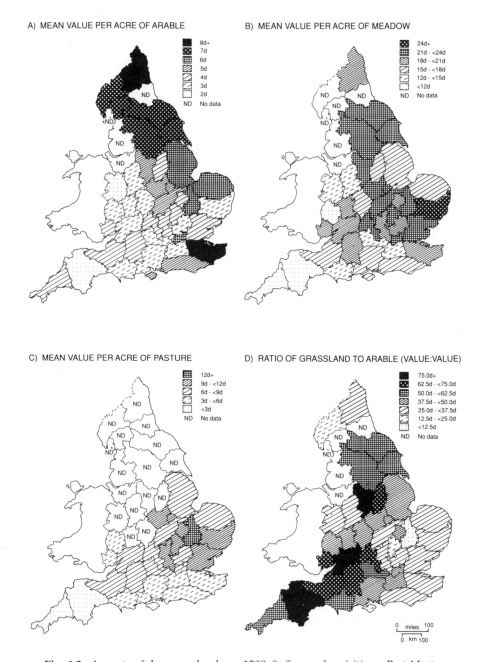

Fig. 4.2. Aspects of demesne land use 1300–9. *Source*: *Inquisitiones Post Mortem.*

Under these circumstances economic rent came increasingly to displace ecological and institutional factors as the main influence upon the pattern of agricultural production. Economic rent is a function of three things: land quality, population density, and, above all, distance from the market. Thus in a commercialized economy, as Von Thünen long ago demonstrated, economic rent determines the intensity as well as the type of farming systems, both of which vary in a spatially systematic way according to access to the market.[58] The expanding market economy of the thirteenth century consequently began to break down any simple, direct relationship which may once have existed between land use and farm enterprise so that there was no longer any consistent correlation between, for instance, relative supplies of grassland and stocking densities of livestock (compare Figs. 4.2D and 4.4A).[59] The physical environment, of course, continued to present medieval farmers with certain specific opportunities, but it was economic circumstances which increasingly determined how they were exploited. This is borne out by the medieval Breckland where, as Bailey has recently shown, a favourable market location more than compensated for difficult environmental conditions.[60] In this case a region of extremely poor, sandy soils, was located within the heart of one of the most prosperous and developed regions in the country and enjoyed convenient riverine access to the important trading port of King's Lynn. Presented with these commercial opportunities, and with no serious institutional obstacles in the form of rigid field systems or inflexible manorial structures, Breckland evolved a flexible agricultural regime based on the close integration of arable and pastoral husbandry which permitted the cash cropping of barley and wool without destabilizing the fragile ecological equilibrium of the area.

Yet whilst it might be possible to triumph over difficult environmental conditions where they were geographically well placed, a remote and inconvenient location was an entirely different matter. This especially applied to regions which were landlocked and far removed from substantial markets, as in the case of Shropshire and adjacent portions of the West Midlands, where arable land values were among the lowest in the country and arable and pastoral husbandry both remained comparatively undeveloped (Figs. 4.2A, 3, and 4). In contrast, the most advantaged regions of all were those where economic, ecological, and institutional circumstances were all favourable, as in the case of eastern Norfolk and eastern Kent.[61] Here, to a unique degree, rich and easily worked loam soils combined with convenient coastal and riverine access to domestic and overseas markets, a weak manorial structure, enterprising and individualistic peasantry, and field systems which imposed few communal constraints upon cultivators. Economic rent accordingly attained a medieval maximum (with arable land consistently valued at well over two-and-a-half times the national average) and was matched by a level of physical productivity which was correspondingly high. The techniques which produced these impressive yields were both advanced and intensive, which demonstrates that medieval agriculture was by no means as incapable of progress as has sometimes been claimed. Indeed, there were three possible avenues of advance: technological innovation, technological involution (the intensification of established methods of production), and increased specialization.

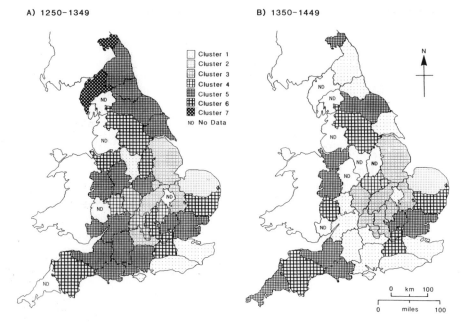

Fig. 4.3. Types of demesne crop combination by county. (For mean characteristics of cluster groupings, see Table 4.1.)

Table 4.1: Types of crop combination: mean characteristics of cluster groupings (percentage of total sown acreage).

Cluster	No. of counties	Wheat	Rye	Barley	Oats	Grain mixtures	Legumes
(A) *1250–1349*							
1	4	31.22	1.72	19.04	24.93	1.10	21.99
2	1	15.92	11.07	40.66	15.74	1.52	13.50
3	5	30.18	5.57	16.63	21.23	17.16	9.23
4	4	41.57	1.81	4.64	17.07	22.94	11.99
5	15	43.13	1.81	8.10	37.42	3.87	5.67
6	8	25.62	9.30	8.12	47.90	3.60	5.47
7	2	20.56	0.24	7.33	71.41	0.00	0.47
Overall	39	34.64	3.98	10.76	35.31	6.93	8.34
(B) *1350–1449*							
1	12	31.95	1.26	23.93	19.16	6.17	17.53
2	1	15.10	5.99	48.69	15.10	1.82	13.20
3	7	32.22	3.28	7.74	10.27	29.24	17.25
4	2	37.52	14.29	19.41	2.23	3.29	23.27
5	9	41.74	0.81	8.33	40.69	1.11	7.31
6	6	27.43	8.19	17.26	39.11	2.04	5.98
Overall	37	33.50	3.49	16.42	24.92	8.36	13.31

For method of derivation see: B. M. S. Campbell and J. P. Power, 'Mapping the agricultural geography of medieval England', *Jnl. of Historical Geography*, **15** (1989), pp. 24–39.

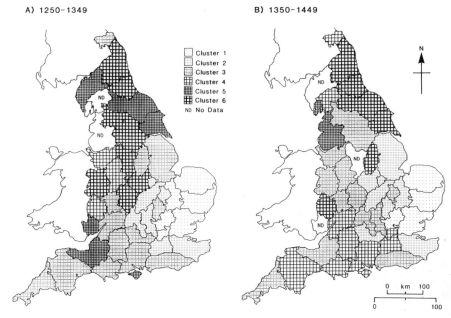

A) 1250-1349   B) 1350-1449

Cluster 1
Cluster 2
Cluster 3
Cluster 4
Cluster 5
Cluster 6
ND No Data

Fig. 4.4. Types of demesne livestock combination by county. (For mean characteristics of cluster groupings, see Table 4.2.)

Table 4.2: Types of livestock combination: mean characteristics of cluster groupings (percentage of total livestock units: horses × 1.0; oxen and adult cattle × 1.2; immature cattle × 0.8; sheep and swine × 0.1).

Cluster	No. of counties	Horses	Oxen	Adult cattle	Immature cattle	Sheep	Swine
(A) *1250–1349*							
1	6	22.05	22.13	25.53	12.03	15.57	2.69
2	7	19.33	32.74	14.75	11.33	16.77	5.08
3	13	9.67	41.13	14.17	9.55	23.17	2.32
4	3	6.70	55.74	16.09	5.50	10.30	5.68
5	5	8.03	68.76	8.98	5.39	8.22	0.62
6	8	16.23	69.35	4.30	3.51	3.60	3.02
Overall	42	13.89	46.72	13.53	8.26	14.59	3.00
(B) *1350–1449*							
1	4	17.59	8.52	33.09	8.68	29.34	2.79
2	7	20.67	26.45	13.82	8.27	25.23	5.56
3	12	9.54	39.53	18.65	12.04	16.43	3.81
4	10	5.39	24.68	13.62	8.93	45.89	1.50
5	6	13.97	70.08	5.50	3.98	3.99	2.48
6	1	2.51	21.58	10.22	49.92	13.44	2.32
Overall	40	11.74	34.56	15.81	10.00	24.68	3.20

For method of derivation see: B. M. S. Campbell and J. P. Power, 'Mapping the agricultural geography of medieval England', *Jnl. of Historical Geography*, **15** (1989), pp. 24–39.

Technological Change

The range of new techniques available to medieval cultivators was limited and their pace of diffusion was painfully slow. Nevertheless, the twelfth and thirteenth centuries did witness several significant technological advances.[62] Among the most important of these was the growing substitution of the horse for the ox in draught work of all kinds which has been documented by Langdon.[63] At the time of Domesday horses provided little more than 5 per cent of total animal draught force on the demesne, and no more than 10 per cent in any of the regions for which there are figures. In contrast, by the beginning of the fourteenth century horses accounted for at least 20 per cent of the animal draught force on demesnes and almost 50 per cent on peasant farms, and these figures exceeded 50 per cent and 75 per cent respectively in certain regions (Table 4.2). The changeover from oxen to horses was greatest for hauling, to the extent that horses easily dominated the carriage of goods by vehicle by the end of the thirteenth century, especially in East Anglia, the East Midlands, and the Home Counties. These were the regions most intimately involved in the growing internal trade in agricultural produce and it is in that context that the rise of horse hauling should be viewed, since it facilitated the more rapid transit of goods and thereby extended the sphere of the market.[64] The horse's adoption into ploughing was less spectacular: mixed teams gained in popularity and some all-horse farms emerged, with the greatest advances occurring on the smallest holdings. Progress assumed the form of a diffusion process, with Norfolk in particular standing in the van, but its pace was slow and must to some extent have been conditioned by the supply of animals. Substitution of the horse for the ox was also associated with a shift from natural to produced fodder and an increase in the intensity of production, since the greater cost of the horse needed to be offset against higher productivity. The latter derived in the main from the fact that, since horses worked faster than oxen, fewer resources needed to be reserved exclusively for the maintenance of the plough. Fodder and especially forage could therefore be diverted to the use of other stock allowing higher stocking densities and the development of more specialized forms of livestock production. Thus in certain parts of East Anglia and the Home Counties diffusion of the plough-horse was associated with the evolution of a distinctive arable-based pastoral economy in which cattle, and especially dairy cattle, assumed a unique prominence (Fig. 4.4).[65] This sometimes gave rise to stocking densities which were actually higher than in some grassier and more traditionally pastoral parts of the country. Such developed mixed-farming systems naturally incurred considerable costs; hence they only developed when justified by the prevailing level of economic rent. This helps to explain why they mostly remained restricted to East Anglia and the South-East, within range of the main centres of urban demand, as well as why diffusion of the plough-horse likewise remained so circumscribed.

Parallel with wider application of horse-power to haulage and traction went the harnessing of wind-power to milling, itself an important adjunct of the agrarian economy. The mechanization of milling offered major gains in labour productivity and water-power had long been used for this purpose. Its availability, however, was uneven and on the evidence of Domesday Book, the East Riding of Yorkshire,

Cheshire, Norfolk, Suffolk, Essex, Hertfordshire, Middlesex, Buckinghamshire, Kent, and Sussex possessed disproportionately small numbers of mills compared with their populations and must have placed considerable reliance upon the use of hand querns. Within these counties it was the windmill which subsequently provided the solution to this unsatisfactory state of affairs. The first recorded reference to a windmill is in 1185 and within a century of its introduction it had become a common sight in many parts of England.[66] The spread of the windmill appears to have followed a classic diffusion pattern, with a slow period of initial adoption giving way to a spate of intense windmill-building activity in the 1230s and 1240s, after which the rate of diffusion gradually slackened. Geographically windmill-building spread from east to west, numbers continuing to rise in the west and north after 1300 when they had long since stabilized in the east. By the mid fourteenth century no region was entirely without them and in the drier and flatter parts of the country they had become the predominant source of milling power. To the north and west of Cambridge, for example, in the Hundreds of Chesterton, Papworth, Northstow, and Longstow, the two watermills recorded in 1086 had both disappeared by 1279 to be replaced by 39 windmills. Elsewhere they provided a supplement to water-power, since the later's greater strength and consistency ensured that it was preferred when both options were available. The windmill thus affords a clear illustration of medieval technological progress and because of the substantial capital sums involved—a new windmill cost about £10 to erect in the late thirteenth century—it was from the start an almost exclusively seignorial inno-vation.[67]

Other technological advances of the period were more modest but nonetheless contributed towards a steady improvement in the tools and techniques of hus-bandry. Unlike the sixteenth and seventeenth centuries, there were few new crops as such, although considerable changes were made in the relative importance and distribution of existing crops, as well as in the ways that they were combined. Wheat was substituted for rye and in certain favoured localities barley began to displace oats as the principal spring-sown grain: maslin (a mixture of wheat and rye) and dredge (a mixture of barley and oats) also grew in importance and helped to diversify the range of crops available to medieval farmers.[68] Most significant of all, however, was the wider cultivation of legumes. They helped to restore the nitrogen level of the soil which was so essential for plant growth and were thereby crucial to the evolution of more intensive forms of rotation. They also helped to upgrade the qualtiy of fallow grazings and supplied a protein-rich source of fodder to the specialized mixed-farming systems which began to evolve during the thirteenth century and which, in the most intensive systems, more than compensated for the reduction in fallow grazings. Peas and beans had long been known and the former were widely grown as a field crop. Vetches were a more recent arrival and appear to have spread northwards and westwards from Kent and adjacent portions of the south coast during the course of the thirteenth century, reaching Norfolk a decade or so before its close.[69] At that time legumes as a group accounted for an estimated 6.3 per cent of the total demesne sown acreage, although in certain districts, such as eastern Norfolk and eastern Kent (where they formed an integral component of an intensive and productive cycle of cropping), this proportion rose to as much as a fifth or a quarter of the total. Yet by themselves legumes were no panacea to the problem of maintaining productivity in an exclusively organic age since much hinged upon how they were incorporated into the overall system of husbandry.

These various technological developments allowed the evolution of more specialized and intensive systems of husbandry and in the latter respect they were reinforced by the application of greater labour inputs to a whole range of old and well-tried techniques. Ploughing, weeding, and harvesting were all undertaken more carefully so that the seed-bed was better prepared, weed-growth more fully controlled, and as little as possible of the crop lost at harvest-time.[70] Greater effort and initiative were expended fertilizing and improving the soil. Manuring, marling, liming, and sheep folding were all employed to this end and were greedy in their consumption of labour.[71] Livestock were increasingly fed on produced rather than natural fodder and there was a shift towards the more labour-intensive forms of pastoralism, cattle rather than sheep, and dairying rather than fattening. There was also undoubtedly an increase in the cultivation of such labour-intensive industrial crops as flax, hemp, madder and saffron, especially on the smallholdings of the peasantry. Simply by employing labour in greater quantities husbandry was elevated to a greater pitch of intensity and although labour productivity eventually suffered, the most intensive husbandry systems could boast an impressive level of physical productivity.[72] The highest recorded medieval yields are those obtained on the rich loam soils of eastern Norfolk, where intensive but flexible rotations were employed which virtually eliminated fallowing. Here, in the late thirteenth and early fourteenth centuries, gross yields per acre averaged 19.5 bushels for wheat, 19.4 bushels for barley, and 17.2 bushels for oats, and on the most productive individual demesnes sometimes averaged as much as 22.6, 20.6, and 20.7 bushels respectively.[73] On peasant farms, where the potential for heavy labour inputs was even greater, levels of physical productivity may have been yet higher. When due account is also taken of the high frequency of cropping and the disproportionate emphasis upon the higher value crops (wheat as opposed to rye, and barley as opposed to oats), arable husbandry in eastern Norfolk emerges as approximately three times more productive than on the Hampshire demesnes of the Bishops of Winchester, which were less labour intensive in their methods and mostly adhered to a two- or, occasionally, a three-course rotation.

Obviously the type of rotation could make a considerable difference to productivity levels and during the thirteenth century rotations came to assume an increasing variety of forms. Over much of the country, of course, regular two- and three-field systems provided a basic framework from which it was difficult to deviate. As Fox has persuasively argued, the fallow field was the organizing principle of this system and apart from the sowing of an occasional inhok with legumes, it had to remain inviolate.[74] Nor, contrary to popular opinion, was there much changeover from two- to three-field systems in this period.[75] Yet within the confines of the system there was considerable scope for flexibility, since the range of crops could be as narrow or broad as was desired. Thus, in the predominantly three-field country of the East Midlands, in Cambridgeshire, Northamptonshire, Rutland, and South Lincolnshire, there was a decided preference for diversity, and full advantage seems to have been taken of the option to plant different crops in the various furlongs of the sown fields (Table 4.1 and Fig. 4.3).[76] Nevertheless, it was outside the bounds of these regular

commonfield systems that the greatest variety of rotational forms was
East Anglia and the Home Counties afford examples of flexible rotatio
different cropping schedules were applied to different parts of the ara
in which fallowing was reduced to one year in four or less, rotatio
fallowing simply took place as and when necessary, and rotatins in which land
alternated between arable and grass on a three or four year cycle in a classic
convertible-husbandry regime.[77] Such rotational diversity helped to bring about a
greater differentiation in the intensity of farming systems.

Regional Specialization

Medieval farmers were confronted by a variety of physical, institutional, and
economic conditions. The country's diverse climate, topography, and soils meant
that different parts of the country were suited to different kinds of agricultural
activity. Field systems varied regionally and so, too, did estate structures, both of
them imposing a particular stamp upon husbandry.[78] But increasingly during the
thirteenth century producers came under the influence of a whole hierarchy of
markets with overlapping hinterlands, of which London was merely the largest and
most central. Indeed, corn and, especially, wool were both traded internationally.
The extent to which individual regions were drawn into this burgeoning commercial
nexus varied considerably and even highly commercialized regions like the East
Midlands might contain major estates with large households to support, such as that
of Peterborough Abbey, which remained more concerned with production for
consumption than production for exchange.[79] Nevertheless, the growth of market
demand coupled with a growing insistence by the feudal classes that rents and taxes
be paid in cash rather than kind meant that landlords and peasants alike found it
both advantageous and necessary to dispose of at least part of their produce on the
market. The result was a growing differentiation of husbandry types as agriculture
became more closely attuned to commercial opportunities. Such specialization
brought gains in economic efficiency and productivity as each region exploited its
comparative advantage in climate, soil, location, and experience (a development
which is expressed both in terms of the particular choice of crops and animals that
were produced and in the intensity of their production).[80]

Research into the agricultural geography of medieval England still has a long way
to go but at a macro-level it is already clear that six broad agricultural types can be
identified and ranked in descending order of intensity as follows:[81]

(1) *Intensive arable farming systems*—these were confined to a few favoured localities
in East Anglia and the south-east. Their distinguishing features were the intensive
use of both labour and land and the reconciliation of a sustained high level of yield
with a low incidence of fallowing. Livestock husbandry was often similarly intensive, with an emphasis upon dairying. These systems were technologically advanced and highly commercialized and supported extremely high rural population
densities which supplied the cheap labour required to sustain them.

(2) *Mixed farming systems of intermediate intensity with an emphasis upon dairying*—
these were more widely distributed and tended to be orientated towards the more
populous and developed parts of the country, particularly those which lay outside
the bounds of the regular common-field system, and were favourably positioned

ɪelative to major markets. They were especially characteristic of much of East Anglia and the Home Counties. Their arable husbandry was only moderately productive and was usually based on a three-course rotation or equivalent. Their pastoral husbandry (which was in large part arable-based) was, however, much more intensive and productive and was geared towards the commercial production of cheese and butter from carefully managed dairy herds.

(3) *Extensive common-field arable systems*—these dominated much of central and southern England and collectively represent the most widespread of all medieval husbandry systems. Because of their geographical extent there has been a tendency to regard them as the norm from which all other farming systems were deviations, although they were considerably less productive of food per unit area of land than some other contemporary systems of husbandry. Since they were often land-locked and remote from major towns and centres of demand their main commercial products tended to be non-perishable crops of high value, such as wheat and wool. These were produced by methods which were extensive rather than intensive in their use of labour and land. Within the broad confines of the common-field system, however, three broad production zones can be identified:

(a) *Commercialized grain production*—this prevailed in the counties of the East Midlands: Lincolnshire, Rutland, Northamptonshire, Bedfordshire, Huntingdonshire, and, above all, Cambridgeshire. In much of this area the arable had been expanded to such an extent that permanent grassland was in extremely short supply. Stocking densities accordingly were low and the emphasis throughout was on grain production. Wheat was everywhere the leading crop followed by either barley or dredge (the main malting grains) in Lincolnshire, Cambridgeshire, and Bedfordshire, and oats in Northamptonshire and Rutland. The more intensive three-field system tended to prevail over the less intensive two- and the productive capacity of the system was developed to the full. Land values indicate an above average level of productivity and the various navigable waterways of the region—the Trent, Welland, Nene, and Ouse—ensured access to markets outside the region.

(b) *Extensive livestock rearing for cash*—in contrast to the East Midlands permanent grassland was relatively abundant in much of southern and south-western England where it was combined with arable land of average or below average value. Yields were likewise inclined to be low and were depressed by low seeding rates and a generally low intensity of cultivation, which was itself partly a function of the prominence of two-field systems. Nor was livestock production, which was often on quite a large scale, much more intensive: oxen were preferred over horses and sheep over cattle, and stocking densities were lower than the abundant supplies of pasture might have led one to expect. Sheep rearing was nevertheless the main commercial activity since wool was better able than grain to bear the costs of carriage from a region which, outside the Thames Valley, did not enjoy ready access to major markets.

(c) *Systems mainly geared towards self-sufficiency*—common-field agriculture was least commercialized in Somerset, the Welsh borderland, much of the West Midlands, and parts of north-eastern England and it was here that it assumed its least intensive and productive form. Many of the counties concerned stood on or near the western boundary where the two- and three-field system merged with various less regular forms. Stocking densities were low since sufficient livestock were kept to service the needs of the arable but no more, replacement animals being readily procured from the upland regions to the north and west. Nor was grain production particularly well developed. The range of crops grown was narrower than elsewhere in lowland England and some combination of wheat and oats or rye and oats invariably predominated. Two-field systems were the norm and low land values imply a correspondingly low level of productivity. These regions were distant from major markets and, since many of them were land-locked, the bulk carriage of grain did not present a viable proposition. The monotonous character of their common-field agriculture, their technological backwardness, and the emphasis upon extensive rather than intensive methods of production are all indicative of an economy still rooted in self-sufficiency rather than exchange and, by implication, a low level of economic rent.

(4) *Extensive pastoral systems with limited crop production*—north and west of the great zone of common-field agriculture crop production ceased to be the primary economic activity and its place was taken by extensive livestock production on permanent grassland. This was the most land and labour extensive husbandry system of all and, appropriately, it prevailed in the remotest locations where it was also favoured by a natural land-use bias towards grassland. The upland pastures of Devon and Cornwall, Wales and the Welsh borderland, the eastern and western flanks of the Pennines, and southern Scotland supported substantial flocks and herds whose demographic profile indicates a strong bias towards breeding. These areas acted as reservoirs of surplus stock for the more livestock deficient regions to the south and east and there is some evidence that major inter-regional transfers of animals were an integral feature of the agrarian economy of the day.[82] In contrast, where arable husbandry took place it was on a relatively small scale and was clearly intended to satisfy immediate consumption requirements only.

This broad categorization subsumes a great deal of more detailed variation, as case studies of individual farming regions are beginning to reveal. Moreover, the economics of arable and pastoral production were very different on account of their contrasting transportation requirements. Grain had to be carried to market whereas livestock could walk; also, compared with grain, livestock products, such as wool, butter, and cheese, were high in value relative to their bulk and consequently better able to withstand the costs of carriage. Commercial grain production was thus strongly influenced by easy access to cheap riverine and coastal communications. Hence the prominence of northern and eastern Norfolk and northern and eastern Kent as the foremost arable farming districts in the country, producing substantial quantities of wheat and barley for sale in a variety of domestic and overseas markets. Hence, too, the above average land values and semi-intensive cropping regimes of coastal Sussex, parts of the Thames valley, and those parts of the East Midlands penetrated by the rivers Ouse, Nene, and Welland which plied an important trade in grain via the coastal ports of Boston and, especially, Lynn. Where there was no such access to cheap water carriage and markets were remote, as in the West Midlands and parts of southern England, land values were generally lower and cropping systems much simpler. The overall pattern is complex and strongly regional in character and contrasts with the pattern exhibited by pastoral husbandry, which is more zonal than regional (Figs. 4.3 and 4).[83] Thus, it was in the south and east that the most intensive pastoral systems prevailed, with a gradation of types of decreasing intensity radiating outwards in a series of concentric zones towards the north and west, where pastoral husbandry assumed its most extensive form. In the most intensive pastoral systems horses made a significant contribution to draught power, cattle predominated over sheep, herds were demographically skewed towards adults (indicative of a specialist interest in dairying), draught were subordinated to non-draught animals, and there was a heavy reliance upon produced as well as natural fodder. This is essentially a labour-intensive, arable-based pastoralism and in the late thirteenth century it was especially typical of the immediate environs of London and parts of Norfolk and Suffolk. If affords a direct contrast with the grass-based pastoralism of much of the north and west, in which livestock schedules of lowland arable farms were dominated by working animals, primarily oxen, and the maintenance of breeding and back-up herds was reserved to specialist stock farms on the upland margins.[84] With cheap land, a reliance upon forage rather than fodder, and correspondingly low labour inputs, the latter were low-cost livestock producers and their surplus animals were consequently at a premium in this livestock-deficient age, both for draught and for meat. Major inter-regional transfers of animals must therefore be envisaged, although this is not a subject which has as yet received systematic investigation. Certainly, much of the wool produced by these remote, upland districts (an increasingly high-valued product) was traded over remarkably long distances.[85]

Overall, there was a strong tendency for the intensity and sophistication of husbandry to increase towards the south and east. It was here that the spatial differentiation of husbandry systems—arable, pastoral, and mixed—was most pronounced and here that arable and pastoral husbandry both assumed their most developed forms. This is a pattern which reflects economic much more than environmental or even institutional influences and it testifies to the role of the market as an arbiter of agricultural production. Nor was this pattern static. Changes occurred as a result of the diffusion of new technology and in response to shifts in relative prices between products.

The Limits to Growth

During the second half of the thirteenth century reserves of colonizable land were gradually exhausted. Expansion was reaching its physical limits and yet there were no signs that the demographic tide was turning. Of itself this would not have mattered had the rate of economic growth been adequate to compensate, but it was not. Increases in agricultural production were becoming increasingly dependent upon the application of additional labour inputs to a finite area of land and the marginal productivity of labour inevitably suffered. Accordingly, agricultural labour became less well remunerated and the living standards of a majority of the population progressively deteriorated, reaching their nadir in the opening decades of the fourteenth century in one of the two lowest points on the entire Phelps Brown/ Sheila Hopkins index (the other being the 1590s).[86] This failure of rural purchasing power, along with agriculture's reduced relative capacity to produce food surpluses, frustrated the growth of a non-agricultural sector with the result that economic growth stagnated. Under these circumstances only individuals able to maintain their economic strength through control of the means of production were able to gain from the situation, and none more so than the landlords. For them the late thirteenth century was a golden era as they reaped high profits from the widening gap between prices and wages. The high farming which many of them came to practise on their estates yielded some impressive results but it should not be overlooked that it was sustained by an inflationary price rise and subsidized by cheap labour and took place against a background of growing landlessness and destitution. Wealth became more polarized and if the demesne lords were the winners the peasantry were emphatically the losers.[87]

The Problem of Excessive Population Growth

Part of the reason for this mounting imbalance between population and resources, as Postan has forcibly argued, was the rate of population growth itself.[88] As Malthus predicted and modern research has demonstrated, pre-industrial populations possess a much greater potential for growth than do their economies. Few pre-industrial economies have sustained rates of economic growth in excess of 0.5 per cent per annum and under medieval social and technological conditions the rate of economic growth was probably much lower.[89] Yet rates of population growth were often twice as great. Thus, Wrigley and Schofield have shown that for England as a whole population growth rates rarely fell below 0.5 per cent between 1541 and 1611 and at their peak, in the 1580s, reached in excess of 1.0 per cent per annum.[90] Equivalent national rates for the early Middle Ages can only be guessed at, although local evidence points to rates which may have been just as rapid. Thus, on the Bishop of Winchester's manor of Taunton annual tithing-penny payments indicate that the adult male population grew at a mean annual rate of 1.3 per cent between 1209 (when it numbered 612) and 1268, and then at an annual rate of 0.5 per cent until 1311 (by which time it had risen to 1448).[91] This compares with a mean annual growth rate of 0.8 per cent for the adult male population of the manor of Halesowen in Worcestershire between 1270 and 1315, as calculated by Razi in a controversial court-roll based reconstitution study.[92] These are impressive rates of population growth by pre-industrial demographic standards, although allowance has to be made for the fact that these figures relate to adult males only and take no account of gains and losses brought about by migration. As Titow and Razi demonstrate, they placed a severe strain upon their respective local economies and if replicated at a national scale for even a few decades would have had dire economic consequences. Real as thirteenth-century economic growth undoubtedly was, it was incapable of absorbing such a rapid expansion in the workforce.

Taunton and Halesowen were both large manors in ecclesiastical ownership and were located in the west of England well away from the main areas of heavy population pressure further east. Taunton was an anciently settled manor and had virtually no colonizable resources left to it by the mid thirteenth century, with the result that population growth generated the most intense competition for land.[93] This shows up in the spiralling level of entry fines which the Bishop of Winchester was able to demand from incoming tenants. The problem was compounded by the fact that the bishop kept a tight control on the supply of villein holdings, whose integrity he was anxious to preserve for the allocation of rents and services. At the same time widows were entitled to inherit their husband's holdings outright; hence for many men marriage with a widow became the only way of obtaining a holding, approximately one in ten of all holdings being acquired in this way during the period 1270–1315. Nevertheless, there still remained far too few holdings to go round and many peasants either had to content themselves with sub-letting land from one of the manor's main tenants (something about which the documents are silent) or had to eke out a livelihood labouring on the holdings of their better-off neighbours. The poverty squeeze experienced by the growing numbers of village poor emerges very clearly from Razi's reconstitution study of Halesowen.[94] Here, too, after 1270 land reclamation neither enlarged significantly the area under crops nor satisfied the growing demand for land with the result that by the opening of the fourteenth century approximately 43 per cent of tenants had insufficient land to support their families. Economically penalized, these smallholders and cottagers exhibited lower rates of replacement than their wealthier neighbours so that a strong demographic differential existed within village society. The better-off villages more than reproduced themselves and it was their surplus children who fuelled population growth and compensated for the heavy loss of life among the poor.

These two studies illustrate some of the adverse consequences of population pressure and show how its impact varied according to local circumstances. Ecological opportunities were certainly important and seignorial policy also made a difference, but of especial significance, as Homans long ago pointed out, were customs governing the descent and transference of land.[95] Whether inheritance custom was partible or impartible, whether widows inherited outright or merely had a life interest in their husband's holding, and whether there was an active peasant land market or not, all served to shape the precise response to population pressure. For instance, on the Norfolk manor of Martham, where partible inheritance and an active peasant land market both prevailed, the effect of mounting population pressure was entirely different from that at Taunton: holdings soon lost their original integrity and were rapidly reduced in size.[96] At some unspecified time in the mid twelfth century 107 tenants had held 1066 statute acres of land, ten of them holding more than 20 acres and 22 of them holding 5 acres or less. By 1292 the same 1066 statute acres were held by 376 tenants, only one of them holding more than 20 acres and no less than 310 of them holding 5 acres or less. Vigorous population growth during the thirteenth century had reduced virtually the entire tenant population to the status of smallholders. Nor did fragmentation end there for over the same period there was a 50 per cent increase in the number of open-field strips as land parcels as well as holdings became subdivided. In some cases this led to the incorporation within the open-field area of land which had originally been held in consolidated blocks, in others existing strips simply got smaller. A similar process has been identified by Bishop in Yorkshire and Baker in Kent and it demonstrates that although the origins of the open-field system were undoubtedly much older it was in the late thirteenth century that many open fields attained their maximum physical development, both in terms of their extent and their physical subdivision.[97] Outside the Midland common-field system such an extreme degree of fragmentation was hardly conducive to the efficiency of agriculture, although McCloskey believes that plot scattering may have helped peasants to minimize the risk of crop failure.[98]

Some localities coped with the problem of population pressure by diversifying their economy and this certainly seems to have endowed them with a greater relative power of survival. In eastern Norfolk, for example, where population densities reached their medieval maximum, smallholding was combined with wage labouring on intensively farmed seignorial demesnes, domestic cloth manufacture, fishing, coastal trading, and a host of other miscellaneous activities. Its peasantry were a hard-bargaining, individualistic, and enterprising lot, yet as their numbers steadily rose so they became more and more vulnerable to fluctuations in the harvest. This shows up in the behaviour of the land market on the manor of Hakeford Hall in Coltishall, where bad harvests increasingly precipitated a spate of land sales as peasants sold off land to buy food, and good harvests elicited a spate of purchases as peasants endeavoured to make good their losses.[99] The problem was that in bad years they sold land in a buyer's market and bought grain in a seller's and vice versa in good years, so the gains never quite made up for the losses and their plight steadily deteriorated. Compared with much of the rest of the country this was a prosperous and well-endowed locality, and it shows up as such in the 1334 Lay Subsidy, but life for its smallholding peasantry was tough and getting tougher.[100]

Ecological Constraints

In any situation of acute population pressure there is a very real danger that natural ecological limits will be exceeded and environmental degradation will set in. The whole expansion of the early Middle Ages ultimately rested on the productivity of the soil and that was easily exhausted. Technologically, this was a predominantly animate and organic age and adequate numbers of livestock were required to till the soil and provide the manure to maintain its fertility. Yet, according to Postan and Titow, grain production expanded too far: pasture was converted to arable and stocking densities reduced, with the result that yields deteriorated.[101] Thus, it was not just, as in the normal Malthusian equation, that food production failed to keep pace with population growth; it was worse than this: production of essential bread grains could not even be maintained at its existing level. Part of the problem, in Postan's view, derived from the very process of colonization, which had brought a great deal of poor quality land into cultivation whose stored up fertility was rapidly exhausted; but even on the older-settled lowland soils he and Titow believe that soil fertility was declining during the course of the thirteenth century. They cite as evidence the low yield ratios obtained by many manorial demesnes and place particular stress upon the declining yield ratios of spring-sown crops recorded on the estates of the Bishops of Winchester during the second half of the thirteenth century.[102] Titow blames these low yields on what he believes to have been a chronic state of under-manuring born of shortage of livestock, a view endorsed by Farmer who employs much the same explanation to account for the similarly low yields on many of the demesnes of Westminster Abbey.[103] Postan has also drawn attention to the low stocking densities on peasant holdings in such traditionally pastoral areas as the Suffolk Breckland and Wiltshire downland and infers that if yields on the demesnes were poor those on peasant holdings must have been even worse.[104]

The situation was, however, more complex than any of these authors suggest. In the first place, plausible though it is to suppose that ecologically marginal land was prone to exhaustion, the evidence does not always support this. The sandy Breckland of north-west Suffolk has often been cited as a classic example of such an area but recent detailed research by Bailey has failed to bear this out and shown, if anything, the opposite, i.e. a state of ecological equilibrium.[105] Secondly, the evidence of declining yield ratios on the Winchester estates is itself ambiguous. Yield ratios are themselves an inadequate measure of yield and reflect a variety of variables, human and physical, of which soil fertility was but one.[106] It will therefore take a great deal more detailed research before it can be established with any degree of certainty whether the decline in yield was due to soil exhaustion as opposed to other factors.[107] That is not to deny that yields on many of the Winchester manors, as on those of Westminster Abbey, were low in both relative and absolute terms, but that is as likely to have been a function of a low intensity of cultivation arising from low levels of economic rent, as of soil exhaustion per se. Many of the lowest-yielding Winchester manors, along with several of those belonging to Westminster Abbey, lay in precisely those parts of southern and western England where agricultural systems were more extensive than intensive. These areas were isolated by high transport costs from the main centres of demand and the proficiency and productivity of their agriculture were correspondingly depressed.

Nor are Titow and Farmer right in supposing that stocking densities were unduly low on the Winchester manors for a national survey of demesne stocking densities shows that they lay towards the upper end of the range.[108] Indeed, an analysis of yields and stocking densities in Norfolk shows that, contrary to established opinion, there was little correlation between the two. High stocking densities did not necessarily guarantee high yields and vice versa. In fact, by the late thirteenth century agricultural systems had evolved which successfully reconciled a sustained high level of arable productivity with stocking densities well below those on the Winchester estates.[109] Their keynote was the close integration of arable and pastoral husbandry and a reliance upon systematic spreadings of farmyard manure and other fertilizing agents rather than the random droppings of grazing livestock. Such methods were, however, expensive of labour and were only viable where economic rent was high and the scope existed to develop an appropriately flexible system of cropping and grazing. A modest supply of permanent grassland was also a help. Given the crucial importance of labour inputs it may thus have been the peasant sector which had the advantage over the demesne sector when it came to the physical productivity of the soil since the former undoubtedly possessed a more favourable ratio of labour to land. Several recent studies have also suggested that the peasant sector may sometimes have been the more innovatory.[110]

Nevertheless, for all that arable productivity may have been more economically than environmentally determined, the ecological constraints upon agriculture were real enough to judge from the difficulties experienced by certain localities during the first half of the fourteenth century. According to the *Nonarum Inquisitiones* of 1342 land lay untilled in scores of parishes in southern Cambridgeshire, north-eastern

Hertfordshire, Bedfordshire, and Buckinghamshire because of declining village populations, the impoverishment of the tenants, a shortage of seed-corn, and inadequate numbers of plough animals.[111] This was the core area of the two- and three-field system where the demographic and commercial pressures upon that system were at their most acute. Many of these common-field townships were also desperately short of permanent grassland and were almost wholly reliant upon the forage available on the fallow arable. The relative availability of grassland (meadow, pasture, and other grazings) can be measured for the demesne sector using the valuations given in *Inquisitiones Post Mortem* (Fig. 4.2D).[112] The picture obtained is only a partial one, since common pasturage is omitted from the equation, but with certain notable exceptions, such as the counties of the north and west, the broad regional pattern is much as might be expected. Thus, grassland was at its most abundant in parts of the north and much of the west and became progressively less so towards the south and east. It was, however, in parts of East Anglia and the East Midlands that it was scarcest of all, and nowhere more so than in Norfolk, and, above all, Bedfordshire and Cambridgeshire. This scarcity of grassland is reflected in the high value placed upon meadow and pasture in these counties (Figs. 4.2B and C) as well as the extremely low stocking densities prevalent on many demesnes. The latter had obvious consequences for the supply of manure to these arable soils. As Fox has argued, the common-field system may have offered considerable advantages under conditions of low population density but it was singularly ill-equipped to cope with the rising population and growing commercialization of the thirteenth century.[113] These communities were thus locked into a system which was incapable of feeding a growing population without incurring seriously diminishing returns to both labour and land. Their deficiency of grassland left them particularly vulnerable to ecological breakdown; hence the signs of economic distress and demographic retreat which are so apparent in the early 1340s.

Yet even in these hard-pressed localities it is far from clear whether the ecological breakdown was cause or effect. Did these common-field communities over-reach themselves and demand too much from the soil, thereby undermining the precarious equilibrium upon which they depended for survival? Or were the resources which they required to maintain the established course of husbandry eroded by external pressures upon the system which were non-ecological in origin? The shortage of seed-corn and livestock which formed the crux of the problem could have resulted in either way, although in both cases a contraction in the area under cultivation (4870 acres of arable were lying untilled in Cambridgeshire in 1341) would have been the same inevitable result. In this context it is important to remember the demands which were constantly being made upon the rural population by its feudal superiors for these may have been the indirect cause of the impoverishment and depopulation which the *Nonarum Inquisitiones* so frequently report. Maddicott has shown that the early fourteenth century was a time of exceptionally heavy royal taxation (the *Nonarum* was itself a tax equivalent to one-ninth of the net production of corn, wool, and lambs, after the deduction of tithes) and that this adversely affected the reproductive capacity of the agricultural system.[114] Not all areas would have been affected equally and under these circumstances it is easy to see how those villages which were ecologically most vulnerable may have suffered most.

Feudalism as a Brake to Progress

For a number of leading historians it is the nature of feudal social and property relations which ultimately negated medieval economic growth and eventually precipitated the crisis which the feudal economy experienced in the fourteenth century. This school of thought derives from Karl Marx and is now associated with Dobb, Hilton, Bois, Brenner and Dunford and Perrons.[115] These authors subscribe to different opinions on a number of issues but all agree that it was the structure of class relations, of class power, which determined the manner and degree to which demographic and commercial changes affected long-term trends in the distribution of income and economic growth, and not vice versa. For them a feudal economy was one in which economic growth was bound to be impeded since at its core lay the rigorous subordination and exploitation of one class by another. Thus the economic vitality of the largest social and economic group, the peasantry, was sapped by the continuous expropriation of a substantial proportion of its surplus product. This hindered them from raising the technical level of their farming and from using their land in a free and rational manner and may eventually, in Brenner's view, have led to the exhaustion of peasant production, since for him it was the surplus-extraction relations of serfdom which left peasant holdings inadequately provided with seed-corn, under-stocked, and prone to soil exhaustion due to the shortage of manure.[116] The feudal system also put peasants at a disadvantage in relation to the market, constrained their social, occupational, and geographical mobility, created an oppressive atmosphere of insecurity both of their persons and of their property, and threatened any reserves they might accumulate. The resentment which they felt at the injustices of this system is expressed in their continual passive resistance to seignorial authority, in sporadic violent protest, and eventually, in 1381, in outright rebellion.[117] Nor was the capital which was extracted from them put to more efficient and productive use by the feudal lords.

The labour that was appropriated to work the demesnes proved costly to monitor and was characterized by low work motivation and efficiency. It was for that reason that many lords found it more expedient to commute their labour services for cash and replace them with a permanent waged labour force, retaining only their harvest works to help cope with the season of peak labour demands and some boon works to deal with various miscellaneous tasks during the course of the year. Nevertheless, although the result was a gain in efficiency few of the profits which this generated were reinvested in the processes of production. When investment levels can be calculated they were invariably very low. Hilton has calculated investment levels for a range of late-thirteenth-century estates and found that, even on estates such as that of Canterbury Cathedral Priory with a reputation for technological progress and good management, they were commonly less than 5 per cent of total cash receipts.[118] In his view the interest of late-thirteenth-century landlords in their estates did not go much further than the exaction of maximum profit, whilst the idea of reinvesting profit for the purpose of increasing production seems to have been present in few minds if any. Rather, as the French historian Duby has emphasized, the feudal aristocracy preferred to devote its wealth to various forms of conspicuous consumption: building, feasting, fighting, and indulging its taste for rich and beautiful objects.[119] As he has written, one of the time honoured virtues of the feudal aristocracy by which their status was measured in society was largesse—the pleasure of being spendthrift—with the result that such surpluses as were produced by the workers were rapidly squandered. This was not without economic spin-offs, but it was only a very narrow sector within the economy which benefited: the building trades, luxury crafts, and certain types of services.

It was, in fact, the lords' consumption which constituted one of the most important determinants of expansion within the feudal economy. With the rise of fashion and the growing sophistication of medieval material culture so the lords' demands for revenue grew. So, too, did the aspirations and ambitions of medieval kings and the scale and authority of government administration, the combined effect of which was to increase the incidence and the burden of royal taxation. Above all the crown levied taxes to fight wars and when it embarked upon major campaigns of territorial conquest in Wales, Scotland, and France in the late thirteenth and early fourteenth centuries that tax burden became onerous in the extreme.[120]

During the course of the thirteenth century English kings became increasingly interested in asserting their power throughout the British Isles. At the same time significant changes took place in the structure of political power within the countries of the Celtic periphery—Ireland, Scotland, and Wales—which were eventually to bring them into direct conflict with England. Within Ireland Gaelic resistance to the Anglo-Normans stiffened and in 1258 a confederation of Gaelic lords was formed with the object of repelling further Anglo-Norman advances and recapturing some of the territory which had been lost.[121] The Scottish monarchy also became more secure and Scotland began to emerge as a recognized European state power of the middle rank with the result that the claim of the English crown to overlordship became increasingly irksome.[122] The Welsh princes, too, led after 1267 by Llywelyn ap Gryffydd, were trying to build up a united principality centred on Gwynedd in north-west Wales.[123] From 1276 Llywelyn was in open rebellion against the English crown and Edward I, who harboured imperialist ambitions, set about the final military subjugation of Wales. Following two successful military campaigns in 1277 and 1282, during which he deployed forces on a scale unprecedented in the history of medieval British warfare, Edward I finally united and annexed Wales into the English crown in 1284. Twelve years later he embarked upon the conquest of Scotland and the drive was on to create a single kingship of the British Isles. The Scottish campaigns were more protracted and less successful than those which had been waged in Wales but were fought on much the same scale. Their combined cost was enormous. To finance them Edward I bled the Irish exchequer white, leaving the Lordship of Ireland permanently impoverished and weakened and prey to attacks from an increasingly aggressive native population.[124] In England it was individuals rather than the country as a whole who were bankrupted. It was the already hard-pressed peasantry who bore the brunt of the increasingly heavy tax burden and who supplied the royal purveyors with the goods demanded to provision the royal armies.

Purveyance was a system by which the king's representatives exercised a prerogative right to purchase compulsorily the victuals and means of transport which the royal household required. It was arbitrary in its incidence and prone to private profiteering, the seizure of goods without payment or consent, and payments either made inadequately or after long delays. To compound matters, it was frequently imposed in conjunction with taxes on movables. But whereas taxes were nation-wide in their incidence purveyance was geographically more restricted and also more oppressive in the areas which it most affected. As Maddicott has shown, purveyance fell most often and heavily upon the counties of the east coast and the East Midlands, with Lincolnshire, Cambridgeshire, and Huntingdonshire being afflicted most regularly and heavily, followed by Norfolk, Suffolk, Yorkshire, and Essex.[125] This reflected the commercialized nature of their agriculture and the convenience of their situation for sending provisions up the east coast to the Scottish border. Such syphoning off of large quantities of goods dislocated established patterns of internal trade whilst the forstalling activities of purveyors threw markets into chaos. Moreover, the success of the Welsh campaigns was bought at the cost of permanently weakening the English colony in Ireland, whilst the Scottish cam-paigns proved extremely destructive to the whole northern economy which had hitherto enjoyed considerable peace and security.[126] Here, the permanent break-down of security may have undermined the north's involvement in the long-distance supply of cattle, with wider repercussions for the economy at large. There were, of course, some individuals, some trades, and some towns which profited from the heightened warfare of the period, but for the bulk of the population and most of the country it was a disaster. In a sense it was a natural outcome of the preceding phase of demographic and economic expansion and the resurgent nationalism with which this was associated. Nevertheless, there is no mistaking the fact that these wars of territorial aggrandizement, with all their direct and indirect costs, disrupted a fragile economy and drove it irrevocably down the path towards crisis.

Crisis

By 1300 the imbalance between population and resources had become such that the economy was ill-equipped to cope with extreme events, yet the next half century delivered a succession of them. In 1315 torrential rain meant that the harvest was a disaster and grain prices soared to five or six times their normal average. By the spring and summer of 1316 Britain, along with much of the rest of western Europe, was in the throes of a famine of major dimensions, which was accompanied by a virulent and widespread epidemic, perhaps typhoid, which greatly increased mortalities.[127] The following harvest was no better and hence the two years 1315–16 and 1316–17 mark a rate of inflation in grain prices without parallel in English experience. The hardship and suffering were terrible—23 prisoners in Northampton gaol died simply for want of food—and in the country as a whole living standards sank to a nadir exceeded only in 1597, another year of terrible dearth.[128] To make matters worse, cattle and oxen were ravaged by a severe outbreak of murrain—probably rinderpest—in 1319 and 1320 which depleted plough-teams and reduced the ability to cultivate the land, and this was followed in 1321–22 by renewed harvest failure. Dearth recurred in 1330–31 but was succeeded by a run of above average harvests during the remainder of that decade which gave some respite to the hard-pressed rural population.[129] In fact, the high yields exacerbated deflationary tenden-cies within the economy, partially provoked by a contraction in the money supply, so that grain prices actually registered a sustained fall for the first time since inflation began almost 150 years earlier.[130] This was good news for subsistence farmers but for their commercialized counterparts it inaugurated a short phase of acute agrarian depression, during which production was curtailed and many landlords began to consider alternatives to direct demesne management. Towards the end of the decade renewed tax demands accompanied the declaration of war with France in 1337 and these culminated in the punitive tax equivalent to the tithe on corn, wool, and lambs levied in 1341. This bit more deeply into the peasants' resources than any previous tax. Harvests were again bad in 1346–47 and then, in 1348–49, bubonic plague struck. The mortality which it precipitated dwarfs that of the Great Famine, large though that had been, and is without subsequent parallel. Within the space of just two years an estimated third of the country's population had died and in the worst hit communities mortality rates reached 60 per cent.[131] Meanwhile various parts of the country suffered additional setbacks of a geographically more specific nature. Thus in the northern counties much damage was wrought by Scottish raiding parties during the decades after the Scottish victory at Bannockburn in 1314 and the border was never to be entirely secure again for the remainder of the Middle Ages. At the opposite end of the country a minor marine transgression flooded the broadland peat cuttings and much of the reclaimed land in the Fens and along the south coast, with serious consequences for the local economies concerned.[132] This can be related to a heightened incidence of storm surges within the North Sea which was itself a manifestation of a change to a cooler and wetter climate.[133]

So many extreme and unfortunate events coming in such close succession naturally exacted a heavy toll. Nevertheless, the impact of crisis was not everywhere the same and the responses of different localities, communities, and social groups likewise varied. In Ireland, for instance, the Anglo-Norman colony was already exhibiting signs of decay before the close of the thirteenth century. Similarly, London—very much the pulse of the kingdom—appears to have peaked demographically and commercially *c.* 1300 and thereafter stagnated.[134] In several exceptionally well-documented Essex communities reported by Poos the onset of population decline can be dated to the Great Famine, which elicited an excess mortality of approximately 15 per cent, and it continued thereafter, so that numbers had already fallen by on average 30 per cent before the Black Death lowered them yet further.[135] On the estates of the Bishops of Winchester a similar trend is implied by the marked deterioration in life expectancy which Ohlin has calculated from the evidence of heriots paid by the heirs of deceased tenants.[136] In contrast, at Halesowen in Worcestershire a 15 per cent decline in population during the Great Famine was followed by recovery so that on the eve of the Black Death numbers had virtually regained their pre-famine level.[137] The tenantry of the manor of Hakeford Hall in the Norfolk village of Coltishall were even more resilient in the face of adversity and managed to maintain and even increase their numbers right up to the outbreak of plague in 1348.[138] The population of the city of Norwich likewise appears to have been growing for at least part of this period so that here too, it was very much the Black Death that reversed the established population trend.[139] Nationally, there has been much debate as to which crisis marks the more decisive turning point but this misses the essential geographical point that there was not one turning point but several.

Although the bold outlines of crisis are clear enough its detailed anatomy is harder to read so that until further research is undertaken no diagnosis of its cause or causes can be entirely satisfactory.[140] Many have been tempted to read into these events the working out of deep-rooted processes of historical development but reality was more complex and diverse than any Malthusian or Marxist model will admit and involved a unique conjunction of exogenous and endogenous factors.[141] Human agencies were hardly responsible for the heightened climatic variability of the period, the rise in sea level, or the build-up of animal infection to explosive force among the rodent population, although social and economic conditions did plainly determine both their impact and the response to them. On the whole the areas which fared best were those which had always done so, namely those with a favourable environment which were well placed and possessed a diversified economy. But the spatial pattern was complex and contraction is apparent at a relatively early date at both periphery and core. The former represents a pulling back from areas which were politically, environmentally, and economically marginal and is, perhaps, only to have been expected; the latter reflects the reduced productivity of the economic system as a whole coupled with the diffusion of a new demographic order. The essential point, however, is that the integrity of thirteenth-century trends was broken as, with the opening of the new century, change began to flow down a number of quite disparate channels. Some areas undoubtedly continued to gain in population but there was no longer a decisive overall increase in numbers, settlement which had hitherto been advancing now—in the face of military, economic, and environmental setbacks—began to be forced into retreat, demesne farming no longer enjoyed unqualified prosperity, the cultivated area was curtailed, and landlords began to turn to leasing as a more secure alternative. This half century of famine, war, and pestilence thus stands out as one of history's great turning points: the rising tide of the early Middle Ages reached its high-water mark and now began to recede. It is a key period and yet there is much about it that remains enigmatic.

Contraction, Rationalization, and Realignment

If the first half of the fourteenth century was a period of transition, it was the second half of that century which brought far-reaching change. The population's failure to recover from the plague outbreak of 1348–49 inaugurated a century and a half of demographic stagnation and malaise. Many of the developments which dominate this period are consequently the opposite of those that had prevailed before: the area under cultivation contracted, the ratio of land to labour improved, living standards rose, there was a retreat from marginal land, and settlements shrank and many were abandoned. Spatially, there was a return to regionalism and politically a drawing-in from the periphery to the core, with a weakening of English control over the Celtic lands of the periphery. In Ireland this is represented by the progressive retreat of the Pale with the loss of territory to the Irish, in Wales by the Glŷn Dŵr rebellion, and in Scotland by the successful defence of Scottish independence: all were assisted by civil war in England.[142] Yet at the same time feudal social and property relations were gradually dissolved, paving the way for a wholly new socio-economic order—

capitalism—which was ultimately to transform the very fabric of society, so that in a very real sense contraction was accompanied by rationalization and realignment.

The Demographic Dimension

The bulk of the medieval population decline took place within the period 1315–75. In the space of just two generations famine and plague wiped out most of the accumulated increment of the preceding 200 years. So great had been the press of numbers on the eve of the Black Death that few holdings remained untenanted for long in the aftermath of that initial disaster, but as successive plague outbreaks culled the population the problem of finding suitable tenants steadily mounted and the records of manor after manor register a dramatic decline in tenant numbers. Labour, too, was becoming scarce and, notwithstanding government legislation in the form of the Statute of Labourers, wage rates steadily rose, providing an indirect index of the decline in population. Replacement rates calculated for a variety of manorial populations provide more graphic evidence that the population was gradually wasting away and for a remarkable group of 13 Essex manors studied by Poos this can be charted directly from the dwindling number of adult males enrolled within the frankpledge system and paying the hundred-penny fine.[143] By 1377, when the Poll Tax provides a vital documentary benchmark, the population numbered at most a little over 3 million, and there can be no doubt that it subsequently declined still further.

Cash wages continued to rise up to the middle of the fifteenth century and real wages increased until almost its close. Between the beginning of the fourteenth century and the end of the fifteenth real wages for agricultural employment rose by a staggering 236 per cent, with the relative gain for unskilled labour being greater than that for skilled. For Thorold Rogers this was the golden age of the English labourer and the Phelps Brown and Sheila Hopkins Index shows that living standards reached a level which was not to be exceeded until well into the nineteenth century.[144] Yet these high living standards were bought at a high demographic price: for much of the later Middle Ages there was a recurrent failure of male heirs at all levels of society, village populations dwindled to the point at which, in many cases, their communities ceased to be viable, and everywhere there is abundant evidence of a scarcity of people rather than of land. The nadir was probably reached sometime in the second half of the fifteenth century, by which time the population may have approximated in size to that prevailing at Domesday and numbered barely 2 million, but this is very much the dark age of medieval population studies due to the increasingly stereotyped nature of court rolls and other manorial sources on which we are reliant for much of our knowledge about the common people. Nevertheless, as late as the mid 1520s Muster Rolls and Lay Subsidies indicate an early Tudor population which is unlikely to have exceeded 2.92 million and may well have been substantially less.[145] That demographic malaise should have persisted for so long and in the face of countervailing influences, such as rising real wages, low prices, and an abundance of cheap land, is remarkable. In its scale and duration it is virtually without later historical parallel and was the product of a demographic regime in which mortality assumed a quite exceptional degree of dominance.

Confronted by a persistent failure of fathers to be succeeded by sons in both town and country, Thrupp dubbed the fifteenth century 'the golden age of bacteria'.[146] For her the low replacement rates were a product of high infant and child mortality rates arising from the unhealthiness of the times, and there is a good deal of evidence to suggest that this problem was general throughout society.[147] For instance, at Halesowen in Worcestershire Razi argues that recurrent outbreaks of plague exacted a higher toll of life among children than among adults with the result that replacement rates were depressed, producing a steady decline in the number of young adults in the village after 1370.[148] This altered the age structure of the population in such a way that nuptiality and natality were both in turn depressed, thus dooming the population of the parish to a long period of stagnation and decline. Plague is arguably the most virulent and fatal disease ever to have affected England's population, producing a death toll of 25–40 per cent in 1348–49, 13.5 per cent in 1361–62, 16.0 per cent in 1369, and 11.7 per cent in 1375. Moreover, it was responsible for a high background mortality throughout the later Middle Ages during which it remained endemic in England, as can be seen from the fact that possibly 25–30 per cent of the monks of Christchurch Cathedral Priory, Canterbury (a relatively well cared for social group) died from plague during the second half of the fifteenth century.[149] Nor was plague the only infectious disease current at this time for public health in general appears to have been exceptionally bad. Many of the Christchurch monks died of tuberculosis although in many other cases an accurate diagnosis of the cause of death is precluded by the inadequacy of contemporary descriptions. Indeed, there is still considerable debate as to the precise epidemiology of plague itself.[150] Nevertheless, if there is still uncertainty as to the exact cause, there is no dispute as to the high absolute level of mortality in the late fourteenth and fifteenth centuries. At this time, and for all the relatively high material well-being of most people, human life was particularly transient and this finds expression in the morbid preoccupation with death displayed by much of the art and literature of the period.[151] This conjunction of high mortality with high living standards lends support to those such as Chambers and Lee who argue for the paramount influence of an autonomous death rate upon population trends in pre-industrial Europe.[152]

Yet mortality did not operate in isolation and closer attention is now being paid to the concomitant changes which may be presumed to have taken place in fertility, especially in the light of Wrigley and Schofield's observation that variations in fertility, largely mediated through variations in nuptiality, were primarily responsible for fluctuations in English population trends after 1540.[153] As long ago as 1912 Tawney speculated that the late-medieval rise in mortality may have been reinforced by a reduction in fertility.[154] He hypothesized that a wider incidence of property ownership, coupled with greater usage of a system of apprenticeship, operated to delay the age of marriage (property owners tending to marry later than wage-earners). Recent research by Smith and Goldberg has cast some light upon these kinds of relationship.[155] Smith uses the evidence of the Poll Tax returns to argue that a European marriage pattern characterized by a relatively late age at marriage and high incidence of permanent celibacy was already in place in much of lowland England by the late fourteenth century. Furthermore, this pattern may have become more pronounced during the following century as rising wage rates and a swing towards pastoral husbandry encouraged greater use of unmarried, living-in farm

servants. Smith's findings are echoed by those of Goldberg who detects an improvement in the economic opportunities available to women over this same period,
especially within the towns, which made it easier for them to remain unmarried and
independent. At the same time, selective rural–urban migration produced a sexual
imbalance in favour of females in the towns and males in the countryside, the effect
of which would have been to heighten the proportions of both sexes who remained
permanently celebrate.

Migration not only redistributed population from the countryside to the town
(and hence from areas of lower to higher mortality), it also redistributed population
locally and regionally. This accentuated the demographic recession in some townships and localities and alleviated it in others. The selective nature of village
desertion—those that were abandoned invariably being neighboured by others that
survived—bears clear testimony to the impact of these kinds of processes.[156] At this
very local level the precise soil conditions of a township, its manorial structure, the
policy of its lord, or other specific circumstances, were probably what determined
whether people stayed or left. Perhaps inevitably, it was the most marginal areas
which suffered most. There was some return migration from the beleaguered Anglo-
Norman territories in Ireland, and a pulling back of settlement from the upland
margins and most intractable and infertile soils (Fig. 4.1D). Settlements were not
necessarily abandoned completely but a single farm might survive where formerly
there had been a hamlet or village.[157] As in the early Middle Ages, areas of weak
lordship tended to fare better than those where lordship was strong, and in this era
of contracting markets it also helped to be in the hinterland of a major town or city,
whilst the presence of industrial employment in some form or other was a further
bonus. Somewhere like north-eastern Norfolk, which combined easily worked soils
with a weak manorial structure, flexible land market, good market access, and the
opportunity for substantial employment in the local worsted cloth industry, thus
fared reasonably well and, as McKinley has demonstrated from an ingenious use of
surname evidence, seems to have received a significant influx of migrants from other
parts of the county and further afield.[158] Migration is, however, a notoriously
difficult thing to trace from historical sources, but the evidence of chevage fines paid
by servile tenants to live off the manor, the high turnover of individuals revealed by
reconstitutions of manorial populations, and the changing composition of successive listings of tax payers, all confirm the strong impression that late medieval society
was geographically highly mobile.[159]

The net effect of all these moves, as a comparison between the 1377 Poll Tax and
the 1525–25 Lay Subsidies makes clear, was to boost the proportion of the total
population resident in eastern, south-eastern, and especially south-western England at the expense of that in the Midlands and the North.[160] As in other respects, the
south-west and its semi-industrial economy excepted, there was a pulling back from
the periphery (Fig. 4.1D).

Agricultural Developments

The decline in population meant a greatly reduced demand for bread at the same
time as rising real incomes boosted the demand for meat and other animal products.
The net result was a progressive swing during the course of the fourteenth and early

fifteenth centuries from arable to pasture. On seignorial demesnes (the only sector for which reliable statistics are available) this manifested itself in the first instance in a reduction of the mean area under cultivation, which had reached a peak at the turn of the thirteenth and fourteenth centuries under the stimulus of unprecedentedly high grain prices. Landlords were already curtailing their cereal acreage during the decades of depressed grain prices prior to the Black Death, either withdrawing the land from cultivation or leasing it out piecemeal to the land-starved peasantry. By the middle of the fourteenth century the mean demesne cereal acreage had shrunk by an estimated 12 per cent and it shrank by a further 20 per cent during the following half century to produce a 30 per cent decline over the century as a whole.[161] For a while after the plague the sheer amount of money in circulation relative to the greatly diminished population sustained prices and provided a final Indian summer for demesne producers, but this was abruptly terminated in the late 1370s as grain prices collapsed and wages continued their inflationary climb. Under these circumstances the seignorial response was less the curtailment of cultivation than its abandonment altogether as the time-hallowed policy of direct management was replaced by one of leasing and landlords became the rentiers which they have remained ever since.[162] Nevertheless, it was not until the second half of the fifteenth century that direct management was completely extinguished as an institution.

The fourteenth-century contraction in cultivation was, however, far from uniform, varying with the policy of the estate, the quality of the land, the readiness with which it could profitably be converted to pasture, and accessibility to markets.[163] On northern demesnes the contraction is scarcely apparent: arable land had never been so abundant that much could now be allowed to lapse from production and its prime function remained, as it has always been, to provide for immediate consumption needs on the estate and within the region. Nor was their cattle-based pastoral economy a particularly expanding one. The contraction was also well below average in the eastern counties, and especially in Norfolk, which were still able to command a market for much of the grain which they produced, albeit a less profitable one, and whose chief competitive advantage lay in arable rather than grass-based husbandry systems. For them the conversion of arable to pasture was generally not a particularly viable proposition and costs were increasingly against their highly intensive form of pastoralism. It was in the central and southern counties that environmental and commercial scope for the development of grass-based pastoral farming was greatest and accordingly here that the sown acreage contracted most markedly, that contraction being most pronounced of all in the sheep-farming districts of southern England where it approached 40 per cent over the century as a whole. Piecemeal leasing diverted some of these arable resources to the peasant sector but for the most part it was the pastoral sector which was their principal beneficiary as is borne out by the fact that it is in precisely these counties that the concomitant rise in livestock numbers was greatest.

The measurement of total livestock numbers, taking due account of the various ages and types of animal, poses considerable methodological problems. Nevertheless, no matter how measured, there is no doubting that demesnes carried on average a significantly greater number of animals at the beginning of the fifteenth century than they had done a century earlier, the scale of that increase within the country as a whole ranging from 10 to 20 per cent according to the method of weighting. Moreover, the bulk of that rise occurred after 1350, which indicates that it was only then that a direct transfer of resources took place out of arable and into pastoral production. The rise was smallest in those counties which were already well endowed with permanent grassland, notably in northern England, where livestock numbers if anything fell (partly because of the demise of sheep farming as northern wool deteriorated in quality), and in the counties of the south-west, where it was well below average. Much the same was true of the traditionally arable counties of the east, Norfolk registering scarcely any change in mean livestock numbers and its neighbouring eastern counties only a relatively modest one. Instead it was in the counties which lay between these two extremes—the traditionally pastoral and the traditionally arable—that the rise in livestock numbers was greatest (between two and five times the national average), notably in the Midlands and above all the south-east. Here more than anywhere else arable was being converted to grassland with obvious consequences for both the look and the management of the land. In these counties the ratio of livestock to crops more than doubled over the course of the fourteenth century, whereas in the country as a whole it increased by 50–60 per cent.

Associated with this swing from arable to pasture went a general lowering in the intensity of husbandry methods. This shows up most clearly in the intensive high-farming systems which had emerged during the boom conditions at the end of the thirteenth century. These reduced their seeding rates, fallowed land more frequently, and generally expended less effort preparing the ground, tending their growing crops, and gathering in the harvest, with the result that although costs of production were economized, output per acre fell.[164] On the whole it was the systems of intermediate intensity which did not rely upon lavish inputs of labour which fared best during the difficult economic conditions of the later Middle Ages. These systems grew in relative importance and benefited from both the wider diffusion of legumes, whose share of the cropped area rose three-fold between the late thirteenth and early fifteenth centuries, and a disproportionate reduction in the acreages occupied by rye and oats, as the poorer soils upon which they were sown were withdrawn from cultivation and barley proved itself a more profitable alternative. These changes helped to diversify cropping systems, raised the unit value of production, and in conjunction with higher stocking densities possibly even enhanced productivity, yet all without any significant increase in the costs of production. Likewise, on the pastoral side it was the more extensive forms of pastoralism which expanded most: meat rather than dairying and sheep rather than cattle.

The horse as a draught animal consolidated its hold upon those areas where it was already well established, in eastern and south-eastern England, but from the mid fourteenth century its wider adoption for ploughing was effectively halted. Indeed, the ox, the slower but cheaper of the two animals, began to stage something of a comeback and in certain localities re-established itself as the pre-eminent beast of traction.[165] Cart horses, the Rolls Royce of medieval road transport, continued to grow in importance down to the 1370s, as more resources became available for their support, but thereafter they too declined as their high maintenance costs increasingly counted against them in the worsening economic climate. With less land under the plough and more resources available for the support of other animals, draught animals as a group declined in relative importance. They had accounted for over 40 per cent of all demesne livestock in the late thirteenth century but this proportion was reduced to less than 30 per cent by the beginning of the fifteenth century. Cattle maintained their importance over this period, and in parts of the Home Counties and East Anglia with access to the valuable London market dairying and fattening appear to have prospered, but it was sheep which were the principal beneficiaries of the general expansion in the pastoral sector.

Sheep farming on permanent grassland is the most extensive form of pastoralism and was therefore well suited to an economic climate in which land was becoming cheaper and labour dearer. In the late thirteenth and early fourteenth centuries high wool prices had encouraged landlords to expand their flocks but during the later Middle Ages, as Lloyd has shown, wool prices were depressed and the chief attraction of sheep farming lay in its low production costs.[166] Between the late thirteenth and the early fifteenth centuries the ratio of sheep to sown acres increased by a factor of three and sheep increased their share of an expanding livestock sector from approximately a fifth to a third. More demesnes were keeping sheep and they were keeping them in larger numbers. For instance, the Norfolk estates of the Prior of Norwich carried two-and-a-half times as many sheep at the close of the fifteenth century as they had done two centuries earlier. The rise of sheep farming is one of the most striking features of the later Middle Ages. In much of lowland England this took place within the context of a sheep–corn system of husbandry, whereby sheep fed upon permanent pastures by day were folded on the arable at night whose soil was thereby enriched by their treading, dung, and urine.[167] These systems grew to become the predominant husbandry type in much of southern England and were ideally suited to conditions in which pasture was abundant, labour both scarce and dear, and uncertain markets favoured those who could produce a range of products, in this case grain, meat, and wool.

The cumulative effect of all these developments was a subtle transformation of the geography of demesne agriculture and the progressive reorientation of a number of regional economies. On the arable side the greatest changes occurred in parts of the Midlands and the north as rotations were adapted to incorporate increased sowings of barley and legumes. On the pastoral side, however, it was the south whose husbandry systems registered the greatest change and it was here that stocking densities rose most dramatically. The net result was a greater regional articulation of farming systems as agriculture became more firmly aligned along regional rather than zonal lines. The husbandry of East Anglia, the Midlands, the southern counties, the West Country and Welsh Borders, the north-east, and the north-west, emerges as possessing an increasingly distinctive regional identity. This reflects the growing provincialism of economic life and represents a retreat from the spatially more integrated economy of the late thirteenth century.

How far the peasantry participated in these developments is, however, a moot point. Direct evidence of peasant agriculture is scarce and fragmentary and attempts to study it have been correspondingly few. That it was characterized by a similar swing towards pastoralism is not seriously in doubt, Dyer has demonstrated as much for Warwickshire.[168]. What is at issue is the precise nature and timing of this change. McIntosh, in a pioneering analysis of social and economic conditions on the manor of Havering in Essex, has shown just how diverse and commercialized late medieval peasant farming could be, as well as how much remains to be known and understood about it.[169] For all the difficulties posed by depressed price contracting markets, the later Middle Ages was a time of unprecedented opportunity for the peasantry and it is plain that its more enterprising members took full advantage of this. Their labour requirements were smaller than those of their feudal superiors and did not pose the same problems of supervision. Land was becoming increasingly abundant and they enjoyed improved access to working capital through the leasing of demesne livestock, buildings, and equipment. Only in the case of sheep farming were the peasantry sometimes penalized by a seignorial prerogative of folding, an institution which was to become a source of friction and agrarian discontent in the early sixteenth century as lords sought to expand their flocks at the expense of those of their tenants.[170]

Within the peasant sector changes in agricultural enterprise were nevertheless of far less moment than structural and tenurial developments, which transformed the size and layout of holdings and the conditions on which they were held in ways which were to be of enduring significance for the evolution of agriculture. In the first place, mean holding size grew substantially during the later Middle Ages. With the decline in population there was more land to go round within the peasant sector and to this was now added much of the land which had formerly been reserved to the demesne sector. The low replacement rates meant that inheritance now operated to amalgamate rather than partition holdings, although increasingly land and holdings changed hands *inter vivos* rather than *post mortem*.[171] This serves as a reminder that the growth of holdings was not a fortuitous process but the product of a series of conscious decisions. Farming was a risky business and many tenants preferred to sell up and avail themselves of the high wages which their labour could command in the towns and the expanding rural cloth industry. Land which no-one was prepared to take reverted to the lord and on some manors its acreage steadily mounted, obliging the lord to manage it himself either by incorporating it into his demesne or, when labour was scarce, by converting it to sheep walk. The piecemeal leasing of demesnes offered further opportunities for those who wished to accummulate land but this too was hazardous, as the many cases of tenants who got into serious arrears of rent bears witness. As the agrarian depression depended in the middle decades of the fifteenth century suitable tenants proved increasingly hard to find and lords found themselves in a weaker and weaker bargaining position when it came to letting their land. The difficulties experienced by the Paston family in the 1460s in the formerly prosperous north-east of Norfolk, as described in the correspondence between various members of the Paston family and their receiver Richard Calle, provide a particularly vivid example of this problem.[172]

By its nature the growth of holding size was therefore a selective process. Peasants varied in their willingness to take on land and in the resources available at their disposal. The result was a growing differentiation of holding size as some individuals built up much more substantial holdings than others. At Martham in Norfolk, where in 1292 there had been no-one much above the status of a near-landless smallholder, the process of engrossing made such progress that by 1497 there were at least eleven holdings of more than 18 acres, including four of more than 30 acres, with the result that just under a fifth of all the tenants held half of the total area.[173] Similarly, at Chippenham in Cambridgeshire the 143 tenants recorded in 1279 (all but two of whom held less than 30 acres) had been replaced by 45 tenants in

1544, eleven of whom held more than 50 acres and one of whom held more than 100 acres.[174] In these and in many other townships an incipient yeoman class was emerging with the experience and the resources necessary for the management of substantial holdings. Behind this transformation lay a long and complex history of land transfers as acre was laid on acre and holding upon holding. Detailed case studies of the late medieval land market are beginning to reveal the dynamics of this process and the extent to which it varied locally according to idiosyncracies of custom and tenure and regionally according to economic and other related factors.[175] It is also becoming clear that it was the land market much more than inheritance or any other process which was primarily responsible for this restructuring of land ownership. Indeed, customary inheritance increasingly fell into abeyance as testamentary bequests gained legitimacy and tenants transferred land to their heirs in their own lifetime by means of *inter vivos* transfers. Individuals were gaining more control over the disposal of their land and if this meant the lapsing of time-honoured custom there were few who lamented its passing.

Associated with these changes in holding size went changes in their layout. As land was concentrated into fewer hands it was almost inevitable that individuals would acquire adjacent parcels and consolidate them into larger blocks. Frequently, however, this process of consolidation became an end in itself and was actively promoted via the selective purchase, sale, and exchange of individual plots within the open fields. This substantially modified and simplified the layout of open fields and along with the parallel reduction in landowners created a very different decision-taking environment from that which had existed at the close of the thirteenth century, when heavily subdivided common fields were managed by a large community of cultivators. It was a slow and painstaking process, but one which tended to gather momentum during the fifteenth century as the number of individual owners and parcels both fell. The many tiny parcels containing just a fraction of an acre were eliminated first and it was only then that more substantial parcels were built up capable of being enclosed. On the supremely fertile soils at Hemsby in Norfolk, which had been heavily parcellated at the end of the thirteenth century, the size of individual plots grew by 20 per cent between 1422 and 1500 to reach a mean of 0.85 acres. Just a few miles away at Hevingham, on rather poorer soils, plot size increased by 39 per cent between 1382 and circa 1500–10, to reach 0.9 acres.[176] In less populous townships where consolidation began from a higher base and the growth of pastoralism placed a premium upon the creation of closes, progress was more rapid, as at Walsham-le-Willows in Suffolk which was effectively enclosed by the end of the fifteenth century.[177] The same was true of many other townships in eastern and south-eastern England, where there were strong commercial incentives behind the consolidation of strips and engrossing of holdings and few institutional obstacles of a communal or manorial nature. Much has been made of the enclosing activities of the early Tudor flockmasters in the Midland shires of England, to the point at which this more peaceful transformation of the countryside has tended to be overlooked.[178] The latter was peasant-based and demonstrates the capacity for change to emerge from within rural society rather than to be imposed from above.

These structural changes—the leasing of demesnes, concentration of land into fewer hands, and consolidation of strips—represent a fundamental departure from the highly polarized agricultural structure of the early Middle Ages with its plethora of tiny, open-field, peasant farms juxtaposed with substantial seignorial demesnes. Such a structure depressed the efficiency of agriculture and was inimical to long-term economic progress. That which replaced it was not. The structural changes which took place during the later Middle Ages paved the way for the emergence of capitalist agriculture in the sixteenth and seventeenth centuries. These changes nevertheless took time to bring about and it was time which the prolonged demographic and economic recession of the fourteenth and fifteenth centuries provided.

Changes in the Prevailing Social Order

No society could have withstood such demographic and economic changes and itself remain unchanged. On the Ramsey Abbey manor at Upwood in Huntingdonshire Raftis has shown that the established socio-economic status quo was maintained for about a generation after the Black Death.[179] That catastrophe and its subsequent visitations precipitated the demise of 18 of the families which had formerly occupied prominent positions within the village, but it was only slowly that lesser families and new tenants from beyond the village rose to prominence. Eventually half-a-dozen formerly insignificant villagers came to hold substantial lands and positions of responsibility and influence. In this way a surface equilibrium was maintained up to the 1390s, but thereafter the village succumbed to the deepening economic and demographic recession and the way was opened for development along new lines. Other detailed reconstitutions of village society using the socio-economic information contained in court rolls and related manorial records have identified a similar breakdown in the established rural social order at some point in the late fourteenth or early fifteenth centuries.[180] Village communities as they had evolved and reproduced themselves over a period of several centuries finally disintegrated and opportunities opened up for new individuals, new families, and, eventually, the emergence of an entirely new social order. The demise of the traditional village community hastened the decay of custom and helped to engender new attitudes to, among other things, proprietorship.

At the same time the power of lords and the nature of feudal tenures also changed. Feudalism in its original form represented a devolution of power and authority where the state was weak, yet this was increasingly anachronistic in late medieval England with its sophisticated and highly developed machinery of central government and powerful royal courts. The jurisdictional power of local lords was waning, more and more of their tenants sought redress in the royal courts, and the

These structural changes—the leasing of demesnes, concentration of land into fewer hands, and consolidation of strips—represent a fundamental departure from resented institution and it had been one of the demands of the Peasants' Revolt of 1381 that all bond men be set free. Lords were naturally reluctant to part with a captive labour force when the alternative was becoming both scarcer and dearer, yet although the revolt of 1381 was quashed and did not itself do much to advance the cause of tenant freedom there was little in the long run that lords could do to arrest the decay of serfdom.[181] With the growth of the royal courts they lacked the necessary coercive powers and, possibly, the will to exercise them.

To some extent servility died out of its own accord: many customary tenants died in the epidemics of the period, others won their freedom by fleeing their native manor, some, in an era of rising peasant incomes, purchased their freedom, and yet others were granted theirs by lords who foresaw the inevitable.[182] But its decay was also hastened by the decline of demesne farming as an institution. The decision to lease rather than manage demesnes had two immediate effects: it promoted the development of leasehold tenures and led to the commutation of labour services for money rents. Many demesnes, of course, had long been worked using a permanent staff of farm servants, but even when this was the case there was a strong temptation to retain boon works for weeding, marling, and other such supplementary tasks for which it would otherwise have been necessary to hire casual labourers, and harvest works always tended to be retained to the bitter end, since the harvest was a time of peak labour demands and was reflected as such in wage rates. If a manor was leased entire the labour services normally went with it and it was then up to the farmer whether he collected them or their money equivalent. If the demesne was split up and leased piecemeal, as was most often the case, the labour services were invariably commuted and replaced by a cash rent. The progress made by the leasing of demesnes and commutation of labour services varied greatly from estate to estate and region to region.

Some estates, such as the Duchy of Cornwall, were already leasing their demesnes at the beginning of the fourteenth century, and with each new crisis the number leased out tended to increase until, by the end of the fourteenth century, it was the exception rather than the rule for the demesne to be retained in hand. The exceptions tended to be institutional estates with substantial households to support, especially those of ecclesiastical houses which, as Kosminsky has shown, were precisely those on which servile dues tended to be heaviest.[183] For example, although Norwich Cathedral Priory first began leasing its demesnes in the 1330s and from the 1350s set a number of its demesnes permanently at farm, it kept a hard core of demesnes in hand until the early 1420s to provision the community in Norwich. In southern England the Bishops of Winchester only abandoned direct management of their demesnes in 1453, whilst in remote Devon Tavistock Abbey kept several of its demesnes in hand throughout the fifteenth century.[184] A few minor lay landlords, such as the De Yelvertons at Rougham in Norfolk, also found it expedient to do likewise. As these examples intimate, it was paradoxically in the more commercialized south and east that direct management of demesnes and their associated labour services lingered longest, and in the north and west, where demesne farming had always been less strongly developed and less viable, that it was replaced soonest by freer and more monetized social and property relations. Dodgshon has drawn attention to this spatial dichotomy and argued that the tensions which it generated ultimately acted as a solvent upon the feudal economy at large.[185]

As bondage declined new types of tenure evolved. Often customary tenancies were converted to leasehold. Spufford has demonstrated that this was the case at Chippenham in Cambridgeshire where, from 1381 to 1446, the majority of holdings of 7 acres or more which passed through the manor court were leased for a term of years.[186] The same was true of many other manors and when combined with the leasing of demesnes it served to make leasehold one of the most common forms of tenure by the close of the Middle Ages. Elsewhere copyhold tenure emerged as the lineal descendant of customary tenure but without its taint. Copyhold tenants held at the will of the lord by copy of the court roll and the lord was entitled to levy an entry fine every time a holding changed hands. As a type of tenure it long outlived the decline of feudalism. By the close of the Middle Ages England had therefore ceased to be a country of peasant proprietors and become one in which the majority of tenants held land at lease or at the will of the lord. This quiet revolution was to have momentous consequences for it opened the way to the emergence of a new set of social and property relations within the countryside based upon the control of capital rather than the control of labour.[187] In that respect the ending of the Middle Ages heralded the dawning of a new epoch.

Conclusion

The England of Henry VIII was not much more populous than the England of William I 450 years earlier, yet socially and economically it was a very different country and possessed an entirely different human geography. The era of expansion and growth in the early Middle Ages possessed one spatial order, the era of contraction and realignment in the later Middle Ages another. The former bequeathed a tamed countryside, a host of new settlements, a commercialized and technologically more advanced and diversified agriculture, a partially colonized and annexed Wales, and a partially colonized and partially conquered Ireland. The latter thinned out and rationalized the settlement network, realigned agriculture, trans-formed the size and layout of farm units, saw the demise of feudal class and property relations, and witnessed a reassertion of native resistance in Ireland and Wales. Together they made a formative contribution to the emergent human geography of both England and Wales (and were not without their repercussions for Scotland and Ireland) and set the tone for patterns of development within the ensuing early modern period, when demographic and economic expansion were again, belatedly, resumed.

References

1. For example, J. Alexander and P. Binski (eds.), *Age of Chivalry: Art in Plantagenet England*, (London, 1987).
2. P. Fowler, *The Farming of Prehistoric Britain*, (Cambridge, 1983), pp. 33–4.
3. R. A. Dodgshon, *The European Past: Social Evolution and Spatial Order*, (London, 1987), pp. 269–86.
4. J. C. Russell, *English Medieval Population*, (Alberqueque, 1948), p. 54; H. E. Hallam, *Rural England 1066–1348*, (London, 1981), p. 247.
5. H. C. Darby, *Domesday England*, (Cambridge, 1977), pp. 87–91; S. Harvey, 'Domesday England', pp. 45–138, in H. E. Hallam (ed.), *The Agrarian History of England and Wales, II, 1042–1350*, (Cambridge, 1988), p. 49. For a more detailed review of the evidence relating to medieval population see R. M. Smith, 'Human resources', in A. Grant and G. Astill (eds.), *The Countryside in Medieval England* (Oxford, 1988), pp. 188–212.
6. J. Hatcher, *Plague, Population and the English Economy 1348–1530*, (London, 1977), pp. 13–14.
7. Russell, *English Medieval Population*, p. 88; Hallam, *Rural England*, pp. 246–48; E. Miller

and J. Hatcher, *Medieval England: Rural Society and Economic Change 1086–1348*, (London, 1978), p. 29; Smith, 'Human resources', p. 191.

8. Cited in R. R. Davies, *Conquest, Coexistence, and Change: Wales 1063–1415*, (Oxford, 1987), p. 147.

9. B. M. S. Campbell, 'Population change and the genesis of commonfields on a Norfolk manor', *Economic History Review*, 2nd ser., **XXXIII** (1980), pp. 178–9.

10. M. J. McIntosh, *Autonomy and Community: The Royal Manor of Havering, 1200–1500*, (Cambridge, 1987), pp. 126–30.

11. J. B. Harley, 'Population and agriculture from the Warwickshire Hundred Rolls of 1279' *Economic History Review*, 2nd ser., **XI** (1958), pp. 8–18.

12. Compare, for example, the divergent trends noted by B. M. S. Campbell, 'Population pressure, inheritance and the land market in a fourteenth-century peasant community' and R. M. Smith. 'Families and their land in an area of partible inheritance, Redgrave, Suffolk 1260–1320', respectively pp. 87–134 and 135–196 in R. M. Smith (ed.), *Land, Kinship and Lifecycle*, (Cambridge, 1984).

13. Darby, *Domesday England*, pp. 90–4.

14. A. R. H. Baker, 'Changes in the later Middle Ages', pp. 186–247, in H. C. Darby (ed.), *A New Historical Geography of England*, (Cambridge, 1973), p. 191.

15. Darby, *Domesday England*, p. 127.

16. B. M. S. Campbell, 'The extent and layout of commonfields in eastern Norfolk', *Norfolk Archaeology*, **XXXVIII** (1981), pp. 18–20.

17. H. C. Darby, 'Domesday woodland', *Economic History Review*, 2nd ser., **III** (1950–51), pp. 26–7; J. M. Lambert, J. N. Jennings, C. T. Smith, C. Green, and J. N. Hutchinson, *The Making of the Broads: A Reconsideration of their Origin in the Light of New Evidence*, (Royal Geographical Society Research Series, 3, London, 1960), pp. 82–107.

18. H. C. Darby, R. E. Glasscock, J. Sheail, and G. R. Versey, 'The changing geographical distribution of wealth in England 1086–1334–1525', *Jnl. of Historical Geography*, **5** 1979, pp. 249–56.

19. P. F. Brandon, 'Medieval clearances in the East Sussex Weald', *Transactions of the Institute of British Geographers*, **48** (1969), pp. 135–53; E. C. Vollans, 'The evolution of farmlands in the central Chilterns in the twelfth and thirteenth centuries', *Transactions of the Institute of British Geographers*, **26** (1959), pp. 197–235; Harley, 'Population and agriculture from the Warwickshire Hundred Rolls of 1279'; B. K. Roberts, 'A study of medieval colonization in the Forest of Arden, Warwickshire', *Agricultural History Review*, **16** (1968), pp. 101–13; G. H. Tupling, *The Economic History of Rossendale*, (Manchester, Chetham Society, 1927); E. M. Yates, 'Dark Age and medieval settlement on the edge of wastes and forests', *Field Studies*, **2** (1965), pp. 133–53.

20. J. A. Sheppard, 'Pre-enclosure field and settlement patterns in an English township: Wheldrake, near York', *Geografiska Annaler*, **XLVIIIB** (1966), pp. 59–77; J. S. Moore, *Laughton: A Study in the Evolution of the Wealden Landscape*, (Occasional Papers, Department of English Local History, University of Leicester, XIX, (1965).

21. R. I. Hodgson, 'Medieval colonization in northern Ryedale, Yorkshire', *Geographical Jnl*, **135** (1969), pp. 44–54.

22. J. McDonnell, 'Medieval assarting hamlets in Bilsdale, north-east Yorkshire', *Northern History*, **XXII** (1986), pp. 269–79; A. J. L. Winchester, *Landscape and Society in Medieval Cumbria*, (Edinburgh, 1987), pp. 37–44.

23. Davies, *Conquest, Coexistence and Change*, pp. 147–51.

24. L. F. Salzmann, 'The inning of Pevensey Levels', *Sussex Archaeological Collections*, **LII** (1910), pp. 32–60; S. G. E. Lythe, 'The organization of drainage and embankment in medieval Holderness', *Yorkshire Archaeologicial Journal*, **XXXIV** (1939), pp. 282–95; R. A. L. Smith, 'Marsh embankment and sea defence in medieval Kent', *Economic History Review*, **X** (1940), pp. 29–37; N. Harvey, 'The inning and winning of the Romney Marshes', *Agriculture*, **LXII** (1955), pp. 334–38; B. E. Cracknell, *Canvey Island: The History of a Marshland Community*, (Occasional Papers, Department of English Local History, University of Leicester, XII, 1959); M. Williams, *The Draining of the Somerset Levels*, (Cambridge, 1970).

25. H. C. Darby, *The Medieval Fenland*, (Cambridge, 1940).

26. H. E. Hallam, 'Population density in medieval Fenland', *Economic History Review*, 2nd ser., **XIV** (1961), pp. 71–81.

27. H. E. Hallam, *Settlement and Society: A Study of the Early Agrarian History of South Lincolnshire* (Cambridge, 1965), p. 17.

28. R. E. Glasscock, 'The distribution of wealth in East Anglia in the early fourteenth century', *Transactions of the Institute of British Geographers*, **32** (1963), pp. 118–23.

29. T. A. M. Bishop, 'The Norman settlement of Yorkshire', in E. M. Carus-Wilson (ed.), *Essays in Economic History*, *II*, (London, 1962), pp. 1–11; Darby, *Domesday England*, pp. 248–59; W. E. Wightman, 'The significance of 'Waste' in the Yorkshire Domesday', *Northern History*, **X** (1975), pp. 55–71.

30. J. A. Sheppard, 'Medieval village planning in Northern England: some evidence from Yorkshire', *Jnl. of Historical Geography*, **2** (1976), pp. 3–20.

31. On the contribution of the Cistercians to the human geography of the Middle Ages see, R. A. Donkin, *The Cistercians: Studies in the Geography of Medieval England and Wales*, (Toronto, 1978).

32. T. A. M. Bishop, 'Monastic granges in Yorkshire', *English Historical Review*, **51** (1936), pp. 193–214.

33. On external migration in Europe at this date see C. T. Smith, *An Historical Geography of Western Europe before 1800*, (London, 1967), pp. 170–82. See also A. R. Lewis, 'The closing of the mediaeval frontier, 1250–1350', *Speculum*, **33** (1958), pp. 475–83.

34. R. Fox, 'Urban development, 1100–1700', pp. 73–92, in G. Whittington and I. D. Whyte (eds.), *An Historical Geography of Scotland*, (London, 1983), pp. 76–9.

35. Davies, *Conquest, Coexistence and Change*, pp. 97–100.

36. B. J. Graham, *Medieval Irish Settlement*, Historical Geography Research Series, 3, (Norwich, 1980).

37. Davies, *Conquest, Coexistence and Change*. pp. 370–3.

38. On the impact of large-scale emigration upon marriage rates in the seventeenth century see E. A. Wrigley and R. S. Schofield, *The Population History of England 1451–1871: A Reconstruction*, (Cambridge, 1981), pp. 224–6, 262–3, and 469–71.

39. Much has been written on the nature of medieval feudalism, for a useful introduction see G. Duby, *The Early Growth of the European Economy*, (London, 1974), pp. 162–77.

40. The nature of feudal rent is discussed in R. H. Hilton, 'Introduction', *idem* (ed.), *The Transition from Feudalism to Capitalism*, (London, 1976), pp. 9–30.

41. J. Hatcher, 'English serfdom and villeinage: towards a reassessment', *Past and Present*, **90** (1981), pp. 26–8.

42. R. V. Lennard, *Rural England 1086–1135: A Study of Social and Agrarian Conditions*, (Oxford, 1959), pp. 230–1.

43. Hatcher, 'English serfdom and villeinage', p. 5.

44. R. H. Hilton, *The Decline of Serfdom in Medieval England*, (London, 1969), pp. 17–18; Dodgshon, *The European Past*, 272–4.

45. Hatcher, 'English serfdom and villeinage', p. 7.

46. M. M. Postan, 'The famulus: the estate labourer in the twelfth and thirteenth centuries', *Economic History Review Supplement*, 2 (1954).

47. Darby, *Domesday England*, pp. 338–45.

48. R. A. Dodgshon, 'The early Middle Ages, 1066–1350', pp. 81–118, in *idem* and R. A. Butlin (eds.), *An Historical Geography of England and Wales*, (London 1978), pp. 84–5.

49. E. A. Kosminsky, *Studies in the Agrarian History of England in the Thirteenth Century*, (Oxford, 1956).

50. For a case study of one such manor see B. M. S. Campbell, 'The complexity of manorial structure in medieval Norfolk: a case study', *Norfolk Archaeology*, **XXXIX** (1986), pp. 225–61.

51. *Ibid.*, pp. 227–32; Kosminsky, *Studies in the Agrarian History of England*, p. 73.

52. Kosminsky, *Studies in the Agrarian History of England*, p. 79.

53. F. Stenton, *Types of Manorial Structure in the Northern Danelaw*, (Oxford, 1910).

54. Duby, *The Early Growth of the European Economy*, pp. 177–80.

55. K. G. Persson, *Pre-industrial Economic Growth: Social Organization and Technological Progress in Europe*, (Oxford, 1988).

56. R. S. Lopez, *The Commercial Revolution of the Middle Ages, 950–1350*, (Englewood Cliffs, 1971); see also Chapter 5 in the current volume by P. T. H. Unwin.

57. D. Keene, *Cheapside before the Great Fire*, (London, 1985).

58. M. Chisholm, 'Johann Heinrich von Thunen', in *Rural Settlement and Land-use: An Essay on Location*, (London, 1962), pp. 20–32.

59. The relationship between land use and farming systems will be discussed in detail in my forthcoming book, *The Geography of Seignorial Agriculture in Medieval England*, (Cambridge).

60. M. Bailey, *A Marginal Economy? East Anglian Breckland in the Later Middle Ages*, (Cambridge, 1989).

61. B. M. S. Campbell, 'Agricultural progress in Medieval England: Some evidence from eastern Norfolk', *Economic History Review*, 2nd ser., **XXXVI** (1983), pp. 26–46; R. A. L. Smith, 'Arable farming', in *Canterbury Cathedral Priory*, (Cambridge, 1943), pp. 128–45; M. Mate, 'Medieval agrarian practices: the determining factors', *Agricultural History Review*, **33** (1985), pp. 22–31.

62. Technological progress in this period is discussed in Persson, *Pre-industrial Economic Growth*, pp. 24–31.

63. J. L. Langdon, *Horses, Oxen and Technological Innovation: The Use of Draught Animals in English Farming from 1066–1500*, (Cambridge, 1986).

64. J. L. Langdon, 'Horse hauling: a revolution in vehicle transport in twelfth- and thirteenth-century England?', *Past and Present*, **103** (1984), pp. 37–66.

65. B. M. S. Campbell, 'Towards an agricultural geography of medieval England', *Agricultural History Review*, **33** (1988), pp. 95–7.

66. R. Holt, *The Mills of Medieval England*, (Oxford, 1988), pp. 17–35.

67. *Ibid.*, pp. 86–87.

68. M. M. Postan, *The Medieval Economy and Society: An Economic History of Britain in the Middle Ages*, (London, 1972), pp. 51–2; Campbell, *The Geography of Seignorial Agriculture*.

69. B. M. S. Campbell, 'The diffusion of vetches in medieval England', *Economic History Review*, 2nd ser., **XLI** (1988), pp. 193–208.

70. W. Harwood Long, 'The low yields of corn in medieval England', *Economic History Review*, 2nd ser., **XXXII** (1979), pp. 464–69; Campbell, 'Agricultural progress in medieval England', p. 38.

71. *Ibid.*, pp. 32–6; Smith, *Canterbury Cathedral Priory*, pp. 128–45.

72. The relationship between labour imputs and physical productivity is discussed in E. Boserup, *The Conditions of Agricultural Growth: The Economics of Agrarian Change under Population Pressure*, (Chicago, 1965).

73. B. M. S. Campbell, 'Arable productivity in medieval England: some evidence from Norfolk', *Jnl. of Economic History*, **XLIII** (1983), pp. 379–404.

74. H. S. A. Fox, 'The alleged transformation from two-field to three-field systems in medieval England', *Economic History Review*, 2nd ser., **XXXIX** (1986), p. 528.

75. *Ibid.*, pp. 538–48.

76. This diversity of cropping is possibly reflected in the proliferation of furlong divisions noted by D. Hall at about this date: in D. Hooke (ed.), *Anglo-Saxon Settlements*, (Oxford, 1988).

77. Campbell, 'Agricultural progress in medieval England', pp. 28–9; T. A. M. Bishop, 'The rotation of crops at Westerham, 1297–1350', *Economic History Review*, 2nd ser., **IX** (1938), pp. 38–44; P. F. Brandon, 'Agriculture and the effects of floods and weather at Barnhorne during the later Middle Ages', *Sussex Archaeological Collections*, **CIX** (1971), pp. 69–93; E. Searle, *Lordship and Community: Battle Abbey and its Banlieu, 1066–1538*, (Toronto, 1974), pp. 272–323.

78. H. L. Gray, *English Field Systems*, (Cambridge, Mass., 1915); A. R. H. Baker and R. A. Butlin (eds.), *Studies of Field Systems in the British Isles*, (Cambridge, 1973); Kosminsky, *Studies in the Agrarian History of England*; B. M. S. Campbell, 'Commonfield origins—the

regional dimension', in T. Rowley (ed.), *The Origins of Open-Field Agriculture*, (London, 1981), pp. 119–29.

79. K. Biddick, *The Other Economy: Pastoral Husbandry on a Medieval Estate*, (Los Angeles, 1989).

80. Persson, *Pre-industrial Economic Growth*, pp. 30–1.

81. This classification is based upon a systematic analysis of a national sample of 1,179 demesnes with land-use information recorded by *Inquisitiones Post Mortem* for the period 1300–9 and 721 demesnes with production information provided by manorial accounts drawn from the period 1250–1349. Preliminary results from the latter are summarized in B. M. S. Campbell and J. Power, 'Mapping the agricultural geography of medieval England', *Jnl. of Historical Geography*, **15** (1989), pp. 24–39. A full discussion of the classification and its rationale will be given in Campbell, *The Geography of Seignorial Agriculture*.

82. R. Cunliffe Shaw, *The Royal Forest of Lancaster*, (Preston, 1956), pp. 359–69; R. R. Davies, *Lordship and Society in the March of Wales 1281–1400*, (Oxford, 1978), pp. 115–16; H. P. R. Finberg, 'An early reference to the Welsh cattle trade', *Agricultural History Review*, **II** (1954), pp. 12–14; C. Skeel, 'The cattle trade between Wales and England from the fifteenth to the nineteenth century', *Transactions of the Royal Historical Society*, 4th ser., **IX** (1926), pp. 137–8.

83. Campbell and Power, 'Mapping the agricultural geography of medieval England', pp. 30–8.

84. I. S. W. Blanchard, 'Economic change in Derbyshire in the late Middle Ages, 1272–1540' (unpublished Ph.D. thesis, University of London, 1967), pp. 168–74.

85. E. Power, *The Wool Trade in English Medieval History*, (Oxford, 1941), pp. 20–40.

86. E. H. Phelps Brown and S. V. Hopkins, 'Seven centuries of the prices of consumables, compared with builders' wage-rates', in Carus-Wilson (ed.), *Essays in Economic History*, II, pp. 179–196.

87. C. Dyer, *Standards of Living in the Later Middle Ages*, (Cambridge, 1989).

88. Postan's population-based interpretation of the period is most fully elaborated in M. M. Postan, 'Medieval agrarian society in its prime: England', in *idem* (ed.), *The Cambridge Economic History of Europe, I*, (Cambridge, 1966), pp. 548–632. See also H. E. Hallam, 'The Postan thesis', *Historical Studies*, **XV** (1972), pp. 203–22.

89. K. G. Persson and P. Skott, *Growth and Stagnation in the European Medieval Economy*, (London School of Economics and Policital Science, S.T.I.C.E.R.D. economics discussion paper, 1987).

90. Wrigley and Schofield, *The Population History of England*, pp. 183–4.

91. J. Z. Titow, 'Some evidence of thirteenth-century population growth', *Economic History Review*, 2nd ser., **XIV** (1961), pp. 218–23.

92. Z. Razi, *Life, Marriage and Death in a Medieval Parish: Economy, Society and Demography in Halesowen, 1270–1400*, (Cambridge, 1980), pp. 27–32. For a critique of Razi's methods see L. R. Poos and R. M. Smith, '"Legal windows onto historical populations"?: recent research into demography and the manor court in medieval England', *Law and History Review*, **2** (1984), pp. 129–52.

93. Titow, 'Some evidence of thirteenth-century population growth'; J. Z. Titow, 'Some differences between manors and their effects on the condition of the peasant in the thirteenth century', *Agricultural History Review*, **X** (1962), pp. 1–13.

94. Razi, *Life, Marriage and Death in a Medieval Parish*.

95. G. C. Homans, *English Villagers of the Thirteenth Century*, (Cambridge, Mass., 1941); R. J. Faith, 'Peasant families and inheritance customs in medieval England', *Agricultural History Review*, **XIV** (1966), pp. 77–95.

96. Campbell, 'Population change and the genesis of commonfields on a Norfolk manor'.

97. T. A. M. Bishop, 'Assarting and the growth of open fields', *Economic History Review*, 2nd ser. **VI** (1935–6), pp. 13–29; A. R. H. Baker, 'Open fields and partible inheritance on a Kent manor', *Economic History Review*, 2nd ser., **XVII** (1964), pp. 1–23.

98. On the benefits of scattering see S. Fenoaltea, 'Transaction costs, Whig history, and the

common fields', *Politics and Society*, **16** (1988), pp. 190–3; D. N. McCloskey, 'English open fields as behavior toward risk', in P. Uselding (ed.), *Research in Economic History, 1*, (Greenwich Conn., 1976), pp. 124–71.

99. Campbell, 'Population pressure, inheritance and the land market in a fourteenth-century peasant community'.
100. Glasscock, 'The distribution of wealth in East Anglia in the early fourteenth century', pp. 72–6.
101. Postan, 'Medieval agrarian society in its prime: England', pp. 553–9; J. Z. Titow, *English Rural Society 1200–1350*, (London, 1969), pp. 52–4.
102. J. Z. Titow, *Winchester Yields: A Study in Medieval Agricultural Productivity*, (Cambridge, 1972).
103. D. L. Farmer, 'Grain yields on the Westminster Abbey manors, 1271–1410', *Canadian Jnl. of History*, **XVIII** (1983), pp. 331–47.
104. M. M. Postan, 'Village livestock in the thirteenth century', *Economic History Review*, 2nd ser. **XV** (1962), pp. 219–49.
105. Bailey, *A Marginal Economy?*
106. Campbell, 'Arable productivity in medieval England', pp. 396–400.
107. For a detailed analysis of the determinants of yields on one Winchester manor see C. Thornton, 'The determinants of land productivity on the bishop of Winchester's demesne of Rimpton, 1208–1403', in B. M. S. Campbell and M. Overton (eds.), *Land, Labour and Livestock: Historical Studies in European Agricultural Productivity*, (Manchester, 1991).
108. Campbell, *The Geography of Seignorial Agriculture in Medieval England*.
109. Campbell, 'Agricultural progress in medieval England', pp. 29–31.
110. On the enterprise of peasant cultivators see, Langton, *Horses, Oxen and Technological Innovation*, pp. 172–253; McIntosh, *Autonomy and Community*, pp. 136–78; Campbell, 'The diffusion of vetches in medieval England', pp. 204–5.
111. A. R. H. Baker, 'Evidence in the '*Nonarum Inquisitiones*' of contracting arable lands in England during the early fourteenth century', *Economic History Review*, 2nd ser., **XIX** (1966), pp. 518–32.
112. Kosminsky, *Studies in the Agrarian History of England*, pp. 46–67; J. A. Raftis, *Assart Data and Land Values: Two Studies in the East Midlands 1200–1350*, (Toronto, 1974); H. S. A. Fox, 'Some ecological dimensions of medieval field systems', pp. 119–58, in K. Biddick (ed.), *Archaeological Approaches to Medieval Europe*, (Kalamazoo, 1984), pp. 121–4; Campbell, *The Geography of Seignorial Agriculture in Medieval England*.
113. Fox, 'The alleged transformation from two-field to three-field systems in medieval England', p. 548.
114. J. R. Maddicott, *The English Peasantry and the Demands of the Crown 1294–1341*, *Past and Present* Supplement 1, (Oxford, 1975).
115. The views of several of these authors are usefully summarized in T. H. Aston and C. H. E. Philpin (eds.), *The Brenner Debate: Agrarian Class Structure and Economic Development in Pre-Industrial Europe*, (Cambridge, 1985). See also M. Dunford and D. Perrons, *The Arena of Capital*, (London, 1983), pp. 97–109.
116. R. Brenner, 'Agrarian class structure and economic development in pre-industrial Europe', *Past and Present*, **70**, (1976), p. 23.
117. R. Hilton, *Bond Men Made Free: Medieval Peasant Movements and the English Rising of 1381*, (London, 1973).
118. R. H. Hilton, 'Rent and capital formation in feudal society', in *The English Peasantry in the Later Middle Ages*, (Oxford, 1975), pp. 174–214.
119. Duby, *The Early Growth of the European Economy*, pp. 166–8.
120. Davies, *Conquest, Coexistence and Change*, pp. 334–59; Maddicott, *The English Peasantry and the Demands of the Crown 1294–1341*, pp. 1–7.
121. A Cosgrove (ed.), *A New History of Ireland, II, Medieval Ireland 1169–1534*, (Oxford, 1987), pp. 240–74.
122. G. W. S. Barrow, *Kingship and Unity: Scotland 1000–1306*, (London, 1981).
123. Davies, *Conquest, Coexistence and Change*, pp. 308–32.

124. M. D. O'Sullivan, *Italian Merchant Bankers in Ireland in the Thirteenth Century*, (Dublin, 1962).

125. Maddicott, *The English Peasantry and the Demands of the Crown 1294–1341*, pp. 17–18. Within the south-east the impact of purveyance is discussed in M. Mate, 'The estates of Canterbury Cathedral Priory before the Black Death, 1315–1348'. *Studies in Medieval and Renaissance History*, **VIII** (1987), p. 20.

126. J. A. Tuck, 'War and society in the medieval North', *Northern History*, **XXI** (1985), pp. 33–52.

127. I. Kershaw, 'The Great Famine and agrarian crisis in England 1315–1322', *Past and Present*, **59** (1973), pp. 3–50.

128. B. A. Hannawalt, 'Economic influences on the pattern of crime in England, 1300–1348', *American Jnl. of Legal History*, **XVIII** (1974), p. 291.

129. D. G. Watts, 'A model for the early fourteenth century', *Economic History Review*, 2nd ser. **XX** (1967), pp. 543–7; Campbell, 'Population pressure, inheritance, and the land market in a fourteenth-century peasant community', pp. 115–16.

130. Phelps Brown and Hopkins, 'Seven centuries of the prices of consumables, compared with builders' wage rates'; M. Prestwich, 'Edward I's monetary policies and their consequences', *Economic History Review*, 2nd ser., **XXII** (1969), pp. 406–16; M. Mate, 'High prices in early fourteenth-century England', *Economic History Review*, 2nd ser., **XXVIII** (1975), pp. 1–16.

131. J. F. D. Shrewsbury, *A History of Bubonic Plague in the British Isles*, (Cambridge, 1971), pp. 54–125; G. Twigg, *The Black Death: A Biological Reappraisal*, (London, 1984), pp. 58–74.

132. Lambert *et al.*, *The Making of the Broads*, pp. 99–102; A. R. H. Baker, 'Some evidence of a reduction in the acreage of cultivated lands in Sussex during the early fourteenth century', *Sussex Archaeological Collections*, **104** (1966), pp. 1–5; Brandon, 'Agriculture and the effects of floods and weather at Barnhorne during the later Middle Ages'.

133. M. Bailey, '*Per impetum maris*: natural disaster and economic decline in eastern England, 1275–1350', in B. M. S. Campbell (ed.), *Before the Black Death: Studies in the 'Crisis' of the early Fourteenth Century*, (Manchesterr, 1991).

134. Keene, *Cheapside before the Great Fire*, pp. 19–20.

135. L. R. Poos, 'The rural population of Essex in the later Middle Ages', *Economic History Review*, 2nd ser., **XXXVIII** (1985), pp. 521–4.

136. G. Ohlin, 'No safety in numbers: some pitfalls of historical statistics', in R. Floud (ed.), *Essays in Quantitative Economic History*, (Oxford, 1974), pp. 59–78. There are, however, problems with the heriot data, B. F. Harvey, 'The crisis of the early fourteenth century', in Campbell (ed.), *Before the Black Death*.

137. Razi, *Life, Marriage and Death in a Medieval, Parish*, pp. 27–32.

138. Campbell, 'Population growth, inheritance and the land market in a fourteenth-century peasant community', pp. 96–9.

139. E. Rutledge, 'Immigration and population growth in early fourteenth-century Norwich', *Urban History Yearbook* (1988), pp. 26–8.

140. Campbell (ed.), *Before the Black Death*.

141. Aston and Philpin (eds.), *The Brenner Debate*; Campbell (ed.), *Before the Black Death*.

142. Cosgrove (ed.), *A new History of Ireland*, pp. 533–56; Davies, *Conquest, Coexistence and Change*, pp. 443–59; A. Grant, *Independence and Nationhood: Scotland 1306–1469*, (London, 1984), pp. 55–7.

143. Poos, 'The rural population of Essex in the later Middle Ages', pp. 515–30.

144. J. E. Thorold Rogers, *History of Agriculture and Prices in England, I.* (Oxford, 1884); Phelps Brown and Hopkins, 'Seven centuries of the prices of consumables compared with builders' wage rates'; Dyfer, *Standards of Living*.

145. B. M. S. Campbell, 'The population of early Tudor England: a re-evaluation of the 1522 Muster Returns and 1524 and 1525 Lay Subsidies', *Jnl. of Historical Geography*, 7 (1981), pp. 145–54.

146. S. Thrupp, 'The problem of replacement rates in late medieval English population', *Economic History Review*, 2nd ser., **XVIII** (1965), pp. 118.

147. J. Hatcher, *Plague, Population and the English Economy 1348–1530*, (London, 1977); R. S.

Gottfried, *Epidemic Disease in Fifteenth Century England: The Medical Response and the Demographic Consequences*, (Leicester, 1977).

148. Razi, *Life, Marriage and Death in a Medieval Parish*, pp. 114–51.

149. J. Hatcher, 'Mortality in the fifteenth century: some new evidence', *Economic History Review*, 2nd ser., **XXXIX** (1986), pp. 19–38.

150. Twigg, *The Black Death*.

151. T. S. R. Boase, *Death in the Middle Ages: Mortality, Judgement and Remembrance*, (London, 1972), pp. 97–106.

152. J. D. Chambers, *Population, Economy, and Society in Pre-industrial England*, (Oxford, 1972); R. D. Lee, 'Population homeostasis and English demographic history', pp. 75–100 in R. I. Rotberg and T. K. Rabb (eds.), *Population and Economy: Population and History from the Traditional to the Modern World*, (Cambridge, 1986).

153. See Chapter 6 below.

154. R. H. Tawney, *The Agrarian Problem in the Sixteenth Century*, (London, 1912), p. 105.

155. R. M. Smith, 'Some reflections on the evidence for the origins of the "European Marriage Pattern" in England', in C. Harris (ed.), *The Sociology of the Family: New Directions for Britain*. (Keele, 1979), pp. 74–112; Smith, 'Human resources', pp. 210–11; P. J. P. Goldberg, 'Female labour, service and marriage in the late medieval urban north', *Northern History*, **22** (1986), pp. 18–38.

156. M. W. Beresford and J. G. Hurst, *Deserted Medieval Villages*, (London, 1971).

157. C. C. Dyer, 'Deserted medieval villages in the west midlands', *Economic History Review*, 2nd ser., **XXXV** (1982), pp. 19–34.

158. R. A. McKinley, *English Surnames Series, II, Norfolk and Suffolk Surnames in the Middle Ages*, (London, 1975), pp. 98–9.

159. F. G. Davenport, 'The decay of villeinage in East Anglia', *Transactions of the Royal Historical Society*, new ser., **XIV** (1900), pp. 123–41; J. A. Raftis, *Tenure and Mobility, Studies in the Social History of the Medieval English Village*, (Toronto, 1964); Campbell, 'The population of early Tudor England', pp. 151–2.

160. J. Sheail, 'The distribution of taxable population and wealth in England during the early sixteenth century', *Transactions of the Institute of British Geographers*, **55** (1972), pp. 111–26; Darby *et al.*, 'The changing geographical distribution of wealth in England 1086–1334–1524', pp. 256–61.

161. Campbell, *The Geography of Seignorial Agriculture in Medieval England*.

162. On the leasing of demesnes see F. R. H. Du Boulay, 'Who were farming the English demesnes at the end of the Middle Ages?', *Economic History Review*, 2nd ser., **XVII** (1965), pp. 443–55; B. Harvey, 'The leasing of the Abbot of Westminster's demesnes in the later Middle Ages', *Economic History Review*, 2nd ser., **XXII** (1969), pp. 17–27; R. A. Lomas, 'The Priory of Durham and its demesnes in the fourteenth and fifteenth centuries', *Economic History Review*, 2nd ser., **XXXI** (1978), pp. 339–53; J. N. Hare, 'The demesne lessees of fifteenth-century Wiltshire', *Agricultural History Review*, **29** (1981), pp. 1–15; M. Mate, 'The farming out of manors: a new look at the evidence from Canterbury Cathedral Priory', *Jnl. of Medieval History*, **9** (1983), pp. 331–44,

163. The observations contained in this and the ensuing five paragraphs are based upon an analysis of a national sample of 392 demesnes drawn from the period 1350–1449. For a fuller discussion of this evidence see Campbell, *The Geography of Seignorial Agriculture in Medieval England*.

164. Campbell, 'Agricultural progress in medieval England', pp. 38–9; Campbell, 'Arable productivity in medieval England', pp. 387–9.

165. Langdon, *Horses, Oxen and Technological Innovation*, p. 212.

166. T. H. Lloyd, *The Movement of Wool Prices in Medieval England*, Economic History Review Supplement 6, (Cambridge, 1973).

167. K. J. Allison, 'The sheep-corn husbandry of Norfolk in the sixteenth and seventeenth centuries', *Agricultural History Review*, **V** (1957), pp. 12–30; R. Scott, 'Medieval agriculture', pp. 7–42 in R. B. Pugh (ed.), *Victoria History of the County of Wiltshire, IV*, (London, 1959), pp. 19–21; J. N. Hare, 'Change and continuity in Wiltshire agriculture in the later Middle Ages', pp. 1–18, in W. Minchinton (ed.), *Agricultural Improvement: Medieval and*

Modern, (Exeter Papers in Economic History, 14, 1981), pp. 4–9; M. Mate, 'Pastoral farming in south-east England in the fifteenth century', *Economic History Review*, 2nd ser., **XL** (1987), pp. 523–36.

168. C. C. Dyer, *Warwickshire Farming 1349–c.1520: Preparations for Agricultural Revolution* Dugdale Society Occasional Papers 27, (Oxford, 1981), pp. 9–16.

169. McIntosh, *Autonomy and Community*, pp. 137–52.

170. K. J. Allison, 'Flock management in the sixteenth and seventeenth centuries', *Economic History Review*, 2nd ser., **XL** (1958), pp. 98–112; S. T. Bindoff, *Kett's Rebellion 1549*, (Historical Association Pamphlet 12, London, 1949), pp. 3–10; M. Bailey, 'Sand into gold: the foldcourse system in west Suffolk, 1200–1600', *Agricultural History Review*, **38** (1990), pp. 40–57.

171. Campbell, 'The extent and layout of commonfields in eastern Norfolk', pp. 26–9; C. C. Dyer, 'Changes in the size of peasant holdings in some west midland villages 1400–1540, in Smith (ed.), *Land, Kinship and Life-cycle*, pp. 277–94.

172. R. H. Britnell, 'The Pastons and their Norfolk', *Agricultural History Review*, **36** (1988), pp. 141–2.

173. Campbell, 'Population change and the genesis of commonfields on a Norfolk manor', p. 190.

174. Spufford, *A Cambridgeshire Community*, pp. 39–41.

175. For examples see Smith (ed.), *Land Kinship and Life-cycle*.

176. Campbell, 'The extent and layout of commonfields in eastern Norfolk', p. 29.

177. D. P. Dymond, 'The parish of Walsham-le-Willows: two Elizabethan surveys and their medieval background', *Proceedings of the Suffolk Institute of Archaeology*, **XXXIII** (1974), pp. 195–211.

178. A. R. H. Baker, 'Changes in the later Middle Ages', pp. 186–247, in Darby (ed.), *A New Historical Geography of England*, pp. 211–13.

179. J. A. Raftis, 'Changes in an English village after the Black Death', *Mediaeval Studies*, **XXIX** (1967), pp. 158–77.

180. E. B. Dewindt, *Land and People in Holywell-cum-Needingworth: Structures of Tenure and Patterns of Social Organization in an East Midlands Village 1252–1457*, (Toronto, 1972); Razi, *Life Marriage, and Death in a Medieval Parish*; C. Howell, *Land, Family and Inheritance in Transition: Kibworth Harcourt 1280–1700*, (Cambridge, 1983).

181. For a fuller discussion of the significance of these developments see R. Brenner, 'The agrarian roots of European capitalism', *Past and Present*, **70** (1976), pp. 61–75.

182. Hilton, *The Decline of Serfdom in Medieval England*, pp. 26–59.

183. Kosminsky, *Studies in the Agrarian History of England*, pp. 103–16.

184. D. L. Farmer, 'Grain yields on the Winchester manors in the later Middle Ages', *Economic History Review*, 2nd ser., **XXX** (1977), pp. 555–66; H. P. R. Finberg, *Tavistock Abbey: A Study in the Social and Economic History of Devon*, (Cambridge, 1951).

185. Dodgshon, *The European Past*, pp. 270–86.

186. Spufford, *A Cambridgeshire Community*, pp. 32–4; Hilton, *The Decline of Serfdom in Medieval England*, pp. 44–7.

187. The geographical consequences of this transformation are explored in Dunford and Perrons, *The Arena of Capital*.

5

Towns and Trade 1066–1500

Tim Unwin

Medieval Towns and Trade: The Contours of Change

Trade at the Edge of Europe

In the late eleventh and early twelfth centuries, England and Wales lay at the periphery of the complex organization of European trade. There was nothing to compare with the emerging Italian city states, such as Pisa and Lucca, which Dodgshon has described as 'the dominant force behind a new territorial structuring of the political landscape' of southern Europe.[1] Over the next four centuries, though, as England came to play a more prominent role in the political and economic life of Europe, the countryside experienced an efflorescence of urban growth and commercial activity. Exports of wool and then cloth were exchanged for imports of luxury items such as silks, spices and wine; the major ports of London, Bristol, Lynn, Boston and Southampton became the loci of exchange for these commodities; and numerous small towns and markets emerged to facilitate their redistribution throughout the breadth of the realm.

It is with the processes underlying these changes that this chapter is concerned. The introductory section considers the problems of urban definition and outlines the broad economic and demographic context of the period 1066–1500 to provide a framework against which detailed changes in trade and the urban economy can be explored. The following section then establishes a chronology of urban and commercial change, before the chapter examines in turn the economy, society and morphology of towns in medieval England and Wales.

Between 1066 and 1500 England and Wales experienced the full flowering of feudalism, its crisis in the mid fourteenth century, and the subsequent social and economic reorganization which laid the basis for the eventual rise to dominance of the capitalist mode of production. In each of these three phases towns played a crucial role, and one of the core themes explored in this chapter is the role of urban life and commercial activity in this transformation of feudalism. A second issue which the chapter addresses is the relationship between urbanization and demographic change. While it is difficult to gain an accurate impression of precise changes in population levels betwen 1066 and 1500, the broad chronology of a period of population growth until the early fourteenth century, followed by a dramatic decline and then some recovery, is well established. The implications of these demographic trends for urban life, and indeed the converse implications of urbanization for demographic change, still remain the subject of considerable debate. Above all, though, the towns and trade of medieval England and Wales cannot be studied in isolation. The changing political and economic linkages between England and the rest of Europe provide an important key to our understanding of the reorganization of urban life and mercantile activity in the period 1066–1500.

Definitions and Origins: Boroughs, Markets and Fairs

By the eleventh century clearly identifiable non-agricultural settlements had emerged in England, some based around royal residences, others developing from earlier *wic* trading settlements, and yet others deriving from the defended *burhs* constructed at the time of the ninth century Viking invasions.[2] These illustrate that already during the Anglo-Saxon period towns had begun to take on a variety of different functions. In Domesday Book there was no one term used to describe them: urban settlements were referred to indiscriminately as *civitas*, *burgus* or *villa*.[3] This emphasizes the difficulty in attempting to define the nature of medieval towns in any precise way. Towns were primarily places where groups of people had obtained, or been granted, some of a range of specific rights or privileges, and it was not until the thirteenth century that any degree of uniformity was to be found in the definition of urban status.[4] In considering these privileges, it is useful to distinguish between the social, political, economic and ideological functions served by the medieval town. Urban settlements thus possessed a specific type of tenure, their inhabitants strove for a degree of political independence, they maintained a particular type of non-agrarian economy, and they often provided the central locale for the ideological power of the Church.

Reynolds has drawn attention to three types of privilege acquired by towns during their campaign towards 'independence' during the twelfth century: burgage tenure, customs and guilds.[5] Central to an understanding of the medieval town was the distinction that evolved between rural *villein* tenure and urban *burgage* tenure. Under the former, *unfree* villeins held a standard unit of land within a manor in return for performing labour services on the lord's demesne. In addition, villeins owed other feudal dues to their lords, and were, at least in theory, bound to inhabit the manor of their birth.[6] In contrast, burgage tenure evolved as a form of *free* tenure by which burgesses held small parcels of land at fixed rents.[7] The linking together in the twelfth century of the words *liberum* and *burgagium*, uniting the concepts of 'freedom' and 'borough', was central to the rise of relatively independent urban communities. This was well expressed in the customs granted to Newcastle upon Tyne in the reign of Henry I, when unchallenged residence by an individual in the town for a year and a day was deemed to preclude any claims by a former lord upon that person.[8] However, a clear cut distinction between burgage tenure and villein tenure was slow to emerge, and labour services survived in some boroughs as late as the end of the twelfth century.

When a place was granted borough status, either by the king or, in the case of seigneurial boroughs, by a secular or ecclesiastical lord, it was usually also granted a series of customs and liberties, often based on those of a well-established borough. Thus, when John, Bishop of Norwich, granted to the *villa* of Lynn the status of a free borough in 1204 he gave it the same liberties and customs as those enjoyed by the borough of Oxford.[9] The customs granted to new boroughs were often based on those of London, and included such privileges as the right to defence against criminal charges by oath rather than battle, and regulations concerning payments for, and the collection of, debt.[10] These emphasize the importance to the burgesses of their own court, which, in Ballard's words, provided them with a 'jurisdictional oasis' isolating them from the rest of the country.[11]

The third of Reynolds' key borough privileges was the right conferred on burgesses to form a merchant guild. While privileges were also granted to particular craft guilds, such as the weavers of London and York, most charters during the twelfth century granted such privileges more generally to the community of the 'merchant guild' and conferred on them the monopoly of trading within their borough. Freedom from the payment of tolls and from a variety of other restrictions on trade was often granted along with these rights. Ballard thus cites the example of Maldon, which was granted a charter in 1171 specifying that the burgesses were to be 'quit of carriage and sumpter service and scutage, of tallage and stallage and lastage and of every toll in every market and in every fair, and in every crossing of bridges and seas and throughout our whole realm'.[12]

Such trading privileges were closely related to the granting of charters for markets and fairs. Boroughs usually possessed the right to hold both markets and fairs, and most settlements in which there were markets also had an annual fair. In this context, it is important to stress that many settlements which were granted market charters were essentially rural in nature and had few pretensions to urban status.[13] These charters usually granted to a lord, or a group of burgesses, the right to hold a market at their manor or borough on a given day of each week. Fairs were larger annual events lasting several days and they were normally initially associated with religious feasts.

These privileges each had their particular manifestation in both time and space. Thus within boroughs and market villages the place and hours at which exchange could take place became tightly controlled. New market places and commercial streets were laid out, not only in most boroughs, but also in a number of villages that had been granted market charters.[14] There was considerable theoretical restriction of trading in space–time, but in practice it seems that commercial activity was never totally confined to the market place. While numerous cases of forestalling were brought before local borough courts, it is nevertheless apparent that much trade avoided the official marketing system altogether. Thus Donkin has shown how many Cistercian monasteries had long-standing contracts with foreign merchants for the export of their wool, and that they 'were frequently obliged to carry their wool to the staple ports or to some point convenient to the buyer'.[15] In many instances wool was thus taken directly from the abbeys or granges to the ports, without entering the regulated official local markets.

Towns and Feudalism: Crisis and Change

Dodgshon has emphasized that the urban functions of boroughs 'had a feudal basis in that the right to hold a fair or market was held off the king or a lord'.[16] However, the contrast between burgage tenure and villein tenure meant that towns were, to an extent, oases of relative freedom within a generally 'unfree' feudal rural society. Dunford and Perrons have emphasized this source of tension within the feudal mode of production, noting that 'while towns were in some ways dependent upon and conditioned by the rural society in which they developed, in other ways urban development was dependent upon exemption from some of the restrictions characteristic of rural feudalism'.[17]

An analysis of this tension is fundamental to our understanding of the role of towns and markets within the economy and society of medieval England and Wales. As Hilton has made clear, it is not possible to see towns simply as being 'external' to feudalism.[18] The growth of 'free' towns can not be seen as being directly responsible for the collapse of 'unfree' feudalism. However, the role of towns and the commercial activity within them, was crucial to the transformation of feudalism that took place between 1300 and 1500. In Hilton's words, 'In the end merchant capital did become invested as industrial capital, when other features (such as the development of wage labour or its proto-industrialization half-way house) emerged. But this could hardly have happened without the spread of simple commodity production throughout the largely self-subsistent economy at the base of society. It is this spread that is reflected in the history of the small market towns'.[19] In relating the empirical evidence concerning the numbers and organization of towns and markets to the underlying structure of feudalism, an issue which must be addressed is the extent to which the growth, crisis and decline of feudalism were reflected in the growth and change of towns and commerce between 1066 and 1500.

Population: Expansion, and Decline

Another issue which has received much attention from historians and geographers has been the relationship between demographic and urban change in the medieval period.[20] A dearth of accurate information on the populations of medieval towns means that this is likely to remain an issue for considerable debate, and as Hilton has emphasized 'playing with numbers may well be a fruitless occupation'.[21] However, it does seem clear that between 1066 and 1300 there was a considerable increase in population, and that this coincided with the foundation of numerous new towns and markets. Darby has estimated that the total population of England recorded in Domesday Book was probably in the order of 1.5 million, of which a possible unrecorded urban total 'might be about 120,000'.[22] Between then and 1300 the total population may have risen by some 300 per cent, although estimates based on the Hundred Rolls of 1277–79 and the Poll Taxes of 1377 vary widely as to the likely population level at this time.[23] The precise role played by the towns in enabling this population increase to be sustained is a matter for some conjecture. It seems likely, though, that increased specialization of production in different parts of the country, associated with improved systems of exchange for livestock and grain through the new network of markets and towns, went some way to enabling higher levels of population to be sustained.

Estimates of the percentage of the population that died during the Black Death of 1348–49 vary widely from 20 to 50 per cent, although some authorities put the figure as low as 5 per cent.[24] On balance, it seems that the major plagues and other outbreaks of disease that occurred during the second half of the fourteenth century reduced the population of England and Wales by about one-third. This highlights a further issue for debate, since bubonic plague was principally an urban disease, requiring relatively high levels of population to sustain it. Towns therefore probably suffered higher death rates as a result of plague than did the surrounding country-side, and it seems that seaports were struck hardest of all. The consequent vitality of urban life during the second half of the fourteenth century and over the fifteenth century can thus be seen to depend much on the levels of rural to urban migration then pertaining. However, the paucity of accurate data concerning urban population levels has meant that it is extremely difficult to reach any firm conclusions concern-ing the effects of the mid fourteenth century demographic crisis on the urban economy.[25] On balance, it seems that there was a substantial fall in urban population between 1300 and 1500, but as Hadwin has argued 'life, even in those towns whose share of national taxable wealth was definitely declining, like Boston and Lincoln, still had a vigour and vitality that gave the resilience to withstand critical press-ures'.[26]

The Chronology of Change: Boroughs and Market Centres

The Boroughs of Eleventh-century England

By the eleventh century a wide range of factors, many of which were not primarily economic in nature, had led to the emergence of *burhs* throughout southern England.[27] Domesday Book thus records 112 places that seem to have been boroughs (Fig. 5.1).[28] However, in contrast to rural areas where information is recorded in a systematic manner, the details of these urban settlements are both incomplete and unsystematic. The largest and most important borough must have been London, but Domesday Book contains no detailed entry for it. Its population may have been around 10,000, with that of its nearest rivals in 1086, York, Lincoln and Norwich, each being somewhere in the order of 5000.[29] Other important towns included Thetford, Oxford, Winchester and Gloucester, and it is probable that the county towns of the Midlands such as Nottingham, Derby and Leicester all had populations of around 2000. In contrast to these important administrative and commercial centres, there were also a number of tiny boroughs at the other end of the scale. The smallest, Hurpston in Dorset, was only recorded as having five inhabitants in 1086.

Domesday Book enables us to catch a glimpse of the short-term effects of processes initiated between 1066 and 1086. Several towns, such as Oxford, York, Lincoln and Norwich, appear to have lost population over this period. In some cases, as in York, Norwich and Shrewsbury, this was as a result of houses being destroyed to make way for the building of castles, but in others there is evidence that disruption in the wake of the Conquest had given rise to a brief recession in urban life. At Lincoln, Exeter and Norwich we read of fires having destroyed some messuages; others were empty as a result of people fleeing; and yet others were simply recorded as being waste, with no reason being given. Altogether castles were constructed at 27 Domesday boroughs, and although in the short term this may have led to some destruction of urban fabric, it is evident that this centralization of military and

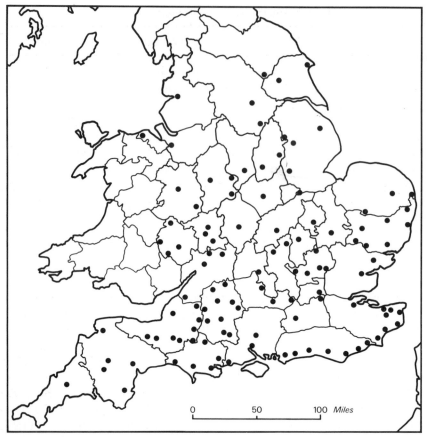

Fig. 5.1. Boroughs mentioned in Domesday Book, 1086. *Source*: derived from H. C. Darby, *Domesday England* (Cambridge, 1986), p. 297.

administrative feudal authority in its turn led to a resurgence of commercial activity around many castles.[30]

Medieval New Towns: the Foundation of Boroughs

Domesday Book only recorded one urban settlement in Wales, that of Rhuddlan, but in the ensuing three centuries Wales was also to see considerable borough foundation. By 1300 Beresford and Finberg record that the total number of boroughs in England had risen to 448, with a further 98 being established after 1300, and there being an additional 63 medieval boroughs for which the date of foundation is unknown.[31] Many of these boroughs resulted from the granting of borough charters to villages that already existed, but Beresford has also chronicled how 166 new planted towns were established in England between 1066 and 1310, at a time when a further 83 such planted towns were constructed in Wales.[32]

Beresford and Finberg have traced the chronology of borough foundations in

Table 5.1: English medieval boroughs by type of foundation.

	Royal		Ecclesiastical		Secular	
	Number	Cumulative total	Number	Cumulative total	Number	Cumulative total
Before 1066	55.5	55.5	7	7	0.5	0.5
1067–1086	25	80.5	11	18	14	14.5
1087–1200	27	107.5	28	46	39.5	54
1201–1250	28.25	135.75	37.5	83.5	67.25	121.25
1251–1300	17.25	153	28.5	112	57.25	178.5
1301–1500	11	164	34.5	146.5	49	227.5
Unknown			71			

Source: derived from M. W. Beresford and H. P. R. Finberg, *English Medieval Boroughs: a Handlist* (Newton Abbott, 1973).

England prior to 1500, and three broad conclusions can be drawn from their work.[33] The first is that there were distinct phases in the granting of borough status, and the role of royal, secular and ecclesiastical lords as founders of boroughs changed through time. As Table 5.1 indicates, the earliest boroughs were mainly royal in foundation, with 83 per cent of all royal boroughs having been founded by 1250. The majority of secular and ecclesiastical borough foundations took place between 1200 and 1300, and indeed in overall terms the most common boroughs by 1300 were those of lay seigneurial foundation, which accounted for 40 per cent of the total.

A second broad conclusion concerns the distribution of boroughs in different parts of England and Wales. Fig. 5.2 illustrates the extent of borough foundation after 1086, and when compared with Fig. 5.1 it indicates the spread of such foundations to the west and the north. Perhaps more interestingly, though, Fig. 5.2 also reveals the great diversity in the density of borough foundation between the different parts of the country. Within England, densities vary from 217,000 acres per borough in Norfolk to as little as 22,000 acres per borough in Devon.[34] These figures must be treated with some caution in view of the difficulties concerning the precise definitions of boroughs, but they do nevertheless indicate the great diversity in borough density that was to be found. It is difficult to explain this distribution, but the activities of individual secular lords in establishing settlements as boroughs in the south-west must have been important. Devon and Cornwall were relatively late to develop economically, and it may therefore have been much easier to create new boroughs here than it was in the already densely settled counties such as Norfolk, Cambridgeshire and Lincolnshire.[35]

However, the size of boroughs must also be taken into acount in any consideration of their distribution. The vast majority of the boroughs of the south-west were very small, and the major medieval towns lay elsewhere. There are numerous problems associated with the sources such as the Lay Subsidies and Poll Taxes, which can be used for a reconstruction of urban wealth and population in the fourteenth century,

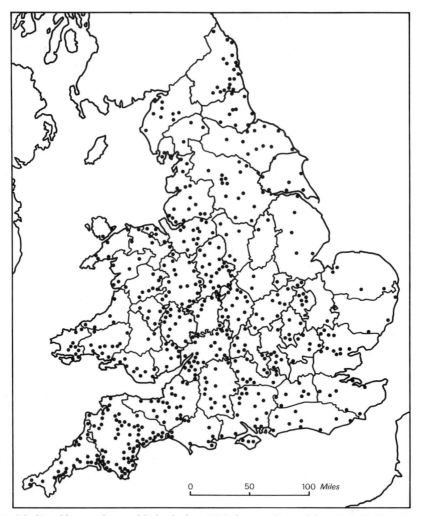

Fig. 5.2. Medieval boroughs established after 1086. *Source*: derived from M. W. Beresford and
H. P. R. Finberg (eds.), *English Medieval Boroughs: a Handlist* (Newton Abbott, 1973) and M. W.
Beresford, *New Towns of the Middle Ages*, (London, 1967).

but they do give us some general indications of the relative sizes of a selection of
urban settlements.[36] In the 1334 Lay Subsidy boroughs and ancient demesnes were
taxed at one-tenth of their assessed movable wealth, and rural areas at one-fifteenth.
This should therefore provide an indication of urban wealth prior to the demographic decline of the mid fourteenth century, but as Glasscock has commented 'the
selection of boroughs by the taxers does not seem to have conformed to any
consistent rules'.[37] Of the major towns in the country, only London, Boston and
Coventry were not considered as taxation boroughs, and if their assessment at the
rate of a fifteenth is taken into consideration, it is possible to obtain an approximate
ranking of towns in 1334. This reveals that London was by far the most wealthy city

in the country with an assessed wealth of £11,000. The next most wealthy town was Bristol (£2200), followed by York (£1620), Newcastle upon Tyne (£1333), Boston (£1100), Great Yarmouth (£1000) and Lincoln (£1000). The towns with assessed wealths between £750 and £1000 were Norwich, Oxford, Shrewsbury, Lynn, Salisbury and Coventry.[38]

Markets and Marketing

In addition to these borough foundations, the period between 1066 and 1350 saw a dramatic increase in the number of markets. Indeed, between 1199 and 1483 more than 2800 grants of the right to hold a market were made in England and Wales. Britnell has drawn a useful distinction between the markets established before and after the year 1200.[39] Prior to 1200 there seems to have been no policy to restrict the establishment of markets, and hundredal markets became a prominent feature of English trade. After 1200, however, Britnell argues that the king's right to license new markets became more effective.[40] This found its expression in the granting of royal charters for new market foundations. In addition lords of well-established, prescriptive, markets also sought charters to confirm their rights to hold markets.

Based on an analysis of market foundations in 21 English counties before 1349, Britnell has shown that the peak period of market foundation came between 1250 and 1275, and it seems that there may well have been local regional differences in the frequency of such market foundations.[41] Many of these markets were granted to small rural settlements, which, as Hilton comments, 'were rather ephemeral'.[42] Thus more than three-quarters of the markets founded between 1200 and 1349 failed to survive into the early modern period. This suggests that the proliferation of medieval markets reflected a transient phase in the economic change of England and Wales, and it exhibits many of the more general characteristics of periodic marketing in different parts of the world throughout history.[43] The growth in local trade reflected in this surge of market foundations coincided with a period of considerable expansion in the rural economy, reflecting increased interaction between food producers, merchants and craftsmen. However, Hilton has also seen the development of small and medium-sized market towns during this period as 'a good indication of the progressing commercialization *and* urbanization of a medieval economy'.[44]

By the end of the thirteenth century a complex series of rents, tolls and legislation had been developed to regulate the processes of market trade. Each market had its summary court of justice at which disagreements in the market place were brought to trial. Strict controls over the weights and measures at which standard goods, such as bread, ale and wine, were to be sold were established, and forestalling was legislated against through tight controls of the times at which trading could take place. Not only did traders have to pay rents for plots of land in the market place, but they also had to pay dues such as stallage if they wished to put up a stall, and picage if they dug holes in the ground for posts. Produce going both into and out of the market was subject to tolls. Typical examples of the costs incurred by merchants at the turn of the fourteenth century can be found from the records of the fair at Lenton in Nottinghamshire: all booths were to be eight feet long and eight feet wide; each type of produce had to be sold in a specific part of the fair; cloth merchants, apothecaries and pilchers paid 12d for the duration of the fair, but those selling iron only paid 4d; and differential rents were to be charged for covered and uncovered stalls.[45] Records of tolls are more extensive than those for rents, and those recorded in the *Placita de Quo Warranto* for Blyth, also in Nottinghamshire, are typical: cartloads of timber and bread were taxed at 1d; cartloads of other goods at 2d; packhorse loads of most goods were taxed at $\frac{1}{2}$d; merchandise carried on a man's back at $\frac{1}{4}$d; horses, oxen and cows at $\frac{1}{2}$d; sheep or pigs at $\frac{1}{4}$d; and if a sack of baled wool was sold at Blyth a tax of 4d was to be paid on it.[46]

Fourteenth-century Crisis and Urban Change

The rate at which borough and market charters were granted began to decrease at the beginning of the fourteenth century, but new markets and boroughs were still being created after the demographic crisis initiated with the famine of 1315–17 and culminating in the series of plagues following the Black Death of 1348–49. There is unfortunately no single source which provides accurate information concerning the dates when markets ceased functioning, but by 1600 it would appear that only perhaps a quarter of the markets of medieval England had survived.

There is considerable debate on the levels of wealth and population in the towns of England and Wales in the period following 1350. The populations of the major towns must all have declined between 1348 and the Poll Tax of 1377. At this date London was by far the most densely populated town, with around 23,000 taxpayers, followed by York with just over 7000, Bristol with around 6000, Coventry with 5000 and Norwich with 4000. Based on the evidence of the Poll Tax, Baker argues that during the latter part of the fourteenth century the 'largest towns were those associated with agricultural markets and the cloth industry or with overseas trade'.[47]

However, all was not doom and gloom for the towns of England and Wales. Bridbury has thus suggested that 'despite the competition of other places and other occupations, life in the old chartered boroughs was still very sweet in the later Middle Ages'.[48] He sees squalor and splendour existing side by side in towns throughout the country. Provincial towns did include numerous derelict buildings, and did petition regularly to have their tax burdens reduced, but at the same time their merchants and citizens were able to lay on extravagant banquets and civil processions. Against this view, Rigby has drawn attention to the difficulties of using ratios based on the taxes paid by towns in 1334 and 1524, which at face value show that the proportion of urban wealth was larger in 1524 than it had been in 1334. He argues that 'the possibility that the lay subsidy returns may exaggerate the growth of urban wealth renders this evidence for the reality of such a trend of dubious value'.[49]

On balance it seems that the period between 1350 and 1500 was one of 'urban vigour amid demographic decline'.[50] Many towns had lost considerable numbers of people, but they remained essential to the commercial economy. Much industry had indeed migrated to the countryside, but the towns still retained a major share of the finishing trades.[51] In explaining this chronology of change, it is essential to focus on the functioning of the urban economy, and it is therefore to a consideration of trade, crafts and industry that the following section now turns.

The Urban Economy

Trade: the International and Local Contexts

Between 1066 and 1500 the structure of English and Welsh trade was transformed in both quantitative and qualitative terms. This was as true of their position with respect to the wider European organization of trade as it was of internal trade within them, and indeed it is this relationship between international and local trade that lies at the heart of an understanding of the role of towns and cities within the medieval economy. In the eleventh century, England and Wales played but a small part in the wider commercial economy of Europe; foreign, alien merchants dominated the import and export of merchandise. By the fourteenth century this situation had begun to change. England was exporting greater quantities of finished products rather than raw materials, tighter restrictions were being placed on the activities of foreigners, and English merchants were beginning to play a greater role overseas. These changes in turn were also closely associated with the increasing importance of craft industries within the towns of England and Wales.

During the eleventh and twelfth centuries the main foci for European trade were the fairs of northern Italy, Flanders and Champagne. These provided the locales of exchange for the two great economic systems of, on the one hand, Italy and the Mediterranean, and on the other, northern France and Flanders. Between these two systems, the main arteries of trade were across the Alps, or along the river systems of the Rhone, Saône and Seine.[52] England and Wales lay well outside these lines of interaction and communication. Likewise, they did not provide a major source of supply or demand for the chief items of trade such as silks, spices, furs, salt and wine. However, during the latter part of the twelfth century, as international demand for grain and wool grew, England and Wales became increasingly drawn into the wider European commercial economy.

By the fourteenth century the great fairs of Champagne, such as those of Troyes and Provins, were on the decline, being replaced in importance by industrial and commercial towns such as Frankfurt, Zurzach, Linz and Deventer. The entire structure of medieval trade had altered to give greater dominance to towns throughout the urban hierarchy. These towns imported food and industrial raw materials, particularly wool, from the surrounding countryside. They were the focus for the importation of goods that had travelled over long distances, such as grain, luxury items, and specialist industrial requirements, and they also functioned as centres for the redistribution of manufactured products and luxuries.

Pounds has commented that 'high quality wool was by far the most important industrial raw material in medieval trade', and much of the highest quality wool came from England.[53] With Flanders and northern Italy being the main centres of cloth production during the thirteenth and fourteenth centuries, a considerable export trade in English wool was generated. During the twelfth and thirteenth centuries Italian urban merchant families had come to dominate much of European trade. As Carus-Wilson has noted, Italian merchants travelled throughout England collecting the ecclesiastical taxes owed to the Pope and then using them to buy up the wool production of the numerous religious houses of the country.[54] She estimates that by 1300 English merchants handled only about one-third of the wool trade. Foreigners also dominated other branches of international trade in which England was involved, most notably the wine trade, the greater part of which was in the hands of Gascon merchants.[55]

The early fourteenth century saw a change in this pattern of international trade, with English merchants, supported by the Crown, beginning to play a more dominant role in the country's international trade. Alien merchants had previously been treated with an ambivalent attitude: they were needed but they were not liked.[56] In 1303 the *Carta Mercatoria* had provided alien merchants with a wide range of privileges, in exchange for increased taxation on their imports. This was modelled on the so-called Gascon Charter of 1302 which had attempted to regulate wine trade disputes between the merchants of Gascony and London. These charters gave aliens the right to be free from murage, pontage and pavage throughout the king's dominions, and also to be free to trade among themselves and with denizens. In exchange aliens were to pay additional customs duties, including 2s on every tun of wine, 3s 4d, on each sack of wool and 6s 8d on each last of hides.[57] These regulations caused considerable resentment, particularly from the London merchants, and in 1311 both the liberties previously granted to aliens and the additional customs were cancelled. Growing antagonism to alien merchants during the fourteenth century, associated with the increased economic strength of the English merchants, led to a substantial fall in alien imports. This was exacerbated in the middle of the century when in 1345 Edward III defaulted on his loans from the Florentine bankers, the Bardis and the Peruzzis.[58]

The greatest change in the medieval trade of England and Wales, however, came during the late fourteenth and fifteenth centuries, when cloth replaced wool as the countries' main export. The extent of this change has been summarized by Carus-Wilson in the following terms: 'during the second half of the fourteenth century England's wool exports shrank by nearly half—from an average 32 thousand sacks per annum in 1350–1360 to an average 19 thousand in 1390–99. Meanwhile cloth exports increased more than sevenfold—from an average 5 thousand cloths per annum in 1350–60 to an average 37 thousand in 1390–99'.[59] This change is illustrated in Fig. 5.3, which shows the importance of the period 1420–80 in the transition. By the mid fifteenth century English merchant adventurers marketing cloth abroad had the great advantage that they did not have to ship their goods to a single port as had the wool merchants of the Company of the Staple who were restricted to the shipment of wool to Calais. In Carus-Wilson's words: 'English merchants marketing English woollens were from the middle of the fifteenth century the most substantial men of affairs in the country, of more consequence than the merchants of the Staple, of more consequence even than the Germans and Italians together'.[60]

By 1500 English and Welsh merchants had achieved three important things. The bulk of the country's trade was in their hands, thus ensuring that merchant profit would accrue to them rather than to foreigners. Secondly, the transformation of raw materials into finished products was also in English hands, thus ensuring that profits from the addition of value remained in England, and thirdly, they had captured foreign markets, thus enabling further profits to be gained from England's exports.

These changes were associated with profound effects in the urban landscape, and nowhere more so than in East Anglia. Between 1086 and 1334 one of the parts of

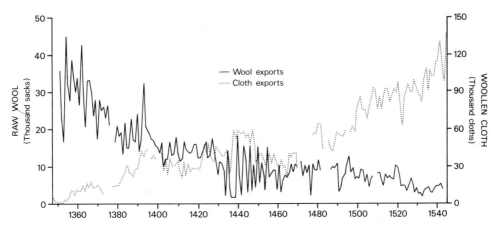

Fig. 5.3. English wool and cloth exports, 1347–1544. *Source*: derived from E. M. Carus-Wilson, *English Merchant Venturers*, (London, 1954), facing p. xviii.

England that appears to have had the greatest economic expansion was the region around the Wash.[61] During the twelfth and thirteenth centuries, the main ports of the Wash, Boston and Lynn, grew appreciably in importance. Lynn mainly exported salt, corn, malt and ale, and from the twelfth century Boston became a major exporter of wool, as well as salt and lead. At the end of the thirteenth century, Boston accounted for one-third of all England's wool exports, and it was the country's premier port in terms of volume of exports. The main import to the region was wine, predominantly from Gascony, but fish, timber and cloth were also imported.[62] During the fourteenth century, however, the decline of the wool export trade, and its replacement by cloth exports, led to a shift in the relative importance of the east coast ports. There was little cloth production in the hinterland of Lynn and Boston, and other ports were better suited to export the produce of the rapidly growing cloth industry. Yarmouth thus emerged as the major port for Norwich's worsted industry and Ipswich and Colchester handled exports of cloth from Suffolk and Essex. Other factors, such as the increasing strength of the Hanse in the North Sea, and the wars with France which led to a slump in wine imports from Gascony, also influenced the decline of the ports of the Wash, but it was the shift in emphasis from wool to cloth that was the main factor in generating a new pattern of trade which was to favour Ipswich, Colchester and Yarmouth at the expense of Boston and Lynn.

Guilds, Crafts and Industrial Change

There were two fundamental waves of change in the organization of crafts and industry between 1066 and 1500: urban industrial production grew and then declined, and this was paralleled by the waxing and waning of the power of the guilds. The main industries of eleventh-century England and Wales were salt-making, iron-working, lead-working, quarrying and pottery production.[63] However, through the twelfth and thirteenth centuries a wide range of craft industries grew up in most towns. Dodgshon has thus recorded how 'Thirteenth-century records for Gloucester list tradesmen as varied as ironmongers, bell foundry workers, cloth makers, leather workers, shipsmiths, parchment makers, needle-makers, hoopers, goldsmiths, glasswrights, soapmakers, girdlers, mercers and drapers'.[64] Quarrying, mining, and salt production remained largely rural in nature, but the processing crafts were primarily urban in location. Cloth production at the beginning of the thirteenth century was thus centred on the major towns of southern and eastern England, such as London, Oxford, Lincoln, Northampton, Norwich, Stamford, Bristol, York and Winchester.[65]

The fortunes of urban industry were closely tied to those of the guilds, whose role, according to Braudel, 'was to bring together the members of a single trade which they defended against all others, in quarrels that were often petty but which had an impact on everyday life. The eagle eye of the guilds was trained above all on the town's markets, of which every trade wanted its fair share. This meant security of employment and profit and "liberties" in the sense of privileges'.[66] During the economic expansion of the twelfth and thirteenth centuries the guilds operated restricted practices of entry into their ranks, they were able to raise prices for the products they sold, and they were able to maintain a close control of the processes of craft production.[67]

However, during the thirteenth century there was an increasing shift of industry away from urban areas to the countryside. This was not only in the industries that had always maintained a rural location, such as iron smelting and charcoal burning, but it was also to be found in the textile industry. The growth of a rural cloth industry was partly enabled by the development and spread of the fulling mill, but a rural location also permitted cloth producers to take advantage of cheap labour away from the prohibitive restrictions of the guilds.[68] Indeed, it seems that some urban merchants were actually taking advantage of opportunities to develop a rural cloth industry. As Miller has argued, 'the very existence of craft guilds or endeavours to establish them might encourage merchants to transfer their entrepreneurial activities to the countryside. Textile skills were traditional there; and rural overpopulation made labour available, often endowed with some small allotment of land as an additional source of livelihood.'[69]

These factors came to play a much more significant role following the mid-fourteenth-century economic crisis. Dodgshon has emphasized 'the contrasts and ultimate conflicts between urban and rural labour, or to put it another way between the regulated forms of the urban guild structure and the freer forms of the countryside'.[70] From the late fourteenth century craft specific guilds were desperately trying to hold on to their privileges and liberties, at a time when these were being eroded by changes in the economic structure of the country. As industry became increasingly rural in location, the spatially specific guild privileges became less and less relevant, and one way in which merchants tried to overcome these problems was through the creation of companies which combined different trades and crafts. Kramer sees these as a defensive move which aimed to restrict foreigners and exert greater control over trade and economic production.[71] By 1500, though, the power of the urban guilds was on the wane, and the restructuring of industry had laid the foundations for the new systems of production which were to provide the basis of the capitalist mode of production.

Re-organization of the Market Economy

Between 1066 and 1300 a complex network of markets had emerged throughout England and Wales, but as Hilton has noted 'The nature of the documentary evidence makes it difficult to find out about the day-to-day economic and social contacts between town and country'.[72] It is nevertheless possible to deduce something about the functioning of this system of markets from their spatial and temporal distribution. Fig. 5.4 illustrates the known markets of Lancashire and Nottinghamshire. These maps indicate that there was a wide dispersal of markets held on different days of the week throughout each county. In general, Thursdays were the most common market days, and most Thursday markets were held in small settlements. In contrast the Saturday markets were usually in the larger settlements, such as Liverpool, Manchester and Southwell. Important towns, such as Nottingham, had the right to hold daily markets. Moreover it is evident that there was some attempt to regulate the days of the week on which markets were to be held. The thirteenth-century lawyer Bracton argued that markets would adversely affect each other if they were less than six and two-thirds miles apart, and although the way he calculated this figure is open to dispute, it is apparent that markets held on the same day were generally further apart than were those with any other temporal separation.[73] Thus the average distance between nearest markets on any day of the week in the four counties of Derbyshire, Lancashire, Nottinghamshire and Staffordshire was 3.7 miles, whereas the average distance between markets held on the same day was 11.6 miles.

These late-thirteenth- and early-fourteenth-century markets, many of which were located in comparatively small villages, played a crucial role in articulating the economic interaction between town and countryside. Britnell has noted that the returns to the lords from market rents, tolls and fines were probably not that large, and he suggests that many lords may well have established markets in order to sustain a growing population who could make their livelihoods from non-agricultural occupations.[74] However, these periodic markets also served other sectors of the population in a variety of ways. For the peasantry they provided an outlet for any surplus production, the income from which they could use to pay taxes and rents, and to buy goods that were not produced on the manor where they lived. For merchants they formed an outlet for the growing craft products of the towns, they provided sources of grain and wool for resale either locally or on the international market, and they were also an outlet for luxury imported goods such as wine.

By 1500 the entire marketing structure had changed, and what little evidence there is suggests that this was not simply the result of the demographic collapse of the second half of the fouteenth century. There had been a qualitative, as well as a quantitative, change in the nature of trade and commerce. The majority of small, rural markets had disappeared, and those that survived were mainly situated in towns at important nodes in the communication network of roads and rivers. In the fifteenth century the increasing ability of the peasantry to obtain higher wages and freer personal status meant that they no longer needed to sell so much grain for taxation purposes, and the returns to the lords from market dues had probably been substantially eroded by inflation. In 1500 four broad types of town existed in England

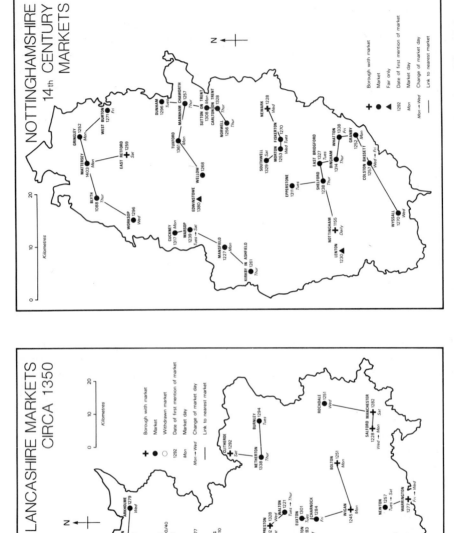

Fig. 5.4. Medieval boroughs and markets: Lancashire and Nottinghamshire. *Source:* derived from G. H. Tupling, 'The origins of markets and fairs in medieval Lancashire', *Transactions, Lancashire and Cheshire Antiquarian Society*, **49** (1933), pp. 75–94; T. Unwin, 'Rural marketing in medieval Nottinghamshire', *Jnl. of Historical Geography*, **7** (1981), pp. 231–51.

and Wales. At the bottom of the urban hierarchy were the 600 or so towns with population of between 500 and 1500, which served as local market centres. Then there were the regional centres, such as Chester, Leicester and Preston, with between 1500 and 5000 inhabitants, and above these were the major towns and cities such as Norwich, York and Newcastle upon Tyne with populations of between 5000 and 10,000.[75] Commerce, administration and justice were all increasingly becoming centralized and integrated at a national level through this urban hierarchy. At the top, with a population of perhaps 60,000, was London, and by the beginning of the sixteenth century the old regional medieval marketing systems of the country had begun to be subordinated to the ever growing demands of the capital for food and raw materials.

Urban Society

Throughout the period in question urban society was complex, diverse, changing, and unequal. Its diversity can be glimpsed from the 29 sundry folk encountered by Chaucer in the Tabard hostelry at Southwark where he lay ready to go on pilgrimage,[76] and in the numerous lists of burgesses recorded for the purposes of urban taxation. People from all walks of life made up urban society; anyone who took to the road would sooner or later come to a town. In this context it is useful to distinguish three categories of medieval society on the basis of place of residence: rural dwellers, who would often visit towns for reasons of commerce, entertainment or justice; urban merchants and traders, who would travel to the countryside to buy and sell goods; and 'outsiders', who included mendicant friars, itinerant pedlars, lepers and criminals.[77] Attention here will focus primarily on those who lived for most of their lives in the towns, and within this very diverse urban society it is possible to identify four main groups: the secular and ecclesiastical nobility; the richer merchants and burgesses; the poorer hucksters and ale-wives; and the employed labourers at the bottom of the social hierarchy.

This social division was, to an extent, reflected in the spatial organization of the medieval town. Centrally located cathedrals or castles formed the focus of attention in many medieval cities, as at Lincoln, Winchester and York. A key feature of most medieval towns was the concentration of crafts and trades by quarter, with burgesses usually living in the same buildings in which they worked. Some trades that were deemed to be noxious, such as tanning and fishmongering, were banished to peripheral locations, particularly in the later medieval period. Other trades sought specifically well-endowed physical locations, with fullers and dyers frequently being found at riverside locations. However, it was not only these trades that were grouped by street or quarter, and in many of the larger towns separate markets existed for the sale of different types of produce. Alien merchants also had their own specific trading quarters, with the merchants of the Hanse, for example, living and trading in the Steelyard or Stalhof on the bank of the Thames in London.[78]

The Urban Nobility

> There was a *Knight*, a most distinguished man,
> Who from the day on which he first began
> To ride abroad and followed chivalry . . . he possessed
> Fine horses, but he was not gaily dressed.
> He wore a fustian tunic stained and dark
> With smudges where his armour had left mark.

(Chaucer)[79]

Such was Chaucer's knight, and many of the towns of medieval England and Wales were established around the castles of his ancestors, the descendants of the great Norman nobles who crossed with William of Normandy in 1066. Others grew up associated with the numerous monastic foundations that emerged during the twelfth century. Indeed, as Table 5.1 indicates, it was the secular and ecclesiastical nobility who obtained borough charters for over two-thirds of the urban settlements of medieval England. The nobility, though, were few in number, and by the time of Chaucer's knight, when most towns had achieved their independence, the role of the nobility in urban society and political organization had diminished in importance. The large monastic foundations probably played a more important role in urban life than did the secular nobility, and in cathedral cities the power of the Church was also not to be ignored. However, by 1500, with the Reformation and the dissolution of the monasteries just around the corner, even the power of the Church had begun to wane in urban life.

Merchants and Burgesses

> There was a *Merchant* with a forked beard
> And motley dress; high on his horse he sat,
> Upon his head a Flemish beaver hat
> And on his feet daintily buckled boots.
> He told of his opinions and pursuits
> In solemn tones, he harped on his increase
> Of capital. . . .

(Chaucer)[80]

Here, with Chaucer's merchant, can be found the real ruler of urban life at the end of the twelfth century. However, as Hilton notes in the context of the West Midlands, surprisingly little is known about the urban ruling elite during the thirteenth century: 'That they were merchants rather than craftsmen seems certain, but although . . . we get some glimpses of their participation in the trade in commodities such as wool and wine, a full picture of their social and economic rule does not emerge.'[81] This conclusion applies to much of medieval England and Wales, but by the early fourteenth century, taxation records enable some idea of the social distribution of urban wealth to be gained. The main conclusion that can be drawn from these records is that there were extreme inequalities in wealth in terms of the figures recorded for movable goods. The leading administrative positions in most towns were usually in the hands of a small number of wealthy merchants, who between them held the various ranks of mayor, steward and bailiff. There was, though, considerable diversity in the social organization of different towns in the early fourteenth century, and Hilton has drawn attention to the way in which some towns, such as Bristol and Gloucester, were dominated both politically and economically by a small merchant oligarchy, whereas others, such as Worcester, seem to have been ruled politically by the apparently less wealthy taxpayers.[82]

The survival of a ledger belonging to Gilbert Maghfeld, an ironmonger and merchant of London, from the reign of Richard II, provides what is probably a typical account of a London merchants's activities in the 1390s. James has traced his life and activities in detail: from 1383 he was often in the service of the King; in 1392 he emerged as sheriff and alderman; and from 1385 to his death in 1397 he regularly held office as royal customer at Southampton, Boston and then London.[83] Maghfeld traded in a range of goods, as did most merchants of his time, but his main overseas interests lay in the iron of the Bayonne–Bilbao area. To obtain this he shipped out quantities of grain and cloth to Bayonne, with the return cargoes consisting mainly of iron, together with subsidiary ladings of wine, beaver, saffron, licorice and other local products. He also traded elsewhere in Europe, exporting cloth in exchange for herrings from Skania, obtaining woad from Genoa, and also collecting cargoes of wine from La Rochelle. Much of this trade was based on credit, and James notes that 'anything from 75 per cent of his merchandise was sold on terms of deferred payment'.[84] This reflects the wider development of new types of credit throughout Europe, which Braudel has seen as being fundamental in introducing new systems of exchange by which the old organization of fairs and markets was confronted by a new anti-market system of private trading involving warehouses and the development of the wholesale trade.[85]

By the end of the fifteenth century urban society had changed once more. Rentals, such as that for Gloucester in 1455, which has been analysed in detail by Langton, enable us to catch a glimpse of the social context of late medieval towns.[86] In this rental, occupations were mentioned for 185 people, representing approximately one-third of the recorded heads of household in the town in 1455. Of these, only two (1.1 per cent) were classified as being of high social status, and twenty (10.8 per cent) were professionals, including apothecaries and lawyers. The largest category of occupations included the 107 people (57.8 per cent) involved in manufacturing and retailing, with the greatest numbers being corvisers, tailors and cutlers. The rental also provides a glimpse of the distribution of occupational groups in different parts of Gloucester in the later Middle Ages, and illustrates a clear tendency towards spatial zoning of economic activity. Central sites on the main streets were occupied by specialist retailers and victuallers, with manufacturer-retailers being located further towards the edge of the town. Langton thus notes how 'those in the cloth clothing trades were strung out along Westgate . . ., while those in the leather clothing trades were scattered along Northgate, Eastgate and Southgate, with notable concentrations of cordwainers by the South and North gates and of glovers along Eastgate and up against the High Cross'.[87]

Hucksters, Ale-wives and the Poor

And you Mayors and Officers who uphold the Law, are the chief link between king and people, be sure that you punish all fraudulent tradesmen, the brewers, the bakers, the butchers and the cooks, in your pillories and ducking-stools. For these are the men who do most harm to the poor, poisoning them with adulterated food, at extortionate prices.

(Langland)[88]

At the bottom of the urban social hierarchy were the small traders and the urban poor, described in Langland's words above. Hucksters, those responsible for the provision of food, drink and other basic commodities, were a particularly prominent feature of small and medium-sized market towns, and regularly feature in the accounts of proceedings in urban courts. The extensive list of offences commonly charged against the traders of Nottingham, and recorded in the records from the Great Tourn of 1395, closely parallels Langland's late-fourteenth-century comments: 'The brewers are charged because they brew against the assize and sell with cups and dishes. The bakers take too much from the common people for the baking of bread, to wit 1¼d for a bushel, that is 6d for a quarter of a gallon, whereas they ought only to take 4d for a quarter. The butchers sell meat which has been kept too long and is corrupt. The fishermen keep their fish too long, and are commonly forestallers of fish. The taverners do not set the assize according to the proclamation of the mayor. Other traders sell garlic, tallow candles, butter and cheese too dear, against the provisions of the statute, and as common forestallers stand outside in the roads where such things come to be sold.'[89] These trades were regulated more than any others by the town authorities in their anxiety to maintain low food prices and labour costs, and it is mainly for this reason that they figure so extensively in the documentation. However, it was activities such as these that made up the day-to-day life of the towns of late-medieval England and Wales. In Hilton's words: 'However great the concentration of wealth in landed property and mercantile profits at the top, the late medieval world was dominated by petty production— peasants and artisans. The small scale of production was reflected in the sphere of circulation by the petty retail trader, as often as not—or perhaps even more often than not—a woman. Langland's world was not a world of low life, but of normality.'[90]

Rural–Urban Migration

Much of the population of medieval towns was sustained by immigration from the surrounding countryside. This was as true of the fourteenth century as it was of the sixteenth, but the distances travelled by migrants varied through time and between towns. Platt has emphasized the problems of identifying the origins of urban inhabitants, but using surname evidence it is possible to make some general conclusions concerning the distances people travelled. He thus notes the success of York and Hull in attracting immigrants from far afield in the late fourteenth century based upon the profits of the Hanseatic trade, and the way in which London attracted the best talents of people from regions well beyond its neighbouring counties.[91]

A detailed study by McClure (Table 5.2) illustrates the diversity and extent of rural–urban migration to be found in towns of different sizes and in different parts of the country, based on the names found in court rolls, subsidy rolls, tallage rolls and the poll taxes.[92] Using non-ambiguous names he illustrates that most migrants to Leicester and Nottingham came from within a 10–15 mile radius, as a result of competition between the two neighbouring towns which offered much the same kind of opportunity without a great amount of national or international trade. In contrast, Norwich and York had peaks at around 20 miles, reflecting their regional

Table 5.2: Early-fourteenth-century urban immigration.

Distance in miles	Leicester (% of 49 names)	Nottingham (% of 86 names)	Norwich (% of 164 names)	York (% of 149 names)	London (% of 238 names)
1–10	47.0	37.1	26.9	20.2	8.9
11–20	22.5	18.6	42.0	30.8	12.2
21–30	12.2	11.6	14.0	13.4	15.2
31–40	0	7.0	6.7	5.3	11.3
41–50	8.2	6.9	0.6	3.3	9.3
51–60	0	3.5	2.4	5.4	8.9
61–70	2.0	1.2	0.6	1.4	4.1
71–80	0.0	2.3	2.4	3.3	2.9
Over 80	8.1	11.6	4.2	16.8	27.2

Source: derived from P. McClure, 'Patterns of migration in the late Middle Ages: the evidence of English place-name surnames', *Economic History Review*, 2nd ser., **32** (1979), pp. 167–82.

economic and administrative dominance. London's attractiveness was of a different magnitude altogether, and it drew people from a wide range of distances throughout the country.

Urban Morphology and Fabric

The economy and society of medieval towns found expression in a particular kind of built fabric and lived experience for their inhabitants. This was as true of the specifically planned towns of England and Wales as it was for those that grew by organic accretion. Burgage tenure carried with it specific implications for urban morphology.

The Morphology of Medieval Towns

Medieval towns reflected a wide range of influences in their morphology, including those of surviving elements from Roman towns, the constraints of geomorphology, the military requirements of castles and walls, the convergence of routeways, and the economic requirements of the market place. The clearest examples of medieval planning are found in the 'new towns' of the late thirteenth and early fourteenth centuries, and particularly those associated with Edward I, such as New Winchelsea and his ten planted towns in north Wales: Flint, Rhuddlan and Aberystwyth, which were constructed following the end of the war in 1277; Conway, Caernarvon, Harlech, Criccieth and Bere, built after the defeat of Llewelyn in 1282; Beaumaris, built after the Welsh rising in 1294; and Caerwys, which seems to have been the only one built primarily for economic reasons. Most of these towns were laid out with their street and burgage plots set out at right angles in the shadow of the castles which dominated the surrounding landscape.[93]

However, it was not only these new, 'planted' towns which exhibited such regular characteristics. Taylor has noted how replanning of villages often took place when they were granted market charters,[94] and this was also true of the many settlements that were granted the status of boroughs. In this context Slater has traced how the expansion of many medieval towns was associated with very precise measurements concerning the size and alignment of burgage plots. The foundation charter of Stratford-upon-Avon, for example, specified that each plot should be 12 perches long and $3\frac{1}{2}$ perches wide.[95] This was typical of the newly developed towns of Warwickshire and Worcestershire, and Slater contrasts such wide and shallow plots with the longer and narrower ones derived from former village tofts as in the Bondgate suburb of Nuneaton.[96] Two other features were typical of these burgage series in the West Midlands: many incorporated back-lane access ways as an integral part of their structure, and the vast majority of the plots were arranged at right angles to the roads upon which they fronted.

Through time these initially regular features of medieval boroughs became subdivided and re-organized, and the 1455 rental of Gloucester already referred to, illustrates how, by the fifteenth century, 'the buildings on the burgage fronts were already considerably subdivided and extended. They were occupied almost exclusively by tenants, who often shared lodgings in what were usually cramped quarters.'[97] Other parts of Gloucester, such as the area from Satires lane past the castle to the quay, lay empty, and numerous smaller plots were vacant, reflecting the population decline of the fourteenth and early fifteenth centuries.

Roads and Rivers: the Arteries of Trade

Remarkably few studies have been undertaken on the transport network of medieval England and Wales. This is surprising given the importance that it played in influencing the costs and patterns of trade, the locations of markets, and the development of towns. The high density of markets that emerged during the thirteenth century implies that there must have been a considerable network of tracks and small roads upon which merchants, hucksters and the rural population travelled to market. Only the most important routes were recorded on maps such as that drawn by Matthew Paris about 1250 and the anonymous map from about 1360 named after Richard Gough who first noted its existence in the eighteenth century.

Parts of the four main Roman roads of Watling Street, Ermine Street, Fosse Way and Icknield Way appear to have survived in reasonable form into Norman times, but the majority of early medieval 'roads' were little more than routes which were maintained through the regular passage of people along them.[98] Most long distance transport was undertaken by water, either on navigable stretches of river or around the coasts. The Thames, the Severn, the Ouse and the Trent provided the main arteries of river transport, but it is evident that by the fourteenth century many smaller rivers and even streams were used to move bulky goods of low value.[99]

Hindle has reconstructed the likely distribution of roads in England and Wales in the middle of the fourteenth century, based on the evidence of maps, royal itineraries, and archaeology.[100] This information is illustrated in Fig. 5.5, which also shows the main navigable rivers. While many other routes must also have been

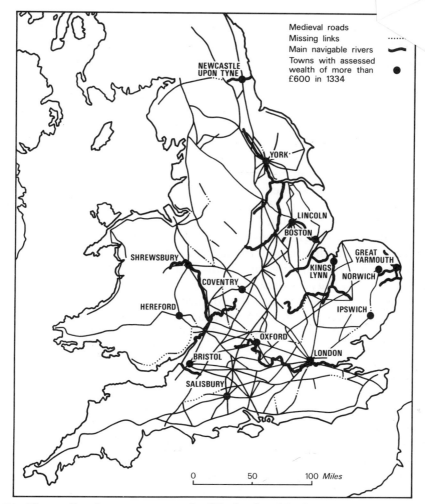

Fig. 5.5. The medieval transport network of England and Wales. *Source*: derived from B. P. Hindle, 'The road network of medieval England and Wales', *Jnl. of Historical Geography*, **2** (1976), pp. 207–21; B. P. Hindle, *Medieval Roads* (Aylesbury, 1982); and R. E. Glasscock, 'England *circa* 1334', in H. C. Darby (ed.), *A New Historical Geography of England before 1600* (Cambridge, 1976), p. 184.

used, the overall focus of the communication network upon London is apparent, as is the high density of road links in the area betwen Southampton, Bristol and Oxford. Another interesting feature is the clustering of routes radiating out from the main towns, such as York and Lincoln. Certain parts of the country were apparently poorly served by the transport network, most notably Wales, Devon and Cornwall, the north-west, and to a lesser extent the south-east and East Anglia. These roads and rivers thus provided the infrastructure of medieval trade. By 1500 all of the most important towns were located at nodes in this emerging transport network, and the markets that survived were likewise those that lay on the main roads and rivers.

⟩nclusion

The period between 1066 and 1500 saw considerable change in the nature of towns and trade. Although a cycle of demographic expansion and decline can be identified, it is not possible to see this simply reflected in a pattern of urban growth and recession. The critical point is that there was a qualitative change in terms of commercial activity and urban society between 1066 and 1500. This is intimately connected with the way in which English and Welsh towns and merchants became increasingly involved in the wider European network of trade. Expansion of international and local trade at a time of demographic growth in the period prior to the fourteenth century generated an increase in the number of towns and markets throughout the realm. Subsequent to this, while population declined, the structure of the urban economy became increasingly subordinated to the demands of the inhabitants of the capital, London. This was associated with the introduction of new systems of credit, changing relationships between supply and demand, and with the development of new industrial enterprises. The implications of the changes in rural society and economy during the fourteenth-century crisis of feudalism were not to be lost on the towns. The emergence of a freer peasantry, able to sell its labour power more readily in either the towns or the countryside, and the development of new acquisitive aspirations amongst the merchant community, laid the way for the emergence of the capitalist relations of production which are explored in subsequent chapters.

References

1. R. A. Dodgshon, *The European Past: Social Evolution and Spatial Order*, (Basingstoke, 1987), p. 213; see also M. M. Postan and E. Miller (eds), *The Cambridge Economic History of Europe, Volume II; Trade and Industry in the Middle Ages*, (2nd edn.), (Cambridge, 1987).
2. J. Haslam (ed.), *Anglo-Saxon Towns in Southern England*, (Chichester, 1984); H. R. Loyn, *The Governance of Anglo-Saxon England*, (London, 1984).
3. H. C. Darby, *Domesday England*, (Cambridge, 1977).
4. C. Platt, *The English Medieval Town*, (London, 1976).
5. S. Reynolds, *An Introduction to the History of English Medieval Towns*, (London, 1977).
6. I. H. Adams, *Agrarian Landscape Terms: a Glossary for Historical Geography*, (London, 1976).
7. M. M. Postan, *The Medieval Economy and Society: an Economic History of Britain in the Middle Ages*, (London, 1972); J. Tait, *The Medieval English Borough*, (Manchester, 1936).
8. Reynolds, *English Medieval Towns*, p. 100.
9. A. Ballard, *British Borough Charters 1042–1216*, (Cambridge, 1913), p. 32.
10. Reynolds, *English Medieval Towns*, p. 101.
11. Ballard, *British Borough Charters*, p. liii.
12. *Ibid*, p. 185.
13. T. Unwin, 'Rural marketing in medieval Nottinghamshire', *Jnl. of Historical Geography*, **7** (1981), pp. 231–51; Royal Commission on Market Rights and Tolls, *Final Report XI*, (London, 1891); I. Starsmore, *English Fairs*, (London, 1975); O. S. Watkins, 'The medieval market and fair in England and Wales', *Y Cymmroder*, **25** (1915), pp. 211–74.
14. C. C. Taylor, 'Medieval market grants and village morphology', *Landscape History*, **4** (1982), pp. 21–28.
15. R. A. Donkin, 'The disposal of Cistercian wool in England and Wales during the twelfth and thirteenth centuries: I', *Citeaux in de Nederlanden*, **8** (1957), p. 115.

16. R. A. Dodgshon, 'The early Middle Ages', in R. A. Dodgshon and R. A. Butlin (eds.), *An Historical Geography of England and Wales*, (London, 1978), p. 105.
17. M. Dunford and D. Perrons, *The Arena of Capital*, (London, 1983), p. 126.
18. R. H. Hilton, 'Lords, burgesses and hucksters', *Past and Present*, **97** (1982), pp. 3–15; R. H. Hilton, 'Medieval market towns and simple commodity production', *Past and Present*, **109** (1985), pp. 3–23.
19. Hilton, 'Medieval market towns', pp. 22–23.
20. T. H. Aston and C. H. E. Philpin (eds.), *The Brenner Debate: Agrarian Class Structure and Economic Development in Pre-Industrial Europe*, (Cambridge, 1985); A. R. Bridbury, 'English provincial towns in the later Middle Ages', *Economic History Review*, 2nd ser., **34** (1981), pp. 1–24.
21. Hilton, 'Medieval market towns', p. 3.
22. Darby, *Domesday England*, p. 89.
23. J. C. Russell, *English Medieval Population*, (Albuquerque, 1948); M. Postan, 'Some economic evidence of declining population in the later Middle Ages', *Economic History Review*, 2nd ser., **2** (1950), pp. 221–46; B. F. Harvey, 'The population trend in England between 1300 and 1348', *Transactions of the Royal Historical Society*, 5th ser., **16** (1966), pp. 23–42.
24. J. F. D. Shrewsbury, *A History of the Bubonic Plague in the British Isles*, (Cambridge, 1971), p. 123; J. Hatcher, *Plague, Population and the English Economy 1348–1530*, (London, 1977), pp. 17–18.
25. Bridbury, 'English provincial towns'; S. H. Rigby, 'Urban decline in the later Middle Ages: some problems in interpreting the statistical data', *Urban History Yearbook*, 1979, pp. 53–5; C. Phythian-Adams, *Desolation of a City: Coventry and the Urban Crisis of the late Middle Ages*, (Cambridge, 1979).
26. J. F. Hadwin, 'From disonance to harmony on the late medieval town', *Economic History Review*, 2nd ser., **39** (1986), p. 426.
27. Haslam, *Anglo-Saxon Towns in Southern England*.
28. Darby, *Domesday England*, p. 289.
29. *Ibid.*
30. D. F. Renn, *Norman Castles in Britain*, (2nd edn.), (London, 1973).
31. M. W. Beresford and H. P. R. Finberg (eds.), *English Medieval Boroughs: a Handlist*, (Newton Abbott, 1973).
32. M. Beresford, *New Towns in the Middle Ages: Town Plantation in England, Wales and Gascony*, (London, 1967).
33. Beresford and Finberg, *English Medieval Boroughs*.
34. *Ibid*, p. 50.
35. H. C. Darby, R. E. Glasscock, J. Sheail and G. R. Versey, 'The changing geographical distribution of wealth in England: 1086–1334–1525', *Jnl. of Historical Geography*, **5** (1979), pp. 247–62.
36. M. Stanley, 'The geographical distribution of wealth in medieval England', *Jnl. of Historical Geography*, **6** (1980), pp. 315–20.
37. R. E. Glasscock, 'England *circa* 1334', in H. C. Darby (ed.), *A New Historical Geography of England before 1600*, (Cambridge, 1976), p. 177.
38. *Ibid.*
39. R. H. Britnell, 'English markets and royal administration before 1200', *Economic History Review*, 2nd ser., **31** (1978), pp. 183–96.
40. R. H. Britnell, 'The proliferation of markets in England, 1200–1349', *Economic History Review*, 2nd ser., **34** (1981), p. 211.
41. Britnell, 'English markets and royal administration'.
42. Hilton, 'Medieval market towns', p. 5.
43. R. H. T. Smith, 'Periodic market places and periodic marketing: a review and prospect', *Progress in Human Geography*, **3** (1979), pp. 471–505 and **4** (1980), pp. 1–31; Unwin, 'Rural marketing in medieval Nottinghamshire'.
44. Hilton, 'Medieval market towns', p. 5.
45. *Records of the Borough of Nottingham I*, (Nottingham 1882), p. 61.

46. *Placita de Quo Warranto* (London, 1807), p. 616.
47. A. R. H. Baker, 'Changes in the later Middle Ages', in H. C. Darby (ed.), *A New Historical Geography of England before 1600*, (Cambridge, 1976), p. 192.
48. Bridbury, 'English provincial towns', p. 13.
49. S. H. Rigby, 'Late medieval urban prosperity: the evidence of the Lay Subsidies', *Economic History Review*, 2nd ser., **39** (1986), p. 416.
50. Hadwin, 'From disonance to harmony', p. 426; see also J. C. K. Cornwall, *Wealth and Society in Early Sixteenth Century England*, (London, 1988).
51. P. Clark and P. Slack (eds.), *Crisis and Order in English Towns*, (London, 1972).
52. N. J. G. Pounds, *An Historical Geography of Europe 450 B. C.–A. D. 1330*, (Cambridge, 1973); R. H. Bautier, 'The fairs of Champagne', in R. Cameron (ed.), *Essays in French Economic History*, (Homewood, 1970), pp. 42–63.
53. Pounds, *An Historical Geography of Europe*, p. 429; see also Donkin, 'The disposal of Cistercian wool'.
54. E. M. Carus-Wilson, *English Merchant Venturers*, (London, 1954).
55. M. K. James, *Studies in the Medieval Wine Trade*, (Oxford, 1971); Y. Renouard, 'The wine trade of Gascony in the Middle Ages', in R. Cameron (ed.), *Essays in French Economic History*, (Homewood, 1970), pp. 64–90.
56. T. H. Lloyd, *Alien Merchants in England in the High Middle Ages*, (Brighton, 1982).
57. *Ibid.*, p. 28.
58. F. Braudel, *Civilization and Capitalism 15th–18th Century: the Wheels of Commerce*, (London, 1985); see also R. A. Goldthwaite, 'The Medici bank and the world of Florentine capitalism', *Past and Present*, **114** (1987), pp. 3–31.
59. Carus-Wilson, *English Merchant Venturers*, p. xvii.
60. *Ibid.*, p. xxiv.
61. Darby, Glasscock, Sheail and Versey, 'The changing geographical distribution of wealth'.
62. E. Carus-Wilson, 'The medieval trade of the ports of the Wash', *Medieval Archaeology*, **6–7** (1962–1963), pp. 182–201.
63. Darby, *Domesday England*, pp. 260–88.
64. Dodgshon, 'The early Middle Ages', p. 111.
65. E. M. Carus-Wilson, 'The English cloth industry in the late twelfth and early thirteenth centuries', *Economic History Review*, **14,** (1944–1945), pp. 32–50.
66. Braudel, *Civilization and Capitalism*, p. 315.
67. Dunford and Perrons, *The Arena of Capital*; see also H. Swanson 'The illusion of economic structure: craft guilds in late medieval English towns', *Past and Present*, **121** (1988), pp. 29–48.
68. E. M. Carus-Wilson, 'An industrial revolution of the thirteenth century', *Economic History Review*, 2nd ser., **2** (1941), pp. 41–60.
69. E. Miller, 'The fortunes of the English textile industry during the thirteenth century', *Economic History Review*, 2nd ser., **18** (1965), pp. 73–4.
70. Dodgshon, *The European Past*, p. 308.
71. S. Kramer, *The English Craft Gilds: Studies in their Progress and Decline*, (New York, 1927).
72. R. H. Hilton, *A Medieval Society: the West Midlands at the end of the Thirteenth Century*, (London, 1966), p. 177.
73. H. de Bracton, *De Legibus et Consuetinibus Angliae Book* **5,** ed. J. Twiss (London, 1880), pp. 583–87; H. S. A. Fox, 'Going to town in thirteenth century England', in A. R. H. Baker and J. B. Harley (eds.), *Man Made the Land*, (Newton Abbot, 1973), pp. 69–78.
74. Britnell, 'The proliferation of markets'; R. H. Britnell, 'The making of Witham', *History Studies*, **1** (1968), pp. 13–21.
75. P. Clark and P. Slack, *English Towns in Transition 1500–1700*, (Oxford, 1976), p. 9.
76. G. Chaucer, *The Canterbury Tales*, (Harmondsworth, 1977).
77. C. Philo, 'Hue and cry from town to town: towards a social geography of outsiders in medieval England', (Unpublished paper, Cambridge, 1987).
78. J. Schildhauer, *The Hansa: History and Culture*, (Leipzig, 1985); A. D'Haenens, *Europe of the North Sea and the Baltic: the World of the Hanse*, (Antwerp, 1984).

79. Chaucer, *The Canterbury Tales,* p. 20–1.
80. *Ibid,* p. 26.
81. Hilton, *A Medieval Society,* p. 205.
82. *Ibid.*
83. James, *Studies in the Medieval Wine Trade.*
84. *Ibid,* p. 203.
85. Braudel, *Civilization and Capitalism.*
86. J. Langton, 'Late medieval Gloucester: some data from a rental of 1455', *Transactions, Institute of British Geographers,* new ser., **2** (1977), pp. 259–77.
87. Langton, 'Late medieval Gloucester', pp. 273–4.
88. W. Langland, *Piers the Ploughman,* (Harmondsworth, 1966), p. 47.
89. *First Report of the Royal Commission on Market Rights and Tolls I,* (London, 1888), p. 21.
90. Hilton, 'Lords, burgesses and hucksters', p. 15.
91. Platt, *The English Medieval Town,* pp. 96–8.
92. P. McClure, 'Patterns of migration in the late Middle Ages: the evidence of English place-name surnames', *Economic History Review,* 2nd ser., **32** (1979), pp. 167–82.
93. Beresford, *New Towns of the Middle Ages,* pp. 3–4.
94. Taylor, 'Medieval market grants'.
95. T. R. Slater, 'The analysis of burgage patterns in medieval towns', *Area,* **13** (1981), pp. 211–16; see also P. Crummy, 'The system of measurement used in town planning from the ninth to the thirteenth century', in S. C. Hawkes, D. Brown and J. Campbell (eds.), *Anglo-Saxon Studies in Archaeology and History,* (Oxford, 1979), pp. 149–64.
96. T. R. Slater, 'Urban genesis and medieval town plans in Warwickshire and Worcestershire', in T. R. Slater and P. J. Jarvis (eds.)., *Field and Forest: an Historical Geography of Warwickshire and Worcestershire,* (Norwich, 1982), pp. 173–202.
97. Langton, 'late medieval Gloucester', p. 275.
98. B. P. Hindle, 'The road network of medieval England and Wales', *Jnl. of Historical Geography,* **2** (1976), pp. 207–21.
99. J. F. Willard, 'Inland transportation in England during the fourteenth century', *Speculum,* **1,** (1976), pp. 361–74.
100. B. P. Hindle, 'The road network of medieval England and Wales'; B. P. Hindle, *Medieval Roads,* (Aylesbury, 1982).

6

Geographical Aspects of Population Change in England 1500–1730

R. M. Smith

The last quarter century has witnessed an enormous, indeed unprecedented, growth in our knowledge of matters to do with the population of early modern England. Until the late 1970s it was possible to encounter two approaches by scholars to discussions of population trends for the nation at large; one was based on estimates and fragmented 'guesstimates' of population numbers for widely separated years;[1] the other utilized the highly problematic estimates of population numbers, fertility and mortality that could be derived from John Rickman's gallant attempt in the early nineteenth century to create counts of baptisms, marriages and burials provided for him by parish incumbents beginning in 1569 and available every tenth year to 1751.[2]

While not all the evidence that figured so prominently in these earlier discussions has been jettisoned, it assumes a subordinate role to the new estimates that were presented in 1981 as a result of more than a decade of meticulous and highly sophisticated research, based upon a sample of 404 English parish registers, by the Cambridge Group for the History of Population and Social Structure. The very considerable complexities of this research are described elsewhere and in this chapter only limited reference is made to the detail of the techniques upon which this attempt at national demographic reconstruction was based.[3] The reconstruction involved assembling a sample of parish registers that were chosen initially because of their quality regarding completeness and accuracy. Substantial corrections to these data were required to take account of a number of short-comings they displayed. Re-weighting of the sample was required in so far as it was not randomly drawn and contained too many large parishes and too few small ones. Further corrections were required because changing baptismal customs led to an extension of the interval between birth and christening which caused babies dying before baptism to be omitted from the register.[4] Such developments caused both the burial and baptismal record to be deficient although this is a problem for the eighteenth-century rather than sixteenth- and seventeenth-century data. In addition, non-conformity grew after 1700 and events in non-conformist registers had to be incorporated into the sample by an increasing factor as the eighteenth century progressed. Finally, to secure a 'true' national data set the total events relating to London had to be included. These data are in every sense estimates although the

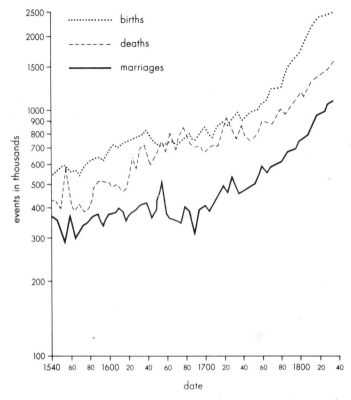

Fig. 6.1. Five-year totals of births, marriages and deaths in England 1540–1837. *Source:* Wrigley and Schofield, *The Population History of England*, pp. 779–80.

procedures and assumptions underpinning their collection and adjustment have been clearly specified. They do allow students of population history to comment with very considerable confidence on the gross trend in English population for most of the period covered by this chapter.[5]

It can be seen in Fig. 6.1 that the growth rates in the series of births, marriages and deaths were not constant through time. In certain phases deaths were increasing faster than births and vice versa. It is possible to detect two very clearly defined phases in the period from 1540 to 1710 and a more ambiguous phase in the final two decades with which we are concerned in this chapter. From 1540 to 1640, with the exception of the first two decades, births, deaths and marriages are all moving upwards and apart from the years 1556–60, births greatly exceeded deaths. In the final decade of this 'century' the gap between the two series was narrowing sharply. From 1640 to 1710 the annual frequencies of births and marriages fell and then oscillated with no obvious trend. The annual pattern of deaths is more variable than births, continuing to rise for a further 40 years after 1640 before stabilizing at the end of the seventeenth century. After 1710 births begin to move on an upward course although their continued growth may be a reaction to the exceptionally severe mortality of the 1720s.

While a consideration of national population growth rates in terms of birth/burial surpluses is suggestive it is hardly a reliable guide to the nation's demographic buoyancy. Only if the unrealistic assumption that there was no net migration is made will these statistics provide an estimate of intrinsic population growth rates. The conversion of these data relating to births and deaths into a time series yielding national population estimates and hence a variety of demographic rates required a major technical innovation in demographic history. The innovation came in the form of 'inverse projection' which takes as a starting population, that of 1871 with a known age structure. If the English population had been closed over the period of 330 years leading up to 1871 and if the mortality of each birth cohort over this period was known, then successive inflation of survivors of a cohort at any census by an estimate of mortality over the cohort's life course should recreate the original birth cohort. If the estimated size of the birth cohort by this process is actually smaller than observed births, deaths must have taken place outside the 'system' under observation. In fact these missing deaths would relate to persons whose deaths occurred outside England and constitute a measure of net migration. These migrants within the framework of 'inverse projection' are allocated to each time period by using a fixed age schedule of migration which assumes that the greatest propensity to migrate was between ages 20 and 35. Inverse projection yields estimates of population size at five-year intervals. It is also possible to proceed to estimate age structures and to relate the estimated numbers of deaths, births and marriages to these population totals to produce birth, marriage and death rates. The technique of inverse projection has excited considerable interest among historical demographers and is generally thought to be a robust device.[6]

National Population Trends

English quinquennial population totals are presented in Fig. 6.2 from 1541 to 1750. They reflect three phases that were also identified in Fig. 6.1. From an estimated population of 2.774 million in 1541 population rose to a high point of 5.281 million in 1656, almost doubling over the course of 115 years. A decline ensued in the 1670s which caused the population in 1686 to be over 400,000 persons smaller at 4.864 million. While a slow growth of numbers occurred thereafter it was not until 1721 that the population total of 1656 was surpassed. The 1720s witnessed the national population briefly falling again below the mid-seventeenth-century high point before sustained and increasingly rapid growth came to distinguish the remainder of the eighteenth century. It is doubtful whether the population growth that took place in the late sixteenth and early seventeenth centuries achieved a national population that equalled the total reached after the last major period of sustained growth in the century before 1300. Indeed the sixteenth century begins with an English population that was at a very low level and there is little evidence to suggest that there had been much sustained prior growth in numbers during the later fifteenth century. In fact, recent findings from counts of adult males over the age of 12 from a small number of Essex manors show numbers sagging slightly in the late fifteenth and early sixteenth century to their lowest point for the whole period from 1270.[7] These data do show signs of strong growth after 1530. However, at their lowest point in the early sixteenth century, Essex manorial populations were almost a third of their pre-Black

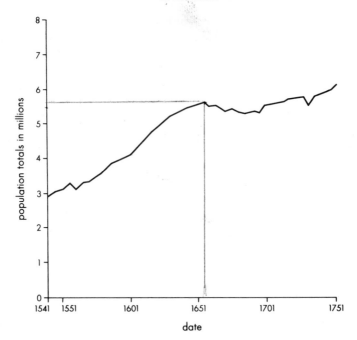

Fig. 6.2. Population of England (excluding Monmouth), 1541–1751. *Source:* Wrigley and Schofield. *The Population History of England,* p. 207.

Death maxima. Rapid growth after 1524–25 that was sustained into the late 1550s is consistent with both Cornwall's estimates of a population of 2.3 million in 1524–25 and intrinsic growth rates of 0.8 to 1.0 per annum over the following 30 years.[8] Whether our data are derived from national or local demographic estimates they strongly endorse the perception of contemporaries such as Thomas Starkey who could reflect in 1535 on 'the grete lake of pepul and skarseness of men'[9] Furthermore, what is noteworthy is that over the period from 1500 to 1730 the phases during which net population occurred were of relatively brief duration. For instance quinquennial intrinsic growth rates in excess of 0.9 per cent per annum were mostly confined to the quarter century after 1560. In 14 of the 38 quinquennia after 1541, concentrated in particular after 1650, growth rates were either negative or below 0.2 per cent per annum.

Mortality 1500–1730

Changes in the Structure of Mortality

The apparent smoothness of the curve of national population size might be thought surprising in view of the relatively volatile pattern displayed by the annual numbers of deaths and births. Indeed much has been written of the very evident 'instability of mortality' through the early modern period and some historians on observing the sudden dramatic peaks of the death rate have gone so far as to suggest that 'the intensity and frequency of the peaks controlled the size of agricultural societies'.[10] There is reasonable support for the view that mortality stabilized through this period. English parish registers reveal a diminution in short-run variability in mortality from the seventeenth century. The English national totals based on the sample of 404 parishes studied by Wrigley and Schofield indicate that the mean deviation of the series of annual crude death rates declined, falling from 17.7 per cent in the years 1550–74 to reach 8.3 per cent in 1700–24.[11] The fall was not smoothly distributed through time and quarterly deviation from 1725 to 1749 saw a rise to 12.3 per cent before the preceding decline was resumed through the remainder of the eighteenth century. Another indicator of the reduced volatility of year-to-year death rates is a consideration of so-called 'crisis' years defined as those in which the percentage deviation above the annual crude death rate from a 25-year moving average exceeded 10 per cent. Wrigley and Schofield distinguish between one-, two- and three-star crises in terms of whether the death rate of the year in question was respectively 10 per cent, 20 per cent or 30 per cent or more above trend.[12] On such a statistical basis 34 'crisis' years were identified between 1541 and 1730. Sixteen of these two- and three-star crises occurred before 1665/66 and only four in the remaining years prior to 1730. Likewise, monthly 'crises' fell from a mean frequency of 1.46 per cent in 1550–74 to 0.98 per cent in 1750–74, although the fall was interrupted in the quarter-century 1725–49 when the incidence of crisis months rose to 1.62 per cent, largely because of the very turbulent phase from 1727–30.

The most striking finding from this research into the stability of mortality concerns the absence of synchroneity in the year-to-year movement of crude death rates and life expectation at birth. In fact, the stabilization of mortality occurred simultaneously with a general decline in life expectancy. Mortality certainly stabilized but it did so at a lower rather than higher level of life expectancy. Indeed 'background' life expectancy measures derived from 'inverse projection' were at their highest level in the late Tudor and early Stuart periods when expectation of life at birth exceeded 40 years before falling over the first two-thirds of the seventeenth century to a low point which was very close to 30 years. The 1690s and early 1700s display some improvement in life expectancy but this was short-lived as the late 1720s saw life expectancy dropping to levels that had previously been experienced in the late 1550s during what may well have been the most severe 'crisis' period since the fourteenth century.

Of particular interest are the apparently discrepant trends in life expectancy and real wages over the seventeenth and early eighteenth centuries. Real wages fell sharply in the late sixteenth century while life expectancy was at its highest level for the whole of the early modern period and even after wages began to rise in the second third of the seventeenth century background mortality continued to worsen (see Fig. 6.3). As Schofield has pungently commented these data provide 'little evidence that long-term trends in scarcity and plenty as captured by the real wage caused marked differences in mortality levels in early modern England.'[13]

While no long-term relationship can be identified showing a strong link between mortality and economic well-being, it is necessary to review the evidence bearing on mortality's sensitivity to short-term variations in the size of the harvest and hence the price of food. Although England may have avoided the long-term operation of the 'positive check' it may have been vulnerable in the sixteenth and early seven-

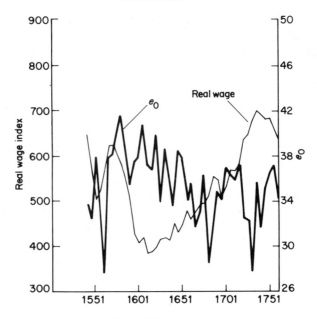

Fig. 6.3. Quinquennial expectations of life at birth (e_0) data compared with an 11-year moving average of a real wage index. *Source:* Wrigley and Schofield, *The Population History of England,* p. 414.

teenth centuries when real wages were falling and increasing numbers of landless individuals were dependent on the market for food purchases. Investigation of systematic relationships between fluctuations in food prices and mortality requires very careful statistical analysis entailing not only a calculation of the magnitude of the association in the year in which the fluctuation occurs but also in the four subsequent years so that lagged relationships can be considered. R. D. Lee has undertaken important work of this kind on English data after 1541 and found that while there was a systematic relationship between fluctuations in wheat prices and mortality it was very weak.[14] In fact only 16 per cent of the short-run variation in mortality was associated with price changes and the bulk of this was the product of effects registered in a relatively small number of years with extreme upward price fluctuations such as 1596/7, 1597/8 and 1545/6. Lee's finding that the cumulative response of mortality to prices fell in the period 1641 to 1745 to a third of the level obtaining in 1548–1640 has been questioned by Galloway who attributed this finding to an unexpected negative association between prices and mortality between 1641 and 1674.[15] Walter and Schofield have recently commented that 'although the connection between food price fluctuations and mortality was always weak, it was not until the mid-eighteenth century that it was entirely broken'.[16] It is noteworthy, however, that the very high food prices of the 1690s were not reflected in any mortality rise. In fact, while real wages in 1697/8 and 1698/9 were 22 and 21 per cent respectively below a 25-year moving average, the death rate in both years was marginally below rather than above average. Food prices in other parts of northern and north-western Europe rose to great heights in the 1690s and while mortality crises were conspicuously absent in England they were readily detectable in Scotland and France.[17] Indeed, it would seem that for the period from 1677–1734 when comparisons can be made with England, 46 per cent of French deaths over age 5 were associated with grain price movements. Only 24 per cent of non-infant deaths for the period 1675–1755 were associated with grain price changes in England.[18] Furthermore, in the year of the price shock, mortality was 30 per cent greater in France compared with 11 per cent in England.

Much of the above research, although undertaken with highly sophisticated econometric techniques , is potentially precarious. While the association between long-run starvation and death is reasonably clearcut the links between malnutrition and the capacity to combat infection is far more complex. An individual's 'nutritional status' is a function both of nutritional intake and energy expended.[19] Disease itself can help to determine nutritional status which can help to influence susceptibility to disease. Consequently, changes in level of energy expenditure connected with alterations to work patterns, shifts in climate and the overall incidence of disease can in unison or independently work to influence nutritional status. If nutritional status deteriorated thereby leading to a rise in mortality it is not possible to know whether this occurred because of food shortages or fluctuations in climate or a shift in the incidence of disease. There has been an accumulation of evidence to suggest that the immune system failed only in conditions of extreme malnutrition. Furthermore, certain diseases of the early modern period such as bubonic plague, smallpox, typhoid and malaria were so virulent that chances of survival did not depend strictly on nutritional status.

Complexities of the kind considered above have turned many historians away from simple-minded searches for the 'positive check' and have led to suggestions that long- and short-run shifts in the level of mortality, although shaped to some degree by economic change as reflected in real wages and the size of the harvest, appear to have been determined primarily by shifts in the pattern of disease rather than living standards. The notion that mortality was in a very real sense autonomous or exogenously determined in early modern England has received much support. In particular it has been forcefully promoted in the writings of R. D. Lee who sees the demographic history of England from the fourteenth to the early nineteenth centuries as largely the acting out of exogenous changes in the independent variable, mortality, which in turn determined changes in fertility, population size and living standards.[20] It is an approach which some historians have been reluctant to endorse in so far as it implicitly marginalizes mortality.[21] Changes in the death rate then require no explanation in terms of human agency.

Geographical Aspects of Crisis Mortality

As units of a smaller spatial scale of analysis are chosen it seems harder to accept mortality as an autonomous variable. The central experience of 'crisis' in the 404 parishes in the Cambridge Group's sample, comprising half of the parishes, lay between 5 and 17 monthly crises per century over the period 1541 to 1871. Of course, at the extremes of this distribution there were five parishes that experienced no crisis whatsoever, and forty-two which suffered 30 or more crisis months per century. Multi-variate analysis of crisis experience in the complete set of 404 parishes reveals distance from market towns and altitude to have been particularly influential in determining a parish's susceptibility to crisis. Susceptibility was high in communities close to market towns and was also high in communities below 50 feet above sea-level and low in those at altitudes above 300 feet. The farming regime of the parish appears to have had little effect on the frequencies with which parishes experienced crisis. An independent regional influence is also observable with parishes over much of Midland England experiencing average crisis frequencies, those in south-east England and the East Midlands below average. Above average frequencies are found in parishes close to the east coast running from the Wash to the Tees estuary, the north-west of England and especially the south-western counties.

Of course this variability, which in part reflects the influence of population density, vulnerability to specific infections and possibly the local effectiveness of welfare provisions, is difficult to comprehend without specific information on the causes of death in identified crises. Before the mid seventeenth century Appleby argued with respect to the issue of a community's vulnerability to famine that there were ' . . . two Englands, one subject to trade depression and harvest failure, but able to avoid widespread starvation, the other pushed past the edge of subsistence by the same dislocations'.[22] Indeed dearths which were associated with the doubling or trebling in death rate in the north-west in 1596/7 and 1622/3 were barely visible in the south and south-east of England.[23] Such an 'ecology of famine' was explained by Appleby in terms of the impact of population growth in the north-west which created, partly through inheritance and encroachment on the wastes, a large smallholder population in environments that were climatically marginal for grain production.[24] In addition, the predominantly pastoral character of the region's farming, exacerbated by a long-term decline in the cloth industry, pushed these areas into severe difficulties as the demand for their specialized products fell and as overall purchasing power in the other English regions plummeted in high-price years. In fact Walter and Schofield have suggested that the farmers in this region may in the late sixteenth and early seventeenth centuries have paid a price for precocious specialization before distributional means were adequate to move grain from areas of surplus to areas of deficit.[25] Furthermore, it may have been that the lowlands of the south and east were better endowed with local social structures and administrative institutions capable of ensuring that surpluses would be redistributed to those who lacked the means to enter the market. The geography of welfare and political institutions may have been a key factor in determining such regional contrasts. Walter and Schofield have also suggested that susceptibility to crisis may have become geographically more restricted in the first quarter of the seventeenth century.[26] For in 1596/7 and 1597/8 mortality rates were 21 and 26 per cent above trend. In 1623/4 mortality was 18 per cent above trend, but only 16 per cent of parishes registered at least one crisis month compared with 19 per cent in 1597–8. What is more many parishes of the south-west and the Welsh Borders that had previously suffered a crisis were not among the crisis-prone of 1623/4 (see Fig. 6.4). Palliser has gone so far as to suggest that susceptibility to famine may have been a declining 'national' tendency from at least the mid sixteenth century, arguing that 1555/7 was a famine-induced crisis as severe as 1596/8 although population had by the latter date increased by more than 25 per cent.[27] By the mid seventeenth century even the north-west had secured the means to avoid famine. The sharp rises in food prices during the difficult years of the 1690s, years which saw mortality rising

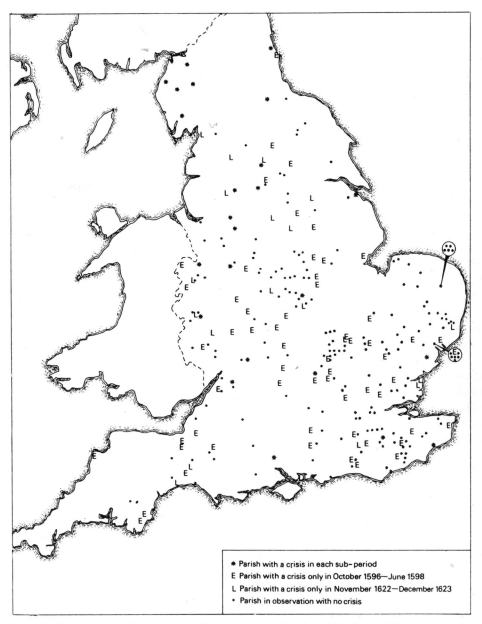

Fig. 6.4. Geographical distribution of local crises in October 1596–June 1598 and November 1622–December 1623. *Source:* Walter and Schofield, *Famine, Disease and the Social Order in Early Modern Society*, p. 35.

sharply in Europe and in nearby Scotland, left this previously vulnerable region unscathed.[28]

If famine may have been a more spatially-restricted cause of death in crisis years, bubonic plague was throughout the period very largely in its short-term appearances a disease of the town. Plague is principally a disease of small mammals, such as rats, and man is an occasional, indeed accidental, host. Consequently the factors influencing the probabilities of the disease spreading to rats and thereafter to humans are of central significance in understanding the extent of the disease. It is generally supposed that plague was not endemic in the rat population, but continually re-imported as a result of overseas trade contacts. In his authoritative study Slack observes that in the sixteenth and seventeenth centuries plague epidemics originated in ports and spread to market centres with only sporadic outbreaks in the countryside.[29] The 1563 plague in London moved to Reading in the following year and on to Bristol in 1565. The foreign origins of the plague most probably explains why ports and towns in the east of England were much more frequently visited by plague than settlements in the north and west, and why outside of London plague was a much more destructive demographic force in Norwich than it was in Exeter. If plague tended to be concentrated in its impact at a macro-geographical level, because of the very restricted movement of *Rattus rattus* and its fleas, it was distinguished by geographically highly clustered patterns of death in family groups at a micro-geographical scale. Schofield and Bradley found this to be the case in their studies of Colyton's and Eyam's plague epidemics in 1646 and 1660 when two-thirds of households suffered no deaths and 40 to 60 per cent of all deaths occurred in clusters of three or more per household.[30] This is in marked contrast to influenza which, according to Slack, rarely produced death clusters in households of three or more that accounted for over 25 per cent of all fatalities in the sixteenth century.[31]

Within towns over the course of the seventeenth century plague became increasingly concentrated in those parts of the urban environment with the poorest housing conditions and where overcrowding was most severe. Slack has documented these developments in London, Bristol, Exeter and Norwich, and speculates that it may reflect an increasing social polarization of rich and poor in the growing seventeenth-century towns and considerable rebuilding within the high status parishes.[32]

While attitudes towards plague were certainly altered through this period by a variety of intellectual and political changes there is reason to suppose that changes in the chronology and spatial patterning of plague outbreaks encouraged a shift in perceptions of the acceptability of human intervention to limit the extent and occurrence of the disease. The increasing concentration in towns and in the suburbs along with a tendency for plague not to occur simultaneously with years of high food prices made it easier to view the disease as a social disease closely associated with the poor. Measures against plague have to be seen as part of the wider attempts by Tudor and early Stuart governments to tackle poverty, vagrancy and urban social disorder. After rather piecemeal local endeavours to control the infected and to prohibit contact with them, in 1578 the Privy Council published a Book of Orders to be implemented whenever outbreaks of plague occurred.[33] A central plank in these orders was that JPs were to be responsible for ensuring that infected houses in towns were completely shut up for at least six weeks, with all members of the family, whether sick or healthy, still inside. While these orders did not enable JPs or customs officers to restrict the movement of goods and people out of infected towns or into infected ports, central government increasingly responded by restraining specific ships or vessels sailing out of specific ports from entering into London and elsewhere. Slack believes that these moves, while far from wholly effective, served to reduce the probability of occurrence of a plague epidemic amongst rats or humans in a specific place to a low level.[34] In fact, unlike Appleby, who argued that the disappearance of plague from England in the late seventeenth century was a chance product of rats with a higher resistance to the plague bacillus, Slack considers that quarantine control in England and elsewhere in Europe reduced the risks of initial infection, until in the end they were negligible.[35] However, in the absence of an understanding of the epidemiology of plague, contemporaries were unable to be sure of their success in controlling what was without a doubt the most frightening cause of death in the early moden period.

Mortality, Mobility and Economic Integration

If the diminution of famine and the total disappearance of plague can be regarded as determinants of crisis mortality whose impact lessened on account of the conscious intervention of men, some historians would argue that there is little reason to suppose that human agency can claim other 'successes' in determining the course of life expectancy over this period. Indeed the disappearance of plague and famine would seem to have coincided with a general worsening of national life expectancy over the course of the seventeenth century.[36] Deterioration of life expectancy is largely the product of rising mortality rates among infants and young children.[37] Evidence for this deterioration in rates derives largely from family reconstitution studies which show that this worsening of life chances among the very young was common to a wide range of communities. In fact, a deterioration in mortality rates among children aged 1–4 is visible through the period from 1550 to 1730 with the sharpest rises in mortality rates occurring before 1650. Infant mortality apparently worsened at first only minimally but then displays quite a sharp rise in the late seventeenth and early eighteenth centuries. Pooled rates for thirteen English parishes indicate a rise in mortality for the 1–4 year-olds from 72 to 102 per thousand between 1550 and 1700. Infant mortality rates at 160 to 170 per thousand through much of the seventeenth century rose to almost 200 per thousand in the early eighteenth century.[38] Of particular interest is the finding that these trends are common to the infants and young children of the English peerage.[39] In fact these privileged groups experienced even higher mortality than the bulk of lower status parochial populations as well as displaying a deterioration in the life chances of their young that preceded that occurring in the wider population; mortality for these infants peaked in 1650–74 at almost 200 per thousand for males, and for the 1–4 age group at 149 per thousand for both sexes.

While these rises in mortality for infants and young children were superimposed upon pre-existing and noteworthy differences between social groups there were also striking contrasts between communities that depended greatly on whether the parishes concerned were located in 'healthy' or 'unhealthy' environments. Low-lying, marshy areas were, for example, much less healthy than well-drained uplands. Fenland parishes like Wrangle in Lincolnshire experienced infant mortality rates that greatly exceeded 200 per thousand,[40] and the marshy coastal estuarine districts of southern and eastern England with death rates two, three, or four times the national average experienced infant mortality rates frequently in excess of 300 per thousand.[41] Such communities were no doubt constantly subject to water-borne infections but suffered in particular from the adverse demographic consequences of their exposure to *vivax* malaria. Furthermore small market towns such as Gainsborough in Lincolnshire or Banbury in Oxfordshire whose populations were *c.* 2000 in 1600 experienced infant mortality rates of 200–250 per thousand with life expectancies at birth of thirty years or less.[42] Such settlements should be compared with isolated communities of which Hartland in north Devon is a particularly good example where between 1600 and 1749 infant mortality rates were frequently below 100 and life expectation exceeded fifty years. Isolation, relatively low population density, and a reasonable distance from a market town combined to explain why Hartland could throughout the sixteenth and seventeenth centuries experience infant mortality rates that were not to be achieved nationally until 1920.[43] It was, of course, in London where the disadvantages of high density living were more dramatically experienced. By the late seventeenth century infant mortality rates of 200 to 350 per thousand were relatively common, although they too would seem to have risen during this period from levels which while considerably more severe than in rural areas were in the early seventeenth century generally below 200 per thousand,[44] In fact in the half-century after bubonic plague disappeared from London, infant mortality appears to have increased by more than a third.

Because of the contrasts in mortality rates between urban and rural locations there are good reasons for supposing that a certain part of the worsening of national life expectancy in the seventeenth century could have been due to the very considerable growth in England's urban population.[45] There is now a consensus that London's share of the national population rose from 5 per cent to almost 12 per cent between 1600 and 1700. Other urban centres with populations of 5000 or more increased their share of the national total from 3 to 6 per cent, resulting in the growth of total urban populations (defined as proportions living in settlements of 5000 or more) from *c.* 8 to *c.* 18 per cent over the course of the seventeenth century.[46] For that reason there was a concomitant increase in the proportion of the population living in 'unhealthy' environments which most certainly helped to depress national life expectancies by two years.

Nonetheless Landers has criticized the commonly encountered tendency to view the contrast between metropolitan mortality regimes and their more thinly populated 'hinterlands' in 'naturalistic' terms by focusing on the former's physical environment, emphasizing in particular the problems of water supply, sanitation and sewerage disposal. Such an approach, he claims, gives water- and food-borne gastric diseases a primacy in determining the character of mortality regimes of large urban centres.[47] Rather than conceptualizing such centres as 'demographic drains' into which those who moved from hinterlands were destined to sink, Landers has recently argued that it is more appropriate to regard the distinctive character of metropolitan regimes as resting on quantitative differences in the incidence of infections common to both metropolis and hinterland. Metropolitan centres therefore acted as endemic reservoirs of infections which spilled over to the latter in the form of recurrent epidemics, spread by commercial or migratory contacts. Consequently, metropolitan populations experienced high mortality but tended to display death rates which were more stable in the short-term than those in the hinterland where mortality was much more volatile from year to year.[48] Landers has compared short-term movements of deaths in the London bills of mortality from 1675 to 1750 with those in the 404 parishes of the Cambridge Group's sample and shows that in the latter mortality was much less stable.[49] Nonetheless the two 'regimes' were not independent of each other in so far as burial surpluses created in London led to a dependence in the capital on migrants whose epidemiological characteristics differed considerably from native-born and long-term metropolitan residents. Immigrants lacked immunity to many infections that were ever-present in London.

For instance, Galloway has analysed the relationship between grain price fluctuations and mortality from various causes of death in the London bills of mortality after 1670.[50] He presents two noteworthy findings fully consistent with Lander's position.[51] Firstly, he found that deaths from typhus responded quite markedly to price fluctuations but with a lag of one year. Typhus, being associated with crowding and dirt, led Galloway to conclude that this lag was a consequence of the crowding of rural poor into London in the period following national conditions of dearth.[52] Galloway's other finding was that smallpox varied significantly in response to grain prices in the same year: this appears to complement Landers's discovery that smallpox deaths were heavily concentrated in early- and mid-eighteenth-century London among adolescent and young adult immigrants who gravitated towards London in economically difficult times.[53] Such a discovery is consistent with the view that price rises pushed adolescents and young adults into London where they suffered as a consequence of their lack of immunological protection from a disease that was endemic in the metropolis.

Another finding that rests uncomfortably with the naturalistic reading of metropolitan mortality stems from the analysis by Landers and Mouzas of the seasonality of deaths in London between 1670 and 1750. They note that there was a striking shift over the course of this period from a situation in which there was a summer peak strongly centred on August to a 'cold weather plateau' stretching from November to April. The disappearance of the summer peak coincides exactly with the virtual elimination of 'griping of the guts' as a cause of death in the London bills of mortality. The lack of any obvious improvement in the physical environment in this period inclines Landers and Mouzas to seek explanations in climatic change or a mutation of the responsible pathogens. In seeking an explanation for the rise in the importance of winter mortality, they believe that typhus and possibly mortality associated with respiratory infections were primarily responsible causes of death. However, they find this difficult to explain given that real wages appear to have been rising through the period in which the seasonality of deaths alters. They are doubtful, however, whether real wages are a reliable indicator of material well-being during this period.[54] Certainly there is evidence to suggest that London's economy went through recurrent difficulties in the 1690s and the early 1700s when the nation was at war. It is interesting to note that Fildes has very recently attempted to show that there was a rise of child abandonment to almost 7 per cent of all baptisms in a sample of London parishes between 1690 and 1730.[55]

Just as London's demography was susceptible to changes that were intricately linked with its connections to the hinterland through migration and movements of

goods and services, so the country at large also experienced considerable epidemiological changes. Steady urban growth and the intensification of market networks
throughout the seventeenth century may have entailed a more effective distribution
of diseases as well as personal skills and commodities. Walter and Schofield suggest
that because of the increased degree of contact between communities, infections
would have become more fully endemic on a regional or national scale, increasing
total exposure and hence reducing life expectancy.[56] This greater exposure of the
population would mean that proportionately fewer persons in individual communities would have been susceptible leading to a reduction in the intensity of national
epidemics. In fact they are inclined to confine their reflections on the longer-term
consequences of this 'endemicization' of diseases to those that were air-borne. Those
most at risk to infection would, so they argue, have been children beyond the age of
weaning and lacking maternal antibodies. Indeed these were the age groups whose
mortality rates, as we have seen, rose most markedly over the course of the
seventeenth century. Walter and Schofield note that

> ... while greater mobility is likely to have progressively reduced the intensity of both
> national and local epidemics over a longer period of time, its *initial* effect already visible in
> the seventeenth century would have been to increase exposure to air-borne infections and
> raise the general level of mortality, offsetting any gains from a reduction in mortality
> connected with plague and typhus.[57]

This thesis is challenging and still requires testing with careful attention to
regional variation and location. One recent consideration of the stability of mortality
in the south-east corner of England in the seventeenth and early eighteenth
centuries by Dobson does not rest easily with Walter and Schofield's interpretation.[58] Having studied in some detail almost 600 parishes in Essex, Kent and East
Sussex, she is unable to identify a stabilization of mortality rates in the late
seventeenth century. Instead she finds that a particularly sharp rise in mortality
occurs in the 1670s and 1680s in association with geographically very extensive but
'mild' crises. 'Fevers', in particular a set of gastric diseases transmitted by flies,
contaminated food, water, animals and human contacts that were seasonally
concentrated in autumn months following hot dry summers, are singled out by
Dobson as largely responsible for this deterioration in life chances.[59] However, like
Walter and Schofield, she is at pains to stress that overseas migrations and the
increasing movements of pathogens associated with migrants provided the energy
that drove these mortality changes in the south-eastern counties.

Fertility 1500–1730

Changes in the Structure of Fertility

The work of the Cambridge Group enables us to distinguish between the short- and
long-term responses of fertility to changes in the economic and demographic
context. In the short-term birth and nuptiality rates were much more responsive to
changes in real wages than was the death rate.[60] For instance, in the twenty years in
which real wages were most above trend marriage rates were, in all but two years,
and the birth rate in all but five years, above trend. In the twenty years when real

wages were most below trend, in only two years were birth and marriage rates not also below trend. The death rate was by no means as responsive. In only nine of the twenty most economically difficult years was the death rate above trend and in the twenty best years in only five did the death rate drop below trend.

Annual fluctuations in wheat prices accounted for 41 per cent of the short-run timing of marriage.[61] The relationship between the two series was symmetrical, high prices inhibiting marriages and low prices encouraging them. The annual fluctuations in wheat prices also had a marked impact on fertility independent of effects working through nuptiality. The main impact of prices on fertility occurred in the same year and in the following year. It is likely that the price effect is not purely one that worked upon fertility, for a certain part of the decline in baptisms may have been the product of fetal mortality in the first two trimesters of the pregnancy.

In the case of fertility there was limited change in its responsiveness to price trends over the period. There were, of course, interrelationships between mortality and fertility that operated through the incidence of marriage.[62] Marriage in the short-term might be supposed to have been enabled by deaths creating 'vacancies' in the economy for young adults seeking access to farms and craft workshops. Some 'new' marriages may have been remarriages after existing marriages had been broken by the death of one of the partners. In the period before 1640 after a mortality crisis in which mortality was 100 per cent above normal, in the ensuing five years, marriages would have been 47 per cent above normal. But for the period from 1641 to 1745 comparable mortality increases stimulated only a 16 per cent increase in marriages in the following quinquenium.[63] This represents a marked decline in the responsiveness of marriages to stimuli from mortality surges and is thought to indicate a significant drop in the incidence of remarriage and probably a lengthening of remarriage intervals.[64] One might speculate that remarriage changes reflected a diminishing importance of landholdings as a basis for marriage and a drop in demand for landed widows as material conditions improved in the later seventeenth century.

Just as the 'background' levels of mortality followed a long cyclical course over the period so too did fertility.[65] Inverse projection has yielded remarkable evidence bearing upon the gross reproduction rate (GRR). The GRR tells us the average number of female births produced by women aged 15–44 who survived through the whole thirty year period. It fell from 2.8 in the mid sixteenth century to slightly less than 2 in 1651 where it stayed until 1681 (see Fig. 6.5). Thereafter the GRR rose to levels that had previously applied in the late sixteenth century, but for much of the first three decades of the eighteenth century there was little net increase in fertility. Between the mid sixteenth and the mid seventeenth century women on average move from a situation where they were having marginally more than five births to one where they had slightly fewer than four offspring.

A number of influences could potentially have determined the course of the GRR. The most important are likely to have been the fertility of married women, the proportion of women ever-marrying, the average age of female marriage, and the extent of illegitimacy. It should be stressed that notwithstanding some intriguing evidence presented in the earliest English study utilizing the technique of family reconstitution, suggesting resort to family limitation among the married women of the east Devon parish of Colyton in the late seventeenth century, the technique has

Fig. 6.5. Quinquennial GRRs in England 1541–1751. *Source:* Wrigley and Schofield, *The Population History of England,* p. 231.

produced no evidence of such practices in other English communities.[66] In fact family reconstitution studies show, for all English communities so far investigated, total marital fertility ratios of approximately 7.4, which remained remarkably constant through time and across space.[67] Indeed the geographical homogeneity of marital fertility rates is as remarkable as the lack of variation through time and distinguishes early modern England from most of her European continental neighbours where regional variations in fertility within marriage could be quite striking.[68] Marital fertility in England was actually very modest in the early modern period, reflected in birth intervals of approximately 2.5 years for women in their twenties and early thirties. There are strong reasons for supposing that such widely spaced births owed a great deal to the ubiquitous practice of breastfeeding for periods of a year or perhaps longer.[69] There were, however, notable exceptions to this pattern. The aristocracy did not breastfeed and employed wet nurses.[70] Their relatively high infant mortality would seem to owe a great deal to this disinclination to breastfeed their infants. Also high status sections of London society would seem not to have breastfed—a behavioural trait that most probably accounts for their short birth intervals, reflecting the somewhat restricted periods of post-partum non-susceptibility.[71] Such a reluctance to breastfeed may have been more widespread in London society. For instance, Landers has shown that infant mortality among the London Quakers in the late seventeenth century was particularly high in the first month of life. This mortality also displayed a noteworthy summer peak which most likely indicates that infants were not fed at their mother's breast.[72]

If there is limited reason to suppose that marital fertility altered in such a way as to determine the course of the GRR, evidence relating to the marriage rate suggests that it was far from invariant during this period. Indeed the first-marriage rate was relatively high in the mid-sixteenth century, falling particularly in the first three decades of the seventeenth century and sagging thereafter to low levels that continued into the 1660s.[73] The rate recovered hesitantly at first but by 1700 there is reason to suppose that marriage was on the increase. However, by 1730 the rate was still considerably below the levels present in the late Tudor period. The crude first-marriage rate reflects the impact both of shifts in the age at first marriage and the proportions ever-marrying. Recent research by Weir and Schofield confirms that for persons born before 1700 most of the changes in the marriage rate were produced by shifts in the proportion ever-married, with mean age at first marriage varying little between 26 and 27.[74] However, these changes in marital incidence were dramatic. Five per cent of those born in 1556 Schofield estimates never married, whereas for the birth cohorts between 1616 and 1641 almost one in five avoided marriage altogether.[75] This low propensity to marry is made all the more remarkable by the fact that in the mid seventeenth century the illegitimacy ratio (the proportion of all baptisms recorded out of wedlock) dropped to its lowest point for the whole period after 1537.[76] Indeed while there were obviously more single women at risk to bear bastards, they showed a greater reluctance to do so than when marriage was more nearly universal. Overwhelmingly the changing proportions of the female population ever-marrying had the dominant influence on the fertility rate in this period.

It is noteworthy that unlike the changing level of life expectancy the crude first-marriage rate displays a far better fit with changes in real wages through this period (see Fig. 6). The sharp drop in the real wage rate after 1600 appears to be mirrored by an equally sharp fall in the incidence of marriage. However, through the middle and later seventeenth century these two trends moved in opposite directions. By the early eighteenth century it is possible to see these two time series once again moving

Fig. 6.6. Real wage trends and crude first-marriage rates (both 25-year moving averages centred on dates shown). *Source:* E. A. Wrigley and R. S. Schofield, *The Population History of England 1541–1871: A Reconstruction*, (2nd edn, 1988), p. xxii.

in the same direction. Wrigley and Schofield have argued forcefully (using this evidence and that relating to the short-term responsiveness of marriages to price changes) that early modern England exemplifies the working of the Malthusian 'preventive check'.[77] Marriage, they conclude, was unambiguously economically determined.

The seasonal pattern of marriage throughout this period strongly reflected seasonal demands for agrarian labour.[78] Monthly marriage levels displayed two major peaks; one in the late spring or early summer, the other in the autumn. A noteworthy trough occurred in July and August, and March and December were unpopular months for marriage. The two latter months reflect the timing of the ancient ecclesiastical prohibitions on marriage during Lent and Rogationtide which although no longer prohibited periods after the Reformation customarily continued to be avoided. The deep summer trough in marriage coincided with the major crop-gathering period of the year, and the autumn and early summer peaks fell in the slack periods after the grain harvest and the lambing season. In England the two peak periods for marriage also coincided with the seasons in which servant hiring fairs were usually held, which marked the beginnings and ends of the servant 'years'. To leave service and to enter marriage was a very common transition for young adults of both sexes in this period. Ann Kussmaul has shown that the seasonality of marriage and the geography of agriculture were closely correlated. In the early seventeenth century when grain farming was geographically more wide-spread, it is noticeable that the bulk of the country was distinguished by a seasonal marriage regime in which the autumn months of October and November were most popular (see Fig. 6.7). However, by the period 1681 to 1720 there had been a remarkable regional bifurcation in preferred seasons for marriage. Broad sections of western England had come to be dominated by spring and early summer peaks reflecting a regional specialization in pastoral farming, whereas the autumn season of marriage was now confined to the eastern regions (see Fig. 6.8).[79]

Such evidence as we have considered bearing on the timing and incidence of marriage is likely to be pleasing to the convinced Malthusian. But why did changes in nuptiality throughout this period operate primarily through shifts in the incidence, rather than the timing of marriage? Goldstone has suggested that it is plausible to divide the labour market into those with reasonably assured prospects of employment such as apprentices with a skill or with strong expectations of inheriting property and those dependent upon the uncertain demand for wage labour.[80] For the former, changes in economic circumstances are likely to be reflected in age at marriage (the accumulator model), while for the latter, the nuptiality response is likely to be one of changes in the proportions ever-married (the future-earnings prospect model). Data relating to proportions ever-married suggest that they reached a low point (77.9 per cent) for the 25-year cohort centred on 1616, which would have been a group whose prime earnings years coincided with real wages which were at their lowest point for the whole period from 1500 to 1730. The proportions ever-married were only marginally higher for the 25-year cohort centering on 1641 whose prime earnings period extended from 1641 to 1680. In this evidence one might suppose that there is strong support for a marriage pattern that was responsive both to the possibilities open to wage earners to save to obtain the

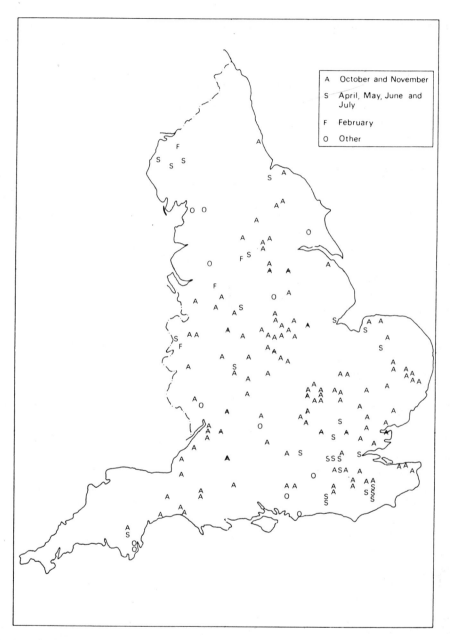

Fig. 6.7. Peak marriage seasons 1561–1600. *Source:* Kussmaul, 'Time, space, hoofs and grain', p. 198.

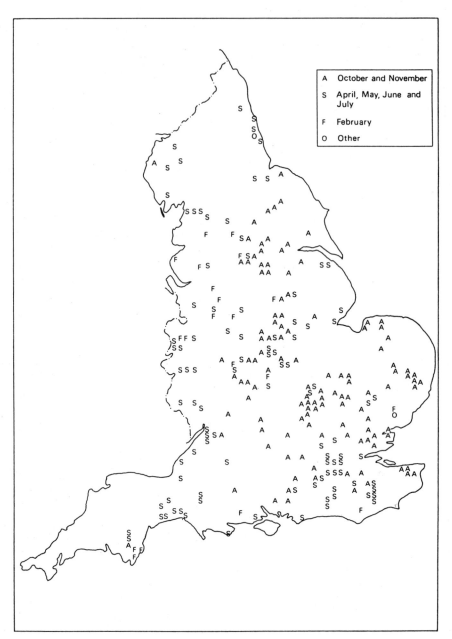

Fig. 6.8. Peak marriage seasons 1681–1720. *Source:* Kussmaul, 'Time, space, hoofs and grain', p. 199.

necessary resources to establish a new household, and to the prospects of continuous earning opportunities after the marriage had taken place. That marital incidence
increased after this low point in the real wage series had passed is apparent from the
substantial rise in the proportion ever-married in the 1660 cohort to 90 per cent.[81]
Such evidence would seem to be consistent with a Malthusian interpretative model
of nuptiality. However, the growth displayed by the proportions ever-married
between the cohorts of 1641 and 1666 was not sustained by the cohorts centred on
1691 and 1716, although real wages continued to grow quite sharply (making the
accumulation of the marital 'nest-egg' easier and the expectation of continued
employment after marriage more assured). In fact, the GRR remains intransigently at
2.1 to 2.2 through the birth cohorts centred on 1691 and 1716. In this latter period
Malthusian theory may not be so relevant as in the later sixteenth and early
seventeenth centuries.

If swings in the proportions ever-married show some inconsistencies with respect
to their responses to change in real wages, there would appear to have been
somewhat greater consistency in the relationship between marriage age and the
social and economic status of brides and grooms. Studies of such matters are still
quite rare but those that have been undertaken indicate that high status grooms
married the youngest brides of all and that labourers and the poor, who married
somewhat earlier than their social and economic superiors, are found entering
marriages with the oldest brides of all. For example, in Colyton in 1600–49 gentry
grooms of 26 took brides who were 24 while the poor of that parish married at 25–26
to women who at 26–27 were often marginally their senior.[82] Elliott in her study of
persons marrying by licence in London between 1598 and 1619 shows that in general
the higher the social status of the groom, the younger was the bride and the greater
the difference in age between partners.[83] Earle finds much the same pattern in a
sample of marriages in London for the late seventeenth and early eighteenth
centuries.[84] For instance, men with fortunes at death in excess of £5000, who on
average married at 30, chose wives of 20 years, while grooms with fortunes of less
than £1000 married at 25 to women who at 22 years were close to them in age.

A striking feature of Elliott's study was that she showed that the average age of
London-born women married by licence was only 20.5, nearly four years younger
than women who were immigrants to the metropolis.[85] In fact, it would seem that
native-born London women, while not marrying at puberty, married in the early
seventeenth century at ages that were considerably younger than was normal. In the
later sixteenth and early seventeenth centuries evidence from the burials in London
parish registers suggests that the sex ratio of the city's population favoured males.[86]
This sexual balance was to change markedly over the course of the seventeenth
century, reflecting perhaps a change in the economic structure of the capital city.
Indeed, Gregory King put the ratio of males to females in the 1690s at 10:13 and notes
the surplus of spinsters to bachelors and widows to widowers.[87] Whether the ages at
marriage of native-born women rose as females became numerically dominant is not
yet known, although it is evident that the chances overall of ever-marrying in the city
fell quite sharply. The probabilities of remarriage for women certainly dropped. For
instance, in the London parish of Stepney remarriages fell from *c.* 48 per cent to *c.* 25
per cent between the early sixteenth and early eighteenth century as the sex ratio at

death fell from 113 in 1610–19 to 79.5 in 1700–15. In this case we can observe how dramatic was the effect of the sexual balance which was evidently the product of changed migration patterns in disturbing the marriage market. In the young adult age groups the sex ratio at death had changed even more dramatically. In Stepney in 1610–19 in the age group 20–24 there had been 162 male for every 100 female deaths but by 1700–15 there were 85 males dying for every 100 females.[88]

Migration 1500–1730

Emigration and National Demographic Change

There is now a large body of published research that has shown how geographically mobile were the people of early modern England.[89] Much less has been written on the wider consequences of this behavioural trait. We have already considered in an earlier section of this chapter how this restlessness may have had considerable epidemiological consequences in our discussion of mortality changes. We are now aware that England was not a closed demographic system because of certain findings that have emerged from 'inverse projection' relating to net migration.[90] It is important to note that during this period net migration was always the product of an excess of emigrants over immigrants. In the late sixteenth and earliest years of the seventeenth century migrants left principally for Ireland. From the 1630s and 1640s the colonies in North America and the West Indies became home for most emigrants. We are able to attach some reasonably reliable pointers to migration from seventeenth-century England that can place into pespective what might appear to be alarmist remarks about the scale of overseas departures; for example, Carew Reynel in the early 1670s believed that 200,000 people 'had been wasted in repeopling Ireland' and a similar number had departed for 'the plantations'.[91] Between 1630 and 1700 Gemery has estimated that some 380,000 British emigrants crossed the Atlantic.[92] The peak decade for departures appears to have been the 1650s although large numbers left in the 1640s and the 1660s. Numbers declined especially after the 1670s. These totals can be supplemented by Wrigley and Schofield's estimates of emigration which encompass all destinations and persons dying at sea or in wars abroad.[93] They indicate a loss of almost half a million people between 1630 and 1700 and confirm that the 1650s were the peak decade for departure, with a net annual loss of 2.4 per 1000. This was a rate which would not be exceeded again until the middle of the nineteenth century. This level of emigration had important demographic implications. Between 1656 and 1686 the English population fell from 5.28 to 4.86 million. Of this fall, approximtely 58 per cent was directly attributable to emigration. Most of the mid-seventeenth-century migrants went to the West Indies, Virginia and Maryland, where because of environmental conditions life expectancies were particularly low.[94] A high proportion went as indentured servants in the rough ratio of three males to one female.[95] What is noticeable is that of the migrants leaving in the mid seventeenth century, few were skilled, and it is significant that the level of departures reached the greatest height at the end of the period of sharply falling real wages in the 1640s and 1650s.[96]

Internal Migration: Patterns and Trends

Clark and Souden in generalizing about this period have summed up developments in these terms:

> What seems fairly clear is that the pattern of physical movement in England shifted from one of muzzy, relatively undifferentiated migration activity before the Civil War to one increasingly overlaid by specialist, and in some measure institutionalized, flows in the later seventeenth and eighteenth centuries. This shift paralleled, and was almost certainly related to structural change in the nature of national economy and society.[97]

Mobility rates in Tudor and early Stuart England were high, and evidence from those who functioned as witnesses before church courts suggests 70 to 80 per cent had moved at least once in their lives.[98] Men moved further afield than women, although no less frequently. The poor and labourers moved further than the affluent and yeomen. This period of falling real wages and relatively frequent harvest failures was one in which long distance movements were particularly notable. Especially striking were the flows of poverty-stricken migrants that had moved from the far north into the southern lowlands.[99] Many urban centres in the south were continually concerned at the presence in their communities of vagrants, who as long distance, single, young adult, male migrants appeared to be very threatening to local order and stability.[100]

Towns were not the only locality that attracted the mobile poor in the late Tudor and early Stuart period. Many detailed regional and community case studies have identified a shift of persons into marginal woodland and pastoral areas, where limited regulation of their right to reside and to practise unlicensed trades was a factor in their attractiveness.[101] In the late sixteenth century it is possible that urban centres became increasingly attractive to the 'subsistence' migrant, where on account of the destruction wrought by frequent epidemics, work might be found as well as more opportunities for crime, prostitution, begging and, of growing importance, access to poor relief which in its early phases was better organized in urban centres.

The second half of the seventeenth century presents a very different picture. The volume of intra-rural migration seems to have fallen; fewer people were making very long distance moves, and most were moving less often.[102] In the rural areas the decades after the Restoration came to be the 'great age of the servant in husbandry'. Servants were being kept in large numbers, moving every spring or autumn as they changed their employers.[103] In this period farmers preferred to have live-in servants paid largely in board and lodging, as labour costs were rising, but the price of agricultural produce and food were in relative terms steady or declining. Under these conditions it made more sense for farmers to utilize live-in servants rather than hire expensive and itinerant labourers.[104] Service in husbandry came to be effectively administered by the laws of settlement after the 1690s and the hiring fairs helped to match supply with demand. This meant that with possibly 15 to 18 per cent of the whole population in service, geographical movements for a substantial section of the population were institutionalized and highly localized.[105] Servants were rarely likely to have moved more than three to five miles between employers. In the late seventeenth century men in particular were moving shorter distances between rural communities. Males in the professions and distributive trades, which were thriving in the rapidly expanding late-seventeenth-century urban centres, and women in general, proved significant exceptions to the general trend. In fact women in the countryside moved as far and as often as they had done previously, and actually moved further, and in greater numbers, into the towns.[106]

Certain of these features left a startling impression upon the evidence that is to be found relating to a wide variety of communities that have survived in the lists of their population drawn up under the Marriage Duty Act of 1695. The most important finding to emerge from this research is the frequent occurrence of extreme skewness of the sex ratios in these populations. We have already noted the dramatic feminization of London's population in the late seventeenth century. Comparable developments were occurring throughout the whole urban system. Souden has discovered that sex ratios at death in English towns in the 1690s and 1700s were often between 80 and 90.[107] This feminization of urban populations was most likely exacerbated by the fact that more of the emigrants in the late seventeenth century left from the towns than had been the case earlier. Indeed the sex ratio at death for England as a whole became skewed. In 1700 there were 100 female deaths for every 98 males, which should be compared with a ratio at birth of 105 males for every 100 females.[108] Outmigration to Ireland and North America had significantly unbalanced the ratio of men to women.

Throughout this period London's growth has been widely acknowledged by scholars as a vital force in the overall migration patterns of early modern England.[109] The capital required large flows of people into it, although its migration field became less expansive after 1600 than it had been before. London's claim upon the demographic fodder of its hinterland had very significant consequences for overall demographic trends, both at the level of the nation and its constituent regions. It has already been suggested that from the middle of the seventeenth century, England's increasingly urbanized population saw the relocation of large numbers of persons into 'unhealthy' environments with notable consequences for national life expectancy. Wrigley and Schofield have revealed in their startling statistics how, because London's growth was faster than that of the nation at large, it exerted a progressively damping effect on the natural surplus created in extra-metropolitan areas.[110] From 1550–74 when London accounted for 5 per cent of the nation's burials, the percentage rose more than threefold, so that by 1724–49 over 17 per cent of all English burials were taking place in the metropolis. At no point between 1500 and 1730 was there not an extra-metropolitan surplus of baptisms over burials. While that surplus certainly fell to very low levels in the half century 1650 to 1700, through the combined effect of lowered fertility, enhanced mortality and periodic high rates of outmigration, the huge surpluses of burials over baptisms in London (227,828 in the period 1650–74 and 181,465 in 1675–99) ensured that national demographic decline took place.

In this period it was the fate of areas close to London to suffer sharp falls in their population. Dobson has recently estimated that the three counties of Essex, Kent, and East Sussex with a population of approximately 380,000 in 1670 lost at least 50,000 by 1720. More geographically extensive work of this kind is clearly needed, if the spatial implications of these national changes in the period are to be better understood.[111]

The second half of the seventeenth century remains a fascinating period in so far as at the national level it represents a period which in general terms experiences both a decline in life expectancy, and a fall and only very slow recovery in fertility. These are not the attributes of a perfectly functioning homeostatic demographic system. Indeed, positive rather than negative feedback is readily detectable. Serious consideration must be given to the possibility that geographical mobility was fulfilling the role of principal destabilizer. The movement of males from England to North America, the shift of people from healthy to unhealthy communities, and in particular the redistribution of males and females so as to create significant regional imbalances in the sexes, are key developments in creating this apparent demographic anomaly. Indeed regional variations in the balance between the sexes may turn out, as Souden has tentatively suggested, to override the spatial homogeneity that so many other demographic variables appear to have displayed.[112] There are strong reasons to suggest that migration was the most formidable demographic differentiator of early modern England.

If that is so, it could be further argued that although fertility was, over this period, the most important proximate demographic determinant exerting influence on national intrinsic growth rates, both mortality and fertility were in their turn being influenced by geographical mobility. Measures of intrinsic growth rates that depend on the interplay of the expectation of life at birth and the GRR provide a seductive, two-dimensional account of demographic processes that owe a very great deal to migratory trends. The third and most important dimension is to be sought in the restlessness of the English population through this period as individuals and families moved increasingly within and outside the nation.[113]

References

1. For example, J. Thirsk, 'Sources of information on population', *Amateur History*, **iv** (1959), pp. 129–33, 182–5; see also T. Hollingsworth, *Historical Demography*, (London, 1969), pp. 78–88, 111–26.
2. M. W. Flinn, *British Population Growth, 1750–1850*, (London, 1969).
3. Described in detail in E. A. Wrigley and R. S. Schofield, *The Population History of England 1541–1871: A Reconstruction*, (London, 1981, and 2nd edn, Cambridge, 1988).
4. R. S. Schofield and B. Midi Berry, 'Age at baptism in pre-industrial England', *Population Studies*, **15** (1971), pp. 281–312.
5. For important critical evaluations of this work see the following: M. Anderson, 'Historical demography after *The Population History of England*', in R. I. Rotberg and T. K. Rabb (eds), *Population and Economy: Population and History from the Traditional to the Modern World*, (Cambridge, 1986); M. W. Flinn, '*The Population History of England, 1541–1871*, essays in bibliography and criticism', *Economic History Review*, **XXXV** (1982), pp. 443–57; M. P. Gutmann, 'Gold from dross? Population reconstruction for the pre-census era', *Historical Methods*, **17** (1984), pp. 5–19; L. Henry and D. Blanchet, 'La population de l'Angleterre de 1541 à 1871', *Population*, **38** (1983), pp. 781–826.
6. R. D. Lee and D. Lam, 'Age distribution adjustments for English censuses 1821–1931', *Population Studies*, **37** (1983), pp. 445–64; R. D. Lee, 'Inverse projection and back projection: a critical appraisal, and comparative results for England, 1539 to 1871', *Population Studies*, **39** (1985), pp. 233–48 and K. Wachter, 'Ergodicity and inverse projection', *Population Studies*, **40** (1986), pp. 257–87.
7. L. R. Poos, 'The rural population of Essex in the later Middle Ages', *Economic History Review*, **XXXVIII** (1985), pp. 522–3.
8. J. Cornwall, 'English population in the early sixteenth century', *Economic History Review*, **XXIII** (1970), pp. 54–69; Wrigley and Schofield, *The Population History of England*, pp. 563–8.

9. S. H. Herrtage (ed.), *England in the Reign of Henry the Eighth,* Early English Text Society, extra ser., **XXXII** (1878), p. 72.

10. M. W. Flinn, 'The stabilization of mortality in pre-industrial Western Europe', *Jnl. of European Economic History,* **III** (1974), pp. 285–318; C. Cipolla, *Economic History of World Population,* (London, 1962), pp. 76–77.

11. Wrigley and Schofield, *The Population History of England,* pp. 317–18.

12. *Ibid.,* pp. 332–6.

13. R. S. Schofield, 'The impact of scarcity and plenty on population change in England', in R. I. Rotberg and T. K. Rabb (eds.), *Hunger and History: The Impact of Changing Food Production and Consumption Patterns on Society,* (Cambridge, 1983), p. 79.

14. R. D. Lee, 'Short term variations in vital rates, prices and weather', in Wrigley and Schofield, *The Population History of England,* pp. 371–84, 392–401.

15. P. R. Galloway, 'Basic patterns in annual variations in fertility, nuptiality, mortality and prices in pre-industrial Europe', *Population Studies,* **42** (1988), p. 291, note 37.

16. J. Walter and R. Schofield, 'Famine, disease and crisis mortality in early modern society', in J. Walter and R. Schofield (eds.), *Famine, Disease and Social Order in Early Modern Society,* (Cambridge, 1989), p. 41.

17. M. W. Flinn *et al., Scottish Population History from the Seventeenth Century to the 1930s,* (Cambridge, 1977); D. R. Weir, 'Markets and mortality in France, 1600–1789', in Walter and Schofield, *Famine, Disease and Social Order.*

18. Galloway, 'Basic patterns', appendix, table 1, column headed 'R-Sq'.

19. N. S. Schrimshaw, 'Functional consequences of malnutrition for human populations: a comment', in Rotberg and Rabb (eds.), *Hunger and History,* pp. 211–14, and R. W. Fogel *et al.,* 'Secular changes in American and British stature and nutrition', in Rotberg and Rabb (eds.), *Hunger and History,* pp. 247–84.

20. R. D. Lee, 'Population homeostasis and English demographic history', in Rotberg and Rabb (eds.), *Population and Economy,* pp. 75–100, and 'Population dynamics of human and other animals', *Demography,* **24** (1987), pp. 443–65.

21. J. Landers, 'Mortality and metropolis: the case of London 1675–1825', *Population Studies,* **41** (1987), p. 60.

22. A. B. Appleby, 'Disease or famine? Mortality in Cumberland and Westmorland, 1580–1640', *Economic History Review,* **XXVI** (1973), p. 430.

23. Wrigley and Schofield, *The Population History of England,* pp. 672–3, 676–7.

24. A. B. Appleby, *Famine in Tudor and Stuart England,* (Liverpool and Stanford, 1978).

25. Walter and Schofield, 'Famine, disease and crisis', p. 24.

26. *Ibid.,* pp. 31–2.

27. D. M. Palliser, 'Tawney's century: brave new world and Malthusian trap', *Economic History Review,* **XXXV** (1982), pp. 346–7.

28. Appleby, *Famine in Tudor and Stuart England,* p. 156.

29. P. Slack, *The Impact of Plague in Tudor and Stuart England,* (London, 1985).

30. R. Schofield, 'An anatomy of an epidemic: Colyton, November 1645 to November 1646', in P. Slack (ed.), *The Plague Reconsidered,* (Matlock, 1977), pp. 95–126; L. Bradley, 'The most famous of all English plagues: a detailed analysis of the Plague of Eyam 1665–6', in Slack (ed.), *The Plague Reconsidered,* pp. 63–94.

31. Slack, *The Impact of Plague,* p. 175.

32. *Ibid.,* pp. 111–72.

33. *Ibid.,* pp. 207–11.

34. P. Slack, 'The response to plague in early modern England: public policies and their consequences', in Walter and Schofield (eds.), *Famine, Disease and the Social Order,* p. 179.

35. *Ibid.,* pp. 184–7.

36. Wrigley and Schofield, *The Population History of England,* pp. 228–30.

37. R. Schofield and E. A. Wrigley, 'Infant and child mortality in England in the late Tudor and early Stuart period', in C. Webster (ed.), *Health Medicine and Mortality,* (Cambridge, 1979), pp. 61–95; E. A. Wrigley and R. Schofield, 'English population history from family reconstitution: summary results 1600–1799', *Population Studies,* **37** (1983), pp. 157–84.

38. Wrigley and Schofield, 'English population history from family reconstitution', p. 177.

39. T. H. Hollingsworth, 'Mortality in the British peerage families since 1600', *Population*, numéro spécial (1977), p. 327.
40. F. West, 'Infant mortality in the East Fen parishes of Leake and Wrangle', *Local Population Studies*, **13** (1974), p. 43; M. Dobson, 'Mortality gradients and disease exchanges: comparisons from Old England and colonial America', *Social History of Medicine*, **2** (1989), pp. 265–6.
41. M. Dobson, '"Marsh fever"—the geography of malaria in England', *Jnl. of Historical Geography*, **6** (1980), pp. 357–90.
42. Wrigley and Schofield, 'English population history', pp. 178–80.
43. E. A. Wrigley, 'No death without birth: the implications of English mortality in the early modern period', in R. Porter and A. Wear (eds.), *Problems and Methods in the History of Medicine*, (London, 1987), pp. 136–7.
44. J. Landers, 'Age patterns of mortality in London during the "long eighteenth century": a test of the "high potential" model of metropolitan mortality', *Social History of Medicine*, **3** (1990), pp. 38–40.
45. Wrigley and Schofield, *The Population History of England*, p. 415.
46. E. A. Wrigley, 'Urban growth and agricultural change: England and the Continent in the early modern period', in Rotberg and Rabb (eds.), *Population and Economy*, pp. 123–68.
47. J. Landers and A. Mouzas, 'Birth seasonality and causes of death in London 1670–1819', *Population Studies*, **42** (1988), pp. 59–60.
48. Landers, 'Mortality and metropolis', pp. 60–1.
49. *Ibid.*, pp. 67–8.
50. P. R. Galloway, 'Annual variations in death by age, deaths by cause, prices and weather in London 1670–1830', *Population Studies*, **39** (1985), pp. 498–500.
51. Landers, 'Mortality and metropolis', and 'Mortality, weather and prices in London, 1675–1825: a study of short-term fluctuations', *Jnl. of Historical Geography*, **12** (1986), pp. 347–64.
52. Galloway, 'Annual variations', p. 499.
53. Landers, 'Mortality and metropolis', pp. 72–5, and 'Mortality, weather and prices', pp. 356–61.
54. Landers and Mouzas, 'Burial seasonality', pp. 76–80.
55. V. Fildes, 'Maternal feelings re-assessed: child abandonment and neglect in London and Westminster, 1550–1800', in V. Fildes (ed.), *Women as Mothers in Pre-Industrial England* (London, 1990), pp. 152–8.
56. Walter and Schofield, 'Famine, disease and crisis mortality', pp. 60–1.
57. *Ibid.*, p. 67.
58. M. Dobson, 'The last hiccup of the old demographic regime: population stagnation and decline in late seventeenth and early eighteenth-century South-east England', *Continuity and Change*, **4** (1989), pp. 395–428.
59. *Ibid.*, p. 418.
60. Wrigley and Schofield, *The Population History of England*, pp. 313–32.
61. *Ibid.*, pp. 368–9, 375, and 383–4.
62. R. Schofield, 'The relationship between demographic structure and environment in pre-industrial western Europe', in W. Conze (ed.), *Sozialgeschichte der Familie in der Neuzeit Europas* (Stuttgart, 1976).
63. Wrigley and Schofield, *The Population History of England*. p. 376.
64. R. Schofield and E. A. Wrigley, 'Remarriage intervals and the effect of remarriage on fertility', in J. Dupâquier *et al.* (eds.), *Marriage and Remarriage in Populations in the Past*, (London, 1981), pp. 211–25.
65. Wrigley and Schofield, *The Population History of England*, pp. 228–36.
66. E. A. Wrigley, 'Family limitation in pre-industrial England', *Economic History Review*, **XIX** (1966), pp. 82–109.
67. C. Wilson, 'Natural fertility in pre-industrial England', *Population Studies*, **38** (1984), pp. 225–40; Wrigley and Schofield, 'English population history', pp. 168–75.

68. R. M. Smith, 'Natural fertility in pre-industrial Europe', in P. Diggory, *et al.* (eds.), *Natural Human Fertility: Social and Biological Determinants*, (London, 1988), pp. 70–88.

69. C. Wilson, 'The proximate determinants of marital fertility in England 1680–1799', in L. Bonfield *et al.* (eds.), *The World We Have Gained: Histories of Population and Social Structure*, (Oxford, 1986), pp. 203–30.

70. V. Fildes, *Wet Nursing: A History from Antiquity to the Present*, (Oxford, 1988), pp. 79–100.

71. R. Finlay, *Population and Metropolis: The Demography of London 1580–1650*, (Cambridge, 1981), pp. 133–50.

72. Landers, 'Age patterns of mortality in London', pp. 45–51.

73. Wrigley and Schofield, *The Population History of England*, pp. 426–8.

74. D. R. Weir, 'Rather never than late: celibacy and age at marriage in English cohort fertility', *Jnl. of Family History*, **9** (1984), pp. 340–54; R. Schofield, 'English marriage patterns revisited', *Jnl. of Family History*, **10** (1985), pp. 2–20.

75. R. Schofield, 'Family structure, demographic behaviour and economic growth', in Walter and Schofield (eds.), *Famine, Disease and the Social Order*, pp. 296–97.

76. R. M. Smith, 'Marriage processes in the English past: some continuities', in Bonfield *et al.* (eds.), *The World We Have Gained*, pp. 78–92.

77. R. Schofield and E. A. Wrigley, 'Introduction', in Rotberg and Rabb (eds.), *Population and Economy*, p. 4.

78. Wrigley and Schofield, *The Population History of England*, pp. 298–305.

79. A. Kussmaul, 'Time and space, hoofs and grain: the seasonality of marriage in England', in Rotberg and Rabb (eds.), *Population and economy*, pp. 195–218.

80. J. Goldstone, 'The demographic revolution in England: a re-examination', *Population Studies*, **40** (1986), pp. 5–33.

81. Schofield, 'Family structure', p. 296.

82. P. Sharpe, 'The total reconstitution method: a tool for class-specific study?', *Local Population Studies*, **44** (1990), pp. 46–50.

83. V. B. Elliott, 'Single-women in the London marriage market: age, status and mobility, 1958–1619', in R. B. Outhwaite (ed.), *Marriage and Society: Studies in the Social History of Marriage*, (London, 1981), p. 84.

84. P. Earle, *The Making of the English Middle Class: Business, Society and Family Life in London 1660–1730*, (London, 1989), pp. 180–5.

85. Elliott, 'Single-women in the London marriage market', pp. 85–6.

86. Finlay, *Population and Metropolis*, pp. 139–42.

87. J. Thirsk and J. P. Cooper, *Seventeenth-century Economic Documents*, (Oxford, 1972), p. 773.

88. Findings reported in a seminar delivered by Dr, Jeremy Boulton at All Souls College, Oxford, May, 1989.

89. A useful collection of key essays is collected in P. Clark and D. Souden, (eds.), *Migration and Society in early Modern Europe*, (London, 1987).

90. Wrigley and Schofield, *The Population History of England*, pp. 219–28.

91. Thirsk and Cooper, *Seventeenth-century Economic Documents*, p. 758.

92. H. A. Gemery, 'Emigration from the British Isles to the New World 1630–1700: inferences from colonial populations', *Research in Economic Theory*, **V** (1980), pp. 179–231.

93. Wrigley and Schofield, *The Population History of England*, p. 224.

94. J. Horn, 'Servant emigration to the Chesapeake in the seventeenth century', in T. W. Tate and D. L. Ammerman (eds.), *The Chesapeake in the Seventeenth Century: Essays in Anglo-American Society*, (Chapel Hill, 1979), pp. 51–95.

95. D. W. Galenson, *White Servitude in Colonial America* (Cambridge, 1981): D. Souden, '"Rogues, whores and vagabonds"? Indentured servant emigration to North America and the case of mid-seventeenth century Bristol', in Souden and Clark (eds.), *Migration and Society*, pp. 150–71.

96. D. Souden, 'English indentured servants and the trans-Atlantic colonial economy', in S. Marks and P. Richardson (eds.), *International labour Migration: Historical Perspectives*, (London, 1984), pp. 19–33.

97. Clark and Souden (eds.), *Migration and Society*, p. 29.

98. *Ibid.,* p. 29.

99. P. Clark, 'The migrant in Kentish towns, 1580–1640', in P. Clark and P. Slack (eds.), *Crisis and Order in English Towns 1500–1700*, (London, 1972), pp. 117–63; J. Kent, 'Population mobility and class: poor migrants in the Midlands in the early seventeenth century', *Local Population Studies,* **27** (1981), pp. 35–51.

100. P. Slack, 'Vagrants and vagrancy in England, 1598–1664', in Clark and Souden (eds.), *Migration and Society,* pp. 49–76; A. L. Beier, *Masterless Men: the Vagrancy Problem in England 1564–1641,* (London, 1985).

101. P. A. J. Pettit, *The Royal Forests of Northamptonshire,* Northants Record Society, **XXIII** (1968), pp. 142 ff.; V. Skipp, *Crisis and Development: An Ecological Case Study of the Forest of Arden,* pp. 151–60; M. Spufford, *Contrasting Communities: English Villagers in the Sixteenth and Seventeenth Centuries,* (Cambridge, 1974), pp. 151–60.

102. D. Souden, 'Movers and stayers in family reconstitution populations', *Local Population Studies,* **33** (1984), pp. 11–28; P. Clark, 'Migration in England during the late seventeenth and early eighteenth century', in Clark and Souden (eds.), *Migration and Society,* pp. 221–7.

103. A Kussmaul, *Servants in Husbandry in Early Modern England,* (Cambridge, 1981).

104. R. M. Smith, 'Fertility, economy and household formation in England over three centuries', *Population and Development Review,* **7** (1981), pp. 602–5.

105. Clark and Souden (eds), *Migration and Society,* p. 33.

106. D. Souden, 'Migrants and the population structure of later seventeenth century provincial cities and market towns', in P. Clark (ed.), *The Transformation of English Provincial Towns 1600–1800,* (London, 1984), pp. 133–68.

107. *Ibid.,* pp. 143–4.

108. D. Souden, '"East, west—home's best"? regional patterns in migration in early modern England', in Clark and Souden (eds.), *Migration and Society,* p. 298.

109. The classic paper is, of course, E. A. Wrigley, "A simple model of London's importance in changing English society and economy, 1650–1750', *Past and Present,* **37** (1967), pp. 44–70.

110. Wrigley and Schofield, *The Population History of England,* pp. 166–70.

111. Dobson, 'The last hiccup of the old demographic regime', pp. 399–414.

112. Souden, '"East, west—home's best"', p. 317.

113   An argument that is developed further in R. M. Smith, 'Exogenous and endogenous influences on the "preventive check" in England 1600–1750: Some specification problems', *Economic History Review* (forthcoming).

7

Agriculture 1500–1730

J. Yelling

In the last thirty years successive texts have stressed the significance of agricultural change in the early modern period. Developments in agrarian structures, in commercialization, and in productive techniques, were all much greater than once foreseen, finally removing the idea that an agricultural revolution began suddenly in the eighteenth century. Probably, these trends have been carried far enough, and the need is now for greater precision which will, *inter alia*, place more stress on the difficulties and limitations of advance. In this chapter I shall consider this in four main sections each devoted to important processes of change : common land and enclosure, landholding, markets and land use, and agricultural production.

Common Land and Enclosure

The related topics of common-field systems and enclosures were among the earliest to attract the attention of geographers to this period. Such agrarian systems were closely linked to the development of settlement and landscape and to the regional distinctiveness of the country's rural areas. Whilst the origins of varying common-field systems lay much earlier than 1500, the more abundant evidence of the early modern period could be used for detailed examination of their workings, so providing a more accurate account of regional types. In turn, the related and very distinctive spatial patterns of enclosure provided an obvious incentive to geographical investigation.[1]

As with other features of agricultural change, emphasis has been given to the extent to which enclosure was achieved before the traditional onset of economic development in the mid eighteenth century. Wordie has recently estimated that at most 45 per cent of the country was enclosed by 1500 and at least 75 per cent by 1760.[2] Turning aside from the large degree of enclosure achieved by 1500, he stressed that the seventeenth century was the main period of enclosure in England and, going on to associate this with substantial increases in productivity, drew the conclusion (with some qualifications) that the incidence of enclosure is an index of economic development. Dahlman and McCloskey, too, though differing in their theories of common-field origins, both regard its demise as an uncomplicated product of the rise of the market.[3] There is a widespread acceptance of Gonner's view that enclosure took place first where it was most profitable 'owing either to a change in its use or to a considerable increase in yield . . . because the profit would compensate for the loss incurred'.[4]

Since the importance of the economic motive in enclosure is not to be denied, such a view seems very persuasive, but it gives rise to some curious results. The implication would seem to be that nearly half the land in the country had been profitable to enclose before 1500 whilst more than a quarter was unprofitable to enclose until after 1750. The latter, apparently remained apart from the pressures of economic change for another two centuries or more, despite the evident importance of such pressures from an early date. Moreover, leaving aside the common waste-lands, the villages that were unprofitable to enclose until after 1750, lay almost exclusively in a broad belt running across the country from Yorkshire to Dorset. What seems striking when put this way is not just the replacement of common lands by enclosure but their co-existence over a very long period. This has become all the more relevant since Gonner's time because of the greater emphasis placed on agricultural change. At the very least what can be said is that no one has properly faced up to the major implications of accepting Gonner's proposition. I myself believe that the incidence of enclosure cannot be explained in these terms alone, and that regional differences in the ease with which enclosure could take place also need to be taken into account.[5]

This is not to deny, however, that there may be some contexts in which general economic pressures against the common lands were overriding. In the north-east of England, Hodgson has placed the development of enclosure of both common waste and common field in the context of an early industrial revolution, promoted particularly by London's demand for coal, which produced an economic transform-ation of the area so overwhelming as to reduce other factors to a subsidiary role.[6] Again, the enclosure of common land in the form of upland wastes, fens, moorlands and forest was limited by existing property rights and usages, but it appears frequently as a response to population pressure and demand for increased pro-duction on land not yet intensively used. Such enclosures were major features of the period, reaching their peak of importance in the extensive fenland schemes of the seventeenth century. Improved techniques of reclamation and farming also had their part to play in bringing about increased production on such lands through the medium of enclosure.[7]

The more limited claim that enclosure was associated with changes in land use is certainly a strong one, and seems to fit better with the incidence of the movement. Although common fields have been portrayed as mixed and relatively unspecialized systems of land use, they survived into the modern era as predominantly arable systems. The early removal of common fields from the western half of the country would seem a natural corollary. Moreover, conversion to pasture has long been associated with the well-known enclosures in Midland counties from the fifteenth century. Any stress on the association of enclosure with a particular land use, however, must diminish the competitive model of enclosures versus common fields, and tend to promote an alternative model in which the two systems appear more complementary to each other. It could be argued then that common fields survived in certain areas because they were able to improve their production in the sector to which those areas were most suited. This would certainly enable us to reconcile the co-existence of common fields and enclosures with a view of the early modern period as one of major economic transformation. However, whilst the complementary model deserves equal consideration to the competitive, it should not I think be simply substituted for it.

The Midland examples just referred to may be used to introduce a key factor in considering the ease with which enclosure could take place. In general, they involved a substitution of livestock fattening for arable production, which was seen to be profitable only on large farms so that enclosure was associated with a reduction in the number of landholdings. The unequal effects of the process on participants then became a potential source of opposition to enclosure; indeed, particularly so in some instances in which the profitability of the process was most apparent. In Leicestershire, Northamptonshire, south Warwickshire and north Buckinghamshire, the classic areas for such enclosure, common fields survived typically as arable-orientated communities alongside enclosed pastoral systems dominated by a few men.[8] Such a pattern is partly one of co-existence of different systems of production, but it is also one of competition, for the enclosed systems are more commercially orientated and more profitable users of land. What keeps enclosure in check is also the opposition which the movement itself engenders.

By what mechanisms could such opposition be made effective? One possibility lies in general methods of political protest—from appeal to public opinion, complaints to Parliament or riotous assembly. Such protest was a notable feature in the Midlands, culminating in the riots of 1607, and probably had some effect in slowing the enclosure movement. Popular protests were also effective in preventing the enclosure of Kings Sedgemoor in Somerset, and in destroying many enclosures in the East Anglian fenlands during the Civil War.[9] Opposition to enclosures of such common land was particularly strong because of its adverse effects on the numerous users of common rights. In general, however, whilst these forms of potential opposition were always a factor to be weighed in the balance, their effectiveness was limited, particularly after the mid seventeenth century when protesters lost their previous support from the state.

The principal method by which opposition to enclosure could be expressed was therefore through the right of landowners to participate in the decision to enclose. Indeed, in a common-field system, communal decision-making might be regarded as a central feature, and a decision to enclose as its final and most important act. In highly integrated common-field systems, the most usual model of the type, this was indeed the case; enclosure resulted from a decision taken together by the whole body of landowners, and there was one particular point in time at which the common-field system was ended. There are some exceptions to this, notably in the earlier part of our period when demesne lands were often taken into enclosure separately, but usually enclosure involves the whole constituency of landowners.

If we consider that at a single point in time a varied constituency of landowners had to agree to such a major change, and to meet all the costs and uncertainties of enclosure, one might imagine that the rewards expected had to be both great and widely spread. This, however, ignores the unequal distribution of land and power in such communities. At the very beginning of our period general enclosures were often achieved where manorial lords came to possess all the land of a small township, so achieving enclosure by 'unity of control'. Later on many enclosures by agreement were achieved by manorial lords negotiating from a position of strength with only a few other landowners. It was in these circumstances that striking contrasts emerged between enclosed townships of pastoral land use and few landowners and more populous peasant communities organized around their common arable fields. However, there were also circumstances in which landowners as a body, though still probably excluding some common-right users, could agree to enclosure. Such enclosures occurred particularly in the mid seventeenth century and later. The balance between coercion and free agreement in 'enclosures by agreement' has yet to be established and certainly varies from one region to another.[10] Free agreement, however, did require a relatively wide distribution of the spoils, and this explains why in a county such as Leicestershire, where pressure for enclosure had been so intense for more than three centuries, 45 per cent of the land and the majority of the communities still remained to be enclosed by Parliamentary Act.

The 'general enclosures' so far considered were not, however, the only type of enclosure. Equally important were 'piecemeal enclosures'. These had two distinguishing features: (1) enclosure did not proceed from a single collective decision but from the activities of individuals or small groups, and (2) enclosure took place piece by piece, the common land disappearing gradually, often over a long period of time. In districts which were enclosed 'piecemeal', portions of common fields of various sizes were surrounded and eaten into by small hedged closes to provide what contemporaries described as a 'woodland' landscape. Holdings still often consisted of small parcels, somewhat scattered in location. Settlement was loosely structured, and often not restricted to a single point, but involving hamlets and individual farms as well.[11] This contrasted with the much more open and rational landscape of general enclosure. Early enclosures, dominated by the manorial lord, had extremely large fields, whilst some of the later enclosures by agreement were allotted by commissioners, resulting in planned divisions similar in general terms to parliamentary enclosures.[12]

In the geography of common fields there is a striking regional division between piecemeal and general enclosure: the latter corresponds to the Midland belt from Yorkshire to Dorset in which parliamentary enclosure was later concentrated, and the former predominates in the remaining areas. This division is of immense importance in agricultural history, but it does not derive from the developing economic geography of the period 1500–1730 either in terms of markets or land use. Instead it originates in the much earlier development of common-field systems, piecemeal enclosure occurring in the less integrated systems which had developed on either side of the Midland belt. We are therefore faced with two distinct regimes of enclosure. In each, the primary motives for enclosure are probably economic, and in this later period they are certainly profit-orientated and related to markets and land uses. But in regions of piecemeal enclosure common fields disappear much more readily, without any decisive moment at which costs, uncertainties, and the differential effects on landowners, have to be weighed. In regions of general enclosure the push required is much stronger and often generates countervailing opposition. The large-scale geographical patterns of enclosure, therefore, are not just the product of economic pressures : these pressures act on a varying surface and the way in which common fields disappear reflects the manner in which they had been developed.

The importance of this regional distinction is still often underestimated. Thus whilst Wordie maintains that 'it was during the seventeenth century that England swung over from being a mainly open field country to a mainly enclosed one; [13] this result is largely achieved by conflating one area mostly enclosed afterwards with another mostly enclosed before. Clearly, too, the division between enclosure regimes is central to any interpretation of the movement in terms of its economic effects or the resistance to enclosure. Finally, there is the important implication that if one of the two regimes had everywhere predominated, then the resultant chronology and geography of enclosure would have been totally different, and this would have affected most other aspects of the agriculture of the period.

Landholding

In contrast to the many studies of landed estates by historians, no large-scale geographical work on this period has so far made landholding its principal focus of interest. Nevertheless, the 'Brenner debate' has recently attracted attention and empirical work has continued at local level. [14] The time is now ripe to bring the study of landholding more centre-stage, probably by linking agrarian concerns to wider social processes. Difficulties are created, however, by the complex nature of landed property, and by the laborious methods required to establish empirical results, usually working from local sources. Landholding occurred at various levels: manorial lords, their tenants, occupying farmers, as well as owners and occupiers of common rights. Landholding distributions, normally established in terms of the acreage of holdings, need to be examined both from an economic point of view (the proportion of land held in units of various size), and in social terms (the proportion of landholdings of various sizes and number of landless).

Beginning with the landlords, historians have usually divided this period into two main eras. The first of these, lasting through to the Restoration, is dominated by the break-up of the estates of the Church and Crown. These estates, occupying perhaps 25–33 per cent of land in the early sixteenth century were reduced to some 5–10 per cent by the 1680s. [15] Economic, social and demographic factors determined that the principal beneficiaries of this change were middling and lesser manorial lords, hence the 'rise of the gentry'. After the Restoration it was the great estates which tended to flourish, again for a variety of reasons, including the practice of strict settlement. The processes at work here flowed, largely, from the affairs of state, the position of the Crown, and later the political dominance of the great landowners. Otherwise, much depended on family histories and other contingent factors rather than any more fundamental geographical structuring, although a metropolitan influence on the size and type of ownership of landed estates can be discerned. There was nonetheless some differential regional impact, and change at the local level was important. Clay points out, for instance, that it was because of the 'rise of the gentry' that the resident squire became a typical feature of the English countryside, and this has obvious links with the type of differentiation of settlements advocated by Mills. [16]

It is, however, the landlord's control of the tenancies on their estates which has the larger geographical implications. Brenner argued that England was exceptional in the degree of control which landlords exercised, and correspondingly in the failure of the peasantry to achieve independent tenure. [17] This was the outcome of a class struggle much determined before our period but continuing through at least until the peasant revolts of the early seventeenth century. The landlord used his power over tenancies, first on demesne and then on copyhold land, to introduce rack-rented or short lease holdings, and to create larger holdings serviced by agricultural labourers. In effect the landlord intervened more directly in the production process to obtain a pattern of tenancy favourable to increased profit, and at the same time his rents became more directly linked to agricultural performance. This direct and capitalist relationship between landholding and profit then became the key factor in agricultural development.

Tawney in his work on the sixteenth century also emphasized the manner in which landlords used their political power to effect the development of landholding. He claimed that small freeholders, unlike copyholders and leaseholders, showed no diminution in numbers and that 'the decisive factor that causes the fortunes of the former class to wax and those of the two latter to wane is to be found in the realm not of economics but of law . . . the freeholders stand firm because their legal position is unassailable'.[18] Since then Kerridge's work has strengthened the view that copyhold of inheritance was also a relatively secure tenure even in the sixteenth century.[19] However copyhold for lives required a periodic renewal by the landlord, so that the extent to which engrossment was linked to security of tenure is still an issue. Tawney's and Brenner's arguments are also useful in underlining two features which might otherwise be taken for granted. One of these is that capitalist structures were created out of an inherited set of unequal property relationships. The distinctive position of demesne land, for instance, is still important in our period, particularly its earlier part. The other is that these adaptations took place within a political framework which if it had been otherwise could have produced a different outcome—a much greater enfranchisement of copyhold for example.

However, too much emphasis should not be placed on tenure as a single factor. The landholding structure of this period did not come about simply by a whittling away of a structure of peasant farming existing in 1500. It is important to take a more dynamic view of landholding, to examine the creation of holdings as well as their demise. During the sixteenth and early seventeenth centuries, demographic factors may have brought about an increase in small farms, especially where population was rising fastest.[20] This does not mean that large farms were subdivided, indeed a process of polarization may have occurred in some areas. Thus Spufford has shown how at Chippenham (Cambs.) between 1534 and 1636 there was a sudden collapse of the middle range of landholders and a major shift towards domination by large units.[21] She found no evidence of seigneurial action to explain this, and attributed it to economic pressures. The larger landholders were more successful in riding out crises and orientating their production to market trends. After the middle of the seventeenth century, demographic as well as economic factors were favourable to engrossment. The fall in corn prices was particularly significant, and many commentators have seen this as a crucial period in the decline of the small landowner.[22]

Such economic factors have a clear geographical structuring relating to the nature of the farming enterprise. Thus mainly arable farming and certain types of livestock fattening favoured larger holdings in contrast to dairying or livestock rearing which were more labour intensive. This would be most apparent at the level of farm occupancy, but it would also affect the landowning structure at its lower levels.

During our period there was therefore a widening contrast in landholding patterns between the arable–sheep farming district of Chalkland Wiltshire, and the dairying district in the north-west of that county. At a larger scale, the more pastoral farming of the western parts of the country favoured a greater survival of smaller holdings there. There was no sudden emergence of a new pattern, but a gradual sharpening of regional differentiation, with many local variations in the pace and scale of change. So far it has not been possible to chart these developments with any accuracy, but by the end of the period the principal features of the geography of farm size depicted by Grigg for mid-nineteenth-century Britain would probably have been recognizable.[23]

So far, no techniques have been developed which might be capable of showing how tenure may have affected the shaping of these regional patterns. It is known that there were important regional differences in the prevalence of different tenures. East Anglia, for instance, had a large proportion of freeholds and copyholds of inheritance, whereas the west of the country had many copyholds for lives.[24] It seems clear that such tenurial patterns had no overriding effect—districts of independent tenure were not necessarily districts of smaller holdings. It remains possible that in a region like East Anglia greater security of tenure may have reduced the engrossment that economic factors would otherwise have produced, but this has yet to be demonstrated. In most parts of the country there was certainly a significant reduction in copyhold tenure through the period, although not always in favour of short leases. Landlords were often motivated by a desire to protect their revenues against inflation, but they did not relentlessly use their powers to achieve drastic tenurial re-organization. One might explain this by the retention of more traditional attitudes by many estate owners, by the fact that capitalism in agriculture still had a long way to go. On the other hand, the mere presence of copyhold tenure did not preclude a market orientation of farming enterprise—such copyholds could indeed be sublet at rack rents. Some weight should therefore be given to the way in which development was possible within existing structures, and certainly we should include the activities of the peasants here as well as manorial lords.

It is interesting that Brenner does not mention the common fields as providing any 'protective shell' against engrossment, a view which was once popular. Enclosure could sometimes be associated with dramatic shifts in landholding and a replacement of peasant subsistence farming by capitalist agriculture. It did not always have this effect, however, whilst engrossment also occurred within the common fields— as at Spufford's Chippenham, which remained unenclosed right through this period. The common fields were therefore not isolated from economic and social processes affecting the country generally, and the regional geography of enclosure does not correspond with any distinctive type of landholding pattern. Paradoxically, the arable orientation of common fields may even have encouraged engrossment. Special mention should be made, however, of common rights. Whilst the most important of these were individually appropriated, and even cottage common rights could be engrossed, it is likely that in practice common usages provided the cottager and other smallholders with an important resource.

Some of the most interesting geographical features associated with landholding are observable at the purely local level, in the variety of landholding patterns from parish to parish. Striking instances of this arose in connection with the 'depopulating' enclosures of the sixteenth and early seventeenth centuries: as at Cotesbach

(1603) in Leicestershire, where sixteen farms were 'decayed'.[25] Their incidence amongst other communities which remained in common field was much related to manorial ownership and policy, as well as sometimes to previous engrossment and economic differentiation amongst the peasantry. Indeed, inter-parish differences in landholding were important throughout the country, and not explainable by purely economic factors. The presence of varying tenures, division of manors and family histories are factors thought to have played a part in this development.

Whatever the relative importance of economy and law, landlord and peasant, in changing landholding patterns, one paramount feature of the period was the increased numbers of the landless, the cottager and the smallholder. Wrigley has calculated that the population of England rose from 2.4 million in 1520 to 4.98 million c. 1670, of which the rural share was 2.28 million and 4.3 million respectively.[26] Even allowing for some creation of farms in the sixteenth century, it is quite clear that the bulk of the additional numbers must have fallen into the groups just mentioned. And although the rural population ceased to increase in the last sixty years of this period, the enhanced engrossment at that time meant that there is unlikely to have been any relief (in numerical terms) at the bottom of the scale. Such a differentiation necessarily had important effects on the social structure of communities, and the living standards and social relations of their constituent classes.[27]

However, whilst the growth of these social groups is partly a corollary of processes already discussed, their geography is much affected by migration and the location of alternative employment. The growth of 'dual economies' in pastoral regions with a large smallholding base has been discussed by Thirsk.[28] She particularly emphasized the complementarity of such agricultural and industrial activities in terms of their labour demands. The relative importance of industry and agriculture varied. During the seventeenth century industries developed particularly strongly in certain poor agricultural districts of the north and Midlands, such as the Black Country.[29] Where successful, such economies drew in migrants from surrounding areas, and became increasingly dependent on industry rather than agriculture. In all cases, however, regions of dual economy grew faster, and drew population from the arable areas, some of which underwent a marked relative decline in population density.

It is interesting that such pastoral and largely enclosed regions often exhibited a smallholding structure, perhaps even a 'farming ladder', once uniquely associated with the common arable fields. Even the landless might find some resource in hedges and thickets, and of course in the common wastes, large and small, which were also a feature of such regions. In the latter part of this period, however, industries were also developing in some arable areas where large numbers of cottagers or landless provided a cheap source of labour. Here a quite different type of relationship to the agricultural economy tends to appear. One well-known case is the Leicestershire hosiery industry, which was frequently attracted to common-field arable townships. In such cases the most important determinant was the control of cottages, industry and migration by landlords, related to the contrasting patterns of 'open' and 'closed' villages studied by Mill.[30]

Markets and Land Use

The extent to which farmers entered into trade is one of the most difficult agricultural parameters to assess, and the evidence allows only very general conclusions. However fragile, such conclusions affect our whole way of thinking about the agriculture of the period. Growing commercialization has a general significance in promoting organizational change and technical advance. But there is also a more specifically geographical role; for increasing areas of the country are brought into a connecting system in which the various parts relate through competition and co-operative linkages. Developments in one part of a market area affect, to varying degrees, all other parts; whilst the nature of production in any one part is shaped by the comparative advantages that area possesses *vis à vis* other regions. These advantages may lie in the physical nature of soils or climate, conducive to a certain type of agricultural enterprise, or they may lie in proximity to markets, or in the existence of an agrarian organization better equipped to take advantage of those markets.

The changes in population outlined in the last section must form the starting point for any examination of factors governing the growth of trade. The sheer increase in numbers must have some effect on its absolute volume. Opportunities for trade are, however, much dependent on specialization. The growth of cities or industrial areas reliant on more agricultural districts for their food is important. Specialization also occurs within agriculture as trade develops, sometimes in response to urban demands. The regional variety of agricultural conditions (physical and organizational) prevailing in Britain was itself a major stimulus to trade. Transport is another important field, for innovations in its equipment or organization can encourage trade and specialization by bringing producer and market closer together, and increased efficiency in the marketing process itself can have a similar effect.[31]

Taking these factors together, it is easy to see how they might link together to create an 'ascending spiral' of progressive development. Once a certain degree of specialization is present (including urban and industrial economies), then developments in the means of trading can promote increased specialization calling forth more trade, in turn promoting developments in transport and marketing. Indeed, in general terms such a model might be applied to this period, with the usual substantial qualification that it must not be seen as a well-oiled mechanism moving swiftly through its motions. There is, however, one further factor whose effects on trade in this period are less easy to estimate. Wealthier populations, other things being equal, demand a wide range of goods, and hence promote more specialization and trade than poorer ones. In this respect, the growth of population in the sixteenth century may be seen as an inhibiting factor, since the population as a whole was certainly poorer in 1600 than it was in 1520, perhaps by as much as 40 per cent.[32] Such a reduction in living standards was, of course, not equally shared by all classes or places, and specifically not by those landholders who benefited from rising agricultural prices. Even so, it may well be that growth in trade was relatively slow in relation to production before 1650. After the Civil War, the changing demographic situation produced a rise in living standards favouring increased specialization, particularly seen in the growth of London and new industrial areas. Landholders, whose own incomes were far less buoyant, came under pressure to respond to these opportunities by increased specialization and commercialization of their production.

The concentration of urban growth in the largest centres, and the development of important industrial districts, was related to a widening of market areas of agricultural produce. By the 1720s, Defoe could note of the West Riding, that 'their corn comes up in great quantities out of Lincoln, Nottingham and the East Riding, their sheep and mutton from the adjacent counties every way; their butter from the East and North Riding, their cheese out of Cheshire and Warwickshire, their black cattle also out of Lancashire'.[33] Economic concentration was most spectacularly exhibited in the growth of London, and the impact of London's demands on agricultural production has been a central theme. Gras attempted to delimit the various market areas for grain from a study of prices. He included some discussion of von Thünen but noted that his work contained 'little or no appreciation of the historical development from the local to the metropolitan market'. This began to develop in the sixteenth century, and by c, 1700 covered most of England south of a line from the Wash to the Severn. Within this region 'prices diminish as the distance from the centre is increased'.[34] Recent studies have extended the metropolitan grain market to virtually the whole country by this date. It is agreed that any regional autonomy in the market for livestock products disappeared much earlier and 'prices everywhere were closely tied to those obtaining in the capital'.[35]

It should be emphasized that regional distinctions in the level of commercialization were not clear-cut. In any one region there were great variations between individual landholders and between localities. It is often thought that peasant landholders who could meet their own subsistence needs may have been less affected by the market than smallholders. In any event, the large landholders are usually seen as the major participators in commercial farming, and this meant, of course, that a greater percentage of land rather than of owners or occupiers were involved in relatively high levels of trade. Some authors suggest a deep divide between commercially orientated estates and farms and other producers.[36] My own view, however, is that increased commercialization should be seen, usually, as a change in the balance of categories rather than an abrupt and decisive transition, and this would apply to regional and chronological development also.

There was, however, variable access to wider markets, caused not only by distance from towns and industrial areas, but also by the ease of moving grain and other products. The geography of water communications was important in controlling access to major grain markets. London received supplies by ship from Kent, and later from East Anglia and much of the east and south coasts. Inland, river navigation along the Thames was a key factor. But although water transport was first choice, there was also considerable overland movement of grain. Defoe mentions Cambridgeshire, Bedfordshire, Northamptonshire and Hampshire as counties which supplied barley and wheat to a string of marketing towns around London. In these centres, such as Royston, Ware, Marlow and Guildford, the grain was usually processed into meat or malt.[37]

A large tract of western England from south Lancashire to Somerset was primarily associated with the dairying industry, mainly for cheese. This was marketed over considerable distances by water and land carriage, allowing Defoe to maintain that

Cheshire, 'however remote from London is one of those (counties) which contributes most to its support'.[38] Further west the repercussions of the wool trade had reached into the Welsh uplands before the sixteenth century. Such areas also strengthened their traditional breeding and rearing industries, supplying sheep and cattle to the surrounding lowlands. The driving of stock from the uplands for fattening in the Midlands, East Anglia and around London was a particularly striking feature of this trade, especially after 1650. In general, the lack of internal restrictions on trade, and the excellence of water communications, must be stressed as factors favouring the commercialization of agriculture in England. However, the lack of any really radical innovation in transport necessarily restricted the extent of geographical re-organization. Overland movement of grain was still difficult, and not until the railway 'did the business of fattening move back into the lowland fringes of the great rearing areas'.[39] The growth of dairying in the west did not dislodge the large dairying district in Essex and Suffolk.

In view of this slow development of the market, one of the most striking features of the early sixteenth century is the presence of strongly contrasting regional economies. John Leland's distinction between the champion parts of the West Midlands and the more pastoral woodland parts seems as clear as any existing at the end of this period.[40] Perhaps such a distinction reflects a greater degree of trade than is normally accorded this early period; certainly it was sustained by some regional interchange of products. The nature of agrarian organization was also, however, a major influence, for whilst the champion regions managed some adaptation to the favourable market for pastoral products in the late medieval period, they remained substantially arable producers and land-use change had therefore been principally accommodated in the more enclosed regions. Differences in land use between adjacent arable common field and enclosed pastoral parishes remained notable through the period. It is more difficult to assess the effect that the continued and sharpening division between champion and woodland regions had on the geography of land use. This depends of course on arguments rehearsed in the first section. If common field easily gave way to enclosure whenever subject to economic pressure then the geography of land use is simply a function of physical conditions, techniques and market opportunities. If it did not, then the geography of land use could have been substantially altered, favouring, for instance, the survival of corn production in the champion districts and of pastoral production outside them.

Whilst some enclosed regions seem to have continued and strengthened their pastoral specialisms, in other cases there was a spread of arable production and convertible husbandry. This was notably the case in the woodland areas of the West Midlands, reducing the impact of Leland's distinction, and leading to the demise of districts using rye rather than wheat, oxen rather than horses. Other more specialized crops were, however, being added. Thirsk has shown that throughout the country the increased use of crops such as woad or hops contributed to employment and to the value of agricultural production.[41] Market gardening made a similar contribution, and its spread around London and other centres of consumption was a notable feature of the period.[42] Above all, although mixed farming was now more prevalent, products varied considerably in type and quality, being prepared for a variety of market outlets, and occupying differing places in the farm economy. Edwards has shown, for instance, that horses were increasingly prepared for various specialized markets.[43] Similarly, cash crops such as wheat and barley received more attention, the malt market being important in the latter case.

Relatively sophisticated information on farm economies is, therefore, required to reveal important individual, local and regional specializations. Glennie has recently shown a development of sheep–corn and dairying specialities in different parts of Hertfordshire. He has also emphasized that increased individual specialization need not always be expected to produce marked regional divisions.[44] Some stress should also be given to the development of linkages between producers, bringing together the themes of individual and regional specialization. The growth of dairying in a region, for example, might be regarded as a linked operation, developing mutually sustainable production, knowledge of the trade, and market outlets, in a way similar to the specialist domestic manufacturers. Another type of linkage developing to an important extent in this period brought together areas of differing land use. Livestock rearers in the uplands thus supplied stock both to lowland enclosures, for fattening, and to the sheep flocks of arable common fields.

Production

Ernle thought that the Tudor farmer devoted himself exclusively to either tillage or pasture. He did not 'combine the two and by the introduction of new crops at once grow more corn and carry more stock'.[45] Searchers after technical innovation in our period have generally accepted this framework for advance, and sought to show that a successful combination of the two branches of agriculture had been achieved earlier than Ernle believed. Agricultural improvement, in this model, came through an initial introduction of increased amounts of fodder. As a result, livestock numbers increased, yielding greater quantities of manure, which in turn raised yields of crops and grass, so starting the 'expanding circle' again. One group of workers have looked particularly to the introduction of short grass leys and new fodder crops such as clover and turnips, particularly in the late seventeenth and early eighteenth centuries.[46] The most radical case for such a circle of improvement was, however, stated by Kerridge. He not only pushed forward the initial introduction of new fodder crops to the mid seventeenth century, virtually completed by 1720, but also brought into the discussion a less intensive rotation of grass with arable which he called 'up and down husbandry'.[47]

Kerridge regarded 'up and down husbandry' as the backbone of an agricultural revolution in the sixteenth and seventeenth centuries. He recognized that practices involving temporary grass tend to be concealed in records which (as in later periods) insist on referring either to arable or pasture. Nonetheless he believed that in the early sixteenth century this form of convertible husbandry 'was confined to the north-west and a few farms elsewhere. It expanded and spread rapidly after 1560, and fastest between 1590 and 1660, by which time it had conquered production and ousted the system of permanency from half the farm land.'[48] The best known form of 'up and down husbandry' occurred on former enclosed pastures in the Midlands in the late sixteenth century. Closes began to be broken up for short tillage intervals followed by long leys of six to twenty years' duration. Under such a system 'three quarters of the farm was grass, and the main object was animal produce'.[49] This was evidently a very specialized system of production, but it seems likely that more intensive convertible systems (usually yet to be specified) were used in the woodland districts during the seventeenth century. Kerridge expected spectacular improvements in productivity from such a system. Crop yields were double those in common fields and 'substituted for mere grazing . . . (it) . . . doubled and replacing common fields quadrupled rates of stocking'.[50]

A noticeable feature of Kerridge's work was that he made little attempt to seek statistical support for his conclusions. The most important source of such statistics lies in probate inventories, and the analysis of complete inventory collections for statistical purposes has largely been developed by geographers. In particular, three large-scale studies of Worcestershire, Norfolk/Suffolk, and Hertfordshire have been completed by Yelling, Overton and Glennie. The information most readily provided by the inventories concerns the composition of farm livestock and crops, and measures of productivity are achieved with more difficulty. One possibility was to measure the numbers of livestock, perhaps aggregated into livestock units, and to make certain assumptions about the size of farm to which the inventories as a body relate. Overton then introduced a major advance in the form of a statistical method which allowed the calculation of crop yields from inventories.

The records of livestock numbers produced for Worcestershire and Hertfordshire show a similar trend.[51] Livestock numbers per inventory begin at a high level in the mid sixteenth century, and fall steadily until the last quarter of the seventeenth. They then rise again, reaching new high levels by the early eighteenth century. In Worcestershire this pattern was produced both in the champion and woodland regions. If, as seems likely, the recorded falls in inventory numbers were partly caused by a declining mean size of farms, the long downward trend need not necessarily reflect declining numbers of livestock per unit area, but it certainly reflects declining numbers per person. Moreover, the rising trend at the end of the period also owes much to increasing mean farm size. Overall, there seems little scope for any large increase in livestock numbers over the period 1550–1730, certainly nothing on the scale that Kerridge suggested. The record of crop yields available for Norfolk/Suffolk and Hertfordshire has shown, however, that these were substantially higher in the early eighteenth century than in the mid sixteenth. Overton's results, covering 1587–98, 1628–40 and 1660–1735 suggested that there was considerable long-term improvement in both the late sixteenth and early seventeenth centuries.[52] Afterwards, barley yields continued to improve, but not those of wheat. Glennie's study of a continuous series from 1550 to 1699 shows some small rise in yields in the late sixteenth century, which was reversed in the early seventeenth century, and followed by a substantial increase in the mid and late seventeenth century, particularly in barley yields.[53]

It is clear that although Overton's and Glennie's results are broadly comparable, there remain important differences over the timing of improvement. Substantial improvement between the beginning and the end of the period is, however, apparent, whereas this is not the case in livestock numbers. The numbers are not, however, a direct measure of productivity—it is possible that increased wool, dairy produce and meat could be produced from the same numbers. At the very least, however, the 'expanding circle' model stands in need of substantial revision. This is not to deny the importance of mixed farming, but it serves to remind us that forms of such farming were already present at the beginning of the period, and that subsequent developments (right up to the 'high farming' of mid-Victorian Britain) built on this at higher technical and economic intensity. We must not assume that systems present in the sixteenth century had reached the limit of their development. Common-field systems, for instance, incorporated grass leys but probably did not systematically rotate them with the arable.[54] Nonetheless, the amount of livestock they carried did not necessarily impose a complete block on yield improvement.

It has become apparent that new crops and innovative techniques in this period should not be regarded as features which suddenly released farming from all previous constraints. They had a contribution to make, but need to be examined in an economic context of prices and markets, and concurrently with changes in farm size and management. Both Overton and Glennie, for example, have been sceptical about the contribution which new fodder crops such as clover and turnips could have made to improved yields in view of the relatively low proportion of the cropped acreage which they occupied. Overton has shown that the turnip first appears as a fodder crop in Norfolk inventories of the 1630s, and by the end of our period was being grown by half the farmers. Turnips were, however, usually grown in small quantities as a fodder supplement on arable farms, and the Norfolk four-course system post-dates this period.[55] Turnips were less widely used in Hertfordshire, still less in the northern and western parts of the country. Clover and other grass substitutes had achieved a wider geographical distribution by the early eighteenth century, even being introduced into common fields alongside the valuable pulse crop. Even so, they were also used on a limited scale, and although these crops provided important fodder resources, there is no reason to believe that they could have been responsible for any major increase in crop yields. Glennie prefers to explain rising yields at the end of his period by improved cultivation practices.[56]

The manner in which innovations were diffused socially and geographically is an important theme of the period. Ernle thought that agricultural progress was inhibited by resistance to innovation, particularly among small farmers and in common fields, a resistance only broken down when the owners of large landed estates began to take a practical interest in agriculture. Few would now place such an extreme emphasis on aristocratic participation, but social differentiation amongst farmers has become an even more important theme since he wrote because of the increased awareness of landholding changes in this period. The emergence of larger farms is indeed commonly thought to reflect an ability of large-scale farmers to innovate and to adapt production to market opportunities. Ernle's prime innovative symbol was the turnip and, fortunately, Overton's inventory analysis has now provided a precise account of its diffusion in Norfolk and Suffolk.[57] He makes use of the titles of gentleman, yeoman and husbandman ascribed to farmers when inventories were made. There was a clear tendency for its diffusion to move down the social scale, probably because gentlemen and yeomen had wider social contacts than husbandmen, whose information was derived from neighbourhood practice. Nonetheless, 42 per cent of husbandmen were growing turnips by the end of this period, far from the total rejection of progress which Ernle tended to assume. Moreover, it may well be that the turnip was especially linked to top-down social diffusion. Social distinctions (though still present) appear to have played a lesser role in the spread of clover. In sixteenth-century Worcester-shire, the replacement of oxen by horses was achieved more quickly in the common fields and on smaller farms.[58] This example shows that particular attention has to be given to the way in which innovations fitted into farming systems—oxen were more suited to large farms and to a cattle economy.

During the period to the mid-seventeenth-century population growth required increased agricultural output, particularly of arable products. Growth began, however, from a position in which arable production was at a relatively low level in the woodland regions, where attention had switched to more profitable forms of livestock husbandry. It seems certain that increased production in these districts made a large contribution to raising arable output. This provided an economic context very suitable to forms of convertible husbandry. Conversely, there is little evidence of radical system change in the champion districts, which remained major contributors to crop production. It seems likely that the demands on agriculture also served to protect traditional forms of production, provided they could make some adjustment. Recently, 'optimistic' and 'pessimistic' views of output in the period have been put forward, although neither supports catastrophe on the one hand or cornucopia on the other.[59] Changes in real income, themselves problematic, form an important part of such assessments. Real income is thought to have fallen, particularly in the late sixteenth century, indicating that agricultural output was not keeping pace with population. If Glennie's yield series turn out to be widely replicated then this, together with the evidence on livestock numbers, will strengthen the 'pessimistic' case. Even then, however, it would be necessary to bear in mind that more marked improvements from the mid seventeenth century must have been based on an agricultural system which had adapted reasonably well to the changes of the previous period.

After the mid seventeenth century, population pressure ceased to be a predominant factor, and farm prices weakened, particularly for some arable products like wheat and rye.[60] However, this reversal of fortunes in terms of prices did not produce any simple return towards previous patterns of land use and production. Many areas strengthened the arable side of their production, although usually in conjunction with some type of livestock production, often sheep farming. The range of fodder crops was widened, and crop yields probably increased, although the strongest evidence for this concerns barley, a crop more resistant than most to price weakness. Markets and competition in price and quality play a greater role in this period, sharpening inter-sectoral differences. Key cash crops emerge—barley in the east, wheat in Worcestershire—on which attention is focused, and around which farming systems are organized. The evidence suggests that cultivation practice on light soils was particularly improved, extending the range of crops grown, and probably increasing fodder and livestock output. Conversely, heavy soil users came under greater pressure. Elements of improvement in production can therefore be more certainly identified in this part of the period, but this should be qualified by the fact that agriculture seems to have been subject to familiar strains once population growth took off again later in the eighteenth century.

Review

The predominant theme of each of the above sections is that despite the achievement of the past much remains to be discovered. Not only do each of the main motors of development require more precise analysis, but their interaction can only be discussed in a tentative manner. It is possible to give primacy to one of them—as Brenner did to landholding changes—but in my view the difficult study of reciprocal action is likely to prove more rewarding. Nor should it be simply assumed that there was one single key to agricultural success—this is one of the more unfortunate by-products of thinking in terms of 'agricultural revolution'. It has to be remembered that agriculture was not a single industry but a series of linked enterprises each with differing combinations of inputs and outputs. This is one major reason why geography is central to its understanding, in the sense both of the geographical structure of the country and of geographical method. The variety of agricultural conditions prevailing in Britain and the linkages between varying agricultural regimes were essential factors of development. At the same time, there is an obvious advantage in the geographical method of using precise regional distinction at various spatial scales to isolate particular combinations of events and causes.

References

1. A. R. H. Baker and R. A. Butlin (eds.), *Studies of Field Systems in the British Isles*, (Cambridge, 1973); J. A. Yelling, *Common Field and Enclosure in England 1450–1850*, (London, 1977); R. A. Butlin, 'The enclosure of open fields and extinction of common rights in England c. 1600–1750: A review', in H. S. A. Fox and R. A. Butlin (eds.) *Change in the Countryside: Essays on Rural England, 1500–1900*, (London, 1979), pp. 65–82.
2. J. R. Wordie, 'The chronology of English enclosure, 1500– 1914', *Economic History Review*, 2nd ser., **36** (1983), pp. 483– 505.
3. D. N. McCloskey, 'The persistence of English common fields', in W. N. Parker and E. L. Jones (eds.), *European Peasants and their Markets*, (Princeton, 1975), pp. 73–119; C. J. Dahlman, *The Open Field System and Beyond*, (Cambridge, 1980).
4. E. C. K. Gonner, *Common Land and Inclosure*, (London, 1912, 1966), p. 199.
5. J. A. Yelling, 'Rationality in the common fields', *Economic History Review*, 2nd ser., **35** (1982), pp. 409–15; Yelling, *Common Field and Enclosure in England 1450–1850*.
6. R. I. Hodgson, 'The progress of enclosure in County Durham 1550–1870', in Fox and Butlin (eds.), *Change in the Countryside*, pp. 83–103.
7. H. C. Darby, *The Changing Fenland*, (Cambridge, 1983); M. Williams, *The Draining of the Somerset Levels* (Cambridge, 1970); J. Porter, 'Waste reclamation in the sixteenth and seventeenth centuries: the case of south-east Bowland 1550–1630', *Transactions of the Historical Society of Lancashire and Cheshire*, **127** (1978), pp. 1–23.
8. M. W. Beresford, *The Lost Villages of England*, (London, 1954); Yelling, *Common Field and Enclosure*, pp. 46–71; M. Reed, 'Enclosure in north Buckinghamshire 1500–1750', *Agricultural History Review*, **32** (1984), pp. 133–144.
9. J. E. Martin, *Feudalism to Capitalism*, (New Jersey, 1983), pp. 159–213; K. Lindley, *Fenland Riots and the English Revolution*, (London, 1982).
10. Yelling, *Common Field and Enclosure*, pp. 16–26; Butlin; 'The enclosure of open fields'; Reed, 'Enclosure in North Buckinghamshire'.
11. Yelling, *Common Field and Enclosure*, pp. 5–10, 26–9, 71– 94, 125–7; Baker and Butlin, *Studies of Field Systems*, passim.
12. H. Thorpe, 'The lord and the landscape', in D. R. Mills (ed.), *English Rural Communities*, (London, 1973), p. 58; Beresford, *The Lost Villages of England*, Yelling, *Common Field and Enclosure*, pp. 127–34; Reed, 'Enclosure in north Buckinghamshire'.
13. Wordie, 'The chronology of English enclosure', p. 495.
14. T. H. Ashton and C. H. E. Philpin (eds.), *The Brenner Debate: Agrarian Class Structure and Economic Development in Pre-Industrial Europe*, (Cambridge, 1985); R. A. Butlin, *The Transformation of Rural England c. 1580–1800*, (Oxford, 1982), pp. 32–41.
15. C. Clay, *Economic Expansion and Social Change: England 1500–1700, Volume 1* (Cambridge,

1984), pp. 142–64; C. Clay, 'Landlords and estate management in England', in J. Thirsk (ed.), *The Agrarian History of England and Wales Vii Agrarian Change*, (Cambridge, 1984), pp. 119–245; J. V. Beckett, 'The pattern of landownership in England and Wales 1660–1800', *Economic History Review*, **37** (1984), pp. 1–22.

16. Clay, *Economic Expansion and Social Change*, pp. 57–8; D. Mills (ed.), *English Rural Communities* (London, 1973); D. Mills, *Lord and Peasant in Nineteenth-Century Britain*, (London, 1980).

17. R. Brenner, 'Agrarian class structure and economic development in pre-Industrial Europe', and 'The agrarian roots of European capitalism', in Ashton and Philpin (eds.), *The Brenner Debate*, pp. 10–64, 213–327.

18. R. H. Tawney, *The Agrarian Problem in the Sixteenth Century*, (London, 1912), p. 34.

19. E. Kerridge, *Agrarian Problems in the Sixteenth Century and After*, (London, 1969).

20. R. B. Outhwaite, 'Progress and backwardness in English agriculture 1500–1650', *Economic History Review*, 2nd ser., **39** (1986), pp. 7–12.

21. M. Spufford, *Contrasting Communities: English Villages in the Sixteenth and Seventeenth Century*, (Cambridge, 1974), p. 91.

22. A. H. Johnson, *The Disappearance of the Small Landowner*, (London, 1909, 1963); G. E. Mingay, 'The size of farms in the eighteenth century', *Economic History Review*, 2nd ser., **14** (1961–2), pp. 469–88; Beckett, 'The pattern of landownership in England and Wales;.

23. D. B. Grigg, 'Small and large farms in England and Wales: their size and distribution', *Geography*, **48** (1963), pp. 268– 79.

24. Clay, *Economic Expansion and Social Change*, pp. 85–91;

25. L. A. Parker, 'The agrarian revolution in Cotesbach 1501– 1612', in W. G. Hoskins (ed.), *Studies in Leicestershire Agrarian History*, (Leicester, 1949), pp. 41–76.

26. E. A. Wrigley, 'Urban growth and agricultural change', in E. A. Wrigley, *People, Cities and Wealth*, (Oxford, 1987), pp. 157– 93.

27. Recent surveys are R. W. Malcolmson, *Life and Labour in England 1700–1780*, (London, 1981); K. Wrightson, *English Society 1560–1680*, (London, 1982); and K. D. M. Snell, *Annals of the Labouring Poor: Social Change in Agrarian England 1660– 1900*, (Cambridge, 1985).

28. J. Thirsk, 'Industries in the countryside', in F. J. Fisher (ed.), *Essays in the Economic and Social History of Tudor and Stuart England*, (London, 1961), pp. 70–88.

29. P. Frost, 'Yeomen and metalsmiths: livestock in the dual economy of South Staffordshire 1560–1720', *Agricultural History Review*, **29** (1981), pp. 32–4.

30. Mills, *Lord and Peasant in Nineteenth-Century Britain*. For case studies of the Leicestershire villages of Shepshed and Bottesford see D. Levine, *Family Formation in an Age of Nascent Capitalism*, (London, 1977).

31. Wrigley, 'Urban growth and agricultural change', J. A. Chartres, *Internal Trade in England 1500–1700*, (London, 1977).

32. According to the Phelps Brown and Hopkins index. Figure taken from Wrigley, 'Urban growth and agricultural change, p. 159.

33. D. Defoe, *A Tour Through the Whole Island of Great Britain 1724–6*, Vol. 2, (London, 1974), p. 199.

34. N. S. B. Gras, *The Evolution of the English Corn Market*, (Cambridge, Mass., 1915), pp. 97, 43, 95.

35. A. H. John. 'The course of agricultural change 1680–1760', in L. S. Presnell (ed.), *Studies in the Industrial Revolution*, (London, 1960), p. 128; see also J. A. Chartres, 'The marketing of agricultural produce', in (ed.) Thirsk *The Agrarian History of England and Wales*, pp. 406–501; and E. A. Wrigley, 'A simple model of London's importance in changing English society and economy 1650–1750', in Wrigley, *People, Cities and Wealth*, pp. 133–56.

36. Notably Clay *Economic Expansion and Social Change*, pp. 57– 72.

37. F. J. Fisher. 'The development of the London food market 1540–1640', *Economic History Review*, 1st ser., **5** (1935), pp. 46–54, reprinted in E. M. Carus-Wilson (ed.) *Essays in Economic History*, Vol. 1, (London, 1954), pp. 135–51.

38. Defoe, *A Tour through the Whole Island of Great Britain*, p. 72.

39. R. Trow-Smith, *A History of British Livestock Husbandry 1700–1900*, (London, 1959), p. 12 See also his *History of British Livestock Husbandry to 1700*, (London, 1957).

40. On this division and its subsequent development see V. Skipp, *Crisis and Development, An Ecological Case Study of the Forest of Arden*, (Cambridge, 1978); Yelling, *Common Field and Enclosure*, pp. 175–92.

41. J. Thirsk, *Economic Policy and Projects: The Development of a Consumer Society in Early Modern England*, (Oxford, 1978).

42. Fisher, 'The development of the London food market', M. Thick, 'Market gardening', in J. Thirsk (ed.), *The Agrarian History of England and Wales*, pp. 503–75.

43. P. R. Edwards, 'The horse trade of the midlands in the seventeenth century', *Agricultural History Review*, **27** (1979), pp. 90–100.

44. P. Glennie, Continuity and change in Hertfordshire agriculture 1550–1700 : 1 Patterns of production', *Agricultural History Review*, **36** (1988), pp. 55–75.

45. (Lord) Ernle, *English Farming Past and Present*, (London, 1912, 1961), p. 57.

46. M. A. Havinden, 'Agricultural progress in open field Oxfordshire', *Agricultural History Review*, **9** (1961), pp. 73– 88; E. L. Jones (ed.), *Agriculture and Economic Growth in England 1650–1815*, (London, 1967), pp. 152–71.

47. E. W. Kerridge, *The Agricultural Revolution*, (London, 1967).

48. *Ibid.*, p. 194.

49. *Ibid.*, p. 202.

50. *Ibid.*, p. 211.

51. J. A. Yelling, 'Livestock numbers and agricultural development 1540–1750: A study of East Worcestershire';, in T. R. Slater and P. J. Jarvis (ed.), *Field and Forest: An Historical Geography of Warwickshire and Worcestershire*, (Norwich, 1982), pp. 281–99; P. Glennie, 'Continuity and change in Hertfordshire agriculture.'

52. M. Overton, 'Estimating crop yields from probate inventories: an example from East Anglia 1585–1730', *Jnl. of Economic History*, **39** (1979), pp. 55–75.

53. P. Glennie, 'Continuity and change in Hertfordshire agriculture 1550–1700, Part II: Trends in crop yields and their determinants', *Agricultural History Review*, **36**, (1988), pp. 145–61.

54. Yelling, *Common Field and Enclosure*, pp. 148–56.

55. M. Overton, 'The diffusion of agricultural innovations in early modern England: turnips and clover in Norfolk and Suffolk 1580–1740', *Transactions of the Institute of British Geographers*, new ser., **10** (1985), pp. 205–22.

56. Glennie 'Continuity and change in Hertfordshire agriculture'. (Part II).

57. Overton, 'The diffusion of agricultural innovations in early modern England'.

58. J. A. Yelling, 'Probate inventories and the geography of livestock farming: a study of East Worcestershire 1540–1750', *Transactions of the Institute of British Geographers*, **51** (1970), pp. 111–26.

59. D. M. Palliser, 'Tawney's century; brave new world or malthusian trap?', *Economic History Review*, 2nd ser., **35** (1982), pp. 339–53; R. B Outhwaite, 'Progress and backwardness in English agriculture'.

60. P. J. Bowden, 'Agricultural prices, wages, farm profits and rents', in Thirsk (ed.), *The Agrarian History of England and Wales*, pp. 1–118.

8

Industry and Towns 1500–1730

P. D. Glennie

Contemporaries described early-sixteenth-century England for a variety of motives, but both foreign and English writers recognized the peripheral position of the British Isles in European life. Britain was not only geographically peripheral, but also marginal in economic, technological and cultural developments. Two centuries later, this view was unthinkable. In 1726 Defoe claimed England 'the most flourishing and opulent country in the world':[1] the most industrial country in Europe, more urbanized than any but the Netherlands, and central in transformed networks of international trade.

To recognize the relative rapidity of English industrial and urban expansion, though, is easier than to quantify or map it. Most information about industry is qualitative. Often we can identify areas of significant industrial production from contemporary writers or fiscal, legal and business records, but we cannot define the precise extent of a locality dependent on particular industrial livelihoods, nor the exact size of the workforce, nor quantify output.

Calculating how many people engaged in industry or lived in towns poses two major difficulties. First, lacking comprehensive occupational surveys, it is necessary to work with source materials compiled for other purposes. Such sources are usually in some way selective of the population they cover, and patchy in geographical coverage, which makes it dangerous to argue from negative evidence. Secondly, households performing industrial work were not simply 'industrial households', since many incorporated both agriculture and one or more types of industry. Within these multi-task households, industrial work was often of seasonally varying intensity, and was balanced against the labour demands of other activities performed within the household. But even though counting occupations is an imperfect measure of industrial activity, the trends towards greater industrialization and urbanization are indisputable. The figures in Table 8.1 represent the best current guesses.[2]

In analysing the dramatic transformation from economic backwater to pre-eminence, industry and towns cannot be considered self-contained sectors. Industrial growth cannot be explained solely by changes within industry, and the dynamic of the urban system was not wholly internal. At macro-scales, both industrial and urban developments were intimately related to greater agricultural productivity, and to the trading profits of successful colonialism. At micro-scale, much industry took place in small domestic units alongside agricultural pursuits. Interactions

Table 8.1: Approximate composition of English population *c.* 1520–1700.

	c. 1520	*c.* 1600	*c.* 1670	*c.* 1700
National population ('000)	2400	4110	4980	5060
Total non-agricultural population ('000)	575	1235	1970	2280
As percentage of national population	24	30	40	45
Rural non-agricultural population ('000)	450	900	1290	1430
Rural non-agricultural as percentage of rural	20	24	30	34
Urban population ('000)	125	335	680	850
London ('000)	55	200	475	575
Urban population excluding London ('000)	70	135	205	275
Number of towns >10,000	2	4	4	6
Other towns >5000	7	15	21	25

between agriculture and industry within households continued to influence industrial change.[3]

These linkages have been recognized by major models of industrial geographical change, which have stressed the ecological and agricultural settings of industry, and the increasing penetration of market economy channelled through urban centres, as influencing the changing geography of the industrial economy.[4]

This chapter first considers regional and local occupational structures to highlight major features of the geography of early-modern industry. An outline of changes in the vital textile industries leads to consideration of the lively debates concerning theories of 'proto-industrialization'. Attention then shifts to mining, metallurgy and related activities, and to the growing range of 'consumer goods' industries. We turn next to urban growth, and the dominant role of London in national economy and society, before highlighting the growth of urban specialization within an increasingly integrated national urban system. The final section is devoted to changing consumption patterns and their impact on urban landscapes.

Estimating Occupational Structure

The political arithmeticians first hazarded guesses of national occupational structure in the late seventeenth century. Gregory King estimated in 1688 that 110,000 households depended on craft and trade, of a national total of 1,390,586.[5] This is now regarded as a massive underestimate. With contemporary estimates of occupational structure scarce and sometimes demonstrably inaccurate, historians and geographers have turned to analysing occupational evidence from various documentary sources.

In this pre-census period, most sources of occupational information are socially biased in their coverage and available for only a limited number of places. Probate records or lists of urban freemen, for example, deal only with the relatively wealthy, but not necessarily for groups of equivalent wealth in different probate jurisdictions or towns (so that only crude comparisons between areas are possible). As indicators of major economic specializations, these and similar sources are invaluable and have been widely used. However, they help little in estimating an area's overall occupational composition.

This section will focus on sources that appear to provide near-comprehensive, unbiased listings of (adult male) populations, and on parish registers. Although not legally required to do so, some incumbents recorded the occupations of bridegrooms or men being buried, and of fathers whose children were baptized or buried. For all sources, however, the apparent neatness of occupational data may be illusory. Caution in interpreting occupation counts, and geographical patterns of recorded occupations, is necessary for three reasons.[6]

First, men were usually ascribed a single occupation, even if their household depended on income from several part-time activities rather than one full-time occupation. Most occupations were becoming more specialized, but the pace of change varied among industries and regions. After *c.* 1540, analysis of probate inventories (lists of a testator's movable possessions) may shed light on whether crafts were practised on a part-time basis.

Second, familiar occupational terms like weaver or bricklayer could cover wide variations in forms of work, and obscure major changes in work relations. A carpenter could be an independent artisan, based on a domestic workshop or working at customers' premises, or might be a wage-labouring employee. Conversely, a proliferation of new terms could reflect either real occupational diversity, or mere fashion. Again, ancillary documentation can illuminate the activities behind novel terms. In making inter-regional comparisons of occupations, the use of relatively broad occupational groups which can accommodate a range of suspected meanings of terms has much to recommend it.

Finally, most sources of occupational data refer mainly to men, and reveal comparatively little about women's work. The importance of women in industrial work is clear from qualitative sources such as diaries and commentaries, but to quantify female labour is virtually impossible. Some textile tasks like spinning and, later, lacemaking, were largely female preserves. It was not uncommon in many trades for a widow to take over the business of her late husband. In some urban sectors, especially petty trading, women were more important than men, and in the larger towns female migrants outnumbered males, attracted by work as domestic servants and in the victualling trades.[7]

Recent work underscores the range of manufacturing industries in which women worked. The stereotype of pre-industrial women's 'domestic passivity' owes much to nineteenth-century sensibilities, and conceals an eighteenth-century narrowing of female roles. Many trades became progressively limited to men, whereas, more than one-fifth of seventeenth century adolescents apprenticed by Southampton parish authorities were girls, and their masters included weavers, tailors and joiners.[8] There was a social class dimension to the sexual division of labour. Female participation in industrial work and trading was highest among the lowest social classes, in part because the family persisted longer amongst the poor as the basic unit of production.

Changing Occupational Structures

There had been striking concentrations of industrial occupations in the Middle Ages. Some were still prominent in *c.* 1500. The scale of the textile industry in south-west Suffolk, for example, is clear from surviving military survey returns for Babergh Hundred in 1522.[9] Occupations are specified for 1570 of 1886 named men, of which 315 (17%) were textile-related. Moreover, many seem to have been full-time workers. Whereas most (99 of 119) of the relatively wealthy clothiers and cloth-makers owned land, the corresponding figures for the poorer textile crafts were much lower (27 of 112 weavers, seven of 41 fullers, and two of 27 shearmen). Amongst craftsmen such as carpenters, bakers, butchers and shoemakers about 25 per cent owned land. While some may have rented land, it is likely that many depended largely on their craft. Only 7 per cent of those designated 'labourer' held land (41 of 562).

Another document resembling an 'occupational census' is a list of able-bodied men in Gloucestershire in 1608.[10] It ascribes industrial or trading occupations to 43·8 per cent of men listed — not dissimilar to the proportion at the 1831 census, although the county's population was then larger. Some localities exhibited intense specializ-ation. Around Stroud, Minchinhampton, and Dursley several parishes had a majority of men listed as weavers or clothworkers, besides various other crafts. Local industrial specializations of this intensity were rare, but even the arable-dominated lowland countryside was far from exclusively agricultural. Many types of craftsmen and tradesmen were widely distributed. In the south-eastern counties making up the Assizes Home Circuit, more than a quarter of men mentioned were ascribed craft or trade occupations (Table 8.2).[11]

From the 1750s a new source of occupational information is available for some areas, the parish lists from which men were balloted for militia service. These lists recorded able-bodied males aged 18–45, and specified their occupations. Although

Table 8.2: Percentage composition of non-agricultural sectors *c.* 1600.

	Gloucestershire 1608	Home Counties 1575–1603
Mining and quarrying	2.5	0.0
Textiles	35.3	10.7
Leather	2.7	4.2
Woodworking	9.1	13.2
Metalworking	7.5	8.9
Construction	4.6	3.8
Food and drink	5.2	8.1
Clothing and footwear	16.9	20.1
Dealing and retailing	9.5	24.0
Carriage and transport	3.7	3.9
Other crafts	0.9	1.9
Professions and services	1.8	1.2

Table 8.3: Occupational data from selected militia lists.

| County (date) | Percentages of occupations among listed men | | | | |
	Agriculture	Textiles and mining	Crafts and trade	Labourers	Servant
Herts (1759)	11.0	1.0	29.4	35.1	19.9
Bucks (1759)	14.4	1.0	32.0	28.9	23.7
Kent (1765)	14.7	0.8	24.1	21.2	38.5
Northumberland (1762)	33.8	13.5	25.7	8.7	16.9
Northamptonshire (1777)	15.3	12.9	30.9	19.1	20.9

analysis of the lists is complicated by various permitted exemptions, the broad outlines of regional occupational structures can be reconstructed (Table 8.3).[12] The use of county units understates specialization in particular communities since there were non-industrial areas in even the most industrial counties. Even so, the mining and textiles presence in Northumberland and Northamptonshire respectively was substantial. By comparison with the southern counties, the textile/mining workforce had the net effect of drawing men from the labouring group. The proportion of men assigned non-agricultural occupations other than in textiles and mining was fairly similar everywhere. The independent artisan was an almost universal figure throughout the period, particularly in south-east England. Indeed, in many areas it was only much later that the village craftsman became less ubiquitous.[13]

Textile and mining communities again appear very distinct in occupational composition. The most specialized parishes in the Northumberland and Northamptonshire militia lists were markedly more specialized than their southern counterparts. In Northamptonshire villages like Crick, Corby, Rothwell and Rockingham, more than 40 per cent of listed men were weavers. Several southern Northumberland townships were dominated by similar proportions of coal miners. In Hertfordshire parishes, single occupations (in the leather, wood and malting trades) rarely accounted for even 10 per cent of listed men.

Broadly similar contrasts can be drawn among parishes for whom earlier data are available from parish registers (Table 8.4).[14] In parts of western and northern England, single activities could dominate occupational profiles. The diversity of urban occupations provides a notable contrast, as to a lesser extent, do rural and small market parishes around the capital. Very different were the much more isolated parishes of rural Shropshire and Lincolnshire. Here the scarcity of full-time non-agricultural occupations was striking.

Thus when historians write that 'rural industry was not a feature of every part of the country'[15] this is true only so far as we take 'industry' to mean what eighteenth-century Englishmen called 'manufactures'—principally textiles, mining and metal-working. By a broader definition including artisan crafts and trades, industry was much more widespread. A substantial proportion of households depended on non-agricultural livelihoods even in areas without 'manufactures' for national and overseas markets.

Table 8.4: Occupations recorded in early modern parish registers.

Parish	Dates	Gentlemen	Farming	Mining	Textiles	Clothing and footwear	Food, dealers and transport	Metal-work	Other craft and services	Labourers	(n)
Tottenham, Middlesex	1574–92	2	24	—	1	6	5	8	5	43	(178)
Myddle, Shropshire	1540–99	9	61	—	2	6	—	1	7	15	(254)
	1600–60	7	49	—	5	5	—	1	7	26	(277)
Colyton, Devon	1609–12	9	11	—	12	5	4	6	11	42	(154)
Clee, Lincolnshire	1609–40	4	24	—	—	2	2	—	—	68	(126)
Layston, Herts.	1618–33	5	12	—	4	14	24	3	15	25	(155)
Bishops Stortford,	1616–27	1	6	—	3	18	22	6	18	19	(120)
Hertfordshire	1685–98	2	6	—	3	12	31	6	22	17	(285)
Newcastle upon Tyne	1660–69	3	1	7	3	13	38	4	26	5	(998)
Sheffield, South Yorks.	1655–59	4	13	—	----10---- (Textiles + Clothing)		4	50	14 (+)	9 (—)	(311)
	1700–09	2	6	—	----8---- (Textiles + Clothing)		6	55	8 (+)	15 (—)	(2681)
Rochdale, Radcliffe, Middleton, Lancs.	1653–59	—	46	2	33	----------17---------- (Clothing → Other)				3	(376)
Middleton, Lancs.	1730–34	—	17	—	62	----------20---------- (Clothing → Other)				1	(357)
Up Holland, Lancs.	1700–03	—	15	—	20	----29---- (Clothing → Other)				37	(178)
	1720–33	—	16	6	29	----31---- (Clothing → Other)				12	(434)
Oldham, Lancs.	1725–27	—	8	6	57	----19---- (Clothing → Other)				11	(536)
Saddleworth, West Yorks.	1722–34	—	11	—	79	----10---- (Clothing → Other)				------	(869)
Otley, West Yorks.	1721–40	2	27	—	12	8	6	----28---- (Metal + Other)		17	(1614)
Wharfedale, West Yorks.	1721–40	2	40	4	7	8	4	----18---- (Metal + Other)		16	(2100)

Percentage of men recorded in occupational groups

Source: See endnote 14.

The significance of particular industries was not just a matter of the size of their workforces. Both contemporaries and most economic historians have judged the relative importance of types of industry primarily in terms of exports. On this criterion there is no disputing the pre-eminence of the various branches of the textile industry. Although manufacturing became much more diverse, expanding production of textiles remained the lynch pin of the export economy.

Textiles Industries

Beneath their continued dominance of exports, textile production was characterized by considerable dynamism. Instability stemmed from depressions in export markets and shifts in foreign and domestic demand for cloth of various types. Some production regions were much more durable than others, either because demand for their staple products was robust, or because they switched production to fabrics for which demand was buoyant, applying new techniques or using new fibres. Both environmental and social obstacles to innovation might need to be overcome: raw material availability, production skills, labour willing to adopt changed work practices, wages sufficiently low for competitive pricing, and access to markets. All these factors varied, and as a result the expansion of the cloth industries was uneven in its chronology and uneven in its geography.

'Textiles' covers an enormous, sometimes bewildering, variety of cloth types, which contemporaries used a wide range of terms to describe.[16] Some names referred to the type and quality of raw material, others to variants of weaving technique, while still others related to particular finishing techniques. Yet other cloth names were general descriptions of quality, colour and appearance, which need not directly relate to production techniques or raw material. Moreover, contemporaries' use of terminology varied across the country and over time. Some modern typologies portray a rigid and intricate system of terminology, but these over-formalize the distinctions between cloth types that contemporaries seem to have made.

Bearing these difficulties in mind, Fig. 8.1 identifies the major locations of textile production in *c.* 1500 and *c.* 1700. Within the areas indicated, the intensity of textile employment and production varied. In national terms, the major producing areas changed more than Fig. 8.1 indicates, because the identity of the most important producing and exporting areas changed. Whereas in *c.* 1500 the dominant areas were East Anglia and the West Country, two centuries later the former had been outstripped by the latter and, increasingly, parts of northern England.[17] The major textile regions, like metalworking regions, contained very local specializations which are glossed over on generalized maps of 'textile areas'. Changes in the location of production were often rapid and on these occasions local specializations could be short-lived.

Organizational Change: the Proto-industrialization Debates

The term refers to a collection of notions concerning the organization and location of industries in the centuries prior to the late-eighteenth-century emergence of factory

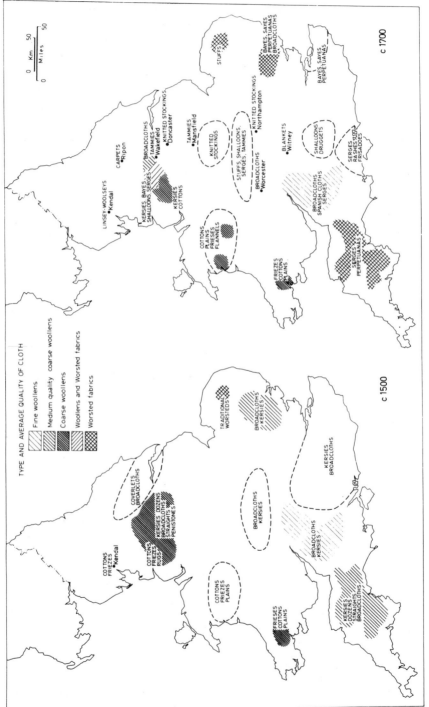

Fig. 8.1. Distribution of major textile specializations, *c.* 1500 and *c.* 1700.

TYPE AND AVERAGE QUALITY OF CLOTH

Fine woollens

Medium quality coarse woollens

Coarse woollens

Woollens and Worsted fabrics

Worsted fabrics

c 1700

STUFFS

BAYES, SAYES
PERPETUANAS
BROADCLOTHS

BAYES, SAYES
PERPETUANAS

CARPETS
•Ripon

BROADCLOTHS
TAMMIES
•Wakefield
KNITTED STOCKINGS,
•Doncaster

LINSEY-WOOLSEYS
•Kendal

TAMMIES
•Mansfield

KNITTED
STOCKINGS

STUFFS, SHALLOONS,
SERGES, TAMMIES

KERSIES, BAYES,
SHALLOONS, SERGES
KERSIES
COTTONS

KNITTED STOCKINGS,
•Northampton
BROADCLOTHS
•Worcester

BLANKETS
•Witney

SHALLOONS
DRUGGETS

COTTONS
PLAINS
FRIESES
FLANNELS

BROADCLOTHS
SPANISH CLOTHS
SERGES

SERGES
RASHES
FRISADOES

FRIESES
COTTONS
PLAINS

SERGES
PERPETUANAS

c 1500

TRADITIONAL
WORSTEDS

BROADCLOTHS
KERSIES

COVERLETS
BROADCLOTHS

COTTONS
FRIEZES
•Kendal

KERSIES DOZENS
BROADCLOTHS
STRAIGHTS
PENISTONES

COTTONS
FRIEZES
RUGS

BROADCLOTHS
KERSIES

KERSIES
BROADCLOTHS

COTTONS
FRIEZES
PLAINS

BROADCLOTHS
KERSIES

FRIESES
COTTONS
PLAINS

KERSIES
DOZENS
STRAIGHTS
BROADCLOTHS

0 Km 50

0 Miles 50

industrialization. There is insufficient space here to differentiate the various approaches in detail, or to develop criticism at length,[18] but the central foci of the theories can be summarized briefly. Naturally, some versions have placed more stress on particular points than others, but nuances of emphasis will not be discussed here.

The key components of proto-industrialization theories fall into three groups. First, the identification of key factors affecting the initial location and subsequent development of early-modern industry. Second, the identification of an inherent dynamism in organizational change in industry. Third, the claim that these organizational changes paved the way for the emergence of 'modern' factory industry, by establishing features often incorrectly regarded as products of factory industrialization rather than as precursors of it.

It has long been commonplace that late-medieval and early-modern industry was often found in rural areas, but particularly in certain types of rural locations.[19] Several factors appear to have been preconditions for this, though not sufficient causes in themselves. First, the availability of free-time in households where gaining subsistence from a smallholding was not a full-time undertaking. Whether free-time was available daily (in most branches of pastoral agriculture) or seasonally (in arable-based mixed farming) was initially less important than that it was available at all.[20] Second, partible inheritance practices (in which family holdings became fragmented through division amongst heirs) prompted families to engage in by-employments such as spinning and weaving to augment subsistence incomes. Third, where landownership was divided amongst several manorial lords, especially if these were absentees, there was less scope for direct manorial restriction of tenants' activities.

Several sources of dynamism in proto-industrial production systems have been discussed. First, the relationships between population growth, subdivided landholdings and industrial employment embodied positive feedback. In-migration and earlier marriage amongst proto-industrial producers led to population growth which exacerbated fragmentation of landholdings, hence increasing households' commitment to industrial work. Meanwhile, growing industrial employment encouraged further in-migration. Second, and especially in Marxian formulations, merchants have an intrinsic 'need' to intensify production so as to appropriate more of the value produced by proto-industrial workers. In its crudest versions, this is merely an expression of 'the innate tendency of capital to accumulate'. Third, technological change put pressure on all proto-industrial systems to produce more intensively in order to remain competitive. Technological innovations such as the knitting machine provided opportunities for entrepreneurs to exert pressure on out-workers. Being beyond the means of domestic workers, they were provided by entrepreneurs who, with the possible sanction of removing machinery, thereby gained control over the pace of production. They were thus better able to co-ordinate output with the state of national and international markets.

A further dynamic originated from the demand side. Demand for the major proto-industrial products—clothing, household fabrics and metalware—was growing. On domestic markets, consumption patterns were changing as the large middling groups in English society devoted a growing part of their rising income to consumer goods. International demand grew as English products achieved dominance in expanding world, especially colonial, markets. While fashion changes (such as the replacement of pewter by earthenware) brought about some absolute declines in demand for certain products, the context for most proto-industry was one of expansion.

Where proto-industrialization had developed to its fullest extent, industrial organization possessed many 'modern' features. Some enterprises were large (even if production was dispersed), and wage-labour and substantial task specialization were widespread (the latter depriving individual producers of the skill to alone transform raw materials into finished products). Workforces were co-ordinated by entrepreneurs in whose hands substantial capital was accumulating. These long-term developments, it is argued, smoothed the way to factory industrialization, which consequently appears less revolutionary a break with past experience than was thought by early-twentieth-century economic historians.

The proto-industrial literature has been criticized at several levels: empirical generalizations are questioned, theoretical categories are dissected, and underlying assumptions scrutinized.[21] Evaluating the criticisms is complicated because the theory consists of several 'targets' (for example, neo-classical and Marxist versions, both with functionalist and non-functionalist formations) rather than a single entity. Moreover the 'targets' are moving, in that recent authors have attempted to remedy unsatisfactory elements in early theories. The critical literature needs careful reading, since criticisms of particular versions have sometimes been used to argue that the whole concept of a proto-industrial theory is invalid.

Central to the views of certain critics who believe that concepts of proto-industry should be abandoned is a particular belief about the role of theory in historical explanation. This is most explicit where Clarkson writes that the 'purpose of a model is to provide a set of generalized explanations of historical developments. This is done by observing regularities in the data and then, by a process of induction, establishing reasons for them.'[22] Not only is this sort of inductive approach thoroughly discredited by debates on the philosophy of both the natural and social sciences over the last quarter century, but is explicitly rejected in even the early elaborations of proto-industrialization theory,[23] which stress the theorization of *processes* of industrial change rather than their geographical *outcomes* (such as 'the geographical pattern of factories').

This affects how the theory is to be 'tested'. Coleman argues that the theories fail an empirical test because not all proto-industrial regions later developed factory industry and because some prominent regions of early factory industrialization had not been significant locations for proto-industry.[24] This is unnecessarily naive, since theorists have stressed (a) that proto-industrial regions were often competing with one another, leading to 'unsuccessful' regions being 'deindustrialized', and (b) that contextual factors such as political stability, access to financial expertise, and exogenous developments on world markets, and the outcome of colonial wars, could be crucial to the survival of regional industries.[25]

The problem with Coleman's argument may be clarified by a biological analogy. An equivalent argument would reject evolutionary theory on the grounds that not all ancestral primate lines have developed into *homo sapiens*. But biologists would hardly claim that the 'failure' of Neanderthal man meant that evolutionary theory should be rejected. Rather it demonstrates the influence of contingent exogenous factors (such as environmental change), and of competition between primate lines to survive.

Calls for abandonment of the proto-industrialization debates are premature: the usefulness of proto-industrial concepts is still an open question. This is not to deny that important problems need to be addressed, of which four will be mentioned here. First, there is a tendency to see urban industry and rural industry as competitive categories, with dominance of overall production moving from one to the other over time. This underplays the degree of integration between town and country, which increased markedly over the period, as well as the numerous examples of proto-industries in towns.[26]

Second, advocates of proto-industrialization have consistently exaggerated the 'non-modernity' of artisan crafts, which are discussed as relics of feudal economies, awaiting technical and organizational changes to release them from stagnation to factory forms. Their potential role as dynamic elements in local economies is neglected in proto-industrial theories, yet the handicraft sectors were major sources of employment growth.[27] A more satisfactory treatment of them is Jan De Vries' specialization model.[28]

Third, the focus on industrial organization has overshadowed the topic of productivity gains, which have been asserted rather than demonstrated. However, the issue of productivity gains is central to debates about the impacts of increases in scale or of more specialized divisions of labour. There is very little direct evidence about the productivity of labour, capital, or raw materials. Attempts to build models incorporating estimates of output, and estimated volumes and costs of all inputs to an activity (raw materials, fuel, labour, time, capital, depreciation), remain highly speculative. The proto-industrial sectors and large-plant industries were probably the main settings for productivity improvements, but even comparatively small changes in work pattern in the artisan trades, may have generated considerable productivity improvements. The whole topic of productivity patterns needs further research.

Fourth, too little is said of industries with altogether different forms of organization. Some activities were incapable of being split into a series of mobile production stages. Shipbuilding, for instance, was large-scale by its very nature, and Royal dockyards may have been the largest of all early-modern industrial concerns, with highly specialized proletarian workforces. Some chemical processes were only technically feasible in relatively large-scale plant. Other activities were locationally constrained to a far greater extent, being dependent on materials found only in particular places. The most obvious and important of these was mining, although industries involving the processing of bulk colonial foodstuffs at major ports were locationally constrained in a parallel way.

Mineral-based Industries

Whether mineral deposits were exploited depended on both environmental and economic factors. Technology, communications and capital availability all influenced the geography of coal and metal mining. The major coalfields also became the pre-eminent sites for a host of industrial processing and metalworking activities. By the 1730s, coal had been substituted for charcoal or wood in most major industrial processes, except the smelting of ores.

In the 1550s coal output was of more than local significance only in north-eastern England, where it is estimated that output from the Tyneside industry reached about 40,000 tons annually. The north-east retained its leading position through a massive and sustained expansion. Coal output is estimated to have reached about 800,000 tons by the early seventeenth century, and about 1,400,000 tons by the early eighteenth.[29] Large-scale production combined with relatively easy movement of coal on waggonways to the Tyne and along the river to Newcastle and Tynemouth for transfer to sea-going craft enabled the north-east to dominate coal supplies around the North Sea. Above all, vast quantities were shipped to London, where sea-coal became the major domestic and industrial fuel. Along the Tyne, lower quality coal sustained fuel-hungry industries like salt extraction from seawater. The production costs of evaporating sea water were several times those of purifying rock salt, but inland rock-salt sites faced such high overland transport costs that the Tyneside industry enjoyed an overall cost advantage.[30]

The Tyneside coal industry became dominated by producers able to invest heavily in tunnelling and pumping technology. From the 1720s several coal-owners organized a cartel known as the 'Grand Alliance'. The cartel maintained prices by restricting output and shipments to London, bought up actual or potential rival collieries in order to suspend production there (so-called 'Dead Rent' collieries), and bought land in order to deny rival pits direct access to the Tyne. The geography of investment and production within the coalfield thus reflected the organizational character of the industry as much as it did the overcoming of environmental constraints by new technology.[31]

By c. 1700 several coalfields, even some lacking proximity to navigable water, were foci for important industrial concentrations. Coal extraction became widespread in Warwickshire and elsewhere in the West Midlands, in Nottinghamshire, in south-west Lancashire, around Whitehaven in Cumbria, in South Wales, in the Forest of Dean and in Somerset. Initially, the characteristic unit of production in all these areas was the small, independent pit, with a comparatively unspecialized workforce numbering less than a dozen. Steam engines were widely used for pumping by 1730, although the large-scale deep mines that dominated Tyneside mining remained atypical. Many early engines were very inefficient, but a coal mine was one location where high fuel consumption was not a significant handicap! The combined output of these fields probably exceeded a quarter of a million tons by 1730, with most destined for local industrial use.[32]

Output of metal ores also grew markedly, particularly of iron, lead, tin and copper. Although smelting was the major activity in which coal had not replaced charcoal, important innovations had nevertheless occurred. In the mid sixteenth century, blast furnaces were introduced, and by 1600 the iron industry had expanded beyond its traditional Wealden centres to the ore-fields of Yorkshire, south Wales and the West Midlands.[33] The larger production units enabled by blast furnaces provided significant economies of scale since fuel accounted for 60–75% of smelting costs. As the scale of production grew, the iron industry became characterized by highly capitalized plants employing proletarian workers. Large-scale works were also the norm in the refining of copper, lead and glass, in the extraction of salt from seawater, in papermaking and in shipbuilding.[34]

The metal industries provided materials for a host of manufacturing processes. Coal became the usual fuel for metalworking and smithing much earlier than for smelting, and metalworking arose wherever coal and metal deposits were found in proximity. Major specializations meeting national markets developed around Birmingham and its satellite towns, and in South Yorkshire. Several metalware trades provide examples of proto-industrial developments.[35] Smaller concentrations of metalworking were widely distributed throughout the coalfields, meeting local demands for items such as tools, horseshoes, nails, pins, cutlery, pewter and brass.[36]

New and 'Consumer Goods' Industries

The broadening of England's industrial base involved more than exploiting newly accessible resources and shaping them into tools or consumer goods. Three additional considerations stimulated industrial imitation and innovation. First, government saw English dependence on continental industries as threatening political security and national wealth. Governments grants of monopolies encouraged domestic production of commodities such as alum (important in dyeing) and gunpowder. Second, stimulation of small-scale manufacturers (notably textiles) was viewed by landowners and town corporations as a means of alleviating poverty. This social engineering had two goals: to diminish the charge of the underemployed poor on local ratepayers, and to stabilize a potentially volatile social group.[37]

Finally, numerous consumer industries were stimulated by shifting consumer preferences and by long-term population growth (augmented by the expanding North American colonies, which obtained most of their manufactured goods from Britain). These factors led to significant increases in demand for cheap utility goods and for more luxurious clothes, furniture and ornaments. As fashion in dress, food and domestic decoration became a major arena of competition for social status, so the links between cultural change and economic change became more tightly drawn. Changing tastes and new opportunities produced by colonial expansion were combined in the raw material processing industries that became concentrated at the major international ports of London and Bristol: sugar refining, and tobacco, coffee and tea processing. By the 1730s, consumption of these refined foods was geographically widespread, well beyond the London area (Fig. 8.2).

London was overwhelmingly the most important centre for these new industries. As social trends diffused down the urban hierarchy from the capital so, at a lag, did many of the industries and trades that met them. Hardly a market town in the country escaped the proliferation of artisan trades: joiners, bakers, cabinet makers, brass workers, confectioners, clockmakers and jewellers. Where production was not yet widespread by the early eighteenth century, the parallel proliferation of retail shopkeepers and itinerant sellers brought new consumer goods almost literally to the doorsteps of millions of consumers (Fig. 8.2).[38]

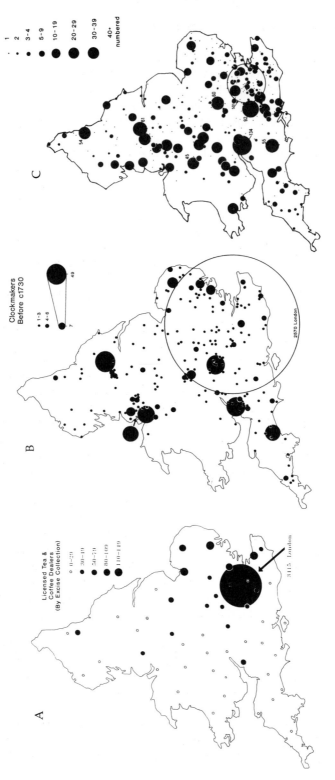

Fig. 8.2. Aspects of the supply of consumer goods. (A) Dealers in tea and coffee, 1736–37. *Source:* Chartres, 'Food consumption', p. 176 and personal communication. (B) Location of clockmakers recorded 1560–1730. Compiled from names listed in B. Loomes, *Directory of British Clockmakers before 1750*, (1982). (C) Licensed chapmen in 1697–98. *Source:* Spufford, *Small Books*, p. 119.

Urban Growth and the Growing Urban System

Urban historians and geographers have debated whether analysis of the urban system is best pursued through investigating the almost universal urban functions of marketing, handicraft, victualling, and services, or whether 'it is by concentrating upon key functions, rather than common features, that most insight is likely to be gained into the nature of pre-industrial urban economies and the reasons for their rise or decline.'[39] However, there is no need to choose one approach exclusively. Most questions about the geography of urbanization require consideration both of factors affecting the urban system in general and of the particular features and contexts of individual localities.

Contemporary usage of the term 'town' embraced places varying hugely in size, setting, functions, and composition. Even some settlements with populations under one thousand were clearly regarded as towns, distinct from surrounding villages and hamlets. Their physical appearance and non-agrarian functions, rather than size, were key features in the perception of places as urban. Even the smallest towns were important in familiarizing potential migrants with novel features of urban life. In Corfield's words 'small towns constituted accepted and acceptable access points to the urban network.'[40]

Differentiating towns by size, role and character, four 'levels' of towns in the urban system are conventionally distinguished: London, which stands alone in size and range of functions throughout the period, then the provincial capitals (such as Norwich, Bristol and Newcastle), then the country towns (forming the backbone of provincial urban society), and finally the several hundred small markets (without corporate urban status, but with some central place functions).[41] The latter two categories can be subdivided to reflect the distinctive experience of particular types of town, especially as urban functions became more specialized. For example, the growths of dockyard towns and leisure towns (such as spas) have been analysed in terms of particular influences on their major functions, which could override general trends in urbanization.

As is clear from Table 8.1, urban and national population totals followed divergent paths. Late-medieval demographic decline, the consequent contraction of urban marketing, and the rise of rural industry left most early-sixteenth-century towns comparatively depressed. London's population, possibly over 100,000 in *c.* 1300, was less than half this number of two centuries later. In Bristol, a Crown enquiry into the falling yield of taxation found 900 houses (nearly half of the housing stock) 'desolate, vacant and decayed.' In Coventry, the decline of staple textile industries precipitated social stress, prompted gild regulations which restricted urban living, and increased the burden of maintaining institutions and infrastructure.[42] Coventry was an extreme case, but illustrates towns' minor share in sixteenth-century population growth. The suburban poverty typical of Elizabethan and Jacobean towns reflected both the strength of socio-economic forces driving people from the land in some areas, and the inability of urban employment to absorb them.

It is simplistic to see urban decline as wholly the outcome of rural industrial growth, but it was a significant factor. Several other major towns suffered from declining staple industries, usually textiles: including York, Winchester, Canterbury, Gloucester, and Salisbury (the latter two losing out to the rural cloth industry of the Cotswolds and Wiltshire respectively). There were other specific causes of relative urban decline. The dissolution of the monasteries was a severe blow to towns which had been centres of pilgrimage and ecclesiastical administration. Towns like St Albans, Bury St Edmunds and Abingdon lost economic assets as well as centres of power and culture when major religious houses were suppressed. Many ports lost trade to London's growing dominance of overseas shipping. Only those which developed independent overseas links (such as Bristol and Hull) or which shipped large volumes of local produce (such as Newcastle) prospered against the trend.

Although only a few towns maintained prosperous medieval manufacturing specializations, others were boosted by new industries. A striking example is the introduction of 'New Draperies' at Norwich and Colchester.[43] Dutch refugees from religious persecution provided a skilled and experienced workforce for the production of new types of worsted which more than offset the diminishing market for traditional East Anglian cloths. Such examples are the exception rather than the rule. Lacking staple manufacturing industries, most town economies depended on processing industries such as tanning, metalworking and malting, together with victualling and retail trades.

London has already been discussed as a town where import processing and consumer goods industries flourished, but to contemporaries, well aware of the huge volume of food and other goods sucked into metropolitan markets, the capital was outstanding for consumption rather than production. Several feared the capital was parasitic on national wealth, or 'a monstrous head grown too big for body of the country of England'. More moderate commentators were still impressed: 'when we are at London', wrote an awestruck Defoe, 'and see the prodigious fleets of ships which come constantly in with coals for this increasing city, we are apt to wonder where they come, and that they do not bring the whole country away'.[44]

Functional heterogeneity was the key to London's continuous economic expansion. The presence of the Court, Parliament and central law courts has long been recognized as a major factor in London's phenomenal growth, but this stress has obscured the range and growth of manufacturing industry (Table 8.4). Beier recently estimated that in *c.* 1700, about 200,000 Londoners depended on manufacturing livelihoods, more than ten times as many as in *c.* 1560, in spite of the departure of framework knitting to the East Midlands.[45] Industrial expansion was a particular feature of the rapidly expanding suburbs.

But if London embodied several distinct economic specializations, the most striking feature of most sixteenth-century urban economies was precisely their very unspecialized character. A substantial proportion of urban livelihoods came from providing the basics of urban life: food and drink, clothing and footwear, and buildings or accommodation. This proportion varied, but was almost everywhere higher in *c.* 1600 than in *c.* 1700. The contrast is indicative of significant changes in urban economies.

Urban growth accelerated as national population growth was petering out in mid-century. London, as before, accommodated the greater part, but outside London the pattern changed (Fig. 8.3). At first, increases were evenly spread through the traditional urban hierarchy, but increasingly, the most dramatic growth was in younger towns: Birmingham—the centre of the West Midlands metalware trades,

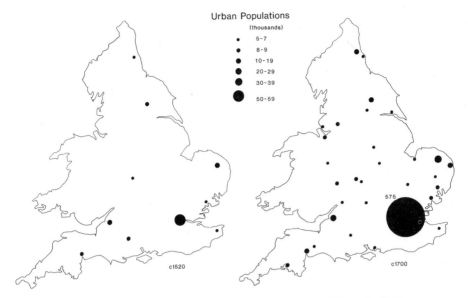

Fig. 8.3. Towns with populations over 5000 in *c.* 1520 and *c.* 1700.

Leeds—hub of the West Riding wool textile areas, Liverpool and Manchester—commercial capitals of the Lancashire and Cheshire cloth industry. This reflected both the central role of commercial towns in proto-industrial regions, and a revival in urban manufacturing. Among older centres, Bristol retained its prominence through trade-related industries such as food refining and metallurgy, but was atypical.

Although not numerically the major contributors to urbanization, many of the older county and provincial centres were crucial to the developing urban system. They were major centres for increased spatial integration, possessing the marketing, service, informational and transportation functions which integrated the space-economy. At both national and local scales improved road and river communications played an enabling role in spatial integration. By 1730 there were extensive turnpike road networks in south-east England and in West Midlands manufacturing districts. New transport arteries were important not only for the movement of commodities, but also for information and news. The movement of capital and information (for example, about prices and markets) was a pre-requisite for commercial agriculture or industry, and the movement of ideas about status and fashion was central to changing patterns of consumption.

Over time, urban functions became more specialized and differentiated as the urban system became an integrated hierarchy of economic and social flows. In the towns came new employment in specialized manufacturing, and in luxury crafts, professions and services. Many towns developed particular product specializations, such as the leather and footwear trades at Northampton. They were the focus for 'occupational regions', and supplied large, even national, markets.[46]

County towns had long been administrative centres. With the law becoming more and more the province of professionals, attorneys (like physicians and private schoolmasters) were almost exclusively urban. The role of county towns as cultural centres was reinforced by the publication there of local newspapers, which encouraged a sense of regional identity, both through news coverage and advertising. Cultural changes also underlay the unprecedented importance of some larger urban centres as arenas of public consumption. Catering for genteel visitors during urban 'seasons', became a lucrative activity. Indeed, several 'leisure towns' developed considerable specialization in servicing leisure and elite culture, especially where administrative and political centrality already provided a social focus.

In turn, spending on buildings by the gentry and professionals stimulated construction. They constituted a growing market for consumer goods, thereby supporting local artisans. Tailors, shoemakers, furniture makers, and the like may have been more the beneficiaries of rising productivity elsewhere in the economy than its sources, but they further increased demand for one another's products. Occupational diversity made urban economies more robust than proto-industrial communities which depended on a single trade.

With the growing integration of the urban system, some streamlining occurred as older 'multi-role' centres faded from prominence and the number of general markets fell.[47] Where craft specialisms and services developed, or towns became important nodes in re-organized marketing networks, urban economies flourished. That greater integration itself ultimately undermined some county towns cannot detract from their importance in the creation of a national space economy and, for middling and wealthy groups, important elements of a national culture.

Consumption, Urban Landscapes and Intra-urban Geography

Historians and geographers are currently paying increased attention to consumption, partly in response to two wider questions: first, how did changing demand affect the nature and geography of production: and second, what were the relative contributions of 'economy' and 'culture' as causes of long-term societal change? Much work has focused on the eighteenth century,[48] but there were major changes in the size, composition and geography of the domestic market for consumer goods during the previous two centuries.[49]

In the period 1675–1725 there were large differences in household wealth and the possession of various 'consumer goods' in different parts of England. London and its environs formed a vast concentration of 'mass consumption' even though 'mass' in this context refers to perhaps half the population.[50] Wide social diffusion of wealth with which to consume, and of the tastes that shaped forms of consumption were both seventeenth-century developments.[51] Changing consumption patterns did not follow simply from higher incomes, but depended also on new tastes in clothing, furniture, interior decoration, and recreation. Towns were crucial in the diffusion of this new knowledge. They were also the major arenas for the display of material or psychological adornment to demonstrate refinement and status.

Cultural changes also had geographical expression in the growing self-consciousness of architectural design, again especially in towns. Economic expansion financed public, commercial and private building, but the form taken by much new urban building reflected cultural discourses.

In turning to Renaissance architecture contemporaries were rejecting the pull of locali-ty . . . a classical doorcase lifted its owner above the petty provincialism of his neighbours (or if they already owned such a doorcase, protected him from their sneers), and in a manner of speaking made him part of the international community.[52]

Appearance became more important in the construction of many types of build-ings (not just aristocratic or ecclesiastical ones), and was no longer subordinate to building function. In Bourdieu's terms, classical architectural touches were cultural capital, the possession of which helped individuals gain access to wider status and power in early modern society.[53]

Familiar models of 'the pre-industrial city' capture some features of early-modern English towns.[54] Most towns had wealthy central districts (relatively healthy, large households, many servants) and poorer outer districts (higher mortality and rates of population turnover, small households, many broken families, few servants, and many immigrants, especially the unskilled).

Important qualifications to these simple expectations need to be made at both bottom and top if the urban hierarchy. The small markets and some county towns were too small to exhibit significant geographical zoning. Social segregation was at the scale of street and yard rather than the parish or ward. The segregation of high-status street-front houses and the low-status courts and alleys just a few yards behind could be very sharp. Parishes, the smallest areal units for which taxation and occupational data are available, may appear socially heterogeneous, but were not socially unsegregated.[55] Meanwhile, the social topography of London exhibited strong segregation at the parish scale, but had a complex multi-focal pattern reflecting the several factors fuelling the capital's dramatic demographic and economic growth.[56]

Elizabethan urban layouts and street plans were much influenced by the legacy of medieval patterns of building and fragmented property rights, just as their appear-ance reflected local materials and vernacular building traditions. After *c.* 1650 these influences were waning. Now the appearance of towns reflected not just local building materials and individuals' notions of design, but also the rules laid down in Parliamentary Improvement Acts, which to some extent incorporated normative notions of design. Thirty-five Improvement Acts for provincial towns were passed before 1730,[57] dealing with matters such as permitted building materials, street widths, the removal of obstruction and gates, the erection of public buildings, public water supplies, and the laying out of gardens.

The relationship between changing social behaviour and purpose-built urban recreation facilities is exemplified by the rise of the promenade. Promenades and public gardens were two aspects of 'the increasing provision of fashionable public space that accompanied the urban cultural renaissance of the later Stuart and early Georgian periods' (Fig. 8.4).[58] Like other new urban landscape features, such as theatres, assembly rooms, race courses and coffee-houses, promenades were arenas in which social status could be competed for and displayed. 'Cultural renaissance' and the landscape elements that both constituted and reflected it were widely distributed. Where these general cultural developments were expressed particularly intensively in the 'leisure towns', they spawned distinctive landscapes still evident in the likes of Bath, Chichester, Shrewsbury and Tunbridge Wells.[59]

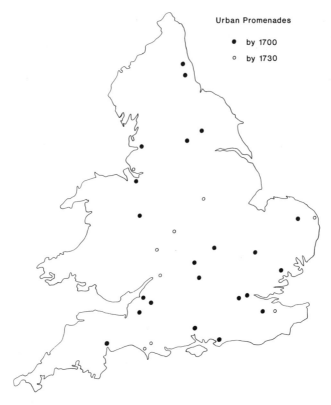

Fig. 8.4. Towns with promenades and public gardens by 1730. *Source*: Borsay, 'Promenade', pp. 135–7 and personal communication.

Concluding Comments

Both industrial and urban growth helped reshape the regional distribution of population and wealth. Midlands metalworking communities like Wolverhampton, Handsworth and Yardley 'had been minor, rural settlements in the early sixteenth century; by the 1670s, they had been transformed, and were crucial in the structure of nascent industrialization.' The proportion of national population and wealth accounted for by towns was increasing. 'Significant regional relocations of . . . [population and wealth in England *c*. 1525–*c*. 1670] . . . were underpinned by the twin themes of urban development and proto-industrialization.'[60]

With increasing spatial integration, both industrial and urban growth were selective developments. Integration encouraged diverse specializations by expanding accessible markets and allowing the freer movement of capital and knowledge, but it could also undermine established industries and towns. High production cost industries, hitherto preserved by a fortuitously accessible location and consequent low transport costs, could rapidly become uncompetitive. When the end came for deindustrializing areas facing more efficient or adaptable competitors, its local impact could be severe. Towns could decline in relative size and status even as England became ever more urban.

Specialization both constituted, and bore witness to, an increasingly integrated economy and society. It remains misleading to speak of integration as though it were one process rather than several: the economy was much more integrated in terms of information (though this was very socially selective) and capital, than it was in terms of commodities or labour. And despite the magnitude of changes between 1500 and 1730, there were much more dramatic changes to come. Yet we can reasonably claim that the specialized regional economies and the nationally integrated urban hierarchy in place by the early eighteenth century largely directed the geography of later events.

References

1. D. Defoe, *A Tour Through The Whole Island of Great Britain*, (1726; Basingstoke, Penguin edition 1971), preface.
2. Calculated from E. A. Wrigley, 'Urban growth and agricultural change: England and the continent in the early modern period' *Jnl. of Interdisciplinary History*, **15** (1984), pp. 686, 688, 700.
3. P. Hudson, 'From manor to mill: the West Riding in transition', in M. Berg *et al.* (eds.), *Manufacture in Town and Country Before the Factory*, (Cambridge, 1982), pp. 124-44.
4. From the ecological standpoint, J. Thirsk, 'Industries in the countryside', in F. J. Fisher (ed.), *Essays on the Economic History of Tudor and Stuart England*, (London, 1961), pp. 70-88, and E. L. Jones, 'The constraints on economic growth in southern England, 1650-1850', *Proceedings of the Third International Conference on Economic History*, (1974) 10, pp. 423-30. For a market-centred model, E. A. Wrigley, 'A simple model of London's importance in changing English society and economy, 1650-1750', *Past and Present*, **37** (1967), pp. 44-70. Although reluctant to engage theoretical issues, C. Clay *Economic Expansion and Social Change: England 1500-1700*, (Cambridge, 1984, 2 volumes), Chapter 8, provides a comprehensive review of individual industries.
5. P. Lindert and J. Williamson, 'Revising England's social tables 1688-1812', *Explorations in Economic History*, **19** (1982) pp. 385-94.
6. J. Patten, 'Urban occupations in pre-industrial England' *Trasactions of the Institute of British Geographers*, new ser. **2** (1977), pp. 259-77; *idem* 'Changing occupational structures in the East Anglian countryside, 1500-1700', in H. Fox and R. Butlin (eds.), *Change in the Countryside: Essays on rural England, 1500-1900*, (London, 1979), pp. 103-21.
7. D. Souden 'Migrants and the population structure of seventeenth century provincial cities and market towns', in P. Clark (ed.), *The Transformation of English Provincial Towns*, (London, 1984), pp. 169-89. It should not be assumed that migrants moved specifically to pursue what eventually became their livelihood.
8. K. D. M. Snell, 'The apprenticeship of women', in *Annals of the Labouring Poor: Social Change and Agrarian England 1660-1900*, (Cambridge, 1985) pp. 270-319, L. Charles and L. Duffin (eds.), *Women and Work in Pre-Industrial England*, (London 1985).
9. J. Pound (ed.), *The Military Survey of 1522 for Babergh Hundred*, Suffolk Records Society, 28 (1986).
10. J. Smith, *A List of Men and Armour for Gloucestershire in 1608*; R. H. and A. J. Tawney 'An occupational census of the seventeenth century', *Economic History Review*, **5** (1934), pp. 25-64.
11. Occupations of indicted men, witnesses, sureties and victims recorded in cases heard at the Home Circuit Assizes calculated from J. S. Cockburn (ed.), *Calendar of the Home Circuit Assizes temp. Elizabeth and James I*, (9 volumes, 1976-80).

12. P. D. Glennie, English Occupational Statistics Before the Census, Historical Geography Research Series, 25 (1990).

13. J. M. Martin, 'Village traders and the emergence of a proletariat in south Warwickshire, 1750-1851', *Agricultural History Review*, **32** (1984) pp. 170-88; G. E. Mingay, (ed.) *The Victorian Countryside* (London, 1980).

14. D. Avery, 'Male occupations in a rural Middlesex parish', *Local Population Studies*, 2 (1969), pp. 29-35; D. G. Hey, *An English Rural Community: Myddle under the Tudors and Stuarts*, (Leicester, 1974), pp. 52-4; E. A. Wrigley, 'The changing occupational structure of Colyton over two centuries', *Local Population Studies*, **18** (1977) pp. 9-21; R. W. Ambler, B. and J. Watkinson, *Farmers and Fishermen: The Probate Inventories of the Ancient Parish of Clee, South Humberside 1536-1742*, (1987), pp. 4-6; Layston and Bishops Stortford parish registers at the Hertfordshire County Record Office; J. Ellis, 'A dynamic society: social relations in Newcastle-upon-Tyne 1660-1760', in Clark (ed.) *Transformation of Provincial Towns*, pp. 217-220; E. J. Buckatzch, 'Occupations in the parish registers of Sheffield, 1565-1719', *Economic History Review*, 2nd ser., **1** (1949), pp. 145-6; A. Wadsworth and J. de L. Mann, *The Cotton Trade and Industrial Lancashire*, (Manchester, 1931), **52**, pp. 314-5; M. Wild, 'The Saddleworth parish registers', *Textile History*, **1** (1969), p. 221; M. F. Pickles, 'Mid-Wharfedale 1721-1812: Economic and demographic change in a Pennine dale', *Local Population Studies*, **16** (1976), pp. 12-44.

15. L. Clarkson, *The Pre-Industrial Economy in England 1500-1750*, (London, 1971) p. 78.

16. P. J. Bowden, *The Wool Trade in Tudor and Stuart England*, (London, 1962); E. Kerridge, *Textile Manufactures in Early Modern England*, (Manchester, 1985).

17. Clay, *Economic Expansion*, II. pp. 13-21.

18. Major statements of proto-industrialization theory are F. Mendels, 'Proto-industrialization: the first phase of the process of industrialization', *Jnl. of Economic History*, **32** (1972), pp.241-61 and P. Kriedte, H. Medick and J. Schlumbohm, *Industrialization Before Industrialization*, (Cambridge, 1981). Useful overviews of geographers include J. Langton and G. Hoppe, *Town and Country in the Development of Early Modern Western Europe*, Historical Geography Research Series, 11 (1983), R. A. Butlin, 'Early industrialization in Europe: concepts and problems', *Geographical Jnl*, **152** (1986), pp. 1-8.

19. Thirsk, 'Industries in the countryside'.

20. The difference could be of greater importance to merchants, to whom the daily availability of free-time in pastoral areas offered a much more regular basis for production.

21. Critical reviews include D. Coleman, 'Proto-industrialization: a concept too many', *Economic History Review*, 2nd ser., **36** (1983), pp. 435-48; R. Houston and K. Snell, 'Proto-industrialization: cottage industry, social change and the industrial revolution', *Historical Jnl*, **27** (1984), pp. 473-92; L. Clarkson, *Proto-industrialization: The First Phase of Industrialization?*, (London, 1985); Berg *et al.*, *Manufacture in Town and Country*.

22. Clarkson, *Proto-industrialization*, p. 9.

23. 'There was nothing unavoidable or automatic in the passage from phase one to the next' Mendels, 'Proto-industrialization', p. 246; Schlumbohm, 'Relations of production—productive forces—crises of proto-industrialization', in Kreidte *et al.*, *Industrialization*, pp. 94-125.

24. Coleman, 'A concept too many', pp. 442-3.

25. Schlumbohn, 'Relations of production', pp. 111-12.

26. A. Everitt, 'Country, county and town: patterns of regional evolution in England', *Transactions of the Royal Historical Society*, 5th ser., **29** (1979), pp. 79-108.

27. E. A. Wrigley, 'Men on the land and men in the countryside: employment in agriculture in early nineteenth century England; in L. Bonfield *et al.*, (eds.), *The World We Have Gained: Histories of Population and Social Structure*, (Oxford, 1986), pp. 296-304, 335-6.

28. J. De Vries, *The Dutch Rural Economy in the Golden Age*, (New Haven, 1974).

29. J. U. Nef, *The Rise of the British Coal Industry*, (London, 1932); Clay *Economic Expansion*, II, pp. 47-50.

30. J. Ellis, 'The decline and fall of the Tyneside salt industry: a re-examination', *Economic History Review*, 2nd ser., **33** (1980), pp. 45-58.

31. P. Cromar, 'The coal industry on Tyneside, 1715-1750', *Northern History*, **14** (1978), pp. 193-207.
32. M. W. Flinn, *History of the British Coal Industry 1700-1830*, (Oxford, 1981).
33. G. Hammersley, 'The charcoal iron industry and its fuel, 1540-1750' *Economic History Review*, 2nd ser., **26** (1973), pp. 593-613.
34. Clay, *Economic Expansion* II, pp. 56-82.
35. M. Rowlands, *Masters and Men in the West Midlands Metalware Trades* (Manchester, 1975); P. Large, 'Urban growth and industrial change in the west midlands', in Clark (ed.), *Transformation of Provincial Towns*, pp. 169-89; D. Hey, *The Rural Metalworkers of the Sheffield Region*, (Leicester, 1972).
36. J. Langton, *Geographical Change and Industrial Revolution: Coalmining in South West Lancashire 1590-1799*, (Cambridge, 1979), pp. 50-4 and 94-100.
37. J. Thirsk, *Economic Policy and Projects*, (Oxford, 1978).
38. M. Spufford, *The Great Reclothing of Rural England*, (London, 1984) discusses itinerant traders; T. S. Willan, *Abraham Dent of Kirkby Stephen*, (Manchester, 1970) shows the range of suppliers to a shop in a small and isolated Cumbrian market town from the 1750s.
39. N. Goose, 'English pre-industrial urban economies', *Urban History Yearbook 1982*, p. 30.
40. P. Corfield, 'Small towns, large implications: social and cultural roles of small towns in eighteenth-century England and Wales', *British Jnl. for Eighteenth-Century Studies*, **10** (1987), p. 126. Even small towns might attract large crowds during fairs and festivals.
41. P. Clark and P. Slack, *English Towns in Transition*, (Oxford, 1977); J. Patten *English Towns 1500-1700*, (Folkestone, 1977); P. Clark (ed.), *Country Towns in Pre-Industrial England 1500-1800*, (Leicester, 1981); P. Corfield, *The Impact of English Towns 1700-1800*, (Oxford, 1982); Clark (ed.), *Transformation of Provincial Towns*; A. L. Beier and R. Finlay (eds.), *London 1500-1700*, (London, 1986).
42. D. Keene, 'A new study of London before the Great Fire', *Urban History Yearbook 1984*, pp. 11-21, C. Phythian-Adams, 'Urban decay in late medieval England', in P. Abrams and E. A. Wrigley (eds.), *Towns in Societies*, (Cambridge, 1978), pp. 168-69; *idem, Desolation of a City: Coventry and the Urban Crisis of the Late Middle Ages*, (Cambridge, 1979).
43. D. Coleman, 'An innovation and its diffusion: the "new draperies"', *Economic History Review*, 2nd ser., **22** (1969), pp. 417-29; U. Preistley, 'The fabric of stuffs: the Norwich textile industry *c.* 1650-1750', *Textile History*, **16** (1985), pp. 183-210.
44. Defoe, *Tour*, p. 535.
45. Beier, 'Engines of manufacture', p. 156.
46. Everitt, 'Country, county and town'.
47. J. Chartres, 'The marketing of agricultural produce' in J. Thirsk (ed.), *Agrarian History of England and Wales, V, 1640-1750*, (Cambridge, 1984) II, pp. 406-502.
48. e.g. N. McKendrick, J. Brewer and J. Plumb, *The Birth of a Consumer Society: the commercialisation of eighteenth century England*, (London, 1978).
49. J. Thirsk, *Economic Policy and Projects*; M. Spufford *Small Books and Pleasant Histories: Popular literature and its Readership in Seventeenth Century England*, (London, 1981); *idem, Great Reclothing*.
50. L. Weatherill, *Consumer Behaviour and Material Culture in Britain, 1660-1760*, (London, 1988).
51. P. Glennie, 'The emergence of a consumer society in early-modern England' (forthcoming).
52. P. Borsay, 'Culture, status, and the English urban landscape', *History*, **67** (1982), pp. 6-7.
53. P. Bourdieu, *Distinction: A Social Critique of the Judgement of Taste*, (Cambridge, Mass., 1984).
54. J. Langton, 'Residential patterns in pre-industrial cities: some case studies from seventeenth-century Britain', *Transactions of the Institute of British Geographers*, **65** (1975), pp. 1-28.
55. Thus it should not be assumed that the smallest spatial unit for which we have data was a coherent community in everyday life.
56. M. J. Power, 'The social topography of Restoration London', in Beier and Finlay, (eds.), *London 1500-1700*, pp. 199-223.

57. Clark (ed.), *Country towns*, p. 21.
58. P. Borsay, 'The rise of the promenade: the social and cultural use of space in the English provincial town *c.* 1660-1800', *British Jnl. for Eighteenth-Century Studies*, **9** (1986), p. 130.
59. A. McInnes, 'The emergence of a leisure town: Shrewsbury 1660-1760', *Past and Present*, **120** (1988) pp. 53-87.
60. C. Husbands, 'Regional change in a pre-industrial economy: wealth and population in England in the sixteenth and seventeenth centuries', *Jnl. of Historical Geography*, **13** (1987) pp. 354 and 356.

9

Regions in England and Wales
c. 1600–1914

R. A. Butlin

In tracing the social and economic development of this country as a whole...we must not expect to find a homogeneous or coherent pattern of evolution, but a piecemeal, localized, and fragmented one: a pattern of regional paradoxes and survivals, in short, where landscapes of poverty and plenty exist for centuries side by side, and where in almost every country the advanced and the primitive, the familiar and remote, remain strangely intermingled until the eve of the railway era. Gradually, moreover, and particularly over the last three or four centuries, this small-scale network of contrasting *pays* has been further complicated, and in places transformed, by the rise of a succession of human regions, if so they may be called, such as the county community, the urban hinterland, the occupational region, the social neighbourhood, the region of religious influence, and so on.[1]

Introduction

The identification or creation of a framework of perceived or real units by means of which the social, cultural and economic arrangements of space in past times have been and may be described is not a simple and straightforward task, but it is important and necessary. The characterization of a variety of regions and localities should be attempted to provide a dynamic framework for the study of the possible geographies of the past that we seek to recover. This chapter, therefore, attempts a substantive analysis of the chronology of regions and regionalism in England and Wales, particularly the ways in which people, from the seventeenth to the early twentieth century, have conceived of, written about, and discussed regions and regionalism. Where possible, the broader cultural, scientific and political contexts within which ideas of regions were located are also discussed.

There is not, and cannot be, of course, an absolute and invariable system of conceptual regions and communities, waiting in a hidden past for rediscovery by the historical geographer or historian. In effect, we create and recreate our own regions and regional structures—as did those groups and individuals from the past whose lived and located experiences and contexts we seek to discover—on the basis of our ideologies, perceptions, and preferences, with recognition of the dynamism of regional processes, economic and cultural. In effect, we write our own geographies of the past for the purposes of the particular analyses, constructions and emphases to which we choose to give priority. A measure of consensus about regions of particular areas at particular periods may emerge from the work of scholars past and present, but there is real danger that these may be regarded as fixed, and the dynamics of regional change ignored, with consequent mismatching of regional divisions and the periods to which an attempt is made to apply them.

A cautionary caveat may be added at the outset. This is the necessary recognition that the majority of conceptions about regions as articulated by writers in the past reflect the values, beliefs, and assumptions of the more literate and powerful, and that their conceptions may depart from those of the silent majority of the population. It is, however, difficult to write the history of regional consciousness of the mass of the population, other than through indirect historical analysis.

Concepts

The Region

Gilbert, in his classic essay on the subject,[2] has outlined, using the schema of Morgan's earlier essay on regional consciousness,[3] a history of the region as a tendency in European thought since the beginning of the nineteenth century, reflected in three trends: the region as a pedagogic device in the teaching and study of geography, incorporating the idea of the 'natural region'; the emergence of regionally specific literature, including the regional novel; and the development of the notion and practice of regionalism for purpose of political and social administration. The development of the various concepts of the region in the history of geographical thought during and since the nineteenth century is of some relevance, since it indicates a fairly rapid intellectual transition from the idea of the natural region to that of the region modified by human action, and an increasing interest in small-scale regions. Thus 'The idea of human activity and its results has become inseparable from the idea of the region. The German geographer Braun considers that the goal of regional geography is the explanation of the transformation of the natural region (*Naturlandschaft*) into a cultivated region or landscape (*Kulturlandschaft*)'[4]

Current views of the region relate to very different intellectual paradigms. Gregory, for example, has indicated the contribution of time-geography and ideas of structuration to the concept of regions and schemes of regionalization, pointing to the region as an heuristic device, involving looser concepts of a region as 'a number of different but connected *settings for interaction*', and the idea of regionalization as a concept of the 'the cluttering of contexts in time-space'.[5] Gilbert has also synthesized the essential features as she sees them of the 'new' regional geography which has developed in the 1980s,[6] specifically in relation to a view of the region as a local response to capitalist processes. She indicates that the current trend is: 'away from visible attributes of an area to its invisible ones, the relations that link individuals and institutions within the region; and toward the interpretation of the region as a process which, once established, is continually reproduced and gradually transformed through practices',[7]

Remarkably few historical geographers have actually attempted the task of identifying and mapping regional schemes. An attempt was made in the regional volumes of Darby's *Domesday Geographies*,[8] (Fig.9.2a) though even here the treatment was uneven, with some authors having chosen not to follow the general arrangement of providing a regional subdivision towards the end of each county chapter. Marshall[9] has also reviewed the geographical and historical literature on the subject of regions and regionalism, and advocated a closer attention to the theoretical and practical difficulties, including those of boundaries, of the historical study of the spatial affiliations and characteristics of past societies.

Of particular importance in this context is the interaction of processes operating at different spatial scales. This has interesting and important implications for a study of the regions of England and Wales, and particularly for the understanding of the effects of economic and political integration and centralization on the nature and strength of regional identities and personalities. Baker, in a short but perceptive observation, has highlighted this point. Indicating the potential view of the region as a mediator between locality and nation, he proceeds to suggest that the process of absorption of communities into wider national polities and societies is quite likely to have been spatially and chronologically uneven, and by no means unilinear. Hence:'. . . while it is possible to detect a process of regional transformation which involved the increasing *economic integration of space*, it might also be possible to detect a process of regional transformation which involved the increasing *spatial disintegration of society*: as the sense of place was transformed from a local to a national consciousness, so the *sense of community* might have ceded to a *sense of class* whose bonds might lie contiguously within a particular geographical region or hierarchically within a certain economic sector, in which case the sense of class would have dominated over any residual sense of place'.[10]

An operable definition of a region might be, therefore, that it is a taxonomic and practical device used for characterizing and identifying, for different purposes and at different points in time, the common cultural, economic and social characteristics of varying communities, in both their local and broader spatial contexts and with some appropriate regard to the association, particularly in essentially pre-industrial times, with their natural environment. It is, in short, about the local and wider associations between people and places and people and people, partly recoverable from written descriptions, and in some cases from maps. The creation of possible regional associations and systems for the past has of course to take into account the dynamic nature of regional change and the difficult but necessary assumption that in theory different means and ends of regionalization are possible for a given piece of territory at any given time or period. This is particularly true of the nineteenth century, when the dynamism of the metropolitan core area effected an intensification of smaller-scale regional patterns and associations.[11]

Regionalism

The question of regionalism is perhaps a clearer one, being more time- and place-specific. The term seems to have begun a period of common currency in Europe in the 1880s and 1890s, with the direct connotation of political movements seeking a greater degree of regional, political, cultural and economic autonomy, a reaction against centralization and metropolitan control. In a perceptive and little-known essay on regional consciousness, F.W. Morgan drew attention to this early form of regionalism:'. . . in much of Europe throughout the nineteenth century, the influence of locality came back, for among most of the small national groups struggling to achieve a more or less separate existence there was a very pronounced consciousness of the individual landscapes of their countries, and a fostering of all the cultural expressions arising out of them. With the movement for political freedom went the preservation of language, dialect, folk-lore, legend, and custom, alike in Bohemia, in Ireland, in Catalonia, in Croatia and Slovenia, and in Wales'.[12] Regionalism in a fairly narrow sense was revived after the First World War, though its aspirations at this later stage seem to have become more confused and in some senses sinister, that is more atavistic, xenophobic, chauvinistic, and even fascist and anti-semitic. Regionalism in the broader sense of a reaction against centralization and standardization of many aspects of life by a national or international state is a limited and late feature of the historical geography of England and Wales, but is an important one.

The Country and the Provincial

These two terms are also time-specific, and help in our understanding of the evolution of concepts about space-relations in Britain, especially England, in the early modern and modern periods. The term *country* has several connotations. One, most obviously, meaning a native land, a national state. Another, a rural (as opposed to an urban) area. This contrasting view of country, as opposed to town, emerged in the sixteenth century, particularly in relation to the growth of London,[13] and Williams has studied the contrast in *The Country and the City*,[14] but it can have a more restricted meaning within the same context: that of a specific region or tract of country with distinct social, economic and landscape characteristics, that is a *pays* in the traditional French connotation of that word. Modern writers, especially on agrarian history, have much favoured this term, especially Everitt[15] and Kerridge,[16] primarily in relation to what would be termed functional regions—in these two cases farming or husbandry regions. Thus Everitt speaks of: '"country" in the old sense of a "countryside" or *pays*. This particular meaning of the word has largely died out in the common speech of English people today, though its disappearance is relatively recent, and still survives in a few special phrases like "the Black Country".'[17] 'Country' was one of a series of terms used in the sixteenth and seventeenth centuries for the purpose of describing a form of natural region, as opposed to the more artificial creation, the county, for example. Other terms included 'stories', 'stages', and 'tracts'.[18] The terminology used by the inhabitants of these small-scale regions in the past to describe their habitats is difficult to recover, and we are dependent on the terminology of educated observers—topographers, chorographers, natural historians and county historians— to give us some idea of contemporary perceptions of place.

The concept of *provincial* and the *provinces* derives from ideas emerging in the late eighteenth and early nineteenth centuries of the contrasts between a growing metropolis and the rest of the country. Four definitions of the term provincial are to be found in Dr Johnson's *Dictionary*, published in 1755, of which the fourth ('not of the mother country; rude; unpolished') is perhaps the most important. As Lucas has indicated, however, Johnson's definition was initially a descriptive rather than a pejorative one, but its transformation to a more comparative and derogatory term came with the nineteenth century and the growth of new towns and cities which, because of their commercial and industrial bases, were thought to lack the culture and style of London.[19] The term had primarily been used in a colonial context until the loss of the American colonies in 1783, but thereafter its connotation changed. Read, in his historical study of the English provinces, draws attention to its introduction in the late eighteenth century and its gradual adoption by such 'provincial' politicians as Cobden, Bright and O'Connor in the early nineteenth century.[20] The provincial energies that were characteristic of the early phases of the Industrial Revolution did, however, strongly contradict the metropolitan assumptions about their inferior economic and cultural status (as they do at the present day), and were reflected in the vigour of local politics, town improvement schemes, the rise of the provincial press, Nonconformity and its associated cultural institutions, notably the Literary and Philosophical Societies, the General Chamber of Manufacturers, founded in 1785, and a host of other economic, political and cultural activities and institutions.[21]

Locale and Locality

As indicated earlier, currents in contemporary geographical thought favour a return to small-scale geographical constructions and analyses, at the level of the locality or locale. While based in part on the classic regionalism of the French school of regional geography of Vidal de la Blache,[22] revision is being attempted by the incorporation of time-geography and theories of structuration. This involves the intensive studies of the life-paths of individuals, families and communities at the level of the parish or group of parishes, the village or hamlet, or small market town, that is the level of the 'locale'. The term 'locale' is much favoured (though not empirically demonstrated) in the time–space theories adapted by Giddens from the work of the Swedish geographer Hägerstrand. Giddens prefers 'locale' to 'place', the former in his view having the broader connotation of the association of a social system with a social space, its space not being permanently fixed (even mobile in the case of nomadic groups) and having only diffuse boundaries.[23] In this type of approach, as Jonas puts it, 'life paths are traced out by delineating how people in their daily, localized practices draw upon the structures and interact with the institutions which govern their lives in a routine, often unintended fashion. While there is recognition of locales . . .beyond the locality and wider systems of interaction (such as capitalism, feudalism, etc.), the meeting of agency and structure is said to be always grounded in localities.'[24] Giddens' broader views on the subject of regions and regionalism suggest that there are different modes of regionalism, distinguished by : the form of their boundaries, their time-spans and spatial scales, and their character. The operational problem with Giddens' notions of regions is, in part, that it is too flexible and elastic, and requires a too frequent zooming of the perceptual lens to give a recognizable picture.[25]

The emphasis therefore is on the structuring and transformation of regions, particularly by the influence of dominant social groups, and especially on small-scale regional social relations and interaction within local regional space. The new type of regional geography is less selective than the old in the range of criteria employed to identify regions, more catholic in its use of theory and employs and recognizes a much wider range of spatial scales at which the processes contributing to the formation or 'becoming' of a region operate.[26]

Regional Writings in the Early Modern Period

Chorographers and Topographers of the Seventeenth Century

According to Emery[27] 'The seventeenth century proved to be an important formative period in the writing of regional geography' and started with a chorographic phase. Chorography was 'a branch of special geography that considered the world "so far forth as it is divided into distinct parts or places", and the chorographer set out to describe 'some one Region . . . (as it) is subdivided into Provinces, Counties and Hundreds'.[28] This ancient chorographic tradition is exemplified and advocated in early-seventeenth-century England in, for example, Peter Heylyn's Microcosmus (1621) and in Carpenter's Geography delineated forth in Two Bookes (1625). It is evident in the regionally specific writings on England and Wales in the late sixteenth and early seventeenth centuries, such as Richard Carew's 'Survey of Cornwall' (1602) and George Owen's 'Description of Pembrokeshire' (1963) in which Owen makes the important distinction between the English and Welsh parts of the county:

> This shire is taken to be divided into two parts, that is to the Englishry and the Welshry . . . The upper part of the shire, which I call the Welshry, is inhabited with Welshmen, the first known owners of the country, and are such as were never removed by any conquest or stranger that won the country. These are the people of the hundreds of Cemais, Colgerran, Dewisland and part of Narberth, in which hundreds there are of divers ancient gentlemen that to this day do hold and keep their ancient houses and descent from their ancestors for 400, 500, 600 years and more . . . But the countries of Roose, Castlemartin, Narberth and most of Daugleddy hundred, the bishop's lordships excepted, were wholly put to the fire and sword by the Normans, Flemings and Englishmen, and utterly expelled the inhabitants thereof and peopled the country themselves, whose posterity remain there to this day, as may appear by their names, manners and language, speaking altogether the English and differing in manners, diet, building and tilling of the land from the Welshmen.[29]

County Histories

Regional descriptions in the late sixteenth and early seventeenth centuries are part of the beginning of the writing of county history, starting with Lambarde's Perambulation of Kent (1576) and broadened in Camden's Britannia (1586), which was a county-based description of Britain. Single county studies which followed include: Samson Erdeswicke's Survey of Staffordshire (1593), Richard Carew's Survey of Cornwall (1602), and Tristram Risdon's Chorographical Description or survey of the County of Devon (1630). Simmons, in his review of English county historians, sees the county histories of this period as information handbooks on counties, written by gentlemen for gentlemen, and 'concerned primarily with description; only incidentally with history, and then with the main purpose of illustrating the relationships of the gentle families of the county'.[30] In this category are also included some of the more famous accounts of county history and genealogy, such as William Burton's Description of

Leicestershire (1597–1604), William Dugdale's *Antiquities of Warwickshire* (1656), and Robert Thoreton's *Antiquities of Nottinghamshire (1677).*

Camden's *Britannia* deserves further mention. William Camden was born in London in 1551, educated at Oxford, and became a master in Westminster school, in the occupation of which post he was able to follow his keen interest in English topography and antiquity and to develop authority in these subjects. *Britannia* was planned as a survey of the topography and antiquities of Roman Britain, with a view, according to Piggot, of enabling 'Britain to take her rightful place at once within the world of antiquity and that of international Renaissance scholarship. . . . It is for this reason that the framework of *Britannia*, persisting through every edition, is that of the Celtic tribal areas of Britain as recorded in the classical geographers, with the English shires grouped within their accommodatingly vague boundaries.'[31] The initial edition and those editions published before Camden's death in 1623 appeared in Latin, but the 1610 edition was translated into English, the language in which subsequent editions were published in the later seventeenth century. The 1607 edition included maps of English counties by Norden and Speed, and was extensively illustrated with drawings and sketches of sites and artefacts.

Its significance for this essay is that it does attempt a measure of regionalization for each county. Thus, in his description of Cambridgeshire he distinguishes between the north and south regions of the county in the following terms: 'The south and lower part is more improv'd, better planted, and consequently more rich and fertil;. . . . The north and farther apart, by reason of the floods, fens, and the many islands made by rivers, is call'd the *Isle of Ely*; abounds with rich pastures, exceeding fresh and pleasant, but however somewhat hollow and spungy, by reason of the waters that undermine it; which sometimes overflow, and drown the greatest part of it.'[32]

The change in language between successive editions of *Britannia* over the late seventeenth century reveals an important change in the book's cultural context, including its regional descriptions: Piggot suggests that 'We have moved out of that Latin-speaking fraternity of learning which, up to the time of Elizabeth, had carried on the tradition of the scholars' *lingua franca*, and are [by Jacobean times] in the new, self-confident, national state in which, with the increase of literacy, an interest in local history was no longer confined to the learned professions, but was as likely to be found in the merchant or the country squire.'[33] Piggott's analysis of the broader context of antiquarianism in the seventeenth century shows that there is also a change, from the first edition of *Britannia* to the Gibson edition of 1695, from a genealogical and heraldic emphasis in the old to a new scientific and antiquarian approach by the group of scholars from Oxford and London who assisted Bishop Gibson with the enlargement and modifications involved in the 1695 edition.[34]

Natural Histories and the New Science of the Late Seventeenth Century

Emery[35] has suggested that the apparent gap in regional studies in England and Wales between the late-sixteenth-century chorographical work and the late-eighteenth-century reporters to the Board of Agriculture is essentially bridged by the work of a group of writers interested in natural history, such as Aubrey, Plot, Morton and Beaumont. Their work, however, represents more than a new change of direction in what retrospectively might be termed 'regional studies': it indicates, as does the re-edition of Camden's *Britannia*, a major change in approach to science, nature and society, and with them to the antiquities of Britain. The roots of this seventeenth-century scientific revolution go back to and beyond the humanists of the European Renaissance, but are distilled and powerfully influenced in Britain in the works of Francis Bacon, including *The Advancement of Learning* (1605), *Novum Organum* (1620), and the *Sylva Sylvarum* (1627), which advocate a new secular scheme of organization of scientific knowledge based on the theory of induction, that is induction to general theory from a starting-point of empirical experience, observation and experiment, with a strong emphasis on classification. The institution which symbolized and developed this work in England was the Royal Society, chartered in 1662 and 1663, but whose work was really initiated by meetings in London and Oxford from 1645 onwards. Piggot, in his study of the history of antiquarianism in Britain in the seventeenth and eighteenth centuries,[36] suggests that the models for the collection of information by scientists of the Royal Society in the late seventeenth century included Renaissance traditions of aristocratic art collections and mercantile and scientific museums; hence the establishment of the Royal Society's Museum of Natural and Artificial Rarities, the Ashmolean Museum, physic and botanic gardens and the like. The connection with the natural historians or regional scientists is clear: . . . 'the point these collections bring home is that the direct counterpart of these classified museums was the similar assembling of knowledge on paper which produced the county surveys or Natural Histories (including a treatment of antiquities) of Aubrey, Plot, Lhwyd and others . . . To a large extent, these surveys had a practical aim, to describe and assess the natural resources of various regions with a view to their exploitation by agriculture, industries and other ventures in trade, and even in medicine and tourism following the recognition of the appropriate mineral springs.'[37]

The flavour of this new type of survey and regionalization may be tasted from a brief consideration of the *Natural Histories* of Dr Robert Plot (1640–96). Plot's two major publications were *The Natural History of Oxfordshire* (1677) and *The Natural History of Staffordshire* (1686). These were the only two of a projected (but not completed) series of natural histories of all the counties of England and Wales. These works epitomize the new inductive and taxonomic science of those associated with the Royal Society: they had as an organizational basis the classical approach of Pliny's *Natural History*, but rejected the genealogical emphasis of earlier writers such as Camden: 'I take leave to inform him [the reader], before I advance that I intend not to meddle with the pedigrees or descents either of families or lands.'[38] Plot announced in 1674 his intention to journey through England and Wales to investigate at first hand a range of natural and antiquarian features of the landscape, having secured letters of support and commendation from the University of Oxford. In 1674 and 1675 he carried out fieldwork in Oxfordshire, and also used the questionnaire system advocated by the Georgical Committee of the Royal Society.[39] The Oxfordshire volume appeared in 1677, and was well received as an example of the new natural or philosophical history, indicated by Plot's appointment as the first keeper of the Ashmolean museum (then being erected in Oxford to house the antiquarian collections of Elias Ashmole) and as professor of chemistry in the university. He became secretary of the Royal Society in 1682. The *Natural History of Staffordshire* had a similar format to *Oxfordshire*, and included a regional basis for the descriptions of the physiographic and agricultural characteristics of the county. He recognized three main parts or regions: the Moorlands and the Pennine fringe; the rich agricultural area to the west and south of the Trent; and the Woodlands or Middle Part of the county. He again used questionnaires as a basis for investigation, improved on those used for Oxfordshire. These printed questionnaires were circulated to Staffordshire farmers and gentry, asking for details of soil type, crops, farm implements, husbandry, minerals, plants, antiquities, and other natural and artificial curiosities. This work gives valuable details of variations in agricultural practice, and also of the developing industries:'. . . the greatest Pottery they have in this country is carried on at Burslem near Newcastle under Lyme, where for making their general sorts of Pots, they have many different sorts of clay . . .'[40]

Emery has suggested that the importance of Plot's work in the history of the regional method lies in its organizational basis, and its objective use of field survey methods to establish regional identities, a method followed much later by the Board of Agriculture reporters in the late eighteenth century.[41] Similar types of county natural history (see Fig.9.1) were also produced, for example by John Aubrey for Wiltshire (1656) and Surrey (1673), by John Morton (1698) for Northamptonshire, and Edward Lhwyd for Cornwall (1695). Lhwyd, who followed Plot as keeper of the Ashmolean Museum, also produced *A Natural History of Wales* (1693) and was part of the Gibson team which produced the 1695 edition of Camden's *Britannia*. The schemes of regional division by the chorographers, natural historians, county historians, and topographers mentioned above are, of course, of interest in their own right. They have also been used and adapted by modern commentators in a variety of attempts to recover the regional cultures of economies of the past. The best known of such adaptations are those produced for past farming regions by Thirsk, Everitt and Kerridge for England and by Emery for Wales, each of which illustrates the benefits and difficulties of attempting to regionalize the past. In his book *The Agricultural Revolution* (1967) Kerridge[42] produced a scheme of 41 farming 'countries' for England and Wales for the period 1500–1800, some of which seem unhelpfully large, such as the 'Midland Plain'. Wales also is treated largely as one unit. In the *Agrarian History of England and Wales*, Volume IV (1967) dealing with the period 1500–1640, Thirsk[43] advanced a scheme of farming regions based on a classification scheme of three main farming types (mixed, pastoral in forests and pastoral in open pasture), subdivided into twelve sub-types. In the same volume, a slightly different system was adopted for Wales by Emery,[44] who distinguishes between two types of region: mixed farming lowlands (seven sub-regions) and pastoral stock-rearing uplands (three sub-regions, southern, central, and northern). Some further attempt at the reconstruction of farming regions for the period 1640–1750 is made in Part I of Volume V of the *Agrarian History of England and Wales*. (see Fig.9.2c).[45] This involves some modification of the scheme used in Volume IV: three main types of agrarian economy are used (pastoral, intermediate, and arable), the formerly separate wood pasture and open pasture are combined, and the intermediate category is a new one, and more detailed description of the specializations of smaller regions is given by means of a system of capital letters. The regional scheme adopted for Wales conforms to this arrangement.[46]

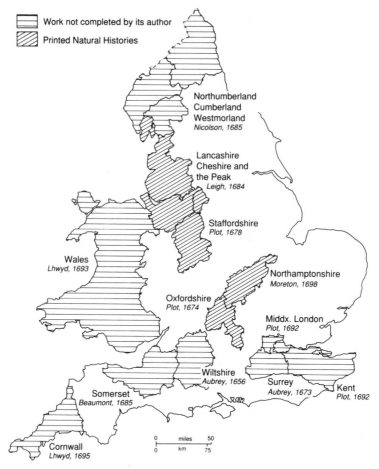

Fig. 9.1. England and Wales: regional studies by natural historians after 1650 (dates are project starting dates). *Source*: F. V. Emery, 'English regional studies from Aubrey to Defoe', *Geographical Jnl.*, **cxxiv**, 3 (1958), p. 320.

A broader scheme of regions for England has been put forward by Everitt, which, while recognizing the essentially dynamic and kaleidoscopic nature of regional change, also recognizes some degree of persistence in the shape of *pays* or 'countries'. His scheme involves a subdivision into eight relatively simple types of region: downland, wold, fielden or champion areas, marshlands, heathlands, forest, fell or moorland, and fenland. A modified map of England based on this scheme has been produced by Thirsk in a recent discussion of the nature of agricultural regions in the period 1500–1750.[47]

The amount of regional identification in the natural histories and county histories had declined by the early nineteenth century. Though the county histories continued into the nineteenth century they increasingly neglected the regional dimension, though they did include maps and topographical illustrations. The quality of scientific investigation of the past and of the landscape seems to have declined markedly in the eighteenth century, with an increasing shift to more romantic views and explanations and more philosophical reflections on the nature of society. Some of the 'Tours' of the eighteenth century, including that of Daniel Defoe, do provide us with useful information on the changing nature of the countryside, but do not set out a systematic system of regions or of methodology. They increase towards the end of the century, with considerable improvements in travel by road, and increasingly incorporate the better maps that are produced after mid-century.

Counties and Communities

The regional schemes advanced as bases for the agricultural and antiquarian studies of the sixteenth, seventeenth, and eighteenth centuries by scholars and scientists, reflect, however, only a limited part of the broad spectrum of possible ways of regionalizing the period. They relate for the most part to matters of topography, agriculture, and various kinds of history, so that, with the possible exception of the natural histories, they take little cognizance of the cultural and social aspects of life, especially those of ordinary people. If one thinks about the way in which individuals and groups of people interacted for a variety of purposes, then it becomes clear that the geographical scales at which social interaction occur in the sixteenth and seventeenth centuries, varied between and within social groups and classes. Much attention, for example, has been paid by historians to the question of the 'county community'. The major debate is between those who contend that the major focus of political loyalty and social and cultural life was the county, often described as 'the country', in contrast to those who argue more traditionally that there was consciousness and awareness of national issues and institutions in the 'provinces'.[48] The county was most certainly an important unit of administration (as evidenced in its predominance on Tudor and Stuart maps) of justice and tax collection, for the election of some Members of Parliament, with the county town an important focus. It is also argued that the county played an important role in the social life, especially that of the gentry, evidenced by the long history of residence and landownership of gentry within a particular shire, and their close-knit patterns of friendship and intermarriage.[49] Against this it has been argued that the social experience of the gentry was, in fact, very much wider than the bounds of a particular county:'. . . and particularly their formal education and their involvement with the national capital, London, ensured that their horizons were not narrowly local. In their participation in local administration, the gentry were continuously reminded that England was a centralized polity, governed by a common law, and they were frequently obliged to confront major constitutional issues directly.'[50] It is also true that the experience of the county was not confined to the gentry, for in respect of the administration of justice non-gentry also participated in Grand Juries, the Quarter Sessions and Assizes.

While the county was one scale of various types of spatial interaction, there were others, including individual parishes, manors, and settlements—often very closely knit communities, micro-regions in themselves. Wrightson in his study of English society in the period 1580–1680 refers to these many thousands of small communities, including villages, parishes, counties, and towns, each of which was a geographical unit and a social system possessing a range of common characteristics and loyalties and a strong sense of place, but which was also, for gentry and peasant, bound up in a wider, national context of direct and indirect experience, including occupational mobility.[51]

A good example both of the use of regional classifications and the study of local communities and associations is that of Underdown in his book *Revel, Riot and Rebellion*,[52] in which he analyses the popular politics and culture of south-central England (Dorset, Somerset and Wiltshire), with specific reference to allegiances in the Civil War, in the period 1603–60. Drawing on the farming regions scheme produced by Joan Thirsk in 1967,[53] and on the work of the topographer John Aubrey, particularly the distinction between arable farming and woodland or pasture areas, Underdown identifies a series of cultural regions to which he ascribes differences of political allegiance during the period 1603–60. A contrast is made between the traditional areas of open-field cultivation and sheep–corn husbandry in the villages of the chalk downlands and the more individual economies and settlement patterns of the cheese and cloth-making country of Wiltshire and north Somerset, and a third intermediate region, the pasture region, with less industrial development, of south-east Somerset and the Vale of Blackmore (see Fig.9.2b). These are reflected in different forms of popular culture. The traditional arable areas retained team sports and older folk customs such as football and church ales and morris dancing, the wood-pasture sports and traditions were more individualistic, and a stronger moral order imposed: bat-and-ball games were played, and charivari—the procession which ritually condemned unfaithful or dominant women—was a common feature. The distribution of allegiance in the Civil War, assessed on the basis of statistical analysis of, for example, pension lists and the Major-generals' returns, indicates that: 'the significance of regional cultural traditions is undeniable. Popular royalism was most widespread in areas where the old festive culture had successfully resisted Puritan attack in the forty years before the civil war—Blackmore Vale, south-east Somerset, the chalk country . . . On the other side . . . we have found fewer Royalists in the north Somerset and north-west Wiltshire clothing districts.'[54] The full implications of this splendid study cannot be explored at length here, but the possibility for more geographically valuable work of this kind is obvious.

The existence of a regional consciousness in the minds of scholars and administrators, and perhaps in the daily lives of ordinary people, especially in rural areas served by small towns, cannot be disputed, though they are difficult to characterize with any precision. The best summary of the difficulty and possibility is probably that by Langton, who has argued that the existence of regions in seventeenth-century England, defined in terms of economic, social and cultural cohesion cannot be doubted, but that the types of regional difference varied according to scale and criteria used to identify them. Hence 'There were different degrees of regional cohesion, even different kinds at different spatial scales. Regional differences were complex and presented different patterns according to different criteria, in terms of different aspects of life, and for different people.'[55] He goes on to contend that although the concept of a region in this period is acceptable, that of regionalism—a conscious sense of adherence and loyalty to a particular territory—was not: this had to await the influence of the industrial revolution.

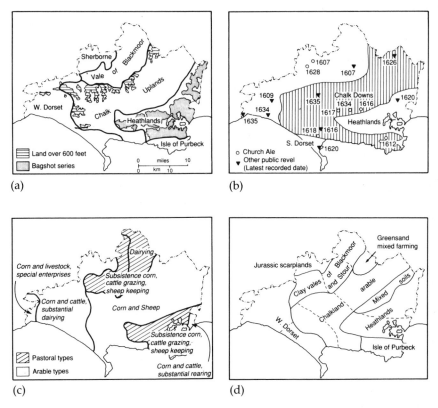

Fig. 9.2. Regional divisions of Dorset. (a) Domesday geography. (b) Regions and popular festivals of the early seventeenth century. (c) Farming regions, *c.* 1640–1750. (d) Modern land-use regions. *Sources*: (a) H. C. Darby and R. Welldon Finn (eds.), *The Domesday Geography of South-West England* (Cambridge, 1962), p. 128. (b) D. Underdown, *Revel, Riot and Rebellion* (Oxford, 1987), p. 92. (c) J. R. Wordie, 'The South and South-West', in J. Thirsk (ed.), *The Agrarian History of England and Wales, Vol. V.1 1640–1750. Regional farming systems*, (Cambridge, 1984) p. 360. (d) L. E. Tavener, 'Changes in the agricultural geography of Dorset 1929–49', *Transactions, Institute of British Geographers*, **18** (1952), p. 96.

Regions in the Eighteenth and Nineteenth Centuries

During the course of the eighteenth century one of the main stimuli to identify regions was the advancement of topographic and geological mapping. This is an extensive subject, which cannot be analysed at length here, but the increasingly widespread production of pre-Ordnance Survey maps such as the many estate surveys and the country topographic maps by the Greenwoods, the Armstrongs, Rocque, Andrews and Cary, for example, undoubtedly encouraged the incorporation of maps into reports on variations in agricultural practice, as ultimately did, of course, the production of maps by the Ordnance Survey, founded in 1791.

Agricultural Writings of the Eighteenth and Nineteenth Centuries

By the end of the eighteenth century, however, another new set of publications arose which are of considerable interest to the historian of regional history and geography in England and Wales. These derive from the foundation in 1793 of the Board of Agriculture and Internal Improvement, and its initiation of a survey of British agriculture on a county basis. The county reports, two for each county, appeared between 1793 and 1815. The first series, published between 1793 and 1796, known from their format as the quarto series, were intended for circulation among farmers in the county, with their comments intended for use in a revised or second edition, known as the octavo edition and published between 1795 and 1815, more frequently by a different author than the one who had written the first edition. They have the title of *A general View of the Agriculture of* . . . (Suffolk, Dorset, etc.).[56]

Although they vary greatly in approach, content and originality, they do for the most part contain maps of the county involved, frequently subdivided into soil or physical regions. Thus Arthur Young's *General View of the Agriculture of the County of Suffolk* (1804) contains a 'Map of the Soil of Suffolk', the major categories being 'Fen', 'Sand' Strong Loam' and 'Rich Loam', the boundaries of each soil region being clearly marked. Each of these regions is described in some detail: 'the western district of sand is a much poorer country, containing few spots of such rich sands as are found on the coast, but abounding largely with warrens and poor sheep-walks: a great deal under the plough *blows*, and consequently ranks among the worst of all soils, black sand on a yellow bottom perhaps excepted. Parts of the district take, however, the character of loamy sand; the whole angle, for instance, to the right of the line from Barrow to Honington, in which no blowing, or even very light sand is found. A more striking exception, though of small extent, is found at Mildenhall, where there is an open field of arable land of capital value, dry yet highly fertile, and friable without being loose; its products almost perpetual, and its fruitfulness almost unvaried.'[57] Thomas Davis, in his account of the agriculture of Wiltshire (1794) divided the county into two parts (see Fig.9.3), the South or Downland region, associated with sheep and corn, and the Northern region, whose principal farming characteristics divided between the dairy produce sub-region of the lower Avon and the Thames valleys, and the Vale of Pewsey, an arable area.[58] A number of problems arise from the attempts at regionalization by the reporters to the Board of Agriculture, including the frequent non-correspondence of soil and land-use regions, and the varying reliability of the sources of information which the reporters used. Nonetheless they do constitute, as Darby has suggested, 'the first large-scale attempt to indicate the regions of England.'[59]

An attempt to remedy some of the perceived defects of the county reports, especially the problem of regions being divided between the individual county volumes, was made by William Marshall, who in his survey of the *Rural Economy of the West of England* suggested that '*Natural*, not *fortuitous* lines, are to be traced; *Agricultural*, not *political*, distinctions, are to be regarded', (Vol. I, p.2), and spoke of 'natural districts' and 'farming districts'. He outlines the practice of these regional beliefs in a series of studies, including *The Rural Economy of Yorkshire* (1788), *The Rural Economy of Gloucestershire* (1789), and the more broadly based studies of the rural economy of the west of England (1796), the Midland counties (1790) and the

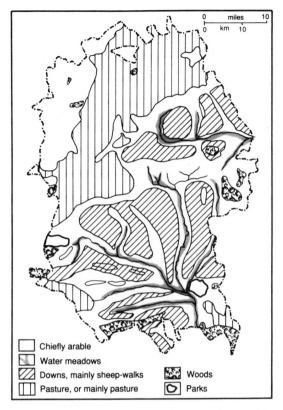

Chiefly arable

Water meadows

Downs, mainly sheep-walks   Woods

Pasture, or mainly pasture   Parks

Fig. 9.3. Regions of Wiltshire, 1794. *Source*: T. Davis, *General view of the agriculture of Wiltshire* (London, 1794).

southern counties (1798). He also abstracted the regional details from the Board of Agriculture county reports in a series of five volumes of abstracts and reviews, the first of which (*the Review and Abstract of the County Reports to the Board of Agriculture*, I, York, 1808) included a map or 'sketch' of the 'Natural Districts' of 'the northern department of England' (see Fig.9.4). In these reviews and abstracts he divided England into six 'departments' (northern, western, midland, eastern, southern and south-western), and further subdivided each of these into natural and agricultural districts.

Regionally based accounts, usually accompanied by maps, of the agriculture of particular counties are also contained in the later Prize Essays, initiated by, and printed in the *Journal of the Royal Agricultural Society*, between 1845 and 1869[60] and provide much more detail than Caird's fourfold division map (published in his *English Agriculture* in 1850–51). Their basis of regional division varies by author and county, and includes geology, crude soil regions, and farming regions. Prince has produced a summary map of agricultural regions of England, 1845–69, which incorporates the main regional ingredients of these prize essays (geology is their dominant feature) based on a classification of six types of region: chalk, sand, clay, upland, fenland and coal. Prince suggests that the consequence of the further

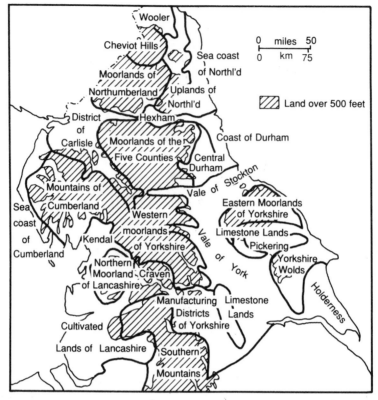

Fig. 9.4. 'Natural districts' of northern England, 1808. *Source*: William Marshall, *The Review and Abstract of the County Reports to the Board of Agriculture, Vol. I* (York, 1808).

involvement of agriculture in England and Wales in international markets produced regional contrasts that were 'sharper and more intricate in 1850 than they had been in 1750'.[61] A detailed analysis of the regional schemes for Warwickshire and Worcestershire advanced in the late eighteenth and the nineteenth century by such agricultural writers as Wedge, Murray, Evershed and Caird has been undertaken by Jarvis, who shows that the perceptions of the 'natural districts' or regions of the two counties varied between the different authors, including the distinction between the Arden and Felden regions of Warwickshire.[62]

The agricultural writers of the later eighteenth century in some respects reflect the views of the new theories of political economy. Change, 'improvement', the efficacy of the hidden hand of 'the market', and the increasing exposure to a developing global economy, were important contextual elements. In economic terms, the increasing demands of the market of an expanding metropolis—London—accelerated the bond between capital and the rest of England and, indeed, Wales. Yet, at the same time, these demands accentuated the market specialisms of particular regions, and thus seem to have accentuated regional economic differences. As Porter puts it, '. . . England was a mosaic in which regional contrasts remained ineradicable. These were partly because of the heterogeneous demands of

London food consumption and, more generally, because England was a market economy with each region specializing in particular commodities. Differences were also environmental responses to variations of latitude, altitude, soil, and climate. Local economies were epicycles in the orbit of the national (partly because some were illicit—for instance the underground distributive networks that poaching, coining and smuggling boosted).'[63]

Regions and Industrialization: the Late Eighteenth and Nineteenth Centuries

Regional Administration

It is a known fact that the geography of England and Wales was changing rapidly in the course of the nineteenth century, the census statistics alone being adequate proof. Change in the distribution of population, notably evidenced in intense urbanization and, later in the century, rural depopulation, together with related changes in the ideologies of power and government, produced new strategies for the solution of problems in such fields of concern as health, sanitation, education, poverty, and law and order.

The regional affiliations and strategies experienced in England and Wales reflect some of these complex changes, both in attempts to preserve traditional ways of life and custom (by the new county archaeological and antiquarian societies, discussed below) and also through the re-organization of the systems of administration which affected many aspects of the daily life of the populace. It is remarkable that very few attempts have been made by historical geographers to trace and analyse the course of the changing geography of administration in England and Wales in the nineteenth century, and T.W. Freeman's *Geography and Regional Administration. England and Wales 1830–1968* (1968)[64] is one of the few analyses of such matters, though its main concern is with twentieth-century reforms.

Some indication of the problems faced by administrators charged with keeping up with the changing regional geography of the nineteenth century is reflected in the sections on units of administration in the Census reports. The first volume of the 1851 Census report contains a long and interesting review of the history of the territorial divisions and subdivisions of Britain, largely, it would seem, to demonstrate the irregularity and inconvenience for census-takers of the historical territorial divisions. 'The old division of the country into parishes, townships, and counties, is open to many of the objections which lie against hundreds. Parishes are, in many instances, almost inextricably intermingled; and they vary in population from single families to tens of thousands of families; in extent from a few hundreds of acres to many thousands of acres. The counties are also irregularly and unequally constituted . . .'[65] A note of frustration eventually creeps in, though modified by Civil Service discretion: 'The inconveniences and perplexities which the variety of ecclesiastical, military and civil, fiscal and judicial, ancient and modern, municipal and parliamentary, subdivisions of the country occasion, have been sensibly felt by us as they were brought under our notice in the enumeration of the population. It is not within our province to reduce them to simplicity and harmony; we call your attention to their existence; and venture humbly to suggest that the task of taking any future Census, the comparison of statistical facts of any kind, and probably all administrative arrangements, would be greatly facilitated by the adoption of a uniform system of territorial divisions in Great Britain.'[66]

An interesting innovation introduced in 1851, essentially for the purpose of creation of uniform statistical divisions, was a system of thirteen new 'Divisions', comprising groups of geographical counties. The divisions were: London; South-eastern (Sussex, Hampshire and Berkshire with non-metropolitan parts of Surrey and Kent); South Midland (Bedfordshire, Cambridgeshire, Hertfordshire, Buckinghamshire, Oxfordshire, Northamptonshire and Huntingdonshire, together with the non-metropolitan parts of Middlesex); Eastern (Essex, Suffolk and Norfolk); South-western (Somerset, Wiltshire, Dorset, Devon and Cornwall), West Midland (Worcestershire, Warwickshire, Gloucestershire, Herefordshire, Shropshire and Staffordshire); North Midland (Nottinghamshire, Lincolnshire, Rutland, Leicestershire and Derbyshire); North-western (Lancashire and Cheshire); Yorkshire; Northern (Cumberland, Northumberland, Durham and Westmorland). Wales was a whole division, and Scotland was two divisions. These divisions, as the Census report indicates, were based in part on historic areas, including Saxon kingdoms, but this historic sensitivity is more than offset by the wish to standardize their areas for statistical purposes. This 'regionalization of 1851', as Freeman calls it,[67] survived into the second half of the twentieth century.

The County

The county remained an important basis of administration of England and Wales, and in mid-century the main county officers, many of whom held honorary, unpaid posts, were the lord lieutenant who was also keeper of the archives, a sheriff, under-sheriff, justices of the peace, and county coroner. The main expenditure by the county was on the maintenance of bridges, gaols, police, prisoners, lunatic asylums and the payment of some county officers.[68] The county was a unit for the administration of large rural areas and their market and county towns, though the growth of large urban areas necessitated the creation of separate units—county boroughs—by the end of the nineteenth century. The role of the county in administration did in some senses change during the nineteenth century, albeit in a complex way. Olney, in his study of *Rural Society and County Government in Nineteenth-century Lincolnshire* (1979) has documented and analysed the changes in a large, mainly rural, county. The major changes reflected a doubling of population, a greater concentration of population in towns, the revolution in communications, much stronger ties with London, and changes in the structure and balance of social classes. Olney shows that in spite of superficial similarity of administrative function within the county between 1880 and 1900, at a deeper level much had changed. Thus, the locational social geography of county society had moved from social activities focused on and around the assizes, Lincoln races, and the colour ball in October and November, to an autumn on the grouse moors of Scotland, continental excursions after the London social season, a January date for the colour ball, and a loss of social importance of the assizes, partly because of the decline in importance and activity of the grand jury and the loss of power of the lord lieutenancy. All this occurred principally at the top of the social spectrum. In contrast, however, the middle classes had effected a renewal of county activities with the foundation of the Lincolnshire Agricultural Society in 1869 and county professional bodies established by lawyers, doctors and land agents. The established church was more in evidence at county level, in contrast to the Methodists, whose circuits ignored county boundaries.[69]

Olney concludes his study with the view that by 1900 the social and administrative unity of Lincolnshire was weaker than it had been early in the nineteenth century, and that county consciousness was in decline. The circumscription of the functions of the lord lieutenant and the gaol sessions (the county had lost its gaol by the end of the century), political fragmentation and the predominance of class feeling over local feeling, and the decline of the position of the greater gentry because of newer elements in local society and declining agricultural rents, all were contributing factors. He suggests that '. . . it is not surprising that county feeling was sapped by the partial urbanization of Lincolnshire in the later nineteenth century, Townsmen found their way onto the bench, and the introduction of the county councils increased their importance. Urban ways of thought were carried into the country-side by newspapers, nonconformist preachers, trade union emissaries, political organizers, and town workers returning to their native villages for the annual feast. During the Boer War national and world events were more closely studied in Lincolnshire than for many years previously. With education came broader hori-zons, and increased mobility meant that the county was becoming ever less self-contained.'[70] In a review of Olney's book, Thompson offers advice to regional historians, relative to Olney's opinion that in 1800 Lincolnshire was too big yet by 1900 it was too small:'It is a message which all regional historians should take to heart: the effective area of a region, which is different at any one time for different social groups and different functions, also changes over time in response to changes in transport and accessibility, which are themselves responses to broad movements in population and economic activity both within and without the region, and outside the nation altogether.'[71]

Regional Identity and Antiquarianism

A particularly interesting feature of the role of the county in cultural matters was the very rapid rise of the county antiquarian and archaeological society from the mid nineteenth century. Piggott has listed some of the reasons for their emergence: 'The impact of the architectural expression of the High Church movement in the 1840s; the new romantic approach to history, the improvement of transport with new roads, and, of course, for long-distance of travel between towns, the railways (the London and Birmingham from 1828); the receptive temper of the times—anxious for self-improvement, socially ambitious; the development of geology and prehistory : all these combined to make the emergence of local archaeological societies inevitable around the middle of the last century.'[72] The earliest of the societies were founded in the 1840s and 1850s. These included those of Northamptonshire and Lincolnshire (1844), Norfolk (1846), Sussex, Bedfordshire, and Buckinghamshire (1848), Lancas-hire and Cheshire (1848), Leicestershire (1855), the Cambrian Archaeological Associ-ation (1847), Wiltshire (1853) and Surrey (1854). Piggot makes the interesting point that the 'earliest societies are practically all in those parts of England dominated by the Anglican church and with an agricultural and squirearchical background, and not in the Midlands and North where Nonconformity of some kind was prevalent',[73] though this thesis has been questioned by Levine,[74] who points out that although during the 1840s and 1850s the majority of such societies were founded in the south-east, from the 1860s onwards when interest broadened from the hitherto dominant interest in Anglican architecture a host of societies was established across the country in both urban and rural areas. The industrial areas additionally had a rather different kind of learned society, such as the Lunar and the Literary and Philosophi-cal societies, themselves significant reflections of the changing hegemony of the eighteenth and early nineteenth centuries, though within the industrializing cities there were recognizable hierarchies of learned societies, with the Literary and Philosophical societies, as Billinge has shown, catering for the upper middle class, various scientific and cultural societies for the middle and lower middle class, and the Mechanics' Institutes for the working class.[75]

The broader significance of the county archaeological and other learned societies has been discussed by Levine, who makes a distinction, *inter alia*, between the county archaeological societies, the printing societies (like the Camden Society and the Hakluyt Society, which published editions of historical documents), and the natural history and field clubs which also blossomed in the mid nineteenth cen-tury.[76] The printing societies rarely had meetings, and membership involved primarily a wish and willingness to subscribe to the societies' publications. In contrast, the archaeological and antiquarian societies had 'a more active and participatory membership',[77] a very distinct class structure, and fierce localist affiliation and sentiment. Membership was generally composed of the propertied and professional middle class, notably the Anglican clergy, whereas the natural history societies and field cubs, having generally a less formal structure and no institutional property (unlike the museums and libraries of the county archaeologi-cal societies), catered for a wider class spectrum.

The geographical import of the avowed purposes of these societies, notably the archaeological and antiquarian societies, is of direct relevance to a search for an understanding of changing regional and local sentiment in the nineteenth century. Levine indicates clearly that the county societies were symbolic of a fierce and militant localism that was determined to resist the erosion of distinctive regional and local differences in culture and tradition, even though it was recognized that the county was a somewhat artificial unit on which to base the operation of such sentiments. Thus: 'The energy that fuelled the success and trenchancy of the county societies was nonetheless channelled into a militant localism which defied the encroachment of a metropolitan culture. Local pride was the driving force behind the activities of the county societies, a localism born not of any sense of inferiority but whose determinant were located very firmly in a sense of place which bore little relation to legal boundaries. . . . It was not merely a simple protest against the loss of a rural way of life or the imposition of an ever more centralized power structure, but an affirmation of the role of provincial culture in a society increasingly prone to defer to the central authority of the urban and the metropolitan. But romantic nostalgia played no part in this. Despite the doubts, pride in modern achievements was common currency and the fruits of civilization were constantly lauded.'[78]

It might be that the county antiquarian societies in their energies and efforts reflected a particular dilemma of the mid nineteenth century, that of a rapidly changing society whose formal and informal sets of apparatus for social and political administration were being stretched, severely tested and found inadequate by such change, which, together with existing local and regional cultural affiliations produced a pragmatic resort to the revival of the role of existing administrative units, including the county, for entirely new or revised purposes. The antiquarian societies were, in effect, reflections of a whole range of new values and interests, including the attempted re-possession of the peoples and places of the past via a powerful sense of both local and national pride, together with the expression of the particular brand of Victorian morality (exhibited in the diplomatic editing of historical documents for publication, particularly personal letters). The symbolism of the spatial patterning of learned societies in the nineteenth century is, however, far from being fully explored and understood, and requires much more attention.

Industrialization and the Intensification of Regional Identity

There is debate on the extent to which the processes of industrialization and urbanization strengthened or weakened regional sensitivity in the period of the Industrial Revolution. Langton[79] has argued that there was in the mid nineteenth century ('the middle forty years') a period of intensification of regional cultural consciousness and cohesion, reflected in the dissolution of national associations of manufacturing and commercial interest pressure groups, a regionally structured disunity of social protest, including Chartism, Owenism and the co-operative movement, and the fragmentation of trade unions. A growing unity of regional character and consciousness, in a more positive sense, was reflected, from the late eighteenth century, in the needs for region-wide co-ordination, for example, of poor relief, and in such matters regional and local newspapers were to play an important role in the dissemination of information. Regional cultures, including dialect and folk culture, strengthened at this time, and regional feeling and activity was also reinforced by the variety of regional economic development, in turn assisted by the role of the canals and early railways in facilitating regional specialization. Langton argues in conclusion that the forces of national integration, especially the railway, which initiated national integration, intensified regional specialization in the short and medium term but extinguished it in the longer term. Reactions to this view are varied, both in general and in detail. Freeman, for example, while not questioning Langton's general thesis, suggests that the role of roads, including turnpikes, in the economic regionalism of early industrial geography of England, is underestimated, as is the regionalizing role of freight-carrying on the railways. Freeman feels that Langton 'has over-stated the case for economic regionalism during the earlier phases of industrialization and under-stated it for the later ones.'[80] Support for the notion of industrialization intensifying regional differences may be found in Dellheim's analysis of Victorian views of the north of England :'The growing concern with the north of England in the early nineteenth century was a by-product of industrialization. The initial impact of industrialization was to accentuate regional differences. In doing so it sparked provincial pride. . . . . In images if not in fact England's centre of gravity had definitely shifted northwards. Victorians explored diverse aspects of the North, including its history, archaeology, landscape, natural history, dialect, literature, industry and humour.'[81]

Gregory entered the debate by questioning the geographical extent of the region-differentiating processes (both outside, and in some cases within, manufacturing districts) and the notion that integration and differentiation are actually different processes. In respect of the latter argument he seeks the support of a number of authors, including Dodgshon,[82] on the experiences of regional specificity of cycles of capital investment in industry, and finishes with two basic propositions: the first that 'Regional systems were now necessarily rather than contingently tied to the world economy and the international division of labour'; secondly, that 'the production of regions became increasingly centralized.'[83] Langton's response[84] opens up some other interesting features of this question, including the notion that the centralizing tendency of government in the nineteenth century was, in fact, a late-nineteenth-century phenomenon and that the effect of the railway system's regional organization and freight rate policy also delayed integration.

The identification of regions and regional characteristics for the nineteenth century is a difficult exercise. Some of the questions and possibilities of solution have been raised in a preliminary way by Langton and Morris, in their introduction to the *Atlas of Industrializing Britain*.[85] They suggest that the period 1820–1914 may be characterized by three basic types of spatial pattern, in turn reflecting different scales and operation of different process: the core-periphery relationship between London and the rest of Britain (reflected in London's centrality in the railway network and its control of commercial and political systems); the development of industrial resource-rich areas, such as Lancashire, Yorkshire and the West Midlands, at the junction of highland and lowland Britain; and the much smaller-scale spatial patterns of the daily lives and horizons of individuals and groups. Such questions as the degree of independence of the new industrial regions and stability and change in cultural patterns in England, Wales and Scotland, remain to be answered. Of particular interest, as Langton and Morris suggest, is that of smaller-scale regions, indicating 'clear differences between the economic bases and cultures of broadly defined regions within the north and the Midlands' and 'hints of smaller-scale distinctions between the four northernmost counties and the rest of northern England, between southeast and southwest Lancashire, between the northern and southern parts of the West Riding of Yorkshire, between the east and west Midlands, and between the champion and wood-pasture regions in the south.'[86] They are entirely correct in their concluding emphasis on both the dialectical nature of processes of reciprocation between the elements and processes of an industrializing country and the different spatial logics of different historical processes. More work needs to be done at regional level to test such broad hypotheses.

There are, however, some recent studies by social and economic historians and by historical geographers which add both theory and empirical substance to the problem of regional identities. One helpful work is D. Smith's comparative study of class formation in Birmingham and Sheffield from 1830–1914, with particular reference to developments in industry, politics and education.[87] The essence of his thesis is that different processes of class formation were at work in the cities of Birmingham and Sheffield, strategically determined by three main sets of contrast: in the modes of social differentiation (Birmingham had a wide range of goods and a complex division of labour; Sheffield a narrower range, an intensive local subdivision of labour and a more specialized position in the national division of labour), in the scale of social organization (there was a disparity between the social organization of Sheffield and its county hinterland, whereas no such contrast was evident in the case of Birmingham and its hinterland), and in nodality and centrality (Birmingham being much better placed in relation to its regional and to national communications networks than was the more isolated Sheffield). In his description of the 'regional context' of social differentiation between the two cities in the period 1830–70, Smith points to the significance of the density of both industrial and rural agricultural villages and settlements in the Birmingham-centred Black Country, in contrast to Sheffield as a more isolated centre of population, contrasts in the 'regional aristocracies'—Sheffield being 'encircled by ermine'[88] (worn by men of great national influence), and although the West Midlands had its share of landed potentates they had much less national influence. The political tradition of Sheffield in the early nineteenth century was revolutionary, utopian and anarchistic. 'In and around Sheffield, the links between the regional aristocracy and the metropolis were very close while the parochial and plebeian character of the industrial population was very marked',[89] though this was to change with the advent of the steel magnates after about 1850. Birmingham, in contrast, had businessmen as leaders in public affairs, but with amicable collaboration with the county gentry. Birmingham, because of its nodal position, its newspapers, and greater percentage of population in professional groups, was a more active centre for broader than parochial political debate and cultural activity.

Regional contrasts, in this case of the manufacturing districts of Lancashire and the West Riding of Yorkshire, are also a central theme of P. Joyce's *Work, Society and Politics*. Joyce's main concern is with the history of popular politics and their links with factory-based production systems and the creation of a factory proletariat from the mid nineteenth century. The transitions to class-based Labour Party politics developed from different bases in Lancashire and the West Riding of Yorkshire, and the outcomes also differed. Hence 'later and less complete mechanization, and thus the more primitive organization of industry and of industrial relations, meant that the culture of the factory cut less deeply to the east of the Pennines, employer paternalism and the operatives' answering response less effectively sealing the society off from class antagonism. A major consequence of these differences was that in the West Riding working-class political organization took precedence over trade union organization, the Chartist political inheritance continuing as a vital presence in a radical tradition which reached more deeply into popular life than was the case in Lancashire.'[90]

The regional characteristics and dynamics of labour processes, production systems, class structures and means and forms of cultural and political expression are themes in D. Gregory's *Regional Transformation and Industrial Revolution*, a study of the woollen industry of the West Riding of Yorkshire in the eighteenth and nineteenth centuries. The development of production in this region, including the changes from the domestic production system to the more advanced capitalistic factory system, are viewed in relation not only to the geography of resources but also the organization and transformation of labour processes (differentially and at different rates between croppers, spinners and weavers) and labour protest at regional and national levels, reflecting in turn changes in class relations of production, political and cultural practice.[91]

A digest of the key ingredients of the better regional studies of the nineteenth century could most certainly incorporate a recognition of the scale factor, of the significance of labour and raw material resources, of the class structures and relations of the region and their interaction with and indication of the complexities of popular and national political and cultural expression. The end product of a synthesis of even many more such studies would not, of course, be a neat map of discrete regional units: more likely a confusing series of maps, Löschian rather than Christallerian in character, which would serve to indicate in an impressionistic way the highly complex and kaleidoscopic spatial patterns of regionality and regional consciousness in the nineteenth century.

Though most of the recent debate about regionalism and industrialization has been concerned with England, similar arguments could be applied to the industrializing parts of Wales. It would be interesting to have a separate analysis and attempted application of the hypotheses stated above for Wales. An additional and crucially important factor in Wales is, of course the question of the Welsh language, whose cultural and regional significance offers some insights into regional culture during the period of industrialization. Pryce[92] has studied this question in detail. The essence of his findings is that before industrialization, three language areas or zones can be identified: Welsh, bilingual, and English. Prior to industrialization of the north-eastern and south-eastern parts of the country, Welsh was the dominant language for the greater part of the country, bilingual zones (in the sense of both languages existing side by side) existing in the borders, the edge of the Vale of Glamorgan, with some outliers in parts of Gower and south Pembrokeshire. English as virtually the sole language prevailed in Radnor, east Monmouthshire, Gower and south Pembrokeshire. By 1900 significant changes had occurred, the Welsh-speaking area having shrunk in a westerly direction as a result of the expansion of the bilingual zone. The main factor was the immigration, especially to the new industrial communities of south-east Wales, by English and Irish immigrant workers. The inner Welsh-speaking core had shrunk considerably by 1900, monoglot Welsh-speaking populations being over half the total population of the counties of Anglesey, Caenarfon, Merioneth and Cardigan, a reduction from the early nineteenth century. The regional cultural implications of such changes are profound, and need further investigation over a wider range of cultural activities, of which language is a crucial and central feature.

The Regional Novel

One aspect of a growing interest in regional character and consciousness was the increase in the nineteenth century of the writing of 'regional' novels. The regional novel has been defined by Phyllis Bentley as 'a novel which, concentrating on a particular part, a particular region, of a nation, depicts the life of that region in such a way that the reader is conscious of the characteristics which are unique to that region and differentiate it from others . . .', and she suggests that the zenith of the regional novel was the period 1840–1940.[93] The merits of such novels for geographical investigation were recognized by Gilbert in the very perceptive section of his essay on 'The Idea of the region', in which he stated the 'English regional novelists display many merits that geographers can recognize and envy. The novel has illuminated the English landscape more brilliantly than any other art. Again many novels present life and work on a clearly marked piece of land with truth. Reality is faithfully shown: it is not lost in the dim twilight of modern geographical jargon.'[94]

The use of the regional novel as evidence of the character of distinctive places in the past is exemplified by Darby's work on Hardy's Wessex.[95] Darby, like Gilbert, sees the regional novel as useful and reasonably reliable geographical evidence, conveying perhaps through the vast array of techniques of description a greater sense of place than a map. In his study of Hardy's Wessex he uses a basis of five regions (Chalk uplands, Vale of Blackmoor, Heathlands, Isle of Purbeck, Hilly Clay lands), essentially the regions of Dorset (see Fig. 9.2), and relates these to the topographic and landscape characteristics of specific novels. Thus '"The Return of the Native" is the main source for the description of the heath country, though there are references to the heaths in many of the other novels. "The Woodlanders" is the main source for the description of the western corner of the Vale of Blackmoor. The action of "The Hand of Ethelberta" is largely centred on the Isle of Purbeck . . . Perhaps the novel that in itself best illustrates the varying countryside of Dorset is "Tess of the d'Urbervilles". Its scenes cover three main elements in Dorset scenery–clay vale, upland, and heathland—and they also give glimpses of the rest of the county.'[96] Barrell[97] examines the Hardy novels from a different perspective: the 'geographies' of the characters and the narrators in *Tess of the d'Urbervilles* and *The Return of the Native*, the former characterized by a circular, 'primal' vision of geography, cartography and the picturesque.

A cautionary view of the wholesale and unqualified use of the regional novel as geographical evidence has been advanced by Freeman, who, in discussion of the problems of understanding the regional geography of industrializing England, has suggested that 'one needs to be wary of seeing the genre of the regional novel as reflecting a singular raison d'être: that is the explication of distinctive regional cultures as they are thrown into sharp relief by various forces of national cohesion. Hardy's Wessex novels fit the genre, but others (for instance those of Arnold Bennett) appear much more as exegeses of *intensifying* regional cultures, springing from the continuing forces of regional differentiation'.[98]

Regionalism in a literary sense, Draper contends, starts in the late eighteenth century, and is a conscious reaction to the growing awareness of changes through industrialization, a broader economy and changes in transportation, manifesting not only a regret for what might be disappearing, but also a recognition of the complexity of regional and local culture and the need for some form of preservation. This affirmation of regional values, he claims, is to be found in Book VII of Wordsworth's *The Prelude*, is 'echoed in the work of Scott, and continues in the work of Mrs Gaskell, the Brontës and George Eliot, culminating in the novels (and also the poems) of Thomas Hardy. Though the "centre" prospered and became increasingly powerful in the nineteenth century, writers such as these resisted its pressures and helped to cultivate in the minds of their readers the notion of a regional/provincial counterbalance to its homogenizing influence', Hardy going further than Wordsworth (both having brought fame to the regions about which they wrote and in which they lived) by 'not merely defending provincial values, but also creating a geographical, mapped regionalism which scarcely exists as such in the work of Wordsworth.'[99]

A chronology of development of the regional novel has been outlined by Lucine

R. A. Butlin

Fig. 9.5. Regional novelists of England and Wales. *Source*: L. Leclaire, *A General Analytical Bibliography of Regional Novelists of the British Isles* (Paris, 1954); see also E. W. Gilbert, 'The idea of the region', *Geography*, **45**, 2 (1960), pp. 157–75.

Leclaire[100], whose maps were the basis of Gilbert's study, and a revised version of which comprises Fig.9.5. The first phase of the regional novel is the period 1800–30, in which predominated 'the novel of national manners and the region', largely confined to Scotland and Ireland. The second phase, 1830–70, is that in which 'the novel becomes localized "into the bargain"', and in which 'we can observe . . . the appearance of writers who fixed upon some part of the country to which they were bound by some circumstances of birth, long residence, family history, — that is to say, in which they took so much interest that it lent to their stories the fittest scenes materially, and above all, sentimentally', with the locale being evolved almost subconsciously.[101] Those whose works are cited in this category include the Brontë sisters, Mrs Gaskell, Charles Kingsley, and George Eliot. Leclaire's third phase is that of 'The regional novel proper', after 1870, and is divided into sub-categories, only two of which concern us here: 'picturesque regionalism' (1870–95), including the novels of Thomas Hardy and Richard Jefferies; and 'sentimental regionalism' (1890–1914), including James Barrie, Arthur Quiller-Couch, Joseph Fletcher and others. Gilmour, in a study of the debate on 'regional' and 'provincial' in Victorian literature, accepts these broad chronological categories, and highlights the contrast between the novels of George Eliot and of Thomas Hardy to illustrate, from the opening chapter of *The Woodlanders* (1887), that 'Hardy's uncertainties of tone reflect a more widespread problematics of the provincial in late Victorian culture, a separation of the provincial from the national which is absent from the work of the great mid-Victorian regional novelists like George Eliot, the Brontës and Elizabeth Gaskell', a fulcrum of the change being Matthew Arnold's 1864 essay on 'the Literary Influence of Academies', in which he critically separates and contrasts the urbane literature of metropolis and the lesser works produced in the provinces.[102]

In order, however, to look into the question of regional identity in the later nineteenth century and beyond through a particular type of novel, much more needs to be done than list, locate, classify and quote selectively. The context is very much broader than this. Thus Raymond Williams in an interesting short essay on 'Region and class in the novel'[103] indicates that there are ideological implications in the possible answers to the question of the distinctiveness of the regions involved. Three different perspectives are offered. The first is that some places are regions, 'with a localized or provincial character, while certain other places are not',[104] reflective from the later nineteenth century onwards of the centralization of national administration and the delegation on a limited basis to areas or regions, that is subordinate local areas. To this apparent administrative discrimination is added a sense of cultural discrimination, reflecting the ideological notion that 'the life and people of certain favoured regions are seen as essentially general, even perhaps normal, while the life and people of certain other regions, however interestingly and affectionately presented, are, well, regional'.[105] The cultural context is clearly that of the emergence of a metropolitan and provincial polity and culture, initiated in the eighteenth and intensifying in the nineteenth century. Williams makes the interesting point that novels about the 'Home Counties' and London are not generally classed as regional, whereas those about more 'distant' parts are.

The second is that 'certain novels are "regional" in the sense that they tell us primarily, or solely, about such places and the life lived in them, rather than about any more general life',[106] with strong implications that the life lived in such regions is an unspoiled relic of a utopian and essentially rural past, having few links with an extra-regional world of urbanization and industrialization. The paradox of variants on this view, as Williams indicates, is that Hardy—regarded as the quintessential regional novelist—is very much more than that: 'To put the matter more generally, the fiction in which to explore and clarify the problem of "regionalism" is, of course, pre-eminently Hardy's. Some metropolitan idiots still think of Hardy as a regional novelist because he wrote about Wessex—that strange, peculiar place—rather than about London or the Home Counties. But at a more serious level, the distinction is very clear inside Hardy's work, as between, on the one hand, *Under the Greenwood Tree* and even *Far From the Madding Crowd*, which can be seen as regional in an encapsulating and enclosing sense, and *The Woodlanders* or *Tess of the d'Urbervilles*, which are set even more deeply in their region but which are not in any limiting sense 'regional': what happens in them, internally and externally—those two abstractions in a connected process—involves a very wide and complex, a fully extended and extensive sense of relationships.'[107]

The third reflection on the distinctiveness of the regions of regional novels has much to do with the specificity of context of the social life therein described, focusing on the way of life of a place or region. The regional novel was written from an internal perspective, the viewpoint of the inhabitants or natives of the region, in contrast, as Williams indicates, to the early forms of working-class industrial novel, which date from the 1840s, written by 'visitors' and 'sympathetic observers', the forms of the novel at the time offering no points of entry to working-class writers, whose energies were directed to different means, including pamphlets, autobiographies and popular and dialect verse.[108] Later, in the late nineteenth and early twentieth centuries, different trends develop in the regional literature. There seems, for example, to have been a marked tendency for the regional and more generally rural literature to be strongly related to a concept of metropolitan bourgeois Englishness, manifest in the work of W. H. Hudson, Edward Thomas and George Sturt, for example. This Englishness was, as Howkins has indicated, associated with 'a specific social formation, the South Country' and thus 'the writings of people like Sturt and Hudson gave a political shape to Englishness', stressing the notions of 'continuity, of community or harmony, and above all a special kind of classlessness',[109] the latter a reflection of the agricultural depression of the 1890s. This 'South Country' image was projected into a national ideology, and paralleled similar images projected by other forms, including music and art.

Several writers have pointed to the effects of increasing facility of travel in the nineteenth century, especially the railway, as an important catalyst in the heightening regional consciousness by novelists of the Victorian period. Keith, for example, instances George Eliot's Adam Bede as an indication of 'feeling towards that sense of regional consciousness which is so important and neglected a development in the Victorian period. Advances in communications, the improvement of roads and the establishment of the railway system, had "opened up" the countryside for exploration and comparison. The Victorians, we might say, learned to recognize not a generalized countryside but a series of different countrysides with their own physical features, history, customs, dialects and ways of living. The Victorian writers, whether of poetry, fiction or discursive prose, had an important role to play in this awakening.'[110] It was this heightening of regional consciousness which also strengthened and intensified the sense of a need to preserve it from erosion by the forces of centralization and standardization, hence, as shown above, the rise of the county antiquarian societies.

The Victorian regional novel has, therefore, much to offer as evidence not only of the specific facts and perceptions of regions and regionalism, but also (and equally important) reflects changes in the relations between metropolis and provincial regions, in turn conditioned by increasing centralization of government and internationalization of economic relations. This was an aspect of change of which Thomas Hardy was fully aware, indicating, as Keith has stated, the importance to him personally of 'the impact of national, non-regional pressures on local regional lives that was to become the central concern of his fiction.'[111]

Conclusion

Those who attempt to identify and construct regions for all or parts of England and Wales for the time-period from the late medieval to the modern era are bound to encounter major conceptual and practical difficulties. Perhaps the most readily committed error is to assume that a scheme of regions is somehow naturally available, determined by some hidden laws of spatial allocation, which can be recovered by assiduous and ingenious scholarly application. Another is the assumption that a scheme of, say, agricultural regions drawn up for the seventeenth century might equally as well apply to the early sixteenth, thus ignoring the dynamics of regional change. Two methods of construction of regions may be positively commended, however. The first, of which some examples are given above, involves the attempt to fathom and interpret the ideas and place perception of those who in the past have exhibited regional sensitivity in their schemes and writings or have drawn up and attempted to implement schemes of regional division for purposes of scientific description or improvement of social, economic and political administration. The second, and probably more important, involves the need to attempt to construct regions and regional systems *de novo* from adequate theoretical bases, and which employ such criteria and elements as class, popular culture and politics, the interaction of social processes at local, national and international scales, together with such resources as land, industrial raw materials and transport systems. The construction of the regional geography of the past need not be constrained by the lack of ready-made systems of regionalization: the real challenge for geographer and historian is that of informed and innovative invention of schemes by means of which spatial patterns of the past may be better understood.

Acknowledgement

I am grateful to David Fussell, Michael Heffernan and Morag Bell for helpful comments and references.

References

1. A. Everitt, 'Country, county and town: patterns of regional evolution in England', *Translations of the Royal Historical Society*, **29** (1979), p.106. See also A. Everitt, *Landscape and Community in England*, (London, 1985).
2. E. W. Gilbert, 'The idea of the region', *Geography*, **45**, 3 (1960), pp. 157–75.
3. F. W. Morgan, 'Three aspects of regional consciousness', *Sociological Review*, **31** (1939), pp. 68–88.
4. *Ibid.*, p. 77.
5. D. Gregory, 'region', in R. J. Johnston, D. Gregory and D. M. Smith (eds.), *The Dictionary of Human Geography*, (2nd edn.) (Oxford, 1986), pp. 394–5.
6. A. Gilbert, 'The new regional geography in English and French speaking countries', *Progress in Human Geography*, **12**, 2 (1988), pp. 208–28.
7. *Ibid.*, p. 212.
8. H. C. Darby, *The Domesday Geography of Eastern England*, (3rd edn.) (Cambridge, 1971); H. C. Darby and I. B. Terrett (eds.), *The Domesday Geography of Midland England*, (2nd edn., Cambridge, 1971); H. C. Darby and E. M. J. Campbell (eds.), *The Domesday Geography of*

South-East England, (Cambridge, 1962); H. C. Darby and I. S. Maxwell (eds.), *The Domesday Geography of Northern England*, (Cambridge, 1962); H. C. Darby and R. Welldon Finn (eds.), *The Domesday Geography of South-West England*, (Cambridge, 1967).

9.   J. D. Marshall, 'Why study regions?(1)', *The Jnl. of Regional and Local Studies*, **5**, 1, (1985), pp. 15–27; J. D. Marshall, 'Why study regions? (2)', *The Jnl. of Regional and Local Studies*, **6**, 1 (1986), pp. 1–12.

10. A. R. H. Baker, in A. R. H. Baker and D. Gregory, 'Some *terrae incognitae* in historical geography: an exploratory discussion', in A. R. H. Baker and D. Gregory (eds.), *Explorations in Historical Geography*, (Cambridge, 1984), p. 191.

11. J. Langton and R. J. Morris (eds.), *Atlas of Industrializing Britain. 1780–1914*, (London, 1986).

12. F. W. Morgan, 'Three aspects of regional consciousness', *Sociological Review*, **31** (1939), p. 69.

13. *Ibid.*, p. 69.

14. R. Williams, *The Country and the City*, (London, 1976).

15. A. Everitt, 'Country, county and town: patterns of regional evolution in England', *Transactions of the Royal Historical Society*, **29** (1979), pp. 79–108.

16. E. Kerridge, *The Farmers of Old England*, (London, 1973).

17. Everitt, 'Country, county and town...', pp. 81–2.

18. F. V. Emery, 'English regional studies from Aubrey to Defoe', *Geographical Jnl.*, **cxxiv**, 3 (1958), pp. 315–25.

19. J. Lucas, *The Idea of the Provincial*, Inaugural lecture, Loughborough University, 1981.

20. D. Read, *The English Provinces c. 1760–1960* (London, 1964), p. 3.

21. *Ibid.*, p. 18 *seq.*

22. See, for example, P. Claval and E. Juillard, *Région et Régionalisation dans la Géographie Française*, (Paris, 1967).

23. A. Giddens, *A Contemporary Critique of Historical Materialism*, Vol. 1, (London 1981), pp. 34–41.

24. A. Jonas, 'A new regional geography of localities', *Area*, **20**, 2 (1988), p. 103.

25. A. Giddens, 'Time Space and Regionalization', in D. Gregory and J. Urry (eds.), *Social Relations and Spatial Structures*, (London, 1985), pp. 265–95.

26. A. Gilbert, 'The new regional geography in English and French speaking countries', *Progress in Human Geography*, **12**, 2 (1988), p. 220.

27. F. V. Emery, 'Irish Geography in the Seventeenth Century', *Irish Geography*, **III**, 5, (1958), pp. 263–76.

28. John Bill, *An Abridgement of Camden's 'Britannia'*, (London, 1626), p.5.

29. Cited by Brian John in *Pembrokeshire*, (Greencroft Books, Newport, 1978 edn.), p. 59.

30. J. Simmons, *English County Historians*, (E. P. Publishing Ltd., Wakefield, 1978), p.7.

31. S. Piggot, 'Introduction' to facsimile edition of Gibson's 1695 edition of *Britannia*, (Newton Abbott, 1971), p. 9.

32. J. Camden, *Britannia*, (facsimile of 1695 edition, Newton Abbot 1971), pp. 402–3.

33. S. Piggott, 'Introduction' to *Britannia*, p. 9.

34. S. Piggott, *Ruins in a Landscape, Essays in Antiquarianism*, (Edinburgh, 1976), p. 111.

35. F. V. Emery, 'English regional studies from Aubrey to Defoe', *Geographical Jnl.*, **cxxiv**, 3 (1958), p. 315.

36. S. Piggot, *Ruins in a Landscape, Essays in Antiquarianism*, (Edinburgh, 1976).

37. *Ibid.*, p. 107.

38. R. Plot, *Natural History of Staffordshire*, (Oxford, 1686) p. 392. See also R. A. Butlin, 'Plot's Natural History of Staffordshire: an appraisal', *North Staffordshire Jnl. of Field Studies*, **2** (1962), pp. 88–95.

39. Emery, 'English regional studies...', pp. 317–8.

40. R. Plot, *Natural History of Staffordshire*, (Oxford, 1686), p. 120.

41. Emery, 'English regional studies', p. 318.

42. E. Kerridge, *The Agricultural Revolution*, (London, 1967).

43. J. Thirsk, 'The farming regions of England', in J. Thirsk (ed.) *The Agrarian History of England and Wales, Volume IV, 1500–1640*, (Cambridge, 1967), pp. 1–112.

44. F. V. Emery, 'The farming regions of Wales', in J. Thirsk (ed.), *The Agrarian History of England and Wales, Volume IV, 1500–1640*, (Cambridge, 1967), pp. 113–60.

45. J. Thirsk (ed.), *The Agrarian History of England and Wales Volume V. 1640–1750. Part I. Regional Farming Systems,* (Cambridge, 1984).
46. F. V. Emery, 'Wales', in J. Thirsk (ed.), *The Agrarian History of England and Wales, Volume V, 1640–1750. Part I. Regional farming systems,* (Cambridge, 1984), pp. 393–428.
47. J. Thirsk, *England's Agricultural Regions and Agrarian History, 1500–1700,* (London, 1987).
48. A review of this debate is to be found in Clive Holmes, 'The county community of Stuart historiography', *Jnl. of British Studies,* **XIX,** (1979–80), pp. 54–73.
49. A. Everitt, *The Community of Kent and the Great Rebellion,* (Leicester, 1966).
50. Holmes, 'The county community', p. 73.
51. K. Wrightson, *English Society 1580–1680,* (London, 1982).
52. D. Underdown, *Revel, Riot and Rebellion,* (Oxford, 1985).
53. J. Thirsk, 'The farming Regions of England', in Thirsk (ed.), *The Agrarian History of England and Wales, Volume IV,* pp. 1–15.
54. Underdown, *Revel, Riot and Rebellion,* p. 206.
55. J. Langton, 'The industrial revolution and the regional geography of England', *Transactions, Institute of British Geographers,* new ser., **9,** 2 (1984), p. 152.
56. H. C. Darby, 'Some early ideas on the agricultural regions of England', *Agricultural History Review,* **11** (1954), pp. 30–47; H. C. Prince, 'England *circa* 1800', in H. C. Darby (ed.), *A New Historical Geography of England,* (Cambridge, 1973), pp. 400–2.
57. A. Young, *A General View of the Agriculture of the County of Suffolk,* (London, 1804; citation from 1813 edition), pp. 5–6.
58. Gordon East, 'Land utilisation in England at the end of the eighteenth century', *Geographical Jnl.,* **1xxxix** (1937), pp. 156–72.
59. Darby, 'Some early ideas...', p. 37. See also, H. C. Prince, 'The changing rural landscape', in G. E. Mingay (ed.), *The Agrarian History of England and Wales, Volume V, 1750–1850,* (1989), pp. 7–15.
60. Darby, 'Some early ideas', pp. 41–7; Prince, 'The changing rural landscape', pp. 76–83.
61. Prince, 'The changing rural landscape', p. 83.
62. P. J. Jarvis, 'The perception of agricultural regions in nineteenth century Warwickshire and Worcestershire', in T. R. Slater and P. J. Jarvis (eds.), *Field and Forest. An Historical Geography of Warwickshire and Worcestershire,* (Norwich, 1982), pp. 301–22.
63. R. Porter, *English Society in the Eighteenth Century,* (Harmondsworth, 1982), p. 55.
64. T. W. Freeman, *Geography and Regional Administration, England and Wales 1830–1968,* (London, 1968).
65. *Census of Great Britain 1851: Population Tables 1, Vol. 1,* p.lxxix.
66. *Ibid.,* p.lxxx.
67. Freeman, *Geography and Regional Administration,* p. 63.
68. *Census of Great Britain 1851: Population Tables 1, Vol. 1,* p. lxii.
69. R. J. Olney, *Rural Society and County Government in Nineteenth-Century Lincolnshire,* (Lincoln, 1979), pp. 172–5.
70. *Ibid.,* pp. 184–5.
71. F. M. L. Thompson, 'Country matters', *History,* **66** (1981), p. 438.
72. S. Piggot, 'The origins of the English county archaeological societies', in *Ruins in a Landscape. Essays in Antiquarianism,* (Edinburgh, 1976), p. 190.
73. *Ibid.,* p. 191.
74. P. Levine, *The Amateur and the Professional. Antiquarians. Historians and Archaeologists in Victorian England, 1838–1886,* (Cambridge, 1986).
75. M. D. Billinge, *Late Georgian and Early Victorian Manchester: a Cultural Geography,* Cambridge University, Ph.D. thesis, (1984); M. D. Billinge, 'Hegemony, class and power in late Georgian and early Victorian England: towards a cultural geography', in A. R. H. Baker and M. D. Billinge (eds.), *Explorations in Historical Geography,* (Cambridge, 1984), pp. 28–67.
76. P. Levine, *The Amateur and the Professional. Antiquarians, Historians and Archaeologists in Victorian England, 1838–1866,* (Cambridge, 1986).
77. *Ibid.,* p. 46.
78. *Ibid.,* p. 59.
79. J. Langton, 'The industrial revolution and the regional geography of England', *Transactions, Institute of British Geographers,* new ser., **9,** 2 (1984), pp. 145–67.

80. M. Freeman, 'The industrial revolution and the regional geography of England: a comment', *Transactions, Institute of British Geographers*, new ser., **9**, 4 (1984), pp. 507–12.

81. C. Dellheim, 'Imagining England: Victorian Views of the North', *Northern History*, **xxii** (1987) pp. 218–9.

82. R. A. Dodgshon, *The European Past: Social Evolution and Spatial Order*, (London, 1987).

83. D. Gregory, 'The production of regions in England's Industrial Revolution', *Jnl. of Historical Geography*, **14**, 1 (1988), pp. 50–8.

84. J. Langton, 'The production of regions in England's Industrial Revolution: a response', *Jnl. of Historical Geography*, **14**, 2 (1988), pp. 170–4.

85. J. Langton and R. J. Morris (eds.), *Atlas of Industrializing Britain*, (London, 1986).

86. *Ibid.*

87. D. Smith, *Conflict and Compromise. Class Formation in English Society 1830–1914*, (London 1982).

88. *Ibid.*, p. 27.

89. *Ibid.*, p. 32.

90. P. Joyce, *Work, Society and Politics, The Culture of the Factory in Later Victorian England*, (Brighton, 1980), p. 331.

91. D. Gregory, *Regional Transformation and Industrial Revolution. A Geography of the Yorkshire Woollen Industry*, (London, 1982).

92. W. T. R. Pryce, 'Wales as a culture region: patterns of change 1750–1971'; *Transactions, Hon. Society of Cymmrodorion*, (1978), pp. 229–61.

93. P. Bentley, *The English Regional Novel*, (London, 1941), p. 7.

94. E. W. Gilbert, 'The idea of the region', *Geography*, **45**, 3 (1960), pp. 157–75. See pp. 163–9, 'The regional novel'.

95. H. C. Darby, 'The regional geography of Thomas Hardy's Wessex', *Geographical Review*, **38** (1948), pp. 426–43.

96. *Ibid.*, p. 442–3.

97. J. Barrell, 'Geographies of Hardy's Wessex', *Jnl. of Historical Geography*, **8**, 4 (1982), pp. 347–61.

98. M. Freeman, 'The industrial revolution and the regional geography of England: a comment', *Transactions, Institute of British Geographers*, new ser., **9**, 4 (1984) p. 511.

99. R. P. Draper, 'Introduction', in R. P. Draper (ed.), *The Literature of Region and Nation*, (London, 1989), pp. 3–4.

100. L. Leclaire, *A General Analytical Bibliography of the Regional Novelists of the British Isles*, (Paris, 1954). Also L. Leclaire, *Le Roman Régionaliste dans les Iles Britanniques 1800–1950*, (Clermont-Ferrand, 1954).

101. Leclaire, *A General Analytical Bibliography*, p. 51.

102. R. Gilmour, 'Regional and provincial in Victorian literature', in R. Draper (ed.), *The Literature of Region and Nation*, pp. 54–6.

103. R. Williams, 'Region and class in the novel', in D. Jefferson and G. Martin (eds.), *The Uses of Fiction*, (London, 1982), pp. 59–68.

104. *Ibid.*, p. 59.

105. *Ibid.*, p. 60.

106. *Ibid.*, p. 59.

107. *Ibid.*, p. 60–1.

108. *Ibid.*, pp. 63–4.

109. A Howkins, 'The discovery of Rural England', in R. Colls and P. Dodd (eds.), *Englishness, Politics and Culture 1880– 1920*, (London, 1986), pp. 74–5.

110. W. J. Keith, 'The Land in Victorian Literature', in G. E. Mingay (ed.), *The Victorian Countryside*, Vol. I. (London, 1981), p. 139.

111. W. J. Keith, *Regions of the Imagination. The Development of British Rural Fiction*, (Toronto, 1988). p. 86.

10

The Changing Evaluation of Space 1500–1914

R. A. Dodgshon

Ideology, Political Economy and Spatial Order

Past landscapes are more than the aggregate patterns generated by countless individual decisions, practices and routines, patterns to be reconstructed and analysed solely at an empirical level. We need to see them as developing within an ideological context that provided ideas on how society should be organized within itself and how it should relate to its resource base. If we are to fully understand a human landscape, then we must clarify its ideological sources of order. In practical terms, this means establishing the broad nature of its ideological context, identifying the various institutional forms through which ideological values were expressed, and then drawing out the different ways in which these institutional forms helped to shape spatial order.

The need to go beyond the mere appearance of landscape and its patterns of spatial order and to consider its changing ideological and institutional context is especially pertinent to the period 1500–1914. Over these four centuries, England and Wales moved from being rural and agrarian societies, still permeated with the decaying institutional forms of feudalism, to being part of an advanced, urban industrial society. Accompanying this profound transformation were far-reaching changes in the ideological and institutional basis of society. Not to appreciate these changes and how they related to spatial order is to content ourselves with appearances and with questions only about how landscapes were formed but not why, and to define them as if they were incidental rather than a considered or substantive product of society and its processes.

Altogether, we can break the problem down into four broad themes. First, we need to briefly remind ourselves of feudalism's character as a source of spatial order and how this affected the geography of change over the late medieval period. Second, we need to understand how the system that replaced it—market capitalism—first developed, both as regards its ideological values and its key institutional forms. Third, we need to clarify the effect which these institutional forms could have on spatial order. Fourth, we need to understand how capital worked to integrate different sectors and regions into a single circuit of capital and the significance which this had for spatial order and its stability.

The Decline of Feudalism: Change from Within or Without?

Recent debate over how feudalism gave way to market capitalism has structured the problem around their differences as modes of production, the one based on lordship and the other on capital. Traditional interpretations of the transition between them stress the effect which the scalar growth of market activity had on the organization of production. More recent contributions to the debate have asserted the case for seeing social relations themselves as the primary locus of change and as determinate of, rather than responsive to, market activity. If there is a geographical perspective to this debate, then it lies in establishing whether the forces of change affected particular areas and sectors sooner and more profoundly than others.

Feudalism generated a qualitatively distinct system of spatial order. An essential part of its character was the way in which the king used his lordship or superiority over all men and all land to create a control system that was both regulatory and exploitive in a territorial as well as social sense. As explained in Chapters 4 and 5, three types of relationship can be identified here. First, the king secured political and military control by granting out of land and powers of lordship to his lordly vassals in return for military services. The second was that between lord and peasant. Once established on large provincial estates, lords had to devise a means of exploiting them. In arable areas, the strategy adopted was for part of the estate to be kept in the lord's hands as demesne and for the remainder to be leased out to tenants in return for labour services on the lord's demesne. Villeinage and slavery were essential props to such a system. A different solution to the problem was for a lord to collect his rent in the form of food rents. Logically, this was a common solution in areas in which arable was limited, such as in the far north of England or in the hillier parts of the Welsh border. The control which the king and later, his lordly vassals, exercised over boroughs and market centres led to a third type of relationship, or that between lords and burgesses.

Being based on grants of jurisdiction, land and rights of trade in return for a definite amount of service or rent, these different forms of relationship needed to be specified or bounded in a geographical sense and anchored to particular points or blocks of land. In effect, feudal relations were mapped into the landscape, their explicit geographical component being part of the way the king both controlled and exploited his realm. Yet despite the king's lordship over all land and all men, feudalization did not produce a uniform or continuous landscape. The extent and intensity of legal jurisdictions devolved varied greatly between lordships. Feudal land tenures added to this unevenness through their emphasis on arable as the basic resource of assessment. Being the sole basis for the calculation of vital feudal dues and obligations, arable needed to be precisely assessed or quantified. The basis for this assessment were the virgates, bovates and carucates that made up customary tenements, customary because they were held by custom of the manor. Other resources—common pasture, meadow, wood, turbary, pannage—were exploited as an appendage of these arable tenements and, therefore, apportioned through them. The sum effect was to produce a patchwork landscape, with a community's right to cultivate land being confined to a core of assessed land represented by customary tenements. Yet even in the heavily feudalized south and east of the country, this core of assessed land could be surrounded by a generous fringe of non-assessed waste.

Towards the north and west, this fringe opened out to form whole regions of non-assessed land, large portions of which were incorporated into hunting forests. Elsewhere, boroughs and other market centres had an equally selective and uneven effect on the economic organization of space not least through differences in the nature and range of their privileges.

The uneven weight of feudal institutions and their prescribed geographical range means that we need to see the feudal landscape as a mosaic ranging from areas that were heavily feudalized to areas only lightly feudalized. Sharpening the significance of this variation is the fact that feudal relationships acquired a strong customary basis. The rights and burdens around which relations had been based in the past were continually invoked as the basis for how they should be defined thereafter. In consequence, the institutional forms of feudal society had a resilience to change, being continually inclined to reproduce the terms of a tenure or office successively as if in a changeless world. Taken together, these two aspects of the feudal landscape— its institutional unevenness and its customary basis[1]—have a bearing on how we interpret feudal decline. On the one hand, we are faced with heavily feudalized areas which, because of feudalism's customary basis, tended to deflect or slow down change. On the other, there existed large areas which were only lightly touched by feudal institutions and which, for this reason, were able to absorb quite radical change easily and quickly. Any assessment of institutional change over the late medieval period must clearly keep these potential differences in mind.

As an instance of how the customary form of strongly feudalized tenures could deflect change, we can cite the way manorial lords took account of the rising pressures on land over the thirteenth century by increasing entry fines, a device which raised the value of land in response to demand without disturbing other customary dues and obligations. The eventual break-up of customary tenure and villeinage was less straightforward. The degree to which the peasant economy, like that of demesnes, was involved in marketing by the thirteenth century, together with the rapidly rising level of demand over the thirteenth and early fourteenth centuries, favoured a shift into free tenures and cash rents. However, the complex role of custom, and the wider institutional rigidities that surrounded feudal tenure, worked against such a shift. Generally speaking, when we survey the heavily feudalized areas of the south and east, the shift away from labour services and unfreedom occurred sooner on smaller than on larger manors. Free tenures and cash rents had developed through manumission and commutation on some of the former by the thirteenth century.[2] The greater ease with which smaller manors could make institutional adjustments and could set aside custom was probably crucial here. Elsewhere, the extent to which the force of custom could retard change contributed to the crisis that enveloped feudalism by the mid–late fourteenth century, a crisis which forced change in even the most conservative areas by the fifteenth century.

Whilst the transformation of lord–peasant relations through manumission and commutation profoundly changed the social context of farming in heavily feudalized areas over the late medieval period, it constitutes only part of the problem. Free tenures held for cash rents appeared in other ways. From as early as the thirteenth century, the colonization of non-assessed land led directly to the creation of cash-bearing free tenures. In livestock-woodland areas like Cannock Chase and Arden and around the fringe of upland-pasture districts, whole new landscapes were created involving not simply cash-bearing tenures but also holdings that were both held in severalty and enclosed. Even where non-assessed land formed only a relatively limited fringe surrounding long-established customary tenements, its colonization was used to change the way land was held and exploited. In effect, the greater flexibility of non-assessed land was seized upon as a means of making critical institutional changes: these changes beginning sooner and proceeding further and more extensively than on assessed land. Indeed, the greater flexibility of tenures created through the assarting of non-assessed land was highlighted by the fact that, though often marginal, they sometimes bore higher rents than the customary holdings on assessed land.[3]

These differences can be taken further. When change came, heavily feudalized areas tended to shift from lord–peasant relations to landlord–tenant relations of a more capitalist sort, with larger farms and rent-driven changes in farm enterprise deepening their commitment to commercial farm production. By comparison, many areas colonized from the thirteenth century onwards followed a different trajectory of development. Livestock-woodland and upland-pasture districts generally had limited opportunities for arable. In the context of the thirteenth century, when pressure to colonize these less fertile environments on a more extensive basis first built up, the introduction of cash rents in place of labour services had the advantage of spreading the rent burden over non-arable as well as arable resources. No less important was the fact that non-arable resources like wool, leather and timber also provided the basis for a wide variety of craft and semi-craft activities. As settlement expanded further into more marginal environments and as holdings became smaller through population growth and subdivision, the extension of livelihood offered by these activities became more necessary. By c. 1500, many farmers and smallholders in livestock-woodland and upland-pasture districts were supplementing the direct subsistence of their holdings with some form of domestic industry, using local resources to support activities like spinning, weaving, hand-knitting, or leather, wood and metalworking. These more diversified economies though, formed only part of their rapidly developing contrast with arable areas. Their concern with the production of use rather than exchange values, or livelihood rather than profits, coupled with their widely dispersed character as a production system and peripherality to the main urban markets, created novel conditions for trade, conditions that merchants were quick to exploit via the putting out system. These same conditions though, together with the lack of strong authoritative control by landlords, were conducive to a more open, less tradition-bound and socially freer society, one that was to express itself through the spread of Nonconformist religion after 1500.[4]

The institutional rigidities surrounding the late medieval urban economy also contributed to this unevenness in society's response to change. The granting of free status to the major boroughs from the late twelfth century onwards gave them greater control over their own affairs. A consequence of this was that their organization took on a more elaborate regulated form. The number of trade gilds multiplied, each enacting its own battery of rules governing apprenticeship, conditions of work, materials and marketing. Confronted with economic problems and a downswing in trade over the fifteenth and early sixteenth centuries, they reacted by becoming more not less defensive, tightening their regulatory control over trade and displaying a concern more with who had access to wealth rather than with producing it. However, as their economy became a regulated, high-cost affair, the more potential it offered to would-be producers who could operate outside their framework of privilege and monopoly. The growth of rural industries in livestock-woodland and upland-pasture districts by *c.* 1500 exploited these differences. Their position outwith the institutional constraints of the urban gilds enabled them to cut costs by using different labour routines, materials and standards of workmanship.

Free Markets, Capitalism and Spatial Order

Given the way in which different areas and sectors responded to change over the later medieval period, we clearly cannot regard the geography of England and Wales *c.* 1500 as the product of a simple or coherent ideology and its associated institutional forms. Though the differential transformation of feudal and customary forms provided part of this diversity, much also derived from the appearance of wholly new areas and sectors of development. The extent to which the latter were contributing to the general pool of new ideological values and institutional forms *c.* 1500 makes it difficult to speak of a simple or linear path of change between feudalism and capitalism. When we come to consider how, after 1500, the organization of society and its spatial order slowly began to acquire a new ideological coherence based on capitalism and its articulation through free market systems, these areas and sectors which had developed *de novo* over the later medieval period were to prove as crucial as those developing out of feudalism.

Defined simply, capitalism can be represented as a system of profit-making in which profit is seen as a return on capital as opposed to labour, a return made up of interest plus a reward for the risk and entrepreneurship involved. If defined as such, then petty forms can be said to have existed throughout the medieval period, wherever merchants and traders were active. However, during the sixteenth and seventeenth centuries, the scale of capital involved in trading and business ventures rose sharply to the extent that we can speak of a commercial revolution taking place. Merchants involved in activities like cloth-making and metalworking began to build up larger, more elaborate networks of trade, linking together the labour of numerous scattered artisans and craftsmen into a single production system. Much of the capital involved in these burgeoning systems of trade comprised circulating rather than fixed capital, that is, raw materials and semi-finished goods—goods whose embodied capital was quickly returned for re-investment—rather than equipment and plant. The trading companies created over the sixteenth and seventeenth centuries to deal in overseas trade (e.g. East India Company, 1600) created equally impressive aggregations of capital. The first voyage sponsored by the East India Company was capitalized at £68,373. Nor were such huge amounts of high-risk capital necessarily offset by high returns. Though early voyages by the East India Company gave returns of 25 per cent, most others gave little more than 10 per cent.

In itself, the emergence of more capitalist forms of trade over the sixteenth and seventeenth centuries did not radically alter the relationship between society and space. This was partly because, by its very nature, the build-up of circulating capital is bound to have a more transient impact on the structuring of space than fixed capital. Besides, unless articulated through free markets, capitalist institutions had a restrained impact on space. Free or price-fixing markets balanced prevailing levels of supply and demand by allocating resources to those users or uses able to bid the most. For a landscape to be fully penetrated and ordered through free markets, land and labour—the so-called 'commodity fictions'[5]—had to be taken to market no less than the commodities actually produced for market by the farmer and artisan. In theory, such markets worked towards a pattern of land use that maximized rent under a given set of market conditions. In actuality, they were constantly changing as new resources or technologies became available, so we can expect the spatial order produced by them to be in a continual flux as capital continually chased after new possibilities for higher returns.

Whilst there is a general agreement about the eruption of more capitalist forms of business and trade over the sixteenth and seventeenth centuries, there is far less agreement over precisely when such forms were combined with free market conditions. For some, free markets actually developed much earlier. Macfarlane, for instance, saw them as in full operation by the thirteenth century. Everything, he declared, 'had its price'.[6] In a more recent contribution, Hodges has gone further back and has dated the emergence of a hierarchical system 'competitive' markets to the tenth–twelfth centuries.[7] By contrast, others have argued with no less authority that 'the institutions, mores, and administrative and legal precepts by which medieval society was structured and governed were inimical to the free play of the market',[8] In fact, altogether, the development of free markets has been variously dated from the tenth down to the eighteenth and nineteenth centuries. On balance, the majority view leans heavily towards the later end of this range.[9]

Clearly, such huge discrepancies over chronology signal fundamental differences of interpretation. However, some apparent differences stem from a failure to define precisely what is being dated. The inception of free markets cannot be seen as a sudden overnight change. Their development was a long drawn out process, one that worked differentially through various sectors and areas, with some phases when they were retarded and others when they moved forward quickly and when their institutional forms underwent rapid evolution. Once we appreciate this, then we can see that there are really two questions to ask about their chronology: first, when did free market activity first appear and, second, when did it become the dominant source of social order. Put in this way, no real conflict need necessarily exist between, on the one hand, those who argue for signs of their *initial* development as early as the thirteenth and fourteenth centures and, on the other, those who argue that they did not become the *dominant* influence on social order until the eighteenth and nineteenth centuries. If we take this sort of *phased* development as our guide, the problem of free markets is best approached by trying to define the conditions which most encouraged their growth. Two lines of argument need to be explored. The first concerns the extent to which we are faced with a state-driven process of political and ideological change, with the state consciously fostering those values and institutions which favoured freer and more enlarged markets, allowing them to penetrate all factors of production and—through the bid-price mechanism—to determine basic matters of reward and status. The second concerns the extent to which there was a degree of spontaneity and self-organization about market capitalism, with the rapidly changing scale, content and pattern of trade during particular periods being sufficient to force change in favour of freer forms simply because, under the circumstances, they proved more responsive and efficient.

Free Markets, Capitalism and Spatial Order: The Ideological and Political Bases of Change

The state's role in establishing and sustaining regulated markets would lead us to assume that it played an equally critical part in their replacement by free markets and in originating a new ideology based on market capitalism. In fact, its role in these matters, though critical, needs careful qualification. A great deal of non-regulated trade developed spontaneously. It required no legislative acts of de-regulation to bring it into being. Indeed, during the sixteenth and seventeenth centuries, when the growth of free markets actually made great strides, the state can be found assembling a framework of regulation at a national scale, passing the various acts that made up the Statute of Artificers (1563), granting monopolies over colonial trade to the various trading companies (e.g. East India Company 1600), and, through the Navigation Acts of 1650 and 60 and Staple Act of 1662, exercising a far-reaching control over English shipping. Such legislation hardly enables us to speak of a government working for freer markets. The thought behind them was mercantilist, the state using its political power to direct and control the benefits of trade.[10]

The idea that trade should still be regulated also permeated contemporary writing on the economy. Tracts on political economy written over the sixteenth and seventeenth centuries treat unalloyed profit- and money-making as a vice, a potential source of social and political disorder. For this reason, the economy could not be allowed to organize itself around the maximization of profit, to institute a self-regulating market, but had to be curbed by prevailing social and political values.[11] Admittedly, some modern commentators have drawn a different conclusion. Macpherson, for example, has argued that Hobbes' *Leviathan*, a work published in 1651, appears familiar with a society already based on 'possessive individualism', one founded around private property in which 'all values and entitlement are in fact established by the operation of the market, and all morality tends to be the morality of the marketplace'.[12] However, in a direct reply, Tribe has drawn attention to the many key concepts which are absent from *Leviathan* yet which are of the essence to a 'possessive market society'. The only conclusion to be reached, reasoned Tribe, was that the economy was 'not yet a separate category of discourse' but still a sphere administered through social and political values.[13]

Yet though we cannot speak of the state simply legislating free markets into existence over the early modern period, it did bring about changes that greatly assisted their development. Progressively, we find property rights being clarified, made more exact and exclusive, and, therefore, more available for exchange, through a range of legislation from the patent laws to enclosure acts. Better policing, larger standing armies and a better-equipped navy made agreements reached in the marketplace more secure. Likewise, the state played an instrumental role in fostering key institutional forms through which early market activity began to expand beyond the resources of the simple merchant. The early dealings of the Stock

Exchange during the 1690s and opening decades of the eighteenth century were based entirely on issues of the Bank of England and on shares in the major colonial trading companies, all state foundations.

Looking at the problem from a different angle, one particularly vital way in which the state aided the growth of freer markets over the early modern period was through the creation of a politically integrated and accessible framework of national space. Seen during the medieval period, England was already more securely integrated as a single polity than other west European states, less susceptible to the fissiparous tendencies that beset feudalism. However, political integration was a complex, ongoing affair, a challenge whose problems altered with the scalar growth of society and economy. Once we grasp this can we can understand why—despite its unity as a feudal state—it was possible for Elton to talk about the progress made under the Tudors in 'reducing all subjects, however great, to the Crown and of consolidating the realm into one unit under the King's sole jurisdiction . . .'[14] and yet, for others to talk of the revolution in government over the mid nineteenth century which, amongst other things, was seen as producing a more integrated state. Far from competing for the same revolution, these different perspectives merely underline the complexities of state integration. The sixteenth-century revolution in government removed the liberties and franchises which had grown up over the medieval period and which had contributed in large measure to the unevenness of feudal space. Important amongst them were the major liberties like the Palatinates of Lancaster and Durham and the Marcher Lordships of the Welsh Border, all of which were now replaced by shires. Additionally, in place of a mixed hierarchy of courts, jurisdictional control everywhere was re-structured around Justices of the Peace appointed by the crown on a parochial basis and representing a direct projection of its authority though, in practice, JPs enjoyed a fair degree of autonomy in how they exercised law. Overall, we can see these changes as attempts by the crown to exercise a more direct and centralized control in response to its own needs and ambitions.

The more uniform political space created by the Tudor revolution in government laid the foundations for a 'national economic space'[15] yet the two have more than a simple cause–effect relationship. The very realization of a 'national economic space' was itself a powerful source of national unification. Hill believes London merchants played a particularly crucial role in this process. The spread of their values, he argues, contributed to the growth of a national consciousness and provided a significant input into the wider process of ideological change. The values which he had in mind were those of Protestantism and what he calls the 'standards and morality of the market-place' which, through the trading activities of London merchants, were 'radiated slowly out from London'.[16] This is an important point but one that needs handling with care. There is a case for arguing that it was the ideas which they imported rather than exported that really mattered. The many new areas and industries that were flourishing by the sixteenth and seventeenth centuries provided a wide range of circumstances under which new institutional forms and social practices could emerge. Their integration via a system of expanding trade largely focused on London provided the latter with a range of new possibilities and opportunities, including forms and practices that were more able to cope with the pressures created by the rapid scalar growth of demand from the late eighteenth century onwards. The greater freedom of these new areas and sectors to respond to subsistence needs and market swings was already apparent by the seventeenth century. Referring to the government-sponsored projects which seemed such a feature of the century, Thirsk noted this paradox. Though initially established by the government, such projects 'flourished best when they passed beyond the pioneer phase, and had entered the deep interstices of the economy, establishing themselves in places that were out of sight of authority and government'.[17] The achievement of London merchants was in linking such 'deep interstices' to the wider economy, their greater adaptiveness to an expanding market being a prime reason why they attracted the control and capital of London's merchants.

By comparison with the Tudor revolution in government, work on the nineteenth-century 'revolution' in government has stressed the extent to which it was a response to the rapid changes taking place in society. As Parris and others have argued, we should view it not as the product of a government thinking in advance, drawing on abstract thought about how an industrializing and urbanizing society ought to be managed, but rather as a *pragmatic* response to changes running ahead of government.[18] We can trace the changes involved back to the late eighteenth century. Having in mind the system of centralized administration supposedly developed around Justices of the Peace back in the sixteenth century, Macdonagh has referred to a 'system of remarkably weak central control, remarkably autonomous local bodies, and remarkably small units of government' now faced with rapid and profound changes in the nature of society and economy.[19] With the passing of the Poor Law Amendment Act (1834), the effectiveness of such a system was greatly reduced. More serious, the growth of population, its urbanization, and the rapid development of factories and workshops after 1780 created wholly new problems for government. In response, government became more involved in governing. It extended its responsibilities and acquired a continuous, systematic interest in the management of society. Four specific areas of response can be noted. First, its need to know about the changes taking place found expression in the first decennial census in 1801, the civil registration of births, deaths and marriages and in the commissions and inspectorates that generated a host of Blue Books on industry, employment, environment and education from the 1830s onwards.[20] Second, it enacted a range of legislation (e.g. Factory Act, 1833, Public Health Act, 1848, Education Act, 1870) that established the state as having ultimate responsibility for defining and maintaining basic standards throughout those spheres of life and work that were most affected by industrialization and urbanization. Third, its extended responsibilities led to the formation of a bureaucracy, a civil service separate in its organization and functions from the political side of government. Even by 1800, the size of this bureaucracy had grown to *c.* 20,000, mostly employed in customs and excise. Over the nineteenth century, their number and range of activities broadened considerably. However, we must keep their growth in perspective. Though the proportion of the total workforce in government employment rose faster over the century than those in industry, they still only constituted 3.6 per cent of the total workforce in 1890 (compared with 24.3 per cent in 1950).[21] Fourth, faced with a rapidly changing distribution of population, the geography of administration was re-structured, partly through the Reform Act (1832) and more substantially through the Municipal Corporations Act (1835) and various late-nineteenth-century Acts

(1882, 1888 and 1892). The Act of 1835 created a new system of borough administration, with elected councils and executive officers. The system thereby created was
extended to all boroughs by the 1882 Act. The 1888 Act is noteworthy because it
created a system of county borough councils, giving cities like London a system of
administration that matched their new extent.

Paradoxically, these changes in the extent of government came about at a time
when thinking on the economy favoured less not more government. This shift in
thought is symbolized for us by Adam Smith's *Wealth of Nations* (1771).[22] Instead of
being subservient to social and political values, the economy—through the agency of
free or self-regulating markets—is now seen as a potential source of order in itself.
Furthermore, the order which it created—with status and reward being determined
in the marketplace—is seen as ideologically acceptable. Market expansion, its
unhindered extension into all areas, sectors and factors of production, was to be
encouraged because it fostered specialization and, through specialization, gains in
productivity. Within such a scheme, the role of the state was considered minimal, a
matter of policing rather than obstructing the efficient working of the market. In
effect, thinking on the economy had moved from seeing it as something embedded
in society to a position in which society was now seen as embedded in the
economy.[23]

The idea that the market should shape the allocation of resources, of laissez faire as
it became known, entrenched itself as the dominant ideology by the second quarter
of the nineteenth century. It found concrete expression through the rise of the Free
Trade Movement, and the eventual repeal of both the Corn Laws (1846) and the
Navigation Acts (1849 and 1850). Although some have questioned the sincerity of the
Free Trade Movement, arguing that its supporters recognized that an industrialized
Britain stood to gain considerably from open markets—with its exchange of industrial products for food imports and raw materials enabling it to create an informal
empire as extensive and as personally advantageous as its formal empire[24]—there
can be no doubting its impact in opening up markets. If we had to select a point at
which free markets were least encumbered by state interference, a point at which
their ability to shape spatial order as per our models of locational theory, then
arguably it would be these middle decades of the nineteenth century. Yet already,
the problems generated by rapid industrialization and urbanization were forcing
economists like Ricardo and Bentham to concede a role for state interference in the
marketplace. Pieces of legislation like the Factory Act (1833), though, were justified
individually rather than seen as deriving from some general principle of state
interference, a necessary evil rather than desirable corrective.

Free Markets, Capitalism and Spatial Order: Sources of Spontaneous Change

In so far as free markets represent an absence of regulation, with prevailing prices
being bid-prices determined by the interaction of supply and demand, then it was
possible for them to come into being by default, either through the growth of trade in
situations or sectors beyond the control of regulated markets or when the sheer
growth and diversification of trade overwhelmed the capacity of established markets. This sort of argument was implicit in what Polanyi had to say about them.

Because regulated medieval markets were subjected to social and political restraints, he contended that free markets could not be seen as a natural development of regulated markets, an inevitable product of their successful expansion. Rather were they an aberration, a sign of their inability to cope or adapt. This was the reason why Polanyi tied their development in with the Industrial Revolution and its rapid expansion of markets.[25] The same point, though, can be used to explain why signs of a marginal shift into a more price-responsive system of markets can be documented for earlier periods.

There were two ways in which regulated markets failed to cope. First, to re-state a point made earlier, the framework of regulation established around medieval trade was anchored to specific towns, areas and activities. This institutional rigidity left them ill-equipped to cope with the rapidly changing pattern and content of trade that was such a feature of the sixteenth and seventeenth centuries. Rural centres of production began to expand rapidly, generating dense, reticulated networks of trade beyond the close control or supervision of urban craft gilds. Not only do we see wholly new industries springing up without any framework of regulation or gild organization, but we also find long established industries undergoing a massive expansion in the countryside, especially in marginal or peripheral areas where regulation was weak or non-existent.[26] The sum effect of all these changes was to spawn areas and sectors of industrial growth which lay beyond the framework of regulated trade that still embraced the more traditional crafts and industries in older urban centres of industry. Not surprisingly, they also spawned new organizational forms of trade that were better able to cope with the range and scale of activity then developing. As Langton and Hoppe observed, below the level of primate cities like London, urban economies—shackled by charters and obsolete institutional forms— tended to crumble over the sixteenth and early seventeenth centuries. By contrast, those rural areas which shared in the growth of new industries fared differently, the coalfields especially offering a 'new frontier of economic life', a success sustained as much by their new organizational forms as by their new products.[27]

A second and probably more powerful solvent of regulated markets was the pressure exerted on regulated forms by the sheer growth of market activity. Increases in the amount of trade, in the amount of information that has to be collated and processed, raise transaction costs and make the switch to more efficient organizational forms attractive. This link between scalar growth and changes in the institutional organization of markets has been noted by a number of writers. It even forms part of Hodges' argument for the emergence of free, competitive markets between the tenth and twelfth centuries.[28] Assuming such an early adjustment to free markets, though, begs the question of what institutional adjustments were left to handle the even greater expansion of trade during the early modern and modern periods. This is the reason why others prefer to bring the switch forward. North, for instance, has argued that the open and licensed nature of medieval markets, with all goods being displayed and their quality and quantity being subject to inspection by market wardens, was appropriate to the level of medieval trade. As the volume of trade expanded over the early modern period, and the problems of bringing sufficient buyers and sellers together to strike a fair price were reduced, he sees the shift to free markets as inevitable, enabling more transactions and larger volumes of goods to be traded at a lower transaction cost. In short, different forms of market organization work efficiently only at different scales so that, as growth takes place, established forms become less efficient, enabling newer forms better adapted to the new scale of operation to gain a cost advantage.[29] Of course, scalar growth can stress institutions in other ways. Greater volumes of goods, more market transactions, having to trade goods over greater distances, and the failure of supply to increase with sharply escalating demand, could all stress regulated markets. What is significant about scalar stress is that we see it operating most forcibly in the larger urban centres. Even in London, for instance, the sheer growth of industrial production by the seventeenth century had led to considerable non-gild trade, a 'usurpation of legitimate authority' as one writer put it.[30]

Likewise, if we look at the urban land market, the combination of burgage tenements and city walls imposed finite limits on the supply of urban land. Even by the fourteenth century, pressure in the more successful boroughs had started to undermine the fixed foundation rents of burgage tenements, universally set at 12d per whole tenement or 6d per half tenement. Outwardly, they remained fixed by custom at 12d and 6d, but beneath these chief rents, the pressure on urban space forced a sub-market into existence as tenements or parts of tenements were sub-let at more advanced rates.[31] By the sixteenth century, traces of customary rents had largely disappeared and pressure on space in the larger towns was sufficient to create a gently contoured land value surface, with town centres and main axes carrying higher ground rents.[32] The extent to which land values in London were becoming shaped by a free land market is highlighted by the degree of factor substitution then evident, with higher site values apparently being traded off against smaller plot size and further offset by site improvements, the latter being manifest through a tendency to build upwards to five or six storeys in high value areas.[33] By the seventeenth century, the extent to which this incipient land value surface had started to affect the use of space is illustrated by the way the differential rent of sites along streets, lanes and alleys was already producing a fine sorting of users through their ability to pay.[34] However, looking at the problem from a slightly different angle, free markets in land require participation if they are to operate efficiently in the sense of allocating sites to those uses yielding the highest rent. This is especially pertinent to the urban land market during the medieval and early modern periods because of the slow rate at which they turned over. In a synthesis of the problem, Vance argued that pre-industrial towns were based around tied housing, with people both living and working on the same site. By comparison, a free market in land and housing required the generalization of housing, that is, the separation of housing and employment so that individuals were forced to bid in a general market.[35] In fact, there are signs that a general housing market of sorts may have been present in London by the sixteenth century with many occupiers holding land on a short lease.[36] Yet this point made, it is doubtful whether early land or housing markets were efficient because of the lags between actual and potential rents. Even in the early nineteenth century, when we might have expected land and housing markets to have become still more active compared with the sixteenth century, contemporaries saw its imperfections as a weakness in a world increasingly dominated by the free market allocation of resources, a weakness explained by the lack of proper institutional forms and the difficulties of maximizing information flow between buyers and sellers.[37]

The potential impact of scalar growth on regulated markets is most dramatically seen in relation to food markets. These were always the most stringently regulated of markets during the medieval period. Phases of rapid growth and, ultimately, the sheer size of towns, though, created practical difficulties for their efficient operation. Needless to say, such problems were acutely felt in London. Even by the thirteenth century, there are clear signs that its rapid growth had pushed the demand for food out far beyond its immediate hinterland and that farmers at a distance were allowing its demands to shape their production decisions (see p. 81). Yet despite these signs of market responsiveness amongst farmers, the evidence suggests that food market-ing within London continued to be closely supervised by the authorities, the role of middlemen being carefully restricted and activities like regrating and forestalling continuing to be punishable.[38] By the seventeenth century, though, more funda-mental changes were starting to take place. The renewed and sustained growth of the capital created a scale of demand for which the organization of regulated markets was ill-suited. The metropolitan effect, already hinted at back in the thirteenth century, now became pronounced, with prices over the country at large being shaped around what could be obtained in the capital.[39] The impact of London's appetite on the pricing structure of agricultural produce was matched by its increasing impact on the actual pattern of marketing, with an ever larger area being tied directly to the provisioning of its needs. Indeed, when we survey the supply of agricultural produce to the metropolitan market between the sixteenth and nine-teenth centuries, we are presented with a remarkable illustration of how free markets injected a dynamic element into the landscape.[40] As demand rose, and prices were adjusted so as to draw in produce from an ever wider area, more and more farmers opted into market production or were forced into it by increases in rent. Once tied to its needs, farmers found that the rapid escalation of metropolitan demand coupled with the development of new areas of production and new transport technologies continually re-configured the geography of locational advan-tage and disadvantage for particular products.

Changes in the scale of London's food supply also had implications for the way it was actually marketed within the capital. Public markets, with their emphasis on the open display and inspection of all produce, were limited in their capacity to handle produce, a capacity soon reached once the volume of produce and number of transactions increased. To a degree, these scalar problems could be accommodated by the duplication and differentiation of market sites. By the late seventeenth century, though, the sheer scale of London's food problem had induced more far-reaching change. The challenge of co-ordinating the collection and transport of larger volumes of produce over greater distances encouraged the emergence of a range of middlemen from the ranks of yeomen farmers, millers, brewers, maltsters, hoymen and carters. At the same time, private dealings had sprung up outside the framework of public markets, paving the way for private bargaining over prices. Initially, the activities of this new breed of middlemen were marginal to the capital's food supply system. By *c.* 1700, though, their capacity and flexibility in handling larger volumes and denser networks had given them a more essential role. Already factors and dealers were openly selling grain to the highest bidder at Bear Quay, the traditional unloading point for grain arriving via the Thames from Kent and East Anglia. By 1750, the auctioning of grain received formal acceptance as the more efficient means of distributing grain between factors, dealers and wholesalers with the foundation of the Corn Exchange. Another consequence of the increasing sale of grain by private agreement or auction was its sale by sample rather than on the basis of a full sighting. By this date also, a great deal of grain was being processed out of London as a means of trimming transport costs, with the emergence in centres like Weybridge, Guildford and Reading of dealers who bought grain, milled it, and then acted as wholesalers and retailers for the flour produced. As trade adjusted to this larger more elaborate form, changes also occurred in how grain, flour and bread were actually sold to the consumer. Just as the sheer scalar growth of trade undermined the factoring and wholesale roles of public markets so also was their retailing role undermined. From as early as 1680 onwards, we find this retailing function being devolved to shops, outlets that were able to provide a dispersed and continuous form of retailing. This decline of the public market for grain was mirrored in other branches of agricultural marketing. Only in the marketing of fruit and vegetables did trade still depend on a significant face-to-face market-centred contact between producer and consumer.[41]

As provincial centres expanded over the eighteenth and nineteenth centuries, they found themselves confronted by similar problems. There too, the solution which emerged involved a greater role for middlemen, and the replacement of open, regulated markets by a factoring and wholesaling trade based on a combination of unrestrained private dealings and auctions, and a retail trade which depended more and more on shops that offered a more continuous form of marketing. As Thompson observed, without this shift to a freer, less regulated system by the late eighteenth century, many provincial centres, especially those away from the main corn-growing districts, would not have coped with prevailing levels of demand. Only during times of crisis did urban authorities step in to re-assert the kind of controls that had once been the norm.[42] In effect, what we are faced with by the end of the eighteenth century is a system of agricultural marketing which, under pressure of growth, had overflowed the narrow bounds and limited capacities of open, regulated markets. Whatever role we ascribe to the middlemen who seized the opportunities offered by these circumstances, there is a sense in which we can see it as a spontaneous shift, a struggle to cope with scalar growth in which an initially small free sector provided a more immediate and flexible response to the problem and which, through its greater effectiveness and efficiency in coping, eventually established itself as the acceptable solution.

Free Markets and Capitalism: their Impact on Industry

The way in which free markets and capitalism combined to shape spatial order can be illustrated by looking in detail at two particular sectors: industry and towns. Their impact on industry passed through different phases. During the early modern period, we find purely domestic systems of industrial production based around independent craftsmen, journeymen and apprentices being slowly penetrated by merchant capital. The linkages worked out between producer and merchant varied. In some cases, merchants provided raw material or semi-finished products like yarn. In other cases, they also provided credit. Eventually, systems emerged in which merchants effectively paid artisans for their labour. An important point to grasp though, is that whilst some merchants may have succeeded in integrating the labour of large numbers of scattered artisans into a single commercial organization, the working unit and, therefore, the proportion of capital wrapped up in buildings and equipment—that is, fixed as opposed to circulating capital—was still modest.[43] Admittedly, one or two industries show signs of capital deepening even at this stage. The average size of mines in the Warwickshire coalfield, for instance, rose significantly over the sixteenth and seventeenth centuries, as did the size of blast furnaces in the Forest of Dean over the seventeenth century. Yet even conceding that some industries saw greater levels of investment in fixed plant or works, the overall feature of the period was of capital broadening, with merchants, companies and business partnerships trying to integrate more units and more labour than by concentrating capital at particular sites. The Foley Partnership is a good instance of a large commercial system developed around a scatter of relatively small units of production, from mines and blast furnaces in the Forest of Dean to forges and workshops in the Black Country.[44]

By the late eighteenth century and the rapid build-up of investment in the factory system from the 1770s and 1780s onwards, both the overall scale of investment and the proportion of fixed capital began to increase significantly. Breaking this investment down, the cost of early factory systems lay more in building than machinery. Early industrialists in the textile industry were initially able to cope with this problem by adapting buildings previously used as mills or warehouses. The entire fixed capital of the Oldham sector of the cotton industry, a major growth point, was valued at only £30,000 in 1795.[45] Only from the 1790s onwards do we start to find custom-built factories. Low entry costs during the early phases of change were further assisted by the fact that early machinery was largely manufactured out of wood. Fully engineered machinery spread only during the closing years of the eighteenth century. These shifts are important when we come to consider the sources of investment capital over these critical early years of the factory system. Though, logically, we might expect merchant capital to have played an essential role, this was not always the case. Certainly, in the cotton industry, merchant capital was vital in funding the pioneering shift into factory spinning during the early decades of change, enabling us to speak of a continuity between merchants of the early modern period and eighteenth-century industrialists.[46] However, the same was not true of the Yorkshire woollen industry. Apart from a shift into factory production by successful wool staplers, it was manufacturers rather than merchants who provided the initial capital outlay.[47]

Once factory production was established by the late eighteenth century investment came from within not without the industrial sector, entrepreneurs simply recycling profits. Though studies suggest that the typical entrepreneur had no clear idea over his costs and profit margins, the returns on capital in the best-practice firms were generally high. It is these profits that we find funding the growth of industry over the closing years of the eighteenth and first half of the nineteenth.[48] Banks were used for working capital and short-term credit but long-term capital—the capital used for plant—was self-generated. This internal source of funding has a bearing on the significance which we can attach to the rising levels of fixed capital. There are two ways of representing this increase. On the one hand, we find some business ventures, especially in textiles, whose proportion of fixed capital was around 40–50 per cent. On the other hand, and a fact which some would see as more important, there was a general increase in fixed capital to around 20–25 per cent. Inevitably, this increased level of fixed capital, and with it, the increasingly specific and non-adaptable nature of such investment, raised the degree to which such investment was committed to particular places an particular forms, just as the growing concentration of capital created communities whose labour skills and cultural practices were equally attuned to particular locations and economies.[49] Yet so long as industrialists acted as their own bankers, entrepreneurs and managers, they were less inclined to see the embeddedness of their capital as creating a conflict.

By the 1830s and 1840s, though, further far-reaching changes began to affect industrial investment. Trade crises and growing competition in its markets lowered the profitability of British industry. New investment led to larger, more integrated factories or units of production. The amount of fixed capital in the cotton industry, for instance, rose from £6.3 million in 1817 to £14.8 million in 1834 and £31 million by 1856.[50] By the 1870s, the continued build-up of investment in new areas of development, like that prompted by the exploitation of Cleveland iron ores, produced spectacular instances of capital deepening, with large volumes of investment concentrated at particular sites. Mergers and expansions in brewing, cotton and chemicals during the 1880s and 1890s produced equally striking examples of capital broadening. The sheer volume of capital demanded by such developments caused industry to draw more long-term credit from banks and the wider capital market. Underpinning this growing reliance on the wider capital market were adjustments in the organization of business ventures. Prior to the 1850s, even a successful sector like the Lancashire cotton industry sustained major investment booms in first, powered spinning, and then powered looms from the capital of individuals and small partnerships. Thereafter, the level of investment capital required by industry began to surge beyond such arrangements. Encouraged also by the Joint Stock Companies Act of 1855, particularly its provisions for limiting liability, many more industrial ventures were incorporated as joint stock companies.[51]

By becoming more closely integrated into the wider capital market over the second half of the nineteenth century, industry became susceptible to its demands and fluctuations. In particular, pressure was created for means by which capital could be dis-invested as well as invested. In addition to interest payments on capital, capital stock was amortized, discounted at a fixed rate so that its freedom to migrate to new areas of investment could be maintained. The cyclical booms which affect industrial capitalism now became compounded by capital migration, with the latter continually migrating in search of high interest rates. The result was that industrial centres passed through phases of growth and stagnation or decline, with an initial build-up of investment in new technologies and labour skills, then a phase of high interest rates but, as these new technologies and labour skills spread and profit rates averaged out, capital gradually moved away in search of rejuvenated profits leaving established centres of production to slowly decline. Herein lies the source of conflict between capital and the physical basis of industrial production. As Harvey put it in a phrase full of meaning for historical geography, 'capitalism increasingly relies upon fixed capital (including that embedded in a specific landscape of production) to revolutionize the value productivity of labour, only to find that its fixity (the specific geographical distributions) becomes the barrier to be overcome'.[52]

Investment in infrastructure and social overhead capital, including roads, bridges, canals, railways, docks, and utilities like gas, water and electricity supply, provided a further dimension to the gross build-up of fixed capital, adding greatly to the institutional and physical rigidity of social and economic forms. The scale of capital involved and the special needs generated by these various forms of investment had considerable impact on the organization of the capital market generally. We can see this clearly in the successive investment booms which slowly integrated national space via a network of turnpike trusts, canals and railways. The development of turnpikes over the eighteenth century relied entirely on local sources of funding provided via trusts or partnerships constituted by Act of Parliament. The construction of canals over the second half of the eighteenth and early nineteenth centuries differed in that, apart from the Duke of Bridgewater's navigation, they were capitalized through joint-stock companies. However, like turnpikes before them, companies tapped local reserves of capital, with landowners and merchants figuring prominently amongst their shareholders. Typically, two-thirds of the subscribers to the Birmingham Canal Navigation 1768–98, for instance, were from Birmingham, whilst half of those subscribing to the Coventry Canal, 1768–90 were from Coventry. The long construction phase of canals, though, allowed for change: the Leeds and Liverpool Canal, 1770–1816, began largely on the strength of subscribers from Liverpool and from the Aire and Colne Valley, but by 1800, less than a half of all shares were held locally. This intrusion of non-local capital occurred primarily during the canal mania of the 1790s when capital from London and commercial centres like Bristol and Liverpool worked towards a wider, national market in shares.[53]

These hints of a national market in shares became more pronounced with the construction of railways from the 1830s onwards. Railways involved much higher levels of capital investment, far higher than any other form of transport, with an average of £4 million per annum during 1830s rising to £15 million per annum during the mania of the 1840s. Between 1841 and 1860, they absorbed 21 per cent of all fixed capital formation in the UK[54] Like canals, railway ventures were funded through joint-stock comanies incorporated by Act of Parliament empowering them to purchase the necessary land and restricting their payment of interest. However, the early life of some companies was characterized by rampant speculation in shares, even before they had been incorporated by Act. Yet despite the speculative atmosphere in which they were born, railways appealed as a relatively safe investment because of the guaranteed interest paid. It is partly for this reason that, once established using a mixture of local and metropolitan capital, most railway companies drew investment from a national market, one that reached beyond the immediate region tapped by particular lines and companies. The changes we can see taking place in the funding of these various transport developments have a wider significance. As forms of investment which affected all regions, their evolution from trusts to joint-stock companies, and from joint-stock companies involving regional capital to joint-stock companies drawing capital from all regions provided the first signs of a truly national market in capital.[55]

Free Markets and Capitalism: their Impact on Towns

A feature of recent debates on urbanization is the stress placed on its role within the general rise of capitalism and free markets. For Harvey, free markets were 'inextricably linked' to eighteenth- and nineteenth-century urbanization through capitalism's 'necessity to create, mobilize and concentrate surplus value'.[56] Like industrial capital, urbanization committed vast amounts of capital to a relatively immobile form, one tied spatially, economically and socially to particular configurations. Feinstein's estimates suggest that investment in residential and other forms of building, much of which represented urban investment, rose from £2million per annum between 1761 and 1790 to £11 million per annum between 1821 and 1860, or from 22 per cent of the gross domestic fixed capital investment to 32 per cent by 1821–40. Though the overall level remained at £11 million per annum between 1841 and 1860, this constituted a lower proportion (20 per cent) of gross domestic fixed capital investment, a fall explained almost entirely by the shift of capital into railways.[57] Quite apart from manifesting society's ability to capitalize a particular site, through the construction of buildings, roads, public utilities, etc., cities 'multiplied the opportunities for realizing rent'.[58] In particular, it imposed a relative evaluation of space based on location, one which had the power to organize city forms through the bid-price mechanism.

Once penetrated by capital, towns were transformed into a vital sector of capitalism whose activities became synchronized with the booms and slumps of the economy at large. During booms in the economy, house construction surged. During slumps, the evidence for the second half of the eighteenth and early decades of the nineteenth centuries suggests that house construction fell away, with houses on the suburban frontier of expansion being left unfinished as the credit of builders ran out.[59] By the mid nineteenth century though, the growing civic consciousness of towns, their increasing ability to act as a developer and the low price of land encouraged some to use slumps to buy up land for extensive uses like schools, hospitals, parks, and cemeteries [60] (see also pp. 421–5). Mediating the impact of these swings in the economy on urban development were the urban landlords, speculators and builders, groups whose potential for profit seeking was modulated by swings in the rate of profit and availability of credit finance. Though activity in the larger cities, with their more generalized economies, tended to mirror national building cycles, towns with more specialized economies had a more individual response. Particular booms and slumps might be accentuated according to the phases of investment and dis-investment in their local economies. Thus, the intensity of the building boom and subsequent collapse in Bristol during the late 1780s and early 1790s reflected the 'idle money' in the south-west and the response of local banks to investment opportunities.[61] In the extreme, towns—like Middlesborough or Barrow in Furness—were largely the product of one or two investment cycles during the mid nineteenth century. In other cases, areas could enjoy prosperity against the national trend. Thus, Liverpool enjoyed its own house-building boom 1844–46 in response to Irish immigration whilst during a boom in coal exports over the early twentieth century, South Wales also enjoyed a house-building boom against the national trend.

The increasingly speculative character of urban development also manifested itself through site improvement, with developers seeking to increase rent yields by improving the site. However, this was not a process that occurred automatically, at least not during the nineteenth century. Any potential increase in rent yield had to absorb replacement costs or the cost of changing the use of the site. For this reason alone, large portions of urban space displayed a gap between their actual and potential rent yield. One analysis also suggests that the inflation of house rents during boom phases of the nineteenth century proceeded at a faster rate than building cost, making replacement less likely. Rather was it the failure of house rents to adjust downwards in step with building costs during times of slump that created speculative conditions for site conversion.[62] However, with burgeoning city economies, city-centre conditions were conducive to conversion at any time. The locational component of land rent was at its most potent here and more than offset the conversion cost of shifting land from residential to commercial use. We can convey the power of this locational component in no more forcible way than by noting that in 1901, London's land rents exceeded the gross of all agricultural land in England and Wales.[63]

Adding to the way urbanization was linked to swings in the national economy was the build-up of investment in public utilities: roads, water, gas and electricity supplies, public transport facilities, bath-houses, wash-houses, gardens and so on. Prior to 1800, the scope for such investment was limited and sustained largely by private capital and opportunism. Additions to the urban road network, for instance, were generally laid out by speculator-developers before letting out plots to speculator builders. With the addition of drainage and house-to-house water supply, they could absorb as much as 50 per cent of the cost of development. The scale of urbanization by the 1800s created a demand for the more organized provision of key utilities like water. The introduction of gas lighting during the 1800s reinforced this demand for a more controlled and co-ordinated provision. Initially, these needs were met by the establishment of private joint-stock companies. At first, these companies operated within a locally competitive framework, with different companies actually bidding for customers in the same street. London, for example, saw the establishment of a number of competing water companies in 1806. It saw its first gas companies in the same decade. By 1850, fourteen separate gas companies competed for lighting up the capital. Generally speaking, though, the early flurry of company formation was followed by a process of thinning through amalgamation. Thus, the two companies that supplied Sheffield's gas were amalgamated in 1844. By this point, the whole context in which public utilities were developed had started to change in another way. The Municipal Corporation Act of 1835 had provided the basis for a new more self-conscious era of civic government. Controlling and developing their public utilities was one dimension to this new-found self-awareness. Slowly, we find utilities being municipalized, taken over by their local authority. The northern industrial towns were the first to respond to this opportunity. London did not act to rationalize control until later. The Metropolitan Water Board was not founded until 1906 when it paid £46.9 million for the various water companies operating within its bounds, a sum which made it one of the most highly capitalized companies in the UK at the time. Local authority interest in utilities was further extended by the Tramway Act of 1870 and the Electric Lighting Act of 1882 which allowed them not only to take over such enterprises but to initiate them. By the eve of the First World War, local authorities controlled most of the national water supply , one-third of the gas supply, two-thirds of the electricity supply and two-thirds of the route mileage of tramways.[64] Taken together it represented a massive investment in social capital, investment that was specific to particular places and what was to be, for many industrial centres, a legacy of more prosperous times.

Spatial Order and the Circulation of Capital

A prime characteristic of mature capitalism is the way capital binds different sectors or regions of an economy into a single interlocking system and allocates investment to those sectors or regions which yield the greatest interest or profit. To this end, it is a system which expands freely, continually seeking to penetrate new areas and their resources. Over and above the penetration of individual sectors, capital seeks to establish a free flow between sectors, to establish a circulation of capital, one that was 'as free as possible from material spatial constraints'.[65] Though elements of this circuit were in place by the seventeenth century, when merchants were already moving capital between sectors, we cannot speak of a fully formed and institutionalized circuit of capital before the mid–late nineteenth century. Activating this circuit was the fact that capitalism's inner workings gave it a cyclical character. Put simply, these cycles comprised phases of innovation and high profit rates, followed by a general diffusion of innovations and an averaging out of profit rates and then eventually stagnation and crisis.[66] All sectors of the economy were affected by these cyclical swings in the rate of investment. However, because of the high levels of fixed capital involved, its geographical specificity and the ease with which the profitability of particular investments could be undermined by newer, more efficient technologies, industry suffered these cycles of growth, stagnation and crisis in a more profound way. At the root of its problems were two kinds of capital movement. First, different cycles of investment involved not only different technologies, but also, different areas of investment, so that we find capital shifting between different regions, as different phases of investment created a succession of new growth areas. We can see this most clearly in the iron industry, with investment cycles shifting between areas over the nineteenth century, from South Wales and the West Midlands to Scotland and then to the north-east and, eventually, the East Midlands. The close link between industrialization and urbanization also meant that the pattern of urban growth likewise varied in step with this movement of industrial capital between areas.[67] Second, different sectors of the capital market—industry, banking and commerce, transport, urban rents, and agriculture—responded to trading cycles in different ways, with a sector like industry being capable of greater gains during investment booms but greater losses during slumps. This encouraged a lateral flow of capital between them during the course of each trade cycle. In effect, capitalism—through the universality of money as a medium of exchange—reduced landscape, urban and rural, industrial and agricultural, to the same terms of value, imposing a common system of order based on the ability of particular sites and resources to yield rent or profit. In the process, all areas became affected by the whim of capital, its tendency to engage and dis-engage particular forms of investment as it sought to maintain the yield of rents and profits.

The growth of an integrated circuit of capital required institutional mechanisms whereby information about areas of investment and rates of profit could be co-ordinated and capital withdrawn from existing uses and re-routed to those offering the greater returns. Like the spread of self-regulating markets, though, the growth of these mechanisms was a slow affair, with institutional forms being slowly adapted to the scale and range of activity involved. If we are forced to select a beginning for the capital market then it would be the creation of joint-stock companies over the sixteenth and seventeenth centuries. Yet though such companies became financed through shares, enabling capital to be dis-invested as well as invested without the company collapsing, early share dealings were limited. Even by 1688, only fourteen joint-stock companies existed: these included trading companies like the East India, a handful of mining and smelting companies and two insurance companies founded in the aftermath of the Great Fire of London (1666). The years immediately following the Glorious Revolution in 1688 saw two key changes. After centuries of royal or government borrowing in a haphazard way, with loans being vouched for on the tally system, the National Debt was created, enabling the government to fund its long-term needs and debt through a system of short-term loans. In 1694, the Bank of England was formed. Together, these changes generated considerable activity in shares and securities, creating a face-to-face market for dealers in and around the coffee houses that lay along Change Alley. However, they also had the effect of giving the London Stock Exchange a bias towards shares and dealings in the major trading companies and government securities.[68] Appropriately, Jonathan's Coffee House, the focus for early dealings in government securities, became the site of the first proper Exchange in 1773 after it had been rebuilt following a fire. Yet as a centre of control over capital flows, it had surprisingly little direct bearing on the growth in industrial output over the eighteenth or, indeed, over much of the nineteenth century. Domestic industrial ventures were seen as too uncertain and speculative.

Opinion is split over whether this standoffishness by the London Stock Exchange actually handicapped industry. To understand how it might have done so, we need to take stock of how the country's wealth was distributed geographically. If we look at the distribution of wealth prior to the eighteenth century, we find that the greatest centres of accumulation were those in which trade and finance were important. Few people made large personal fortunes out of manufacturing. This pattern of wealth creation meant that the greatest concentrations were to be found in London and the south-east, or in commercial centres like Bristol and Liverpool.[69] Remarkably little change occurred to this pattern over the eighteenth and early nineteenth centuries. If we look at the distribution of wealth during the mid nineteenth century, we still find that—with the exception of the great landowners, some of whom gained considerably from the exploitation of mineral wealth on their estate (e.g. Marquis of Stafford)—the greatest concentrations of personal wealth in per capita terms were to be found in the centres of finance and commerce, even in county towns and watering places, rather than in manufacturing towns.[70] London was pre-eminent whilst elsewhere, more people amassed personal fortunes in a commercial centre like Liverpool than in the manufacturing workshops and mills of, say, Manchester. The nineteenth-century saying about Liverpool gentlemen, Manchester men, Bolton chaps and Wigan fellows got it only partly right, for even outlying cotton towns like Bolton had wealthier chaps than Manchester's men.

Given this general dis-association between areas of wealth accumulation and areas of industrial growth, we might expect London's Stock Exchange to have played a major role in shifting capital between them. The fact that so few industrial companies were floated on its Exchange over the eighteenth and early nineteenth centuries suggests that it failed in this vital role. However, industry had other options open to it during these critical years. For venture capital, it relied largely on that provided by individual entrepreneurs or small partnerships and on re-invested profits for the purchase of plant and equipment. To this extent, industry could be described as self-sufficient with regard to investment capital, though we need to remember that the capital provided by some entrepreneurs was mercantile *ab origine*. By comparison, when we come to look at working capital, that used to buy raw materials and meet labour costs, extensive use was made of the short-term credit facility provided by bills of exchange negotiated by local attorneys, money scriveners and bill brokers drawn on London banks though, by the late eighteenth century, local or provincial banks had become involved in the chain. The Lancashire cotton industry, in particular, made very effective use of such bills for its short-term credit needs. Clearly, in this sense, we can speak of industry being drawn into the wider capital market. Even by the mid eighteenth century, the flows involved had started to run along well-defined channels. Capital saved in the south and east, including substantial amounts from agricultural districts, was directed via the London banks to meet the short-term credit needs of industrial areas like Lancashire and the West Riding. In a counter flow though, the growing volume of industrial insurance contracted by these industrial areas helped to provide the London capital market with the funds needed to satisfy its demand for long-term credit facilities, including the growing demand for mortgages from agricultural districts.[71]

Signs of how this pattern was to change first became apparent during the closing decades of the eighteenth century. The building of canals then railways brought a sharp increase in the volume of share dealing. Initially, much of the capital invested in canals was raised through local investors—especially local merchants and landowners—but significantly, the canal mania of the 1790s saw greater volumes of capital moving out of London to tap a range of provincial opportunities. This tendency for London investment capital to become involved with provincial schemes was even more evident with the railway companies formed over the 1830s, 1840s and 1850s. However, even at this stage, the shift to a national rather than regional market in shares was more apparent during the mania of the 1840s whilst there was also a tendency for the flotation and early speculation in shares to involve local investors and for London capital to buy in only after shares had started to give a safer if lower return. The large sums invested in regional canal and railway projects, though, also gave encouragement to the growth of provincial stock exchanges. Though they had not the range or volume of dealings compared with the London exchanges, they were important in providing a market attuned to local needs and more in touch with local information flows about investment. Also, their specializ-ation in response to local needs—with Manchester specializing in cotton and railways, Liverpool in insurance, Cardiff in coal—helped offset their limited scale of activity. Arguably, the growth and independence of such exchanges served to emphasize some of the regional and sectoral divisions still apparent within the capital market *c.* 1850.[72]

As industry turned more and more to the capital market for investment funds over the second half of the nineteenth century, the majority of companies were floated on these provincial exchanges rather than on the industry-shy London Stock Exchange. Indeed, at the very point when the twin processes of capital deepening and broadening over the 1880s and 1890s dramatically increased industry's demands on the capital market for investment funds, the London Stock Exchange witnessed a huge exodus of funds into foreign government securities and railways, a 'spatial fix' that preserved capital's opportunities for a safe but modest return for large investments.[73] The effect of this was to moderate the extent to which it acted as a source of investment funds for industry. Indeed, though more industrial companies were being floated on the London Stock Exchange by the 1900s and though new technologies had created ready communication between London and provincial exchanges, effectively merging their activities, the fact remains that by 1914, trading in domestic mining, transport and industrial shares accounted for only 8 per cent of its total business with, astonishingly, trading in industrial shares being estimated at only 0.5 per cent of all its activity. What this means is that whilst industry was certainly part of a wider capital market by this point, flows in and out of it were not routed in any simplistic way via the London Stock Exchange.[74]

This penetration of finance capitalism into industry and the creation of a single capital market had considerable implications for the forces affecting spatial order in Engand and Wales. Prior to the mid nineteenth century, industrial investment tended to involve manager-entrepreneurs like the Peels, Arkwrights and Crawshays. Though we can speak of new regions of production being created during phases of investment in new technologies, the involvement of such manager-entrepreneurs tended to inhibit easy dis-investment. This is not to say that those involved did not shift profits out of industry. Both Richard Arkwright senior and junior shifted huge sums sideways into land. Indeed, Morris has suggested that beneath the general circulation of capital, there existed a personal cycle, with individual entrepreneurs being net borrowers of capital during the early part of their career, and then lenders during the later part, as they shifted capital into property and forms of rental income. Such shifts though, tended to utilize profits more than capital.[75] Indeed, early industrialists seem to have had a limited notion of obsolescence, firms rarely allowing for fixed capital replacement in their accounts. Like the charcoal-using blast furnaces that continued producing down into the 1790s, long after coke-using blast furnaces had become more economic as producers, there was a tendency for some technologies to be kept in use for their physical working life. In other words, we are faced with an industrial system in which fresh capital was—to a degree—mobile, seeking out new investments, but in which dis-investment was hardly practised. To this extent, commerce and industry were quite different as investments. As the nineteenth century progressed, though, we find a critical change taking place. The penetration of finance capital into new transport technologies and later into industry created pressure for dis-investment once the profit rates from particular investments had been eroded. This pressure for dis-investment became all the greater given the huge amounts of fixed capital sunk into public utilities and manufacturing over the mid–late nineteenth century. The response came as much through change in financial practice as through institutional adjustments. Investments in plant became amortized, written offer at a fixed rate, enabling that devoted to it to be, in effect, re-constituted for re-allocation. In short, the penetration of finance capital into the material fabric of landscape was at a price, that price being the freedom to dis-invest once profits fell below expected or average rates. If there is a geographical dimension to the cyclical swings of growth and stagnation within a capitalist system of spatial order, it is this positive shift of capital from areas of decline to areas of growth.

Adam Smith argued that as industrialization and economic development ran forward, the rate of return from industry would decline but that progressive improvements would raise the rent of land and, therefore, the share of wealth appropriated by the landlord. Neoclassical economists like Ricardo disagreed, arguing that improvements in transport would have the effect of lowering or equalizing rent. This expectation that transport improvements would counter the general tendency for rents to rise with economic progress is known as the Ricardo paradox.[76] Latterly, Harvey has taken a Smithonian view by arguing that, over time, the proportion of capital raised through industry—his primary circuit of capital—will fall behind that generated by speculation, construction and real estate—his secondary circuit—so that we can expect a net shift from one to the other.[77] Such an argument would be consistent with Harvey's further assumption that, over time, cities have formed an increasingly important arena for the expropriation of rent. However, we must handle the point cautiously. The crude analysis of rents over the nineteenth century—an age of major transport improvements—shows that Ricardo may have been right and that the proportion of total national income represented by rents actually fell. The decrease, though, was largely accounted for by the fall of agricultural land rents. By comparison, urban land rents increased their share of national income. Yet significantly, they largely did so over the closing decades of the nineteenth century, when the failure to invest in better transport technologies raised the pressure on urban land. Once this investment was made in the years after 1900, urban rents were depressed relative to national income. However, if we take account of income generated by public utilities as well as land and building rents, then there is no doubt that Harvey's secondary circuit gained a greater share of national income during the nineteenth century.[78] It is equally true, though, that improvements in transport worked to equalize rents and to retard the shift between his primary and secondary circuits.

The Nineteenth Century and Beyond

The relationship between, on the one hand, the dominant ideology of a state system and, on the other, the institutional forms through which society and economy actually function was rarely consonant or perfectly matched. Problems of inertia, or the very opposite, rapid change, could sharply divide the thought embodied in the one from the practice expressed through the other. The historical geographer also needs to take account of a further source of inconsistency. Even where free markets have all the necessary institutional forms and can operate without constraint and where capital is continually being re-constituted for new investment, there is rarely a close accordance between the actual use of resources—raw materials, land and labour—and the potential allocation which, under prevailing market conditions, would yield the highest rent. The reason for this is simple. Resources have to be taken to market, processed by it, if the latter is to determine how they are allocated. For all sorts of reasons, lags inhibit the easy response of resources to market opportunities. At the same time, market conditions are never static but constantly changing. In effect, capital is continually chasing after a moving target, continually trying to dis-engage from the embeddedness of previous investment cycles so as to seize the possibilities offered by changed markets.

Both of these different sources of inconsistency matter to any assessment of the link between ideology and spatial order over the nineteenth century. By the middle decades, state ideology and policy favoured free markets and a range of institutional forms and supporting legislation facilitated the movement of capital. More than at any other time, this was an age when we can speak of free markets organized around the needs of capital. Yet even as the political debate over the economy seemed to resolve itself in favour of free trade, notably through the repeal of the Corn Laws, the social and environmental problems created by rapid industrialization and urbaniza- tion forced the government to adopt a more supervisory and regulatory posture. At the local government level too, we see important shifts being set in motion by the mid nineteenth century. The gradual municipalization of basic public utilities like gas, water, lighting, electricity and transport and the responsibility which municipal authorities slowly acquired for the provision of basic educational and welfare facilities, including schools, hospitals, cemeteries, public baths and gardens, con- tributed enormously to the emerging self-consciousness of provincial cities and towns over the second half of the century. Yet though local politicians, like the Birmingham liberal, Joseph Chamberlain, were arguing the political case for munici- pal authorities as providers and managers of such services by the 1860s, their reasoning was still largely pragmatic—rather than based on ideological notions of 'municipal socialism'.[79] Not until the 1880s do we find the start of a real shift away from this view, with radical thinkers like A. Toynbee and T.H. Green and groups like the Fabian Society (1884+) beginning to argue for state and municipal interference in the management of society and economy as a matter of principle. As their case gained ground, the stage was set for the mixture of free enterprise, centralization and collectivism that was to be such a feature of the British political scene in the twentieth century (see Chapter 19).

We can detect comparable disconformities between the institutional forms of market capitalism and prevailing spatial order during the nineteenth century. The prime reason for this lay in the rapidity with which markets changed over the nineteenth century. The escalating demand for urban food supplies, the outward surges of city bounds and the effect of technical innovation on industrial production functions and on the efficiency and capacity of transport meant that markets were dynamic rather than static. No sooner had the process of adjusting the use of land and resources to a perceived set of market conditions got under way, than market changes altered the calculation. In effect, the landscape of the nineteenth century was never the product of a single, coherent market system, but invariably comprised a patchwork of land uses forged under a variety of market conditions, one which *in toto* was far from yielding optimum rent. Only if we understand the tension created by this discrepancy between the actual and potential uses of land do we understand the character of spatial order when forged under market capitalism.

References

1. For further comment, see R. A. Dodgshon, *The European Past: Social Evolution and Spatial Order*, (London, 1987), Chapters 6 and 7.
2. See, for example, R. H. Hilton, *The English Peasantry in the Later Middle Ages*, (Oxford, 1975), p. 139; J. E. Martin, *Feudalism to Capitalism. Peasant and Landlord in English Agrarian Development*, (London, 1983), pp. 58–78.
3. J. Hatcher, 'English serfdom and villeinage: towards a reassessment', in T. H. Aston (Ed.,), *Landlord, Peasants and Politics in Medieval England*, (Cambridge, 1987), pp. 264–5.
4. This point is best developed in the work of J. Thirsk. See, for instance, 'Seventeenth–century agriculture and social change', in J. Thirsk (ed.), *Land, Church and People: Essays Presented to H. P. R. Finberg*, Agricultural History Review Supplement, vol. 18 (1970), pp. 148–77.
5. K. Polanyi, *The Great Transformation*, (Boston, 1957 edition), p. 68.
6. A. Macfarlane, *The Origins of English Individualism*, (Cambridge, 1978), p. 152.
7. R. Hodges, *Primitive and Peasant Markets*, (London, 1988), pp. 62–95.
8. Hatcher, 'English serfdom and villeinage', pp. 280–1.
9. See, for example, K. Polanyi, *Primitive, Archaic and Modern Economies*, (Boston, 1968), pp. 26–37; D. Harvey, *Social Justice and the City*, (London, 1973), pp. 242–3; F. Braudel, *Afterthoughts on Material Civilization and Capitalism*, (Baltimore, 1977), pp. 40–1.
10. C. Wilson, *Mercantilism*, Historical Association Pamphlet no. 37, (London, 1958), p. 10.
11. Discussion of these points can be found in A. O. Hirschman, *The Passion and the Interests: Political Arguments for Capitalism Before Its Triumph*, (Princeton, 1977), especially pp. 41–2, 56 and 82–3.
12. C. B. Macpherson, *The Political Theory of Possessive Individualism*, (Oxford, 1962), pp. 85–6.
13. K. Tribe, *Land, Labour and Discourse*, (London, 1978), p. 48.
14. G. R. Elton, *The Tudor Constitution. Documents and Commentary*, (2nd edn.), (Cambridge, 1982), p. 31.
15. P. Corrigan and D. Sayer, *The Great Arch. English State Formation as a Cultural Revolution*, (Oxford, 1985), p. 43.
16. C. Hill, *Reformation to the Industrial Revolution*, (Harmondsworth, 1969), p. 27.
17. T. Thirsk, *Economic Policy and Projects*, (Oxford, 1978), p. 133.
18. H. Parris, *Constitutional Bureaucracy*, (London, 1969), pp. 281–2. See also, W. C. Lubenow, *The Politics of Government Growth. Early Victorian Attitudes Toward State Intervention 1833–1848*, (Newton Abbot, 1971), p. 180; O. MacDonagh, *Early Victorian Government 1830–1870*, (London, 1977), especially Chapter 1.
19. O. MacDonagh, *Early Victorian Government*, p. 12. See also, W. C. Lubenow, *The Politics of Government Growth*, pp. 16–17.
20. For a relevant general discussion of this point, see S. Woolf, 'Statistics and the modern state', *Comparative Studies in Society and History*, **31** (1989), pp. 588–604.
21. G. K. Fry, *The Growth of Government*, (London, 1979), p. 2. Taylor's point that nineteenth–century governments strove for a policy of minimum expenditure is relevant here; see A. J. Taylor, *Laissez–Faire and State Intervention in Nineteenth–Century Britain*, (London, 1972), p. 59.
22. A. Smith, *An Inquiry into the Nature and Causes of the Wealth of Nations*, (5th ed.), (ed. E. Cannan), (London, 1930), Vol. 1, pp. 6–7.
23. Polanyi, *Great Transformation*, pp. 68–76; K. Polanyi, *Primitive, Archaic, and Modern Economies*, pp. 158–73.
24. J. Gallagher and R. Robinson, 'The imperialism of free trade', *Economic History Review*, **VI** (1953), pp. 1–15.
25. Polanyi, *Great Transformation*, pp. 68–76; Polanyi, *Primitive, Archaic and Modern Economies*, pp. 158–73.

26. D. C. Coleman, *The Economy of England 1450–1750*, (Oxford, 1977), p. 179; R. H. Hilton, 'Capitalism—what's in a name', *Past and Present*, **1** (1952), p. 35; C. Husbands, 'Regional change in a pre-industrial economy: wealth and population in the sixteenth and seventeenth centuries', *Jnl. of Historical Geography*, **13** (1987), p. 357.

27. J. Langton and G. Hoppe, *Town and Country in the Development of Early Modern Western Europe*, HGRG Research Paper Series, no. 11, 1983, p. 35.

28. Hodges, *Primitive and Peasant Markets*, pp. 104–12.

29. D. C. North, 'Markets and other allocative systems in history; the challenge of Karl Polanyi', *Jnl. of European Economic History*, **6** (1977), pp. 703–16. For a general review of transaction costs and trade, see also, North's *Structure and Change in Economic History*, (New York, 1981).

30. A. L. Beier, 'Engine of manufacture: the trades of London', in A. L. Beier and R. Finlay (eds.), *London 1500–1700. The Making of the Metropolis*, (London, 1986), pp. 160–1.

31. R. H. Hilton, 'Some problems of urban real property in the Middle Ages', in C. H. Feinstein (ed.),*Socialism, Capitalism and Economic Growth*, (Cambridge, 1967), pp. 328–9.

32. J. Langton, 'Late medieval Gloucester: some data from a rental of 1455', *Transactions of the Institute of British Geographers*, new ser., **2** (1977), pp. 266–7.

33. D. Keene, 'A new study of London before the Great Fire', *Urban History Yearbook*, (Leicester, 1984), pp. 14–15.

34. M. J. Power, 'The social topography of Restoration London', in Beier and Finlay (eds.), *London 1500–1700*, pp. 211–212.

35. J. E. Vance, 'Land assignment in pre-capitalist, capitalist and post-capitalist cities', *Economic Geography*, **47** (1971), pp. 101–20, esp. 112–13.

36. Keene, *Urban History Yearbook*, pp. 16–17.

37. F. M. L. Thompson, 'The land market in the nineteenth century', *Oxford Economic Papers*, new series, **IX** (1957), p. 285.

38. S. Thrupp, *The Merchant Class of Medieval London*, (Ann Arbor, 1948), pp. 92–7.

39. N. S. B. Gras, *The Evolution of the English Corn Market*, (Cambridge, Mass., 1926), pp. 121–2.

40. For the sixteenth and seventeenth centuries, see F. J. Fisher, 'The development of the London food market 1540–1640', *Economic History Review*, **V** (1934–5), pp. 46–64. For the eighteenth and nineteenth centuries, see R. Peet, 'The spatial expansion of commercial agriculture in the nineteenth century: a von Thünen explanation', *Economic Geography*, **45** (1969), pp. 283–301; R. Peet, 'Influence of the British market on agriculture and related economic development in Europe before 1860', *Transactions, Institute of British Geographers*, **56** (1972), pp. 1–20.

41. For further discussion. See D. Baker, 'The marketing of corn in the first half of the eighteenth century: North East Kent', *Agricultural History Review*, **18** (1970), pp. 126–50; A. Everitt, 'The marketing of agricultural produce', in J. Thirsk (ed.), *The Agrarian History of England and Wales*, Vol. IV, (Cambridge, 1967), pp. 506–23.

42. E. P. Thompson, 'The moral economy of the English crowd in the eighteenth century', *Past and Present*, **50** (1971), especially p. 88.

43. See, for example, the figures for fixed capital in the early eighteenth-century iron industry in S. Pollard, 'Fixed capital in the Industrial Revolution in Britain', *Jnl. of Economic History*, **XXIV** (1964), pp. 299–314.

44. B. L. C. Johnson, 'The Foley Partnerships: the iron industry at the end of the charcoal era', *Economic History Review*, **IV** (1951–2), pp. 322–40.

45. P. L. Cottrell, *Industrial Finance 1830–1914. The Finance and Organization of English Manufacturing Industry*, (London, 1989), p. 20.

46. *Ibid.*, p. 14. See also, A. P. Wadsworth and J. De Lacy Mann, *The Cotton Trade and Industrial Lancashire 1600–1780*, (Manchester, 1931), pp. 71–96.

47. P. Hudson, *The Genesis of Industrial Capital. A Study of the West Riding Wool Textile Industry, c. 1750–1850*, (Cambridge, 1986), p. 262.

48. Cottrell, *Industrial Finance 1830–1914*, pp. 7, 20 and 23–4.

49. *Ibid.*, p. 5.

50. *Ibid.*, p. 19.

51. G. Ingham, *Capitalism Divided? The City and Industry in British Social Development*, (London,

1984). p. 162. See also, E. V. Morgan and W. A. Thomas, *The Stock Exchange. Its History and Functions*, (London, 1962), p. 131; R. C. Michie. 'The London Stock Exchange and the British securities markets 1850–1914', *Economic History Review*, **XXXVIII** (1985), p. 64.

52. D. Harvey, *The Limits to Capital*, (Oxford, 1982), p. 394.

53. J. R. Ward, *The Finance of Canal Building in Eighteenth-Century England*, (Oxford, 1974).

54. C. H. Feinstein, 'Capital accumulation and the Industrial Revolution', in R. Floud and D. McCloskey (eds.), *The Economic History of Britain since 1700, vol. 1: 1700–1860*, (Cambridge, 1981), p. 133.

55. G. R. Hawke and J. P. P. Higgins, 'Transport and social capital', in *ibid.*, p. 251.

56. D. Harvey, *Social Justice and the City*, (London, 1973), p. 237.

57. Feinstein, 'Capital accumulation and the Industrial Revolution', p. 133.

58. Harvey, *The Urbanization of Capital*, (Oxford, 1985), p. 64.

59. J. R. Ward, 'Speculative building at Bristol and Clifton, 1783–1793', *Business History'*, **XX** (1978), p. 13.

60. J. Whitehand, 'Building activity and intensity of development at the urban fringe: the case of a London suburb in the nineteenth century, *Jnl. of Historical Geography*, **1** (1975), pp. 211–24; J. Whitehand, 'Building cycles and the spatial pattern of urban growth', *Transactions, Institute of British Geographers*, **56** (1972), pp. 39–55.

61. Ward, 'Speculative building', p. 15.

62. H. W. Singer, 'An index of urban land rents and house rents in England and Wales 1845–1913', *Economica*, **IX** (1941), p. 229.

63. A. Offer, *Property and Politics 1870–1914. Landownership, Law and Urban Development in England*, (Cambridge, 1981), p. 255.

64. M. Falkus, 'The development of municipal trading in the nineteenth century', *Business History*, **XIX** (1977), pp. 134– 56.

65. Harvey, *Urbanization of Capital*, p. 386.

66. M. Dunford and D. Perrons, *The Arena of Capital*, (London, 1983), pp. 227–47; P. Hall and P. Preston, *The Carrier Wave. New Information Technology and the Geography of Innovation 1846–2003*, (London, 1988), especially Chapters 1–2.

67. B. T. Robson, 'The impact of functional differentiation within systems of industrialized cities', in H. Schmal (ed.), *Patterns of European Urbanization since 1500*, (London, 1981), pp. 111–30.

68. Ingham, *Capitalism Divided*, p. 147; P. G. M. Dickson, *The Financial Revolution in England. A Study in the Development of Public Credit 1688–1756*, (London, 1967), pp. 486 and 514–15.

69. Ward, *The Finance of Canal Building*, pp. 140–2; R. Grassby, 'English merchant capitalism in the late seventeenth century. The composition of business fortunes', *Past and Present*, **46** (1970), pp. 87–107.

70. A. D. M. Phillips and J. R. Walton, 'The distribution of personal wealth in English towns in the mid-nineteenth century', *Transactions, Institute of British Geographers*, **64** (1975), pp. 35–48; W. D. Rubinstein, 'The Victorian middle classes: wealth, occupation and geography', *Economic History Review*, 2nd ser., **XXX** (1977), p. 610; W. D. Rubinstein, 'Wealth and wealthy' in J. Langton and R. J. Morris (eds.), *Atlas of Industrializing Britain 1798–1914*, (London, 1986), pp. 156–9.'

71. Dickson, *The Financial Revolution in England*, pp. 484–5; L. S. Pressnell, *Country Banking in the Industrial Revolution*, (Oxford, 1956), pp. 36, 45, 77–9 and 84–99; B. L. Anderson, 'The Attorney and the early capital market in Lancashire', in F. Crouzet (ed.), *Capital Formation in the Industrial Revolution*, (London, 1972), pp. 223–55.

72. R. C. Michie, 'The London Stock Exchange and the British securities market 1850–1914', p. 64.

73. Ingham, *Capitalism Divided?*, pp. 146–7. The term 'spatial fix' is taken from D. Harvey, 'The spatial fix—Hegel, von Thünen and Marx', *Antipode*, **13** (1981), pp. 1–12. For a counter view, see M. Edelstein, 'Rigidity and bias in the British capital market 1870–1913', in D. N. McCloskey (ed.), *Essays on a Mature Economy. Britain after 1840*, (London, 1971), pp. 83–111. A critical summary of both views is provided by S. Pollard, 'Capital exports, 1870–1914: harmful or beneficial?', *Economic History Review*, 2nd ser., **XXXVIII** (1985), pp. 489–514.

74. S. Pollard, *Britain's Prime and British Decline. The British Economy 1870–1914*, (London, 1989), p. 93.
75. R. J. Morris, 'The middle class and the property cycle during the Industrial Revolution', in T. C. Smout (ed.), *The Search for Wealth and Stability. Essays in Economic and Social History Presented to M. W. Flinn*, (London, 1979), pp. 91–113.
76. A. Offer, 'Ricardo's paradox and the movement of rents in England, *c.* 1870–1910', *Economic History Review*, **XXXIII** (1980), pp. 236–52. See also, G. S. L. Tucker, *Progress and Profits in British Economic Thought*, (Cambridge, 1960), p. 65.
77. Harvey, *Urbanization of Capital*, pp. 62–89.
78. Offer, 'Ricardo's paradox', p. 248.
79. D. Fraser, 'Joseph Chamberlain and the municipal ideal', *History Today*, **37** (1987), pp. 33–9.

11

Population and Society 1730–1914

R. Lawton

The transformation of Britain from the mainly rural, pre-industrial society of the early eighteenth century to the predominantly urban, manufacturing society of what has been described as the first industrial nation[1] provides a model of the process of modernization, or 'development' against which similar processes in other countries and at other times are often measured. That development process involved several major transitions. First, there was an economic and technological transition from a relatively slowly changing agricultural way of life with widely dispersed handicraft industries in the home and in small workshops to an innovative, increasingly mechanized and regionally concentrated and specialized manufacturing and commercial economy. Secondly, there was a massive social transition from rural to urban living, from small, more cohesive communities, to a new, much less coherent urban society with a quite different class structure and life-style. Thirdly, a demographic transition from relatively slow population growth to a rapid natural increase was accompanied by a major regional redistribution with substantially increased population mobility.

In various ways population change reflects all these transitions and their underlying processes. Change in the total and the structure of the national population reflects demographic changes in the components of population growth. Changes in regional distribution due to differential population growth reflect shifts in the relative economic importance of town and country and of regional economies. At the local scale, changing patterns of population— in terms of both demographic and socio-economic structure—reflect the continuing process of adjustment of society to the changing patterns of life in both town and country. The main emphases in this chapter will be on changes in population growth and distribution at both the national and regional levels, though reference will also be made to contrasts in demographic and social trends in rural and urban areas.

National Population Trends

From the Restoration (1660) to the 1730s, fluctuating population trends ranging from losses of 0.2 to gains of up to 0.4 per cent per annum persisted in England, with high mortality in 1727–31 reversing the slow growth of the previous 50 years.[2] Over the next century accelerated population increases of up to an estimated 0.8 per cent per annum led, in the 1780s to 1820s, to a phase of hitherto unprecedented population growth, averaging 1.45 per cent per annum in England and Wales, and reaching a peak of 1.8 per cent per annum in the census decade 1811–21.[3] Relatively high rates of growth were maintained until the end of the nineteenth century, slackening somewhat after 1851 although total increments grew to an average of 338,000 per annum in England and Wales between 1871 and 1911.[4] Cumulatively, the population increased four-fold from around 9 million in 1801 to 36.1 million in 1911: this was indeed a population revolution (Fig. 11.1).

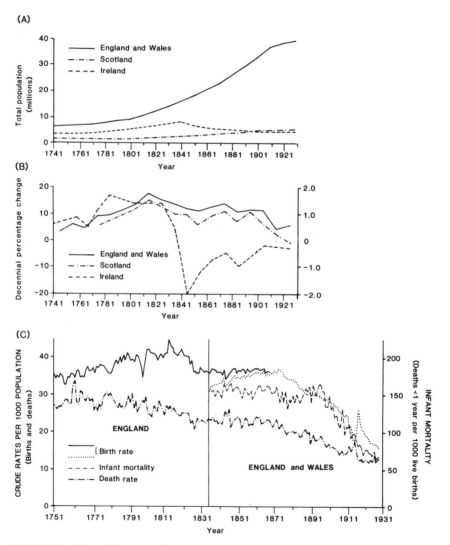

Fig. 11.1. (A) Total population and (B) trends in Great Britain and Ireland, 1741–1926, (C) vital trends in England, 1751–1836 and in England and Wales, 1837–1926. *Sources*: A and B: B. R. Mitchell and Phyllis Deane, *Abstract of British Historical Statistics* (Cambridge, 1962), Tables I.1 and I.2. C: E. A. Wrigley and R. S. Schofield, *The Population History of England 1541–1871* (London, 1981), Appendix 3, Table A3.3, and Mitchell and Deane, Tables I.10 and I.12.

The precise reasons for this relatively rapid growth from the mid eighteenth century have been, and still are, being debated.[5] First, a substantial reduction in mortality was achieved due to better diet, better hygiene, and more effective control of epidemic disease, particularly smallpox. Together these contributed to a substantial reduction in general mortality from 32 per 1000 (ranging annually from 25 to 45) in the early eighteenth century, to 26 per 1000 (annually 21–28) in the early nineteenth (Fig. 11.1C), and raised the expectation of life at birth from 33–35 to 36–37 years.

The onset of the British demographic transition, also saw considerable fluctuations in fertility. A younger marriage age (for women 24 rather than 25.4 as in the early eighteenth century)[6] and somewhat higher marriage rates by the late eighteenth century were reflected in increased birth rates averaging 39–40 per 1000 around the turn of the century, as compared with 33–34 per 1000 in the mid eighteenth and mid nineteenth centuries. These trends were a feature of both rural areas, where they have been associated with the system of outdoor poor relief (the Speenhamland system),[7] and industrial areas, where there was employment for women and children in handicraft and the early factory industry.[8] The gross reproduction rate, which measures the comparative reproduction potential of women, peaked at around 3.0 in the second and third decades of the nineteenth century as compared with 2.5 in the 1770s and 1860s. These trends may have resulted from earlier marriage and reduced maternal mortality rather than increased standardized fertility: Habakkuk has calculated that a reduction of only one year in the mean marriage age would increase family size by 8 per cent,[9] helping to accelerate population growth in the second stage of demographic transition from around 1780 to 1830.

From the 1830s to the 1880s the rates of population increase slackened. Unhealthy conditions in many urban and industrial districts held back improvements in general mortality rates, which remained around 22–23 per 1000 until about 1880.[10] Thus, while life expectancy at birth was around 41 years for the country as a whole, it was below 35 years in the worst areas (for examples Liverpool, Manchester and Merthyr) as compared with over 50 in some rural areas. It was only with improved housing, sanitation and public health, and better scientific medical knowledge, especially of such infectious diseases as cholera and typhoid, that towns become safer places — especially for the working classes — a fact reflected in the rapid improvement in infant mortality after the turn of the century.

A decline in the birth rate from the 1870s initiated the third phase of the British demographic transition.[11] Prior to this, age and incidence of marriage had acted as a regulator of fertility and family size together with the traditional constraint — *coitus interruptus* (see Chapter 6). But, while there had been advocates of birth control, such as Thomas Paine, and powerful arguments for restraint of fertility in Malthus' first (1798) and subsequent essays on the Principle of Population, there is little evidence of birth control in the modern sense of the term until the 1870s. The restriction in the size of middle-class families became evident from the 1880s.[12] Sociological, economic and demographic factors have all been invoked to explain the adoption of family limitation through the spacing of births and progressive restriction of the child-bearing period by means of contraceptive devices.[13] Whatever the causes, it was a social revolution which extended, if unequally, to all classes of society and all regions of Britain by the 1920s. In consequence, whereas around 1860 the average family was nearly seven children for women marrying at between 20 and 24 years of age, after 1870 fewer children were born and there were fewer mothers bearing children in their late 30s and early 40s.[14] Among economic factors were the cost of schooling and caring for middle-class children, while restrictions in the employment of child labour from mid-century in both factory and field and, after the 1870 Education Act, compulsory education began to prevent working-class children from earning. More employment for women (in workshops, factories and offices) may have been a further disincentive to prolonged years of child-bearing. These and other factors caused the average size of family to fall to around 3.5 for women marrying young, by about 1910. However, the British fertility decline is still far from fully analysed or understood. Woods has argued that theoretical considerations, such as the association of the fertility decline with modernization accompanying industrialization and urbanization, do not accord with the spread of family limitation in urban and rural areas alike. Not is it easy to see precisely how fertility decline is related to mortality trends, in particular, to declining child and, later, infant mortality, or to the levels of internal and international migration. Finally, social diffusion from higher- to lower-status groups was uneven, though social and cultural attitudes—rather than wider availability of cheap contraceptive devices—must have been crucial for family formation decisions of individual parents.[15] Certainly there are substantial regional and class differences in fertility in late-nineteenth- and early-twentieth-century Britain, some of which are touched on later (pp. 305 annd 314).

The general growth of population would have been substantially greater in the nineteenth century had it not been for overseas migration. Though the net loss by migration throughout the nineteenth century was relatively unimportant, varying from 0.05 to 0.23 per cent per annum between 1841 and 1910 (Table 11.1A), overseas migration affected both rural and urban areas, the level of overseas emigration rising during periods of economic depression when migration, especially to North America, was an alternative to internal migration to the growing towns and industrial regions.[16]

In all some 10 million people emigrated from Britain between 1815 and 1914 and, at its peak in the 1880s and 1900s, 1.55 and 1.88 million, respectively, left England and Wales for non-European destinations. In the decade 1901–10, the net loss by migration is estimated as half-a-million, only 100,000 below the net loss in the depression period 1881–90.[17] Both are above the 519,000 net loss estimated for eighteenth-century England as a whole by Wrigley and Schofield and match their estimated 621,000 net loss for 1815–1850. Of a total estimated emigration of 2.35 million, 1861–1900—63 per cent male—rather more than one-third came from largely urbanized areas (London, Lancashire and the West Midlands) and another third from mainly rural areas, while 30 per cent were from industrial and partly urbanized areas (such as the Home Counties, Yorkshire, the East Midlands and the North-East and South Wales coalfields). Hence, despite wide variations in rates of emigration most counties sent considerable numbers overseas and some rural counties lost a substantial proportion of their native-born population in the forty years 1861–1900, over 10 per cent in the case of Cornwall.[18] Since a high proportion were aged between 15 and 24 the cumulative demographic impact of heavy losses must have been considerable, especially in rural areas.

Table 11.1A: Population trends, England and Wales, 1701–1921.

	Population		Natural increase		Births		Deaths		Net migration	
	000s	Per cent increase p.a.	000s	Per cent p.a.	000s	Per cent p.a.	000s	Per cent p.a.	000s	Per cent p.a.
1701[a]	5058	—	—	—	—	—	—	—	—	—
1731[a]	5772	0.28	958	0.38	8779	3.47	7821	3.09	−244	−0.10
1781[a]	7042	0.73	1438	0.83	6523	3.76	5085	2.94	−168	−0.10
1801[a]	8597*	1.10	1660	1.18	5787	4.11	4127	2.93	−105	−0.07
1831[b]	13,897	1.73	4975	1.81	13,253[(e)]	4.82	8278[(e)]	3.00	−234	−0.09
1881[b]	25,974	1.74	11,332	1.63	32,362	4.66	21,030	3.03	−745	−0.11
1921[b]	37,887	1.15	14,188	1.37	35,440	3.41	21,252	2.05	−2275	−0.22

*England and Wales (adjusted to include military) 9156. [(e)] Estimated

Table 11.1B: Vital trends, England and Wales, 1841–1920.

(Average annual)[b]	Births/1000	Fertility rate B/F 15–44	Deaths/1000	Infant mortality (D <$/$1000 live births)
1841–50	32.6	136.9	22.4	154
1851–60	34.2	145.1	22.2	153
1861–70	35.2	151.3	22.5	154
1871–80	35.4	153.9	21.4	149
1881–90	32.5	139.3	19.1	142
1891–1900	29.9	123.1	18.2	154
1901–10	27.2	109.3	15.4	127
1911–20	23.8	104.1	14.4	101

Sources:
[a] Estimated rates for England only, E. A. Wrigley and R. S. Schofield, *The Population History of England, 1541–1871* (London, 1981), Tables B.8, A2.1 and A3.3.
[b] B. R. Mitchell and Phyllis Cole, *Abstract of British Historical Statistics* (Cambridge, 1962).

All parts of the country contributed to overseas migration, as did all occupations and social classes. In the mid-Victorian period 50 per cent of emigrants from England were unskilled labourers; but by the late nineteenth century this proportion dropped to one-third or less. Certainly by then four out of five emigrants from England and Scotland were predominantly from large towns and industrial areas, and included a considerable and increasing proportion of skilled handicraft, industrial and tertiary workers who formed nearly half (48.6 per cent) of British passengers in ship lists of vessels arriving in the United States in 1878 and 59.1 per cent in 1897.[19]

The consequences of these various demographic and structural changes for population were two-fold. First, they led to changes in the age structure and, secondly, in the growth potential and size of the workforce. Between the late seventeenth century—a period of relatively low fertility and high average age—and the high-fertility, youthful populations of the mid-1820s, the proportion of children under five probably increased by one-third and that of the 5–14 and 25–59 year-old groups by one-quarter, while older dependants (over 60) fell by one-third.[20] Throughout the early- and mid-Victorian period Britain enjoyed a youthful population structure which changed little until the 1890s (Table 11.2).

While lowering of mortality rates produced more people in the older age groups, a relatively high birth rate maintained a structure favourable to population growth. Nevertheless, until the late-Victorian period there was a high dependency rate. Until the 1880s around 36 per cent of England's population was in the under-15 age group and only 5 per cent in the over-65s. This favoured the growing labour market in a generally expanding economy though in periods of economic depression, as in the 1880s, the inability to absorb labour led to a sharp increase in emigration; moreover, areas of economic decline—both rural and urban—shed labour to a huge internal migration system driven principally by the shifting demand for labour[21] (see below,

Table 11.2: Age structure, England and Wales, 1821–1921.

	Percentage of population aged			
	0–14	15–44	45–64	65+
1821	48	29	16	7
1841	36	46	13	4
1851	35	46	14	5
1861	36	45	15	5
1871	36	45	15	5
1881	37	45	14	5
1891	35	46	14	5
1901	32	48	15	5
1911	31	48	16	5
1921	28	47	19	6

Sources: Censuses of Great Britain (1821–51) and England and Wales (1861–1921).

pp. 302–311). Moreover, as the compulsory education system under the 1870 Act and its successors began to make an impact on child labour, the incentive to restrict families affected all classes of society. By the end of the century a falling birth rate was reflected in the population structure: juvenile dependency fell while improvements in mortality over the late nineteenth century helped to increase the proportion of over-65s.

While these trends show all the features associated with the classic demographic transition model, the passage to phase III from a lengthy phase II in which reduced mortality led to substantially increased natural increase of population was prolonged in England and Wales by rural–urban migration.[22] The decline in rural birth rates is late (in contrast to the situation in France) since early industrial development and urbanization, together with emigration, successfully absorbed surplus rural population. Hence, differentials in regional rates of national increase were offset by even wider contrasts in levels of internal migration: not only did England experience an early *vital* transition, but it embarked early on the second stage of what has been described as the *mobility* transition.[23]

From the later eighteenth century there was a relative and, from the mid nineteenth century, an absolute movement of people from rural to urban and industrial areas[24] permitting natural increase, due largely to a relatively high birth rate, to persist in many rural areas until late in the nineteenth century.[25] Out-migration from the rural reservoirs of very large numbers of young adults—both men and women—provided the stock from which, in the eighteenth century, the large towns, London in particular, were able to sustain relatively rapid growth despite high mortality. During the nineteenth century rural migrants gave momentum over short periods of very rapid growth to individual areas from which subsequently, high rates of growth could be sustained largely by natural increase.

Continuing redistribution of population between peripheral areas and a core of maximum economic and population concentration progressively focused upon the areas of south Lancashire and west Yorkshire, the industrial Midlands and Greater London, together with secondary nodes in north-east England and South Wales, all areas of high levels of urbanization and industrialization by the later nineteenth century (Table 11.3).

In south-east England growth prior to 1851 was focused largely on London, though the south-coast towns—particularly ports and resorts such as Portsmouth and Brighton—experienced rapid growth from the later eighteenth century. In the later nineteenth century the South East's rate of population increase was much above the national level and its share of Britain's population increased markedly reflecting the spreading growth and influence of Greater London. In contrast, the West Midlands experienced early industrialization and rapid population growth up to the 1860s, but the relative decline of the Black Country after 1870 is reflected in the slight fall in the region's share of the national population by 1901.

Despite early developments in coalmining, especially in north-east England, the northern region and Wales did not experience the full impact of mining and heavy industry until the mid nineteenth century. Thereafter high rates of population growth led to an increase in their relative regional importance, though the upsurge of population in the South Wales coalfield in the later nineteenth century is obscured in Table 11.3 by massive migrational losses from rural Wales.

Table 11.3: Comparative regional population trends in Great Britain, 1701–1901.

REGION	Total population (000)						Share of Great Britain (per cent)					
	1701[a]	1751[a]	1801[c]	1851[c]	1901[c]		1701	1751	1801	1851	1901
ENGLAND	5413	5691	8305	16,764	30,515		78.7	76.8	79.1	80.6	82.5
South-East	1609	1690	2503	5111	10,523		23.4	22.8	23.8	24.3	28.4
West Midlands	516	558	858	1713	2987		7.5	7.5	8.2	8.2	8.1
East Midlands	486	472	640	1152	2013		7.1	6.4	6.1	5.5	5.4
East Anglia	516	484	626	1049	1131		7.5	6.5	6.0	5.0	3.1
South-West	1061	1109	1344	2243	2570		15.4	15.0	12.8	10.8	6.9
Yorks/Humberside	409	461	817	1808	3514		6.0	6.2	7.8	8.7	9.5
North-West	339	425	882	2525	5278		4.9	5.7	8.4	12.1	14.3
North	480	494	634	1163	2498		7.0	6.7	6.0	5.6	6.8
WALES	413	449	588	1164	2013		6.0	6.1	5.6	5.6	5.4
SCOTLAND	1048[b]	1265[b]	1608	2889	4472		15.2	17.1	15.3	13.9	12.1
GREAT BRITAIN	6974	7405	10,501	20,816	37,000		100	100	100	100	100

Table 11.3: Comparative regional population trends in Great Britain, 1701–1901 (continued).

REGION	Percentage increase				Percentage regional change Percentage G.B. change			
	1701–51	1751–1801	1801–51	1851–1901	1701–51	1751–1801	1801–51	1851–1901
ENGLAND	5.2	32.6	101.9	82.0	68	72	104	106
South-East	5.0	51.9	104.2	105.9	65	114	106	136
West Midlands	8.1	56.1	99.7	74.3	105	126	102	96
East Midlands	-2.9	47.2	79.9	74.8	-38	104	81	96
East Anglia	-6.3	30.3	67.6	7.8	-82	68	69	10
South-West	4.6	26.1	66.9	14.6	60	57	68	19
Yorks/Humberside	12.6	82.5	121.2	94.4	164	182	123	121
North-West	25.5	109.7	186.4	109.0	331	242	190	140
North	2.8	32.6	83.3	114.9	36	72	85	148
WALES	8.7	34.9	98.0	73.0	113	77	100	94
SCOTLAND	20.7	27.1	79.6	54.8	269	60	81	71
GREAT BRITAIN	7.7	45.4	98.2	77.7	100	100	100	100

The regions are the revised Standard Regions of 1971.

Sources:
a Phyllis Deane and W. A. Cole, *British Economic Growth, 1688–1959*, (2nd edn.) (Cambridge, 1969).
b Figures based on Dr Webster's 1755 estimates and Sir John Sinclair's 1707 estimate from the *Old Statistical Account*. For a discussion of the problems in estimating eighteenth-century population in Scotland, see M. W. Flinn *et al.*, *Scottish Population History from the Seventeenth Century to the 1930s*, (Cambridge, 1977), pp. 241–70.
c Department of the Environment, *Long Term Population Distribution in Great Britain—a study: Report by an inter-departmental Study Group*, (H.M.S.O., 1971), Tables 1.4, 1.5, 1.6 and 1.12.

Other regions south of the Humber–Mersey experienced a relative decline in population, particularly in the later nineteenth century. In East Anglia and the South West the decline and ultimate demise of many rural industries, together with persistent nineteenth-century migration from the land and slow urban growth, led to a marked reduction in their share of the national population. The East Midlands fared better reflecting a more diversified economy which by the later nineteenth century increasingly attracted population to its towns and industries from adjacent and northern areas. This led to an acceleration in population growth reflected in its increased proportion of the national population in the twentieth century.

Similarly, in the North-West and Yorkshire, rapid growth in the specialist textile districts in the eighteenth and early nineteenth centuries led to large population growth, absolutely and relatively. By the late nineteenth century, despite considerable industrial diversification, rates of population growth fell, reflecting out-migration from many of the older industrial areas.

Spatial Patterns of Population Development, 1730–1911

Detailed, exact and directly comparable analysis of vital and migrational components of population change in England and Wales over this period is impossible. Prior to the development of civil registration of vital statistics with the creation of the Office of Registrar General in 1837, vital trends must be calculated from baptismal and burial registers both of which are deficient in a number of ways. Even after the adoption of civil registration, vital data, especially on births, were defective and, despite the much increased census data on age and sex composition from 1841, it is difficult to calculate standardized measures of fertility and mortality.[26] Migration must be estimated indirectly: first, by comparing natural change with total change to give net migration; and, secondly, from the 1841 census onwards by using census information on birthplace to give lifetime migration into a particular area[27] or to estimate inter-censal migration from changes in birthplace figures in successive censuses adjusted for mortality.[28] Changing areal units of enumeration also create problems.

1730–80

From the mid eighteenth century population growth in England and Wales accelerated. The 1730s and 1740s were years of slow growth, continuing the relatively high mortality which kept the general rate of natural growth during the early eighteenth century to a very low level and created a substantial loss between 1727 and 1730.[29] The calculations of Deane and Cole, based on the Parish Register Abstracts of the early censuses, suggest that in London and the south-eastern counties there was a considerable excess of deaths over births, population growth being sustained by considerable in-migration. In a number of rural counties of Midland, southern and northern England natural growth was negligible and, indeed, there were some areas of decline; in many such areas total numbers fell because of out-migration.

From 1732 to 1783 (Rostow's suggested date of economic 'take-off'[30]) national population increased by 36.8 per cent due mainly to a substantial reduction in death rate coupled, perhaps, with a slight increase in birth rate. Rates of natural increase accelerated in all parts of the country outside London, particularly in areas of early industrial development—such as the West Midlands and the textile districts of east Lancashire, west Yorkshire and Notts–Derby—and in adjacent counties where birth rates seem to have been relatively high.[31] Already, it seems, there may have been a demographic gradient from higher fertility and mortality in the north and west to lower rates in the south and east, London—with its very high mortality—excepted.

While Deane and Cole's calculations of net migration from estimates of natural and total change must be regarded as somewhat speculative, the areas of gain seem to have been dominated by the metropolitan counties and the new industrial areas of the West Midlands and textile regions, in keeping with the concept of growing redistribution of population resulting principally from short-range movement. Seasonal migration of labour, local mobility (encouraged by movement of labour from 'closed' parishes to 'open' parishes),[32] annual hirings of farm servants and migrant (including itinerant) craftsmen, all contributed to a less stable rural population than once thought. Comparison of parish 'listings' and persistence of families in parish registers suggest a relatively high turnover.[33] Studies of marriage distance have also confirmed considerable local movement with, among higher social groups and their servants, a considerable element of long-distance migration.[34]

Studies based on apprenticeship registers[35] and Poor Law records also point to considerable migration to a wide spectrum of towns. There were significant long-distance movements of skilled craftsmen in a wide range of industries (for example, in metallurgy, chemicals and glass-making), while textiles and coalmining attracted not only considerable short-range but also medium- and long-distance migration.[36]

Migration, often over considerable distances, sustained the rapid growth of London and the major provincial cities in the early- and mid-Georgian period, and was a key factor in the growth of new towns such as spas and seaside watering places, and the emerging industrial centres. In London, deaths persistently exceeded births until the 1780s and intermittently so—as in large provincial cities—until mid-Victorian times.

At the beginning of the eighteenth century London, with a population of nearly 600,000, already housed one-tenth of the country's population. Over the next half-century, despite an estimated net migration gain of 500,000 to 600,000, population grew only to some 675,000 (due to high mortality).[37] Deane and Cole estimate a migration gain in the metropolitan counties of 404,720 between 1750 and 1780, when London's population had increased to around three-quarters of a million.[38] The demographic as well as the economic attraction of the capital was nation-wide. It drew people from all parts of England and Wales, with town dwellers probably important among long-distance migrants including those from Ireland, Scotland and overseas: indeed, of married people treated at the London Dispensary between 1774 and 1781, one in 11 was Irish-born, one in 15 Scots, and one in 60 foreign.[39] London was at the head of a hierarchical system in which dominance was more pronounced than in the nineteenth century, with a primacy over the next large city of some 20 to 1.

Other large urban and industrial centres drew upon smaller settlements and adjacent rural areas to sustain their accelerating increase, producing a substantial increase in urban growth from the mid eighteenth century, the population and social implications of which for mid- and late-Georgian England have yet to be examined. Urban populations increased from 22 or 23 per cent of the total in 1700 to one-quarter by 1750,[40] and around one-third (over 3 million people) by 1801[41] with a substantial increase in migrants to many towns.

However, not all towns were equally affected. Traditional regional centres, especially in predominantly agricultural districts or which had lost handicraft industry, grew relatively slowly; so did country towns whose modest growth at best paralleled that of surrounding rural areas. But industrial centres, ports, and spas and seaside resorts grew rapidly. The practical problems of rapid population growth in the towns, especially those of health, sanitation and the levying of rates, produced a considerable number of local censuses in the later eighteenth century. Of over 120 counts from 1750 to 1790 listed by Law, 102 related to 81 towns ranging from market centres to major provincial cities.[42] Of the 12 places for which there is more than one listing, some larger ones doubled their population—Manchester from 19,839 in 1758 to 42,821 in 1788; Birmingham from 23,688 in 1750 to 30,804 in 1770; and Nottingham from 10,020 in 1739 to 17,711 in 1779—while the new industrial town of Bolton mushroomed from 5339 to 11,739 between 1773 and 1789. In contrast, the smaller market and county towns grew more slowly: for example, Cambridge with 6422 people in 1728 had reached only 9868 by 1794.

Information on population structure in such local censuses is mainly related to sex and household structure with a few giving age and marital status. The latter indicate fewer children and old people and more young adults in the towns than in rural areas, evidence of active in-migration with a future growth potential already reflected in pressure on housing in the larger towns.

1780–1831

During this half-century population increased sharply by an estimated 86 per cent. The balance between agriculture and industry shifted and levels of urbanization increased with large numbers drawn to London and the big provincial cities.[43] However, natural increase was often highest in rural areas, with their lower death rate. Extensions to the cultivated area and the intensification of farming, together with a wide range of rurally based industries, retained much of the natural increment in the countryside: Deane and Cole believe that 'not until 1800 [was there] a general movement of population to . . . new industrial centres'[44] fed by natural increase and by short-range movement from adjacent areas.

Nevertheless, the 'modern', twentieth-century pattern of population distribution was taking shape by the first census of 1801. Though early-nineteenth-century England was still predominantly rural, with one-third of its population dependent on agriculture, industrial and commercial activity accounted for population concentrations in Greater London, the Black Country, south Lancashire–west Yorkshire and Tyneside and parts of the North-East coalfield (Fig. 11.4). While remote rural areas of upland Wales and northern England and low densities, in much of lowland England population increases rivalled those of many towns. Indeed, 'the man of the crowded countryside was still the typical Englishman'.[45]

Between 1780 and 1830 the highest rates of population increase were, first, in the metropolitan and south-eastern counties, not least the south-coast towns; secondly,

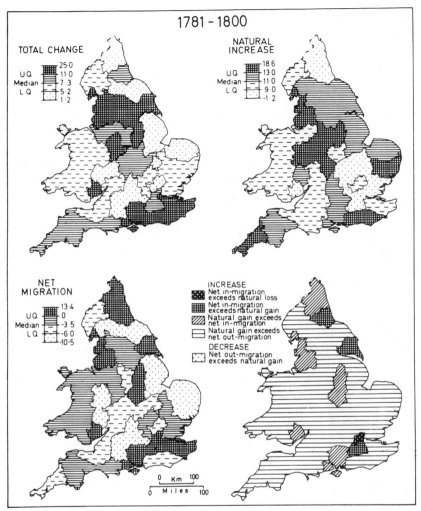

Fig. 11.2. Components of population change in England and Wales by counties, 1781–1800. The average decadal rate of change per 1000 over the period is shown in four quartile groups and is comparable with Fig. 11.3. Based on Phyllis Deane and W. A. Cole, *British Economic Growth 1088–1599* (2nd edn.) (Cambridge, 1969), Table 26 (p. 115).

in the industrial north (especially Lancashire and south Yorkshire), the West and parts of the East Midlands; and, thirdly, the mining and industrial districts of Cornwall, Monmouth and south-east Wales, and north-east England (Figs, 11.2 and 11.3). Low-growth areas included both relatively populous farming districts in East Anglia and the south Midlands and thinly peopled uplands in the South-West, Wales and northern England. All were increasingly dependent on farming and many had suffered a decline in handicraft manufacture, especially textiles. However, in general the rural areas experienced a population growth not dissimilar from the national rate.[46] Enclosure and reclamation often greatly benefited hitherto marginal lands, especially during the plough-up campaign of the Napoleonic Wars,

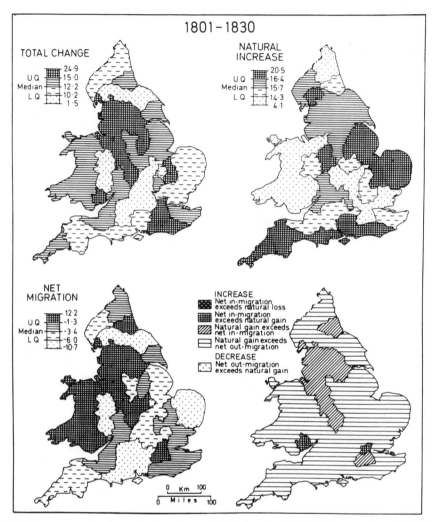

Fig. 11.3. Components of population change in England and Wales by counties, 1801–30. The average decadal rate of change per 1000 over the period is shown in four quartile groups and is comparable with Fig. 11.2. Based on Deane and Cole, see Fig. 11.2.

in both upland and lowland Britain.[47] In many areas of low agricultural productivity, the harnessing of water power and cheap domestic labour to textiles, knitwear and metallurgical industries stimulated a mixed, proto-industrial economy with high rates of natural growth.[48]

Such growth cannot be ascribed solely to natural increase. While deficiencies in parochial registration, especially of births, make analysis of regional fertility and mortality hazardous, above-average rates of natural increase seem to characterize both low-growth areas such as East Anglia, the South Midlands and Wales and also rapidly growing urban and industrial areas such as London, the West Midlands and the industrial north. London's mortality fell in the late eighteenth century, but its birth rates remained low. In contrast in the North-West and the industrial Midlands a rising birth rate and a falling death rate led to acceleration of natural growth. In most rural areas mortality continued to fall and additional births contributed to high local rates of natural increase, notably in the southern and south-western counties, and in parts of East Anglia and eastern England. There were increases in family size in many rural areas, reflected in the substantial increase in the national crude birth rate in the late eighteenth and early nineteenth centuries. But there is little to support the contentions of Malthus and the 1834 Poor Law Commissioners that the so-called Speenhamland system of outdoor poor relief led to earlier marriage and increased families among the rural poor, though it may have contributed to reduced infant mortality.[49]

In sum, increased births were a significant agent of population change in the late eighteenth and early nineteenth centuries. The peak five-year mean crude birth rate of 1813–17 was 41.8 per 1000, 16 per cent above the 36.1 for 1778–82. Nevertheless, crude death rates had fallen by 11 per cent over that period, from 28.2 to 25.2 per thousand. However, between 1815 and 1835, much of that increase in births had been lost; crude birth rates fell to 35.8 in 1830–34, while crude death rates continued to fall to 22.1 per 1000.[50]

Because of high mortality and relatively low fertility the greater part of population growth in London and the metropolitan area during the period 1780–1830 — perhaps three-quarters of a million out of an estimated total increase of 1,364,000 — was contributed by net migration. Although in the industrial regions of England much of the growth came from their own natural increase and that of adjacent counties, the major provincial cities attracted population from farther afield. For example, the numbers of Irish, Scots and overseas-born in the population of late-Georgian Liverpool were substantial and the city's rapid growth depended largely on migration, which accounted for over two-thirds of its population increase between 1790 and 1801.[51] However, while there was a growing volume of short-range movement there was no sudden transfer of population from the south to the Midlands and north of England.[52] Between 1781 and 1830 the greatest migration gains were in the metropolitan region and only Lancashire, Durham and Monmouth appear to have experienced continuous net in-migration while Yorkshire and parts of the West and East Midlands showed intermittent gain. Though such estimates of net migration are certainly defective, they suggest an increasing focus of movement on a relatively few areas. For the most part rural areas suffered net migrational losses, though the local situation was complex: areas with industry often attracted labour from adjacent districts, producing a considerable ebb and flow of population. Nevertheless, the bulk of migration was towards the towns and new industrial regions in what Redford described as 'a complex wavelike motion',[53] with a transfer of some of the natural increase of rural populations to the towns and industrial areas in which migrational and natural increases of population combined to produce rapid total growth.

From the late eighteenth century the acceleration in the growth of urban population was as great as any experienced in modern times and, particularly in London and the larger provincial cities, it led to major health and social problems and to marked changes in the characteristics of the towns and their populations (see Chapter 15). London, with a population of some 960,000 in 1801, was the only truly large city, and continued its dominance, though at a slower rate of growth, to reach 1,776,556 in 1831 in a metropolitan area 'some 8 miles around St. Pauls'. The provincial capitals expanded rapidly and the impact of industrialization spawned new towns, particularly in the textiles and metalworking districts. By 1801 33.8 per cent of the population was urban and that proportion grew rapidly to 44 per cent by 1831, with urban population doubling to absorb 62.8 per cent of the national increase of 5 million, 1801–31.[54]

Compared with the eighteenth century when London dominated the national pattern of urban growth, the gap between the capital and regions was narrowed and the rank order of cities began to assume a more regular gradient. The pattern of urban growth, 1780–1830, points to a number of regional sub-systems with high rates of population increase particularly in the textile areas of south Lancashire and west Yorkshire and the metalworking areas of the West Midlands, while the rapid growth of towns along the south coast was also marked.[55] Many textile towns achieved spectacular growth, up to ten-fold in places like Bury, Bolton, Bradford, and Huddersfield, while of the regional capitals Manchester grew from 27,246 in 1773 to some 182,000 in 1831 and Leeds from 17,121 in 1775 to 123,000. There were similar increases recorded in the metallurgical districts: Birmingham grew from 50,000 in 1781 to 144,000 in 1831; Wolverhampton from 11,368 in 1788 to 25,000; and Sheffield from 26,538 to 92,000. Notable increases were also recorded in many seaports, particularly the large commercial ports such as Liverpool which grew from 34,407 in 1773 to 202,000 in 1831, though specialized ports also boomed—for example, Sunderland increased its population from around 10,000 in 1760 to 39,000 in 1831. Rapid development of naval bases such as Plymouth and Portsmouth, together with resorts such as Brighton, also had much to do with rapid urbanization along the south coast.[56]

In contrast, older regional centres in particular market and county towns often achieved only modest population growth, especially in southern and eastern England. Norwich, one of the largest of pre-industrial cities in England with a population of 40,050 in 1786, had only 62,000 in 1831: Exeter, despite its growing regional functions, suffered from decline of its port and regional textile trade and the population of 28,000 in 1831 was little more than twice that of the late seventeenth century.

Chalklin suggests that the bigger provincial towns added an average of some 500–1000 new migrants to their population every year.[57] Birmingham, where population grew by some 20,000 in the 1780s and 1790s, attracted people from rural Warwick-shire and Matthew Boulton, the founder of the Soho works at Handsworth, claimed that, 'I have trained up many, and am training up more, plain country lads into good workmen.'[58] Many migrants to the growing textile towns came from adjacent handicraft production and from Ireland.[59]

In London and the major provincial cities, among the growing numbers of long-distance migrants the Irish formed the largest group. The 1841 census counted 284,128 Irish-born, 1.9 per cent of the total population of England, over half of whom lived in London, Liverpool and Manchester.[60] Indeed in all three cities over 10 or even 20 per cent of inhabitants of some areas were of Irish origin. In London these included St Giles, Whitechapel and Shadwell.[61] In Liverpool the numbers of Irish increased rapidly after the 1798 uprising, according to contemporaries. Already certain districts in the town centre and in the working-class 'North End' held significant concentrations of Irish, which increased as the proportion of Irish built up to 17.3 per cent of the Borough's population in 1841 and which were reflected in the spread of Catholic churches in the early nineteenth century and in growing overcrowding.[62] Such conditions led to a worsening of living conditions in towns that was reflected in relatively high levels of urban mortality even before the marked deterioration of the 1830s.[63]

Despite growing migration from countryside to town, rural population growth accelerated to a peak in 1811–21, the decade of most rapid increase in the country as a whole.[64] Increased demand for labour, not least on newly reclaimed and enclosed land, usually more than compensated for the decline in small farms and the increase in landless labourers.[65] However, while the numbers of those engaged in primary pursuits continued to rise, they formed a diminishing proportion of the rurally employed, although in 1831 half the population of rural England was still engaged in agriculture, horticulture and forestry.[66] In contrast to widespread depopulation associated with earlier enclosures for pasture (see above, pp. 181–188) there is little evidence of widespread depopulation following parliamentary enclosure. A more likely local cause of slow population growth was the restriction on labourers' cottages in 'closed' parishes,[67] though Yelling,[68] while admitting that there was considerable local variation, has argued that in most parishes involved in enclosure during this period there was—to use the conclusion from one study of the effect of enclosure on 200 parishes in the East Midlands—'no necessary accompaniment of population decline or even of very slow growth'.[69]

Nevertheless, by 1830 rural population growth was slowing down. Though population continued to increase throughout most of rural England, up to mid-century there was early decline in three Welsh counties, slow growth along the Welsh Border, in south-west England and the grazing areas of the Midlands, and very limited increase in much of upland Wales and parts of northern England.

The relatively high rural growth rate was due to relatively high fertility. There is little support for the view that this was directly due to Poor Law family allowances (see above, p. 299) influencing the age or numbers of those marrying and increasing the size of families among the rural poor.[70] However, the restrictive settlement clauses of the Old Poor Law helped to retain surplus labour in remoter rural areas which was released from the 1830s.[71] A more important factor was the continuing diversity of employment offered by the 'dual economy' in many rural areas in the mid nineteenth century: local craft trades in village and market town, and a considerable amount and range of rurally located cottage, workshop and extractive industry gave great diversity to the employment structure,[72] while the turnpike and canal age brought new jobs to the countryside in addition to giving a new nodality to some market towns.

The drift of rural industry towards new industrial regions in fact often contributed to rural—as well as urban—growth in this period. Nevertheless, in promoting accelerated urban increase it was also instrumental in initiating a substantial redistribution of population, the full impact of which was to be experienced only in Victorian times: as Francis Galton later observed 'the population of towns decays and has to be recruited by migrants from the country'.[73]

1831–1911

From the 1830s migration from the countryside accelerated: though rural fertility and natural increments remained relatively high, the surplus was progressively directed towards industrial areas, the coalfields and the rapidly growing towns, particularly London. Much of the transfer of population remained short-range, though the strong pull of major cities reached out to more distant regions. Fed by young adults, most towns and industrial regions provided most of their population increment from their own natural growth by the end of the century.

Although rural depopulation and the fuller concentration of population in the towns and industrial regions continued, from the 1880s new features affected regional trends. As the rural reservoirs were drained of younger people their natural increase declined, due especially to falling births: indeed by 1891 there were many rural areas in which fertility was substantially below the national level (Fig. 11.6) and in which indices of less than 0.6 pointed to controlled marital fertility (I_g) in some agricultural districts and small towns.[74] Larger towns and, especially, the coalfield areas derived more and more of their increment from natural increase to which the rapidly falling death rates of the late nineteenth century largely contributed, though fertility also remained very high in many heavy industrial and mining areas. Changing patterns of industry, including a relative decline of staple industries in areas of early industrialization, shifted the balance of attraction towards areas in which new industries were developing most rapidly, especially the South East and the West and East Midlands. As the rural reservoir drained, the emphasis shifted from mainly short-range rural-urban movements to inter-regional movements of population, much of it urban-urban in character.

In 1851, while half the population of England and Wales still lived in rural areas, only one-fifth was dependent on agriculture. The considerable increases in population since 1801 both in areas of early industrialization and in newer industrial regions such as the North East and South Wales coalfields, produced a marked extension of areas of high population density (Fig. 11.4). In the later nineteenth century, however, widespread decline reduced the rural population to only 21 per cent of the national total with a mere 8 per cent on the land: much rural industry, which had previously given diversity to the countryside, was lost to the towns.

Of the four-fifths who were town dwellers, a high proportion was crammed into large cities and the rapidly expanding conurbations. The most rapid increases, 1851–1911 (Fig. 11.5), were often in areas peripheral to those of earliest industrial growth, many of which were losing population to newer industrial areas. The resultant pattern of population distribution is more complex and reflects varying regional responses to both industrial change and the emergence of a more diversified economy in which building, transport and services of all kinds were growing more rapidly than manufacturing. Many of the features associated with the economic and population trends of the twentieth century were already present from the 1880s: the pull of the coalfields was giving way to the attraction of the large ports and the major urban markets; greater regional concentration of industry in large production units continued to shift the centre of gravity of population north and west; there was a reversal of internal migration and a growing movement of people to the Midlands and south accelerating the countrywide movement to Greater London — 'the drift to

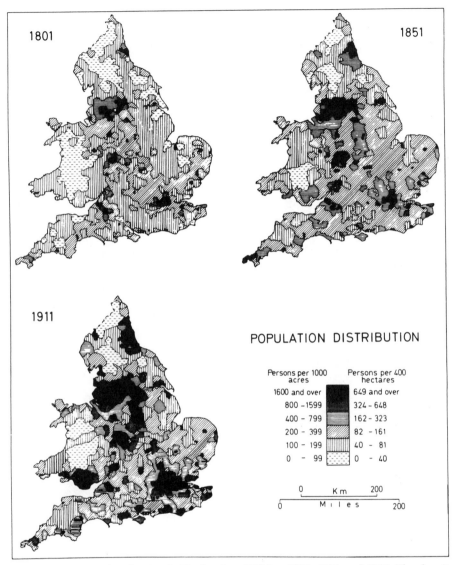

Fig. 11.4. Population distribution in England and Wales, 1801, 1851 and 1911. The density of population is shown for registration districts. Based upon the *Census of Great Britain, 1851* and the *Census of England and Wales, 1911*.

the south-east'—which was a marked feature of regional population trends in Britain from the later nineteenth century.[75]

Regional analysis of natural and migrational components of population change becomes more secure from the 1840s with the more detailed censuses from 1841 and civil registration of vital events from 1837, despite under-registration of births up to mid-Victorian times. Estimates of net migration from a comparison of registered births and deaths with census figures of total change, show regional and intra-regional population trends in some detail from 1841 (Fig. 11.5).[76] The dominant

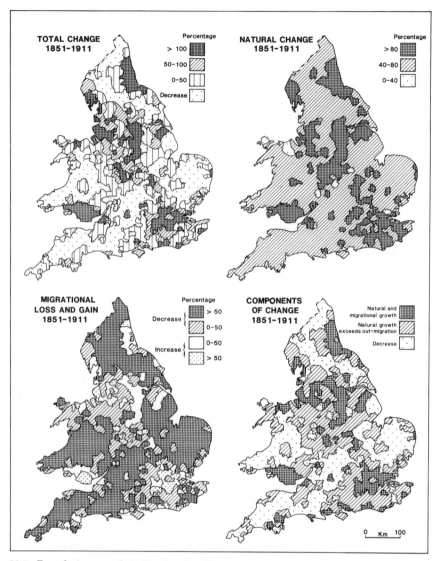

Fig. 11.5. Population trends in England and Wales, 1851–1911: total, natural and migrational. Components of change shows the relative change, 1851–1911: increase (natural and migrational, and where natural growth exceeds net out-migration); and decrease—where net migrational loss exceeds natural growth. *Source*: Censuses of England and Wales, 1851–1911.

features of rapid urbanization accompanied by large-scale out-migration from the countryside are evident in rural migrational losses of over 4.5 million people between 1841 and 1911 which absorbed 85 per cent of their natural increment, while towns and 'colliery districts' gained 3.3 million, about one-sixth of their total increase (Table 11.4). Fluctuations in migration differentials, over time and from region to region, account for a substantial part of the temporal and spatial variations in population trends in this period. While regional variations in birth and death rates contributed to differential growth, during the Victorian period these fluctuated much less than migration, both nationally and regionally.

Rates of natural growth in rural areas were generally lower than those in urban and industrial areas though there were considerable contrasts, for example, between the high natural increase of mining and heavy industrial areas and the low rates in most textile towns and in London. Despite high mortality, which did not begin to approach the national average until the 1880s, cities and industrial areas generally had above-average rates of natural growth. With a youthful population structure, thanks partly to in-migration of young adults, crude birth rates in these areas were generally high, though there was considerable variation in indices of marital fertility (I_g) and of marriage (I_m), between and within them. Thus, while in 1861 the higher I_g values (over 0.7) were mainly in northern and western areas, relatively low marriage tended to hold down the overall fertility indices (I_f), especially in rural areas but also in some industrial districts (e.g. the textile towns).[77] By the end of the century many rural districts, especially in the south and east had both low marital fertility and marriage rates, while in the industrial areas there were sharp contrasts between the lower fertility of the textile districts and the higher fertility in heavy industrial areas. The large migrational gain of the early and mid nineteenth century in the large towns and textile regions gave a built-in predisposition to high natural growth from mid-century. Similarly, heavy in-migration to the coalfields from the mid nineteenth century onwards provided the basis for large families and high natural growth at the end of the century.

While the number of births remained relatively high in rural areas until well into the nineteenth century, prolonged outflow of young men and women, the potential parents of the next generation, reduced their growth potential. Thus despite relatively low mortality, there was a sharp downturn in the natural increase of rural areas after 1891. Rural births peaked in the south of the country in the 1860s and in northern areas in the 1870s and by the early twentieth century rural birth rates were 30 per cent below their nineteenth-century peak, with fertility reduced through decline of both I_g and I_m, whilst an ageing rural population had little potential for natural growth;[78] the draining of the rural reservoir was reflected in reduced levels of out-migration by the First World War.

The vital experience in the urban and industrial areas varied considerably, not least within individual regions. The major cities were areas of relatively high natural growth, though above-average birth rates were offset by relatively high mortality until after 1900; London's slower natural growth came from below-average birth rates until the period 1901–10. However, within the cities there were marked contrasts. Inner areas of high mortality, often relatively low fertility and persistent out-migration showed rapid population decline after the mid-century. The suburbs, on the other hand, gained by in-movement of young people, by relatively high birth rates and moderate to low mortality. Similar contrasts exist between 'residential' districts and poorer-class areas of the industrial regions (Table 11.4). In the textile areas demographic decline came from migrational loss and more rapid decline in births than the national average. In contrast, despite relatively high mortality, colliery districts maintained a strong late-nineteenth-century growth with high natural increase resulting from high fertility, relatively early marriages and large families.[79]

Table 11.4: The growth of population in England and Wales, 1841–1911.

	Population in 1841	Population in 1911	Natural increase 1841–1911	Net gain (+) or loss (−) by migration 1841–1911	Ratio of migrational gain or loss to natural increase (per cent)	Total percentage increase 1841–1911
1. Towns						
(a) Large						
London	2,261,525	7,314,738	3,802,252	+1,250,511	+32.9	223.7
8 Northern	1,551,126	5,191,769	2,747,306	+893,337	+32.5	234.7
(b) Textile						
22 Northern	1,386,670	3,182,382	1,705,779	+89,933	+5.3	129.5
(c) Industrial						
14 Northern	603,214	1,812,219	1,361,999	−152,994	−11.2	200.4
11 Southern	296,009	708,693	428,363	−15,679	−3.7	139.4
(d) Old						
7 Northern	289,819	648,769	343,006	+15,944	+4.6	123.9
13 Southern	664,782	1,375,651	732,973	−22,004	−3.0	107.0
(e) Residential						
9 Northern	206,897	559,022	211,895	+140,230	+66.2	170.2
26 Southern	692,185	1,770,030	750,483	+327,362	+43.6	155.7
(f) Military						
16 Southern	470,821	1,212,413	616,644	+124,948	+20.3	157.5

Northern towns	4,031,725	11,394,161	6,369,985	+986,450	+15.5	188.2
Southern towns	4,385,222	12,381,525	6,331,165	+1,665,138	+26.3	182.3
All towns	8,669,167	23,775,686	12,701,150	+2,651,588	+20.9	174.3
2. Colliery districts 9 Northern	1,320,342	5,334,002	3,363,112	+650,548	+19.3	304.0
3. Rural residues: 12 Northern	2,425,614	2,875,113	2,093,257	−1,643,770	−78.6	18.5
12 Southern	3,740,228	4,085,691	3,208,729	−2,863,266	−89.2	9.2
All rural	6,165,842	6,960,804	5,301,986	−4,507,036	−85.0	12.9
North of England	7,783,682	19,602,876	11,825,942	−7648	−0.1	151.8
South of England	8,125,450	16,467,616	9,540,294	−1,198,128	−12.6	102.7
Total	15,914,148	36,070,492	21,366,236	−1,209,892	−5.7	126.6

Based on Cairncross (1953) using T. A. Welton's classification of 1911 but with a modification in the division between north and south.

The considerable net migrational loss from the rural areas in the late nineteenth century was complemented by massive concentration of population into a relatively few urban and industrial areas. Migrational gain accounted for over one-sixth of the population increase of 15.1 million in the urban areas of England and Wales between 1841 and 1911, one-quarter of London's total increase, and similar proportions in the large northern towns. Yet fluctuations in prosperity in industrial areas tended to off-set phases of high migrational gain, so that while one-quarter (160) of all registration districts gained by migration over the period 1851–1911, in only 53 out of the 160 was there migration gain in every decade. These were confined principally to London and the South-East, the North-West and Yorkshire, parts of the North-East and South Wales coalfields, and the West and East Midlands industrial areas (Fig. 11.5).

Regional cycles of population change reflected fluctuations in growth rates and, particularly, changes in net migration as developing or expanding economies drew much of their labour force from other areas. However, after the initial in-migration population growth was often self-sustaining and, if economic growth and the labour market slackened, people moved to other areas. In the 1890s and 1900s many northern industrial areas, particularly textile towns, lost population, while London and the South-East and Midlands gained. Hence, the relative contribution of migration to total population growth over the period 1841–1911 differed consider-ably from one type of area to another: it was considerable in London and the larger towns; very marked in the residential towns; persistent, but not pronounced, in the colliery districts; and limited and, after 1881, negative in the industrial towns. However, as urban areas expanded rapidly in the late nineteenth century with the assistance of mass transportation (see Chapter 16) movement to the suburbs made for substantial population movements of an intra-urban rather than inter-regional character.

Brinley Thomas has argued that migration is a sensitive index of British economic conditions, in particular as measured by building fluctuations, which are in turn inversely related to those of the United States.[80] When growth was strong in Britain, levels of internal migration were high (as in the decades 1861–70, 1871–80 and 1890–1901) but when growth was weak in Britain, external migration increased, particu-larly to North America, as in the decade 1881–90 and 1901–10. Although differential natural growth helps to account for regional differences in population change, the major determinant of *fluctuations* in the rate of change was migration. In a period when individual economic necessity often compelled movement, migration trends may be seen as one of the best indicators of both short- and long-term shifts in regional economic growth and in the labour market. As growth slackened, many older industrial and coalfield areas lost population by migration. Such areas (e.g. the longer-worked exposed coalfields, the Black Country, parts of east Lancashire and west Yorkshire) experienced migrational loss or fluctuation in migration. In contrast, within many parts of south-east England and the East Midlands, and in Birmingham and north Warwickshire migrational gain in the late nineteenth century followed earlier losses. A summary of natural and migrational components of change in the period 1851–1911 (Fig. 11.5) indicates that in three-quarters of all registration districts natural gain was coupled with migrational loss, with out-migration exceeding natural gain in areas of severe rural depopulation in lowland England, the South-West, rural Wales and the northern Pennines. Natural gain exceeded migrational loss in 41 per cent of all districts which avoided the worst effects of out-migration because of industrial activities or which were affected by late-nineteenth-century suburban growth. In only 20 per cent of registration districts was there both natural and migrational gain over the period 1851–1911, principally in the major conurbations (London, South Wales, the West Midlands, Merseyside, Greater Manchester, west Yorkshire and north-east England) and cities of the East Midlands. Elsewhere the picture is more confused, the concentration of high natural growth and migrational gain in each of the major urban regions as a whole being masked to some extent by complex short-distance migration within them.

Net migration conceals a complex ebb and flow of population movement which, in the absence of population registers recording migration, must be studied from census birthplace tables. First attempted in 1841, these summarize 'lifetime migration'—usually for geographical counties—at each census from 1851. Such birthplace data yield limited information on migration flows.[81] In 1885 Ravenstein drew attention to the complex pattern of internal migrations, mainly short-range dispersion from rural areas, to urban and industrial areas of population absorption.[82] By 1861 most rural counties had lost over 20 per cent of their native-born populations through internal migration. Decadal levels of loss were over 25 per cent in some areas (for example, the south Midlands and parts of mid-Wales) and by the end of the century cumulative loss of over 50 per cent of their natives was experienced in some areas. In contrast, migrants were attracted to a relatively few targets. For example, in 1861, in London, the South Wales and Durham coalfields, the West Midlands and Cheshire, over 30 per cent of the population were born outside the county of residence, while the towns often had much higher proportions of non-natives. By 1911 in much of south-east England over 40 per cent were non-natives and in nearly all the towns of the Greater London area the proportion was over 50 per cent. Allowing for the effect between censuses of death and re-migration of people living outside their native county, estimates of new migration for each decade between 1851 and 1911, disregarding movements between adjacent counties, show that up to the First World War the areas of persistent loss were in rural Wales, northern England, the South-West, East Anglia and, perhaps surprisingly, Staffordshire.[83] The main areas of gain were Greater London and South Wales (especially Glamorgan); Lancashire, Yorkshire and Durham initially gained, then lost from the late nineteenth century; by the end of the century formerly rural counties around London were gaining by overflow from the capital and by direct movement from all other regions of Britain.

The estimated levels of external migration (to Scotland, Ireland and overseas) were often relatively high between 1861 and 1901, especially in the depressed 1880s, from both rural and, increasingly, urban areas. London lost an estimated 135,000 by net emigration, 1881–90, 7.6 per cent of its native-born population. The collapsing mining economy of Cornwall led large numbers of 'hard rock men' to North America and Australia; its net emigration loss of 118,000 (between 16 and 20 per cent of the county's native-born) in the census decades 1861–91 exceeded the net internal migrational loss in the 1860s and 1880s. Though this was exceptional, the increase in external migration and fall in internal migration in the 1880s suggests the complementarity of home and overseas labour markets proposed by Brinley Thomas. Indeed the majority of counties of England and Wales, both agricultural and industrial, lost over four per cent, and a few over ten per cent or more of their native-born in the 1860s and 70s, rising to above 6 per cent in the depression decade 1881–90, with particularly high losses from western agricultural counties and some older industrial regions. Baines has shown that 60 per cent of emigrants were from urban areas—35 per cent from London, the West Midlands and Lancashire. But, whereas fluctuations in internal migration seem to have depended on the relative attractive-ness of urban areas, the permanent net emigration of some 2.33 million English and Welsh between 1861 and 1900—nearly two-thirds of them male—reflects choices made not only on the basis of relatively short-term economic prospects but the pull of a range of factors leading to a considered decision to migrate: there was, Baines concludes, 'no general trade-off between rural-urban migration and emigration'.[84]

Migration greatly influenced the population structure and vital trends in both sender and receiver areas. The break-down by age of persons born and enumerated in selected counties in 1911 indicates that lifetime migrants generally exceeded the proportion of the total adult population under 35 years. Contemporaries were in no doubt that internal migration in Victorian England was to a considerable degree age- and, sometimes, sex-selective and that women were more likely to move then men, unlike the male-dominated emigration. Welton's analysis of the estimated net migration gain or loss by age groups, for the areas listed in Table 11.4 showed that in 1881–1900 towns made considerable gains in the 15–35 groups and the over 65 groups.[85] In the 'old towns' the gains were mainly of young females (mainly for domestic service) and older ages of both sexes. In the colliery and heavy industrial districts the largest gains were of men under 35 and of women between 25 and 40. In residential towns the age-migration gain among men was in the over-35 groups but among women it was found in most age groups, especially in those aged 15–25 and 40 and over. Rural areas lost people in nearly all age groups except the 70–75, but especially men aged 15–30 and women up to the age of 50. Thomas's analysis of a number of urban areas, 1871–1900, reveals the declining attraction of many older industrial regions for the younger adult population (aged 20–44).[86] Within the rapidly expanding urban regions of the mid and later nineteenth century, migrants to inner-city areas tended to be dominated by single persons among the younger age groups. Finally migration towards suburbs often occurred after marriage and at distinctive stages in the family cycle, creating different demographic structures within the urban region which, by the later nineteenth century, were made more distinctive as longer journeys to work developed.

The impact of differential migration, and of variations in both fertility and mortality, on the population structure of Britain has yet to be studied in detail. By mid-century, relatively high male : female ratios characterized heavy industrial areas of strong recruitment of male labour (e.g. South Wales, Durham and Yorks–Derby–Notts coalfields and in the Black Country); and also rural areas of heavy migrational loss of women (such as north and central Wales, Lincolnshire and the south-east Midlands and in the rural South-East). While some of these features persisted until the First World War—especially the male dominance of heavy industrial areas—by 1911 female dominance had become marked in the major city regions, particularly in London and the south-eastern counties, but also in provincial commercial cities such as Liverpool and Manchester.[87]

England's youthful population structure reflected relatively high fertility and, especially in the cities and industrial regions, in-migration of young adults. In 1851 the least youthful areas, with the lowest proportions under 15 years, were rural districts of long-standing migration and low fertility (e.g. parts of mid-Wales and the northern Pennines) and the inner areas of large cities, increasingly characterized by large numbers of single persons and outward family migration to suburbs. Older age groups were still limited nationally, reflecting relatively low life expectancy, while rural depopulation was already seen in the ageing population of parts of mid- and west Wales and of East Anglia and south-west England. By 1911, the onset of fertility decline and enhanced life expectancy was reflected in lower proportions under 15 years and more older adults. Regionally, the loss of young adults by migration from inner cities, areas of industrial decline, and long-standing rural depopulation, together with greater concentrations of in-migration on Greater London and the major provincial conurbations, was reflected in above-average concentrations of younger working age populations (15–44). But residential migration to outer suburbs (especially the outer South-East) gave greater proportions of middle-aged persons (45–64). In contrast to the still-youthful populations of the major industrial regions, rural areas—especially of Wales and southern England—were characterized by ageing populations with relatively high proportions of people over 65.[88]

Rural and Urban Society

One crucial aspect of differential population growth was the movement of labour from rural to urban areas. Growing concentration of industrial employment, the greater mobility permitted by the railways and the relative decline of employment in the countryside led to a reduction in the rate of population increase in agricultural areas from the 1830s perhaps assisted by the easing of settlement regulations under the Poor Law Amendment Act of 1834.[89] From the 1840s, net out-migration became general leading to a general decrease in population after 1851, a fall arrested only in the early 1900s and then only in areas affected by residential growth around the cities. The reasons for those losses, though complex, were basically economic: the decline of employment in agriculture, especially for farm labourers, the loss of craft industries to urban factories and workshops, and the increasing accessibility of the big towns all pushed people from the countryside; higher wages and more varied job opportunities pulled them towards the towns.[90]

Rural out-migration, severe and sustained throughout the period of 1841–1911, fluctuated in intensity from decade to decade. By the 1850s, few places in England were more than ten miles from a railway station and most parts of the country had contact with towns. The short-range currents of migration engendered were directed toward the populous areas and the new industrial and urban centres. As local population declined, small market towns lost business and, by the late nineteenth century, their decay was hastened by improved accessibility to the larger towns. Thus internal migration was analogous to a simple gravity model in which movement to centres of attraction decreased in inverse proportion to distance, though great opportunities in large cities or rapidly growing industrial areas enlarged the migration hinterland and accentuated long-distance movement.

Heavy population losses resulting from the fall in demand for agricultural labour were experienced in all types of farming, arable and stock alike, and in all but the highest quality cash-crop areas. Initial replacement of seasonal labour by machinery was accentuated by agricultural depression from the 1870s, especially in arable districts, and was accompanied by the decline of seasonal migrant labour.[91] Only in those rural areas close to growing towns or industrial regions were losses from the land offset by growth of an adventitious population not dependent upon primary activities.[92]

Even in 1831, 44.3 per cent—6.15 million of the total population of 13.49 million—was urban (Table 11.5). London was by modern standards a great city of 1.78 million but there were five other cities of over 100,000 including their suburbs: Manchester–Salford (235,000), Liverpool (210,000), Birmingham (144,000), Leeds (123,000) and Bristol (104,000).[93] By 1851 just over half the population were town dwellers, with London a giant of 2.5 million and a number of provincial cities exceeding one-quarter of a million. In 1911, even at a conservative estimate, 80 per cent of England and Wales's 36 million people were urban and probably nine-tenths depended on towns for a living. Over half the urban population—15.8 out of 28.5 million—was in 36 large towns of over 100,000 headed by London with 7.25 million within the conurbation.[94] Of the 27 million added to the population of England and Wales, 1801–1911, 94 per cent (25.5 million) was absorbed by towns. The differential growth between urban and rural populations became marked from the 1830s: rural areas added only 13 per cent to their population between 1841 and 1911, but urban dwellers nearly trebled (+182 per cent), nearly one-third of the urban gain coming from net migration (Table 11.4).

Most labour recruited by nineteenth-century cities was unskilled and largely drawn from the immediate rural hinterland though in certain cases, as with both the pre- and post-famine Irish migration, powerful 'push' forces in the home area caused massive long-distance movements. Specialist skilled workers and professional people often moved farther and more directly to new jobs. For example, migration into the West Midlands was dominated by short-distance migration but the greater range, intensity and origins of movement to Birmingham and the Black Country reflected expansion of trade, increased job opportunities and higher wages. Thus, the population of Saltley, an industrial suburb of Birmingham, was dominated in 1851 by those born in the Birmingham area, but the skilled workers in its new railway carriage-building industry were recruited from coach-builders, wheelsmiths and the like born in towns throughout the British Isles.[95] Similarly, technological and economic changes in glass-making in the mid nineteenth century were reflected in considerable movement of skilled labour between glass-making centres; many migrants to the expanding glassworks of St Helens, Lancashire in the 1840s and 1850s came from older established glass makers on Tyneside, Clydeside and Stourbridge.[96]

Selective migration of young adults provided the potential for high urban fertility, while progressively creating a population structure adverse to rural growth. Even in London, the biggest attraction for migrants, three-quarters of the total increase, 1841–1911, came from natural growth. However, fertility varied considerably in Victorian Britain: regionally, between different types of town, and between different social classes and residential areas. In 1861 the highest levels of fertility were in rural

Table 11.5: Urban and rural populations in England and Wales, 1801–1911.

	TOTAL		RESIDUAL			URBAN			Per cent of total in towns of			
Year	Million	Per cent change	Million	Per cent change	Per cent of total	Million	Per cent change	Per cent of total	<10,000	10–50,000	50–100,000	>100,000
1801	8.9		5.9		66.2	3.0		33.8	9.9	9.5	3.5	11.0
1811	10.2	14.0	6.4	9.5	63.4	3.7	23.7	36.6	10.8	8.4	3.7	13.7
1821	12.0	18.1	7.2	11.7	60.0	4.8	29.1	40.0	11.0	9.2	4.3	15.6
1831	13.9	15.8	7.7	7.8	55.7	6.2	28.0	44.3	10.6	11.1	4.0	18.6
1841	15.9	14.3	8.2	6.2	51.7	7.7	25.0	48.3	10.0	12.1	5.5	20.7
1851	17.9	12.6	8.2	1.4	46.0	9.7	25.9	54.0	9.9	13.4	5.8	24.8
1861	20.1	11.9	8.3	0.5	41.3	11.8	21.6	58.7	9.8	14.1	6.1	28.8
1871	22.7	13.2	7.9	-4.5	34.8	14.8	25.6	65.2	10.8	16.2	5.6	32.6
1881	25.9	14.7	7.8	-1.5	30.0	18.2	22.8	70.0	10.5	16.0	7.3	36.2
1891	29.0	11.6	7.4	-5.0	25.5	21.6	18.8	74.5	10.2	16.2	8.6	39.4
1901	32.5	12.2	7.2	-3.3	22.0	25.4	17.5	78.0	8.9	18.0	7.4	43.6
1911	36.1	10.9	7.6	6.2	21.1	28.5	12.2	78.9	8.8	18.3	8.0	43.8

Based on Law, 'The growth of urban population', (1967), Tables V, VI and XI. The urban category is based on three criteria: minimum size, density and degree of nucleation. Hence the 'residual' category is not confined to purely agricultural rural areas. Estimates of the truly rural vary, some arguing that it was as low as one-third in 1841 and one-eighth by 1911: for a summary see Lawton, 'Rural depopulation in nineteenth-century England' (1967).

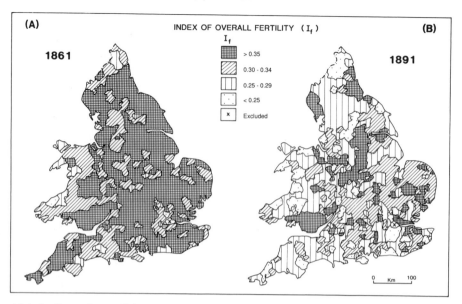

Fig. 11.6. Indices of overall fertility (I$_f$) in England and Wales, 1861 and 1891, by registration district. *Source*: R. Woods, *Theoretical Population Geography* (London, 1982), Figs. 3.13 and 3.14.

and urban/industrial areas (Fig. 11.6). However, within these categories there were substantial differences. For example, fertility was lower in much of rural Wales and parts of the South West and the northern Pennines than in most of the rural lowlands. Very high fertility in heavy industrial regions, particularly the coalfields and metal manufacutring areas, contrasted with much lower levels in London and the textile regions. By the late nineteenth century with the onset of the fertility decline, the position was more complex, and contrasting patterns of nuptiality and differences in the rate of adoption of family limitation affected family size.[97] These cannot be fully explained by a model of progressive diffusion of birth-control practices from higher to lower social classes (see pp. 287–8). As important are the economic circumstances attached to different occupational structures. Thus in rural areas with high levels of living-in farm servants—as in parts of western and upland Britain—marriage was often deferred, and general fertility (I$_f$) restricted, though marital fertility remained high; where agricultural labour lived off the farm, as in much of eastern and southern England, marriage could be earlier but there was need to control marital fertility earlier. In urban areas, too, sex ratios and employment opportunities—in particular for women outside the home—influenced the incidence and age of marriage and shaped marital fertility patterns.[98] Thus high levels of fertility remained longest in areas of mainly male employment, essentially the coalfields, heavy industrial districts (e.g. Sheffield and the Black Country) and northern ports (e.g. Liverpool and Hull). Conversely, areas providing factory or commercial employment for women (as in the Lancashire textile and the London areas, respectively), or where demand for domestic servants was high (London and many of the older towns, resorts and residential centres of southern England, in particular), produced lower levels of general fertility and an earlier decline in marital fertility, especially in middle class suburbs.[99]

However, for most of the nineteenth century, natural increase was restrained by high mortality, especially in the large industrial cities. William Farr estimated that in the 1820s mortality ranged from 17.8 per 1000 in Suffolk to 30.3 in Middlesex for men, but urban rates were much worse than the county rates. Poverty, bad water supply and sanitation and poor housing retained the contrast between 'Healthy Districts', where the average expectation of life at birth in the 1880s was 51.5 years as compared with 43.7 in England and Wales, and the 'Poor Districts' (e.g. Manchester, where life expectation was only 28.8 years).[100] Glass has stressed the continuing gap in the 1840s in male life expectation at birth (e_o) between Liverpool (25 years) and Surrey (44 years) and, in 1911–12, between county boroughs (47.5) and rural districts (56.3).[101] This gap did not begin to narrow until the 1880s and was pronounced at all ages and in both sexes ranging from a ratio of 134 to 74 (England and Wales = 100) for males aged 0–4 between Manchester and the healthiest areas, to 124 to 90 for men aged 15–24 (the most favourable comparison for towns) but deteriorating to 153 as against 78 in ages 55–64.[102]

Recent studies have confirmed the contrasts between the high morbidity and mortality in such urban industrial areas as the North East and South Wales coalfields, Yorkshire and Lancashire, and parts of the Midlands with e_o less than 35 years in 1861, and rural areas of southern England where e_o was over 50.[103] However, the rural/urban gap was not universal, and some areas of eastern England and north Wales had relatively high mortality up to mid-Victorian times. Although improvements in public health, sanitation, water supply, housing and living conditions (including diet) narrowed the range of differential mortality, by the early twentieth century the large cities lagged behind the smaller towns and rural districts (with e_o of 51, 53 and 55, respectively), and the overcrowded working-class areas remained, as in Liverpool, twice as risky as the healthy suburbs.

The slow upward movement of life expectancy from the 1860s must be sought in improvements in the control of such epidemic diseases as cholera, typhoid and typhus, in some reduction in tuberculosis (especially with better milk supply in the later nineteenth century) and in substantial reduction in child deaths due to scarlet fever and diphtheria.[104] These are reflected in the falling age-specific mortality of all age groups above one year.

But infant mortality remained very high, though fluctuating, until 1900. It was particularly bad in poor urban districts, a class and environmental disparity which may have worsened between the early 1800s and the 1840s when one-quarter of all children died before their fifth birthday. In the late 1890s infant mortality in general was as high as in the early 1860s (Fig. 11.1C). But mortality in industrial towns was markedly worse than in rural counties at all stages during the first year of life: the more crowded the town, the worse the situation. Even small towns in a rural setting had worse infant mortality than their surrounding countryside. The impact varied, of course, with social class and income, and the surroundings and level of care these brought to babies. Thus, although the decline in infant mortality benefited all social classes—and hence all areas of the country—in much the same proportions, class differentials remained, although the decline in urban areas was most marked. Factors initiating that decline were both social and environmental: better housing and sanitary conditions; improvements in water supply, milk and food; better child care, helped by better education and public health, including ante- and post-natal services which benefited the care of both mother and child; and better attention given to infants in the smaller families of the post-fertility transition.[105]

Contrasts in infant mortality are but one, if the major, aspect of the varying general mortality experience within Victorian cities. They directly reflect environment, housing and socio-economic conditions. Armstrong's pioneer study of York stresses the marked contrasts in mortality in the 1840s, which he ascribes mainly to environmental conditions, especially drainage.[106] However, both in the city centre and the suburbs, the highest social classes were longer-lived and less susceptible to epidemic and contagious diseases: whereas the mean age of death in 1844 ranged between 35.3 and 22.6 years in the 'best' and 'worst' parishes in York, it was 49.2 and 20.7 years for gentry and professional people and for artisans, respectively, with little difference between city and suburb. Such contrasts were more marked in the large industrial cities. In London in 1886–9, the general death rate was 19.6 per 1000 and infant mortality 188 per 1000: the poor districts of the East End had rates of 25.6 and 175 respectively, but working-class people housed by the Peabody Trust were below these levels at 18.6 and 141 respectively.[107] Similarly, Woods has shown that in Birmingham, a city with a good health record and near to the national death rate in the 1880s, there were marked internal differences in mortality from such diseases as measles, scarlet fever and typhoid.[108] Such contrasts echo the intra-urban contrasts in the impact of cholera and typhoid epidemics of the mid nineteenth century (see above, p. 287)[109] and support the view that sanitary reform and, especially, improved living standards did most to lower mortality in the late nineteenth century.[110]

Conclusion

Industrialization, urban growth and rural decline were accompanied by distinctive phases and patterns of population development between the mid eighteenth century and the First World War. Long-term trends in fertility and mortality led to an acceleration in population growth during the late eighteenth and early nineteenth centuries which maintained its momentum, despite the problems of high urban mortality in the early-Victorian period, until the 1880s. Thereafter a combination of heavy overseas migration and the onset of fertility decline, through control of marital fertility, led to a slackening of relative (though not aggregate) growth up until the First World War.

In the equally important redistribution of population between town and country, and in the differential growth of individual places and regions, migration played a major role, influencing both the pattern and structure of population. Mobility, both inter-regional and within the city, was also a key factor in the demographic, social and spatial transformation of the population of England and Wales. Within a lifetime the same individual could be a migrant several times over: as an itinerant worker; on moving from a rural to an urban area, usually involving a change of job; as an inter-urban migrant to a larger city with perhaps greater job opportunities; then in a series of short-distance movements within the city of his final choice perhaps occasioned by changes in job, or family status or changing economic fortunes. Clearly the aggregate of such individual decisions produced substantial flows of people from country to town, as reflected in the changing character of both rural and urban communities. The demographic and socio-economic impact on cities was considerable. City centres changed rapidly as transients passed through to more established residential areas; working-class residential areas absorbed newcomers from other regions and by movement from other parts of the city; though some middle-class residential areas persisted throughout the nineteenth century, others were invaded by the poor and deteriorated rapidly; new high-status suburbs were built in the semi-rural periphery to receive those displaced. Thus the restructuring of Victorian cities reflected processes of internal population change which have associated demographic, social and economic characteristics (see Chapter 15). It is appropriate, in a chapter in which the main emphasis has been on demographic characteristics at a regional level, that we should be reminded of the life experience of millions of individuals, for an understanding of their decisions and actions is crucial to an understanding of the fundamental processes of change in population and society experienced during the demographic transition.

Acknowledgement

I wish to acknowledge the support of the Leverhulme Trust, through an Emeritus Fellowship, during the writing of this chapter.

References

1. For general accounts see P. Mathias, *The First Industrial Nation: An Economic History of Britain, 1700–1914*, (London, 1969) and Phyllis Deane, *The First Industrial Revolution*, (Cambridge, 1965).
2. E. A. Wrigley and R. S. Schofield, *The Population History of England 1541–1871. A Reconstruction*, (London, 1981), App. 3 and 5.
3. M. W. Flinn, *British Population Growth, 1750–1850*, (London, 1970).
4. Rosalind Mitchison, *British Population Change since 1860*, (London, 1977).
5. T. McKeown, *The Modern Rise of Population*, (London, 1976) ascribes the main changes in natural growth to reduced mortality. The significance of an upward trend in births in the late eighteenth and early nineteenth centuries is indicated by J. T. Krause, 'Changes in English fertility and mortality, 1781–1850', *Economic History Review*, 2nd ser., **XI** (1985), pp. 52–70, and Wrigley and Schofield, *The Population History of England*, Chapter 10 and App. 3.
6. E. A. Wrigley and R. S. Schofield 'English population history from family reconstruction 1600–1790', *Population Studies*, **37** (1983), pp. 157–84.
7. For a detailed examination of this question see M. Blaug, 'The Poor Law Report re–examined', *Jnl. of Economic History*, **XXIV** (1964) pp. 229–45 and for a detailed case study see J. P. Huzel, 'Malthus, the Poor Law, and population in early nineteenth-century England', *Economic History Review*, 2nd ser., **XXII** (1969) pp. 430–52.
8. See J. D. Chambers, 'The Vale of Trent, 1670–1800: a regional review of economic change', *Economic History Review*, Supplement No. 3, (London, 1957) for an example of the impact of early industrial development on family size. The wider context is given in his *Population, Economy and Society in Pre–industrial England*, (London, 1972).
9. H. J. Habakkuk, *Population Growth and Economic Development since 1750*, (Leicester, 1971).
10. R. Woods and J. Woodward (eds.), *Urban Disease and Mortality in Nineteenth–century England*, (London, 1984).
11. R. Woods and P. R. A. Hinde, Mortality in Victorian England: models and patterns', *Jnl. of Interdisciplinary History*, **18** (1987), pp. 27–54.
12. J. A. and Olive L. Banks, *Feminism and Family Planning in Victorian England*, (Liverpool, 1964).

13. For general view see N. L. Tranter, *Population and Society 1750–1940. Contrasts in Population Growth*, (London, 1985), Chapter 4.

14. W. V. Hole and M. J. Pountney, *Trends in Population, Housing and Occupancy Rates*, (HMSO, London, 1971), pp. 13–19.

15. R. I. Woods, 'Approaches to the Fertility Transition in Victorian England', *Population Studies*, **41** (1987), pp. 283– 311.

16. B. Thomas, *Migration and Economic Growth: a study of Great Britain and the Atlantic Economy*, (Cambridge, 1954), and *Migration and Urban Development*, (London, 1972), especially Chapter 2.

17. D. Baines, *Migration in a Mature Economy. Emigration and Internal Migration in England and Wales, 1861–1900*, (Cambridge, 1985), Tables 3.1 and 3.3

18. *Ibid.*, Tables 6.1 and 6.2.

19. Charlotte Erickson, 'Who were the English and Scots immigrants to the United States in the late-nineteenth century', in D. V. Glass and R. Revelle (eds.), *Population and Social Change*, (London, 1972), pp. 347–81; *idem*, 'Emigration from the British Isles to the U.S.A. in 1841, Pt. 1, Emigration from the British Isles, *Population Studies*, **43** (1989). pp. 347–67.

20. Tranter, *Population and Society*, pp. 178–9.

21. E. H. Hunt, *British Labour History 1815–1914*, (London, 1981), especially Chapter 5.

22. This point has been stressed by D. Friedlander, 'Demographic responses and population change', *Demography*, **6** (1969), pp. 359–81.

23. W. Zelinsky, 'The hypothesis of the Mobility Transition', *Geographical Review*, **61** (1971), pp. 219–49; five stages were outlined in such a transition.

24. J. Saville, *Rural Depopulation in England and Wales, 1851– 1951*, (London, 1957).

25. R. Woods, *Theoretical Population Geography*, (London, 1982), pp. 112–24.

26. See D. V. Glass, 'A note on the under-registration of births in Britain in the nineteenth century', *Population Studies*, **5** (1951–2), pp. 70– 88; J. T. Krause, 'The changing adequacy of English registration, 1690–1837', in D. V. Glass and D. E. C. Eversley (eds.), *Population in History, Essays in Historical Demography*, (London, 1965), pp. 379–93; and M. S. Teitelbaum, 'Birth under-registration in the constituent counties of England and Wales: 1841–1910',*Population Studies*, **28** (1974), pp. 329–43.

27. The classic study is E. G. Ravenstein, 'The laws of migration', *Jnl. of the Statistical Society*, **XLVIII** (1885), pp. 167–235.

28. See D. Friedlander and F. J. Roshier, 'A study of internal migration in England and Wales, Part 1', *Population Studies*, **19** (1966), pp. 239–79; and D. E. Baines, 'The use of published census data in migration studies', in E. A. Wrigley (ed.) *Nineteenth–Century Society*, (Cambridge, 1972) pp. 311–35.

29. Wrigley and Schofield, *The Population History of England*, Table A3.3.

30. W. W. Rostow, *The Stages of Economic Growth*, (Oxford, 1960).

31. Phyllis Deane and W. A. Cole, *British Economic Growth, 1688–1959*, (2nd edn.) (Cambridge, 1969): Chapter 3 is a concise and careful review of population changes in England and Wales in the eighteenth and early nineteenth centuries. For a critique of their estimates see L. Neal, 'Deane and Cole on industrialization and population change in the eighteenth century', *Economic History Review*, 2nd ser., **XXIV** (1971), pp. 643–7.

32. D. R. Mills, *Lord and Peasant in Nineteenth Century Britain*, (London, 1980).

33. Such listings are discussed by P. Laslett, *The World We Have Lost*, (London, 1965). For a case study see N. Tranter, 'Population and social structure in a Bedfordshire parish: the Cardington Listings of Inhabitants, 1782', *Population Studies*, **21** (1967), pp. 261–82.

34. W. J. Edwards, 'National Marriage Data: A Re-Aggregation of John Rickman's Marriage Returns', *Local Population Studies*, **17** (1976), pp. 25–41 and 'Marriage Seasonality 1761–1810: An Assessment of Patterns in Seventeen Shropshire Parishes', *Local Population Studies*, **19** (1977), pp. 23–7.

35. E. J. Buckatzsch, 'Places of origin of a group of immigrants into Sheffield, 1624–1799', *Economic History Review*, 2nd ser., **II** (1950), pp. 303–6.

36. For textile workers, see H. A. Randall, 'Some aspects of population geography in certain rural areas of England during the eighteenth and early nineteenth century', for a case study of Kettering (Northants), unpublished Ph.D. thesis, University of Newcastle upon Tyne (1971); and for miners see J. Langton, *Geographical Change in the Industrial*

Revolution, the South-West Lancashire Mining Industry, 1590–1799, (Cambridge, 1978). B. Trinder, *The Industrial Revolution in Shropshire*, (London, 1973), discusses migration to an early centre of the metallurgical industry. For a general review see P. Spufford 'Population mobility in pre-industrial England', *Genealogists Magazine*, **17** (1973), pp. 420–9; 475–81; and 537–43.

37. M. Dorothy George, *London Life in the Eighteenth Century*, (London, 1925), following the contemporary estimates of Dr Price (1779), gives the total for the Metropolis (the area covered by the Bills of Mortality together with five out-parishes) as 674,350 in 1700 (George, *London Life*, p. 329). In a recent review G. Rudé, *Hanoverian London 1714–1808*, (London, 1971), follows E. A. Wrigley, 'A simple model of London's importance in changing English economy and society, 1650–1750', *Past and Present*, **37** (1967), pp. 44–70, in estimating the population of the area as 575,000 in 1700, 675,000 in 1750 and 900,000 in 1800.

38. Deane and Cole, *British Economic Growth*, Table 25 (pp. 108–9) and p. 111.

39. George, *London Life*, p. 111. The great majority of London's 14,000 Roman Catholic households listed in the Returns of Papists of 1767 and 1789 were Irish, while many of the recent overseas immigrants were German and Polish Jews, according to Rudé (*Hanoverian London*, p.7).

40. C. W. Chalklin, *The Provincial Towns of Georgian England. A Study of the Building Process 1740–1820*, (London, 1974), Chapters 1 and 2, reviews population trends from 1700 to 1820.

41. C. M. Law, 'The growth of urban population in England and Wales, 1801–1911', *Transactions, Institute of British Geographers*, **41** (1967), pp. 125–43.

42. C. M. Law, 'Local censuses in the eighteenth century', *Population Studies*, **23** (1969), pp. 87–100.

43. *Ibid.* See also T. A. Welton, 'On the distribution of population in England and Wales and its progress in the period of ninety years from 1801–1891', *Jnl. of the Royal Statistical Society*, **LXIII** (1900), pp. 527–89.

44. Deane and Cole, *British Economic Growth*, p. 113.

45. J. H. Clapham, *An Economic History of Modern Britain*: Vol. I *The Early Railway Age, 1820–1850*, (2nd edn.) (reprinted, Cambridge, 1967), p. 66.

46. Deane and Cole, *British Economic Growth*, pp. 130–33.

47. See, for example, D. Thomas, *Agriculture in Wales during the Napoleonic Wars. A Study in the Geographical Interpretation of Historical Sources*, (Cardiff, 1963).

48. D. R. Mills (ed.), *English Rural Communities: The Impact of a Specialized Economy*, (London, 1973), Part Two: 'Specialization in Industry'; D. Gregory, *Regional Transformation and Industrial Revolution . . . the Yorkshire Woollen Industry*, (London, 1982).

49. For the debate on the level of poor relief under this system see M. Blaug, 'The myth of the Old Poor Law and the making of the New', *Jnl. of Economic History*, **XXIII** (1963), pp. 151–84. Case studies include D. A. Baugh, 'The cost of Poor Relief in south-east England, 1790–1834', *Economic History Review*, 2nd ser., **XXVIII** (1975), pp. 50–68, and J. P. Huzel, 'Malthus, the Poor Law, and population' (1969).

50. Wrigley and Schofield, *The Population History of England*, Table A3.3.

51. P. Laxton, 'Liverpool in 1801: a manuscript return for the first national census of population', *Transactions, Historic Society of Lancashire and Cheshire*, **130** (1981), pp. 73–113.

52. Deane and Cole, *British Economic Growth*, pp. 106–22, argue that the view of A. K. Cairncross that 'the north triumphed over the south mainly by superior fertility (and not . . . by attracting migrants)', *Home and Foreign Investment, 1870–1913*, (Cambridge, 1953), p. 79, is as true of the eighteenth and early nineteenth century as of the period from 1840.

53. A. Redford, *Labour Migration in England, 1800–1850*, (Manchester, 1926).

54. Law, 'The growth of urban population in England and Wales, 1801–1911', pp. 125–43.

55. B. T. Robson, *Urban Growth: An Approach*, (London, 1973), especially p. 30 and pp. 63–89.

56. See Chalklin, *Provincial Towns of Georgian England*, pp. 32–54, for a general description of late-Georgian urban expansion.

57. *Ibid.*, p. 54.

58. Quoted by R. Lawton, 'Population movements in the West Midlands, 1841–1861', *Geography*, **XLII** (1958), p. 168.
59. See Redford, *Labour Migration in England* for a full analysis using the Poor Law records. The social impact of the change from handicraft to factory industry is discussed by N. J. Smelser, *Social Change in the Industrial Revolution, and application of theory to the Lancashire Cotton Industry*, (London, 1959).
60. T. W. Freeman, *Pre-famine Ireland. A Study in Historical Geography*, (Manchester, 1957), pp. 37–46.
61. L. H. Lees, *Exiles of Erin*, (Manchester, 1979).
62. J. Papworth, 'The Irish in Liverpool 1835–1871', Unpublished Ph.D. thesis, University of Liverpool (1982).
63. R. Woods and J. Woodward, *Urban Disease and Mortality in Nineteenth-century England*, (London, 1984).
64. R. P. Williams 'On the increase of population in England and Wales', *Jnl. of the Royal Statistical Society of London*, **XLIII** (1880), pp. 462–96.
65. A. H. Johnson, *The Disappearance of the Small Landowner*, (London, 1909).
66. S. W. E. Vince, 'The rural population of England and Wales', 1801–1951', unpublished Ph.D. thesis, University of London, (1955).
67. B. A. Holderness, 'Open and Closed parishes in England in the eighteenth and nineteenth centuries', *Agricultural History Review*, **XX** (1972), pp. 126–39; and Mills (ed.), *English Rural Communities*.
68. J. A. Yelling, *Common Field and Enclosure in England 1450–1850*, (London, 1977), Chapter 11.
69. R. H. Osborne, 'A general view of the population changes in the middle Trent counties, 1801–1861', *East Midlands Geographer*, **5** (1970), pp. 39–51.
70. J. M. Martin, 'Marriage and economic stress in the Feldon of Warwickshire during the eighteenth century', *Population Studies*, **31** (1977), pp. 519–35, rejects the notion of 'associating imprudent marriage with Poor Law practice'.
71. W. Hasbach, *A History of the English Agricultural Labourer*, (Translated by Ruth Kenyon) (London, 1908).
72. See Mills, *English Rural Communities*, Part Two; and R. Hall, 'Occupation and population structure in part of the Derbyshire Peak District in the mid-nineteenth century', *East Midland Geographer*, **6** (1974), pp. 66–78.
73. F. Galton, 'The relative supplies from town and country families to the population of future generations', *Jnl. of the Statistical Society of London*, **XXXVI** (1873), pp. 19–26.
74. R. Woods and C. W. Smith, 'The decline of marital fertility in the late nineteenth century: the case of England and Wales', *Population Studies*, **37** (1983), pp. 207–25.
75. R. H. Osborne, 'Population', Chapter 8 of J. W. Watson and J. B. Sissons, *The British Isles*, Chapter 18, (London, 1964).
76. For a review of spatial changes see R. Lawton, 'Population changes in England and Wales in the later nineteenth century: an analysis by Registration Districts', *Transactions, Institute of British Geographers*, **44** (1968), pp. 55–74.
77. R. Woods and C. W. Smith, 'The decline of marital fertility in the late nineteenth century', pp. 212–15 and Figures 4–6.
78. The effect of rural depopulation on population structure is discussed by J. Saville, *Rural Depopulation in England and Wales, 1851–1951*, (London, 1957).
79. M. Haines, *Fertility and Occupation. Population patterns in industrialization*, (London, 1979), Chapter V.
80. Thomas, *Migration and Urban Development*, Chapter 2.
81. See D. E. Baines in E. A. Wrigley (ed.), *Nineteenth-Century Society*, (1972).
82. E. G. Ravenstein, 'The laws of migration', *Jnl. of the Statistical Society of London*, **XLVIII** (1885), pp. 167–227. For a review of his work see D. B. Grigg, 'E. G. Ravenstein and the "laws of migration"', *Jnl. of Historical Geography*, **3** (1977), pp. 41–54, Appendix 1.
83. D. Friedlander and R. J. Roshier, 'A study of internal migration in England and Wales, Part 1', *Population Studies*, **19** (1966), pp. 239–79.
84. Baines, *Migration in a Mature Economy*, p. 281, Table 7.3 and Appendix 1.

85. T. A. Welton, *England's Recent Progress . . . in the twenty years from 1881 to 1901*, (London, 1911), Appendix B.
86. Thomas, *Migration and Urban Development*, (1972).
87. R. Lawton, 'Population', in J. Langton and R. J. Morris (eds.), *Atlas of Industrializing Britain*, (London, 1986), pp. 14–15.
88. *Ibid.*, pp. 16–18.
89. For a critical case study see Anne Digby, 'The labour market and the continuity of social policy after 1834: the case of the eastern counties', *Economic History Review*, 2nd ser., **XXVIII** (1975), pp. 69–83.
90. From the considerable literature on rural depopulation in Victorian Britain, see Saville, '*Rural Depopulation in England and Wales*'; and, for its effects on society and regional population trends, see R. Lawton, 'Rural depopulation in nineteenth-century England', in R. W. Steel and R. Lawton (eds.), *Liverpool Essays in Geography: A Jubilee Collection*, (London, 1967), pp. 227–55.
91. E. J. T. Collins, 'Harvest technology and labour supply in Britain, 1790–1870', *Economic History Review*, 2nd ser., **XXII** (1969), pp. 453–73.
92. See Vince, 'Rural population of England and Wales' (1955).
93. B. R. Mitchell and Phyllis Deane, *Abstract of British Historical Statistics*, (Cambridge, 1962), Table 8.
94. J. T. Coppock, 'The changing face of England, 1850–c. 1900' in H. C. Darby (ed.), *A New Historical Geography of England*, (Cambridge, 1973), p. 655.
95. R. Lawton, 'Peopling the Past', *Transactions, Institute of British Geographers*, new ser., **12** (1987), pp. 159–83.
96. J. T. Jackson, 'Long–distance migrant workers in nineteenth-century Britain: a case study of the St Helens' glass makers', *Trans. Hist. Soc. of Lancs. and Cheshire*, **131** (1982), pp. 113–37.
97. R. Woods and C. W. Smith, 'The decline of marital fertility in the late nineteenth century: The case of England and Wales', *Population Studies*, **37**, (1983), pp. 207–25.
98. R. I. Woods and P. R. A. Hinde, 'Nuptiality and age at marriage in nineteenth-century England', *Jnl. of Family History*, **10** (1985), pp. 119–44.
99. These features emerge both from the past major survey of fertility in England and Wales, D. V. Glass, pp. 161–212 of L. Hogben (ed.), *Political Arithmetic*, (London, 1938), and from more recent studies: M. S. Teitelbaum, *The British Fertility Decline*, (Princeton, 1984) and R. I. Woods 'Approaches to the fertility transition in Victorian England', *Population Studies*, **41** (1987), pp. 283–311.
100. Weber, *The Growth of Cities*, p. 347. The mortality experience of these areas, designated by the Registrar General, is analysed by W. Farr, *Vital Statistics*, (London, 1885).
101. D. V. Glass in J. Ferguson (ed.), *Public Health and Urban Growth*, (London, 1964).
102. T. A. Welton, 'Local death-rates in England and Wales in the ten years 1881–90', *Jnl. of the Royal Statistical Society*, **LX** (1897), pp. 33–75.
103. R. I. Woods and P. R. A. Hinde, 'Mortality in Victorian England, models and patterns', *Jnl. of Interdisciplinary History*, **XVIII** (1987), pp. 27–54.
104. T. McKeown, *The Modern Rise of Population*, (London, 1976), Tables 3.1–3.5
105. R. I. Woods, P. A. Watterson and J. H. Woodward, 'The causes of rapid infant mortality decline in England and Wales, 1861–1921, *Population Studies*, **42** (1988), pp. 343–66 and **43**, pp. 113–32.
106. A. Armstrong, *Stability and Change in an English County Town. A Social Study of York 1801–51*, (Cambridge, 1974), especially Chapter 5.
107. Weber, *The Growth of Cities*, p. 352. For a fuller discussion of health in relation to housing in London, see A. S. Wohl, *The Eternal Slum, Housing and Social Policy in Victorian London*, (London, 1977).
108. R. Woods, 'Mortality and sanitary conditions in the "best governed city in the world" — Birmingham 1870–1910', *Jnl. of Historical Geography*, **4** (1978), pp. 35–56.
109. E. W. Gilbert, 'Pioneer maps of health and disease in England', *Geographical Jnl.*, **CXXIV** (1958), pp. 172–83.
110. G.M. Howe, *Man, Environment and Disease in Britain, A Medical Geography through the Ages*, (Harmondsworth, 1976), Chapters 11 and 12.

12

Agriculture and Rural Society 1730–1914

J. R. Walton

Towards the end of the eighteenth century, T.R. Malthus exposed the cyclical character of the relationship between the numbers of people and the supply of their means of subsistence. Low population levels and relatively cheap food meant increasing real wages, earlier marriage, higher fertility, and sustained population growth, which, in its turn, led to increasing food costs and declining real wages. The mounting pressure of population on the means of subsistence was released in either a cataclysmic mortality surge, brought on by one or other of the 'positive' checks to population growth, principally famine and disease, or more sedately via the 'preventive' mechanisms of delayed marriage and declining fertility. Thus the way was cleared for population growth to recommence.

The Malthusian model, in one or other guise, stands vindicated by much that historians have told us of economic and demographic conditions in the past. The effects of population pressure loom large in the standard accounts of both late medieval England and early modern France. Age at marriage, marching to the distant rhythm of previous real wage shifts, emerges from Wrigley and Schofield's monumental analysis as the primary determinant of England's pre-industrial demographic regime[1]. But, Wrigley and Schofield further reveal, Malthus' diagnosis more or less coincided with the decay of the relationships which it identified. From the late eighteenth century onwards, there occurred 'changes in productivity so profound that an increase in poverty was no longer the price of an increase in numbers'.[2]

This chapter examines eighteenth- and nineteenth-century agriculture in the context of its contribution to and interaction with the ebbing of the Malthusian tide. The discussion will focus on sources of productivity growth within agriculture. We will therefore be concerned with the changes in organization and technique which brought about major increases in the domestic farming sector's absolute contribution to output. However, the various aspects of interaction between the agricultural and industrial sectors will not be ignored, for it was the growth of the industrial sector, above all else, which so expanded the dimensions of economic activity as to destroy the foundations of the Malthusian world.

Changes in the Demand for Food, 1730–1914

The best context for a survey of eighteenth-and nineteenth-century agriculture is an estimate of change in the demand for its principal product, food. By how much would domestic agricultural production have had to increase were it seeking to supply no other market than the home market, and the home market were seeking no other source of supply than the domestic agricultural sector? The answer is a function of two variables: population and per capita demand.

Adjustment of Wrigley and Schofield's eighteenth-century English population totals to include the population of Wales, and revised nineteenth-century census figures provide the necessary demographic information.[3] The population of England and Wales was 5,636,000 in 1731. By 1781 it had increased by more than a third, to 7,541,000, and by 1831, at 14,224,000, it showed a two-and-a-half-fold increase on the original 1731 figure. By 1911, at 36,070,000, population had increased more than six-fold since the start of our period. Even had no other factors contributed to enhanced demand, these figures are sufficient evidence of the need for considerable output growth in agriculture.

But the likelihood is that simple growth in numbers was not the only source of upward pressure on the country's capacity to produce food. Shifts in per capita demand are notoriously difficult to determine, especially in so far as they depend on changes of a cultural rather than economic character. The incorporation of potatoes into the working-class diet was as much driven by the changing tastes of consumers and the changing attitudes of potential producers as by economic forces.[4] The gradual substitution of wheat for oats and barley in the northern and western diet during the nineteenth century reflected not only rising real incomes and the converging prices of wheat and less costly cereals but the cultural consequences of increasing urbanization.[5] As these and other instances reveal, changing dietary preferences are not something which can be understood in detail by reference to economic considerations alone.

Nevertheless, economics can be helpful if we are content to view matters more generally. It is a reasonable assumption that average household income increased in real terms during the period in view; indeed, this much is implicit in the notion that Malthusian constraints were shattered. If, let us assume, income doubled between 1730 and 1911 and the demand for food increased in the same proportion (in other words, the income elasticity of demand for food, that is the ratio of change in demand for food to change in income, was exactly one), then it follows that by 1911 consumer demand for food was not approximately six and a half times its 1730 level, as the population statistics would imply, but had in fact increased more than twelve-fold. Evidently, population statistics are not in themselves necessarily sufficient to capture the essence of changing demand.

No exaggerated claims can be made for the accuracy of the real wage series presented in Table 12.1. The figures up to 1791 derive from the largely southern wage and price data collected by Phelps Brown and Hopkins, as recently converted to a real wage series by Wrigley and Schofield, and from data on the real wages of Lancashire labourers, collected by Gilboy.[6] The figures given are mean averages of the ten years centred on each decadal year, indexed to the ten-year mean for 1726 to 1735. The contribution of the Gilboy data to the overall series has been weighted

Table 12.1: Real wages and potential demand, 1731–1911.

Year	Real wages	Potential demand	Years	Real wages	Potential demand
1731	100	100	1821	121	265
1741	100	106	1831	169	425
1751	100	110	1841	213	612
1761	92	107	1851	247	799
1771	96	118	1861	209	757
1781	102	136	1871	255	1044
1791	102	150	1881	321	1477
1801	103	169	1891	400	2059
1811	101	189	1901	456	2630
			1911	406	2598

Source: see text.

according to the changing proportion of the population of England and Wales which might be defined as 'northern'.[7]

The figures from 1791 onwards, which I have spliced on to the earlier data and indexed to the same 1731 base, derive from the recent work of Lindert and Williamson.[8] Linear interpolation has been used to generate decadal values up to 1851 from the original data, which refer to a number of relatively well-documented but erratically distributed benchmark years.[9] The figures from 1851 onwards required no adjustment. In the final column in Table 12.1, labelled 'potential demand', I have attempted to derive a crude index of changing potential demand within England and Wales by multiplying each real wage value by the corresponding proportionate change in population since 1731. These results suggest that the growth of demand up to the second decade of the nineteenth century was no more than that implied by the rate of growth of population, but began to exceed it thereafter, in general by an increasing margin. Taking up our earlier hypothesis of unitary income elasticity of demand for food leads to the suggestion that by 1911 demand had increased to about 26 times its 1731 level, as compared with a six-fold increase in population. About 60 per cent of the increase occurred during the last 40 years of the full 180 year period. Our problem is to determine whether actual aggregate demand for food came anywhere near the extraordinary levels suggested by these figures, and whether supplies matched requirements.

Demand–Supply Interactions

Fig. 12.1 represents a simple model of the entire demand–supply system for food during the eighteenth and nineteenth centuries. The direction of the relationship between variables is indicated by the signs, positive for direct and negative for inverse. Where two signs are shown, the larger indicates the dominant relationship, the smaller a possible short-term response. As in all models of this kind, detail has been sacrificed to clarity. For instance, deliberate exclusion of the non-food sector of agricultural output makes this less complete as a model of the nation's agricultural

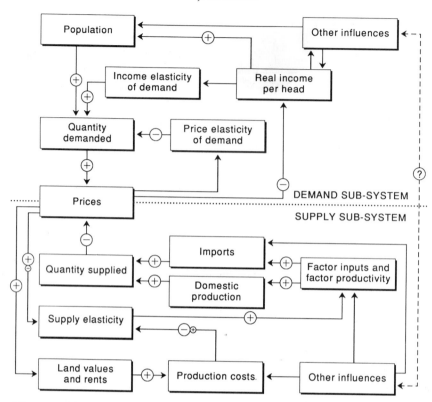

Fig. 12.1. The demand–supply system for food in England and Wales, 1730–1914.

system than it is as a model of its food-supply system, albeit correspondingly easier to comprehend. Rough calculations suggest that the major non-food demand of the late nineteenth century (the supply of oats and hay to the urban horse population) placed a much heavier load on the system than the major non-food demand of the early eighteenth century (the supply of charcoal to the iron industry).[10] However, as most other non-food users did not consume agricultural products in a way which completely precluded their parallel use for food, perhaps one should not imagine too great an excess of additional non-food demand within the system as our period progressed. The brewing and distilling industries returned spent grains as feed for cattle and pigs.[11] Processors of wool, tallow, soap and hides provided a supplementary market for the livestock sector. And the relatively limited and declining domestic use of peat, furze and fuelwood (even by the early part of our period London and many other ports were heavily dependent on coastwise shipments of coal)[12] appears to have imposed no exclusive or inalienable claims on the more or less marginal areas responsible for producing a large proportion of these fuels. The boxes marked 'other influences' circumvent the need to specify a multiplicity of variables lying at or beyond the periphery of the agricultural sector, like, for example, the political forces which led the nation to embrace free trade. The growth of food imports and significant consequential effects on domestic production systems and their geography inescapably followed.

Other simplifications within the model arise from the specific circumstances of the period concerned. Thus, in present-day Britain one would not hypothesize a positive association between changes in real income per head and changes in the size of the population. Yet this was the relationship prevailing throughout much of our period, as Wrigley and Schofield have shown. Likewise, where land is owner-occupied, as is the greater part of agricultural land today, even if the upward pressure of rising product prices on land values[13] works its way through into production costs it is highly unlikely to exert downward pressure on supply elasticity. A large rented sector may present a different case, depending on the conditions of tenure and the social relations of production under which it operates.

Before 1750

So far, our discussion has focused on the upper part of Fig. 12.1, and particularly on the likely effects on demand of changes in population and real wages. So extraordinary was the scale of real income and population growth that we are not encouraged to look much further for the major driving force of the supply–demand system. But for the 80 or 90 years between the Restoration and 1740 or 1750, and especially the early decades of the eighteenth century, we might well be mistaken. Evidence derived from national yield and marketing data suggest that between 1695 and 1750 the marketable surplus of grain rose by 21 per cent, while the increase in the production of mutton probably exceeded 40 per cent.[14] Overton's analysis of the probate inventories of Norfolk and Suffolk draws attention to substantial increases in output, especially of barley and of cattle, during the first three decades of the eighteenth century.[15]

The reworkings of Deane and Cole's economic growth estimates by Cole, Crafts and most recently Jackson, shown in Table 12.2, support the idea of strong output growth during the first half of the eighteenth century. All three of the more recent estimates invert Deane and Cole's rank ordering. Whereas Deane and Cole's

Table 12.2: Estimates of annual agricultural output growth (%).

Years	Crafts	Cole	Deane and Cole
1700–60	0.60	0.62	0.24
1760–80	0.13	0.43	0.47
1780–1800/01	0.75	0.70	0.65
1801–31	1.18		1.64
		Jackson	
		(Income elasticity of demand 0.5)	
		(Price elasticity of demand −0.6)	
1660–1740		0.61	
1740–90		0.04	

Sources: W. A. Cole, 'Factors in demand 1700–80', in Floud and McCloskey (eds.), *Economic History of Britain I*, p. 64; N. F. R. Crafts, *British Economic Growth During the Industrial Revolution* (Oxford, 1985), p. 42; R. V. Jackson, 'Growth and deceleration in English agriculture, 1660–1790', *Economic History Review*, 2nd ser., **XXXVIII** (1985), p. 346.

assumptions led to the suggestion of successive increases in the rate of output growth throughout the century, the work which has followed Crafts' demonstration of inconsistencies in those assumptions indicates that the first half of the century experienced more rapid output growth than the period immediately following it. The major uncertainties in the new estimates concern the output trends of the second half of the century, a problem to which we shall return.[16] Increasing quantities of food supplied to a population which was stable or declining in number suggests downward pressure on both food prices and producer's returns, especially in the cereals sector, notwithstanding official efforts to support farm incomes by subsidizing the export of grain and malt. The relatively high real wage levels prevailing at the beginning of the period 1730–1914 reflect the upward influence on real incomes of falling food prices.[17]

Two explanations are offered for agricultural change during this period. Either output increased because producers attempted to maintain constant net incomes in the face of stable or declining demand and stable or falling prices, or declining demand and falling prices were a function of a drive towards higher output which had its roots deep within the supply sub-system. If the first is true, the relationship between price and supply elasticity could be inverse in the short-term as well as direct, as Fig. 12.1 indicates. In other words, downward pressure on prices might have a temporarily positive impact on supply, generating a reverse supply curve. If the second is true, then clearly the entire system, and possibly the wider economy which lay beyond it, were being energized from the supply sub-system in the bottom half of Fig. 12.1, not from the demand sub-system at the top. In other words, we would be mistaken in making the assumption that the supply of agricultural commodities has always borne a close relationship to its demand environment.

Although one may detect in recent scholarship more emphasis on the second interpretation and less on the first, which was that favoured by both John and Jones when they originally argued the case for significant output growth during the period before 1750,[18] there is no reason to make any pronouncement on their relative merits, except perhaps to point out that we should not presume that they are mutually exclusive and non-interactive, especially over a period of time as lengthy as this. In any event, whether one takes supply or demand to be the driving force, the components of growth are likely to be the same.

Had population continued on its upward course of the early seventeenth century, then sustained per capita real income growth would have required much greater increases in the supply of food than in fact occurred. The forces which kept population steady despite early evidence of rising real incomes, most importantly the response delays which ensured that real income growth was not instantly translated into earlier marriages and increasing fertility, have thus to be treated as a material aid to the performance of the agricultural sector during this period.[19] We should also not ignore the constraining effects of high excess mortality in the major towns. Of greater importance, however, were changes within the food supply sub-system itself involving changes in the inputs or the productivity of land, labour and capital, the three factors of production. There is evidence that agriculture derived benefit from the extension of the total acreage, largely an effect of reclamations on fen, coastal and upland margins mostly initiated during the period of population growth prior to 1650.[20] But this was less significant than improvements in the productivity of both land and labour, partly through the application of greater quantities of capital but more importantly through changes in the organization of land and in the agricultural techniques applied to it.

It would be trespassing too much on a period which is more prelude than focus to this chapter to examine these in great detail. Nevertheless, we should note new evidence of considerable enclosing activity in the seventeenth century: Wordie suggests as much as 24 per cent of the total land area of England, although this is likely to be an over-estimate.[21] Doubtless enclosure assisted (though we now know that open field did not completely preclude) the introduction of cropping innovations which were expressly intended to take advantage of relatively favourable livestock prices. Even in an area as progressive as Norfolk and Suffolk, Overton finds little evidence that turnips and clover were fully integrated into cereal rotations before the middle decades of the eighteenth century. Indeed, it seems likely that even thereafter the growth of root crops as a full course in four-course systems was more the exception than the rule in most parts of the country. But new fodder crops and legumes were adopted on a smaller scale before the mid eighteenth century, both in East Anglia and elsewhere.[22] The livestock sector drew further support from the conversion of significant acreages of arable to temporary grassland on the lighter lands and to permanent pasture on the heavy clays.[23] The chalk downlands of central southern England saw intense investment in watermeadow systems designed to promote early season grass growth and heavier crops of hay.[24] Already, by the mid eighteenth century, new techniques of selective cattle breeding pioneered in Lancashire were being taken up in the Midlands and beyond, extending qualitative improvements in cattle to new areas.[25] One inevitable consequence of such intense activity in the livestock sector was an increased supply of manure, with beneficial effects on the output of cereal crops. However, mixed farming was not spread across the land with blanket uniformity. The level of regional specialization which had emerged by the early eighteenth century allows us to draw broad contrasts between a pastoral north and west and an arable south and east. This is revealed most cogently in Kussmaul's ingenious derivation of regional shifts in farming practice from changes in the seasonality of marriage. In emphasizing the role of London's growth in shaping the country's agricultural geography, Kussmaul also reminds us of another important element in the equation.[26] Although increases in total population were small, the growth of the urban proportion of the population was not. The major towns and cities, especially London, expanded as increasing purchasing power generated demand for non-food goods and services.[27] If we accept that the real income growth which fostered urban growth was itself in part a function of the increased supply of food, then we cannot regard urbanization as a primary cause of agricultural advance. But at the very least we can say that it imposed direction and order on early-eighteenth-century agriculture and its development. The most dynamic agricultural regions of the early eighteenth century were those that enjoyed easy access to urban markets, especially that of London.[28]

1750–1815

We can afford to take a more expansive view of the period after 1750. In recent years, much additional light has beeen shed on some of the opacities of late-eighteenth-

and nineteenth-century agriculture by several projects on the major cross-sectional sources of the period, notably by 1801 crop returns and other Home Office enquiries for the years 1795 to 1800, the surveys conducted under the Tithe Commutation Act of 1836, the agricultural statistics collected by Poor Law Unions in 1854, as well as the annual June returns, beginning in 1866.[29] Three of these serve as the basis for a valuable set of maps depicting change at county level over the nineteenth century.[30] In addition, our understanding of the acreages affected by parliamentary enclosure has been extended by the posthumous completion of Tate's 'domesday', based largely on act and award summaries, and by Chapman's survey of a 10 per cent sample of English and Welsh enclosures, which painstakingly sums the acreages allotted to each individual in the detailed apportionments to the awards.[31] However, the inconsistent estimates of the Tate and Chapman projects suggest that intense scrutiny of a problem does not necessarily guarantee its instant resolution, while mapping the mappable can only offer partial insights into the economic and social processes which shape changing patterns on the ground. Sources which provide episodic snapshots of the geographical patterning of certain variables supplement rather than supplant the economic and sociological reasoning which are the keys to the logic of agrarian change and the essential context to its geography.

As already observed, the performance of agriculture appears to have worsened during the second half of the eighteenth century. By quite how much depends on one's judgement of the different estimates given in Table 12.2. Jackson's figures (those presented here are based on the most plausible of several elasticity assumptions) are the most recent. Those of Crafts next so, with the estimates of Cole and of Deane and Cole predating them. To the extent that more recent figures have the advantage of better input data, including the fruits of recent work by Wrigley and Schofield, Lindert and Williamson, and O'Brien, they deserve greater emphasis. Associated with an improved understanding of the history of economic growth, are successive downward revisions of the significance of the second half of the eighteenth century. Indeed, Jackson's most favoured scenario implies negligible agricultural output growth (>0·04 per cent per year) in the face of a population growth of 0·66 per cent per year over the period 1741 to 1791.

The only possible flaw that I can detect in Jackson's reasoning is that demand may have been inelastic downwards to a greater extent than his elasticity assumptions suggest. It is not impossible that although mean per capita demand did decline the downward drift of real wages was not matched by commensurate reductions in per capita demand for food among those segments of the population who had always lived at or close to susbsistence levels. This effect might have been reinforced by divergent real wage and real income trends such as could be brought about, for example, by the widespread adoption of methods of poor relief which were intended to match labourers' resources to the minimum subsistence needs of their families by supplementing wages from the rates.[32] The redistributive effects of taxation and poor relief should have a place in the equation. But such speculations are more a plea for further research than an attempt to rehabilitate the largely discredited claims of late-eighteenth-century agriculture.

None of these recent interpretations offers any support for the once accepted view that the second half of the eighteenth century was a period of unprecedented agricultural progress. Broadly, in the first half of the century, agriculture supplied in excess of demand; in the second, rising prices testify to the sluggishness of agriculture's supply response. Such fragmentary evidence as is available on yield is consistent with the national estimates. At least, in relatively well-documented, well-investigated and progressive East Anglia, the upward movement in wheat yields during the period between 1730 and 1760 was succeeded by 40 years of decline.[33] Price rises for food contributed to the stagnation in real wage levels revealed in Table 12.1.

The excess capacity which had enabled England to be a net exporter of grain throughout the half century up to 1760 was soon absorbed, and the country began to develop a degree of import dependence.[34] It was fortunate, especially in the context of the Napoleonic blockade, that the Celtic periphery was able to make a substantial net contribution throughout the second half of the eighteenth century and into the nineteenth. The Scottish livestock sector saw massive increases in activity and profitability in response to enhanced demand from English markets.[35] But the most striking additions to English needs came from Ireland, whose contributions of beef, butter and pork went up three-fold, six-fold and seven-fold, respectively, between 1760 and 1790. Thomas estimates that, by the 1830s, the supply of grains, butter, meat and livestock available to the English population would have been smaller by at least one-sixth had it not been for imports, mainly from Ireland.[36]

The deceleration of domestic output growth during the second half of the eighteenth century admits no easy explanation. Certainly, we cannot rule out the fortuitous effects of an exceptional run of good harvests during the 1730s and 1740s, contrasted with an unusually large number of bad ones during the 1750s and 1760s. On the other hand, severe outbreaks of cattle plague in the 1740s, and the return of subsistence crises to many parts of the country during the bad harvests of the late 1720s indicate that even in the earlier period nature was not entirely benign in its effects.[37]

Not only do climatic factors present an unconvincing general argument for agriculture's relatively indifferent performance during the second half of the eighteenth century, they do nothing to help us better understand how we should now regard those features of late-eighteenth-century agriculture which were once seen as either manifestations or causes of its success. The links between agriculture and the industrial sector, traditionally viewed as a source of industrial growth and a manifestation of agricultural advance, and the effects of parliamentary enclosure, once treated as a central cause of output growth in agriculture, deserve to be examined in greater detail in the light of the evidence just presented. In both cases, it is central to a correct understanding of their later eighteenth-century functions that we should first acknowledge the considerable advances which had been made prior to 1700. Those relating to enclosure have already been noted. Evidence for early growth of the commercial and industrial sectors is provided by revisions of the social table of Gregory King which suggest that as early as 1688 the proportion of families engaged in agriculture was probably no greater than 55·6 per cent of the total.[38] England and Wales had an essential advantage over most European rivals in the early growth of sectors outside agriculture and early structural reorganization within it.

Agriculture and the Rise of the Industrial Sector

It is not plausible that the growth of the market within the agricultural sector was sufficient to generate the kind of demand for manufactures which the eighteenth- and nineteenth-century expansion of manufacturing industry implies. Current thinking about the period before 1750, when agricultural output was growing rapidly and food prices were declining or stable, is that reduced incomes for farmers and landlords, especially pronounced among cereal producers,[39] and improved real wages for both agricultural and non-agricultural labour resulted in a net change in the demand for manufactures which, while positive, was not greatly in excess of zero.[40] During the period after 1750, neither agriculture's indifferent supply re- sponse nor its generally modest contribution to the additional tax burdens of the nation, which weighed disproportionately on the non-agricultural sectors,[41] suggests an appreciable contribution to a widening of the market for manufactures. O'Brien claims that industrial growth owed rather more than most scholars have been disposed to believe to the contribution of foreign trade.[42] Indeed, it is arguable that, throughout the entire period surveyed in this chapter, thanks to the perverse effects of foreign trade, agriculture may have contributed rather more to the growth of the economy by its supply failures than by its supply successes. The argument refers to the symmetries which are an essential feature of a developing global trading economy. Exports of manufacturers gave Britain the income necessary to import an increasing proportion of its food and raw material requirements. Equally, income from exports of food and raw materials gave the overseas suppliers of those commodities the ability to buy British manufactures. One might well say that the growth of an exporting sector would not have been possible without the growth of an importing sector. In its unique position as initiator of the large-scale global trading economy, Britain could only export those items in which its global comparative advantage was high (i.e. manufactures), if it was prepared to provide cashflow to potential export markets by importing from them those items in which its global comparative advantage was low (i.e. certain foodstuffs and raw materials).[43] How- ever, this argument is most readily sustained in the context of agriculture's acqui- escence in a fully fledged free-trade system during the second half of the nineteenth century, which we shall consider in due course. For the period presently in view, we would do rather better to focus our attention on two other, more positive features of agricultural–industrial interaction.

The first is concerned with the emergence of specialist agricultural and industrial regions as a consequence of the sub-national as opposed to global workings of comparative advantage. The argument, which owes most to the work of E. L. Jones, is as follows. Regional differentiation in patterns of economic activity was slight as long as production systems and market demand were so structured as to give no region any distinctive form of comparative advantage. Broadly, Jones argues, this was the situation which existed during the early part of the seventeenth century. By the end, however, urban growth and changing agricultural technologies had conferred particular advantages for advanced agricultural production on some regions, notably the lighter soil uplands of the south and east, putting the disparate textile industries which existed within those areas at a competitive disadvantage with their agriculture. A southern landowner with capital in southern industry suffered the penalty of high opportunity costs unless he redirected his industrial efforts to agriculture. Thus the deindustrialization of southern Britain was a corollary of its agricultural growth.[44] The regions which came to specialize in industry were, so to speak, selected from among those which were less suitable for technically-advanced agriculture. At the macro-scale, the 'selection' depended on a host of factors, of which some form of industrial tradition was among the most important. At the micro-scale, the shape and form of industry could be determined by narrow variations within the local, even the parochial, agrarian economy. Hence, as Hudson has shown, woollen manufacture developed in those parts of the West Riding where fertile soils, strong manorial control, late enclosure and the persistence of small estates provided conditions appropriate for the rise of master clothiers. By contrast, the worsted sector, with its early dependence on artisan systems of production, came to the fore in those places where poor soils, weak manorial control, early enclosure and partible inheritance had brought into existence a large, landless labour force.[45]

The second theme concerns agriculture's capacity to release labour. Although the rate of output growth in late-eighteenth-century agriculture was modest, the growth of labour productivity within agriculture was appreciable. Crafts estimates that between 1688 and 1759, the agricultural labour force contracted at the rate of 0.05 per cent per year, while during the period of rapid population growth in the second half of the eighteenth century it increased by the modest annual rate of 0.06 to 0.35 per cent.[46] O'Brien suggests that if labour productivity in English agriculture had remained at its 1700 level, then the domestic agricultural output of 1800 would have required a labour force larger by almost 90 per cent than England's agricultural labour force of that year.[47] Although such estimates are not unproblematic,[48] they do imply a level of labour-force growth within agriculture substantially lower than the rate of growth of the population at large, and therefore a rate of increase in labour productivity within agriculture which draws our attention to the possibility of effective productivity improvement through technological, organizational and other change which is not implicit in the modest rates of overall output growth. The large average size of farms, high rates of capital investment, and high average densities of livestock, including the relatively free use of horses to displace humans, have been suggested as underlying causes of England's good and improving levels of labour productivity.[49]

The results also pose questions, as yet impossible to answer with any certainty, about who, exactly, among the agricultural labour force were 'released', where they went, and whether they were happy to go there. It may suffice to observe that a massive release of labour to new or 'revolutionized' industries would poorly accord with our understanding that as late as 1841 no more than about 19 per cent of Britain's labour force were employed in that sector, and that much labour-force growth within the industrial areas is explained by the high fertility of those areas.[50] The rapid growth of employment in traditional rural handicraft and retail trades, which we know was occurring during the early decades of the nineteenth century, may or may not be a useful indication as to where we might look for the 'released' in this earlier period.[51]

Parliamentary Enclosure and the Social Relations of Production

In the years since Kerridge pleaded that 'the hoary fable of the supreme importance of parliamentary enclosure should be relegated to limbo',[52] it has become more and more apparent that there is less and less which parliamentary enclosure need be called upon to explain. It cannot be invoked as the single most important cause of agricultural output growth when, as we now know, output grew faster before the late-eighteenth- and early-nineteenth-century period in which enclosure by parliamentary act was concentrated. We must be similarly circumspect in treating the promoters of parliamentary enclosure as a kind of 'capitalist press-gang' responsible for ejecting labour from the countryside into the factories, when, at least on Crafts' evidence, the most rapid rates of labour release from agriculture appear to have taken place before rather than during the era of parliamentary enclosure.[53] Likewise, the social distribution of land before 1750 was already unequal to an extent that rules out parliamentary enclosure as a major instrument of redistribution and concentration.[54] Parliamentary enclosure rounded off a long-running process of land reorganization and re-allocation; it did not initiate it. Hence, its social and economic consequences are to be sought more in the local and regional histories of the areas which were affected than in an impact at the national scale. In this context, relegation to limbo would be much too severe a judgement.

Two kinds of agricultural region were particularly affected by parliamentary enclosure: areas of surviving open field, mostly in Midland and eastern England, and wastes and commons scattered throughout the whole of England and Wales but of particular importance in the upland areas of the north and west. In the most recent attempt to determine the areas involved, Chapman suggests that if land which was re-allocated by award but already enclosed is excluded the acreages were 7.25 to 7.35 million in England and 1.17 million in Wales.[55] About 40 per cent of the English total comprised 'field land', that is open fields normally in arable cultivation. Conversely, less than 2 per cent of the Welsh total was in this category, the bulk of the residue being 'common waste and pasture', in the uplands for the most part. The temporal and spatial separation of the enclosure of open-field arable and of pasture commons was a distinctive feature of the process. Not only were most enclosures either predominantly of arable or predominantly of pasture commons, but for any given region the predominantly arable enclosures tended to occur earlier than those which were predominantly pasture. Taking a succession of concentric bands centred on the early core area of Midland parliamentary enclosure in north Northamptonshire, Chapman shows that not only was enclosure generally later in each successive distance band but that in all distance bands the median date of arable enclosure preceded the median date of pasture enclosure. In the outer bands, corresponding with the uplands of northern England, Wales and the West Country, enclosure was late and exclusively pastoral.[56] One implication of this recent work is that open field did not dominate Midland enclosures to the extent once thought. But there still appear to have been two enclosure movements, one Midland-focused, occurring very largely between 1760 and 1830 and involving substantial areas of open field, the other northern and western in orientation, which only started to gather pace from the turn of the century and involved the enclosure of substantial areas of commons and waste. Each deserves to be treated separately.

The first thing to be explained in the Midland case is why so much open field remained to be enclosed in 1750. After all, these were relatively productive areas not in any sense distant from urban markets and their associated demand pressures. The most likely reason is the susceptibility of pre-enclosure field systems. In areas where these were incoherent or irregular then enclosure by agreement was relatively easily accomplished and surviving areas of open field more readily obliterated.[57] In the Midland core area, where such irregularity was exceptional, large-scale enclosure could only occur once it had been discovered that statute provided a mechanism which successfully circumvented the common-law requirement that agreement must be unanimous.[58] In one sense, then, the timing of enclosure by private parliamentary act is a matter of legal history. But this history has as its context the economic environment of the second half of the eighteenth century. Rising prices set farmers searching for ways of increasing production. Equally, landowners and tithe-owners began to think more seriously about the adequacy of their own returns. Enclosure acts were first sought in parishes where ownership structures presented fewest difficulties. More problematic cases were tackled as the high price inflation of the late eighteenth and early nineteenth centuries increased the likelihood of significant net returns despite ever-higher capital costs.

In recent years, attention has been given to the social distribution of enclosure's benefits. The question is not, as it has sometimes been formulated, efficiency versus equity, did parliamentary enclosure increase output or redistribute income, but who were the beneficiaries of known efficiency gains? Few scholars now doubt that output improvements occurred. Although available data are few, cereal yields on former open-field lands show varying increases, but often of the order of 10 per cent.[59] In addition, enclosure created opportunities for the further pursuit of comparative advantage, whether on heavy-soiled former Midlands open fields, which were converted to pasture and could thus benefit from relatively favourable livestock prices, or on the chalk and limestone scarplands where one-time heaths and rabbit warrens were converted to technically-advanced arable mixed-farming systems.[60] Were the benefits of enclosure and its consequent developments distributed equitably?

The answer has to be that they were not. Allen's manipulations of data collected by Arthur Young during the 1760s show that enclosure was more effective in boosting the incomes of those who owned the land than the incomes of those who farmed it.[61] In other words, enclosure provided an opportunity for owners, or at least large owners, to extract a greater proportion of the surplus. Much remains to be done on this subject. Possible interconnections between enclosure and changes in tenancy custom and practice have barely been explored. Preliminary work on the archives of some of the major institutional landowners does not suggest that rack-rented leases and regular renewals were the immediate outcome of parliamentary enclosure, and customary leases one of its victims. But it does indicate that enclosure occurred during a period of mounting dissatisfaction among large, absentee owners at the difficulties they faced whenever they attempted to value their holdings as a preliminary to possible rent review. Several Oxbridge colleges, whose interest might be in land or tithes, found implacable opposition in parishes where grudging acceptance of 'ocular survey' did not extend to surveyors wishing to use any of the more exacting tools of their trade.[62] In these circumstances, parliamentary enclosure could hardly be resisted. Detailed surveys at shared cost, negotiations conducted through a network of professional agents and in a parliament dominated by landed interests ensured that the whole process was structured to the advantage of larger landowners.[63] Small wonder that recent research reveals that the smaller tenants and occupying owners, and those enjoying customary use-rights on the commons but without formal entitlement to field land are among enclosure's palpable if not always clearly visible victims.[64]

The enclosure of commons and wastes presents a rather different set of problems. At the root of this is the difficulty of knowing whether enclosure merely altered the ownership of commons and waste or resulted in reclamation. Was commons enclosure only a legal instrument or did it bring about permanent conversion to more intensive forms of agricultural production? Such slender evidence as is available suggests differences between lowland and upland commons in this respect. In general, the enclosure of lowland commons and waste was associated with reclamation, which continued until the price collapse of the late 1870s. In the uplands, on the other hand, there is less reason to associate enclosure with reclamation and improvement of a permanent kind.[65] The uplands had always served as a temporary reservoir of additional resource which could be called upon whenever price and climatic conditions provided an appropriate combination of stimuli.[66] An enclosure award did not greatly alter this position. Indeed, on the North York Moors a large proportion of the area allotted by award was not subject to normal fencing requirements even though it might eventually be reclaimed. Conversely, many of the areas where fencing obligations did apply reverted to rough grazing during the years following enclosure.[67] One can only concur with Turner's observation that commons enclosure was not 'a once and for all process which- . . . can be catalogued and locked away in a chronological time capsule,'[68] and counsel against the over-literal interpretation of land-use statistics which assume that commons enclosure necessarily meant an extension of agricultural activity.[69] Having said that, it should be emphasized that the surge in upland enclosure during the war years of the late eighteenth and early nineteenth centuries coincided with a period when conditions favoured reclamation for both cereals and livestock production.[70] Underlying the conventional pieties of the act and award preambles, with their references to the need for improvement, there is, as in lowland enclosure, also a strong hint that more powerful interests were trying to extract a greater proportion of the associated gains.[71] The overall effects of enclosure may have been more modest than once thought, but they cannot be considered wholly neutral, either in economic or social terms.

1815–1914

Prior to 1750, the impetus for agricultural change appears to have resided largely within the supply sub-system. During the second half of the eighteenth century, agriculture responded with difficulty to the pace of increasing demand. Admittedly, labour productivity in agriculture followed a remarkable upward course. But the great changes of parliamentary enclosure may well have been more effective in redistributing surplus than in increasing its overall size. Sluggish supply-side responses provided the seed-bed in which the ideas of Malthus and like-minded contemporaries germinated. As O'Brien has put it, 'Malthusian theories of population, Ricardian concepts of rent and laws of diminishing returns reflect the fears of intelligent and observant men who, for nearly a century, expected economic progress to founder against serious supply constraints from agriculture.'[72]

If the 60 years prior to Waterloo were notable for providing circumstantial support for Malthusian doctrines, the 85 years between the conclusion of hostilities and the end of the century were equally notable for their apparent demonstration that these doctrines did not have the force of inevitability. The growth of economic activity outside the agrarian sector lay at the heart of the process. But agriculture's own contribution was not negligible, and may be summarized under three separate headings. First, the extension and intensification of cultivation, which had proved barely adequate as a response to the buoyant demand conditions of the Napoleonic Wars, showed something of its true potential during the difficult process of adjustment which followed the onset of peace. The country began to have a keener sense of the scope of changes which had already occurred. Second, the continuation and elaboration of technological innovations and improved agricultural practices brought about further possibilities for additions to domestic agricultural yields and output. The notion of 'improvement', a term not innocent of ideological content, was first canvassed and then pursued as a means whereby landowners might best fulfil the responsibilities of their position and distance themselves and their tenants from the worst effects of unrestricted free trade in agricultural commodities. Third, despite the growth of domestic output, higher net demand was satisfied to an increasing extent from imports, which contributed about one-fifth to total foods consumed in 1820, one-third by mid-century, and more than one-half by 1914.[73] The producers' antidotes to free trade ultimately proved no panacea affording cheap food for the masses without cost to the producers' own prosperity.

Post-war Uncertainties

The history of domestic agriculture post 1815 may thus coveniently be broken down into three separate phases. The first, the period of post-war adjustment and difficulty, lasted approximately until the Repeal of the Corn Laws in 1846. During this period, farmers and landlords suffered declining incomes as better harvests and less pressing demand conditions brought producers' returns down from their wartime peak. As in all boom and slump cycles since the early eighteenth century, cereal producers suffered more volatile market conditions than livestock producers,[74] an effect exacerbated by their initial insistence on responding to less favourable prices by producing more rather than less. Backward sloping supply conditions for wheat appear to have lasted until about 1835, when more marginal producers began to withdraw from cereal production altogether.[75]

In such circumstances, one might expect net benefits to flow to consumers, agricultural labourers included. But the combined effects of demography and policy ensured that their effective gains were few. High fertility consequent on an earlier upswing of the Malthusian cycle and exacerbated by the release of military manpower onto the general labour market meant that labour could only apply leverage to wage rates in places where vigorous industrial growth created enclaves of labour scarcity. Whereas in the late 1760s the highest agricultural wages had been paid in the south-eastern counties, by the late 1790s the highest paid counties were mostly in the north. The poverty of southern labour persisted until the last quarter of the nineteenth century.[76] Adverse policy responses produced both a devalued social wage, as the less-eligibility principle enshrined in the Poor Law Amendment Act of 1834 gradually replaced a variety of *ad hoc* systems offering relief in aid of wages by the undesired workhouse,[77] and a higher effective cost of living, as the Corn Laws continued to place more or less insurmountable obstructions between the British consumer and the potential benefits of the importation of less costly grain from overseas sources of production. Small wonder that the period up to the mid-1840s has been identified as one when the benefits of economic growth flowed unequally in the direction of those who were already well-off.[78] We may suspect that the expansion of rural trading during these years, which we have already noted, was a response to these desperate economic circumstances, not least because traders were disproportionately represented among those who were the first to leave the countryside during the great migrations of the second half of the century, possibly suggesting economic marginality.[79]

Reactions to the difficult post-war years varied according to circumstance. Acquiescence intermingled with action, the latter taking a variety of forms. So far as labour is concerned, three are notable. First, there were various riots and disturbances, including the Swing protests of 1830–1, which affected large areas of southern and eastern England and were directed particularly against threshing machines. Less wide-ranging collective action against a variety of grievances, including the New Poor Law, also affected various parts of both England and Wales.[80] Second, there was a certain amount of utopian grassroots support, more sentimental than practical in character, especially widespread among Chartist sympathizers but not wholly confined to the Chartist movement, for the idea that labour could be rescued from the indignities to which Malthus had condemned it and agricultural production scale unmalthusian heights of abundance if land were returned to the people. Under 'rational' smallholding cultivation based on spade husbandry, produce became 'superabundant', the radicals believed. This contrasted with Malthus' own more sceptical view of 'systems of equality' which destroyed 'those stimulants to exertion which can alone overcome the natural indolence of man'.[81] The failed Chartist land schemes testify more to the fertility of an idea than to that of its associated practical agriculture.[82] In fact, the concept was never entirely absent from radical thought throughout the nineteenth century, and came closest to entering upon its inheritance as liberal governments antipathetic to the landed interest began to heap misery on traditional repositories of landed wealth and deference towards its close. Last, and by no means least, there was the campaign for Corn Law Repeal, more vigorously pursued by urban and industrial interests than by any other, it is true, but attracting among agricultural labour occasional recognition that herein also its own best interests lay.[83]

So far as landowners and farmers were concerned, the single issue of Repeal came to engross their own debates during the period of post-war uncertainty. If by 1846, Repeal had become a political inevitability in an economy increasingly dominated by industrial and commercial interests, there were many agriculturalists who saw the loss of protection as a source of opportunity rather than an unmitigated catastrophe.[84] 'Improvement' was both an expression of faith in the productive potential and inherent competitiveness of a technically-advanced agriculture under conditions of high investment, and a political label worn by those who stood in opposition to the unbending advocates of protection. The newly founded English (later Royal) Agricultural Society, with its motto 'Practice with Science' promoted the message of High Farming and improvement, standing in intellectual opposition to organizations like the anti-league and the local agricultural associations which put up a dogged defence of the protectionist case.[85]

High Farming and the 'Golden Age'

Many of the improvements which the 'improvement party' saw as an answer to the problems of competition were already familiar to progressive farmers of the pre-Repeal period, including, so it has been argued recently, the possibility of extending more lucrative livestock enterprises on to lowland arable farms through the use of mixed farming methods. East Anglia was in the vanguard of these developments.[86] The 30 years or so which followed Repeal, a period which came to be referred to as the 'Golden Age' of English agriculture, saw both the wider popularity of these newly established techniques and the acceptance of additional novelties. Some were associated with the specific circumstances of Repeal, including the government loans which sought to win converts to the cause of improvement by providing funding for new capital investment, notably for field drainage. These may or may not have been effective in extending advanced agricultural methods to the hitherto intractable clays.[87] Many owed rather more to other circumstances of the time. The increasing industrialization of the economy, the extension of the railway network, the greater dissemination and considerable cheapening of print, the extended provision of capital, and the wider distribution of imported inputs like linseed and guano afforded a host of new possibilities.[88]

Mid-century improvements in the yield of wheat, often regarded as the Cinderella of high farming, suggest a solid basis of achievement. Judicious reading of the results of surveys made by a firm of Liverpool corn merchants indicate an increase from 21.7 to 34.7 bushels per acre between the 1820s and the 1850s, as compared with a national average yield for the first decade of the present century of only 33.0 bushels.[89] That increasing domestic demand was to a large extent supplied from domestic sources testifies to the general achievements of the 'golden age'. And yet, the whole edifice of high farming was erected on foundations which were far from secure. The supposed flexibility of its mixed farming systems proved to be illusory when confronted by rising production costs at home and steeply declining prices resulting from increased import penetration by low-cost producers overseas.[90]

To understand the domestic aspect of its difficulties, we need to know something of the underlying contradictions of the society in which high farming had taken root. Tenant farmers were only able to show a good return on high farming activities, especially when product prices were under pressure, if they could rely on reasonableness in both landlords' rent and labourers' wage expectations. Tenants hoped that the relatively low monetary returns traditional of landownership would continue even though the capital required of landlords had increased.[91] For their part, landlords were inclined to view their returns in both broad and narrow terms. Rental income represented the narrow return. Beyond it lay broader returns from the pleasures of rural life, patronage, influence and peer-group approval which were among the indirect benefits of landed proprietorship. In theory, there should have been some possibility that reductions in the narrow return might be counterbalanced by improvements in the broad return. In practice, tenants increasingly regarded landlords' attentiveness to the broader return as at best irrelevant and at worst inimical to their own interests.

During the nineteenth century, the issues of compensation for tenant improvements (itself given a new dimension by the enlarged amounts of tenant capital demanded by high farming), the preservation of game, and the expectation that tenants would defer to their landlords' political inclinations were sources of, at best, difficulty, at worst, antagonism.[92] Notwithstanding the extravagant claims sometimes made for home-farm agriculture,[93] tenants were equally unimpressed by many of the landlords' direct interventions in farming, especially when undertaken with the primary aim of impressing social equals and betters. The landowners' interest in pedigree cattle breeding, more attentive to the rhetoric of utility than to utility itself, was a case in point.[94] Stallion owners able to recognize utility when they saw it gained a good livelihood by touring their charges round the country from mare to mare, a process effective in transmitting the benefits of the shire breed to the agricultural horse population by the end of the century.[95] By contrast, the breeders of pedigree Shorthorn cattle, caught up in a world of hobby farmers, the perverse judging points of the show ring, the inflated returns of speculative investment in fashionable blood lines, and the social exclusivity of the upper ranks of landed society, had greater difficulty both in establishing an improved breed with desirable utility characteristics and in disseminating it to the farming population.

Of course, none of this denies the benefits to agriculture which arose from sustained landlord investment in fixed capital items like farm buildings, from landlords' readiness to rebate rents when times turned sour, or from their insistence, through the mechanism of lease covenants, that tenants adhere to the minimum decencies of good practice.[96] Nor does it argue against the proposition that as long as the indirect returns to landownership continued at some level, then there were likely to be net financial benefits for the tenantry, however much they might resent its social cost. It should also be emphasized that the level of alienation and tension was not uniform across the country but varied according to the circumstances of individual estates and localities. Indeed, many larger tenants expected rather more deference from their social inferiors than did some of the smaller landowners.[97] Even so, as the odds were increasingly stacked against adequate direct returns from landownership so the indirect returns also started to lose much of their appeal. Those landowners who were able to draw on fortuitously acquired sources of industrial and commercial income could regard themselves as fortunate.[98] Landless individuals who had built professional, commercial or industrial fortunes no longer saw the acquisition of land as an obligatory passport to social advance.[99] The traditional functions of landlordism were steadily being undermined, and with them one of the supports of high farming.

So too, if rather more gradually, was the equally important support of cheap labour. Whatever their differences, landowners and tenant farmers had a shared interest in keeping labour cheap. Labour itself had no such interest, but its stubbornly high fertility and long-standing reluctance to take the escape route of migration ensured that labour long remained in excess supply and pauperized in southern England, its standards of living well below those achieved in the more competitive labour market of the industrializing Midlands and North.[100] For the landowning gentry and aristocracy, a congested and pauperized countryside was neither comfortable to live with nor much of a visual tribute to enlightened proprietorship, even if the cheap labour which it offered was highly desirable in other respects. Their solution was to create a small coterie of 'constant men', locked into the obligations of deference, an arrangement epitomized by the model or estate village which the landowner owned and controlled.[101] A less visible but more numerous casualized labour force was left as a residuum in villages of fragmented ownership, where housing conditions could be as dire as in any urban slum. These 'open' villages became the target of reformist Victorians, their conditions exposed in a host of reports on a variety of subjects from the employment of women and children in agriculture to the reform of Poor Law settlement provisions.[102]

Banks has recently argued that the practice of drawing a rigid distinction between the two types of settlement, characterizing one as 'close' and the other as 'open', is rooted in the rhetoric of nineteenth-century moralizing, and that its unquestioning use by present-day historians to describe an objective reality of nineteenth-century social geography is therefore mistaken.[103] While it is true that the problem was only severe in labour-flush southern England, and even there it is impossible to pigeon-hole all villages, or even the majority, into one or other of the categories 'open' and 'close', the distinction still has its attractions. It draws attention to the existence of a rural reserve army of labour, which helped delay the adoption of new labour-saving, capital-consuming technologies in agriculture.[104] It also underlines the considerable importance of micro-scale variations in the economic and social geography of the Victorian countryside which partly arose from the pattern of landownership. Differences between villages in economy, social structure and culture were considerable, although incompletely and often inaccurately captured by the necessarily crude distinction between open and close.[105]

Agriculture in Crisis, 1878–1914

The narrow tolerances of high farming were fully exposed during the last part of our period, when, ironically, demand was growing most rapidly. Every circumstance conspired against it. First, the Second Reform Act of 1867 ushered in a unique era, only finally terminated by the steady increase in home ownership following the conclusion of the Second World War, when the majority of the British electorate had no personal stake in and were therefore inclined to be antipathetic towards the special pleadings of realty. The markedly unequal distributions revealed by the New Domesday of Owners of 1873 could only fuel the reformist zeal of people like Lloyd George, whose attitudes may be gauged from his description of the great landed peers as 'five hundred . . . ordinary men chosen accidentally from among the unemployed', and whose actions included the progressive taxation of income and estates in the famous People's Budget of 1909–10.[106] Second, labour began to improve its position, partly as a result of the modest successes of the newly founded agricultural trades unions, partly because of the effects of migration, some of it organized by the unions themselves, both to British and to overseas destinations. The resulting imbalances in the age and sex structures of the residual agricultural labour force contributed to its reducing fertility.[107]

Third, and most important, agriculture was obliged to contend with reduced returns arising from the delayed effects of free trade. The relative importance of west European sources of imports, including Ireland, declined as new supplier areas, notably the vast un- or under-exploited acreages to the west of the Appalachians and in Prussia and western Russia, came on stream.[108] No less significant than the land itself were the resources applied to its exploitation. These included immigrant human capital, in the American case largely European in origin and including among its number some individuals identifiable as refugees from the post-Repeal adversities of English agriculture,[109] as well as the fruits of technological progress in land and sea transport which brought dramatic reductions in transfer costs wherever they reached. The domestic cereals sector was the first to feel the draught, which became successively a gale and a hurricane after the conclusion of the American Civil War and the disastrous domestic harvest of the late 1870s and 1880s. By 1910, overseas suppliers were meeting 80 per cent of domestic demand for wheat.[110]

Livestock producers were somewhat better protected from competitive pressure. Indeed, in view of high income elasticities of demand for their principal products, the intrinsic suitability of most of England and Wales to pastoral systems of production, and the close proximity of major markets, it is arguable that in the buoyant market conditions of the later decades of the nineteenth century (see Tables 12.1 and 12.3), they should not have experienced competitive disadvantages of any kind. And yet, as Table 12.3 shows, from mid-century up to the outbreak of the First World War, the increase in the domestic production of meat, which, it will be noted, includes net additions from Scottish and Irish sources, was barely sufficient to keep pace with the increasing per-capita consumption of the 1850s population, let alone the massive increase in the number of consumers. The liquid milk trade, market gardening and poultry production, all serving expanding markets and more or less

Table 12.3: Indices of average annual meat consumption, United Kingdom (1851–60 = 100).

Years	Domestic	Imported	Imported as % of total	Consumption per head
1851–60	100	100	4	100
1861–70	103	298	11	103
1870–74	127	478	14	124
1875–79	126	777	21	127
1880–84	122	1018	26	126
1885–89	127	1114	27	128
1890–94	135	1531	32	140
1895–99	134	2120	40	150
1900–04	139	2307	41	151
1905–09	139	2389	42	147
1910–14	142	2480	42	145

Source: Richard Perren, *The Meat Trade in Britain, 1840–1914* (London, 1978), p. 3.

protected from foreign inroads by the nature of their products, were the only untarnished bright spots of late-nineteenth-century agriculture. The districts which specialized in these commodities comprised both the urban margins and, increasingly, dairying areas and more concentrated pockets of specialist market gardening strung along the main railway routes.[111]

The domestic agricultural scene towards the end of the century was not uniformly gloomy, therefore, although even the more favoured producers knew something of adversity.[112] But the most striking thing about it was that the gloom was most intense among those who had succumbed to the technologically-advanced farming systems of earlier times. The latent non-linear characteristics of 'progress' were clearly revealed in the resilience of agriculture in areas like the urban fringes and the pastoral north and west where high farming had made limited inroads. Small-scale, often owner-occupied, undercapitalized, non-innovative farmers, some of whom still preferred to employ living-in farm servants where they could not wholly depend on family labour and had no truck with non-resident day labour, found that they were not quite so marginal as they had been led to suppose.[113] What remained of an English and Welsh 'peasantry' and 'yeomanry' enjoyed something of a Renaissance during the closing years of our period.[114]

Conclusion

Following an early-eighteenth-century period when agricultural output increased in excess of demand and a late-eighteenth-century period when it lagged rather seriously behind it, the nineteenth century appears to have fallen into three distinct phases, each dominated by a different response to the problem of reconciling the needs of consumers and suppliers. The loss of protected markets was alleviated by the pursuit of technological advance until this solution was itself undermined by a surge of cheap imports. The sequence of events in nineteenth-century agriculture might therefore be crudely characterized as protection, innovation and capitulation. It took two world wars, the loss of Empire, the emergence of powerful farming lobbies within Britain and the European Community, and tremendous progress in all branches of agricultural science to reinstate the arguments against excess import dependence and in favour of a vigorous, technologically-advanced domestic agriculture, protected as necessary, although as much by subsidies supported from general taxation as by price guarantees and tariff barriers. In the second half of the twentieth century technological advance, protection, and importation have provided a simultaneous rather than a sequential solution to the problems of agricultural production and food supply.

As a consequence, the Malthusian threat seems more remote than ever. A veritable lattice of safety nets appears to protect our essential subsistence. When food expenditure absorbs a relatively small proportion of personal income and huge surpluses clog the intervention stores we do not sensibly contemplate the prospect of starvation. Should the increments from technological advance ever fade, and so far there is little sign of their doing so, or consumers rebel at the high cost of subsidized production, then imports could again be called upon to supply the deficiency.

And yet, one might well consider whether our supposed escape from the Malthusian world has not taken us on a course which must eventually lead back to it. A nation may make a good living by focusing its efforts on its industrial and commercial sources of income as long as its competitors are few and its comparative advantages in those areas clearly defined. Neither is any longer true in the British case, it might be argued.[115] Further, agriculture itself is capable of making ever-greater improvements in factor productivity only if it has access to relatively cheap sources of energy. Many of the most technically-advanced production systems require an energy input greater than the energy they produce. Conversely, the highest energy ratios are invariably found in pre-industrial agriculture.[116] The ultimate environmental cost of high-intensity agriculture represents a further unknown. Did the process of economic transformation which dates back before the early eighteenth century merely suspend the Malthusian system rather than suppress it? Time alone will tell.[117]

References

1. E. A. Wrigley and R. S. Schofield, *The Population History of England 1541–1871; a Reconstruction*, (London, 1981).
2. R. S. Schofield and E. A. Wrigley, 'Population and economy: from the traditional to the modern world', in R. I. Rotberg and T. K. Rabb (eds.), *Population and Economy: Population and History: from the Traditional to the Modern World*, (Cambridge, 1986) p. 1.
3. R. D. Lee and R. S. Schofield 'British population in the eighteenth century', in R. Floud and D. McCloskey (eds.), *The Economic History of Britain since 1700, I 1700–1860*, (Cambridge, 1981), p. 21: Wrigley and Schofield, *Population History of England*, pp. 577, 595; C. M. Law, 'The growth of the urban population in England and Wales, 1801–1911', *Transactions, Institute of British Geographers*, **XLI** (1967), p. 130.
4. R. N. Salaman, *The History and Social Influence of the Potato*, (Cambridge, 1949).
5. E. J. T. Collins, 'Dietary change and cereal consumption in Britain in the nineteenth century', *Agricultural History Review* **XXIII** (1975), pp. 97–115.
6. Wrigley and Schofield, *Population History of England*, pp. 638–44. Gilboy's data from B. R. Mitchell and P. Deane, *Abstract of British Historical Statistics*, (Cambridge, 1971), pp. 346–7.
7. County totals from P. Deane and W. A. Cole, *British Economic Growth, 1688–1959*, (Cambridge, 1969), p. 103. Definition of 'northern' in Wrigley and Schofield, *Population History of England*, p. 433.
8. P. H. Lindert and J. G. Williamson, 'English workers' living standards during the industrial revolution: a new look', *Economic History Review*, 2nd ser., **XXXVI** (1983), p. 13; J. G. Williamson, *Did British Capitalism Breed Inequality?*, (London, 1985), pp. 17, 30.
9. M. W. Flinn, 'English workers' living standards during the industrial revolution: a comment', *Economic History Revew*, 2nd ser., **XXXVII** (1984), pp. 88–92; P. H. Lindert and J. G. Williamson, 'Reply to Michael Flinn', *Economic History Review*, 2nd ser., **XXXVII** (1984), pp. 93–4.
10. Assuming a 20 year coppice rotation, the early eighteenth century iron industry would have needed 440,000 acres: G. Hammerlsey, 'The charcoal iron industry and its fuel', *Economic History Review*, 2nd ser., **XXVI** (1973), p. 606; J. M. Lindsay, 'Charcoal iron smelting and its fuel supply; the example of the Lorn furnace, Argyllshire, 1753–1876; *Jnl. of Historical Geography*, **I** (1975), pp. 288–9. At its late-nineteenth-century peak, the urban horse population is estimated to have consumed 2,169,000 acres of oats and 2,112,000 acres of hay per annum. F. M. L. Thompson, 'Nineteenth-century horse sense', *Economic History Review*, 2nd ser., **XXIX** (1976), pp. 60–79; and, 'Horses and hay in Britain, 1830–1918', in F. M. L. Thompson (ed.), *Horses in European Economic History: a Preliminary Canter*, (Reading, 1983), pp. 50–72.

11. P. Mathias, 'Agriculture and the brewing and distilling industries in the eighteenth century', in E. L. Jones (ed.), *Agriculture and Economic Growth in England 1650–1815*, (London, 1967), pp. 80–93.

12. M. W. Flinn, *A History of the British Coal Industry, II 1700–1830*, (Oxford, 1984), pp. 212–25, 273–85.

13. On gross product and land values see C. Clark, *The Conditions of Agricultural Progress*, (3rd edn.) (London, 1957), pp. 637–40.

14. J. A. Chartres, 'The marketing of agricultural produce', in J. Thirsk (ed.), *The Agrarian History of England and Wales, V 1640–1750, II Agrarian Change*, (Cambridge, 1984), pp. 443–5.

15. M. Overton, 'Estimating crop yields from probate inventories: an example from East Anglia, 1585–1735', *Jnl. of Economic History*, **XXXIX** (1979), pp. 363–78; 'Agricultural revolution? Development of the agrarian economy in early modern England', in A. R. H. Baker and D. Gregory (eds.), *Explorations in Historical Geography: Interpretative Essays*, (Cambridge, 1984), p. 130.

16. Deane and Cole, *British Economic Growth*, pp. 66–78; N. F. R. Crafts, 'English economic growth in the eighteenth century: a re-examination of Deane and Cole's estimates', *Economic History Review*, 2nd ser., **XXIX** (1976), pp. 226–35; 'Income elasticities of demand and the release of labour by agriculture during the British industrial revolution', *Journal of European Economic History*, **IX** (1980), pp. 153–68; 'British economic growth, 1700–1831; a review of the evidence, *Economic History Review*, 2nd ser., **XXXVI** (1983), pp. 177–99.

17. P. J. Bowden,'Agricultural prices, wages, farm profits and rents', pp. 1–118, and 'Statistics', pp. 850–6; J. Thirsk, 'Agricultural policy: public debate and legislation', pp. 305–11, 328–38, all in J. Thirsk (ed.), *Agrarian History, V. II*.

18. E. L. Jones, 'Agriculture and economic growth in England, 1660–1750: agricultural change', A. H. John 'Agricultural productivity and economic growth in England 1700–1760', both in *Jnl. of Economic History*, **XXV** (1965).

19. E. A. Wrigley, 'The growth of population in eighteenth-century England: a conundrum resolved', *Past and Present*, **XCVIII** (1983), p. 142.

20. E. Kerridge, *The Agricultural Revolution*, (London, 1967), pp. 222–39; H. C. Darby, *The Changing Fenland*, (Cambridge, 1983); J. Porter, 'Wasteland reclamation in the sixteenth and seventeenth centuries: the case of south–east Bowland', *Transactions of the Historic Society of Lancashire and Cheshire*, **CXXVII** (1978), pp. 1–23; C. G. A. Clay, *Economic Expansion and Social Change: England 1500–1700 I People, Land and Towns*, (Cambridge, 1984), pp. 107–12.

21. J. R. Wordie, 'The chronology of English enclosure, 1500–1914', *Economic History Review*, 2nd ser., **XXXVI** (1983), pp. 483–505; J. Chapman, 'The chronology of English enclosure', and J. R. Wordie, 'The chronology of English enclosure: a reply', *Economic History Review*, 2nd ser., **XXXVII** (1984), pp. 557–9, and 560–2.

22. Overton, 'Agricultural revolution', pp. 129–30; 'The diffusion of agricultural innovations in early modern England: turnips and clover in Norfolk and Suffolk, 1580–1740', *Transactions, Institute of British Geographers*, New ser., **X** (1985), pp. 205–21; R. Morgan, 'The root crop in English agriculture, 1650–1870', Ph.D. Thesis, University of Reading, 1978; R. J. P. Kain, *An Atlas and Index of the Tithe Files of Mid-Nineteenth-Century England and Wales*, (Cambridge, 1986), pp. 460–1; P. Brassley, 'Northumberland and Durham', pp. 53–6, and F. V. Emery, 'Wales', pp. 412–14, in J. Thirsk (ed.), *The Agrarian History of England and Wales, V 1640–1750 I. Regional Farming Systems*, (Cambridge, 1984).

23. B. A. Holderness, 'East Anglia and the Fens', in J. Thirsk (ed.), *Agrarian History V.I.*, pp. 224–5; J. Broad, 'Alternate husbandry and permanent pasture in the Midlands, 1650–1800', *Agricultural History Review*, **XXVIII** (1980), pp. 77–89.

24. Kerridge, *Agricultural Revolution*, pp. 251–67; G. G. S. Bowie, 'Watermeadows in Wessex—a re-evaluation for the period 1640–1850', *Agricultural History Review*, **XXXV** (1987), pp. 151–8.

25. N. Russell, *Like Engend'ring Like: Heredity and Animal Breeding in Early Modern England*, (Cambridge, 1986), pp. 138–54.

26. A. Kussmaul, 'Agrarian change in seventeenth-century England: the economic historian as palaeontologist', *Jnl. of Economic History*, **XLV** (1985), pp. 1–30.

27. E. A. Wrigley, 'A simple model of London's importance in changing English society and economy', *Past and Present*, **XXXVII** (1967), pp. 44–70.

28. J. A. Chartres, 'Food consumption and internal trade', in A. L. Beier and Roger Finlay (eds.), *The Making of the Metropolis: London 1500–1700*, (London, 1986), pp. 168–96.

29. M. Turner, 'Arable in England and Wales: estimates from the 1801 crop returns', *Jnl. of Historical Geography*, **VII** (1981), pp. 291–302; 'Agricultural productivity in England in the eighteenth century; evidence from crop yields', *Economic History Review*, 2nd ser., **XXXV** (1982), pp. 489–510; R. J. P. Kain and H. C. Prince, *The Tithe Surveys of England and Wales*, (Cambridge, 1985); Kain, *Atlas of Tithe Files*; J. T. Coppock, 'Mapping the agricultural returns: a neglected tool of historical geography', in M. Reed (ed.), *Discovering Past Landscapes*, (London, 1984), pp. 8–55.

30. M. Overton, 'Agriculture', in J. Langton and R. J. Morris (eds.), *Atlas of Industrializing Britain, 1780–1914*, (London, 1986), pp. 34–53.

31. W. E. Tate, *A Domesday of English Enclosure Acts and Awards*, (Reading, 1978), (M. E. Turner, ed.); M. Turner, *English Parliamentary Enclosure*, (Folkestone, 1980); J. Chapman, 'The extent and nature of parliamentary enclosure', *Agricultural History Review*, **XXXV** (1987), pp. 25–35.

32. P. H. Lindert, 'English population, wages and prices: 1541–1913', in Rotberg and Rabb (eds.), *Population and Economy*, pp. 60–1. On methods of relief see K. D. M. Snell, *Annals of the Labouring Poor: Social Change and Agrarian England, 1660–1900*, (Cambridge, 1985), Chapter 3; J. G. Williamson, 'Did English factor markets fail during the industrial revolution?'. *Oxford Economic Papers*, **XXXIX** (1987), pp. 641–78.

33. M. Turner, 'Agricultural productivity in eighteenth-century England: further strains of speculation', *Economic History Review*, 2nd ser., **XXXVII** (1984), pp. 256–7. Because Overton's figures are net while the figures for the 1760s are gross, the second quarter of the eighteenth century may have witnessed even less significant yield improvements than direct comparison of the two data-sets suggests: R. C. Allen, 'Inferring yields from probate inventories', *Jnl. of Economic History*, **XLVIII** (1988), pp. 117–25; P. Glennie, 'Continuity and change in Hertfordshire agriculture, 1550–1700: II—Trends in crop yields and their determinants', *Agricultural History Review*, **XXXVI** (1988), pp. 148–9, 159–61.

34. A. H. John, 'English agricultural improvement and grain exports, 1660–1765', in D. C. Coleman and A. H. John (eds.), *Trade, Government and Economy in Pre-Industrial England*, (London, 1976), pp. 45–67; E. L. Jones, 'Agriculture 1700–80', in Floud and McCloskey (ed.), *Economic History of Britain I*, p. 68; Chartres, 'Marketing of agricultural produce', pp. 448–54.

35. R. A. Dodgshon, 'The economics of sheep farming in the southern uplands during the age of improvement, 1750–1833', *Economic History Review*, 2nd ser., **XXIX** (1976), pp. 551–69.

36. B. Thomas, 'Escaping from constraints: the industrial revolution in a Malthusian context;, in Rotberg and Rabb (eds.), *Population and Economy*, pp. 182–5.

37. J. Broad, 'Cattle plague in eighteenth-century England', *Agricultural History Review*, **XXXI** (1983), pp. 104–5; Wrigley and Schofield, *Population History of England*, pp. 681–5.

38. Crafts, *British Economic Growth*, p. 14.

39. J. V. Beckett, 'Regional variation and the agricultural depression, 1730–50', *Economic History Review*, 2nd ser., **XXXV** (1982), pp. 35–51.

40. R. A. Ippolito, 'The effects of the agricultural depression on industrial demand in England, 1730–1750', *Economica*, **XLII** (1975), pp. 298–312; D. N. McCloskey, *Econometric History*, (London, 1987), pp. 20–1.

41. P. O'Brien, 'The political economy of British taxation, 1660–1815', *Economic History Review*, 2nd ser., **XLI** (1988), pp. 1–32.

42. P. K. O'Brien, 'Agriculture and the industrial revolution', *Economic History Review*, 2nd ser., **XXX** (1977), pp. 166–81; 'Agriculture and the home market for English industry, 1660–1820', *English Historical Review*, **C** (1985), pp. 773–800.

43. Crafts, *British Economic Growth*, especially pp. 135–7. Intermediate parties and commodities (e.g. slaves) might be involved.

44. E. L. Jones 'Agriculture and economic growth in England, 1660–1750: agricultural change'; 'Agricultural origins of industry', in E. L. Jones (ed.), *Agriculture and the Industrial Revolution*, (Oxford, 1974), pp. 67–84, 128–42; 'The constraints on economic growth in southern England, 1650–1850', *Contributions V*, Third International Conference of Economic History, Munich 1965, (Paris, 1974).

45. P. Hudson, *The Genesis of Industrial Capital: a Study of the West Riding Wool Textile Industry c. 1750–1850*, (Cambridge, 1986).

46. Crafts, *British Economic Growth*, pp. 15–16.

47. O'Brien, 'Agriculture and the home market', p. 781.

48. N. F. R. Crafts, 'British economic growth: some difficulties of interpretation'; J. G. Williamson, 'Debating the British industrial revolution', *Explorations in Economic History*, **XXIV** (1987), pp. 245–68, 269–92, 320–5.

49. R. C. Allen, 'The growth of labour productivity in early modern English agriculture', *Explorations in Economic History*, **XXV** (1988), pp. 117–46; P. O'Brien and C. Keyder, *Economic Growth in Britain and France 1780–1914*, (London, 1978), pp. 102–45; N. F. R. Crafts, 'British industrialization in an international context', *Jnl. of Interdisciplinary History*, **XIX** (1989), pp. 415–28; E. A. Wrigley, *Continuity, Chance and Change: The Character of the Industrial Revolution in Britain*, (Cambridge, 1988), pp. 34–43, 72; G. Clark, 'Productivity growth without technical change in European agriculture before 1850', *Jnl. of Economic History*, **XLVII**, (1987). pp. 419–32.

50. Crafts, 'British Economic Growth, pp. 4–5; D. Levine, *Family Formation in an Age of Nascent Capitalism*, (London, 1977).

51. E. A. Wrigley, 'Men on the land and men in the countryside: employment in agriculture in early-nineteenth-century England', in L. Bonfield, R. Smith and K. Wrightson (eds.), *The World We Have Gained: Histories of Population and Social Structure*, (Oxford, 1986), pp. 295–336.

52. Kerridge, *Agricultural Revolution*, p. 24.

53. N. F. R. Crafts, 'Enclosure and labour supply revisited', *Explorations in Economic History*, **XV** (1978), pp. 172–83.

54. C. Clay, 'Landlords and estate management in England', in Thirsk (ed.), *Agrarian History V. II*, pp. 162–4.

55. J. Chapman, 'The extent and nature of parliamentary enclosure', pp. 27– 8.

56. *Ibid.*, p. 32–4.

57. J. A. Yelling, *Common Field and Enclosure in England 1450–1850*, (London, 1977), Chapters 2 and 3; 'Rationality in the common fields', *Economic History Review*, 2nd ser., **XXXV** (1982), pp. 409–15.

58. D. N. McCloskey, 'The economics of enclosure: a market analysis', in W. N. Parker and E. L. Jones (eds.), *European Peasants and their Markets: Essays in Agrarian Economic History*, (Princeton, 1975), pp. 127–33.

59. M. Turner, *Enclosures in Britain 1750–1830*, (London, 1984), pp. 40, 44; *English Parliamentary Enclosure*, pp. 95–7.

60. Yelling, *Common Field and Enclosure* pp. 194–5; A. Harris, *The Rural Landscapes of the East Riding of Yorkshire 1700–1850*, (Oxford, 1961); H. C. Darby, 'The age of the improver, 1600–1800', in H. C. Darby (ed.), *A New Historical Geography of England*, (Cambridge, 1973), pp. 340–4.

61. R. C. Allen, 'The efficiency and distributional consequences of eighteenth-century enclosures', *Economic Journal*, **CII** (1982), pp. 937–53.

62. See, for example, Trinity College, Cambridge, Muniments. Box 14 Survey of Kellington, Yorks 1774; Box 16 (B.8.CC./DD.) Correspondence concerning valuation of tithes of Coxwold, Yorks, 1770–1772; Box 36 III Surveys, valuations, drainage, enclosure and tenancy changes at Skidby, Yorks; Box 41. Ocular and other surveys and valuations, tithes of Heversham, Westmorland, 1777– 1784.

63. J. M. Martin, 'Members of parliament and enclosure: a reconsideration', *Agricultural History Review*, **XXVII** (1979), pp. 101–9.

64. J. M. Neeson, 'The opponents of enclosure in eighteenth-century Northamptonshire', *Past and Present*, **CV** (1984), pp. 114–39; J. M. Martin, 'The small landowner and parliamentary enclosure in Warwickshire', *Economic History Review*, 2nd ser., **XXXII** (1979), pp. 328–43; M. Turner, 'Cost, finance and parliamentary enclosure', *Economic History Review*, 2nd ser., **XXXIV** (1981), pp. 236–48; J. M. Martin, 'Village traders and the emergence of a proletariat in south Warwickshire, 1750–1851', *Agricultural History Review*, **XXXII** (1984), pp. 179–88; Snell, *Annals of the Labouring Poor*, Chapter 4.

65. Kain and Prince, *Tithe Surveys*, pp. 196–200.

66. Kerridge, *Agricultural Revolution* p. 24; M. L. Parry, *Climatic Change, Agriculture and Settlement*, (Folkestone, 1978).

67. J. Chapman, 'Parliamentary enclosure in the uplands: the case of the North York Moors', *Agricultural History Review*, **XXIV** (1976), pp. 1–17.

68. Turner, *Enclosures in Britain*, p. 23.

69. This may underpin the increase in agricultural land-use suggested by D. Grigg, *The Dynamics of Agricultural Change*, (London, 1982), pp. 184–5.

70. M. Williams, 'The enclosure and reclamation of waste land in England and Wales in the eighteenth and nineteenth centuries', *Transactions, Institute of British Geographers*, **LI** (1970), p. 57; S. Macdonald, 'Agricultural response to a changing market during the Napoleonic Wars', *Economic History Review*, 2nd ser., **XXXIII** (1980), pp. 59–71.

71. Chapman, 'Parliamentary enclosure in the uplands', p. 4; D. J. V. Jones, *Before Rebecca: Popular Protests in Wales 1793–1835*, (London, 1973), pp. 35–66.

72. P. K. O'Brien, 'Agriculture and the industrial revolution', p. 172.

73. Crafts, *British Economic Growth*, pp. 126–7; C. O Gráda, 'Agricultural decline 1860–1914', in Floud and McCloskey (eds.), *Economic History of Britain II*, p. 197.

74. A. K. Copus, 'Changing markets and the response of agriculture in south west England 1750–1900', Ph.D. Thesis, University of Wales (1986), pp. 50–5.

75. A. R. Wilkes, 'Adjustments in arable farming after the Napoleonic Wars', *Agricultural History Review*, **XXVIII** (1980), pp. 90–103.

76. E. H. Hunt, 'Industrialization and regional inequality: wages in Britain, 1760–1914, *Jnl. of Economic History*, **XLVI** (1986), pp 935–66.

77. A. Digby, *Pauper Palaces*, (London, 1978); A. Digby, 'The rural poor', in G. E. Mingay (ed.), *The Victorian Countryside*, (London, 1981), pp. 591–602; W. Apfel and P. Dunkley, 'English rural society and the New Poor Law: Bedfordshire, 1834– 47', *Social History*, **X** (1985), pp. 37–68; Snell, *Annals of the Labouring Poor*, Chapter 3.

78. Williamson, *Did British Capitalism Breed Inequality?*

79. Wrigley, 'Men on the land'; A. Armstrong, *Farmworkers: a Social and Economic History 1770–1980*, (London, 1988), p. 113.

80. A. Charlesworth, 'Social protest in a rural society: the spatial diffusion of the Captain Swing disturbances 1801–1831', *Historical Geography Research Series*, I, (Norwich, 1979); J. Lowerson,'Anti poor law movements and rural trade unionism in the south-east 1835', A. Digby, 'Protest in East Anglia against the imposition of the New Poor Law', D. J. V. Jones, 'The Rebecca Riots', all in A. Charlesworth (ed.), *An Atlas of Rural Protest in Britain 1548–1900*, (London, 1979); Snell, *Annals of the Labouring Poor*, Chapter 3; R. Wells, 'Rural rebels in southern England in the 1830s', in C. Emsley and J. Walvin (eds.), *Artisans, Peasants, and Proletarians, 1760–1860*, (Beckenham, 1985), pp. 124–65.

81. M. Chase, *The People's Farm: English Radical Agrarianism 1775–1840*, (Oxford, 1988), especially p. 133.

82. D. Thompson, *The Chartists*, (London, 1984), pp. 299–306.

83. J. P. D. Dunbabin, *Rural Discontent in Nineteenth Century Britain*, (London, 1974), pp. 16, 71.

84. D. C. Moore, 'The Corn Laws and High Farming', *Economic History Review*, 2nd ser., **XVIII** (1965), pp. 544–61.

85. Travis L. Crosby, *English Farmers and the Politics of Protection, 1815–52*, (Hassocks, 1977).

86. Copus, 'Changing markets', Chapters 7 and 8; F. M. L. Thompson, 'Free trade and the land', in Mingay (ed.), *Victorian Countryside*, p. 106.
87. A. D. M. Phillips, *The Underdraining of Farmland in England during the Nineteenth-Century*, (Cambridge, 1989).
88. F. M. L. Thompson, 'The second agricultural revolution', *Economic History Review*, 2nd ser., **XXI** (1968), pp. 62–77.
89. E. L. Jones, *Agriculture and the Industrial Revolution*, (Oxford, 1974), pp. 184–90; E. H. Whetham, *The Agrarian History of England and Wales VIII 1914–1939*, (Cambridge, 1978), p. 3. Seasonal fluctuations in bushel weight make comparisons based on annual bushel yields suspect.
90. E. J. T. Collins, 'Agriculture in a free trade economy: Great Britain 1870–1930', *Transformazioni delle società rurali nei paesi dell'Europa occidentale e mediterranea*, pp. 70–1.
91. D. Spring, *The English Landed Estate in the Nineteenth Century: its Administration*, (Baltimore, 1963), pp. 48–50; F. M. L. Thompson, *English Landed Society in the Nineteenth Century*, (London, 1963), pp. 251–3.
92. R. J. Colyer, 'Limitations to agrarian development in nineteenth-century Wales', *Bulletin of the Board of Celtic Studies*, **XXVII** (1978), pp. 602–16; J. R. Fisher, 'Landowners and English tenant right, 1845–1852', *Agricultural History Review*, **XXXI** (1983), pp. 15–25; J. H. Porter, 'Tenant right: Devonshire and the 1880 Ground Game Act', *Agricultural History Review*, **XXXIV** (1986), pp. 188–97; D. C. Moore, *The Politics of Deference: a Study of the Mid-Nineteenth Century Political System*, (New York, 1976); J. R. Fisher, 'The limits of deference: agricultural communities in a mid-nineteenth century election campaign', *Jnl. of British Studies*, **XXI** (1981), pp. 90–105; J. Obelkevich, *Religion and Rural Society: South Lindsey 1825–1875*, (Oxford, 1976), pp. 23–61.
93. J. V. Beckett, 'Absentee landownership in the later seventeenth and early eighteenth centuries', *Northern History*, **XIX** (1983), pp. 88–9; *The Aristocracy in England 1660–1914*, (Oxford, 1986), pp. 158–64.
94. H. Ritvo, *The Animal Estate: the English and Other Creatures in the Victorian Age*, (Cambridge MA, 1987), pp. 45–81.
95. K. Chivers, 'The supply of horses in Great Britain in the nineteenth century', in Thompson (ed.), *Horses in European Economic History*, pp. 31–49.
96. T. W. Beastall, 'Landlords and tenants', in Mingay (ed.), *Victorian Countryside*, pp. 428–38; C. S. Orwin and E. H. Whetham, *A History of British Agriculture, 1846–1914*, (Newton Abbot, 1971), pp. 152–64.
97. R. J. Olney, *Lincolnshire Politics 1832–1885*, (Oxford, 1973), p. 39.
98. Spring, *English Landed Estate*, pp. 128–9; T. Raybould, 'Aristocratic Landowners and the industrial revolution: the Black Country experience c. 1760–1840', *Midland History*, **IX** (1984), pp. 59–86; M. Sill, 'Landownership and industry: the East Durham coalfield in the nineteenth century', *Northern History*, **XX** (1984), pp. 146–66; D. Cannadine, 'The landowner as millionaire: the finances of the Dukes of Devonshire, c. 1880–c. 1926', *Agricultural History Review*, **XXV** (1977), p. 92; Beckett, *Aristocracy*, pp. 200–37.
99. W. D. Rubinstein, 'New men of wealth and the purchase of land in nineteenth-century England', *Past and Present*, **XCII** (1981), pp. 125–47; R. C. Allen, 'The price of freehold land and the interest rate in the seventeenth and eighteenth centuries', *Economic History Review*, 2nd ser., **XLI** (1988), pp. 1–32.
100. Armstrong, *Farmworkers*, pp. 110–55; W. A. Armstrong, 'The influence of demographic factors on the position of the agricultural labourer in England and Wales, c. 1750–1914', *Agricultural History Review*, **XXIX** (1981), pp. 71–82; E. H. Hunt, *British Labour History 1815–1914*, (London, 1981), especially pp. 32–116, 144–57.
101. M. A. Havinden, 'The model village', in Mingay (ed.), *Victorian Countryside*, pp. 414–27.
102. B. A. Holderness, 'Open and close parishes in England in the eighteenth and nineteenth centuries', *Agricultural History Review*, **XX** (1972), pp. 125–39; D. R. Mills, *Lord and Peasant in Nineteenth Century Britain*, (London, 1980).
103. S. J. Banks, 'Nineteenth-century scandal or twentieth-century model? A new look at "open" and "close" parishes', *Economic History Review*, 2nd ser., **XLI** (1988), pp. 51–73.

104. E. J. T. Collins, 'The rationality of "surplus" agricultural labour: mechanization in English agriculture in the nineteenth century', *Agricultural History Review*, **XXXV** (1987), pp. 36–46.

105. Banks, 'Nineteenth-century scandal', pp. 64–71.

106. D. Spring, 'Land and politics in Edwardian England', *Agricultural History*, **LVIII** (1984), pp. 17–42; P. H. Lindert, 'Who owned Victorian England? The debate over landed wealth and inequality', *Agricultural History*, **LXI** (1987), pp. 25–51.

107. Armstrong, *Farmworkers*, pp. 108–55; D. Baines, *Migration in a Mature Economy: Emigration and Internal Migration in England and Wales 1861–1900*, (Cambridge, 1985); J. P. D. Dunbabin, *Rural Discontent*.

108. J. R. Peet, 'The spatial expansion of commercial agriculture in the nineteenth century: a von Thünen interpretation', *Economic Geography*, **XLV** (1969), pp. 283–301; R. Peet, 'Influences of the British market on agriculture and related economic development in Europe before 1860', *Transactions, Institute of British Geographers*, **LVI** (1972), pp. 1–20.

109. W. E. van Vugt, 'Running from ruin?: the emigration of British farmers to the U.S.A. in the wake of the repeal of the Corn Laws', *Economic History Review*, 2nd ser., **XLI** (1988), pp. 411–28.

110. Thomas, 'Escaping from constraints', p. 188.

111. P. J. Perry, *British Farming in the Great Depression 1870–1914*, (Newton Abbot, 1974), p. 23; O Gráda, 'Agricultural decline', pp. 175–97; Collins, 'Agriculture in a free trade economy', p. 66; D. Taylor, 'Growth and structural change in the English dairy industry, c. 1860–1930', *Agricultural History Review*, **XXXV** (1987), pp. 47–64; G. M. Robinson, 'Late Victorian agriculture in the Vale of Evesham', School of Geography, University of Oxford, *Research Papers*, **XVI** (1976); B. Short, '"The art and craft of chicken cramming": poultry in the Weald of Sussex 1850–1950', *Agricultural History Review*, **XXX** (1982), pp. 17–30; P. J. Atkins, 'The growth of London's railway milk trade, c. 1845–1914', *Jnl. of Transport History*, **IV** (1978), pp. 208–26; 'The charmed circle: von Thünen and agriculture around nineteenth-century London', *Geography*, **LXXVII** (1987), pp. 129–39.

112. A. Mutch, 'Farmers' organizations and agricultural depression in Lancashire, 1890–1900', *Agricultural History Review*, **XXXI** (1983), pp. 26–36; G. Rogers, 'Lancashire landowners and the Great Agricultural Depression', *Northern History*, **XXII** (1986), pp. 250–68.

113. D. Grigg, 'Farm size in England and Wales, from early Victorian times to the present', *Agricultural History Review*, **XXXV** (1987), pp. 183–7; E. J. T. Collins, 'The Economy of Upland Britain, 1750–1950; an Illustrated Review', Centre for Agricultural Strategy, University of Reading, *Paper IV*, (1978), pp. 14–17; M. Roberts, '"Waiting upon chance": English hiring fairs and their meanings from the 14th to the 20th centuries', *Jnl. of Historical Sociology*, **I** (1988), pp. 120–1, 130–1.

114. J. V. Beckett, 'The peasant in England: a case of terminological confusion?' *Agricultural History Review*, **XXXII** (1984), pp. 113–23; J. K. Walton, 'The strange decline of the Lakeland yeoman: some thoughts on sources, methods and definitions', *Transactions of the Cumberland and Westmorland Antiquarian and Archaeological Society*, 2nd ser., **LXXXVI** (1986), pp. 221–33.

115. Thomas, 'Escaping from constraints', pp. 171.

116. Grigg, *Dynamics of Agricultural Change*, pp. 79–80.

117. The author would like to thank Richard Moore–Colyer and Tony Phillips for their helpful comments on an earlier draft of this chapter.

13

'A New and Differing Face in Many Places': Three Geographies of Industrialization

Derek Gregory

Introduction

The dominant image of the Industrial Revolution is probably still one of blackened tubs of coal clanking to the pit-head and tipping into waggons and barges; of brooding factories shrouded in steam and smoke and echoing with the clang and clatter of machines; of bales of cotton piled high in warehouses and swung down into the holds of high-masted sailing ships. It is not an altogether misleading picture, but it fails to capture the complexity—the multiple historical geographies—of industrialization.[1] In this chapter I want to describe three of these geographies (there were others) which were put in place in the course of the eighteenth and nineteenth centuries.

In doing so, I prefer to avoid the term 'Industrial Revolution' for two reasons. First, until the 1830s 'industry' usually meant 'work' rather than a separate sector of the economy. Changes in the world of work were by no means narrowly economic, of course: they were connected to changes in society, culture and politics. Exactly how they were connected is a matter for debate. Different theoretical systems will provide different answers. Some of them will want to privilege the economy—to insist, for example, on the primacy of the logic of capital—whereas others will prefer to grant a greater measure of independence (and causal power) to other spheres of social life. But it seems clear that it was not until the 1830s that the concept of 'industry' in anything like its modern form came to dominate economic discourse. Apart from one or two early surveys, it was also during that decade that the barbed reports of Arthur Young and the regional inventories prepared for the Board of Agriculture were matched by similar inquiries into the manufacturing districts.[2] What this implies—and my second reason for caution about an 'Industrial Revolution'—is that many of the changes that had taken place during the eighteenth century and the first decades of the nineteenth were, in a sense, remarkably traditional. Most historians now agree that industrialization was a long-drawn-out process and that it is inappropriate to think of it as a cataclysmic transformation. Certainly, the idea of an industrial 'revolution' only became a commonplace during the 1830s. And for good

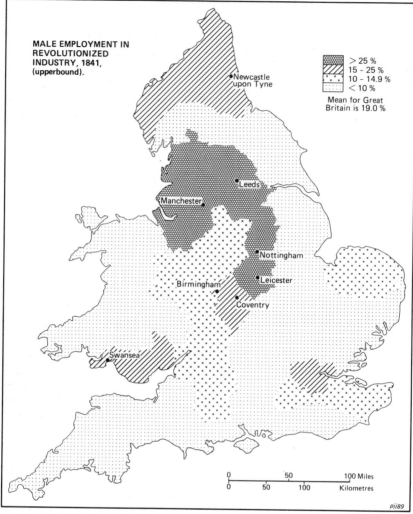

Fig. 13.1. The distribution of male employment in 'revolutionized' industry, 1841 (after Crafts).

reason: even with a deliberately exaggerated definition of 'revolutionized industry' only one worker in five would have been employed in those branches as late as 1841. Most of them would have been concentrated in a narrow band of counties (Fig. 13.1) and, even within those manufacturing districts, many industries would have been reliant upon the strength and skill of the individual worker rather than the repetitive movements of machines.[3]

Let me begin, therefore, with a geography of industrialization which was in place before the 1830s, which transformed the meaning of 'work' in quite fundamental ways, but which was largely unaffected by the advance of steam power.

The Geography of Proto-industrialization

'Proto-industrialization' was a term coined by Franklin Mendels to describe the first phase of the industrialization process: one which 'preceded and prepared for' full-scale industrialization through 'the rapid growth of traditionally organized but market-orientated, principally rural industry.'[4] The existence of industries in the countryside had long been a commonplace of historical inquiry, but Mendels' vocabulary brought with it a series of new and theoretically informed questions.

Models of Proto-industrialization

Models of proto-industrialization can be grouped into two main sets. They obviously overlap, but it is nevertheless possible to distinguish broadly 'ecological' models (concerned largely with the origins of proto-industrialization) and essentially 'economic' models (concerned largely with the transformation of proto-industrial systems).

The various *ecological models* start from the central importance of the relations between people and the land on which they lived. It was through that basic grid, so it is claimed, that social life in pre-industrial Europe was produced and reproduced. Labour in such an agrarian economy is intrinsically seasonal, Mendels argued, and so 'the adoption of industry by a growing number of peasants . . . meant that labour previously unemployed or underemployed during a part of the year [could be] put to work on a more continuous basis.' Such a logic would locate proto-industrialization in the arable regions, of course, but Thirsk had already drawn attention to the importance of the pastoral regions. Her argument was based on daily rather than seasonal time-budgets and she showed that farmers and labourers were not tied to the cow's tail 24 hours a day and that they (too) could find time to make cloth, perhaps dig coal or work metal. There seems little reason to promote one logic over another, therefore, and to expect any simple relationship between proto-industrialization and the agrarian economy.[5] What was perhaps more significant were differences in the sexual division of labour between arable and pastoral regions. In arable regions male and female labour cycles generally moved more or less together, peaks and troughs coinciding throughout the year. In the longer term, however, women were gradually being displaced from the agricultural labour force and many of them turned to spinning, lace-making, straw-plaiting or glovemaking. The earnings which could be stitched together from these and other sources were an essential component of the household budgets of most labouring families in arable regions. In pastoral regions, by contrast, male and female labour cycles alternated throughout the year and this allowed the involvement of the whole family in cloth-making and the development of a detailed division of labour within the household.[6]

But there were other, still more powerful reasons for drawing on the whole family. Children were not just mouths to feed but hands that could be put to work, at least in the preparatory stages of the production process, and from a very early age daughters helped their mothers spin and sons joined their fathers at the loom. In circumstances like these couples had every incentive to marry early and, as they were drawn ever more completely into domestic production, so they had no need to wait until they inherited or bought sufficient land to support a family. As the age of marriage tumbled and the child-bearing period lengthened, so—in the absence of family limitation strategies—population developed a self-sustaining impetus which fed back into the extension of the domestic system.[7]

Yet if proto-industrialization produced a labour-*surplus* economy in this way, how could it conceivably 'prepare for' labour-*saving* technical change? The various *economic models* seek an answer to exactly this question.[8] They suggest that the progress of proto-industrialization was determined by the intersection of two basic circuits. At the micro-level, the artisan household strove to maintain a precarious balance between production and consumption. Both labour discipline and pro-duction schedules were oriented towards use-values: towards meeting the needs of the family. When cloth prices fell during one of the crises that plagued the expanding world-economy, production would have to be stepped up to boost the short-fall in receipts if consumption were to be held steady. But, obviously, if everyone did the same the recession would become deeper and wider, so that this circuit of 'petty commodity production' was peculiarly vulnerable in a crisis.[9]

At the macro-level, the products of the domestic labour process were brought together and consigned to distant, often overseas markets by merchants whose transactions were organized around exchange-values. They were committed to the pursuit of profit and the accumulation of capital as ends in themselves; but at the very moments when the opportunities for them to reap profits were at their greatest—when the market boomed and prices rose steeply—artisan households could satisfy their immediate consumption needs most easily and so cut back on production. Once they had found their means of subsistence they were free to divert their energies out of the labour process and into feasting, dancing and playing: the familiar celebrations of what E. P. Thompson once called the 'moral economy'.[10] Merchants who sought to control the circuit of mercantile capitalism were thus ever liable to be frustrated during a boom.

When these two circuits are linked up they constitute a 'contradiction': that is to say, each circuit depends on the other and yet at the same time each circuit operates in opposition to the other. According to the basal logic of the economic model, this contradiction was resolved by merchants seizing hold of the sphere of production: gathering up what Marx called the 'invisible threads' of 'capital's other army', the artisans scattered across the countryside, and binding them together in the factory system. To be sure, many mill-owners used outworkers, either for particular stages in the production process or to meet unexpected or specialized orders, but these people were so dependent on the factory system that they were as much a part of it as if they were confined within its walls. Artisans and outworkers were no strangers to technical change, but the progress of mechanization not only broke the bargaining power of the skilled artisan and reduced labour costs; it was also a vital instrument in what Marx identified as the subordination of labour to capital. Many of the new skills which were now required could not be put to work outside the factory gates. They depended on machines which could scarcely be installed in a domestic workshop or an upstairs attic. If workers were to feed their families, therefore, they had little choice but to accept—at least outwardly—the new labour discipline and with it the new calculus of political economy in which everything was weighed on the scales of profit and loss.

But in practice matters were rarely as simple as these models make out. Although they accentuate the importance of the regional geography of proto-industrialization—Mendels has repeatedly claimed that it was at the regional scale that the rhythms of industry and agriculture could be integrated most effectively—these models do not adequately convey the multiplicity of pathways to industrial-ization (and de-industrialization) that existed in eighteenth-century Britain and neither do they open much of a conceptual space for the contingencies which were involved in the processes of regional transformation.[11] There is no space to develop these criticisms in detail, so let me sketch in just two qualifications of particular importance.[12]

First, far from the tie to the land being broken by proto-industrialization, it was often of continued and strategic importance through its role in determining access to credit. Changes in the geography of credit materially affected the geography of proto-industrialization.[13] Credit was needed not only to keep the labour process going in the ordinary course of events but also to cope with sudden fluctuations of fortune: to weather the storms of recession or to take on more hands, buy in more wool and install more machines when the economy picked up again.

Second, merchants were not narrowly economic actors, closeted in the counting-house and the cloth hall: the bearers of some deep-seated logic of capitalism. The usages of the traditional moral economy affected them as well and formed a fragile bridge between the rough-and-tumble life-worlds of the artisans (Thompson's 'plebeian culture') and the larger structures of the dominant 'patrician society'. In some places, in consequence, merchants set their faces against the factory system too, and for profoundly cultural and political reasons. In their eyes, the new regime of accumulation threatened the established social order and their privileged position within it.[14] In short, cultural and political geographies did not simply reflect economic geography: they actively shaped the contours of industrialization.

Taken together, these qualifications—along with the others that might be made—imply that there was no smooth and inevitable progression from proto-industrialization to 'Industrial Revolution'.[15] In some regions, on the contrary, de-industrialization took place. The woollen industry along the Suffolk–Essex border, amongst the most important in Britain in the seventeenth century, was in terminal decline by the mid eighteenth. In other regions, what Levine calls industrial 'involution' was the norm. In the framework-knitting villages of the East Midlands, for example, the existence of local labour-surplus economies prompted a deepening division of labour dependent upon a labour-intensive, low-level technology which held its own against the factory system until the middle of the nineteenth century. In the woollen industry of the West Country and the cotton industry of Lancashire, something like the classical transition occurred: merchants seized hold of the means of production and controlled the labour process across the countryside and inside the factory.[16] In the woollen industry of the West Riding of Yorkshire, however, many of the first factories ('proto-factories'?) were established not by merchants but by the clothiers themselves. In contradistinction to the classical model, Marx described this as the *really* revolutionary path to industrial capitalism and it is worth examining in more detail.[17]

The Dynamics of the Domestic System[18]

I want to work with three themes that can be picked out from the preceding discussion: the rhythms which pulsed through the work routines of the local economy; the resources which were drawn upon in domestic woollen production; and the responses of different groups of people to the emergence of the factory system.

We can spin these three threads together within the framework of time-geography. Fig. 13.2 is a schematic representation of the system of interaction of four domestic clothiers (A–D) in the Yorkshire woollen industry during a hypothetical three-week period at the turn of the eighteenth and nineteenth centuries. This must seem unduly abstract, I realize, but the domestic system was in some substantial sense defined through these time–space paths: it depended on a series of transfers and couplings in time and space which were not incidental to its operation. The co-ordination of these activities, precarious as it was, meant that the domestic system had its own internal discipline: different to that of the factory system, to be sure, but none the less decisive. What is more, the system as a whole was far from 'domestic' if that means 'confined within the household': the whole sequence of production was spread out across the landscape and its products were destined for distant markets.

We can hang some flesh on these bare bones and clarify the time–space consti-tution of the domestic system by tracing through the paths of the clothiers. Each of them, working at home with their families and perhaps one or two journeymen, would clean the raw wool, spin it into yarn and weave it into cloth. All of these processes displayed a characteristically seasonal rhythm of production which was

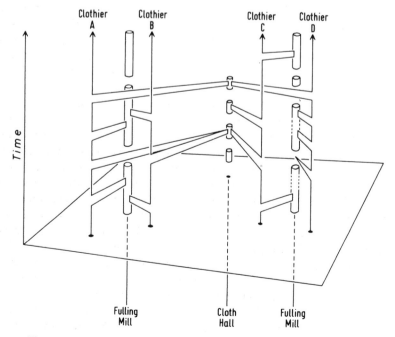

Fig. 13.2. Time–space paths in the domestic woollen industry.

largely independent of the demands of agriculture. Once the days grew shorter and the roads to the cloth halls were blocked by falls of snow, winter could be as slack inside the workshops as it was out in the fields. many of the celebrations of the moral economy were tied to seasonal festivals too: Christmas, Easter, saints' days, wakes weeks. Once the cloth had been woven, it had to be taken to the fulling mill, where it was soaked in water and pounded on huge fulling stocks to make the fibres spring together. Here too seasonal rhythms were pronounced. As more and more mills crowded on to the banks of the Aire, the Calder and their tributaries, so it became more and more difficult to maintain a sufficient head of water in high summer. Clothier D, for example, has to make several trips to his local mill only to find that fulling has been temporarily suspended or that the machinery is working at reduced speed. While he waits to have his cloth fulled, he misses two market days. The markets were themselves seasonal—spring was usually reckoned to be the 'flush time'—but they imposed time-disciplines of their own too. The cloth halls in Leeds, Huddersfield and Wakefield were open only between set times on set days of the week, and all cloth was supposed to be sold to merchants in these highly constrained time–space 'windows'. But the regularity which this implies was disrupted time and time again. By the end of the eighteenth century perhaps 70 per cent of woollen cloth produced in the West Riding was being exported, most of it across the Atlantic to the former American colonies. The overseas market was notoriously uncertain and, by the close of the century, wildly unstable. The price signals transmitted through the cloth halls reverberated back through the production sequence to inform (and, on occasion, to misinform) clothiers about buying more wool, hiring more journeymen or seeking credit for new machines.

These decisions depended upon access to credit. Those few clothiers who had sufficient landholdings, either through inheritance or purchase, were in a privileged position. They could use their resources to secure loans and so take on more workers and purchase or rent more machines. In the last 30 years of the eighteenth century the diffusion of scribbling machines and slubbing billies (which partially mechanized the preparatory processes), of spinning jennies (which increased the number of spindles that could be worked by one person), and flying-shuttles (which allowed looms to be worked single-handed) had together increased production speeds by around 50 per cent.[19] Clothiers who could not obtain credit were often unable to install the new machines and so found themselves in an ever more vulnerable position. Those who could obtain credit often bought into the fulling sector and installed the newer, faster machines in sheds and workshops next to their mills. Some of them used their economic clout to by-pass the cloth halls altogether and sell by sample. In this way, many of the first factories in the woollen industry were established not by merchants, as the models of proto-industrialization would suggest, but by so-called 'opulent clothiers'. And the interlocking structure of capability, coupling and authority constraints was changing in ways which left the vast majority of small clothiers ever more exposed to market failure. In fact the export market collapsed at intervals throughout the Napoleonic Wars (1793–1815), when successive trade embargoes virtually closed off the Atlantic and Continental markets, putting many formerly independent clothiers out of work and plunging whole families and communities into the depths of poverty. Proto-industrialization and proletarianization went hand in hand.

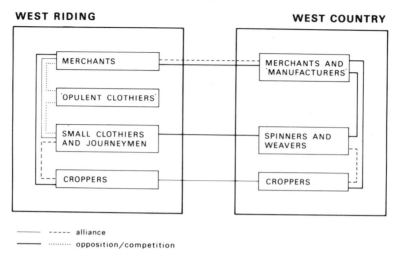

Fig. 13.3. Class alliances in the domestic woollen industry, *c.* 1806.

But the small clothiers and journeymen did not give in without a fight. Their response was three-fold.

At first they used the various trade organizations and benefit societies which had grown up around the cloth halls to petition Parliament to safeguard domestic production by restricting the growth of the factory system and lifting the trade embargoes. In doing so, they tried to forge a series of class alliances, both within the region and between the woollen industries of the West Riding and the West Country (Fig. 13.3). But success was limited. Some local merchants were prepared to endorse the clothiers' case: partly, one suspects, on genuinely moral grounds, but partly too because the rise of the factory-masters threatened their own position and power within the local community. On occasion these men can be glimpsed behind the scenes, lending their support and even orchestrating the appeals to Parliament. But they were not prepared to tolerate the parallel claims made by the croppers—the men and women who finished the cloth for them—and it was not long before the alliance foundered. Inter-regional alliances were, if anything, even harder to sustain. Merchants in the West Riding had little time for their counterparts in the West Country simply because they had been rivals for so long. Similarly, it was difficult for clothiers in the West Riding to make common cause with spinners and weavers in the West Country since their class positions were so different. Small clothiers in Yorkshire were fighting against proletarianization, whereas the divisions between capital and labour had already been etched deeply into the West Country industry. Only the croppers managed to organize themselves on an inter-regional basis, but even their success was short-lived. Parliament threw out the petitions and urged the repeal of all the protective legislation regulating the woollen industry.[20]

Once the constitutional mechanisms had been exhausted, many of the artisans engaged in direct, militant action to press home their case. Although the Luddite campaigns which reached their climax in 1811–12 were by no means confined to the West Riding—Lancashire and the Midlands were also important centres of agitation

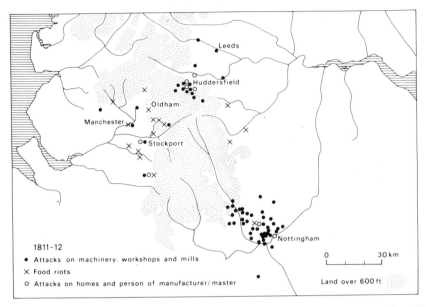

Fig. 13.4. The geography of social protest in the northern counties, 1811–12 (after Charlesworth).

(Fig. 13.4)—it seems unlikely (to me) that inter-regional co-ordination was any more successful on this front. Even so, I think it wrong to dismiss the threatening letters, riots and attacks on machinery as unreflective 'rebellions of the belly'. All of these protests were shaped by the experience of state indifference (sometimes outright hostility) and were informed not only by the conventions of the customary moral economy but also by a defiant critique of the new doctrines of political economy.[21]

But some clothiers had seen the writing on the wall. They pooled their resources and established so-called 'company mills', which retained something of the reciprocity and the mutuality of the domestic system while at the same time realizing some of the economies of scale of factory production. These mills first appeared in the closing decades of the eighteenth century (though it seems clear from their distribution that many of them were the preserve of if not opulent then certainly substantial clothiers); they were still there, and in greater numbers, by the middle of the nineteenth century (by which time it was common for small manufacturers to rent a couple of rooms in a mill).[22]

Landscapes of Fire

In 1850, in one of his first reports from South Wales, the *Morning Chronicle's* special correspondent described the approach to Merthyr Tydfil by night. Still miles away from the town, he wrote, surrounded by the dark shapes of the mountains, 'the very sky seems on fire'; coming closer, he could see 'the lofty blast furnaces of Cyfartha and Ynys-fach project upwards huge volumes of crimson flame; below these, and yielding a yellow light, the tall chimneys of the refineries and of the puddling and balling-furnaces, severally glow with fire'; further down the valley, more furnaces and forges, and 'above, glowing brilliantly, stands the vast circle of furnaces at Dowlais; higher still and perched, as it were, in the very clouds, are the fiery domes of Ivor.' Approaching a furnace in blast, its jets of flame shooting far into the night, he was reminded of nothing less than 'a cathedral on fire': though even that extravagant metaphor scarcely seemed to do justice to the intensity of the scene.[23] Many contemporaries were equally awed by the power of steam and the new industrial landscape which it produced. The first steam engines were called 'fire engines', but once they were released from solely pumping water from the bowels of the earth and began to power machinery directly they lost some of their diabolic associations. When Sir George Head visited Leeds in 1835 he made a point of climbing into the engine-house of a woollen factory. There he found 'the harmony of the movements of the engine altogether was so perfect and free from friction, the brilliancy of the polish bestowed on many of its parts so lustrous, and the care and attention paid to the whole so apparent, that imagination might readily have transformed the edifice into a temple, dedicated by man, grateful for the stupendous power that moved within, to Him who built the universe.'[24] Even those who reversed the imagery and demanded the exorcism of Blake's 'dark, satanic mills' conceded by the very force of their objections the potency of the new industrial order.

It was an imagery which captured the attention of later writers too, who painted a portrait of the Industrial Revolution as 'Prometheus Unbound': an epic narrative of coal and steam powering the economy towards 'take-off'.[25] One of the most accomplished of these modern representations is Wrigley's account of the relations between energy systems and economic growth. I want to discuss this in some detail since it raises a series of important questions about the ecology of industrialization: but it will soon become clear that I have a number of reservations about the thesis in its present form.

Energy Systems and Economic Growth

Wrigley distinguishes three ideal-typical phases of economic growth.[26] The first phase is the *simple organic economy*. In all organic economies, so he argues, land is the basis of economic activity: it is simultaneously the source of food, of heating materials, of building materials and of raw materials. The provision of any one of the four will always conflict with the claims of the other three and so economic growth is necessarily conditional. As more sheep are raised to supply wool for the cloth industry, for example, so (all other things being equal) less land is available to grow corn to feed the growing population. The system as a whole is therefore dominated by *negative feedback*.

The transition to an *advanced organic economy* loosens some of these constraints. In Britain, many commentators gave pride of place to the deepening division of labour. The very first sentence of *The Wealth of Nations*, published in 1776, attributed 'the greatest improvement in the productive powers of labour' to the division of labour and, for all its imperfections, Adam Smith's parable of the pin-makers indicated the gains that could be had through increased specialization.[27] This was not a peculiarly eighteenth-century phenomenon: one observer of the Birmingham metalware trades in 1844 was astonished to find 'that the making of inkstands formed a distinct branch of manufacture' and that the local Trades Directory distinguished 'such trades as coffin nail makers, ring turners, dog collar makers, tooth pick case makers, fishing hook makers, stirrup makers, packing needle makers, &c'. Within such an advanced division of labour, he remarked, 'a man who spends all his life in making coffin nails or packing needles must acquire an astonishing dexterity in his particular department'—which was, of course, precisely Smith's point.[28] But Wrigley considers the gains made in this way to have been exaggerated. His counter-argument consists of three main propositions.

(1) The real diagnostic of an advanced organic economy is, in Wrigley's view, the increased efficiency with which energy flows are utilized. The substitution of animal power for human labour is one example; the development of water power is another.[29] In both cases, however, growth is still conditional. Animals have to be fed and so take up acres that could otherwise provide food for the human population; conflicts between mill-owners and farmers over water-rights were one of the constants of eighteenth-century rural society. And no matter how these conflicts are resolved, they all revolve around the productivity of the land and as such are subject to what the classical economists identified as the law of diminishing returns.

(2) These constraints are real enough, but Wrigley argues that it is the continued dependence upon energy *flows* which is critical because economic growth is still limited by the ability to capture 'some fraction of a flow whose size varies little from year to year and not at all in secular trend.'[30] Local improvements can be made in the short term but no general increase in output over the long term is possible; any concerted attempt to boost production is likely to result in an energy crisis. In a classic study Nef claimed that the shortage of wood in the seventeenth century was so acute as to constitute a national crisis and Clapham drew attention to what he called 'the fuel famine of the eighteenth century'. Although their chronologies were different, both of them were referring, in rather different ways, to the limits to growth of an organic economy.[31]

(3) These limitations are compounded by the predominantly *areal* production characteristic of an organic economy. The volume of grain, wool and wood moved on horseback or in carts was simply too small, Wrigley asserts, to warrant an effective transport network. Again, some improvements are possible (though I think Wrigley says too little about them). In the first place, an extensive and efficient carrying network was in existence by the end of the seventeenth century and the advanced character of the organic economy was attested by the gradual substitution of waggons for strings of packhorses, by the vigorous expansion of road haulage and by the spread of a comprehensive system of turnpike roads during the eighteenth century.[32] In the second place, Adam Smith—on whom Wrigley relies for many of his characterizations of the advanced organic economy—insisted on a causal connected between the division of labour and the growth of water carriage. 'It is upon the sea coast and along the banks of navigable rivers,' he wrote, 'that industry of every kind naturally begins to subdivide and improve itself.'[33] It might be objected that neither of these developments did much for the supply of raw materials and that they were directed principally towards the marketing of finished products. But the

charcoal iron industry, which in so many other ways is supposed to exemplify Wrigley's thesis, provides a graphic illustration of what could be achieved. At the beginning of the eighteenth century it still carted its timber from woodlands close to the furnaces, much as Wrigley's argument would lead one to expect, but pig-iron was often sent considerable distances from furnace to forge by water.[34] Wrigley's thesis depends upon a particularly narrow definition of 'raw materials', therefore, which does not readily allow for sequences of production in which outputs from one sub-system become the inputs to another. These qualifications aside, however, Wrigley maintains that in general 'areal production meant poor communications.'[35]

Taken together these three propositions imply that while positive feedback may exist within an advanced organic economy, it will always be localized in time and space and that the system as a whole will continue to be dominated by *negative feedback*.

The transition to a *mineral-based energy economy*—one based on the exploitation of coal—transforms the situation for three parallel reasons.

(1) It reduces the pressure on the land. Wrigley reckons that 'tapping coal reserves on a steadily increasing scale produced much the same effect as would have resulted from the addition of millions of acres of cultivable land to the landscape of England.'[36] J. G. Kohl had reached the same conclusion in 1844. 'Where wood is burned,' he wrote,

> a vast extent of the country must be occupied by forests and withdrawn altogether from the labours of the husbandman. Coals, on the contrary, a powerfully condensed species of fuel, lie below the surface . . . and leave the soil above for human food to be raised upon it . . . By means of her coal mines Great Britain is able to maintain double the population that she could without them.[37]

Much of the woodland had long been cleared, but Wrigley's argument turns not only on the extension of the cultivated area that took place after 1750 (especially the grubbing up of trees and the enclosure of waste land in the north and west of the country) but also, counter-factually, on the reduction of the cultivated area that would have been necessary had the expansion of industrial output continued to depend upon the resources of the organic economy.[38]

(2) Tapping inorganic *stocks* of energy (rather than flows) allows for a much more rapid expansion of output over the longer term. Coal is a finite resource, of course, but Wrigley insists that its extraction makes possible 'enormous increases in output . . . for a substantial period in a way which has no parallel in the felling of timber.'[39] In Britain the output of coal increased from under 3 million tons in 1700 to over 30 million tons by 1830 and reached 50 million tons by 1850. Annual rates of growth climbed from around 1 per cent during the early eighteenth century to 2 per cent between 1750 and 1800 and reached nearly 3 per cent by 1815; they accelerated in the 1830s to around 4 per cent and again in the late 1840s to reach a peak of around 6 per cent in the 1850s. But these gross figures conceal significant regional differences (Fig. 13.5). The North-East field dominated the industry throughout the period and its production expanded rapidly after 1775, but as other regions stepped up production so its share of total output fell from over 40 per cent in 1700 to under 25 per cent by 1830. Production in the Lancashire field expanded rapidly, at first through the pull of the markets on Merseyside and then from the increasing demand

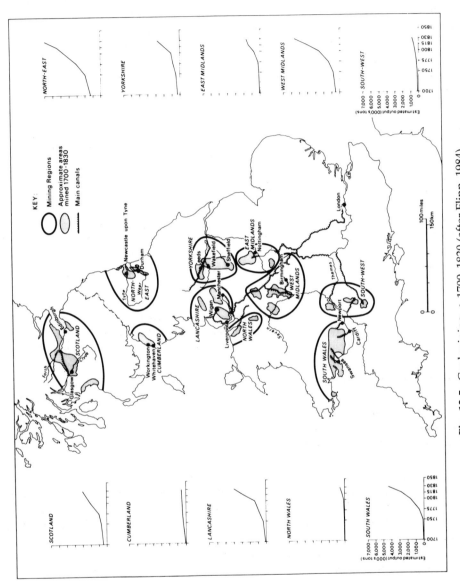

Fig. 13.5. Coal mining, c. 1700–1830 (after Flinn, 1984).

from cotton mills around Manchester, and by 1775 it accounted for 10 per cent of total output. During the last quarter of the eighteenth century production in the West Midlands field expanded, particularly around the Black Country and the Potteries, and the eastern section of the South Wales field was opened up. By 1830 these two regions accounted for 18 per cent and 15 per cent of total output respectively.[40]

(3) With the expansion of coal output the *punctiform* (rather than areal) production of raw materials is generalized and this allows the development of a more effective transport network: instead of small loads of timber being led over a large number of routeways, large tonnages of coal can be funnelled into a small number of high-capacity channels.[41] In the seventeenth century land carriage could double the price of coal within two miles of the pit-head; by the end of the eighteenth century, in the wake of various improvements in overland transport, the price would usually double within ten miles.[42] This was still a high premium, however, and so coal continued to be shipped by water wherever possible. The coastwise trade was still of special importance. Flows along the west coast of Britain were localized and very few cargoes moved more than 50 miles, but almost all ports on the east and south coasts were supplied from the North-East field (which controlled around 80 per cent of the coastwise trade).[43] Towards the end of the eighteenth century the improvement of river navigations and in particular the construction of canals played an important part in opening up the inland fields. By the early nineteenth century Arthur Young reckoned that 'navigable canals have been so greatly extended and the price of coals consequently so much reduced that there are not many situations in which a man's wood is found to be the cheaper fuel.'[44] Coal traffic was in turn the life-blood of most successful canals, and the Duke of Bridgewater had been convinced from the very start that 'a good canal should have coals at the heels of it.' But canal companies were usually local undertakings and most flows were probably under 20–25 miles. Even on the Grand Junction canal, the main trunk route, less than a quarter of the total traffic travelled the whole length of the line and on the Birmingham Canals, the busiest in the country by the early 1830s, almost half the coal was carried *within* the mining districts.[45] While canals undoubtedly made regional economic systems more cohesive, therefore, and canal traffic bound discrete sub-regional resource fields, production sites and markets into what Freeman calls 'a complex, expanding system of symmetric and triangular reciprocities' at a *regional* level, they had little impact on the *inter*-regional coal trade. I suspect Flinn is right to conclude that, with rare exceptions, 'canals did not fundamentally disrupt the regional market economy of the coal industry.'[46] Although Adam Smith had recognized very early on that canals would 'open many new markets' for most commodities, he was adamant that 'the productions of distant coal mines can never be brought into competition with one another.'[47] In 1830, over 50 years later, the Select Committee on the Coal Trade heard detailed evidence from Frederick Page, a proprietor of the Kennet and Avon Canal. In his view,

> The north country coalowners have got the finest means of supply in the world, they have got the sea, and every inch we go by inland navigation we go at great expense . . . We go only 70 or 80 miles from the pit, the north country gentlemen can go 400 or 500 miles at less price.

To support his claims he submitted a map, admittedly imperfect and based on his own observations over the previous seven or eight years, which showed the areas supplied by each of the coalfields. Although the reach of some of the inland fields is impressive, especially when compared with the situation in the seventeenth century when coal was rarely moved more than 10 or 15 miles beyond their boundaries, the continued dominance of the North-East field on the eve of the railway age is striking (Fig. 13.6).[48] By mid-century, however, the railways had effectively captured the inland coal trade; they widened market areas and broke open local monopolies. Even so, the average lead by rail was still only around 30–40 miles. The geography of flows was more complex than this implies, and some companies hauled coal over much longer distances, but most movements continued to be confined to the industrial complexes which had emerged on the main coalfields.[49] These were dense clusters of interacting and interlocking firms: the propulsive centres of the new industrial economy.

For these reasons, Wrigley concludes that the mineral-based energy economy is dominated by *positive feedback*. And in his view, clearly, it was the coronation of King

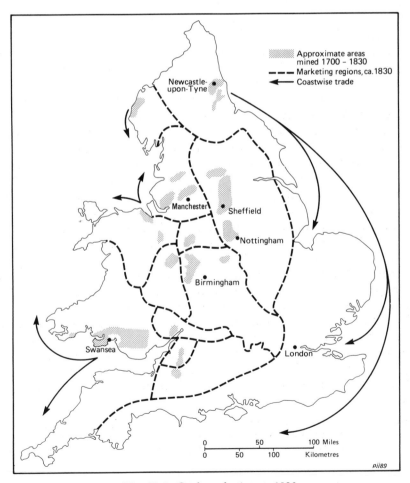

Fig. 13.6. Coal marketing, *c.* 1830.

Coal that made this possible. Indeed, George Stephenson had suggested at the time that henceforth the Lord Chancellor should sit not on a woolsack, the symbol of medieval prosperity, but on a sack of coals.[50]

Innovation Diffusion and the Sinews of Industrialization

The three phases of growth which Wrigley distinguishes are ideal types: in reality they overlapped and the transitions between them were uneven in time and space. In general, however, Wrigley claims that:

> The later eighteenth and early nineteenth centuries . . . emerge as a time of uncertainty when the rising difficulties inherent in organic economies towards the end of a phase of growth threatened to arrest further progress, but were matched by rising opportunities brought into being by the switch to a mineral-based energy economy.[51]

I want to explore this claim in some detail by wiring it to the diffusion of technical innovations. In doing so, I will pay some considerable attention to the economic logic involved, but I do not mean to imply that the calculus of profit and loss was the only consideration to be taken into account. Diffusion was a directed process, to be sure; but it was also a contested one. The new skills and the new divisions of labour which they entailed had important social and cultural implications and the adoption (or otherwise) of these innovations was shaped by a series of struggles around class, gender and status which cannot be reduced to the marionette movements of the economy.

Wrigley's diagnosis presents two possibilities. On the one side, the sector which seems to conform most closely to his chronology is the iron industry. Wrigley presents this as the classic case of being 'saved by the switch', so to speak, but it is by no means open and shut. Some writers have certainly identified an energy crisis in the charcoal iron industry: but they locate it in the seventeenth century, when furnaces were removed from the depleted woodlands of the Weald of Kent and relocated in the forests of South Wales and the north and west of England.[52] Other writers suggest that the increased fuel efficiency of the industry combined with the prudent woodland management policies of inter-regional cartels to at least stabilize the situation on the new sites. Between the end of the sixteenth and the middle of the eighteenth centuries production of pig-iron increased at a rate of around 4 per cent per decade. This may not be spectacular but neither is it the record of an industry in protracted crisis.[53] In the second half of the eighteenth century, however, output soared (from 28,000 tons in 1750–4 to 180,000 tons by 1800) and there is little doubt that this was the result of a switch from charcoal to coal. Abraham Darby had been using a coke-fired furnace to produce pig-iron at Coalbrookdale since 1709, but until the 1750s it was still cheaper to use a charcoal furnace. Darby managed to stay in business through the sale of a new by-product of coke pig-iron, thin-walled castings; he kept his casting technology a closely guarded secret and sold perhaps 70 per cent of his output as cast iron. By the middle of the eighteenth century, however, the cost differential had been reversed: the cost of cutting and coaling wood had increased sharply while the relative cost of coal had fallen. By 1788 there were 53 coke-fired furnaces in operation, heavily concentrated in Shropshire (21) and Staffordshire (7) with secondary clusters in Derbyshire (7) and Yorkshire (6) and in Glamorganshire (6). The balance of pig-iron production had shifted decisively in favour of the coke-

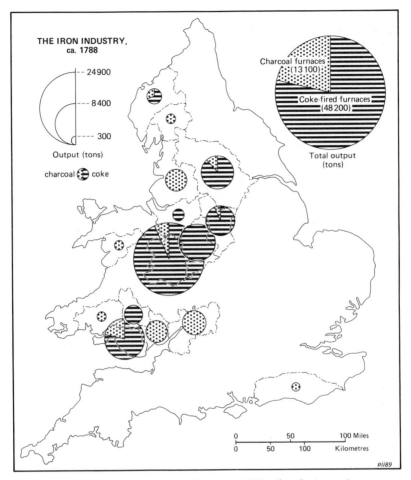

Fig. 13.7. The iron industry, *c.* 1788 (after Scrivenor).

fired furnaces in the West Midlands and South Wales (Fig. 13.7).[54] By this time, too, several ironmasters had successfully used coal in the conversion of pig-iron to bar iron; but it was the rapid diffusion of Henry Cort's puddling process in the 1790s that made the most dramatic impact on the industry.[55] Coal could now be used in both the furnace and the forge and by 1830 the iron industry accounted for almost 20 per cent of total coal sales. This gave a considerable fillip to the coal industry and in particular to the development of the West Midlands and South Wales fields, which were confirmed as the principal seats of the iron industry. To some historians, of course, this is all obvious. 'Drawn by a powerful magnet,' Ashton once claimed, 'the iron industry became localized on the coalfields.' But matters are not quite so simple. It may well be true that by 1820 around 90 per cent of total pig-iron production came from the coalfields: but these same districts were also rich in iron ore so that it is far from easy to sort out the relative locational importance of the two.[56] In fact, there had been a close correlation between furnaces and coal measures ironstone since at least the early eighteenth century, when Johnson claims that most furnaces were within

eight or nine miles of their ore supply.[57] It also seems likely that the 'pull' of coal
lessened from the 1830s—especially once the diffusion of Nielson's hot blast furnace
had reduced coal consumption by around two-thirds[58]—and that the importance of
blackband and coal measures ironstone peaked in the 1840s. From mid-century the
locus of the industry shifted to ore deposits off the coalfields.[59]

Still, the transition at the turn of the century squares reasonably well with Wrigley's
thesis. Yet on the other hand he insists that the key to sustained economic growth
was not the release of *heat* energy (which was the point of both Darby's smelting
process and Cort's puddling process) but a method of deriving *mechanical* energy.[60]
'More than any other single development,' Wrigley contends, the steam engine
'made possible the vast increase in individual productivity which was so striking a
feature of the industrial revolution.'[61] In part, of course, it was the steam engine that
made possible the tremendous expansion of the coal industry. As mines plunged
deeper, so more water had to be pumped out of them. Cutting drainage adits could
be formidably expensive and was often impracticable; horse-gins were slow, expensive to run and not much use beyond 120 feet or so. The first real advance came with
the Newcomen engine, which was first installed in a coal mine in 1712. It could raise
water in vast quantities from far greater depths than any previous technology had
allowed and its diffusion was remarkably rapid (Fig. 13.8). During the 1720s the locus
of innovation was the West Midlands field, the home ground of the most vigorous
salesmen rather than the most obvious market, but soon afterwards the coal-owners
on Tyneside started to invest heavily in the new draining machines. By 1775 a steam
pump was probably a feature of all but the smallest and shallowest collieries in
Britain and the North-East field, with its deep mines and rich reserves, had far and
away the largest share. The vast majority of them were Newcomen engines.[62] Even
after 1769, when Watt patented a steam pump which used a separate condenser to
reduce fuel consumption, the Newcomen engine remained in widespread use.[63]
Although Watt engines became steadily more attractive to coal-owners from the
1790s on, Newcomen engines continued to be installed well into the nineteenth
century. By 1800 there were perhaps as many as 2500 steam engines at work in
Britain and 40 per cent of them were in coal mines.[64]

What fits Wrigley's chronology most convincingly, however, is the invention of a
rotary engine capable of powering machinery directly.[65] The rotary engine had been
developed by 1779, but in 1781–2 Watt patented his Sun and Planet device and
thereafter the Birmingham-based firm of Boulton and Watt took a commanding
lead.[66] For much of the early period Boulton and Watt were not really manufacturers
of steam engines at all: they supplied the plans, the expertise and some of the more
complicated parts but acted more as consulting engineers and middlemen between
their customers and the ironmasters who made most of the parts.[67] The first Sun and
Planet device was applied to an existing engine erected at their own works to power
a forge hammer; the first new engine using the rotative principle was for another
forge hammer, this time at Wilkinson's Staffordshire foundry in early 1783. But
demand from the iron industry was limited and Watt assumed that the main market
would be found in corn mills in London and the south and east of England. As early
as June 1781 Boulton had reported that manufacturers in Manchester (and elsewhere) had gone 'steam mill mad', but Watt expressly asked him 'not to seek for
orders for cotton-mill engines' because 'there are so many mills erecting on powerful

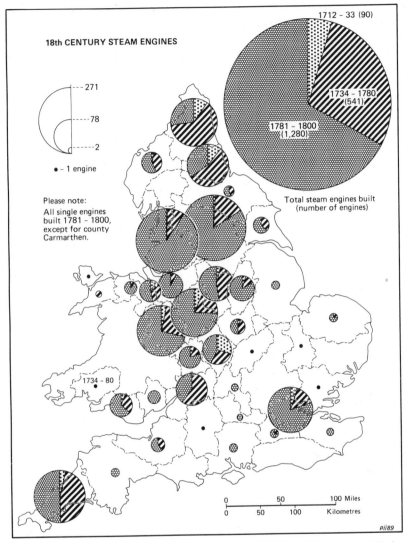

18th CENTURY STEAM ENGINES

1712 - 33 (90)

1734 - 1780 (541)

1781 - 1800 (1,280)

- 271
- 78
- 2

• – 1 engine

Please note:
All single engines
built 1781 - 1800,
except for county
Carmarthen.

Total steam engines built
(number of engines)

1734 - 80

0   50   100 Miles
0   50   100   Kilometres

pjj89

Fig. 13.8. The diffusion of steam engines 1712–1800 (after Kanefsky and Robey).

streams in the North of England that the trade must soon be overdone.'[68] Certainly, the adoption path of the Sun and Planet engine did not follow the familiar S-shaped curve of classical diffusion theory: it showed a steady expansion rather than a dramatic acceleration. And in part this must have been a result of the constraints imposed on the diffusion process by competition from other sources of power.[69] But by 1784 Watt had conceded that his rotary engines were 'applicable to the driving of cotton mills, in every case where the convenience of placing the mill in a town or ready-built manufactory will compensate for the expense of coals and of our premium.'[70] The first Sun and Planet engine was installed in a spinning mill the following year, though even then it was not in the north of England but the Midlands.[71] It was not until 1789 that a Sun and Planet engine was installed in a

Manchester spinning mill, and two years later Boulton and Watt were still complaining that 'Manchester has been backward in adopting our engines.'[72] The situation changed during the 1790s, however, and by the early nineteenth century, when a series of regional clusters of adoption had emerged, Lancashire was easily the most active market, followed by the West Riding, the East Midlands and London (Fig. 13.9).[73] The textile industries constituted the main market—in fact, they contained 1

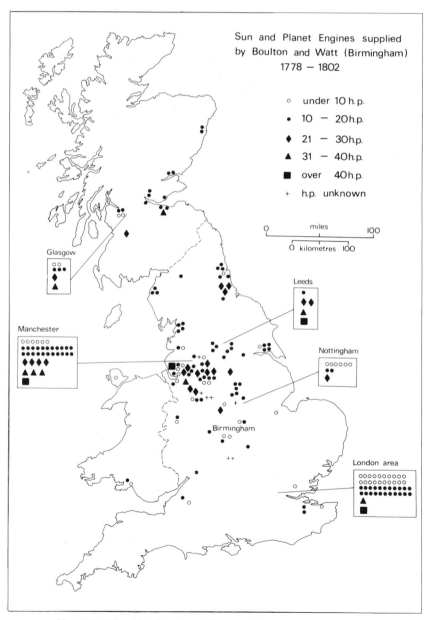

Fig. 13.9. The distribution of Sun and Planet engines, 1802.

in 5 of *all* steam engines in operation by 1800—and there was a clear concentration in the cotton spinning industry.[74]

Yet Wrigley specifically *exempts* the cotton industry from his model—traditionally seen as the pacemaker of the Industrial Revolution—because, like most other textile industries, its expansion coincided with the climax of the advanced organic economy. Its growth involved a deepening division of labour and a widespread application of water-power and so, in many ways, it was 'exploiting old lines of development with a new intensity rather than striking out in a radically different direction.'[75] The cotton industry certainly underwent a spectacular expansion in the closing decades of the eighteenth century.[76] The factory system gained a firm foothold and between 1771 and 1788 over 180 Arkwright-type mills were built in England and Wales alone.[77] Most of them were three or four storeys high, employing between 100 and 200 hands and working 1000 spindles. Yet this tremendous increase in the scale of production required only 10 h.p. per mill, which could be generated by a very modest stream.[78] Larger mills started to appear in the 1790s, running 3000 spindles and requiring 30 h.p., but even some of these relied upon water power. The application of steam power was gathering momentum by then and steam engines were being applied directly to mule-spinning; yet by 1800, on the most charitable of assumptions, steam power was involved in only 25 per cent of all cotton production.[79] Water wheels continued to provide most of the power used in the industry until after 1820 and held their own against steam engines until the late 1830s.[80]

If this means that we have to revise our 'heroic' assumptions about the place of the steam engine in the transformation of the cotton industry, however, it also means that we must revise our assumptions about its role in manufacturing industry more generally. For Musson has shown that 'the "steam revolution" was *predominantly* in cotton' [my emphasis] and that 'British industry [as a whole] had not been revolutionized by the mid-nineteenth century.'[81] To forestall misunderstanding, I should say that this is not to deny the importance of 'the machinery question' which was debated so hotly during the first half of the nineteenth century; the struggles which surrounded it shaped not only the diffusion of many of the technical innovations I have discussed here but also framed the subsequent development of the labour process in other spheres too. The machinery question is usually assumed to have been settled, as a *public* issue at any rate, by the end of the 1840s. But it was by no means settled at the level of the shop floor.[82] There was still considerable space for mechanization (and resistance to mechanization) after 1850:

> As capital-intensive industrialism matured during the first half of the nineteenth century, steam consumption remained at a low level and engine distribution continued to be confined along a narrowly marked frontier.[83]

The frontier moved slowly. By 1879 steam engines supplied 97 per cent of power in the cotton industry and 85 per cent of power in the woollen industry. Yet the textile industries accounted for nearly one-half of all manufacturing horsepower and around one-third of total industrial horsepower.[84] Most manufacturing operations were still unmechanized and whole areas of the industrial economy remained far from the advancing frontier. As mechanization proceeded, it did not so much push back the boundaries of manual labour as create new dependencies between hand-

and steam-powered technologies. In juxtaposing the two in this way, Samuels reminds us, we are speaking 'of *combined* as well as of an *uneven* development. In mid-Victorian times, as earlier in the nineteenth century, they represented *concurrent* phases of capitalist growth, feeding on one another's achievements, endorsing one another's effects.'[85]

Combined and Uneven Development

'New discoveries in metals, mines and minerals,' wrote Defoe in 1726, 'new undertakings in trade, engines, manufactures . . . make England especially show a new and differing face in many places.' In this passage, as elsewhere, Defoe was I think drawing attention not only to changes over time but also to contrasts over space. His remarkable *Tour Through the Whole Island of Great Britain* inaugurated, through its framework of regional circuits and its active sense of process, a distinctively new tradition of topographical writing. Although he said he intended to avoid 'mere geographical description', it is impossible to read his account without recognizing the profound regionalization of the economy: the ways in which, as he put it, some towns 'which are lately increased in trade and navigation, wealth and people' had done so 'because they have some particular trade or accident to trade, which is a kind of nostrum to them, inseparable to the place': the Leeds cloth trade, the Newcastle coal trade and the like.[86] Defoe was obviously not unaware of the advance of industry but, like most writers of his day, he was uninterested in 'pursuing an analysis of the location of industry as the special feature of its progress.'[87] Instead, he regarded trade as the moving force behind the new economic landscape: to G. D. H. Cole the *Tour* was simply 'Britain through tradesman's eyes.' And since no examination of trade could fail to register the signal importance of London, the counterpoint to Defoe's regional thematic was provided by the immense centralizing power of the metropolis, 'this monstrous city' which 'sucks the vitals of trade in this island to itself.'[88]

I now want to show how these two themes were threaded into the industrial space-economy of the late eighteenth and early nineteenth centuries.

Industrialization and Spatial Divisions of Labour

For most of the eighteenth century commentators continued to remark on the growth of specialized manufacturing regions. Adam Smith thought that the most productive and, as it happened, the most recent of these regional economies were the result of a 'natural' (though by no means inevitable) progression from agriculture through manufacturing industry to foreign trade. 'The manufactures of Leeds, Halifax, Sheffield, Birmingham and Wolverhampton' were all, so he said, 'the offspring of agriculture.' Their dynamism exemplified what he took to be the proper symbiosis between town and country: the shuttle between industry in the towns, 'working up the materials of manufacture which the land produces', and agriculture in the countryside enlarged the markets of both and acted as the driving force of economic progress. Other industries had other origins, and in so far as Smith was less sanguine about their long-term prospects he presumably recognized (by implication at any rate) the multiplicity of regional pathways which were opened up or closed off by the growth of specialized manufacturing systems. The parallels between his thesis and modern ecological models of proto-industrialization are, I hope, clear enough.[89] Smith was of course writing before the factory system had secured much of a hold, but the locus of industrialization already coincided with the coalfields. The conjunction was not lost on him. 'All over Great Britain,' he observed, 'manufactures have confined themselves to the coal counties.' But in his view this great confinement was very rarely the direct result of a dependence upon coal. In a few cases, like the iron industry, coal was 'a necessary instrument of trade' and so its availability was a matter of some moment: although even there, as we have seen, its significance was far from straightforward. In all other cases, however, Smith believed that the price of coal affected the location of industry through its effect on the wage bill rather than as a factor of production in its own right. It was coal consumption in the hearths of labouring families that weighed most heavily. 'The price of fuel has so important an influence upon that of labour,' Smith argued, that manufacturers had been attracted to the coalfields by the pleasurable prospect of paying lower wages.[90]

By the mid-1830s and 1840s the spatial divisions of labour brought about by the uneven progress of industrialization and the advance of the factory system had hardened still further. 'Each of the principal branches of English manufacture,' Kohl wrote in 1844, 'has appropriated to itself some particular town or district.' Like most observers, he noticed that 'the limits of the densely peopled manufacturing districts are almost everywhere defined by the extent to which the several coal-fields go.'[91] The coincidence was a leitmotiv in topographical writing of the time and Manchester occupied a central place within the literary landscape. The cotton industry led the way in the application of steam power and the smoke-filled skies of Manchester, of 'Cottonopolis' and 'Coketown', cast a long pall over the contemporary imagination. Napier once described Manchester as 'the chimney of the world' and when de Tocqueville visited the city in the summer of 1835 he found its streets enveloped in 'perpetual fog' and its skies covered by 'a sort of damp smoke':

> The sun seen through it is a disc without rays. Under this half daylight 300,000 human beings are ceaselessly at work. A thousand noises disturb this dark, damp labyrinth . . . The footsteps of a busy crowd, the crunching wheels of machinery, the shriek of steam from boilers, the regular beat of the looms, the heavy rumble of the carts, those are the noises from which you can never escape.

And he had no hesitation in listing among Manchester's many 'favourable circumstances' it having 'close by the largest coal-mines to keep the machines going cheaply.'[92] Modern writers have often said much the same. The steam-powered cotton industry was 'virtually tied to the coalfield'; 'only one [town] beyond the coalfield, Preston, has acquired a substantial cotton industry: only one on the coalfield, St Helens, has failed to do so.'[93] But the smoke sometimes blinds us to the obvious fact that the mills depended upon water to generate the steam (and to facilitate several stages of production). Contemporaries rarely made the same mistake and another portfolio of impressions is readily assembled. Staying in Manchester in 1838, Carlyle was woken at 5.30 a.m. by all the mills starting at once, 'like an enormous mill-race or ocean-tide. The Boom-m-m, far and wide.' Kohl had a similar experience. The clapping of clogs on the early-morning pavements; the striking of the factory clocks; silence. Suddenly:

> All at once, almost in a moment, arose on every side a low, rushing and surging sound . . . It was the chorus raised by hundreds and thousands of wheels and shuttles, large and small, and by the panting and rushing from hundreds of thousands of steam engines.

He remembered standing on a bridge to watch 'the thirsty manufactories' suck up water from the Irwell 'which, dirty as it is, is invaluable to them, and which they pour back into the river in black, brown and yellow currents.' And when he visited one of the most advanced mills in Manchester he found the workmen anxious to show him its 'steam-worked water-engine which commands the whole nine stories of the building and is capable of drenching it with enormous quantities of water in a few minutes.'

> Scarcely, however, had the water entered the pump than numbers of heads were thrust from windows, shouting and gesticulating. We had the steam-engine stopped, and on going in found to our consternation that in a few seconds half a floor had been deluged with water. The plugs of the pipes running through the buildings had been left open, and had thus occasioned this flood among the cotton.[94]

Now I am not suggesting that the one set of images should substitute for the other. Steam-power was obviously important to the cotton industry and there was a marked concentration of cotton mills in areas where the price of coal was low. But, as von Tunzelmann cautions, 'this is far from saying that coal prices were paramount in *determining* [their] location.' In fact, the steam engine did not greatly affect the location of the cotton industry, except in detail: its primary contours had been marked out long before, by the matrix of domestic production and the availability of water power, and the steam engine did little more than etch those outlines in bolder relief, erasing at the margins and thickening at the centre.[95] In other industries, as we have seen, the penetration of steam-power was much more limited and long delayed. In consequence, 'whatever our reconceptions about the great shift of factories from rural hillsides to the city during the industrial revolution . . . they do not correlate with industrial adoption of steam.'[96]

These arguments clearly do not imply the replacement of one explanation by another: spatial divisions of labour were neither produced nor sustained by any central generating mechanism. Indeed, the most important manufacturing city in mid-Victorian Britain fits neither of the two sterotypes sketched in the previous paragraph: most of London's industries relied on hand- or foot-driven machinery. It would have surprised visitors to hear the capital described as a manufacturing city, but if few of them remarked on its industrial importance this was because they had come to see other things. London was dominated by no single industry, and its very heterogeneity contributed directly to the invisibility of metropolitan manufacturing. Yet as late as 1861 more than one in six of all workers in manufacturing industry were employed in London and manufacturing occupied nearly one in three of all workers there. Many of the heavier industries had already moved out, and the most important sectors of the urban economy specialized in second- not first-order production: in clothing not textiles, furniture not timber, printing not paper manufacture. Many of them relied on skilled artisans (London was overwhelmingly a city of small masters) but an increasing number of trades were being casualized: building labourers, shipworkers, dockworkers and others all had to contend with sudden shifts in the demand for their services.[97]

These spatial divisions of labour installed a complex grid of social relations: what Thrift calls 'a patchwork quilt of different but connected production cultures'. That they were *different* is unexceptionable. In Manchester, for example, distinctive working-class cultures had emerged by the middle of the nineteenth century, structured on the one side by a series of accommodations between capital and labour which splintered and eventually subdued the radical movements of the 1830s and 1840s, and on the other by a series of patriarchal assumptions which were sometimes challenged but never seriously threatened by the employment of women in the mills. In London, a more traditional artisan culture persisted, no less patriarchal but increasingly defensive, disturbed by the encroachments of the casual labour market where women were herded into the sweated trades and men fought one another for the half-chance of a half-job.[98] It would no doubt be possible to sieve out still finer gradations: the micro-geographies of the manufacturing districts were far from homogeneous. For this reason the claim that these different cultures were *connected* is more contentious. Several writers have argued that social organization was fractured and divided until the middle of the nineteenth century: that the local community provided the basis for collective action because working people were physically unable to transcend the particularities of place and forge the large-scale systems of indirect relationships supposedly characteristic of class mobilization. Struggles were at best regional, usually local, often personal; the dividing lines were etched more deeply by the uneven development of the industrial economy.[99] I have some sympathy with these claims, and I have already indicated some of the obstacles in the way of inter-regional alliances in the woollen industry. But superimposed over these local discriminations—and to a degree spatch-cocked into them—were more cohesive layers. Production was heavily regionalized and working-class politics firmly rooted in the local milieu: but there were, I think, larger horizons. For many people these must have constituted a largely mental landscape, illuminated by the corresponding societies at the end of the eighteenth century and the spluttering beacons of a radical press in the early nineteenth. But the spatial organization of unions in the 1820s and the contours of Chartism in the 1830s and 1840s (Fig. 13.10) demonstrate that for large numbers of ordinary workers the national scale had a palpable physical reality too, well before the 1850s.[100] They were confronted by a system of domination which, though it too had its local and regional inflections, was also national (and, in quite another sense, international) in its scope. Whatever barriers were in the way of working-class mobilization, we need to remember that many of them were put there by those in positions of economic and political power whose reach was much more extensive than that of the radical artisan or factory-worker.

There is no space to map these dimensions in any detail and I want instead to consider the economic axis around which they were orientated. In doing so, I put on one side some of the most important questions concerning political integration and the territorial structure of the state apparatus: although, as will become obvious, these were affected by (and in turn impacted on) the process of industrialization which remains my primary concern.[101]

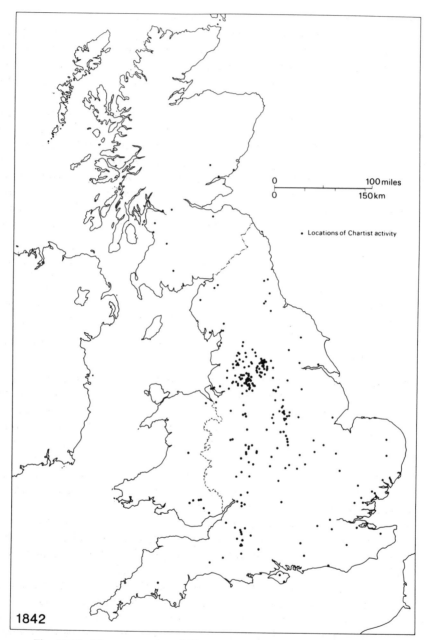

Fig. 13.10. The geography of Chartism, 1842 (after Thompson, 1984).

Industrialization and the Integration of the Space-economy

As Adam Smith knew very well, spatial divisions of labour entail connection as well as difference, integration as well as differentiation. This was not confined to the eighteenth and nineteenth centuries. Specialized regions and systems of inter-regional exchange were two sides of the same early modern coin.[102] But the uneven progress of industrialization restructured pre-existing systems of interaction at a series of different scales.

Towards one end of the spectrum, new city-regions emerged. Like the old county communities, these were integrated through social, cultural and political ties threaded together in the towns, but in the manufacturing districts these were cast in a radically new framework by a mesh of specifically *industrial* linkages. The deepening division of labour and the realization of external economies decisively affected the evolution of interconnected complexes of firms and industries.[103] I have already shown how the domestic system of production spun an intricate network of interdependencies in the West Riding of Yorkshire, and the factory system wove a similar web in Lancashire.

> Manchester, like an industrious spider, is placed in the centre of the web, and sends forth roads and railways towards its auxiliaries, formerly villages but now towns, which serve as outposts to the grand centre of industry . . . An order sent from Liverpool in the morning is discussed by the merchants in the Manchester Exchange at noon, and in the evening is distributed among the manufacturers in the environs. In less than eight days, the cotton spun at Manchester, Bolton, Oldham or Ashton, is woven in the sheds of Bolton, Stalybridge or Stockport; dyed and printed at Blackburn, Chorley or Preston, and finished, measured and packed at Manchester.[104]

If the matrix is extended to include the links with banks and finance houses, with engineering shops and suppliers, then the regional nexus becomes very dense indeed. It was precisely this regional coherence, repeated over and over again, that prompted Langton to argue that the structure of the early industrial space-economy was characterized by 'a growing uniformity of character' within regions—the crystallization of distinctive regional cultures or *mentalités*—and an increasing fragmentation between them. For a time, even London's star was supposedly eclipsed by the rise of these provincial satellites as they began to exert a 'sway over national commerce' hitherto reserved for the capital alone.[105]

Langton's thesis raises two closely connected questions. To what extent is it possible to speak of the integration of the space-economy at scales *other* than the regional between 1750 and 1850? And to what degree did industrialization weaken the centralizing power of London during the same period?

Towards the other end of the spectrum, many of the new industrial economies were integrated into a world market. There may well be room for debate over the direction of causality—whether trade was the offspring of industry or vice versa—but the proportion of industrial output exported rose from 20 per cent (by value) at the opening of the eighteenth century to 35 per cent at its close. These summary figures inevitably understate the importance of export markets for some sectors and some regions, especially the textile industries and the iron industry, but when Wallerstein identifies the period from 1730 to 1840 as the second era of expansion of the capitalist world-economy he is obviously only echoing, in a different vocabulary, what was common knowledge to contemporaries.[106] 'Not an axe falls in the woods of America,' declared one observer in 1812, 'which does not put in motion some shuttle, hammer or wheel in England.' Clothiers in the West Riding looked across the Atlantic with furrowed brow during the American War of Independence and did so again when the wars with France brought Britain into collision with the United States of America. On the Manchester Exchange Kohl was astonished to find that within hours of the arrival of news of the peace with China (in 1842) 'agreements, contracts and purchases of extraordinary number and importance has been transacted . . . upon the strength of it.' Provincial newspapers were full of reports of battles and treaties in these 'far-away places', as Brewer puts it, and institutions like the Manchester Exchange made dozens of newspapers and periodicals available to their members because politics, commerce and credit were increasingly seen to be all of a piece: commercialization (and, with it, the expansion of the world-economy) gave political events an economic importance they had previously lacked. Merchants not only had to attend to fluctuations of the market and read its signals. Together with their clerks and packers they had to know its particularities too. 'Goods must be packed differently for different nations,' Kohl discovered, and 'wares to be carried on the backs of elephants, camels or llamas must be differently packed from those to be conveyed by waggons, canals or railways,'[107] Political and economic geography, of a sort, was thus part of the stock of knowledge drawn on more or less routinely by virtually everyone involved in manufacturing and commerce. If all this indicates that regional consciousness was far from introspective, I suspect that in one sense it simply adds a dimension to Langton's thesis rather than reverses it. The space-economy can still be decomposed into a series of regional systems, now facing outwards through the major estuary ports. But this manoeuvre immediately reveals the central importance of London. It is perfectly true that industrialization gave a tremendous boost to the northern ports, especially Liverpool and Hull, but by the middle of the eighteenth century London had become the warehouse of the world and in the wake of the French wars it pushed aside Paris and even Amsterdam to become, by the early nineteenth century, the financial as well as the physical pivot of the world-economy.[108]

Some commentators thought the same was true of the domestic space-economy. 'If all the interests of England are concentrated in the city of London, which is today the meeting place of all business,' wrote one seasoned French observer in 1815, 'one can say that London is present in the rest of England.'[109] But some historians have argued that the dynamics of the metropolitan economy were so different in character and chronology from those of other regions that a 'deep-seated dualism' came to characterize the space-economy of mid-Victorian Britain. They claim that the industrial economies of the north were increasingly distanced from the booming commercial and financial economy of the metropolitan south and that the latter, autogenerative and by no means dependent on 'transfers and spill-over effects' from the former, became 'the world's first large-scale consumer society.'[110] Strictly speaking, these claims lie largely outside the period with which I am principally concerned, but I think they are overstated and in ways which bear directly on Langton's thesis.[111] For the birth of consumer society belonged to the eighteenth not the nineteenth century; while it owed a great deal to the midwifery of the metropolis, its stirrings were felt far and wide; and although manufacturing in London was increasingly directed towards consumption goods, the consumer society was umbilically tied to the industrial economy.

I cannot develop these propositions in the detail they deserve, and I must confine myself to the principal connections between commercialization and industrialization. In doing so I follow J. H. Plumb, who argued that eighteenth-century England inaugurated 'the first society dedicated to ever-expanding consumption based on industrial production.' If, as he claimed, this 'acceptance of modernity' brought with it a new estimation of 'novelty and newfangledness'—ever-increasing profit is not made in a world of traditional crafts and stable fashions—then, for all the importance of the export market, the wheels of exchange must have been oiled and the friction of distance reduced within the domestic space-economy too. Indeed, several historians have shown that the home market was of strategic importance to the process of industrialization (and, until 1780 at least, perhaps even of greater importance then the export market).[112] London's direct importance varied: for some commodities it was a major centre of distribution, for others it was not.[113] But this is not the sole issue. Commodity flows are clearly of considerable interest; they are the staple of Langton's thesis. But the expansion of industrial capitalism depended not only on the circulation of capital in its commodity form: it also required the constant transformation of capital *between* its commodity and non-commodity forms and the rapid transmission of information to trigger those displacements in time and space.[114] Let me say something about each of them.

Industrialization both depended on and impacted upon the credit system. 'If for much of the eighteenth century Britain was a collection of regional economies,' Brewer remarks, 'then one of the most important ways in which those economies were linked was through the circuit of credit—a route that was inter-regional even if its journey was often via the capital market and mercantile metropolis of London.'[115] In the course of the eighteenth century many of these arrangements were formalized through the correspondent system established between individual country banks and their London agents: according to Pressnell, 'the principal device by which the *underlying economic unity* of the country was given institutional expression' (my emphasis). The system had a primate structure. Inter-regional debts were usually settled through the London account, so that flows short-circuited from the provinces to the metropolitan switchboard and then back out again. The switchboard was rewired in 1773 when the London banks established a joint clearing house to expedite bank to bank transfers. The dominant direction of (short-term) credit movement was from the agricultural counties to the manufacturing districts: what Ashton once famously celebrated as 'the marriage between the thrift of the South and East and the enterprise of the Midlands and the North.' Pressnell considers these connections to have provided a 'considerable degree of structural unity' for what would otherwise have been a peculiarly cellular banking system, but they nevertheless proved to be increasingly vulnerable.[116] After the spectacular financial crisis of 1825–26, when more than 70 banks in England and Wales were forced to suspend payment, the Bank of England established branches in the provinces. Most of them were in the manufacturing districts. Although the Bank retained its monopoly of joint-stock banking until 1833, this was now confined to the metropolitan banking radius which ran 65 miles out of London. Other joint-stock banks were

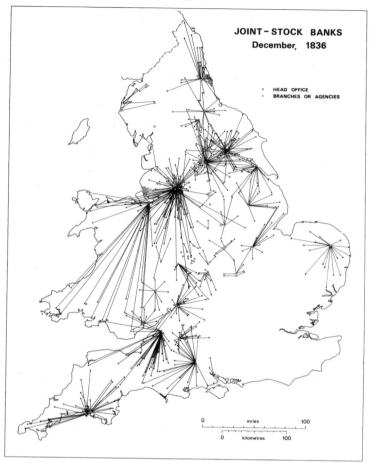

Fig. 13.11. The spatial structure of joint-stock banking, 1836.

allowed to compete with the Bank in the provinces and many of them located close to its branches: hence the locus of joint-stock banking emphatically coincided with the locus of industrialization. Fig. 13.11 shows that the new system had a pronounced regional structure, but a number of banks were already reaching far beyond their home regions—in 1836 the National Provincial Bank (not shown on the map) had 47 widely scattered branches controlled from its London office—and in practice many of the bills of exchange which the joint-stock banks accepted locally were subsequently rediscounted through London.[117] Domestically as well as internationally, therefore, London was the linchpin of the financial system and its institutions were deeply embedded in provincial industrialization.

McKendrick notes that London also 'served as the shop-window for the whole country, the centre of forms of conspicuous consumption which would be eagerly mimicked elsewhere, the place which set the style for the season and saw the hordes of visitors and their retinues of servants carry back those styles to the rest of the country.' This was more than a matter of imitation, of the 'fantastical folly of fashion', because the market was carefully monitored and manipulated by men like Boulton (whose interests lay as much in the intricate 'toy trades' as in the manufacture of steam engines) and Wedgewood (whose eye was fastened as firmly on the mass market for pottery as it was on the aristocratic pursuit of porcelain). Both men depended on rapid information about changes in consumer demand so that production runs could be altered accordingly, and they carefully planned advertising campaigns to launch new lines. The system was so finely tuned that in 1787 Sir John Hawkins reckoned that 'a new fashion pervades the whole of this our island almost as instantaneously as a spark of fire illuminates a mass of gunpowder.' Fashion may have changed with kaleidosopic speed; it may have been ephemeral: but it was far from superficial. 'One must not forget,' McKendrick reminds us, 'that the prosperity of Lancashire cotton manufacturers, London brewers, Sheffield cutlers, Staffordshire potters, the toy makers of Birmingham—and the fortunes of the woollen, linen and silk industries—were based on sales to a mass market.' Those sales depended in turn on the effective transmission of product information and price signals.[118] London was the hub of other kinds of commercial information too. Since 1784 mail-coaches had left the Post Office at eight o'clock every evening and rattled through the night. De Quincey must have indulged his passion for opium to excess to have thought their progress compared with that of 'fire racing along a train of gunpower'—or perhaps he had been reading too much Hawkins—but the speed of communication did accelerate dramatically during the early nineteenth century (Fig. 13.12). Time–space convergence was greater over longer distances and so the manufacturing districts were pulled correspondingly closer to London. This affected more than routine business correspondence because mail-coaches carried more than letters. Inventories and price-lists, orders and invoices, samples and patterns, banknotes and bills were all transmitted by mail. So too were most newspapers. Throughout the eighteenth century the provincial press depended on a regular supply of London newspapers which were systematically gutted for local consumption. Provincial newspapers prided themselves on the 'precisest exactness' of their commercial information. By the middle of the century most of them were regularly printing lists of shipping movements, including arrivals and departures at Bear Quay in London, and from 1756 specialist trade papers started to appear containing detailed extracts from *Lloyd's List*. Provincial newspapers also carried reports on the state of commodity markets in London and elsewhere, including the price of wool, cotton and other industrial raw materials, news of stocks and bankruptcies, together with a high volume of advertisements. All of this has to be kept in proportion: there were cross-posts (which avoided London) and illegal systems of conveyance (which avoided the Post Office); the provincial press fed its readers on more than a warmed-over serving of metropolitan fare and its commentaries often articulated a distinctly different voice. But if the circulation of commercial information was the life-blood of the consumer society, then many of its arteries still radiated from the pulsing heart of the metropolis.[119]

The previous paragraphs have been preoccupied with the connections between London and the rest of England, and yet it is exceptionally difficult to make much sense of the industrialization of England without considering the United Kingdom as a whole. It is not necessary (nor, I think, desirable) to accept the thesis of internal colonialism in its entirety to see that new systems of economic dependency were put in place during the eighteenth and nineteenth centuries and that these were often

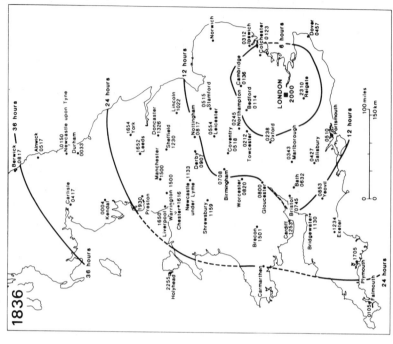

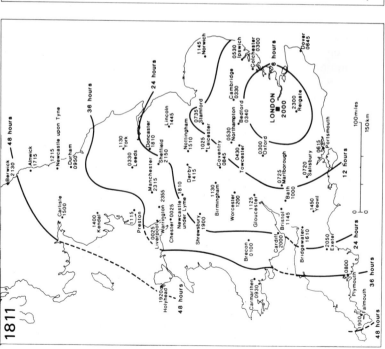

Fig. 13.12. Time–space convergence, 1811–36.

dictated, at first- or second-hand, by London. There were close connections between England and Wales, Scotland and Ireland before then, of course, and the motives behind union were in each case political rather than economic.[120] But Hechter argues that economic integration went cap in hand with political incorporation and that the economic ties between all three countries and England were greatly strengthened by industrialization. Specialized urban-industrial enclaves were established within Wales, Scotland and Ireland which were in many respects more closely tied to the metropolitan core and the world market than to their own hinterlands: Swansea and South Wales; Glasgow and Clydeside; Belfast and east Ulster.[121]

By the eighteenth century Wales was already an export sector of the British economy. For much of the century Williams suggests that the relationship was essentially colonial. English merchant capital penetrated Wales, drawing in profits from the Atlantic slave trade and the Indian empire; the regional economy of North Wales was controlled from Liverpool, that of South Wales from Bristol. But it was a double-edged process. From the 1790s the massive expansion of the coal and iron industries prepared the ground for what Williams calls, only half-jokingly, the 'world empire' of South Wales. In the course of the next century Swansea displaced Bristol and a measure of internal autonomy was secured; eventually South Wales coal would keep the Royal Navy afloat and the din from its clamorous arc of iron- and steelworks would reach around the world. Yet central to the explosive growth of this urban-industrial economy was its profoundly *imperial* character: racked by all the contradictions that such a relationship entails, splintered into multiple fragments by the uneven progress of industrialization, Wales remained bound to the rhythms of an imperial economy orchestrated from London.[122]

The union between England and Scotland was firmly in place by the middle of the eighteenth century. Customs and tariff barriers had been eliminated and patterns of trade reoriented towards England and her colonies. From the 1780s there was a rapid penetration of capitalist industrialization into Scotland, though on a front secured almost single-handedly by the cotton industry, and after 1830 the Scottish economy was increasingly geared to the manufacture of a highly specialized and intricately related mix of heavy industrial products which complemented rather than challenged the industrial economy south of the border. 'The increasing integration or assimilation of Scotland to a system of international trading relations, controlled effectively by the City of London, served to intensify Scotland's distinctiveness as a region of the British economy. Yet the underlying reality of economic clientage remained.'[123]

Ireland presents an altogether different picture. Wales and Scotland were drawn into the British industrial economy in their own right if not exactly on their own terms, whereas the relations between England and Ireland were unequivocally asymmetric. Some writers talk about 'two Irelands' in the eighteenth and nineteenth centuries: one a largely subsistence, rural economy and the other a 'maritime economy' confined to the east coast and closely bound to England by ties of trade and credit. This is a caricature, of course, but like all caricatures it is recognizable. The industrial development of the maritime economy was boosted by the demands of the French wars in the second half of the eighteenth century, only to be cut short by the post-war depression. Belfast alone weathered the storm, through the expansion of linen and flax spinning and, from the middle of the nineteenth century, the spectacular growth of its engineering and shipbuilding industries. But its very dynamism set it still further apart. Those sectors remained directed towards export markets and contemporaries were quick to jibe that Belfast had 'nothing in common with the rest of Ireland': that it was 'in Ireland but not of it.' The most important function of the bulk of the Irish economy was the supply of provisions and labour to buttress the industrialization of the mainland.[124]

To tease out this web of wider connections and to suggest that it was by no means inchoate—that it had a systematic shape, pulled together by the compulsive demands of London—is not to deny the reality of regional economies or the vibrancy of regional cultures. Neither is it to erase the differences etched into the social landscape. Disraeli's Two Nations' were real enough; so was the division between Mrs Gaskell's 'North and South'. But the social topographies mapped by writers like these were, for all their power, simplifications. Behind them was an intricate and changing mosaic of economic interdependencies. Porter is surely right to remark that, in comparison with the rest of Europe, England at the beginning of the eighteenth century was already highly integrated. He is also right to say that it was 'a patchwork of distinctive local communities'; that 'everywhere there were hidden local economies and secret worlds.' Yet in the course of the eighteenth and nineteenth centuries those different worlds increasingly touched, penetrated and transformed one another. 'England was a close-knit country,' Porter claims, 'above all because its economy was interlocking.'[125] To be sure, it will not do to attribute everything to industrialization. But its advance made up a large part of the 'new and differing face' which England displayed in so many places. Many of those places were in England itself; by the close of the nineteenth century many more were not.

References

1. It follows that the inconography of industrialization was equally complex: see Asa Briggs, *Iron Bridge to Crystal Palace: Impact and Images of the Industrial Revolution*, (London, 1979) and Francis Klingender, *Art and the Industrial Revolution*, (London 1947; revised edn, St Albans, 1975).
2. For an early survey see J. Aikin, *A description of the Country from 30–40 miles Around Manchester*, (London, 1795), for a later survey, see Sir George Head, *A Home Tour Through the Manufacturing Districts of England in the Summer of 1835*, (London, 1836; repr. 1968). The only reports on industry which approached the official status of those of the Board of Agriculture were prepared for Select Committees and Commissions in response to specific inquiries on (for example) the hand-loom weavers, factories and social conditions in the mining districts,
3. For a discussion of 'industrialization' and 'Industrial Revolution' as historical categories see Keith Tribe, *Genealogies of Capitalism*, (London, 1981), pp. 101–120. For complementary accounts of the non-revolutionary nature of the Industrial Revolution, drawn from radically different theoretical perspectives, see Raphael Samuel, 'Workshop of the world: steam power and hand technology in mid-Victorian Britain', *History Workshop Jnl*. **3** (1977), pp. 6–72, and N. F. R. Crafts, *British Economic Growth During the Industrial Revolution*, (Oxford, 1985). Fig. 13.1 is derived from Crafts, Economic growth, Table 1.1. The exclusion of women from Crafts' account mirrors their exclusion from the industrial labour force. Female employment in 1841 was concentrated overwhelmingly in domestic service, and many of the new occupations opened up by industrialization (including the better paid jobs in the textile industries) were monopolized by men: see Sylvia Walby, *Patriarchy at work: Patriarchal and Capitalist Relations in Employment*, (Cambridge, 1986), pp. 94–142.

4. F. F. Mendels, 'Protoindustrialization: the first phase of industrialization', *Jnl. of Economic History*, **32** (1972), pp. 241–61.

5. Mendels, 'Proindustrialization'; F. F. Mendels, 'Les temps de l'industrie et les temps de l'agriculture: Logique d'une analyse régionale de la protoindustrialisation', *Revue du Nord*, **63** (1981), pp. 21–33; J. Thirsk, 'Industries in the countryside', F. J. Fisher (ed.), *Essays in the Economic and Social History of Tudor and Stuart England*, (Cambridge, 1961). pp. 70–88. It should also be noted that Mendels' argument was intended to be a general one, although it was based primarily on the geography of proto-industrialization in continental Europe, whereas Thirsk's essay was a more narrowly empirical account of the English case alone. There have been comparatively few studies which have examined these arguments at a regional scale within Britain, but the exceptions include Pat Hudson, 'Protoindustrialization: the case of the West Riding wool textile industry in the eighteenth and early nineteenth centuries', *History Workshop Jnl.* **12** (1981), pp. 34–61 and John Swain, *Industry Before the Industrial Revolution: North-east Lancashire c. 1500–1640*, (Manchester, 1986).

6. K. D. M. Snell, *Annals of the Labouring Poor: Social Change and Agrarian England 1660–1900*, (Cambridge, 1985), pp. 15–66. The domestic system of labour was strongly patriarchal and for all their importance women were invariably assigned to subordinate positions: see Ivy Pinchbeck, *Women Workers and the Industrial Revolution 1750–1850* (London, 1981 edn.) and Maxine Berg, *The Age of Manufacturers: Industry, Innovation and Work in Britain 1700–1820*, (London, 1985), pp. 129–58. That said, industries which went through the proto-industrial phase at least retained some space for female employment, whereas the so-called 'new' industries which developed in the nineteenth century usually excluded women altogether: see Ellen Jordan, 'The exclusion of women from industry in nineteenth-century Britain', *Comparative Studies in Society and History*, **31** (1989), pp. 273–96.

7. Mendels, 'Protoindustrialization'; for a fuller (and correspondingly more sensitive) treatment, see David Levine, *Reproducing Families: the Political Economy of English Population History*, (Cambridge, 1987), pp 111–32.

8. These paragraphs derive from Peter Kriedte, Hans Medick and Jurgen Schlumbohm, *Industrialization before Industrialization: Rural Industry in the Genesis of Capitalism*, (Cambridge, 1981); see also their 'Protoindustrialization on test with the guild of historians: response to some critics', *Economy and Society*, **15** (1986), pp. 254–72. Their arguments depend, in part, upon a reading of Marx and so I should add that Marx made it plain that technical change was only 'labour-saving' in the sense that it increased output per worker and, in so doing, often made whole sections of the labour force redundant (like the hand-loom weavers who lost out to the power loom). But in many (perhaps most) cases mechanization also increased the *intensity* of work for those employed on the new machines. In his speech on the Factories Bill in 1844 Lord Shaftesbury observed that 'machinery has executed, no doubt, the work that would demand the sinews of millions of men; but it has also prodigiously multiplied the labour of those who are governed by its fearful movements.' Marx elaborated Shaftesbury's remarks in *Capital: a Critique of Political Economy*, Vol. 1, (Harmondsworth, 1976 edn.), pp. 533–43.

9. These claims are derived from the Chayanov model of the peasant economy; its (original) application to the Russian peasantry has been heavily criticized and its bearing on the British case is no more straightforward.

10. E. P. Thompson, 'The moral economy of the English crowd in the eighteenth century', *Past and Present*, **50** (1971) pp. 76–136. The moral economy militated against any simple separation between 'work' and 'play' and thereby ensured that the round of daily life was given meaning by more than narrowly material considerations. But the moral economy was by no means monolithic and a careful cultural geography of its conventions and practices is of the first importance: see Dale Williams, 'Morals, markets and the English crowd in 1766', *Past and Present*, **104** (1984), pp. 56–75 and the response by Andrew Charlesworth and Adrian Randall, 'Comment: morals, markets and the English crowd in 1766', *Past and Present*, **114** (1987), pp. 200–20. The horizons of the moral economy reached beyond the eighteenth century and informed (though usually

indirectly) the critical temper of both Owenism and Chartism: see Gregory Claeys, *Machinery, Money and the Millenium: from Moral Economy to Socialism 1815–1860*, (Cambridge, 1987).

11.   Like my summary here, most of the discussion of proto-industrialization has centred on the textile industries. There has been some attention paid to rural metalworkers—see, for example, D. Hey, *The Rural Metalworkers of the Sheffield Region*, (Leicester, 1972), and Marie Rowlands, *Masters and Men in the West Midlands Metalware Trades before the Industrial Revolution*, (Manchester, 1975)—but none of it has bothered much with formal theoretical categories. In the light of the monotonic focus and unilinear logic of existing models of proto-industrialization, therefore, the *variety* of early industrial systems needs some emphasis. For a brilliant review of what she calls 'the polymorphic nature of industrial organization' see Berg, *Age of Manufacturers*.

12.   For more detailed critiques of the concept of proto-industrialization, see R. Houston and K. D. M. Snell, 'Protoindustrialization? Cottage industry, social change and industrial revolution', *Historical Jnl.* **27** (1984), pp. 473–92 and Maxine Berg, Pat Hudson and Michael Sonenscher (eds.), *Manufacture in Town and Country before the Factory*, (Cambridge, 1983), pp. 1–32.

13.   The definitive study is Pat Hudson, *The Genesis of Industrial Capital: a Study of the West Riding Wool Textile Industry c. 1750–1850*, (Cambridge, 1986).

14.   For the general argument see E. P. Thompson, 'Patrician society, plebeian culture', *Jnl. of Social History*, **7** (1974) pp. 382–405, and 'Eighteenth-century English society: class struggle without class?', *Social History*, **3**(2) (1978), pp. 133–65; for a case-study see R. G. Wilson, *Gentlemen Merchants: the Merchant Community in Leeds 1700–1830*, (Manchester, 1971). The argument is not confined to the eighteenth century. Some writers claim that this hostility to manufacturing industry was symptomatic of a much more persistent malaise: that the modernizing impetus of industrialization was shackled by the continued hegemony of an aristocratic and mercantile elite right through the nineteenth and into the twentieth centuries. See, for example, M. J. Wiener, *English Culture and the Decline of the Industrial Spirit 1850–1980*, (Cambridge, 1981) and Perry Anderson, 'The figures of descent', *New Left Review*, **161** (1987), pp. 20–77.

15.   See the simple typology in Charles Tilly, 'Flows of capital and forms of industry in Europe 1500–1900', *Theory and Society*, **12** (1983), pp. 123–42. Again, the examples that follow are all taken from the textile industries, but economic growth and decline affected many other industries in eighteenth-century Britain too. De-industrialization, then as now, was part of a larger restructuring of the space-economy. For a survey see Berg, *Age of Manufacturers*, pp. 108–28.

16.   David Levine, *Family Formation in an Age of Nascent Capitalism*, (London, 1977); Julia de Lacy Mann, *The Cloth Industry in the West of England from 1640 to 1880*, (Oxford, 1971); no modern study of the Lancashire cotton industry has surpassed A. P. Wadsworth and J. de L. Mann, *The Cotton Trade and Industrial Lancashire 1600–1780*, (Manchester, 1931).

17.   Karl Marx, *Capital: a Critique of Political Economy*, Vol. III (New York, 1967 edn.), pp. 334–46.

18.   This section re-works raw materials contained in Derek Gregory, *Regional Transformation and Industrial Revolution: a Geography of the Yorkshire Woollen Industry*, (London, 1982); I have provided a parallel discussion in 'The time-space constitution of the domestic system' (forthcoming).

19.   The sequence of innovation did not correspond to the sequence of production, however, and technical change was characteristically spasmodic; speeding-up one phase of the labour process often produced a bottleneck in another. A smooth sequence could only be restored, in the short term at least, by taking on more hands. In this sense (and, I think, in others) the 'flexibility' of production was as important a structural feature of early industrialization as it seems to be of late-twentieth-century post-Fordist systems of production.

20.   For all that, the fact that clothiers and journeymen from different villages could come together in a concerted regional campaign shows that the domestic system was not incompatible with a supra-local organization: on the contrary, it was precisely because

the time–space constitution of the domestic system entailed extensive transfers and couplings that such close-knit co-operation was possible. What ultimately divided the woollen industry was not distance but different class interests. I have derived the concept of intra- and inter-regional class alliances from David Harvey, *The Urbanization of Capital* (Oxford, 1985), pp. 148–62. The Parliamentary battle and its context is described in detail in Gregory, *Regional Transformation*. The minutes of evidence appended to the *Report of the Select Committee on the State of the Woollen Manufacture in England*, (PP 1806, Vol. III) provide the most vivid testimony of what was at stake and of the state's inability (or unwillingness) to understand the clothiers' concerns. For a discussion of the different discourses involved in those hearings see John Smail, 'New languages for labour and capital: the transformation of discourse in the early years of the Industrial Revolution', *Social History*, **12** (1987), pp. 49–72; and Adrian Randall, 'New language or old? Labour, capital and discourse in the Industrial Revolution', *Social History*, **15** (1990), pp. 195–216. Here too there are parallels to be drawn with Britain in the 1980s.

21. For a narrowly economic interpretation of Luddism, see M. Thomis, *The Luddites: Machine-Breaking in Regency England*, (Newton Abbot, 1970). E. P. Thompson, *The Making of the English Working Class*, (Harmondsworth, 1968) makes the case for a concerted inter-regional campaign which, in places, trembled on the edge of a quasi-revolutionary movement. A more measured view, though one which certainly does not minimize the political significance of Luddism nor its affinities with preceding and succeeding democratic movements, will be found in J. R. Dinwiddy, 'Luddism and politics in the northern counties', *Social History*, **4** (1979), pp. 33–63. Although historians usually confine Luddism to the northern counties, it cannot be completely divorced from earlier disturbances in the West Country: see A. J. Randall, 'The shearmen and the Wiltshire outrages of 1802: trade unionism and industrial violence', *Social History*, **7** (1982), pp. 283–304 and *idem*, 'The philosophy of Luddism: the case of the West of England woollen workers ca. 1790–1809', *Technology and Culture*, **27** (1986), pp. 1–17.

22. See Hudson, *Genesis*, pp. 76–81. For a detailed account of the rise of the factory system see D. T. Jenkins, *The West Riding Wool Textile Industry 1770–1835: a Study of Fixed Capital Formation*, (Edington, 1975), pp. 1–48. Outside the woollen industry the most ingenious co-operative strategy that I know took place in Coventry, where in the middle years of the nineteenth century domestic artisans linked their cottages and workshops to communal steam engines: see John Prest, *The Industrial Revolution in Coventry*, (London, 1960), pp. 96–135 and S. R. H. Jones, 'Technology, transaction costs and the transition to factory production in the British silk industry 1700–1870', *Jnl. of Economic History*, **47** (1987), pp. 71–96.

23. J. Ginswick (ed.), *Labour and the Poor in England and Wales 1849–1851*. Vol. III: *The Mining and Manufacturing Districts of South Wales and North Wales*, (London, 1983), pp. 15–16. The identity of the author is unknown. Other visitors to ironworks used different but no less extravagant metaphors. When the Duke of Rutland visited Cyfartha in 1797 he said he 'never saw anything that gave me more the idea of the infernal regions' and an Italian traveller coming upon Coalbrookdale in the 1820s similarly compared his journey to a 'descent to the infernal regions': Alan Birch, *The Economic History of the British Iron and Steel Industry 1784–1879*, (London, 1967), pp. 58–84.

24. Head, *Home Tour*, p. 184.

25. In Greek mythology Prometheus stole fire from the gods for the benefit of humankind. The two modern authors invoked here are David Landes, *The Unbound Prometheus: Technological Change and Industrial Development in Western Europe from 1750 to the Present*, (Cambridge, 1969), and W. W. Rostow, *The Stages of Economic Growth: a Non-Communist Manifesto*, (2nd edn.) (Cambridge, 1971). It is only fair to add that Landes provides a far more scrupulous account than Rostow.

26. E. A. Wrigley, 'The supply of raw materials in the Industrial Revolution', *Economic History Review*, **15** (1962), pp. 1–16; *idem*, *Continuity, Chance and Change: the Character of the Industrial Revolution in England*, (Cambridge, 1988). There are significant differences of emphasis between these two accounts but I do not think my composite distorts Wrigley's essential thesis.

27. Adam Smith, *The Wealth of Nations*, Vol. 1 (Oxford, 1976 edn.), p. 13.

28. J. G. Kohl, *England and Wales*, (London, 1844; repr. 1968), p. 5; see also Berg, *Age of Manufacturers*, pp. 287–314. Smith's point was subsequently sharpened considerably by Marx who provided an incisive discussion of the detailed division of labour in *Capital*, Vol 1, pp 455–470. For a commentary, see Ali Rattansi, *Marx and the Division of Labour*, (London, 1982).

29. These innovations were not once and for all substitutions: they had their own historical geographies and were themselves subject to continued technical change. Watermills were widely used in medieval Britain, for example, but the scale and speed of transmission increased significantly during early industrialization: see G. N. Tunzelman, *Steam Power and British Industrialization to 1860*, (Oxford, 1978), pp. 164–9.

30. Wrigley, *Continuity*, p. 51. Although Wrigley's basic argument is no doubt correct, water power was subject to considerable seasonal variation which made it difficult for manufacturers to control their supply schedules: see, for example, T. S. Ashton, *Iron and Steel in the Industrial Revolution*, (Manchester, 1963 edn.), pp. 99–100 and Gregory, *Regional Transformation*, pp. 68–70, 208–10.

31. J. U. Nef, *The Rise of the British Coal Industry*, (London, 1932), p. 161; J. H. Clapham, *An Economic History of Modern Britain: the Early Railway Age 1820–1850*, (Cambridge, 1930 edn.), p. 78. Both authors noted that Sombart had previously suggested that early capitalism might have foundered completely as a result of its chronic energy crisis: Werner Sombart, *Der Moderne Kapitalismus*, Vol. 11 (Leipzig, 1902), pp. 1138–40.

32. On road haulage during early industrialization see J. A. Chartres and G. L. Turnbull, 'Road transport', in Derek Aldcroft and Michael Freeman (eds.), *Transport in the Industrial Revolution*, (Manchester, 1983), pp. 64–99; the corrections proposed by Dorian Gerhold, 'The growth of the London carrying trade, 1681–1838', *Economic History Review*, **41** (1988), pp. 392–410 principally concern the carriage of finished products. On the turnpike system see Eric Pawson, *Transport and Economy: the Turnpike Roads of Eighteenth-Century Britain*, (London, 1977).

33. Smith, *Wealth of Nations*, Vol 1, p. 32. The pre-eminent account of river navigation in the pre-canal age is still T. S. Willan, *River Navigation in England 1600–1750*, (Oxford, 1936). Despite its title, J. T. Ward, *The Finance of Canal-Building in Eighteenth-Century England*, (Oxford, 1974), pp. 1–17 also provides an account of river improvements in the seventeenth and eighteenth centuries. Although there were several highly successful schemes (notably on the Aire and Calder), Ward implies that the extension of river navigation was slower and more limited than Willan envisaged.

34. B. L. C. Johnson, 'The charcoal iron industry in the early eighteenth century', *Geographical Jnl.* **67** (1951) pp. 167–77. These flows were greatly facilitated by the existence of a series of interlocking inter-regional cartels within the industry, notably (but not exclusively) the Foley partnerships.

35. Wrigley, 'Supply', p. 7.

36. Wrigley, *Continuity*, p. 57.

37. *Ibid.* p. 57; Kohl, *England and Wales*, p. 78. Some contemporaries had (mistakenly) anticipated a more indirect effect too. The fortunes of most canals were closely tied to coal and as more canals were built, so the argument went, fewer horses would be required and land which had grown hay would then revert to wheat: see, for example, J. Phillips, *A General History of Inland Navigation*, (London, 1803 edn.), pp. 133–4.

38. See H. C. Darby, 'The clearing of the English woodlands', *Geography*, **36** (1951), pp. 71–83; M. Williams, 'The enclosure and reclamation of wasteland in England and Wales in the eighteenth and nineteenth centuries', *Transactions of the Institute of British Geographers*, **51** (1970), pp. 55–69. I suspect the counterfactual argument is the decisive one: so much woodland had been cleared, in fact, that during the eighteenth century extensive forestry projects were encouraged in Cardiganshire, Gloucestershire, Northumberland, Perthshire and elsewhere. For a wider perspective on these developments see Stephen Daniels, 'The political iconography of woodland in later Georgian England', in Denis Cosgrove and Stephen Daniels (eds.), *The Iconography of Landscape:*

Essays on the Symbolic Representation, Design and Use of Past Environments, (Cambridge, 1988), pp 43–82 and Keith Thomas, *Man and the Natural World: Changing Attitudes in England 1500–1800*, (London, 1983), pp. 198–212.

39. Wrigley, *Continuity*, p. 26. Wrigley makes much of W. S. Jevons, *The Coal Question*, (London, 1864) but Jevons was in fact already (albeit prematurely) alarmed at the prospective exhaustion of coal reserves.

40. M. W. Flinn, *The History of the British Coal Industry* Vol. 2: *1700–1830: The Industrial Revolution*, (Oxford, 1984); B. R. Mitchell, *Economic Development of the British Coal Industry 1800–1914*, (Cambridge, 1984); Sidney Pollard, 'A new estimate of British coal production 1750–1850', *Economic History Review*, **33** (1980), pp. 212–35. The regional geography mapped in Fig. 13.5 is complicated still further by sub-regional variations within each coalfield: for a particularly clear illustration see John Langton, *Geographical Change and Industrial Revolution: Coalmining in South-West Lancashire 1590–1799*, (Cambridge, 1979).

41. Wrigley, 'Supply, pp. 3, 7. Coalfields are self-evidently areal resources but Wrigley's point is that their *exploitation* is essentially punctiform. For much of the eighteenth century the ideal-typical case involved coal being raised to the surface at a limited number of pit-heads from which tracks or waggonways led down to water-side staithes. But the reality was shaped by more than the geometry of conventional location theory. On Tyneside coal-owners routinely used their way-leaves to block off their rivals' access to the staithes and so exclude them from the lucrative coastwise trade: see Flinn, *History*, pp. 160–2 and Peter Cromar, 'The coal industry on Tyneside 1771–1800: oligopoly and spatial change', *Economic Geography*, **53** (1977), pp. 79–94. The relations between resource exploitation and transportation were thus often more complex than Wrigley allows. In any event, transport systems are not shaped by the supply of raw materials alone and when it came to marketing finished products Wrigley's thesis could easily be reversed. As the home market grew more extensive, so a transport system was required to serve 'an enormous variety of locations over a multitude of routes': see Michael Freeman, 'Introduction', in Aldcroft and Freeman (eds.), *Transport*, pp. 6–10.

42. Nef, *Coal industry*, pp 101–4. Nef insists that this was not as restrictive as it seems. Over large areas of the interior there was 'scarcely a spot not within a morning's ride of a working coal pit' so that even in the late seventeenth century many towns could (and did) receive coal overland at a lower price than that paid for water-borne coal in London. If Nef's calculations are correct, perhaps 40 per cent of total output in 1700 was marketed overland and around 10 per cent shipped by river (principally along the Tyne and Wear—arms of the North-East coastwise trade—and the Severn and the Trent); the rest went by sea.

43. P. M. Sweezy, *Monopoly and Competition in the English Coal Trade 1550–1850*, (Cambridge, Mass., 1938). At the start of the eighteenth-century London alone accounted for almost two-thirds of coal shipments from the North-East and the metropolitan share was still above half by its close. Much of the coal was burned in domestic hearths and, in consequence, air pollution had been a matter of public concern since at least the seventeenth century.

44. Arthur Young, *Elements and Practice of Agriculture*, Vol. 11 (London, 1818), p. 135.

45. Gerard Turnbull, 'Canals, coal and regional growth during the industrial revolution', *Economic History Review*, **40** (1987), pp. 537–60; Charles Hadfield, *Canals of the West Midlands*, (Newton Abbot, 1966), p. 92.

46. Michael Freeman, 'Transport', in John Langton and R. J. Morris (eds.), *Atlas of Industrializing Britain 1780–1914*, (London, 1986), p. 86; Flinn, *History*, p. 188. The dynamism of these regional economic systems needs some emphasis, and perhaps more than Flinn allows: see Turnbull, *Canals*. For a fine case-study see John Langton, 'Liverpool and its hinterland in the late eighteenth century', in B. L. Anderson and P. M. S. Stoney (eds.), *Commerce, Industry and Transport: Studies in Economic Changes on Merseyside*, (Liverpool, 1983), pp. 1–25.

47. Smith, *Wealth of Nations*, Vol. 1, pp. 163, 185.

48. *Report of the Select Committee on the State of the Coal Trade*, (PP. 1830, Vol. VIII), p. 293. Market areas at the end of the seventeenth century are mapped in Nef, *Coal industry*, facing p. 19; inland collieries with access to the Severn or the Trent could, of course, ship coal much further than 15 miles. Market areas in the early nineteenth century are mapped in PP 1830, VIII which was indeed published on the eve of the railway age: the Liverpool and Manchester Railway opened in 1830.

49. G. R. Hawke, *Railways and Economic Growth in England and Wales 1840–1870*, (Oxford, 1970), pp. 157–86. London continued to depend on the coastwise trade but it was increasingly drawing its supplies by rail from the East Midlands, Yorkshire and South Wales fields; 1867 was the first year in which more coal was carried to London by rail than by sea. For a discussion of market areas in the second half of the nineteenth century see M. J. Freeman, 'Introduction', in Michael J. Freeman and Derek H. Aldcroft (eds.), *Transport in Victorian Britain*, (Manchester, 1988), pp. 1–56, especially Figs. 7 and 8.

50. Brian Lewis, *Coal Mining in the Eighteenth and Nineteenth Centuries*, (London, 1971), p. 15. The dominance of positive feedback presumably does not preclude the spasmodic crises which were a chronic feature of the economic landscape of early-nineteenth-century Britain. I assume that Wrigley's point is double-headed: (i) economic growth was now released from the shackles of the organic economy over the *long* term and (ii) the crises which punctuated the growth curve of the new economy no longer centred on the supply of *energy*.

51. Wrigley, *Continuity*, p. 115.

52. Wrigley, 'Supply', p. 5; Ashton, *Iron and steel*; B. Thomas, 'Was there an energy crisis in Great Britain in the seventeenth century?' *Explorations in Economic History*, **23** (1986), pp. 124–52.

53. M. W. Flinn, 'The growth of the English iron industry 1660–1760', *Economic History Review*, **11** (1938), pp. 144–53; G. Hammersley, 'The charcoal iron industry and its fuel', *Economic History Review*, **26** (1973), pp. 593–613; P. Riden, 'The output of the British iron industry before 1870', *Economic History Review*, **30** (1977), pp. 442–59.

54. Even so, entry barriers to the coke-iron industry were high and while the flow of resources into the coke-fired sector was constrained charcoal ironmasters could continue in production; of the 70-odd charcoal furnaces in operation in the middle of the eighteenth century, 24 were still in blast in 1788 (12 of them in South Wales and the south-west of England). See C. K. Hyde, *Technological Change and the British Iron Industry 1700–1870*, (Princeton, 1977), pp. 53–68, and Harry Scrivenor, *History of the Iron Trade*, (London, 1854; reprinted 1967), p. 87.

55. Hyde, *Technological Change*, pp. 88–92.

56. Ashton, *Iron and Steel*, p. 100; cf. Howard G. Roepke, *Movements of the British Iron and Steel Industry 1720–1951*, (Urbana, Ill., 1956), pp. 24–32.

57. Johnson, 'Charcoal iron industry'.

58. Neilson's original patent was taken out in 1828 but the process was not perfected until 1834. The first successful hot blast took place at the Clyde ironworks and by 1836 all the Scottish ironworks had adopted the process. Its diffusion in England and Wales was much slower. Some ironmasters remained sceptical about its technical merits and in the Midlands in particular there were fears that its wholesale adoption would lead to a bloody price war. But these considerations cannot account for the marked regional variations in its diffusion. Several contemporaries claimed that the rate of adoption was simply a function of the quality of coal. In regions where coal had a low carbon content ironworks using the old process had to consume huge quantities of coal to produce coke: the hot blast used raw coal instead of coke, and so ironmasters in those regions had much more to gain from the fuel savings made possible by the new process. Hence diffusion was most rapid in Staffordshire, Yorkshire and Derbyshire and much slower in South Wales, where one in six blast furnaces had adopted the new process by 1839. See Birch, *Iron and Steel*, pp. 179–86; Hyde, *Technological Change*, pp. 146–59; Scrivenor, *Iron Trade*, pp. 259–64; A. H. John, *The Industrial Development of South Wales 1750–1850*, (Cardiff, 1950), p. 156.

59. Roepke, *Movements*, pp. 39, 48–51. Naturally, these remarks about the locational importance of coal do nothing to minimize its economic significance. In 1873 *Griffiths' Guide to the Iron Trade of Great Britain*, (Newton Abbot, 1967 edn.), pp. 184–5 included this extraordinary paean to coal: 'Our gracious Queen may justly boast of the gold of Australia, the precious diamonds of the Cape, the indigo and opium, and of late the cotton and jute, of India, but her vast dominions, either at home or abroad, are unable to furnish any single staple commodity or manufacture which can compete in value and national importance with the coal annually raised in the United Kingdom.'

60. Some historians insist that the best results from coke smelting and puddling waited on the steam engine to replace the comparatively inefficient water-driven bellows: Ashton, *Iron and Steel*, p. 97 and H. R. Schubert, *History of the British Iron and Steel Industry from c. 450 BC to AD 1775*, (London, 1957), p. 333. Hyde, *Technological Change*, pp. 69–75 thinks these claims are exaggerated, but he does concede that the steam engine 'served to speed diffusion of the new technique.'

61. Wrigley, 'Supply,' p. 12.

62. John Allen, 'The introduction of the Newcomen engine from 1710–1733', *Transactions of the Newcomen Society*, **42** (1969–70), pp. 169–90, **43** (1970–71), pp. 199–202, **45** (1972–73) pp. 233–6; John Kanefsky and John Robey, 'Steam engines in eighteenth-century Britain: a quantitative assessment', *Technology and Culture*, **21** (1980), pp. 161–86; Flinn, *History*, pp. 110–28.

63. In fact Boulton & Watt were reluctant to have their engines erected in coal mines and they concentrated many of their efforts on the Cornish tin-mines instead. The reason was simple: they based their fee (or 'premium') on a one-third share of the savings in fuel achieved by their new engine, and since coal at the pit-head was very cheap the savings and hence the premiums were correspondingly small. Watt once suggested that where coal was cheap the premium should rise to one-half, but nothing came of it. See John Lord, *Capital and Steam Power 1750–1800*, (London, 1923; reprinted 1966), p. 160 and Eric Roll, *An Early Experiment in Industrial Organization: a History of the Firm of Boulton & Watt 1775–1805*, (London, 1930; reprinted London, 1968), pp. 30–1. As a general discussion of the diffusion of steam power Lord's study is now hopelessly dated, but if it is supplemented by Roll's careful account it remains a useful survey of some aspects of Boulton & Watt's operations.

64. Kanefsky and Robey, 'Steam engines'.

65. This is where Wrigley's thesis intersects with Marx's claim that the steam engine 'as it continued to be down to 1780 did not give rise to any industrial revolution. It was, on the contrary, the invention of machines that made a revolution in the form of steam engines necessary': Marx, *Capital*, Vol. 1, p. 497.

66. In fact Watt patented five devices for obtaining rotary motion and used the Sun and Planet version until 1802. The partnership between Boulton and Watt had begun in 1775 and by the end of the eighteenth century the company was responsible for more than ten times as many engines nationally as its nearest rivals, Bateman & Sherratt, but it by no means had a monopoly (cf. Lord, *Capital*, p. 147). There were many other engin-makers, Watt's engines were extensively pirated and the Newcomen engine could itself be converted to rotary motion. By 1800 Boulton & Watt's market share of all engines was around 20 per cent: pumping engines accounted for one-third of their output and rotary engines for the remaining two-thirds. See Kanefsky and Robey, 'Steam engines'.

67. Boulton & Watt usually recommended John Wilkinson, whose firm had foundries at Broseley (Shropshire), Bradley, near Bilston (Staffordshire) and Bersham, near Wrex-ham (Denbighshire); Wilkinson's chief rival was the Coalbrookdale group of firms. For an indication of the wider web of industrial linkages during the early period see Roll, *Early experiment*, pp. 55–6, and Ashton, *Iron and Steel*, pp. 67–68. Boulton & Watt established their own foundry at Soho, on the bank of the Birmingham Canal at Smethwick, in 1795–6. Partly in response to pressure from their customers, they had been making an increasing proportion of the parts themselves for some time. But the impending expiration of Watt's patent imposed a particular urgency: commercial

survival demanded a more substantial movement into production. Even so, they continued to rely on local foundries for some of the smaller parts for at least another five years. See Roll, *Early Experiment*, pp. 149–66.

68. P. Mantoux, *The Industrial Revolution in the Eighteenth Century*, (London, 1964 edn.), p. 334. Their caution meant that Boulton & Watt did not supply the engine for the first Manchester cotton mill to be powered directly by steam. The mill in question was owned by Richard Arkwright, who had made several abortive (and, it must be said, brusque) approaches to Boulton & Watt before he obtained rotary motion from a Newcomen-type engine in June 1783. His success was short-lived, however, and he abandoned the enterprise in October of the same year. Later that month Boulton urged that 'if we were to receive an order for a mill engine at Manchester it would do us no harm as it would show that there are other men in the world almost as ingenious in the engine way as Mr Arkwright and might be a useful example.' Arkwright was not the only one to have his fingers burned: the Peels, the Cartwrights and a number of other manufacturers were also involved in costly failures with early steam engines. See Wadsworth and Mann, *Cotton Trade*, pp. 490–1; Jennifer Tann, 'Richard Arkwright and technology', *History*, **58** (1973), pp. 29–44; S. D. Chapman, *The Cotton Industry in the Industrial Revolution*, (London, 1987 edn.), pp. 18–19.

69. And other engines: one of the reasons it took Boulton & Watt so long to break into the Lancashire market (apart from their initial reluctance to do so) was competition from local engine-makers, most of whom were using pumping engines to return water above an overshot wheel. See A. E. Musson and Eric Robinson, *Science and Technology in the Industrial Revolution*, (Manchester, 1969), pp. 393–426. The diffusion process also reflected major internal constraints on expansion, including a chronically irregular cash flow during the early period and shortages of both skilled workers at the Soho Foundry and engine erectors on site. It seems to have been the sons of the two original partners who finally succeeded in putting the company on a sound basis: Roll, *Early Experiment*, pp. 165, 268–270.

70. Mantoux, *Industrial Revolution*, p. 334. The premium charged for rotary engines was based on horse-power not on coal saved (cf. note 55) and was usually higher for London than provincial customers; Roll, *Early Experiment*, pp. 116, 240–1.

71. Robinsons mill in Popplewick (Nottinghamshire). In fact, this case simply confirms the point about competition from other sources of power. Robinsons only installed the steam engine in case they lost a lawsuit against Lord Byron over water-rights; the engine was not an unqualified success and as soon as the case was settled satisfactorily they tried to sell it. See S. D. Chapman, 'The cost of power in the Industrial Revolution', *Midland History*, **1** (1970), pp. 1–23; Tann, 'Richard Arkwright'.

72. Musson and Robinson, *Science and Technology*, pp. 405, 410.

73. This account is derived from lists contained in Birmingham City Library: Boulton & Watt MSS. Jennifer Tann's superb work has shown that these lists are not entirely reliable, however, so that Fig. 13.9 can only be a rough guide to the geography of adoption. For an excellent regional case-study see Jennifer Tann, 'The employment of power in the West of England wool textile industry 1790–1840', in N. B. Harte and K. G. Ponting (eds.), *Textile History and Economic History: Essays in Honour of Miss Julia de Lacey Mann*, (Manchester, 1973), pp. 196–224.

74. Kanefsky and Robey, 'Steam engines'. Cartwright patented a power loom in 1786–8 but the general adoption of power-loom weaving was delayed until the early 1820s and 1830s. See Duncan Bythell, *The Handloom Weavers*, (Cambridge, 1969).

75. Wrigley, 'Supply,' pp. 12–14; *Continuity*, pp. 78–9.

76. How spectacular is a matter of some debate. Crafts, *British Economic Growth*, pp. 21–3 claims that the rate of growth of the cotton industry was exceptionally fast. He estimates that its real output grew by 4.6 per cent (1760–70), 6.2 per cent (1770–80), 12.8 per cent (1780–90) and 6.7 per cent (1790–1801). The median sectoral growth rate hovered between 1.3 and 1.7 per cent over the same period. Although Chapman, *Cotton Industry*, pp. 54–60, raises some plausible doubts about these figures, he still concludes that the cotton industry made an outstanding contribution to the growth of the British econ-

omy. It counted for comparatively little until the middle of the eighteenth century, but by the opening of the nineteenth it had overhauled the woollen industry, the traditional staple of the industrial economy.

77. At least 44 were built in Lancashire, 36 in Yorkshire, 27 in Derbyshire, 19 in Nottingham-shire and 15 in Cheshire; the rest were widely scattered. Most of the mills are mapped in S. D. Chapman, 'The Arkwright mills—Colquhoun's census of 1788 and archaeological evidence', *Industrial Archaeology Review*, **6** (1981–82), pp. 5–26. The typical Arkwright mill was valued at around £3000; in the domestic woollen industry, by contrast, a fulling mill would usually be valued at around £100–200 and a collection of workshops rarely more than £500. For more general discussions see *idem*, 'Fixed capital formation in the British cotton industry 1770–1815', *Economic History Review*, **23** (1970), pp. 235–66; D. T. Jenkins, *West Riding*, pp. 139–90.

78. In fact the water-frame was originally designed as a small machine working 48 spindles by hand. Berg claims it was only Arkwright's patent that confined it to large-scale production since Arkwright refused a licence to anyone without a thousand-spindle mill. But Arkwright's patents were infringed by a number of manufacturers, suspended in 1781 and, after a protracted series of legal battles, finally set aside in 1785, so that their effect was evidently limited. In any case, the capacity of the water-frame steadily increased: it was using 72 spindles by the late 1780s and 120 by the end of the century. See Berg, *Age of Manufactures*, p. 241; Chapman, 'Arkwright Mills', p. 10; R. S. Fitton and A. P. Wadsworth, *The Strutts and the Arkwrights 1758–1830: a Case Study of the Early Factory System*, (Manchester, 1958), pp. 81–6.

79. Chapman, 'Fixed capital'. The mule was a development of the spinning jenny (which usually worked around 60–80 spindles). It was originally incorporated within the putting-out system and until the late 1780s worked up to 144 spindles by hand. The application of water power in 1790 and of steam power a few years later increased the number of spindles and allowed the machines to be operated in pairs: productivity immediately soared. For a comparison of the costs and benefits involved in the water-frame and the steam-powered mule, see von Tunzelmann, *Steam Power*, pp. 176–9.

80. Chapman, 'Cost of power'; *idem*, 'Cotton industry'. In 1838 steam engines supplied around 75 per cent of power in the textile industries (78 per cent in the cotton industry and 55 per cent in the woollen industry); in 1850 they supplied 80 per cent of power in the textile industries (86 per cent in the cotton industry and 61 per cent in the woollen industry).

81. A. E. Musson, 'Industrial motive power in the United Kingdom 1800–1870', *Economic History Review*, **29** (1976), pp. 415–39; see also von Tunzelmann, *Steam Power*, pp. 179, 224, 289.

82. Maxine Berg, *The Machinery Question and the Making of Political Economy 1815–1848*, (Cambridge, 1980); Samuel, 'Workshop', pp. 9–12. The machinery question is usually framed by notations of class, which were of obvious and continuing importance and which were as much part of the geography of industrialization as any 'logic of capital': see Derek Gregory 'Contours of crisis? Sketches for a geography of class struggle in the early Industrial Revolution in England', in Alan R. H. Baker and Derek Gregory (eds.), *Explorations in Historical Geography: Interpretative Essays*, (Cambridge, 1984), pp. 68–117. But the machinery question also entailed assumptions about gender and sexuality which were no less important in shaping the geography of industrialization: see Jane Humphries, '. . . "The most free from objection": the sexual division of labour and women's work in nineteenth-century England', *Jnl. of Economic History*, **47** (1987), pp. 929–49.

83. Dolores Greenberg, 'Reassessing the power patterns of the Industrial Revolution: an Anglo-American comparison', *American Historical Review*, **87** (1982), pp. 1237–61.

84. These figures are based on Kanefsky's corrections of Musson's original calculations: John Kanefsky, 'Motive power in British industry and the accuracy of the 1870 Factory Return', *Economic History Review*, **32** (1979), pp. 360–75. 'Total industrial horsepower' includes power used in mines, waterworks, gasworks, etc.

85. Samuel, 'Workshop', pp. 57–60; see also Duncan Bythell, *The Sweated Trades: Outwork in Nineteenth-Century Britain*, (London, 1978).

86. Daniel Defoe, *A Tour Through the Whole Island of Great Britain*, (London, 1927 edn.), Vol. 11 p. 535, Vol. 111, Preface. The *Tour* was first published between 1724 and 1726. It was subsequently revised by Samuel Richardson and others—the last edition being published in 1779, long after Defoe's death—but all of these 'revisions' depart substantially from the spirit of Defoe's original and turn it into an antiquarian guidebook. In his introduction to the first edition, G. D. H. Cole remarked that 'No one is likely to accuse Defoe of a passion for accuracy.' Even so, Cole conceded that he could be 'a highly competent observer' and in my view Defoe's account remains an indispensable source for the mood of much of early-eighteenth-century Britain. A rather more sober companion is J. H. Andrews, 'Some statistical maps of Defoe's England', *Geographical Studies*, **3** (1956), pp. 33–45.

87. Maxine Berg, 'Political economy and the principles of manufacture', in Berg, Hudson and Sonenscher (eds.), *Manufacture*, pp. 33–58. As befits the collection in which her essay appears, Berg confines the meaning of 'location' to the division between town and country; although she is more sensitive to the *regional* geography of industrialization than most historians, she does not accord it any systematic analysis: see Berg, *Age of Manufacturers*.

88. Defoe, *Tour*, Vol. 1, p. 43.

89. Smith, *Wealth of nations*, Vol. 1, p. 409; for a modern (and more comprehensive) version, see E. L. Jones, 'The agricultural origins of industry', *Past and Present*, **40** (1968), pp. 128–42. Jones emphasizes inter-regional rather than intra-regional complementarities but the logic is substantially the same. 'The crux was the enlargement of mutual, reciprocal markets: for industrial goods among the cash-cropping farm population and for grain among workers in rural industries.' Smith takes up the story at a later stage and so accentuates the urban orientation of manufacturing industries and the development of distant, often overseas markets.

90. Smith, *Wealth of nations*, Vol. 11, p. 874. There was nothing particularly novel about this claim. At mid-century writers were already noting that the cloth trades had moved 'northward where greater plenty of firing and cheaper rates of other common necessaries of life . . . favour their increase much more than in our southern counties': see Gregory, *Regional Transformation*, p. 48. But the advantage, such as it was, seems to have been short-lived. Between 1760 and 1800 wages rose in the north and, in many cases, overtook those in the south: see E. H. Hunt, 'Industrialization and Regional Inequality: Wages in Britain 1760–1914', *Jnl. of Economic History*, **46** (1986), pp. 935–61.

91. Kohl, *England and Wales*, pp. 18, 78–9. For Napier, Carlyle and other writers on mid-century Manchester see Stephen Marcus, *Engels, Manchester and the Working Class*, (New Haven, 1975), pp. 28–66.

92. Alexis de Tocqueville, *Journeys to England and Ireland* (edited by J. P. Meyer), (New Haven, 1958), pp. 104–7. This edition is based on the diaries he kept during his visit to Britain in 1835. Kohl himself noted that 'the blue heavens are hidden from us by the thick black smoke of the huge factory chimneys which weave a close and impenetrable veil of brown fog between the city and the sky': *England and Wales*, pp. 132–3.

93. H. B. Rodgers, 'The Lancashire cotton industry in 1840', *Transactions of the Institute of British Geographers*, **28** (1960), pp. 135–53.

94. Kohl, *England and Wales*, pp. 121–2, 132, 146.

95. Mantoux, *Industrial Revolution*, p. 337; von Tunzelmann, *Steam Power*, pp. 66–7, 125. The geography of water power during early industrialization merits much more attention than it has received hitherto, but there are considerable difficulties in large-scale reconstructions before the Factory Inspectors' Returns of the 1830s: see Paul Laxton, 'Wind and water power' in Langton and Morris (eds.), *Atlas*, pp. 69–71.

96. Greenberg, 'Power patterns', pp. 1259–61.

97. Peter Hall, *The Industries of London since 1861*, (London, 1962); Gareth Stedman Jones, *Outcast London: a Study in the Relationship Between Classes in Victorian Society*, (Oxford, 1971).

98. For the general argument about the geography of class relations see Nigel Thrift, 'The geography of nineteenth-century class formation', in Nigel Thrift and Peter Williams (eds.), *Class and Space: the Making of Urban Society*, (London, 1987), pp. 25–50; on the geography of gender relations see Linda McDowell and Doreen Massey, 'A woman's place?', in Doreen Massey and John Allen (eds.), *Geography Matters! A Reader*, (Cambridge, 1984), pp. 128–47. For the specific contrasts I draw here see Patrick Joyce, *Work, Society and Politics: the Culture of the Factory in Later Victorian England*, (Brighton, 1980) and Jones, *Outcast London*.

99. Craig Calhoun, 'Class, place and industrial revolution', in Thrift and Williams (eds.), *Class and Space*, pp. 51–72, and John Langton, 'The industrial revolution and the regional geography of England', *Transactions of the Institute of British Geographers*, **9** (1984), pp. 145–67.

100. Humphrey Southall, 'Towards a geography of unionization: the spatial organization and distribution of early British trade unions', *Transactions of the Institute of British Geographers*, **13** (1988), pp. 466–85; Gareth Stedman Jones, 'The language of Chartism', in James Epstein and Dorothy Thompson (eds.), *The Chartist Experience: Studies in Working-Class Radicalism and Culture 1830–1860*, (London, 1982), pp. 3–58; Dorothy Thompson, *The Chartists*, (London, 1984).

101. Flows of information, circuits of capital and movements of people were as vital to the armature of the state as they were to the articulation of the space-economy. Think, for example, of the orders and inquiries sent out to the provinces and the reports and returns which they set in motion; of the collection of taxes and duties and the counter-movements of state expenditure; and of the domestic movements of troops and the rounds of officials administering justice and supervising the excise, inspecting factories and overseeing the Poor Law. There can be little doubt that the eighteenth and nineteenth centuries witnessed an extraordinary increase in the degree of state integration in each of these three registers. See John Brewer, *The Sinews of Power: War, Money and the English State 1688–1783*, (London, 1989), and Philip Corrigan and Derek Sayer, *The Great Arch: English State Formation as Cultural Revolution*, (Oxford, 1985). Yet the state was notably resistant towards nationalism as an ideology and the rhetoric of 'the nation' was often captured and carried off by the radicals: see Linda Colley, 'Whose nation? Class and national consciousness in Britain 1750–1830', *Past and Present*, **113** (1986), pp. 97–117, and cf. Gerald Newman, *The Rise of English Nationalism: a Cultural History 1740–1830*, (London, 1987). That virtually all of these discussions concern *England* requires emphasis.

102. See, for example, Alan Everitt, 'Country, county and town: patterns of regional evolution in England', *Transactions of the Royal Historical Society*, **29** (1979), pp. 79–108 and Keith Wrightson, 'Aspects of social differentiation in rural England, c. 1580–1660', *Jnl. of Peasant Studies*, **5** (1977), pp. 32–47.

103. The theoretical basis for this assertion may be found in Harvey's sketches of the 'structured coherence' that emerges within the tense and turbulent landscapes of capitalist production and in Scott's post-Weberian location theory: see Harvey, *Urbanization*, pp. 35–45, 136–44, and Allen J. Scott, *Metropolis: from the Division of Labor to Urban Form*, (Berkeley, 1988). pp. 26–60. Astonishingly, it remains an assertion since there has been remarkably little investigation of the locational dynamics of industrial complexes in nineteenth-century Britain. An extraordinary lacuna in Richard Dennis's otherwise superb account of *English Industrial Cities of the Nineteenth Century*, (Cambridge, 1984), for example, is any sustained discussion of *industry*.

104. Leon Faucher, *Manchester in 1844: its Present Condition and Future Prospects*, (London, 1844), pp. 15–16 (translation modified).

105. Langton, 'Industrial Revolution', pp. 156, 159, 163. Langton attributes the fragmentation of the space-economy to its reliance upon a disjointed canal system for commodity transfers and suggests that it was not until the coming of the railways that long-term processes of integration were set in motion. In an important commentary Freeman argues that this overlooks the integrative function of road transport during the late eighteenth and early nineteenth centuries; but he also claims that the differential tariffs

subsequently imposed by railway companies in the second half of the nineteenth century frequently sharpened geographical divides and accentuated regional structures. On his reading, it was the *Victorian* rather than the Georgian space-economy that was fragmented. See M. J. Freeman, 'Road transport in the English industrial revolution: an interim reassessment', *Jnl. of Historical Geography*, 6 (1980), pp. 17–28; *idem*, 'The industrial revolution and the regional geography of England: a comment', *Transactions of the Institute of British Geographers*, 9 (1984), pp. 502–12; *idem*, 'Introduction', in Freeman and Aldcroft (eds.), *Transport*, pp. 50–2. See also Derek Gregory, 'The production of regions in England's industrial revolution', *Jnl. of Historical Geography*, 14 (1988), pp. 50–8, and John Langton, 'The production of regions in England's industrial revolution: a response', *Jnl. of Historical Geography*, 14 (1988), pp. 170–4.

106. W. A. Cole, 'Factors in demand', in Roderick Floud and Donald McCloskey (eds.), *The Economic History of Britain Since 1700*, Vol. 1. *1700–1860*, (Cambridge, 1981). pp. 36–65; R. P. Thomas and D. N. McCloskey, 'Overseas trade and empire', in Floud and McCloskey (eds.), *Economic history*, pp. 87–102; Immanuel Wallerstein, *The Modern World System*, Vol. III, *The Second Era of Great Expansion of the Capitalist World Economy, 1730–1840s*, (San Diego, 1989).

107. Gregory, *Regional Transformation*, p. 158; Neil McKendrick, John Brewer and J. H. Plumb, *The Birth of Consumer Society: the Commercialization of Eighteen-Century England*, (London, 1982), pp. 215–16; Kohl, *England and Wales*, pp. 127–9. There were obviously two aspects to the 'geographies' I have in mind here: the compilation of *inventories*—the accumulation and sedimentation of knowledge about topography, resources, peoples—and the transmission of *chronicles*—the communication of day-to-day events around the world. The first of these has received considerably more attention than the second, though few historians display the contextual sensitivity evident in David Mackay, *In the Wake of Cook: Exploration, Science and Empire 1780–1801*, (London, 1985). The lags and biases in the international circulation of information would repay comparably close attention. Until the 1830s, for example, a letter from Britain to India could take up to eight months to reach its destination, and the onset of the monsoon season meant that any reply would be another sixteen months away. Delays of this kind evidently had enormous repercussions on the conduct of political and economic affairs. The two countries were not linked by telegraph until 1865. See Daniel Headrick, *The Tools of Empire: Technology and European Imperialism in the Nineteenth Century*, (New York, 1981), pp. 129–39; *idem*, *The Tentacles of Progress: Technology Transfer in the Age of Imperialism 1850–1940*, (New York, 1988), pp. 97–110.

108. Anderson, 'Figures of descent', pp. 32–5. The rise of merchant-manufacturers in the provinces in the 1780s and 1790s did little to dent London's financial hegemony. One London banker noted in 1802 that London had become 'the trading metropolis of Europe and indeed of the whole world; the foreign drafts, on account of merchants living in our outports and other trading towns and carrying on business there, being made with scarcely any exceptions payable in London.' In this sense, as Chapman remarks, even Liverpool remained financially dependent on its southern rival: S. D. Chapman, *The Rise of Merchant Banking*, (London, 1984), p. 9; see also *idem*, 'British marketing enterprise: the changing roles of merchants, manufacturers and financiers, 1700–1860', *Business History Review*, 53 (1979), pp. 205–34.

109. René Martin Pillet, *L'Angleterre Vue à Londres et dans ses Provinces pendant un Séjour de Dix Années*, (Paris, 1815), p. 23.

110. W. Rubinstein, 'The Victorian middle classes: wealth, occupation and geography', *Economic History Review*, 30 (1977), pp. 602–23; C. H. Lee, 'Regional growth and structural change in Victorian Britain', *Economic History Review*, 34 (1981), pp. 438–52; *idem*, 'The service sector, regional specialization and economic growth in the Victorian economy', *Jnl. of Historical Geography*, 10 (1984), pp. 139–55; *idem*, *The British Economy since 1700: a Macroeconomic Perspective*, (Cambridge, 1986), pp. 125–41. An important attempt to carry a parallel argument down to the present is Geoffrey Ingham, *Capitalism Divided? The City and Industry in British Social Development*, (London, 1984).

111. Part of my disagreement turns on the nature of the evidence which Rubinstein and (in particular) Lee use to secure their arguments: most of it relates to *patterns* from which it is notoriously difficult to make any inferences about *processes*. For a detailed critique of the dualism thesis see M. J. Daunton, '"Gentlemanly capitalism" and British industry 1820–1914', *Past and Present*, **122** (1989), pp. 119–58, which shows, amongst other things, that the City was neither a cohesive bloc nor altogether estranged from industry.

112. McKenrick, Brewer and Plumb, *Consumer Society*, p. 316; D. E. C. Eversley, 'The home market and economic growth in England 1750–1780', in E. L. Jones and G. E. Mingay (eds.), *Land, Labour and Population: Essays Presented to J. D. Chambers*, (London, 1967), pp. 206–59; Ralph Davis, *The Industrial Revolution and British Overseas Trade*, (Leicester, 1979), pp. 62–76.

113. Compare, for example, S. R. H. Jones, 'The country trade and the marketing and distribution of Birmingham hardware 1750–1810', *Business History*, **26** (1984), pp. 24–42, and Lorna Weatherill, 'The business of middleman in the English pottery trade before 1780', *Business History*, **28** (1986), pp. 1–76. London was peripheral to the first of these distribution systems and central to the second, but two notes of caution are necessary. First, although the country trade in needles was not organized through London, the separate London trade was far and away the most important. Second, both distribution systems were more or less national in scope: needle salesmen made regular journeys as far south as Plymouth and as far north as Ripon.

114. David Harvey, *The Limits to Capital*, (Oxford, 1982).

115. McKendrick, Brewer and Plumb, *Consumer Society*, p. 207. The present discussion is confined to the banking system, but there were other sources of credit. The money-scrivening attorney in particular played a central role in mediating the local supply of long-term credit for much of the eighteenth century: see B. L. Anderson, 'The attorney and the early capital market in Lancashire', in François Crouzet (ed.), *Capital Formation in the Industrial Revolution*, (London, 1972), pp. 223–55. But it is wrong to assume that banks played no part in long-term credit: see Peter Mathias, 'Capital, credit and enterprise in the Industrial Revolution', in *idem*, *The Transformation of England: Essays in the Economic and Social History of England in the Eighteenth Century*, (London, 1979), pp. 88–115.

116. L. S. Pressnell, *Country Banking in the Industrial Revolution*, (Oxford, 1956), pp. 105, 115, 126; T. S. Ashton, *The Industrial Revolution 1760–1830*, (Oxford, 1964), p. 74. Private banking was cellular simply because the Bank of England had a blanket monopoly of joint-stock banking until 1826. Its charter ensured that capital for the establishment of a private bank of issue could not be drawn from more than six partners and this naturally restricted the scale of any individual bank's operations. But in many cases the correspondent system was associated with a formal partnership: at the close of the eighteenth century almost one in three of all country banks had partnership connections with one or more of their correspondents. Still, some caution might be advisable. Critics of the early nineteenth-century capital market in London charged that it 'was unable to recognize, let alone meet the legitimate needs of the industrial hinterland': David Moss, 'The private banks of Birmingham 1800–1827', *Business History*, **24** (1982), pp. 79–94. It needs to be remembered, however, that these remarks were made following the financial crisis of 1825–26. In fact one historian argues that this crisis was *exacerbated* by the close integration between London and the provinces. 'While the system was incompletely integrated it was possible for a loss of confidence in one region to end with a few local bank failures'; but as the system became more closely articulated 'it was possible for a state of misplaced confidence to develop a [dangerous] momentum of its own': Phyllis Deane, *The First Industrial Revolution*, (Cambridge, 1979 edn.), pp. 190–7.

117. *Report of the Secret Committee on Joint Stock Banks*, (PP 1836, Vol. IX; PP 1837, Vol. VIV); Edward Nevin and E. W. Davis, *The London Clearing Banks*, (London, 1970), pp. 33–86; S. E. Thomas, *The Rise and Growth of Joint-Stock Banking*, (London, 1934); Hartley Withers, *National Provincial Bank 1833–1933*, (London, 1933). The proposal for a national provin-

cial bank came from Thomas Joplin who had long wanted to transfer the Scottish system of branch banking to England. The prospectus for the Bank was issued in 1833 and hailed the advantages of 'the great metropolitan institutions . . . spread[ing] their branches to the remotest districts.' For an understandably short period the Bank was even called the National Bank of England. Although all of its branches were controlled from London, the Bank had no office in the capital open to the public for over 30 years. There are several histories of individual banks, but the historical geography of joint-stock banking in England has received remarkably little attention: but see the maps in P. L. Cottrell, 'Banking and finance', in Langton and Morris (eds.), *Atlas*, pp. 144–55.

118. McKendrick, Brewer and Plumb, *Consumer Society*, pp. 21, 34–99. On the cultural geography of this 'consumer revolution' in its early stages see Lorna Weatherill, *Consumer Behaviour and Material Culture in Britain 1660–1760*, (London, 1988), pp. 43–69.

119. Jeremy Black, *The English Press in the Eighteenth Century*, (London, 1988), pp. 66–79; G. A. Cranfield, *The Development of the Provincial Newspaper 1700–1760*, (Oxford, 1962), pp. 96–8; Derek Gregory, 'The friction of distance? Information circulation and the mails in early nineteenth-century England', *Jnl. of Historical Geography*, **13** (1987), pp. 130–54. I am currently completing a study of information circulation through the press.

120. The *formal* chronology is as follows: the Principality of Wales was incorporated within Britain between 1536 and 1534; the English and Scottish crowns were united in 1603 and an Act of Union—parliamentary incorporation—was secured in 1707; an Act of Union between England and Ireland was finally forced through in 1801. For a summary see Jim Bulpitt, 'The making of the United Kingdom: the anatomy of English imperialism', in *idem*, *Territory and Power in the United Kingdom: an Interpretation*, (Manchester, 1983, pp. 70–103.

121. Michael Hechter, *Internal Colonialism: the Celtic Fringe in British National Development 1536–1966*, (London, 1975). Hechter's study is immensely suggestive and in fact draws upon a model of uneven development; nevertheless it seems to me both theoretically flawed and empirically insensitive. For a commentary and revision see Tom Nairn, *The Break-up of Britain: Crisis and Neo-nationalism*, (London, 1981 edn.).

122. Gwyn Williams, *When was Wales? A History of the Welsh*, (London, 1985), pp. 143–5, 173–6, 182–97. I should add that Williams is sharply critical of the thesis of internal colonialism. In fastening on relations of exchange, he says it loses hold of the importance of production and so 'mishandles the central reality of uneven development.' He also claims that by the end of the nineteenth century Wales was no mere satellite but 'a central directive force' in the triumph of British imperial capitalism: *idem*, *The Welsh in their History*, (London, 1982), pp. 196–7.

123. Keith Burgess, 'Workshop of the world: client capitalism at its zenith, 1830–1870', in Tony Dickson (ed.), *Scottish Capitalism: Class, State and Nation*, (London, 1980), pp. 137–180. Although Lennan regards eighteenth-century Scotland as 'a classic illustration of internal Hanoverian colonialism', it was by no means a one-sided process of domination. Burgess emphasizes that 'a major part of the task of internal colonialism was accomplished by the Scots themselves' because 'the rich and powerful among them found the compensation so immensely profitable': Bruce Lennan, *Integration, Enlightenment and Industrialization: Scotland 1746–1832*, (London, 1981), p. 55; Keith Burgess, 'Scotland and the first British Empire 1707–1770: the confirmation of client status', in Dickson (ed.), *Scottish Capitalism*, pp. 89–135. Their profits were not limited to activities north of the border, moreover, and Cage argues more generally that in some senses 'the economic development of England [in the eighteenth and nineteenth centuries] was in part a Scottish phenomenon': R. A. Cage, 'The Scots in England', in *idem* (ed.), *The Scots Abroad: Labour, Capital, Enterprise 1750–1914*, (London, 1985), pp. 29–45.

124. J. H. Johnson, 'The two "Irelands" at the beginning of the nineteenth century', in Nicholas Stephens and Robin E. Glasscock (eds.), *Irish Geographical Studies: Essays in Honour of E. Estyn Evans*, (Belfast, 1970), pp. 224–43; T. W. Freeman, *Pre-famine Ireland: a Study in Historical Geography*, (Manchester, 1957); Patrick O'Farrell, *Ireland's English Question*, (London, 1971). For an illuminating comparison between Ireland and Scotland

see T. M. Devine, 'The English connection and Irish and Scottish development in the eighteenth century', in T. M. Devine and David Dickson (eds.), *Ireland and Scotland 1600–1850: Parallels and Contrasts in Economic and Social Development*, (Edinburgh, 1983).

125. Roy Porter, *English Society in the Eighteenth Century*, (Harmondsworth, 1982), pp. 17, 51–62.

14

Towns and Urban Systems 1730–1914

H. Carter

The Urban System 1730–1914

Large-scale urbanization has been a process common to all the countries of the Western world in modern times. More recently it has become characteristic of developing countries. Britain was the first to be subject to this critical transformation, critical not only because it changed the settlement pattern but because it revolutionized the whole socio-economic system. Between 1730 and 1914 England and Wales shifted from being primarily rural to being predominantly urban countries. The significance of the process was immediate and obvious and recognized as much by literati as by those concerned with social welfare.[1] Even before the end of the nineteenth century the first major study of urbanization had been published in Adna Ferrin Weber's book, *The Growth of Cities in the Nineteenth Century*.[2] Weber began by noting that it was a common observation that the most remarkable social phenomenon of the century had been the concentration of population in cities. But on the same first page he poses more pertinent questions: 'What are the forces that have produced a shifting of population? Are they enduring? What is to be the ultimate result?'

There have been numerous attempts since Weber's pioneer work to consider these questions and, in general, they fall into two categories. The first comprises studies directed at the first of Weber's questions. In approach, they constitute a narrative, though explanatory account of the growth of towns related to specific causes. They are usually carried out region by region or according to functional type. A recent example is made up of those chapter sections subtitled 'Towns and Cities' in the volume *A New Historical Geography of England*, edited by Darby.[3] Studies in the second category are more concerned with Weber's last two questions and can be identified as theoretical, national and system based. Their approach is dominated by an attempt to evaluate structural transformations which are related to rank–size relationships of varying descriptions. These works are best exemplified by Robson's book *Urban Growth*.[4] It must be admitted that neither approach has been greatly productive. The first has given rise to a large number of very similar descriptive accounts but little in the way of synthesis, while the second has given some relevant insights into the emergence of size relationships but of a restricted kind.

In this present review of changes in the urban system over some 180 years or so a three-fold division will be adopted. To begin with a general review of the facts of urban growth 1730–1914 will be presented. That will be followed by a review of the regional and functional components of that growth, and finally the possibility of extracting some generalizations will be considered.

In measuring city size and significance one is compelled to use population as the sole criterion, for any more esoteric bases would be far too difficult to develop. The sources available divide themselves in two. Before 1801, and the first census, one is forced to employ a miscellany of sources, standardizing and integrating their material to derive an overall perspective. After 1801, the availability of the census enables one to take sources for granted and to concentrate on the problems of interpretation and analysis. Amongst the various sources used to construct a view of the urban system before 1801, the most valuable include parish registers, bills of mortality, taxation assessments, especially the Hearth Tax, and, when available, local censuses.[5] Most of these imply the use of a multiplier to convert partial information into population. There are problems both of accuracy and of uniformity, for it is unusual to obtain figures relating to all towns at one date. Again, prior to the municipal reforms of the early nineteenth century it is difficult to know what to count as urban. The famous list, *Index Villaris or an Alphabetical List of all Cities Market Towns . . .* of 1680 included a large number of decayed towns where markets were no longer held.[6] Definition is also a problem when the censuses become available. Administrative character has always been used as the identifier of urban status in England and Wales, but that counted for little in a period of rapid change, and especially when the administrative system was itself changing. The early censuses made no attempt to identify urban and rural and it was not until 1851 that the populations of municipal and parliamentary boroughs were added to those of unincorporated places of over 2000 to isolate an urban component. By 1871 figures for municipal boroughs and places with either an Improvement Commission or a Local Board were used and after 1881 the Urban Sanitary Districts provided the basis. Census data, therefore, do not provide the simple foundation which at first might appear to become available in 1801. Fortunately there have been two valuable attempts at providing effective data sets. The first is that by Jan de Vries in his book *European Urbanization 1500–1800*.[7] As the title indicates the scope is wider in extent than the subject matter of this chapter and only covers the period to 1800. But the book includes the data base from which the analyses are derived. It is based on a meticulous review of all the available sources and is of the greatest value. C. M. Law's work is more limited in space and time dealing with England and Wales only during the nineteenth century and is a reinterpretation of published census data.[8] He attempts to provide a uniform set of figures by deriving a definition of urban areas from a combination of a minimum size criterion (2500), a measure of density (over one per acre) and a nucleation principle. Using these bases he has calculated urban populations for each census and his figures will be used in the discussion of the facts of urban growth.

Table 14.1 sets out various measures of change in the urban population of England and Wales for all the census years of the nineteenth century. It reveals the extent and character of change. The urban population itself increased eight-fold during the period, while the proportion living in towns rose from a third in 1801 to over three-

Table 14.1: Urban populations in England and Wales, 1801–1901 (after C. M. Law).

England and Wales

Year	Total population	Urban population	Percentage urban	Percentage urban change in previous decade	Index of urban population, 1801 = 100	Urban change as percentage of total change in previous decade	Number of places with population greater than 2500	Number of places with population greater than 100,000
1801	8,829,536	3,009,260	33.8	—	100	—	253	1
1811	10,164,256	3,722,025	36.6	23.7	124	56.0	302	3
1821	12,000,236	4,804,534	40.0	29.1	160	59.0	352	4
1831	13,896,797	6,153,230	44.3	28.0	204	71.1	397	6
1841	15,914,148	7,093,126	48.3	25.0	256	76.3	450	7
1851	17,927,609	9,687,927	54.0	25.9	322	99.1	522	10
1861	20,066,224	11,784,056	58.7	21.6	392	98.0	577	13
1871	22,712,266	14,802,100	65.2	25.6	492	151.8	697	17
1881	25,924,434	18,180,117	70.0	22.8	604	103.5	754	20
1891	29,002,525	21,601,012	74.5	18.8	718	113.0	845	24
1901	32,527,843	25,371,849	78.0	17.5	843	107.0	908	33

quarters by 1901. In 1801, London was the only city with a population of over 100,000; by the end of the century there were 33 cities with over that figure. If Law's base of 2500 be taken as the threshold of urban status, then the total number of urban places increased from 253 to 908, that is, by over three and a half times. But if the system of cities was extended in number, it was also changed in structure, for the largest towns accounted for an increasingly greater proportion of the total urban population. Thus if the smallest group with populations between 2500 and 10,000 is examined it will be seen that the proportion of the urban population accounted for by them actually fell from 29.1 per cent in 1801 to 11.2 per cent in 1901, while the proportion of the total population accounted for by this size class declined from 9.9 per cent to 8.9 per cent over the same period. In complete contrast, the proportion of the urban population in towns of over 100,000 rose from 32.6 per cent to 55.5 per cent and the proportion of the national population in these largest towns increased from 11.0 per cent to 43.8 per cent. Indeed, the percentage of the urban population accounted for by all size groups below 100,000 fell between 1801 and 1901. The implication is that the hierarchy of towns was taking on a different structure.

In terms of change during the century there was a fairly even decennial increase as measured by the percentage urban change, but with small peaks in the early part in 1821 and in the latter part of the century in 1871, and a tailing off towards 1901. When urban change is related to total change, however, there is a marked dominance in the last quarter of the century when the metamorphosis of the country to an urban basis was completed with the onset of gross rural depopulation, so that urban increase became greater than total increase, with rural losses making up the difference. (see p. 302).

Table 14.1 and the foregoing exegesis of it outline the essential facts of urbanization as a national process. But urbanization did not operate uniformly over the country and a brief account of regional and functional variation is essential to this analysis. Moreover, moving away from the general statistical scale allows a brief review of the situation during the eighteenth century before census figures are available.

In the first half of the eighteenth century the urban system in England and Wales was largely that which had emerged from the late medieval period (see Table 14.2). It reflected local wealth and density of population supported by agriculture, rural industry and the trade based on their products. It also represented political clout as expressed through an administrative system still concerned with the security of the realm and the preservation of a united kingdom. At the lowest level in the urban hierarchy, it is estimated that there were between five and six hundred market towns, many possessing extremely small populations with a minimum about 500 and a maximum about 1800.[9] These were the survivors of that complex web of market towns which had characterized the late medieval period. Change at this level had been considerable as the sorting out process eliminated those less able to compete.[10] Communication, especially along rivers and around the coast, had certainly improved, but to no revolutionary extent and those towns which had been lifted out of this level owed a great deal to the administrative system, both lay and ecclesiastical, based on the counties. For the operation of that system, especially for the administration of justice, designated centres were needed and these were raised to a level above that of the market town. In that designation, advantages in location

Table 14.2: The largest towns of England and Wales in 1650 and 1750 (after de Vries). *Note*. Population estimates are given to the nearest thousand. Below a threshold of 10,000 De Vries gives some populations, but not all, so no attempt has been made to extend the list below that level.

1650		1750	
London	400	London	675
Bristol	20	Bristol	45
Norwich	20	Norwich	36
Newcastle	13	Newcastle	29
Colchester	10	Birmingham	24
Exeter	10	Liverpool	22
York	10	Manchester	18
		Leeds	16
		Exeter	16
		Plymouth	15
		Chester	13
		Shrewsbury	13
		Derby	12
		Ipswich	12
		Nottingham	12
		Sheffield	12
		Portsmouth	10
		Sunderland	10
		Yarmouth	10
		York	10

and size, derived from centrality and agricultural wealth, were critical. But to a large degree the towns which had counties named after them, such as Nottingham, Derby, Leicester, Northampton and Bedford, still retained their status. Raised still farther above this level were those centres which can be termed 'provincial capitals'. All commentators agree that five stood out—Norwich, Bristol, York, Exeter and Newcastle. Moreover these towns maintained this status over a period of some 200 years, suggesting an era of stability, at least in the upper ranges of the hierarchy.[11] It is not possible to consider them individually, but a number of general points can be made. The first and obvious one is that wealth of surroundings and location on navigable rivers or function as ports had played significant roles in enhancing their status. But at the same time there was a political, administrative and ecclesiastical backing. None of these towns lay within competing distance of London. They represent, too, the last phase in the importance of the provincial capitals of less stable areas of the United Kingdom. Newcastle, in particular, was still, at the outset of the period, a major bastion against the Scots. In contrast, towns in closer proximity to London suffered from competition with that primate city at a time when its population was some 20 times that of its nearest in size. There were two provincial areas significantly without capitals at this higher level. The first was Wales where the general poverty of the country, together with its physical nature of a mountain core and a thin periphery, had produced no chief city. The same physical character meant that there was no one focus in the Marchlands. Potential candidates like Chester, Shrewsbury, Hereford, Worcester and Gloucester remained at the county town level. But in the extreme south, Bristol was the effective capital of southern Wales, just as the rapidly growing port of Liverpool was later to become the capital of the north. The Welsh situation was, to a degree, echoed in north-west England. In Lancashire, the county town of Preston and the older capital city of Lancaster, were locally effective but lacked regional command. Chester was in decline and Liverpool growing as was Manchester. A transition situation characterized the area even at this early date. Moreover, Cumberland and Westmorland were as thinly populated and incapable of generating a regional capital as was Wales. It is a significant reflection on the pre-industrial situation that whereas the east coast had three provincial capitals in Norwich, York and Newcastle, in addition to London, the west coast had only Bristol. This contrast reflected their differences of agricultural wealth and the industry and trade derived from its products. Finally, at the head of the hierarchy, there was London, a primate city which was the centre not only of trade and commerce, but pre-eminently of government and administration.

This discussion of towns in the mid eighteenth century is incomplete as Table 14.2 indicates. It fails to include those already characterized by special industry such as Birmingham, which had risen to occupy fifth place in the ranking of towns, and it takes no account of the spas or naval ports. Even so, it represents a system in transition from the medieval inheritance into the basis of the nineteenth century. The completion of those changes is best introduced by a tabulation of the largest towns at the first census of 1801 (see Table 14.3).

From about 1730, a period of stability, at least in the upper echelons of the urban hierarchy, was replaced by one of quite fundamental change. If London is excluded, only Bristol retained its place among the five largest towns in 1801. Norwich had moved down to seventh, Newcastle to thirteenth, Exeter to fourteenth and York to sixteenth. The newcomers which displaced them rested unequivocally on industry for their growth. Appropriately the incoming members epitomize the new areas of urban growth. Manchester and Liverpool, the first a regional centre of commerce

Table 14.3: The largest towns of England and Wales, excluding London, in 1801 and 1851.

	1801		1851
Manchester	84,000	(includes Salford)	367,955
Liverpool	78,000		375,955
Birmingham	74,000		232,841
Bristol	64,000	(includes Barton Regis Hundred)	137,328
Leeds	53,000		172,270
Plymouth	43,000		
Norwich	37,000		
Bath	32,000		
Portsmouth	32,000	(includes Portsea)	
Sheffield	31,000		135,310
Hull	30,000		
Nottingham	29,000		
Newcastle	28,000		
		Bradford	103,310

After Prince and Harley, in H. C. Darby (ed.), *A New Historical Geography of England*, pp. 459, 578.

and the second a port, were the cities being created by cotton textiles: Birmingham was the largest of a group of West Midland towns concerned with metalware and miscellaneous engineering products: Leeds was the capital of the woollen manufacturers of Yorkshire's West Riding. Lower down in the hierarchy, Sheffield, at tenth, was the centre of a steel industry and the other specialized trades such as Sheffield plate, while Nottingham, twelfth in rank, represented in its hosiery and lace industries the growing area of the East Midlands. High in the ranks were Bath, still representing the spas and foreshadowing the resorts, together with Plymouth and Portsmouth, the naval bases. It is necessary to record at this point that in spite of the overturning of the rank order of towns highest in status, nevertheless those coming to supremacy were already settlements of some size with a long-standing industrial tradition based on earlier mercantile activity. Although changes were fundamental even so there was an element of continuity. One of the bases for the successful take-off of the new industrialism would seem to have been a good urban foundation. Industrialization and urbanization would seem to have been mutually reinforcing, rather than to have acted in a simple unilateral cause–effect fashion.

Each of the major industrial cities was associated with an aureole of smaller towns, the sizes of which were closely related to their industrial development. This is best illustrated by Lancashire where the smaller cotton towns grew as rapidly between 1801 and 1821 as the larger centres (see Table 14.4).

Space precludes a narrative description of the causal factors behind the growth of individual members of a hierarchy which was being both extended in length and modified in structure. However, an overall picture can be given in a series of maps derived from a set produced by Robson[12] (Fig. 14.1).

These maps show those towns whose growth in the specified decade was one standard deviation above the mean for its size group. It must be emphasized that these are not absolute growth rates, but rates related to the means for size groups, so that at any one time only a proportion of any size group can appear. The size groups are not identified on the maps but are indicated in the key. The main conclusions which can be drawn from this series of maps reinforce the fairly standard view on the evolution of industrial and urban England and Wales. Even so, some interesting points emerge. The earliest decade from 1801 to 1811 appears transitional between the pre-industrial state and the new order being ushered in by industry. County towns, such as Bridgewater in the South-west, Carmarthen in South Wales and

Table 14.4: Population growth of cotton towns.

	1801	1823
Wigan	10,989	17,716
Bury	7072	10,583
Oldham	12,024	21,662
Blackburn	11,980	21,940
Bolton	12,549	22,037
Preston	11,887	24,575
Stockport (Cheshire)	14,850	21,726

After Chalklin, *Provincial Towns of Georgian England*, p. 35.

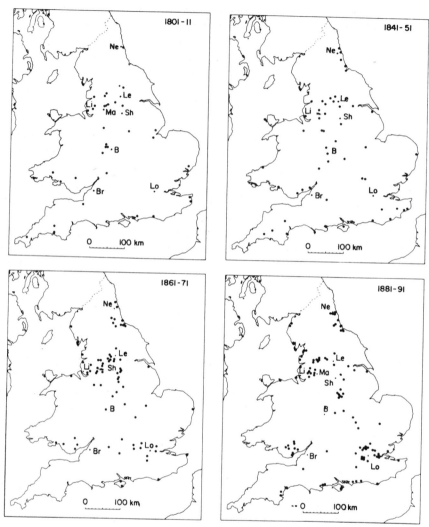

Fig. 14.1. The pattern of urban growth in England and Wales in four selected decades (after Robson). Those cities registering high rates have been abstracted. Standardized growth rates are represented where

$$zi = \frac{Gi.n - \bar{G}n}{\sigma n}$$

where *Gi.n* is the growth rate of the *i*th town the population of which puts it within the *n*th size group of towns: *Gn* and *σn* are the mean and standard deviation of the *n*th size group. Lower limits of size groups used are 2500, 5000, 10,000, 20,000, 40,000, 80,000, 160,000, 320,000. B. T. Robson, *Urban Growth* (1973), pp. 82, 98–111.

Boston in East Anglia, reflect both the significance of the regional centre and the role of the port as a distributor of shop goods, a role which was to continue until the coming of the railway. The Severn Valley has only one representative of high growth but there were others in the West Midlands area generally. The newer seaside resorts such as Ramsgate appear, although the war with France gave a distorted stress to south-east coast ports. But the main growth area was Lancashire. The high growth rate of its towns was sustained into the next decade when a clear dominance is evident in both Lancashire and the West Riding of Yorkshire. Elsewhere the occurrence of high growth is sporadic, apart, perhaps, from the south-coast towns. By 1831–41 and 1841–51 a new influence begins to operate through the development of the railway system and the rapid growth of the ports dealing with the import of raw materials and the export of manufactured goods. The West Midlands appear more firmly as an area of rapid growth once the railway mitigated the problem of distance from the coast, while in the North-East and South Wales the ports themselves show rapid increase. By the decade 1851–61 the main industrial areas of the country were clearly established and marked by growth, the only exception being South Wales. But the North-East, Lancashire, the West and South Ridings of Yorkshire, Nottingham–Derby and the West and East Midlands were outstanding cores of high urban increase. During the decade 1861–71 three features were added to this complex. The first was a distinct scatter of growth in the London basin as Greater London was created out of surburban extension. The second was the appearance of a new generation of seaside resorts created by the demand of the industrial population and of which Blackpool was the epitome. The third was the clear entry of South Wales into the high growth area as coal mining and export expanded. By 1881–91, the patterns of growth show up that axial belt of population lying south-east to north-west from London to Lancashire–Yorkshire which was to be the outstanding feature of the population distribution of England until after the Second World War. High growth can also be discerned in the two major industrial areas outside this dominant belt, North-East England and South Wales.

The crucial issue for the historical geographer is whether the pattern of growth which characterized the period 1730–1914 can be shown to demonstrate any general principles of city-system development. The standard types of analyses have been carried out by Robson for the period when reasonably accurate census data are available.[13] In these rank order was plotted against population size for decennial censuses (Fig. 14.2) and also the rank changes of individual towns between censuses were plotted. The progressive horizontal shift to the right in the rank–size array demonstrates the simple addition of extra members into the array, while the vertical shift indicates the growth of the size of individual members. The general form of the graph remains surprisingly similar, thereby reflecting some form of allometric growth, that is, there is a relationship between the addition of extra cities and the size of cities. This confirms the conclusion drawn earlier (p. 404) regarding the concentration of growth in the upper ranks of the settlement array, but it does not signify that a structural transformation was in progress. As regards those towns which were the largest in 1801, the examination of change in rank supports the view that there was comparatively little shift of rank order amongst the top places, but that fluctuations became greater the farther down the hierarchy of towns one moves. Robson writes,

All of these larger places (London, Liverpool, Manchester, Birmingham), indeed, show relatively little change in their rank order over the whole period. On the other hand, with smaller places there is a tendency for increasingly large fluctuations to occur at smaller city sizes. Some places moved rapidly up the rank hierarchy: Leicester, for example, was 21st in 1801, had moved to 13th by 1891 and retained this rank up to 1911. Other places moved rapidly down the hierarchy: Exeter, for example, began at 20th position, and had fallen to 65th by 1911.[14]

These analyses, therefore, suggest that over a short time period the largest cities captured, in direct and simple terms, a disproportionate amount of growth, thereby maintaining their highest ranking and confirming an allometric growth characteristic. At the lower end of the scale there was considerable change and jockeying for position.

At this point it is appropriate to consider other interpretations of the same problem. Haggett, Cliff and Fry in *Locational Models*[15] briefly review historical changes in city-size distributions. They conclude that although the Industrial Revolution administered a severe shock to the system, there may be a general tendency for the urban system to move towards a dynamic equilibrium, maximum entropy distribution.[16] Presumably this simply means that the rapid creation of new towns during the century shook up the existing hierarchy, but that eventually it settled back to a condition of relative stability after the maximum period of town creation was over. This was largely achieved by towns, constrained by the threshold populations needed to generate services and by the limited range over which they could operate, eventually achieving a settled relationship in the context of the total population distribution. It appears that two forces were at work, in addition to the direct, aggregating influence of industry and mining. The first of these consisted of those agglomeration economies in the offering of goods and services which

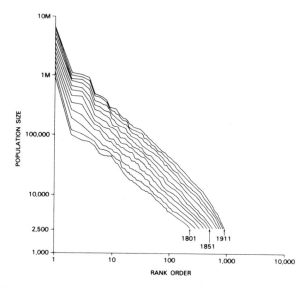

Fig. 14.2. The rank–size array of towns in England and Wales, 1801–1911 (after Robson[4]).

favoured the largest settlements. The second comprised those constraints of the traditional central-place concept, threshold and range, which sorted out the smaller centres. The separation of all these into two distinct influences is, however, quite arbitrary.

The most pertinent contribution to the role of agglomeration economies has been that of Pred.[17] Over a number of years he has developed and extended the notion of cyclical cumulative growth put forward by Myrdal. Fig. 14.3 reproduces his diagram which outlines the circular and feedback process of local urban-size growth for individual large cities during a period of industrialization. It is based on new or enlarged industry providing the most likely environment for invention and innovation. This not only further stimulates industry but generates a multiplier which is

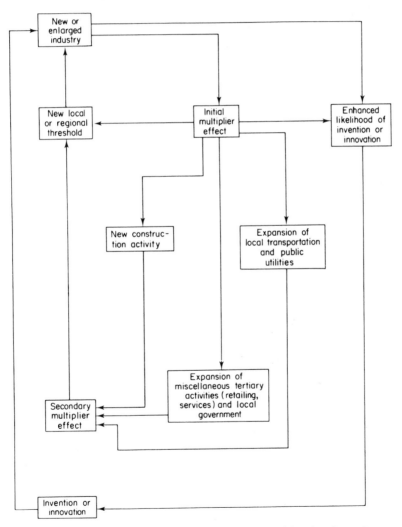

Fig. 14.3. The circular and cumulative feedback process of local urban size-growth for individual large cities during periods of initial modern industrialization (after Pred[17]).

expressed in the extension of construction, transport and public utilities and in tertiary services. These in turn attract new investment and provide a stimulus to further industrial growth. It is this process which explains two distinctive features of urban growth in the period under discussion; most of the large towns were early centres of mercantile activity in which the critical thresholds were met and new activity generated; those towns which grew most rapidly were the largest towns, with few fundamental changes in rank at the top occurring during the nineteenth century. It must, however, be noted that these statements are only true if a limited time span is taken. If reference is made to the hierarchy of towns in the first half of the eighteenth century there is a complete transformation at the top of the size-rank array. By 1801, with the sole exception of London, all of the top towns have disappeared, apart from Bristol (which does not appear in Robson's array). In other words, much of the real transformation at the higher levels is concealed before the first British census of 1801. Again the dominance in growth of the largest towns is lost by the end of the nineteenth century, probably due to the onset of surburbaniza-tion, although that could well be regarded as indistinguishable from the growth of the largest centres. Even so, it must be conceded that viewing the problem over a long time period arouses reservations as to the role of agglomeration economies. But once growth at a point was begun, for whatever reason, then size generated a size increase and encouraged innovation and the achievement of new thresholds. But a further problem arises in a critical review of this notion for it is essentially *ex post facto*, virtually teleological, in its structure. This can be revealed by a review of some of the detail of urban growth in any one area.

South Wales can be regarded as exceptional in the British context of industrial urbanization for its critical development was late; there was no strongly developed urban system, no mercantile capital, and the basic investment came from sources outside the area. It is possibly an example of internal colonialism rather than of growth generated from within. But however it be regarded, a number of problems arise which cut across the idea of agglomeration, innovation and invention as the controllers of the city system's growth. The earliest eighteenth-century core of industry was about Swansea Bay, but that area was rapidly superseded by Merthyr Tydfil, the centre of the iron industry after 1750. Merthyr was the largest town in Wales for most of the period under review, and certainly in all the censuses from 1801 to 1881. Between 1871 and 1881 it lost its supremacy to Cardiff and fell below Swansea and the Rhondda, although to regard the last area as a single settlement demands an array of presumptions. Merthyr did not fall rapidly in population until the present century but even so, according to all the principles, it should have grown apace. In 1821 it was still more than twice the size of Cardiff and Swansea. Moreover, it was the centre of significant innovation in the iron industry and, above all else, in transportation. In 1801 Richard Trevethick's steam engine ran from Penydarren to Abercynon, so inaugurating the age of the steam locomotive. And yet, by 1881 Merthyr had been overtaken by a town which had only 1870 inhabitants in 1801. The success of Cardiff also raises questions, for it never achieved the size and signifi-cance of equivalent capitals of other industrial areas such as Birmingham or Manchester, when, according to the principles of cumulative agglomeration, it should have. The reasons for the situation described are neither obscure nor surprising. Merthyr lost its supremacy in the Welsh hierarchy because the basic local raw material, iron ore, was exhausted and the transport costs of importing ore to an inland and upland location became prohibitive. Again, after 1860 the main characteristic of South Wales was the export of coal and the bulk of this went through the port of Cardiff. But Cardiff failed to generate a real industrial base.[18] This can be attributed in part to the attitude of the Bute family who owned the docks but did little to enhance the facilities which might have attracted shipbuilding. Further, the late development of Cardiff meant that it could not gain a place in the manufacturing sphere and, like a true colonial city, it exported the raw material wealth of the hinterland without establishing raw-material-using industries of its own. This brief review of South Wales reverts to the particular which the chapter has attempted to avoid, but even the shortest study of a particular area throws doubt on the universality of general principles. Innovative centres survived and prospered only when locations remained industrially or commercially advantageous, not simply because they were innovative centres; and if innovation diffused down a hierarchy it was because that hierarchy already existed and not because the diffusion process structured a hierarchy. All this does not mean that the cyclical and cumulative process of city growth did not operate, but that it was only one of a number of processes of great complexity by which a range of pre-existing and new settlements were sorted out and reached a stage of relative equilibrium.

Fig. 14.4 attempts to depict, in an elementary fashion, the forces that shaped the urban system of England and Wales during the period 1730 and 1914. The inheritance was the system of cities which had emerged into the early modern period. If equilibrium be defined as a minimum of rank change, then it was a system in equilibrium, for shifts in rank change had been limited and local for a number of centuries. The onset of a period of rapid fluctuation was characterized by the accumulation and investment of mercantile capital. Growth was fostered particularly where early available capital engendered technical innovation and where economies accrued to the agglomeration process. Thresholds were continuously raised so the innovation became especially associated with the largest centres. A group of regional capitals emerged, very different from those of the early eighteenth century. Within the orbit of these leaders, a whole range of small industrial settlements came into being, some *ab initio*, others through the transformation of older market towns. If initial sizes were determined by the scale of manufacturing and mining enterprises, the need for local government and service provision added an extra basis for discrimination over size. As these administrative and tertiary services became of a more standard character over the century, a countrywide comparative control exerted by thresholds and ranges encouraged the sorting of centres into something approaching a hierarchical order. Within that process, as Robson has effectively demonstrated, the ability of a town to acquire the most general area-serving functions was the key to success.[19] The more highly specialized a city the more prone it was to changing technology and the greater the freedom for entrepreneurs to switch investment to a different point, that is, the easier it was to relocate surplus value. Thus, functional differentiation enters into the process of system evolution and in this context, the pre-existing settlements already involved in administrative and service functions were greatly advantaged.

Also, in the process of sorting, the railway had a major impact. Communications are first established where demand is greatest, that is between the largest towns. The

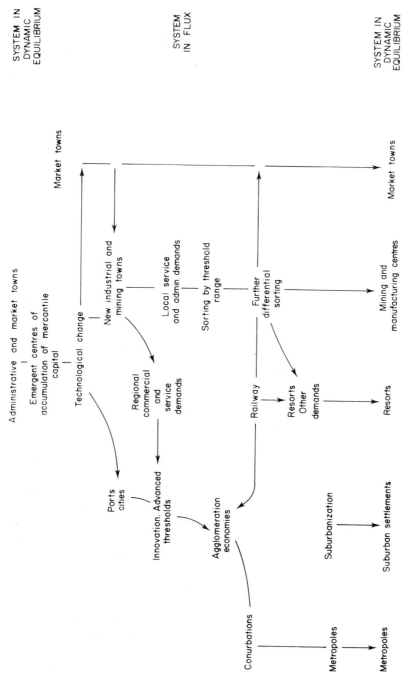

Fig. 14.4. A generalized view of forces shaping the array of towns in the nineteenth century.

result is an addition to the cyclical and cumulative growth which was the basis of the great metropolis. But the railway also created towns such as Crewe and Swindon and acted discriminately on others. Furthermore, industrial populations demanded resorts so that old centres were revived and new ones literally entered the ranks. It is interesting to note that the 1851 census recorded the highest growth rate between 1811 and 1851 in the class called 'watering places' at 254 per cent, as against 224 per cent for 'manufacturing places'.[20] By the latter part of the nineteenth century cumulative growth meant that the largest cities were no longer discrete entities but were associated with a range of separate satellite surburbs. This extended period of flux and change was approaching its end by the year 1900. It had produced a wide range of settlements, both in function and size, but had now reached a situation where rank change was again small. In other words it was in a state of dynamic equilibrium with maximum entropy.

Again, this can be illustrated from Wales. Between 1801 and 1901, the number of towns by formal designation increases from 61 to 112, almost doubling in 100 years. Yet only 12 of the 61 settlements of 1801 do not appear in Beresford's gazetteer of new Welsh towns of the Middle Ages. This suggests that periods of maximum flux or change are exceptional for here is not a system subject to minor influences of morphogenesis and morphostatis, but one subject to catastrophic change. Indeed one is tempted to draw the analogy with the notion of catastrophism in geomorphology and argue that the urban system is subject to short catastrophic periods of change which determine its basic form, and long periods of dynamic equilibrium as the energy injected is dispersed. It might be that much analysis of change in urban systems has not succeeded because of a failure to specify the nature of the time scale being considered. From the broadest point of view the period 1730 to 1900 can be regarded as one of major transformation as new settlements came into being, interacting with the old and achieving relative equilibrium under the twin controls of threshold and range operating at distinctive levels, with agglomeration economies distorting that simple central place resolution into a more unequal pattern.

These conclusions which this review has reached have, however, been challenged by de Vries in his consideration of European urbanization. He writes, 'the medieval city may have had many virtues, but the autarchic structure of the middle ages could not serve as the urban framework of a commercial and industrial society. The industrial city of the factory age was undoubtedly a novel and powerful organism, but it inserted itself into an existing urban system which it modified but did not transform.[21] The last phrase is the critical one. De Vries lays stress on the period between 1600 and 1750 when, he maintains, urban growth was mostly thoroughly concentrated into a handful of the many hundreds of cities comprising the urban system. They were predominantly capitals and ports and it was during this early period that an integrated urban system emerged. Thus his analysis of stability and discontinuity produces, what he terms, an unexpected finding, that post-1800 urban growth displays elements of continuity with the past. 'Regionally dominant cities, particularly those possessing formal political functions, have tended to hold their positions through thick and thin' so that 'the era of the Industrial Revolution was not a unique urban watershed introducing shocks to some systems as to create a new urban system,' and 'it is, therefore, a mistake to regard the rapid growth of industrial towns in the nineteenth century as creating the modern urbanized society of the advanced nations'.[22]

To a degree these conclusions are not new. By 1965 it had been demonstrated that in Wales the medieval separatism had been succeeded before the onset of industry by a hierarchical ordering of towns, 'a balanced pattern of service centres and a nesting system of urban fields . . . a pattern and a system not based on simple distance controls, but ultimately linked to the physical nature of the countryside, the economic needs of the times and the inherited tradition and privileges of settlements'.[23] Again, in England and Wales it has already been shown that industrialism was itself the product of mercantilism which created the system of cities and the flows of capital through it which was a prerequisite of industrial urbanism. But that city system was most certainly transformed as the discussion of agglomeration economies has already demonstrated (p. 411).

It would seem then, however convincing the arguments of Pred and de Vries, they do not fit the facts of change in England and Wales, a statement which, if valid, immediately demands explanation. There seem to be two reasons. The first is simply that of scale. On a Brundel-like European scale it is possible to agree with de Vries that 'the cities of Europe formed a polynuclear urban system in the sixteenth century, but thereafter came to be fashioned into a single-centred system focussed on north-western Europe. The decisive period for this transformation was the first half of the seventeenth century',[24] and yet at the same time it is possible to justify the more local, radical transformation of the city system in England and Wales after 1750. Different scales, as so often in geographical analysis, elucidate different interpretations. The second reason is the uniqueness of England and Wales and a standard precept of elementary geography. In Britain the Industrial Revolution preceded the revolution in transport it brought about, especially the creation of the railway pattern. Elsewhere in Europe the reverse was true and hence the railways were adjusted to the existing urban system and industry followed; just as contemporary industry adjusts to the motorways. The result in England and Wales, however, was a substantial restructuring of the urban system even if many of the lineaments of pre-industrial times can be discerned.

Finally, de Vries suggests that 'a truly iconoclastic interpreter of the data . . . might argue that the post 1820–50 process of urban concentration in large cities has only restored the hierarchical characteristics imparted during the creation of Europe's modern urban system in the seventeenth century'.[25] Again, this is a statement with which one can agree. But it implies a substantial upset took place during the nineteenth century which is only now working itself out. The north–south divide in England and Wales, or the dominance of the South-East, is in this sense no more than the reinstatement of pre-industrial space relations. But it also underlines the extent of the industrial transformation.

The Forms of Towns

The massive increase in urban populations during the period under review resulted in correspondingly great physical extensions of the built-up areas of towns which in turn triggered a fundamental restructuring in terms of urban land uses. That restructuring was highly complex, but if one critical process has to be identified, it was the segregation of uses. During the period there was a progressive separation of the various distinctive uses, and within each broad use category there were parallel processes of change. Again, in general terms, what had been a relatively undifferentiated town centre, only distinctively different on market days, was translated into a permanent shopping and administrative area or Central Business District (CBD). Industry and the railway, often in close association, produced their own city regions. By the end of the century the development of intra-city transportation had metamorphosed the constricted walking city into the extensive tram (or street car) city, thus initiating rapid suburban growth.

The segregation of land uses was only in part a consequence of sheer physical growth, for it was also a response to a series of technological transformations by which uses were changed in nature and driven apart. Three of these revolutions can be briefly examined.

(1) *Industrial technology*. Traditionally this had been regarded as the critical area of change. The older situation had been one of small-scale craft industries based on workshops scattered throughout the town and producing for a local market. Two changes occurred:

(a) Large-scale, factory-based industry came into being demanding extensive areas of land. The urban core location was made inadequate and obsolete. The new sites covered large extents of land. Accessibility to water and rail transport was demanded. The urban industrial region emerged.

(b) The workshop-based craft industries were eventually displaced. Thus, for example, the boot and shoe maker was eventually ousted by mass produced factory goods from the East Midlands; the bespoke tailor became a retailer of centrally produced off-the-peg garments.

Manufacturing was in this way concentrated into larger and distinctive regions within the town. The pit head with all its associated buildings played a similar role.

(2) *Retail technology*. In this context, a whole series of changes took place. They were not complete until the end of the century, that is, they were not immediate and revolutionary, but the end result was a radical change in the whole system.

(a) The weekly market was gradually replaced by, or transformed into, the permanent shopping centre. Very often the first stage which characterized the first half of the century was the building of a market hall. Goronwy Rees in his history of Marks and Spencer noted that the career of Michael Marks epitomized the development of retailing in the nineteenth century.[26] Marks started in Leeds as a pedlar or packman. By 1884 he had a stall in the open market there which operated on two days of the week. From there he moved to the covered market, which had been opened in 1857 and which was open every weekday. The next stage was to open stalls in other markets: by 1890 he had five.

(b) The old core of the town, or part of it, which had been a mixture of land uses became more specialized into retail or professional uses.

(c) As the factory-based mass-produced article appeared, so local crafts were undermined and the old combined workshop-retailing establishments were replaced by specialist retailers of manufactured goods. The railways greatly enhanced this process by providing speedy transport even of perishable commodities.

(d) Part of the specialization process was the wider occurrence of the lock-up shop.

(e) By the 1880s the developments in (b) and (c) had reached a further stage with the appearance both of multiple stores and department stores, the former especially in the grocery trade. Thomas Lipton started a one-man grocery store in Glasgow in 1872; by 1899 he had 245 branches throughout Britain.[27]

(f) The distribution of manufactured goods demanded increasing storage space and such facilities were provided sometimes in separate buildings, but most frequently on the upper floors of retail shops.

(g) With the changes above, and related to urban growth itself, there was a greater demand for professional services. Attorneys and surgeons were among the most obvious of those seeking central locations, but a variety of other users also located themselves here, offering services to business, auctioneers and accountants, or to the public, such as lending libraries.

(3) *Transport technology*. There were two aspects which greatly affected the towns.

(a) The impact of a developing railway system was immediate as it was a significant consumer of urban land. The railways pushed their termini as far as was possible into the town centres, clearing swathes of existing housing, usually of low quality, and creating characteristic sectors. 'Districts divided and confined by the railways tended to be cast finally and irretrievably into the now familiar mould of coal and timber yards, warehousing, mixed light and heavy industrial users and fourth rate residential housing'.[28] Railways themselves took up some 5.4 per cent of central land in London and 9.0 per cent in Liverpool.[29] Shaw has noted two further consequences, the forcing up of land values and the provision of very distinctive boundaries to many central areas.[30]

(b) The century began with what has been called 'the walking city', that is where movement was primarily on foot. The operation of the town at the beginning of the period was organized about highly limited mobility; indeed, its extent and structure was largely determined by it. By the end of the century this had largely been transformed. The carriage was supplemented by the railway, the electric tramcar, the omnibus and eventually replaced by the motorcar. The bonds of immobility which restrained the town into a tightly limited circumstance were effectively broken by the First World War.

It is appropriate to illustrate the impact of these changes on a relatively small town, representative of the many which were transformed during the nineteenth century.

The population of Neath increased from 2512 to 13,720 during the nineteenth century and the impact of this growth upon the evolution of its internal structure can be demonstrated by setting out a series of inter-related developments (Fig. 14.5). The prime mover, in line with the generalized pattern established above, was the growth of a well-defined industrial region built, it is true, on somewhat earlier beginnings. The controls were the transport lines formed by the River Neath, the Neath Canal (1791) and the South Wales railway (1850). The components were predominantly brickworks, steel and tinplate, and chemicals, which built up an elongated region extending south from the medieval core. Adjacent to this region, and with the main

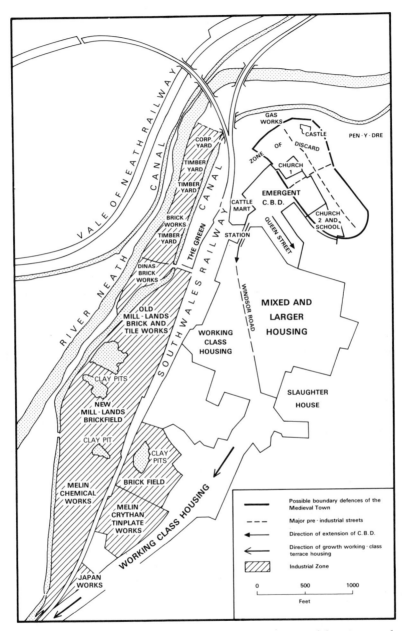

Fig. 14.5. The structure of Neath, Glamorgan in the last quarter of the nineteenth century.

Swansea–Cardiff road as an axis, a series of working-class residential areas grew. Melincrythan and Penrhiwtyn are examples. With the growth of the town (and its hinterland), retail and trading functions also increased and a clear central business district was created. As this occurred, so the whole area shifted south and developed away from the old core so that the old High Street with its Market Hall became no more than a decadent part of the shopping area, a true zone of discard as witnessed by the change of its name to Old Market Street. The streets of the new shopping centre were greatly different from those of the medieval nucleus. The cause of this shift was probably simple demand for the space that was more easily available to the south because of site conditions, but more particularly a closer relation to the southward growth of the industrial region and associated working-class housing.

As the earlier core was partly abandoned, it can be considered a zone of discard, and the space left vacant was taken over by the poorest sections of the population. Two areas of dereliction developed, the one immediately about the castle and locationally coincident with the medieval nucleus, the other in the relict area between railway and river, inappropriately called the Green, but truly on the wrong side of the tracks. Thus another characteristic piece of the central part of the town had come into being, what is now called the inner city.

Neath demonstrates effectively the emergence of a retail core, industrial region and railway zone. But it was never to demonstrate a distinctive financial area since it was too small, though a small but clearly identifiable administrative area was created after the Second World War. Thus both the rapidity and degree of land-use segregation depended fundamentally on the size of the settlement and the rapidity of development. The move towards segregation had appeared much earlier in larger towns. Thus Cardiff, the administrative capital of South Wales, had both a distinctive financial area and especially a very distinctive administrative area in Cathays Park.[31] These testify to the most ubiquitous functions which developed during the nineteenth century, finance as a response to the growing demands of the entrepreneurs and administration due to the growing complexity of local government.

To switch to the largest of scales and consider London may seem somewhat outrageous, but in spite of the contrast the same processes were operative. Because of London's size and significance, most of the basic developments had taken place before 1730. Thus the growth of 'The City' from Tudor times as the core of finance and trading, the Royal Exchange dated to 1570, and the increased land values which were a consequence, had displaced industry northwards to villages like Clerkenwell and Spitalfields, and to the river front, especially down stream of the Tower where it was clearly associated with wharves and warehouses and the processing of imported materials. The industrial East End has thus been created, although it was to grow enormously in size and intensity around a nexus of new docks during the nineteenth century. Since the complexities of London are so great, two characteristic areas only will be considered to demonstrate the process. The first is the development of West End retailing which was already apparent in 1730 but which was greatly transformed after 1815, the other, the growth of Bloomsbury.

Shaw has established three phases in the emergence of the West End as the prime retailing concentration in London.[32] The first was the construction of bazaars in the 1830s and 1840s, virtually the market-hall stage identified earlier. Shaw notes that there were ten in early Victorian London with Oxford Street, a new axis of extension, being one of the major locations. The second phase was the increase in shop size by amalgamation with the intention of establishing 'island' sites dominating a whole block. The third phase after 1880 was the construction of purpose-built stores reaching its peak with the opening of Selfridges in 1909. The major forces behind this developing pattern were the traditional combination of pull and push. It was most clearly pulled by the westward extension of London and by the nature of that extension, dominated as it was by the highest quality residences. It was also pushed out by the City as that became the dominant presence of financial and business services, tied about the major institutions such as the Bank of England, the Royal Exchange and the Stock Exchange. Moreover Kellett has argued that the land values in the City were six to eight times as high as even the most elegant West End residential areas so that for that reason also finance remained fixed and it was residence and retailing which shifted.[33]

The second area, Bloomsbury, also developed around core institutions but they were of a very different character, the British Museum and the University of London. The British Museum was originally the site of Montague House built in 1668 but in 1755 it had been replaced by the Museum and the present building was erected between 1823 and 1847. Because of the University and University College, other institutions were also located in the area such as the Slade School of Fine Art in 1871. The area was early developed, Bloomsbury Square, originally Southampton Square, dating to 1660. But it was with the development of the Bedford estate by builders such as Cubit and Burton that the series of handsome squares were constructed during the early nineteenth century. Lawyers found these houses convenient to the Inns of Court, but it was the influx of intellectuals, writers, painters and musicians which gave the area its particular character and in the early part of the present century it reached its apotheosis in the Bloomsbury group. It is also noteworthy relative to its character that to the south it abutted and overlapped another distinctive region developed about Drury Lane and Soho Square. Here then is an easily identified, highly specialized urban region which had crystallized out of the amorphous scene in a process so characteristic of the period under review. Other distinctive pieces from the resultant mosaic could have been chosen; Soho and Fleet Street are the most obvious. But it needs to be added that these use-areas were never in any sense discrete for not only were there overlaps but most uses could be found somewhere within them.

London, therefore, illustrates in a far more specialized way the same processes that were operative in Neath and Cardiff, the tendency for more and more specialized land-use associations to emerge, more clearly segregated as growth provided the stimulation and changes in technology and government set up new demands.

If internal restructuring of the city was a dominant process, its corollary was the outward extension of the built-up area. The critical concept in this process is that of the urban fringe belt, introduced into British historical geography by Conzen[34] and subsequently developed by Whitehand.[35] This concept is based on the fact that towns do not extend evenly and steadily, but by alternating periods of rapid growth and of quiescence or still-stand; this is clearly evidenced by the numerous studies of building cycles during the nineteenth century.[36] As a result there comes about a distinction between an intensively built-up area, the consequence of a growth phase, and a fringing belt immediately about it which is subsequently only slowly encroached upon. This is most obvious in the contrast between the intra-mural areas of medieval towns where the land was finely divided into burgage lots, and the extra-mural areas where land was usually held in much larger parcels, often by large estates. 'It is' writes Conzen, 'as if such a belt once established created its own environment and imposed its own conditions of further development on its area in terms of shape and size of plots, types of land use, and degree of opening up its streets'.[37] As this statement maintains, the fringe belt differs not only in cadastral but also in land-use characteristics. In simplest terms, the existence of open land, held in large extents, at the margin of the city provides opportunities for extensive consumers of urban land. In the nineteenth century such consumers, greatly enhanced by public health and associated legislation, were the variety of public utilities, cemeteries, waterworks, hospitals which were carefully removed from residential areas. Public parks, urban-related market gardening and large country houses with extensive grounds can also be included. When extension starts again in a new period of economic growth and housing boom, a further belt of housing will surround the inner fringe belt. Indeed, it is more likely that parts of the fringe belt will be absorbed, that is engulfed by the new housing demand, even to the extent that it is occluded, or totally converted. The former market garden or large estate built over for housing is a widely recurring feature. But some of the inner fringe belt will remain and give the city an annular structuring as a consequence of the succession of fringe belts which characterize it. Fig. 14.6 indicates this pattern as identified by Conzen[38] and Whitehand[39] in Newcastle with the inner fringe belt (IFB) surrounding the medieval town and the middle fringe belt as a distinctive nineteenth-century feature.

> Even before the IFB was enclosed by the residential expansion of the Victorian period, late fringe belts were forming at much greater distances from the centre. The eighteenth and nineteenth centuries saw the building of numerous country houses within a few miles of the city. During the Victorian period in particular, various institutions (notably several isolation hospitals and a lunatic asylum), residences standing in their own grounds, cemeteries and waterworks found sites generally within one and a half miles of the built-up area of the time. Where the geology permitted, quarries and brickworks found similar peripheral locations. During the vigorous residential growth of the late Victorian period some of the less distant plots were swallowed up by the house builder, but the majority survived to form a discontinuous belt of varying width. This belt stretched northward from the riverside in the area of Elswick and Benwell and incorporated the open spaces of the Town Moor and Nun's Moor. . . . In the east the belt followed approximately the line of Jesmond Dene (where the gorge had attracted a number of country houses) down to the Tyne near its confluence with the Ouseburn. The modern representative of this fringe belt . . . is termed the Middle Fringe Belt.[40] (Fig. 14.6)

The structuring principle behind this model of a city composed of a sequence of fringe belts is that during times of economic boom and of an upswing in the building cycle, housing with its greater demand for accessibility and more intensive use of land will outbid institutions and utilities for urban land and create a ring of residential development, but the reverse will apply in times of economic recession. A characteristic structuring is thus 'written in' to the internal organization of towns.

In later works, Whitehand had continued to strengthen the basis of the fringe belt concept, especially its necessary footing in economic interpretations of land-use organization within the city.[41] If the extension of land-use types, such as residence or

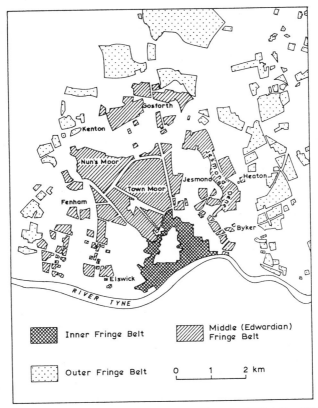

Fig. 14.6. The fringe belts of Newcastle upon Tyne in 1965 (after Whitehand).

institutions, is differentially related to periods of growth and still-stand, then those types must of necessity be related in some way to the traditional bid-rent curves which are used to explain the articulation of land uses. These two elements of urban geography, the fringe belt and the bid-rent curves of uses against distance, have been woven together by Whitehand. Thus Fig. 14.7 demonstrates the relationship between two urban land uses, for argument sake the one simply called intensive (a), and the other extensive (b). The bid-rent curves will differ because to the intensive use accessibility is paramount whereas, although important, it is not as necessary to the same degree to the extensive use which will, therefore, have a gentler slope. In times of boom the situation in Fig. 14.7A will appertain, whereas in a slump, B will be indicative of the situation. The consequence will be a predominance of intensive uses under one condition, of extensive uses under the other. The alternating land-use pattern of the fringe belt sequence is thereby tied into the conventional economic explanations of concentrically-zoned land uses.

But problems do arise from this simplistic notion that a town resembles a tree with the fringe belts analogous to growth rings, clearly identifiable and indicative of successive booms and slumps. It is clear that there is no coincidence in reality between building cycles, the critical reflection of boom and slump, and the age and

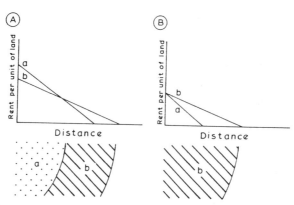

Fig. 14.7. Relationship between bid rents for land-intensive use (a) and land-extensive use (b) and distance from the city centre: (A) during a housebuilding boom, (B) during a housebuilding slump.

character of fringe belts. In addition, the concept of 'absorption' or 'occlusion' has already been introduced to indicate that fringe belts do not remain in their pristine state. The problem of lack of relation in duration between building cycles and fringe belts has been noted by Anthony Sutcliffe[42] who has pointed out that cycles of residential accretion and fringe belt development were much longer than those of house building, whereas if the theory outlined held, they should be exactly coincidental. This Whitehand accepts. 'Between the occlusion of an inner fringe belt in the mid-Victorian period and the present, most British cities have experienced four house building cycles . . . but they are unlikely to have acquired more than two further fringe belts.'[43] This disjunction is not easily explained but is probably part of the standard scale problem of fitting local conditions to a national aggregate. In addition local conditions relating to landholding, as well as the more general issue of the compatibility of uses, are likely to have played a detailed part in individual cities. Again, the significance of a well-defined fixation line can be vital in the formation of belts. Even so, the discrepancy between the direct evidence from housebuilding cycles and that relating to the production of fringe belts must remain disconcerting.

The other difficulty is, perhaps, less fundamental. It is summarized in the statement that 'at first sight the tendency for fringe belts to be perpetuated and augmented long after they cease to be at the edge of the city seems inconsistent with . . . arguments about the relative abilities of institutions and housebuilders to bid for sites'.[44] Thus new relations between distance and bid-rent occur as the city grows, that is as distance increases. So, new patterns should arise and the fringe belt should only be an ephemeral feature eliminated by new land-use arrangements. To a degree this does happen and is subsumed in the concept of absorption. Institutions do relocate farther and farther out as the extensive land held is put under pressure to be redeveloped for more intensive uses. This is not greatly removed from ideas of invasion and succession in land use rather than social terms. But the fringe belt remains identifiable and visible because the value placed on individual buildings and the tradition associated with them, as well as advantages of location inherited rather than having to be bid for, will generate an inertia so that complete transform-

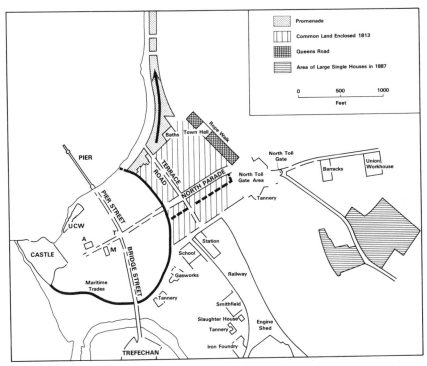

Fig. 14.8. The structure of Aberystwyth in the last quarter of the nineteenth century. A = Assembly Rooms; M = Market Hall; T = Town Hall. The heavy black line shows the former town walls marking the first fixation line. The second fixation line is marked by the Rope Walk and the railway. The heavy broken line marks the rough divide between the higher social status areas of the sea front and the lower status areas adjacent to the railway.

ation of the fringe belt or its elimination is unlikely. It will retain sufficient character to be identifiable and give character to city morphology.

The small town of Aberystwyth in Dyfed can be used to illustrate the issues which have just been discussed.[45] The main lineaments of fringe belts and fixation lines are indicated on Fig. 14.8. The first fixation line was marked by the town wall and effectively operated from 1277, when it was built, to 1813, after it had been demolished, when the area immediately outside it was developed. The outer edge of this inner belt is marked by a second fixation line, which was determined by the change of land ownership from municipal to private, distinctive linear features such as a rope walk and the railway, and to the south by steep valley-side slopes (Fig. 14.8). This second fixation line only lasted until the late 1860s when, with the arrival of the railway, a local boom based on a resort function occurred and residential growth moved beyond it into the middle belt.

Two points can briefly be noted without entering into the complexities of these developments. The translation of the inner fringe belt after some five hundred years of existence was related to local growth and bore no necessary relation to national trends. Indeed, Whitehand uses South Wales, throughout the later period between 1890 and 1915, to demonstrate the clear lack of coincidence between housebuilding

activity in Great Britain and in South Wales,[46] and it was to the latter that Aberystwyth responded.

The second point is that the inner fringe belt, the common land of the medieval
borough, was substantially translated in use after 1813, but its identity remained
quite clear. In that year the land was enclosed and the northern section was used for
residential extension, although after the mid-1860s part was reconverted into an
extension of the central business district. But its grid-like layout means that it stands
out quite distinctively from the block structure of the town within the former walls,
and the linearity of extensions after 1870. The part of the inner fringe belt to the south
still retains its open extensive structure for the plot pattern has been only partly
modified for some sporadic residential development, both public and private. It
might be argued that this survival is simply a function of smallness of size. In relative
terms, however, the town has grown considerably, but away from this southern
section of the inner belt which has been left almost in relict form and clearly
identifiable.

The brief analysis of this example goes some way to meet criticisms of the fringe
belt concept and its utility in morphological analyses. The belts identified are a
response to specific local conditions of growth and the specific impact of fixation
lines, again created by local circumstances. And whilst translation has subsequently
occurred the belts still stand out quite clearly in morphological terms.

Into these schemata of fringe development it is possible to integrate still further
elements in order to move towards a more complete interpretation of townscapes as
it evolved in the nineteenth century. Thus innovation in building technology is likely
to coincide with periods of rapid growth; it is a constituent of a boom. Domestic
living changed substantially during the period under review. The development of
fixed baths and water closets flushing into town drains, of internal hot water systems
and town gas for lighting and cooking, all attracted the increasingly prosperous
middle class into new houses with modern conveniences. But not only did they want
to enjoy these advantages, they wished to emulate the country gentry. A house in its
own grounds was not exactly an estate, but it was an acceptable substitute. The
classic lines of the Regency town house went out of fashion and the turreted gothic
mansion with its lawns, flower beds and monkey puzzle trees unambiguously
displaying social status replaced it—'gabled gothic hard and red, with here a
monkey puzzle tree and there a round geranium bed'.[47]

These new houses filled in the fringe belts, but their growth took place not only at
the margins but also, through conversion, in the extant areas so that innovation
worked its way to the core. To revert to the example of Aberystwyth, Victorian gothic
can be characteristically found in the conversion or translation of the middle fringe
belt which occurred in the late nineteenth century and the beginning of the
twentieth, but conversion also took place in the inner fringe belt, where, for example,
the present Ceredigion Museum, once a theatre, is an admirable example. But still
farther into the core, Nash's Castle House built in the 1790s was remodelled in the
1860s and became simply the core of a projected hotel after a fantasy design by
Seddon. It eventually became the nucleus of the University College of Wales. That
use still remains as 'The Old College', but the newer College has been established on
a new site within what can be called a second middle fringe belt exemplifying an
expected and characteristic outward shift of use needing extensive land. But note

that in keeping with former comment, the earlier location has not been abandoned. All this suggests that an integrated interpretation of urban morphology and land use in the nineteenth century is possible, but as yet it is promised rather than accomplished.

Conclusion

This chapter has been devoted to two aspects of change between 1730 and 1914, mainly during the nineteenth century. The first was the driving force, town growth and the transformation of the urban hierarchy. The second attempted to clarify its consequence in terms of town morphology. All these aspects, and others too of social change, must be integrated in interpretation, as they actually were in reality.

References

1. G. Robert Stange, 'The frightened poets', in H. J. Dyos and M. Wolff (eds.), *The Victorian City: Images and Reality*, (London, 1973), pp. 475–94.
2. A. F. Weber, *The Growth of Cities in the Nineteenth Century*, (New York, 1988).
3. H. C. Darby (ed.), *A New Historical Geography of England*, (Cambridge, 1973).
4. B. T. Robson, *Urban Growth: an Approach*, (London, 1973).
5. P. Clark and P. Slack, *English Towns in Transition*, (Oxford, 1976), Chapter 1, pp. 1–16, and Chapter 6, pp. 82–96; C. W. Chalkin, *The Provincial Towns of Georgian England*, (London, 1974), pp. 4–31.
6. J. Adams, *Index Villaris or an Alphabetical list of all Cities, Market Towns, Parishes, Villages and Private Seats in England and Wales*, (London, 1680).
7. J. de Vries, *European Urbanization 1500–1800*, (Cambridge Mass., 1984).
8. C. M. Law, 'The growth of urban population in England and Wales, 1801–1911', *Transactions, Institute of British Geographers*, Old Ser., **41** (1967), pp. 125–43.
9. Chalklin, *Provincial Towns of Georgian England* p. 5.
10. H. Carter, *The Towns of Wales: a Study in Urban Geography*, (2nd edn.) (Cardiff, 1966), pp. 29–68.
11. For example, H. C. Darby, 'The age of the improver: 1600–1800', in Darby (ed.), *A New Historical Geography of England*, p. 381; Chalklin, *Provincial Towns of Georgian England*, pp. 13–17.
12. B. T. Robson, *Urban Growth*, pp. 98–127.
13. *Ibid.*, pp. 16–127.
14. *Ibid.*, p. 38.
15. P. Haggett, A. D. Cliff and A. Frey, *Locational Models*, (London, 1977).
16. *Ibid.*, pp. 123–4.
17. The most useful summary of this contribution is in A. Pred, *City-systems in Advanced Economies*, (London, 1977).
18. For a review of the problems of Cardiff in the nineteenth century see M. J. Daunton, *Coal Metropolis. Cardiff 1870–1914*, (Leicester, 1977), pp. 15–71.
19. B. T. Robson, 'The impact of functional differentiation within systems of industrialized cities', in H. Schmal (ed.), *Patterns of European Urbanization since 1500*, (London, 1981), Chapter 4, pp. 19–131.
20. *Census* 1851, Vol. 1, p. xiix.
21. J. de Vries, *European Urbanization*, p. 254.
22. *Ibid.*, p. 149.
23. H. Carter, *The Towns of Wales, A Study in Urban Geography*, (Cardiff, 1965), p. 68.

24. J. de Vries, *European Urbanization*, p. 167.
25. *Ibid.*, p. 260.
26. G. Rees, *St. Michael: A History of Marks and Spencer*, (London, 1969).
27. J. B. Jeffreys, *Retail Trading in Britain, 1850–1950*, (London, 1954).
28. J. R. Kellett, *The Impact of Railways on Victorian Cities*, (London and Toronto, 1969), p. 293.
29. *Ibid.*, p. 290.
30. G. Shaw, 'Recent research on the commercial structure of nineteenth-century British cities', in D. Denecke and G. Shaw (eds.), *Urban Historical Geography. Recent Progress in Britain and Germany*. (Cambridge, 1988), Chapter 16, pp. 245–6.
31. H. Carter, 'Cardiff, local, regional and national capital', in G. Gordon, (ed.), *Regional Cities in the U.K.*, (London, 1986), Chapter 10, pp. 182–3.
32. G. Shaw and M. T. Wild, 'Retail patterns in the Victorian city', *Transactions, Institute of British Geographers*, new series, **4** 1979, 278–91.
33. J. R. Kellett, *Impact of Railways*, p. 311.
34. M. R. Conzen, 'Alnwick, Northumberland: a study in town plan analysis', *Transactions, Institute of British Geographers*, **27** (1960).
35. J. W. R. Whitehand, 'Fringe belts: a neglected aspect of urban geography', *Transactions, Institute of British Geographers*, **41** (1967), pp. 223–33. The most useful summary is J. W. R. Whitehand, 'The changing nature of the urban fringe: a time perspective', in J. H. Johnson (ed.), *Suburban Growth. Geographical Processes at the Edge of the Western City*, (London, 1974), Chapter 3, pp. 31–52.
36. J. Parry Lewis, *Building Cycles and Britain's Growth*, (London, 1965).
37. Conzen, 'Alnwick, Northumberland', p. 81.
38. M. R. G. Conzen, 'The plan analysis of an English city centre', in K. Norborg (ed.), *Proceedings of the I. G. U. Symposium in Urban Geography, Lund 1960*, (Lund, 1962), pp. 383–414.
39. Whitehand, 'Fringe belts, a neglected aspect of urban geography'.
40. *Ibid.*
41. J. W. R. Whitehand, *The Changing Face of Cities. A Study of Development Cycles and Urban Form*. Institute of British Geographers, Special Publication no. 21.
42. A. Sutcliffe, Review of J. W. R. Whitehand 'The Urban Landscape', *Journal of Historical Geography*, **9** (1983), pp. 77–9.
43. Whitehand, *'The Changing Face of Cities'*, p. 83.
44. *Ibid.*, 85.
45. H. Carter and S. Wheatley, 'Fixation lines and fringe belts, land uses and social areas: nineteenth century changes in the small town', *Transactions, Institute of British Geographers*, new ser., **4** (1979), pp. 214–38.
46. Whitehand, *'The Changing Face of Cities'*, p. 15.
47. J. Betjeman, 'Thoughts on the Diary of a Nobody', *Collected Poems*, (London, 1958), pp. 259–60.

15

The Social Geography of Towns and Cities 1730–1914

R. Dennis

It is a strange shortcoming of research on the social geography of cities during the age of industrialization that attention has turned only recently to labour and capital processes underlying more measurable and observable features such as residential patterns, housing characteristics and geographical mobility. Parts of this chapter will attempt to redress this imbalance, but, bearing in mind the paucity of empirical work on the geography of employment and finance in nineteenth-century cities, my comments will necessarily be more speculative than definitive.

The period from 1730 to 1914 witnessed several major transitions; from a predominantly rural to an overwhelmingly urban society, from a domestic to a factory system of production, and from mercantile to industrial to the beginnings of finance or corporate capitalism. But these changes varied from place to place in their impact on society, as a comparison of London with 'workshop cities' such as Birmingham and Sheffield, and with 'factory cities' like Leeds and Manchester will seek to demonstrate.

Casual Labour, Poverty and the Inner City

Numerically, London was always the country's foremost industrial city. In 1861, almost 15 per cent of all workers in manufacturing industry in England and Wales were employed in London, a total of 469,000, as many as the entire population of Manchester and Salford; but most of them were working in small workshops or at home. As late as 1851, 75 per cent of employees in London worked in firms with less than five workers, and 86 per cent of industrial employers engaged fewer than ten men. Only 1.6 per cent of employees worked in firms with 50 or more fellow workers, and there were only 17 establishments with more than 250 workers.[1] During the course of the nineteenth century, some of London's largest-scale operations declined. Silk-weaving in Spitalfields collapsed early in the century, in the face of free trade and more efficient factory production in Cheshire; Thamesside shipbuilding collapsed in the 1860s, reflecting the use of new kinds of raw materials and the increasing size of vessels, to which Clydeside and the north-east were more suited.[2] So London became a city of very diverse but mainly small-scale manufacturing, and a city with an enormous range of service activities. In 1861, 903,000 Londoners were engaged in 'service industries', including building, gas and water, transport, distributive trades, banking and insurance, public administration and professional services.[3] The latter offered well-paid and secure employment, but many service activities were seasonal, casual, insecure and poorly paid, especially work in the building industry, in portering (e.g. in wholesale markets like Covent Garden, Billingsgate and Smithfield), and in the docks. London also attracted large numbers of self-employed street traders, particularly during periods of economic depression. So the metropolis became a major focus for casual labour, and many of the city's social problems stemmed from this fact.

The relationship between the labour market and the housing market in London in the second half of the nineteenth century has been explored in a classic work of social history, *Outcast London*, by G. Stedman Jones, but more recently a historical geographer, D. Green, has examined the origins of the labour problem in *early-nineteenth-century London*.[4] Green shows that major changes in industrial organization in trades like clothing and shoemaking were associated with changes in social geography. The eighteenth-century industry had concentrated in small workshops, mostly in the West End, close to the homes of wealthy customers. It was a 'bespoke' form of manufacture, producing clothing, shoes, furniture and other household goods to order; and it provided employment for skilled adult males who had progressed through apprenticeship to the status of journeymen and, ultimately, masters. During the nineteenth century it was superseded by 'slop' manufacture, of lower quality, mass-produced goods, for purchase 'off the peg' by a new clientele of modestly well-off lower-middle-class clerks and by a new urban proletariat. The new forms of production involved a much greater division of labour, each worker responsible for only one stage in the manufacturing process. Associated with this fragmentation and mechanization of manufacturing went deskilling and a greater use of female labour, paid by the piece rather than at an hourly rate. Workers were employed either in sweat-shops or as outworkers, in their own homes, called upon only when demand required them. The location of industry shifted from West End to East End, to exploit a female and juvenile labour force, the wives and children of men casually employed in the docks or in heavy industries such as soapmaking, tanning and, later in the century, chemicals, all concentrated close to the Thames or in the lower Lea valley.

The separation of non-manual from manual, middle class from working class, rich from poor, was reinforced and extended. A new scale of residential segregation developed and, associated with it, a new degree of ignorance and neglect. The rich no longer encountered the poor, except through the sensationalism of the press; out of sight, if not out of mind, the poor could be blamed for their poverty and urged to greater efforts of self-help. Even among philanthropic agencies, a distinction was drawn between deserving and undeserving, and the Charity Organisation Society — an umbrella agency for large numbers of different charities and trusts — was as concerned to restrict aid as to dispense it, in order to ensure that the poor were not demoralized by too generous or too easily available forms of assistance.[5]

Yet most poor people were victims of an economic system that offered few opportunities for self-help. Employers' profits depended on increasing their share of the market, expanding production but avoiding overproduction (which reduced prices once supply exceeded demand) by searching out new markets (in distant locations and among lower-income groups) and new products (thereby creating new kinds of demand).[6] At the same time, it was desirable to reduce production costs and accelerate the circulation of capital so that, even if the rate of profit was reduced, investment would yield its return more quickly than before. In London, costs were reduced, partly by deskilling and the use of female or child labour, partly by casualization—only hiring workers when absolutely necessary, and partly by the use of outwork. As land values and rents increased, so employers limited the size of their permanent workshops, shifting the costs of production-space onto employees who would have to find homes large enough to accommodate a workbench, loom or sewing machine. Tools and machinery could also be charged to the outworker. This, in turn, limited the housing opportunities of workers in at least two ways: they were obliged to live within walking distance of workshops and warehouses where they collected materials and delivered completed pieces; and they were forced to seek accommodation in an uncontrolled and overcrowded privately rented housing market, since they could not afford the relatively high and regular weekly rents (with arrears rarely allowed) for better-quality philanthropic or, from the 1890s onwards, local authority dwellings. Moreover, these new kinds of working-class housing were subject to rules and regulations, prohibiting subletting to help pay the rent, and denying tenants the right to undertake paid work within the home; for example, women were not allowed to take in laundry work, and costermongers were rarely provided with space to store barrows or stock.[7]

By the late nineteenth century, a cycle of poverty had developed in the East End: parents encouraged their children to seek evening and weekend employment, and to leave school at the earliest opportunity, taking jobs which, in the short term proved quite well-paid—as errand boys or newspaper vendors, for example—but which had no future and provided no skilled training for adult life, thereby perpetuating the existence of an unskilled, uneducated 'reserve army' of casual labour.[8]

The casual labour problem was not unique to London's East End. It existed to some degree in all large provincial cities, for example in Liverpool where, as in London, the demand for dock labour combined with the presence of a substantial migrant labour force (in this case mainly Catholic Irish). In Liverpool in 1871, approximately 12 per cent of the adult male workforce was employed in dockside warehouses or docks, where labour was hired on a half-day basis.[9] Men were recruited from 'stands' at fixed times of the day, starting at 6.50 a.m. There were no special lists, giving regular attenders priority, but in practice, men either followed a particular firm or shipping line, or they regularly attended the same 'stand', where in time they were recognized and given preference.[10] This pattern of allegiance, the early start to the day, and the uncertainty that there would be any work at all, meant that dock labourers found lodgings close to their preferred workplace. In 1871, 77 per cent of Liverpool dock workers lived within a mile of a dock. By comparison, only 12 per cent of office workers lived less than a mile from the central business district, where most were employed.[11] In West Ham, to the east of London, more than half of the dock labourers resident in the borough lived in two Thamesside wards ('Tidal Basin' and 'Custom House and Silvertown') which included the Royal Docks within their boundaries. In these wards, dock labourers comprised 4–5 per cent of the *total*

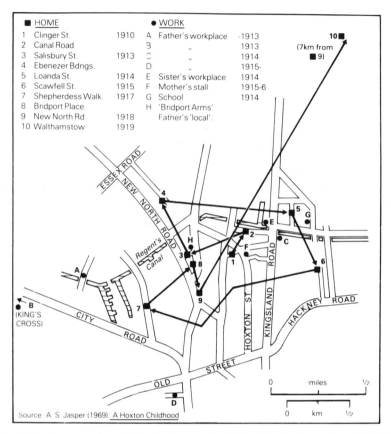

Fig. 15.1. Home and work for the Jasper family in Hoxton, London, 1910–19.

population in 1901 (including women, children and the elderly); by contrast, in the north of the borough, only two miles away, only 0.25 per cent of the population were dockers. Assuming full employment for as many dockers as possible, 20–25 per cent would have had work on less than one day per week; in practice, most dockers worked only three or four days each week.[12] In Liverpool, in 1908, 30 per cent of dockers averaged 30s (£1.50) per week in wages, but 25 per cent received only 7s 6d (37.5p) and 20 per cent 5s (25p) per week. Given house rents of between 5s (25p) and 6s 6d (32.5p) per week, even for three- or four-roomed houses, it is clear that either dockers' families had to 'double up', sharing accommodation even in small houses, or that they depended on the earnings of several family members to pay the rent for a whole house.[13]

Geographically, one consequence was to create necessarily self-sufficient working-class communities, 'mutualities of the oppressed',[14] in which poor families depended far more on one another for help in times of crisis than they did on the beneficence of charity or the state. Working-class families moved house frequently, from one set of rented rooms to another, but they rarely moved far, always remaining close to pubs and corner-shops where they could expect to obtain credit, and to markets and 'houses of call' (informal employment offices, often in pubs, where master craftsmen would recruit labour) where they were known by potential employers. For example, the Jasper family moved nine times in Hoxton, in London's East End, in nine years between 1910 and 1919. Each move reflected a change in the family's circumstances: employment and unemployment, birth and death, family members leaving home or returning home. Moving house was usually easily achieved; because the turnover rate was so high, there were always some vacant dwellings; tenancies were on weekly terms; and removal costs were negligible — 6d (2.5p) for a day's hire of a costermonger's barrow on which possessions could be trundled through the streets to the new home, or 5s (25p) for the luxury of four hours' use of greengrocer's horse and van. Information on vacancies would be supplied by friends, workmates or the rent collector; so families inevitably learnt more about nearby houses to let than about (possibly more suitable) vacancies farther away. Wherever the Jasper family lived, they remained within comfortable walking distance of Wilmer Gardens, where mother ran a clothes stall, and of the 'Bridport Arms', father's favourite 'local' (Fig. 15.1).[15]

Suburbia

At the same time as the London economy created an unskilled, marginal under-class, concentrated in the Victorian equivalent of today's inner-city 'urban priority areas', it also generated other novel elements in class structure: a labour aristocracy of skilled mechanics and engineers, responsible for building and maintaining new machinery, strongly unionized, but also attracted by middle-class values of respectability, self-help and home ownership; and a lower middle class of clerks, book-keepers, bank cashiers, junior managers and schoolteachers, perfectly satirized in the Grossmiths' depiction of Mr Pooter and his family and friends in *The Diary of a Nobody*.[16] Each of these classes found its natural habitat in suburbia in speculatively built, by-law terraced housing, either in places like Camberwell and Hackney, dependent on new forms of public transport — horse trams in the 1870s, cheap fares on suburban railways in the 1880s, electric trams by the early 1900s, or in industrial suburbs like West Ham and Woolwich, where workplaces such as the Great Eastern Railway works at Stratford and the Woolwich Arsenal were on a larger scale, and where the social structure and supporting institutions more closely resembled those of the industrial north.[17] For example, two expressions of working-class self-help — the co-operative retail store and the building society — were successful in Victorian London only in these atypical industrial suburbs.[18]

If the socio-spatial structure of inner districts was a creation of industrial capitalism, so too was suburbia. Marxist geographers have argued that suburban development was one way out of a crisis of overaccumulation of industrial capital which could not be re-invested in existing industries without precipitating problems of overproduction. The 'solution' was to divert profits from manufacturing into a secondary circuit of capital, based on the provision of infrastructure vital for the social reproduction of labour: housing, public utilities, health-care and education. Of course, this is to regard the improvement of living conditions cynically in purely profit-making terms, but it provides a welcome, if exaggerated, corrective to a 'Whig' view of history, in which the heroic and progressive character of Victorian urban development has been emphasized.[19] A little less cynically, advances in the quality of housing and sanitation may be interpreted as middle-class reactions, first to the fear of disease—smallpox, cholera, typhus—spreading from slums into respectable districts, and latterly to the fear of immorality—especially, in London, incest, which was blamed on overcrowding—corrupting even respectable, hard-working labouring families.[20] Improvements in the built environment were assumed to create a healthier, more contented and ultimately more productive workforce, less prone to industrial or political protest, more capable of fighting for their country. Hence, the building of model villages by industrialists in the late eighteenth and nineteenth centuries: Styal in Cheshire, Copley outside Halifax, and Saltaire, outside Bradford, are perhaps the best preserved examples. Hence, too, the first garden suburbs and cities: Port Sunlight, Bournville, Letchworth; and hence the introduction after the First World War of subsidized council housing—'homes fit for heroes'—based on the wartime experience that you could not produce an 'A1 population' out of 'C3 homes'.[21]

But the suburban *lifestyle* was also important, creating demands for new kinds of consumer goods: three-piece suites and pianos, household appliances, flush toilets, lawn mowers, bicycles. So suburbia offered a way out of overproduction of a limited range of goods, by providing the setting and the demand for new products. Yet suburban development was two-edged: in solving one problem, it created others. Capitalism depends on growth, change and development; but established suburban populations, especially once they started to own their homes outright or on mortgages, became anti-growth and anti-change. Suburban owner-occupiers strove to maintain, if not enhance, property values by preserving the status quo, opposing non-residential development, excluding outsiders. Restrictive covenants, originally introduced by ground landlords anxious to ensure high-quality development, were subsequently reasserted by long-term tenants, sometimes contrary to their landlord's own revised assessment of his estate's potential. In Edgbaston, an elite suburb of Birmingham laid out by Lord Calthorpe from the 1820s, tenants argued against relaxing covenants to permit the opening of shops, and they opposed the laying of tramlines through the estate, as much because they promised to make the area *too* accessible as on grounds of environmental pollution.[22] Suburbs tended to increase levels of residential differentiation: most suburbs were one-class and, by attracting the professional middle classes and petty bourgeoisie to live at a distance from their city-centre businesses, they led also to one-class, working-class inner districts. What, at one level, was an efficient use of capital, at another proved threatening to the interests of capital, by providing locales for the development of working-class political movements and a broadly based working-class consciousness, uniting workers in different industries but living as neighbours in solidly working-class communities.

Social Structure and Spatial Structure

In practice, such class consciousness existed more in the fertile imaginations of middle-class observers than on the ground among ordinary working-class households.[23] But it flourished briefly in some textile towns especially in Lancashire and

Cheshire in the first half of the nineteenth century. Here, the industrial structure was very different from London's East End. Units of employment were much larger, particularly in the cotton spinning industry. For example, the *average* number of workers employed in cotton textiles firms in Manchester in 1841 was 264. In Blackburn there were 281 workers per firm: eight firms, each with at least 500 workers, together accounted for 53 per cent of the town's cotton workers; by 1847 the four largest firms employed 42 per cent of the workforce.[24] In these circumstances, some have argued, there was a purely impersonal relationship between master and mill operatives; industrial relations were based on conflict as employees, denied the opportunity to own the means of production, sought to wrest control of the conditions and pace of work.[25]

The classic statements of this argument appear in two sets of contemporary observations by distinguished foreign visitors: Count Alexis de Tocqueville's account of his travels in England in 1835, in which he compared Manchester, the archetypal factory town, with Birmingham, like London a city of small workshops, but unlike London supposedly a city of social mobility, prosperity, health and community; and Engels' passionate analysis of *The Condition of the Working Class in England*, much of it based on his first-hand experience of Manchester in 1844.[26]

De Tocqueville recorded his reactions succinctly: 'At Manchester a few great capitalists, thousands of poor workmen and little middle class. At Birmingham, few large industries, many small industrialists. At Manchester workmen are counted by the thousand, two or three thousand in the factories. At Birmingham the workers work in their own houses or in little workshops in company with the master himself. . . . From the look of the inhabitants of Manchester, the working people of Birmingham seem more healthy, better off, more orderly and more moral than those of Manchester.' The consequence was that the 'separation of classes' was much greater in Manchester than Birmingham.

The geography of class was elaborated by Engels, who described Manchester as a series of concentric zones: a non-residential central business district, surrounded by 'unmixed working-people's quarters', in turn encompassed by the 'regularly laid out streets' of the middle bourgeoisie, and finally, the detached villas of the upper bourgeoisie. The pattern clearly resembled that identified by Burgess in Chicago eighty years later (Fig. 15.2)[27]; and the processes at work were the same free-market forces, creating a land-value surface which excluded relatively low-value residential uses not only from the city centre but also from the main traffic arteries radiating from the centre to the middle-class suburbs. The result was a 'hypocritical plan' which served 'to conceal from the eyes of the wealthy men and women of strong stomachs and weak nerves the misery and grime which form the complement of their wealth'.[28]

Yet in reality no *formal* planning lay behind this zoning of people and land uses: the only *planned* residential segregation in Georgian or Victorian cities occurred on the extensive estates of large landowners. On Lord Calthorpe's Edgbaston estate in Birmingham, zoning was intended 'to keep apart the welcomed wealthy and the tolerated tradesmen'.[29] In late Victorian London, the Duke of Westminster reserved sites for philanthropic model dwellings around the edges of his estates in Mayfair and Belgravia. Whatever the sincerity of the Duke's philanthropy, it is evident that this plan helped to protect the highest-quality parts of his estate from the spread of

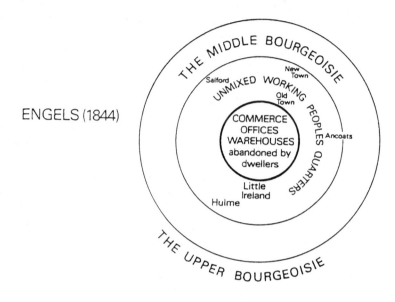

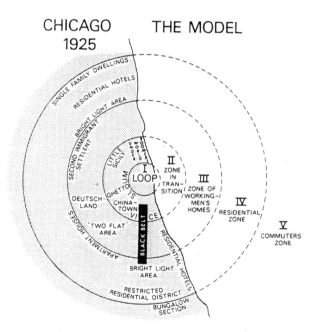

Fig. 15.2. Engels' Manchester and Burgess' Chicago.

surrounding slums. Moreover, the model dwellings also provided orderly accommodation for the army of shop assistants, non-resident servants and service workers, like carpenters and plumbers, whose presence nearby was essential for the maintenance of an aristocratic lifestyle.[30]

An even clearer example of this kind of intra-estate residential segregation occurred earlier in the century in the layout of the Crown estate in Regent's Park by John Nash where, behind the elaborate stuccoed upper-class terraces facing the park, were mews cottages for servants, streets of modest terraced housing for tradesmen and artisans, a canal basin for agricultural produce, and meat, hay and vegetable markets. The Regent's Canal itself skirted the northern edge of the park, functioning not only as a transport artery and a picturesque landscape feature, but also as a barrier between the rich in the park and poorer districts to the north and east. There were few ways into the park between the terraces, and those there were could be carefully policed. And the park itself was only fully opened to the public in 1841, fifteen years after the completion of most of the buildings. To the south, Regent Street also functioned to separate elite estates to the west from lower-class streets in Soho.[31] Yet all these examples were still only *estate planning*, not *town planning*.

In fact, Manchester's social geography was more complex than Engels' 'model' indicated. His own description of different inner-city communities—Little Ireland, Old Town, Ancoats—hints at not only an ethnic dimension to residential differentiation, but also segregation within the working classes, between the respectable, regularly employed factory workers and less secure street traders and casual labourers.

And in every large town, segregation in space was matched by segregation in time. Working-class and middle-class residents might use the same streets, but for different functions and at different times. Social segregation was not only a matter of where people lived—where they were recorded in directories or ratebooks, or enumerated by the census takers—but also of how they *appropriated* space. For example, Harrison has shown how public meetings and processions were located so as 'both to give to and gain from their surroundings an extra representational significance . . . the appropriation of public space gave that space new meanings. The self-confident solidity of Georgian squares became shaky when repeatedly occupied by shabby but sober political aspirants.'[32] The selection of a new route for a procession 'could in itself induce panic among the upper classes because of the implications of a break in routine; established patterns of crowd occurrence made crowd events both more comprehensible and, as importantly, avoidable.'[33] Even the working-class 'rush hour' was a routine crowd event to be avoided by the sensitive middle class, as Mrs Gaskell noted of her heroine in *North and South*. Near her home there were many mills, 'out of which poured streams of men and women two or three times a day. Until Margaret had learnt the times of their ingress and egress, she was very unfortunate in constantly falling in with them.'[34]

If Manchester was not as simple spatially as it was often depicted, this was partly because it was not so simple socially and economically as observers like de Tocqueville implied. Manchester contained a larger and more diverse middle class than smaller factory towns, including foreign merchants and businessmen (like Engels himself!) and 'a very considerable commercial population, especially of commission and "respectable" retail dealers'.[35] Indeed, Billinge has suggested that the class struggle between proletariat and bourgeoisie was less significant than that between old and new middle classes: the landed gentry and the new bourgeoisie. Billinge's emphasis is social rather than territorial: he focuses on institutions, such as the Manchester Literary and Philosophical Society, in which a struggle for cultural and political authority was played out.[36] Studies of the Manchester middle classes have also examined the role of Nonconformist chapels, especially Cross Street Unitarian Chapel, and patterns of intermarriage associated with the consolidation of a business elite. Gatrell argues that 'The very depth of the chasm between rich and poor . . . almost guaranteed in the rich an inward-turning or self-referential mentality.' From a middle-class perspective, 'Manchester's political life in the first half of the nineteenth century was dominated less by overt class conflict than by the competitive pursuit of power by groupings within the middle-class community.'[37]

By comparison with Manchester, contemporary observers viewed Birmingham much more favourably; the literature on Birmingham emphasizes community, class collaboration, harmony and social mobility rather than conflict and class struggle. Thus, Briggs concluded: 'If Engels had lived not in Manchester but in Birmingham, his conception of "class" and his theories of the role of class in history might have been very different. In this case Marx might have been not a communist but a currency reformer.'[38]

These speculations on the nature of class structure in different economic circumstances are of value to historical geographers because they direct us to examine the connections between 'shapes in society' and 'shapes on the ground'. Cannadine suggested a simple model linking the presence or absence of residential differentiation to the degree of class consciousness, eschewing any hint of a crude determinism in the relationship, but emphasizing the variety of ways in which different 'shapes on the ground' could be used and interpreted by urban residents.[39] The absence of large-scale residential differentiation could reflect the 'Birmingham' type of intermixing and mutual dependence of masters and men, or a paternalistic involvement of employers and managers in the everyday lives of their employees, characteristic of 'industrial colonies' in many cotton towns (e.g. Blackburn, Bolton, Ashton-under-Lyne) as well as of the 'model villages' praised by parliamentary committees and in 'social novels' like Disraeli's Sybil;[40] but it could also facilitate the growth of a radical working-class consciousness, as the working classes faced constant reminders of just what they were missing, and as politically aware skilled artisans and little masters could create a proletariat out of their otherwise disorganized neighbours. Indeed, it is notable that Oldham, a cotton town in which the scale of factory employment was much smaller than in Blackburn or Ashton, and where there was a large 'middling class' of small masters and petty bourgeoisie, but where residential differentiation was still limited in the 1840s, has been presented by Foster in his highly influential Class Struggle and the Industrial Revolution, as a classic example of working-class consciousness.[41]

Just as variously, the existence of a high degree of residential segregation between workers and employers could yield an absence of *class* action, as different grades of worker jostled for superiority with one another (much as Gatrell suggested of the Manchester elite), but lacked any local target or symbol of wealth or power against which to rally support; or—left to their own devices—a segregated working class might develop the intensity of revolutionary consciousness feared by the elite but predicted and welcomed by Marx and Engels.

Another version of the Manchester–Birmingham, factory–workshop thesis has been presented by Thrift in the context of the current interest among human geographers in 'locality studies' and 'uneven development'.[42] Thrift compares Leeds, the centre of the woollen textiles industry, with Sheffield, examining the period 1850–70 when, he argues, Sheffield was developing a dual economy and a dual class structure. In the old established 'light trades' like cutlery and file-making, a strongly unionized artisanate negotiated with merchant capitalists, little masters and factors (middlemen), some of whom were also housing landlords, in close-knit communities characterized by artisan institutions like sick clubs, Sunday Schools and Methodist chapels. But this potentially cohesive artisan class was in 'an increasingly marginal position in both the local and national systems of production',[43] as new units of employment in the steel industry came to match the scale of the largest Lancashire cotton firms; the firm of John Brown, for example, employed only 200 in 1856, but 5000 by 1872. Steelworkers constituted a new industrial proletariat, strongly segregated in new housing estates, but—at least until the 1880s—with little sense of class consciousness. Yet this was not simply a replacement of 'Birmingham' by 'Manchester': the steel industry involved a different set of class relationships from textiles, for example, in failing to provide employment opportunities for women. Nor were the 1860s and 1870s, a time of generally improving living standards, comparable with the straitened circumstances of the 1830s and 1840s, when a quarter of the Manchester working class were unemployed, and less than a fifth were in full employment.[44]

Leisure

Manufacturing and industrial services (like dock labour) were not the only bases of urbanization in the eighteenth and nineteenth centuries. Inland spas, like Bath and Cheltenham, and seaside resorts, like Blackpool and Scarborough, reproduced the social geography of production in a social geography of leisure.[45] The contrast between main-street terraces and back-street slums was replicated in that between sea-front hotels and back-of-town boarding houses. In Blackpool, middle-class North and South Shores contrasted with working-class lodgings close to the town centre and the railway station.[46] As living standards improved and more people could afford trips to the seaside by public transport, so ecological processes of invasion and succession affected resorts as much as metropolitan centres. Brighton became a holiday 'zone-in-transition', part working-class, part red-light district, part bohemian upper class; while more conservative middle-class families migrated to farther-flung railway termini like Ilfracombe and Torquay.[47] As one-class residential areas proliferated in industrial cities, so exclusively one-class resorts (as opposed to separate districts within a resort) became desirable.

Leisure activities within cities also divided along class lines. The internal layout of public houses came to mirror the structure of society: a variety of bars—saloon, lounge, public—and private rooms separated different classes of customer, and the behaviour and activities associated with each. The introduction of bar counters separated customers from staff, and the removal of seats from town-centre 'gin palaces' reflected a more commercial attitude, encouraging a greater turnover of customers, and more rapid drinking, just as the conversion of 'free houses' into brewery-owned 'tied houses' indicated the trend to corporate or monopoly capitalism.[48]

The geographical distribution of different kinds of licensed establishments was also significant: beerhouses, licensed under the 1830 Beershop Act to brew and sell beer but no spirits, were concentrated on side-streets in working-class districts; public houses licensed for all kinds of alcoholic drink were located on more prominent sites, often on street corners, but still more frequent in commercial districts or working-class residential areas than on middle-class estates.[49] In fact, pubs were frequently excluded from middle-class areas by restrictive covenants written into the terms of sale or lease of land for building. If any licensed premises existed in middle-class suburbs, they were likely to be 'off licences': better-off people purchased alcohol for consumption in the warmth, comfort and privacy of their own homes, but in the poorest districts the pub was a convivial and attractive substitute for cold, bare and uninviting homes. So, in south London in 1903, working-class north Peckham boasted 35 pubs, one for every 483 inhabitants, but only seven off licences, one per 2416 persons; while nearby Alleyn Ward, containing the exclusive and carefully regulated Dulwich College Estate, offered its 14,631 residents only one pub, but 11 off licences.[50]

In working-class districts pubs were used for far more than drinking—they provided meeting places for building clubs and friendly societies, brass bands and debating clubs, horticultural shows and trade unions; they also functioned as labour exchanges and wages offices. So it is not surprising that the temperance movement tried to create its own brand of non-alcoholic pubs, nor that at least one historical geographer has reconstructed patrons' 'journey to pub', much as others have more conventionally charted the lengthening 'journey to work' in the late nineteenth century.[51]

Churches, too, involved far more than religious observance. They offered sports clubs, dramatic societies, sewing circles and mutual improvement societies.[52] If pubs were 'negative externalities' in middle-class areas, churches were regarded as positive amenities. Georgian and Victorian estate developers reserved or donated sites for churches, just as inter-war suburban developers favoured tennis courts and cinemas.[53] But churches erected to maintain a sense of community, to preserve a parochial structure in the perceived impersonality of big cities, gradually came to undermine ties of neighbourhood and locale. The residentially mobile would retain membership even if they moved to a new neighbourhood; each place of worship would develop its own social and doctrinal character—evangelical or Anglo-Catholic, for example; and, however hard they tried, Victorian church builders could never provide premises for every denomination in every neighbourhood! So, with increased mobility and leisure time, 'journey to church' also lengthened, and helped to erode structures of community that depended primarily on the association of near neighbours.[54]

There were also strong correlations between social class and church membership. The new urban bourgeoisie favoured intellectual or rational dissent, as, for example, Cross Street Unitarian in Manchester, or Highfield Independent (Congregational) in

Huddersfield. New, more evangelical, forms of Nonconformity, such as Wesleyan Methodism, tended to attract the families of tradesmen and the labour aristocracy (the Methodist system of local lay preachers and class leaders provided fertile ground for the nurturing of trade union officials and political activists), while Primitive Methodism was more solidly working class (and less urban, strongest in mining areas such as County Durham and Cornwall). Anglicanism was traditionally associated with the gentry, but the sense of mission among both Evangelical and Anglo-Catholic wings of a broad church also made for a strong Anglican presence in the slums.[55]

Political beliefs and voting behaviour frequently paralleled religious affiliation, although the details of the equation depended on local circumstances. In Huddersfield and Bradford, for example, Nonconformity, free trade, self-help and Liberalism went together, while Conservative voters were more often Anglican and more often professional people than tradesmen.[56] But there were also local neighbourhood effects. Tradesmen in predominantly professional districts were more likely to follow their neighbours and vote Tory; shopkeepers in working-class neighbourhoods were sometimes subject to 'exclusive dealing', tantamount to blackmail, fearing violence to their property if not their person, or at the least the withdrawal of trade if they declined to vote as their unenfranchised customers demanded.[57] In a study of Lancashire mill towns in the late 1860s (after the Second Reform Act of 1867 had widened the franchise to include most adult males, but before the introduction of the secret ballot in 1872) Joyce showed how voters of similar socio-economic status, but living in different neighbourhoods, supported different candidates in line with the politics of local millowners. Not only the mill operatives, who might have feared for their jobs if they had voted otherwise, but also other local residents, following occupations quite unconnected with local mills or with providing services to their neighbours, tended to vote according to the custom of their district (Table 15.1).[58]

Table 15.1: Voting patterns in Park Ward, Blackburn, in 1868.

	Per cent voting Liberal in Liberal area	Per cent voting Tory in Tory area
All voters[a]	67	69
All cotton workers	73	76
supervisory	71	89
skilled	73	78
unskilled	75	69
Other workers	65	64
labourers	61	72
iron and engineering	56	81
craft and skilled	53	66
retailers/dealers	73	73
Total no. of voters[a]	938	678

[a]Voters could each vote for two candidates. Figures exclude 'split voters' who divided their votes between the parties.
Source: P. Joyce, *Work, Society and Politics* (Brighton, 1980).

Community and Segregation

Two organizing concepts have underlain many studies of the spatial structure of nineteenth-century cities: 'neighbourhood' or 'community', the notion that residence involves interaction and influence—dissent and conflict as much as harmony and co-operation—and that therefore geography (i.e. place) matters; and 'segregation', emphasizing the geographical separation of different classes and ethnic groups, and most clearly reflected in a debate among historical geographers since the early 1970s, concerning the 'modernity' of Victorian cities.[59] Contemporary observers usually regarded these concepts as mutually exclusive since, to them, 'community' necessarily involved harmony, social balance and a hierarchical, probably deferential, relationship between classes. The ideal of community was contrasted with their distaste for the emergence of 'two nations', each ignorant of and indifferent to the circumstances of the other.[60] Current interpretations suggest rather the superficiality of territorially defined communities, *except* under conditions of residential segregation. 'Community' and 'class' become almost interchangeable terms.[61]

How much, or how complete, a pattern of segregation is required to make a city modern? As Beresford has shown, 'East End' and 'West End' were already distinctive social areas of Leeds in the late eighteenth century, more by accident than as the result of any preconceived plan.[62] Langton and Laxton, too, have illustrated the existence of distinctive occupational and social patterns in eighteenth-century Liverpool;[63] while Baigent suggests that the structure of eighteenth-century Bristol was transitional between those of pre-industrial and modern cities. 'The central parishes were wealthy and housed many commercial and professional men as they always had done, but they were being eclipsed as the highest status areas of the city by the new residential suburbs.'[64] While there was clearly defined segregation at the scale of individual streets, each parish included both rich and poor, high-value and low-value property.

Geographical segregation *within* the extremes of rich and poor, between the two Manchester middle classes, or between different groups within the working classes (other than on ethnic lines) is difficult to identify before the end of the nineteenth century, especially if *exclusively* one-class neighbourhoods are sought.[65] It seems likely that the larger the city, the more complex and the larger in scale were patterns of residential differentiation. Manchester had one-class neighbourhoods, Huddersfield had one-class streets. But a front street–back yard contrast between rich and poor, evident in small towns such as Merthyr Tydfil,[66] and often attributable to eighteenth-century infilling of the gardens of merchants' houses, as in Leeds,[67] survived to the end of the nineteenth century even in London, as Charles Booth's famous map, depicting the poverty or comfort of each street by different colours of shading, so dramatically demonstrated. In red and yellow (very comfortable) Bloomsbury there were still rookeries shaded dark blue or black (direst poverty); and even some new middle-class suburbs contained pockets of newly created slum housing, such as Sultan Street in otherwise respectable Camberwell.[68] How such patterns developed, and survived or altered, leads us finally to a more detailed examination of Georgian and Victorian housing markets.

Housing

In their system and form of housing provision, eighteenth- and nineteenth-century cities might appear to have been far from 'modern'. A predominantly 'Whig' style of housing history has stressed the 'progress' from insanitary, ill-built and unregulated slums to by-law terraces, blocks of council flats and semi-detached suburbia.[69] Associated with changes in housing conditions there have been equally marked changes in tenure. In the eighteenth century few urban households were owner-occupiers. For the poor, homeownership was economically impossible; for the rich, particularly in metropolitan society, it was an inconvenient irrelevance. Far better to take a year's lease of the most fashionable, or the most lavish house one could afford, moving regularly as fashion or personal circumstances altered. Owner-occupation had few advantages in an inflation-free economy, where there were no tax concessions to benefit homeowners rather than landlords or tenants. By contrast, today homeownership is regarded as a universal goal; approximately two-thirds of all dwellings are owner-occupied and only about one in ten householders rents from a private landlord. The change in attitudes to tenure can be traced to the late nineteenth century, to self-help propaganda and middle-class aspirations for suburbia; but changes in actual patterns of ownership really post-date the First World War.[70]

Some aspects of the development process have already been described. In some cities, a handful of aristocratic ground landlords owned a large proportion of land suitable for development. Edgbaston, on the outskirts of Birmingham, was owned by Lord Calthorpe, who also had an estate near King's Cross in London; Mayfair and Belgravia formed part of the Grosvenor estate, Covent Garden and Bloomsbury belonged to the Duke of Bedford; Cardiff was dominated by three landowning families, the Butes, Windsors and Tredegars; most of Huddersfield was owned by the Ramsdens, a clothier family that had inched ahead of its neighbours over the preceding two centuries; Eastbourne and Barrow-in-Furness, two very different places which each grew rapidly in the later nineteenth century, were both owned by the Dukes of Devonshire.[71] These major landlords attempted to plan the development of their estates by carefully drafting building leases to specify the quality and type of development that was permissible, restricting the construction or at least the location of low-value housing and listing the uses to which buildings could be put. During the nineteenth century, leases of 99 or 999 years became common, the latter giving builders and housebuyers the semblance of freehold ownership, but allowing the ground landlords sufficient rights to impose restrictive covenants with a reasonable expectation that they could be enforced. But in the eighteenth century leases had often been much shorter or uncertain in length — scheduled to run during the lives of named individuals, or for a maximum of 21 years, or simply 'tenancies at will' where the leaseholder depended entirely on the goodwill of the landowner.[72] Short leases without covenants provided ideal conditions for the development of purpose-built slums, as at Sultan Street in Camberwell, and as Engels observed in densely packed and shoddily built rows of back-to-back houses in new suburbs of Manchester. He argued that builders erected houses that would last no longer than the length of their lease.[73] But more frequently, the leasehold system led to an overprovision of middle-class houses, which were then subdivided, usually without any extra sanitary amenities, to provide for lower-income households.[74]

Leasehold development has attracted more than its fair share of attention, probably because large-scale aristocratic landlords kept more detailed and better organized records than more speculative, small-scale and ephemeral enterprises. In practice an increasing proportion of new housebuilding used small plots of freehold land, producing a patchwork quilt of land uses and house types. In Leeds, for example, much eighteenth- and early-nineteenth-century development took place in the yards behind front-street houses and workshops. Working-class back-to-back cottages thus adjoined the houses of woollen merchants and leading tradesmen. Interestingly, Beresford found that this kind of development was more common where the front houses were owner-occupied.[75] Presumably, where middle-class tenants were in residence, owners were fearful of offending their tenants' privacy and reducing the rental value of their dwellings by building on back gardens.

Overall, few people of any social class were owner-occupiers. In 1740 only 7 per cent of buildings (and only 1 per cent of cottages) in Leeds were owner-occupied; a century later, 3.8 per cent of dwellings were reported to be owner-occupied. But at each date the proportion was higher in the affluent and suburban West End than in the city centre or East End.[76] For other towns in the later nineteenth century, figures are recorded in Table 15.2. It seems likely that many more new houses were initially occupied by their owners but that, as houses aged, so they passed into the rental market.[77] Moreover, even among the minority of owner-occupiers, homeownership was rarely perceived as it is today. From the 1770s onwards, building clubs—the local, fixed-term equivalent of later permanent building societies—provided for skilled artisans and tradesmen to acquire a row of cottages or a pair or block of back-to-backs rather than individual house purchase.[78] Such petty proprietors might choose, temporarily, to occupy one of their houses themselves, but they were not *just* owner-occupiers, as most of today's homeowners are; they were also landlords of other people's homes. And many landlords did not own the houses they occupied themselves. It was important for their status and self-esteem, and for their voting rights, that they owned property, not that they owned their own homes.

So most householders rented their dwellings from private landlords, perhaps indirectly via the services of an agent, rent collector or house farmer. Agents were involved in all aspects of property management, selecting and evicting tenants, setting and collecting rents, maintenance and repair. During the nineteenth century agents assumed responsibility for an increasing proportion of the housing stock: in Birmingham, Grimley and Son managed 5000 houses by 1884; in West Ham, thirteen agents between them looked after nearly 6000 houses by 1904.[79] So, although property ownership was generally small-scale, few landlords owning more than 50–100 houses and the vast majority of landlords owning less than 10,[80] control had become much more concentrated by the beginning of this century.

The scale of management is important because we may envisage some tenants moving house between dwellings managed by the same agent, obtaining information on vacancies from their rent collector or through the agent's office; and other blacklisted tenants, once evicted, unable to obtain accommodation in other dwellings under the same management, and forced to go farther afield in search of

Table 15.2: Owner-occupation in selected towns and cities.

Place	Date	Owner-occupied dwellings (%)	range[a]	Source
Leeds	1740–41	6.7	2.3–13.0	Ratebooks (Beresford, 1988)
Leeds	1839	3.8	1.4–6.9	Council survey (Beresford, 1988)
Leicester	1855	4.0		Ratebooks (Pritchard, 1976)
Leicester	1895	—	0.2–17.3	Ratebooks (Pritchard, 1976)
Cardiff	1884	9.6	4.5–16.0	Ratebooks (Daunton, 1976)
Cardiff	1914	7.2		Ratebooks (Daunton, 1976)
Huddersfield	1847	10.7		Ratebooks (Springett, 1979)
Huddersfield	1896	9.3		Ratebooks (Springett, 1979)
Oldham	1906	8.3		Ratebooks (Bedale, 1980)
Brighton	1910	8.3		Lloyd George Valn. (Short, 1989)
Durham	1850	17.0		Ratebooks (Holt, 1979)
Durham	1880	17.5		Ratebooks (Holt, 1979)
Cromer	1910	28.6		Lloyd George Valn. (Short, 1989)
Birmingham	1896	1.3		Ratebooks (Daunton, 1983)—
Blackburn	1895	11.1		figures show the percentage of
Halifax	1901	13.8		*rateable value* occupied by
Middlesbrough	1890	14.0		owners; since high-value
Sunderland	1900	27.3		dwellings were more likely to be owner-occupied, figures probably exaggerate the percentage of *dwellings* that were owner-occupied

[a]Range indicates the percentage of dwellings owner-occupied in the wards with the highest and lowest percentages. For further details see the maps and tables reproduced in Dennis *English Industrial Cities of the Nineteenth Century* (1984).
Sources: M. Beresford, *East End, West End: The Face of Leeds During Urbanisation 1684–1842* (Leeds, 1988); M. J. Daunton, *House and Home in the Victorian City* (London, 1983); B. Short, 'The geography of England and Wales in 1910: an evaluation of Lloyd George's "Domesday" of landownership', *Historical Geography Research Series,* **22** (1989); R. Dennis, *English Industrial Cities of the Nineteenth Century* (Cambridge, 1984), gives full details of Bedale, Daunton (1976), Holt, Pritchard and Springett.

lodgings. Housing management practices therefore impinged upon issues of neighbourhood and mobility discussed earlier in this chapter.

At the bottom end of the market, where dwellings were let by the room, and by the night, house farmers were middlemen who agreed to lease a whole house on the usual terms, probably for three months or a year, and then set about subletting to as many tenants as they could pack into the property. They took the financial risk—the dwelling might prove unlettable, or tenants might abscond without paying—but with the prospect that a full house would yield enormous profits. As important, they provided the means whereby respectable aristocratic or bourgeois property owners could distance themselves from decidedly disreputable slum property, from which they continued to profit.[81]

The rental system evidently suited ground landlords, builders, employers and tenants. The latter could move house easily and cheaply; builders could dispose of new houses, even though the potential occupiers had neither the capital nor the security to buy property themselves; and employers could hire and fire labour confident that the housing market would respond quickly—employees would 'double up' as demand for housing rose, vacancies fell and rents increased, or spread themselves more generously when demand fell, vacancies rose, and landlords were obliged to reduce rents. The cyclical nature of the market, and the interdependence of rent levels, vacancy rates, levels of arrears allowed by landlords, and rates of residential mobility, is clearly illustrated in statistics collected from house agents in West Ham (Fig. 15.3).[82]

But the system depended on a steady supply of investors willing to take on the risks of private landlordism. Recent studies by economic historians have revealed who landlords were and the scale of their operations. For example, Daunton calculated that in Cardiff in 1884 only 5 per cent of landlords owned more than 10 tenanted houses each, but between them they accounted for one-third of all rented dwellings; only six Cardiff landlords owned more than 50 houses.[83] A less systematic, more personalized, survey by Beresford of the owners of cottage property in the East End of Leeds revealed three owners with more than 50 cottages (houses with rateable values of no more than £1 each) in 1805, but another thirteen with at least 20 East End cottages.[84] Landlords included builders, who chose or were forced by the sluggishness of the market to retain ownership of some of the houses they built, lawyers and accountants, whose knowledge acquired investing other people's money helped in their own investments, local shopkeepers and artisans usually owning no more than a single row or block of cottages, and spinsters and widows, for whom a regular income from house rents was equivalent to an annuity or pension. But until the end of the nineteenth century, there were few company landlords apart from semi-philanthropic, limited-dividend companies owning blocks of flats in London, Liverpool and Manchester. And for all the attention devoted to industrialist landlords, such as the Gregs at Styal and Titus Salt at Saltaire, few working-class dwellings were owned by employers in most industrial towns.[85]

In a relatively undeveloped capital market, the acquisition of housing to let was an obvious and generally secure way of investing capital. But with the authorization of limited liability companies, with new outlets for investment in canal and railway companies, and in the colonies and the New World, and with a national banking network transferring funds around the country, housing ceased to be so attractive a destination for savings and legacies. By the early twentieth century, housing landlords found themselves squeezed into accepting lower profits, especially as they faced increasing rate demands from local authorities which they found difficult to pass on to tenants in the form of higher rents. Evidently the housing system was in danger of collapse even before the First World War, which produced rent control, inflation, a housing shortage, and new expectations which the old order could not satisfy.[86]

Two other, related, trends helped to alter the form of the built environment. The increasing acceptability of female employment, in teaching, nursing and office work, meant that some middle-class women were less inclined to a life of household

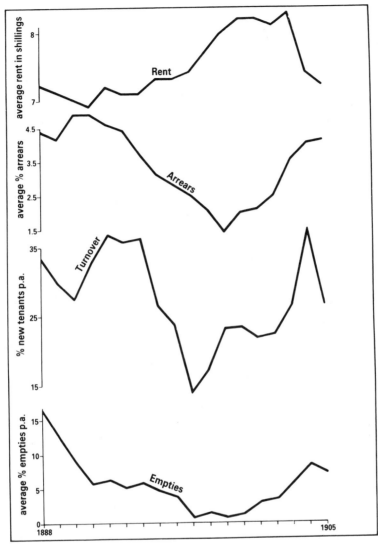

Fig. 15.3. House rents, levels of rent arrears, population turnover and empty houses: privately rented dwellings in West Ham, 1888–1905.

management. But these forms of employment particularly appealed to girls who had previously gone into domestic service, since they offered far more independence than a life 'below stairs': hence the growth of 'the servant problem', the increasing difficulty for the middle classes to obtain reliable domestic help. And hence the demand for smaller, more manageable dwellings, replete with labour-saving devices: suburban villas shed their attics and cellars, and contracted into the Edwardian semi-detached; apartment-living became acceptable for the rich as well as the poor.[87]

Epilogue

This brief résumé may appear to confirm the differences—in development processes and forms of ownership, as well as in basic levels of amenity—between historical and contemporary housing systems. Yet there are parallels, extending beyond the popular resurrection of 'Victorian Values', and including, at least from a 'Whig' perspective, an apparent rolling up of the carpet of welfare provision that began in Victorian cities and gradually extended during the first half of the twentieth century.

Each housing system has been based on the needs of private capital. In each system the beneficiaries of any philanthropic, municipal or central government distortion of the free market have been the respectable, regularly employed working class and lower middle class. In the nineteenth century they became tenants of philanthropic housing trusts, living in carefully regulated blocks of model dwellings; in London and Liverpool, after the 1890s, they became council tenants in either inner-city flats or commuting on workmen's fares from suburban cottage estates; or they climbed into petty proprietorship with the aid of the building society movement.[88] In the 1980s they have been helped into the property-owning democracy by council house sales, mortgage tax relief, and subsidies designed to help first-time buyers and applicants from council waiting lists. In each system the poor have been marginalized, blamed for their poverty and regarded as an irritating distraction from the successes of the free market.

Meanwhile, the direction of 'progress' has been reversed. The nineteenth century saw the strengthening of local government, the regulation and municipalization of urban public transport and vital public utilities, and the introduction of indirectly subsidized housing (through rate subsidies, cheap government loans to philanthropic housing agencies, and the sale of slum-clearance land for housing at below free-market prices).[89] The 1980s closed with deregulation, privatization, the dismantling of metropolitan government, and attempts to revive private landlordism from a century of decline. The relevance of past to present can seldom have been so evident.

References

1. F. Sheppard, *London 1808–1870: The Infernal Wen*, (London, 1971); G. S. Jones, *Outcast London*, (Oxford, 1971).
2. Sheppard, *London*, Chapter 5; G. Weightman and S. Humphries, *The Making of Modern London 1815–1914*, (London, 1983).
3. Sheppard, *London*, p. 159.
4. Jones, *Outcast London*; D. R. Green, 'A map for Mayhew's London: the geography of poverty in the mid-nineteenth century', *London Jnl*, **11** (1985), pp. 115–26; for the full argument see D. R. Green, 'From Artisans to Paupers: The Geography of Poverty in Mid-nineteenth century London', Ph.D. thesis, University of Cambridge (1984).
5. On philanthropy, see A. S. Wohl, *The Eternal Slum*, (London, 1977); for a geographical perspective, see R. Dennis, 'The geography of Victorian values: philanthropic housing in London, 1840–1900', *Jnl. of Historical Geography*, **15** (1989), pp. 40–54.
6. D. Harvey, *The Urbanization of Capital*, (Oxford, 1985), especially Chapters 1 and 2.
7. Wohl, *The Eternal Slum*; see also J. White, *Rothschild Buildings*, (London, 1980).
8. Jones, *Outcast London*; an interesting geographical perspective, focusing on the role of child labour in the cycle of poverty, is the subject of work in progress by D. Gray, Dept of Geography, Queen Mary College, London.

9. C. Pooley, 'Residential differentiation in Victorian cities: a reassessment', *Transactions, Institute of British Geographers*, new ser., **9** (1984), p. 136.
10. J. Smith, 'Class, skill and sectarianism in Glasgow and Liverpool, 1880–1914', in R. J. Morris (ed.), *Class, Power and Social Structure in British nineteenth-century Towns*, (Leicester, 1986), p. 169.
11. Pooley, 'Residential differentiation', p. 136.
12. Calculated from data in E. G. Howarth and M. Wilson, *West Ham: A Study in Social and Industrial Problems*, (London, 1907).
13. Smith, 'Class, skill and sectarianism'.
14. R. Williams, *The Country and the City*, (London, 1973), Chapter 10.
15. A. S. Jasper, *A Hoxton Childhood*, (London, 1969). On residential mobility more generally, see R. Dennis, *English Industrial Cities of the Nineteenth Century: A Social Geography*, (Cambridge, 1984), Chapter 8.
16. G. and W. Grossmith, *The Diary of a Nobody*, (Bristol, 1892); G. Crossick (ed.), *The Lower Middle Class in Britain, 1870–1914*, (London, 1977); R. Gray, *The Aristocracy of Labour in Nineteenth-Century Britain, c. 1850–1914*, (London, 1981).
17. On Camberwell, see H. J. Dyos, *Victorian Suburb*, (Leicester, 1961); on West Ham, J. Marriott, 'West Ham: London's industrial centre and gateway to the world', *London Jnl.*, **13** (1988), pp. 121–42; on Woolwich, G. Crossick, *An Artisan Elite in Victorian Society: Kentish London, 1840–80*, (London, 1978).
18. On the geography of co-operation, see M. Purvis, 'Popular institutions', in J. Langton and R. J. Morris (eds.), *Atlas of Industrializing Britain 1780–1914*, (London, 1986), pp. 194–7; M. Purvis, 'Nineteenth-Century Co-operative Retailing in England and Wales: A Geographical Approach', D. Phil. thesis, University of Oxford (1988); on building societies, see S. D. Chapman (ed.), *The History of Working-Class Housing*, (Newton Abbot, 1971) and M. Doughty (ed.), *Building the Industrial City*, (Leicester, 1986).
19. Harvey, *Urbanization of Capital*; R. Walker, 'The transformation of urban structure in the nineteenth century and the beginnings of suburbanization', in K. R. Cox (ed.), *Urbanization and Conflict in Market Societies*, (London, 1978), pp. 165–211.
20. A. S. Wohl, *Endangered Lives: Public Health in Victorian Britain*, (London, 1983); for some empirical studies of health in Victorian cities, see R. Woods and J. Woodward (eds.), *Urban Disease and Mortality in Nineteenth-Century England*, (London, 1984).
21. S. M. Gaskell, *Model Housing*, (London, 1987); J. N. Tarn, *Five Per Cent Philanthropy*, (Cambridge, 1973); J. Burnett, *A Social History of Housing, 1815–1985*, (London, 1986).
22. D. Cannadine, *Lords and Landlords: The Aristocracy and the Towns, 1774–1967*, (Leicester, 1980); see also M. Spiers, *Victoria Park Manchester*, (Manchester, 1976).
23. Contemporary perceptions are discussed by Dennis, *English Industrial Cities*, Chapter 3, and A. Lees, *Cities Perceived: Urban Society in European and American Thought 1820–1940*, (Manchester, 1985); and illustrated in B. I. Coleman (ed.), *The Idea of the City in Nineteenth-Century Britain*, (London, 1973).
24. D. Gadian, 'Class formation and class action in north-west industrial towns, 1830–50', in Morris (ed.), *Class, Power and Social Structure*, pp. 24–66.
25. J. Foster, *Class Struggle and the Industrial Revolution*, (London, 1974); see also P. Joyce, *Work, Society and Politics: The Culture of the Factory in Later Victorian England*, (Brighton, 1980).
26. A. de Tocqueville, *Journeys to England and Ireland* (ed. J. P. Mayer) (London, 1958), especially pp. 104–8; F. Engels, *The Condition of the Working Class in England*, (London, 1969, originally 1845).
27. Engels, *Condition of the Working Class*, p. 79; E. W. Burgess, 'The growth of the city', in R. E. Park and E. W. Burgess (eds.), *The City*, (Chicago, 1925), pp. 47–62.
28. Engels, *Condition of the Working Class*, pp. 79–80; for a modern interpretation of Engels, see S. Marcus, *Engels, Manchester and the Working Class*, (New York, 1974).
29. Cannadine, *Lords and Landlords*, p. 113.
30. D. J. Olsen, *The Growth of Victorian London*, (Harmondsworth, 1979), p. 145.
31. A. Saunders, *Regent's Park*, (Newton Abbot, 1969); J. Summerson, *Georgian London*, (Harmondsworth, 1969).

32. M. Harrison, 'Symbolism, ritualism and the location of crowds in early nineteenth-century English towns', in D. Cosgrove and S. Daniels (eds.), *The Iconography of Landscape*, (Cambridge, 1988), pp. 195, 210.

33. *Ibid.*, p. 195.

34. E. Gaskell, *North and South*, (London, 1854–5), Chapter 8.

35. Engels, *Condition of the Working Class*, pp. 75–6.

36. M. Billinge, 'Hegemony, class and power in late Georgian and early Victorian England: towards a cultural geography', in A. R. H. Baker and D. Gregory (eds.), *Explorations in Historical Geography*, (Cambridge, 1984), pp. 28–67.

37. V. A. C. Gatrell, 'Incorporation and the pursuit of Liberal hegemony. in Manchester 1790–1839', in D. Fraser (ed.), *Municipal Reform and the Industrial City*, (Leicester, 1982), pp. 15–60; the quotations are from pp. 17–18.

38. A. Briggs, *Victorian Cities*, (Harmondsworth, 1968), p. 116.

39. D. Cannadine, 'Residential differentiation in nineteenth-century towns: from shapes on the ground to shapes in society', in J. H. Johnson and C. Pooley (eds.), *The Structure of Nineteenth Century Cities*, (London, 1982), pp. 235–51.

40. B. Disraeli, *Sybil: or The Two Nations*, (London, 1845).

41. Foster, *Class Struggle and the Industrial Revolution*.

42. N. Thrift, 'Introduction: the geography of nineteenth-century class formation', in N. Thrift and P. Williams (eds.), *Class and Space: The Making of Urban Society*, (London, 1987), pp. 25–50.

43. *Ibid.*, p. 31.

44. Dennis, *English Industrial Cities*, p. 73.

45. R. S. Neale, *Bath 1680–1850: A Social History*, (London, 1981); C. W. Chalklin, *The Provincial Towns of Georgian England: A Study of the Building Process 1740–1820*, (London, 1974); J. Walton, *The English Seaside Resort: A Social History, 1750–1914*, (Leicester, 1983).

46. J. Walton, *The Blackpool Landlady: A Social History*, (Manchester, 1978).

47. F. B. May, 'Victorian and Edwardian Ilfracombe', in J. Walton and J. Walvin (eds.), *Leisure in Britain 1780–1939*, (Manchester, 1983), pp. 186–205; for a superb evocation of Brighton's multifaceted character, see A. Bennett, *Hilda Lessways*, (London, 1911).

48. P. Bailey, *Leisure and Class in Victorian England*, (London, 1987).

49. B. Harrison, 'Pubs', in H. J. Dyos and M. Wolff (eds.), *The Victorian City: Images and Realities*, (London, 1973), Vol. 1, pp. 161–90.

50. Dyos, *Victorian Suburb*, p. 154.

51. W. Bramwell, 'Pubs and localised communities in mid-Victorian Birmingham', *Queen Mary College (London) Dept of Geography Occasional Paper*, **22** (1984).

52. Dyos, *Victorian Suburb*, pp. 156–63; G. Best, *Mid-Victorian Britain 1851–75*, (London, 1971), pp. 170–97.

53. Dennis, *English Industrial Cities*, p. 158; A. Jackson, *Semi-Detached London*, (London, 1973), p. 129.

54. R. Dennis and S. Daniels, '"Community" and the social geography of Victorian cities', *Urban History Yearbook*, (1981), pp. 7–23; Dennis, *English Industrial Cities*, pp. 280–5.

55. H. McLeod, *Class and Religion in the Late Victorian City*, (London, 1974); H. McLeod, 'Religion', in Langton and Morris (eds.), *Atlas of Industrializing Britain*, pp. 212–17.

56. R. Dennis, 'Housing, class and voting behaviour in West Riding textile towns', in Historical Geography Research Group, *Geography of Population and Mobility in Nineteenth-Century Britain*, (Cheltenham, 1986), pp. 46–70; R. Dennis, 'Class, behaviour and residence in nineteenth-century society; the lower middle class in Huddersfield in 1871', in Thrift and Williams (eds.), *Class and Space*, pp. 73–107.

57. Foster, *Class Struggle and the Industrial Revolution*.

58. Joyce, *Work, Society and Politics*, Chapter 6.

59. D. Ward, 'Victorian cities: how modern?', *Jnl. of Historical Geography*, **1** (1975), pp. 135–51; Pooley, 'Residential differentiation in Victorian cities: a reassessment'.

60. Coleman, *The Idea of the City*; Dennis, *English Industrial Cities*, Chapter 3.

61. See, for example, C. Bell and H. Newby, 'Community, communion, class and community action', in D. T. Herbert and R. J. Johnston (eds.), *Social Areas in Cities*, (London, 1976), Vol. 2, pp. 189–207; for an entertaining but also thought-provoking modern gloss on 'two

nations' and 'community', see D. Lodge, *Nice Work*, (London, 1988), especially pt. 1, Chapter 3.

62. M. Beresford, *East End, West End: The Face of Leeds during Urbanisation 1684–1842*, (Leeds, 1988).

63. J. Langton and P. Laxton, 'Parish registers and urban structure: the example of late-eighteenth-century Liverpool', *Urban History Yearbook*, (1978), pp. 74–84.

64. E. Baigent, 'Economy and society in eighteenth-century English towns: Bristol in the 1770s', in D. Denecke and G. Shaw (eds.), *Urban Historical Geography: Recent Progress in Britain and Germany*, (Cambridge, 1988), pp. 109–24; the quotation is from p. 124.

65. D. Ward, 'Environs and neighbours in the "Two Nations": residential differentiation in mid-nineteenth century Leeds', *Jnl. of Historical Geography*, **6** (1980), pp. 133–62.

66. H. Carter and S. Wheatley, 'Residential segregation in nineteenth-century cities', *Area*, **12** (1980), pp. 57–62.

67. Beresford, *East End, West End*.

68. C. Booth, *Charles Booth's Descriptive Map of London Poverty 1889*, (reprinted by the London Topographical Society, with an introduction by D. A. Reeder) (London, 1984); on Sultan Street, see Dyos, *Victorian Suburb* and B. Short, 'The Geography of England and Wales in 1910: an Evaluation of Lloyd George's "Domesday" of Landownership', *Historical Geography Research Series*, **22** (1989).

69. For example, Burnett, *A Social History of Housing* and Wohl, *The Eternal Slum*. For a critique, see M. J. Daunton, *House and Home in the Victorian City: Working-Class Housing 1850–1914*, (London, 1983), Chapter 1.

70. M. J. Daunton, *A Property-Owning Democracy? Housing in Britain*, (London, 1987); P. Williams, 'Constituting class and gender: a social history of the home 1700–1901', in Thrift and Williams (eds.), *Class and Space*, pp. 154–204.

71. On Edgbaston and Eastbourne, see Cannadine, *Lords and Landlords*; on London, D. J. Olsen, *Town Planning in London: The Eighteenth and Nineteenth Centuries*, (New Haven, 1982); on Cardiff, M. J. Daunton, *Coal Metropolis: Cardiff 1870–1914*, (Leicester 1977); on Huddersfield, J. Springett, 'Landowners and urban development: the Ramsden estate and nineteenth-century Huddersfield', *Jnl. of Historical Geography*, **8** (1982), pp. 129–44.

72. P. Aspinall, 'The evolution of urban tenure systems in nineteenth-century cities', *Centre for Urban and Regional Studies Research Memorandum*, **63** (1978).

73. Engels, *Condition of the Working Class*, p. 91.

74. For example, in Cardiff (see Daunton, *Coal Metropolis*) and West Ham (see Howarth and Wilson, *West Ham*).

75. Beresford, *East End, West End*, pp. 95–6.

76. *Ibid.*, pp. 88, 408–9.

77. M. Swenarton and S. Taylor, 'The scale and nature of owner-occupation in Britain between the wars', *Economic History Review*, **38** (1985), pp. 373–92.

78. Chapman, *The History of Working-Class Housing*; Doughty, *Building the Industrial City*.

79. Daunton, *House and Home in the Victorian City*; Howarth and Wilson, *West Ham*.

80. Dennis, *English Industrial Cities*, p. 169.

81. Daunton, *House and Home*, pp. 174–5.

82. Howarth and Wilson, *West Ham*.

83. Daunton, *Coal Metropolis*.

84. Beresford, *East End, West End*, pp. 178–9.

85. Daunton, *House and Home*, Chapter 8.

86. *Ibid.*, Chapter 9.

87. J. N. Tarn, 'French flats for the English in nineteenth-century London', in A. Sutcliffe (ed.), *Multi-Storey Living*, (London, 1974), pp. 19–40; Jackson, *Semi-Detached London*, pp. 44–7; L. Walker, 'Architecture and design', in J. Beckett and D. Cherry (eds), *The Edwardian Era*, (Oxford, 1987), pp. 117–30.

88. Dennis, 'The geography of Victorian values'; R. Dennis, 'Hard to let in Edwardian London', *Urban Studies*, **26** (1989), pp. 77–89; C. Pooley, 'Housing for the poorest poor: slum clearance and rehousing in Liverpool, 1890–1918', *Jnl. of Historical Geography*, **11**, pp. 70–88.

89. Wohl, *The Eternal Slum*.

16

Transport and Communication 1730–1914

N. Thrift

Introduction

Some of the early cinema films from the turn of the century show urban street scenes, usually of London. Through the curtain of ghostly flicker, carts, drays, carriages, motorbuses, cabs and automobiles all mix together in what appears to be a glorious muddle. The films cannot capture the smell of horse manure or oil, the clatter of horses' hooves or the rattle of the early internal combustion engine. But they do still conjure up a history and geography of transport and communication which it is important to know about. For, in the period from 1730 to 1914, that history and geography was central to the making of English and Welsh society.[1]

Two points need to be made right at the start of the chapter. First, transport and communication cannot be split apart. Each relies upon the other in all manner of ways: for example, the development of newspapers is tied up with the history of the Post Office, the railways and the telegraph, the development of the Post Office is tied up with the history of the railways and the telegraph, the development of the railways would have been hindered without the invention of telegraphy and the telegraph's development would have been slower without the railways. Second, transport and communication are wrapped in and wrapped around people's lives. Their chief importance is not as abstract graphs joining one place to another but as a part of the fabric of everyday life: that cold caught travelling on the outside of the stage coach; the frantic poring over a railway timetable to see if the last train was gone; the arrival of the telegram announcing Auntie's death; the final demand before the gas was cut off; the photograph of the family on holiday.

That said, this chapter takes a drier course. It is split into eight sections. The chapter first considers the world of transport and communication in 1730. The next section outlines the main developments on the roads between 1730 and the dawn of railways. The third section is an account of the development of the waterway system. The section after that considers the expansion of the railways. The fifth section refers to the roads. The sixth section recounts the history and geography of communication between 1730 and 1914. The penultimate section considers the world of transport and communication in 1914. The final section then examines what impacts the history and geography of transport and communication had on the making of English society over the whole period from 1730 to 1914.

1730

In the years immediately preceding 1730, England and Wales was already much remarked upon by visitors from the Continent for the sophistication of its transport systems and the effects of these systems on the conduct of social life.[2] The demand for transport which led to this sophistication was fuelled in at least five ways. First of all, this was a highly mobile society by the standards of its time (with the exception of certain sections of the population like farmers and yeomen). Movement between communities was a constant, chiefly the result of labour market factors like the established circuits of adolescent servants and apprentices and seasonal labour, but also of simple life cycle events like marriage.[3]

Second, the wheels of commerce were moving ever faster and, as they did so, so the need for transport became greater. The demand for consumer goods was growing and these goods (and information about them) had to be distributed.[4] Then again, basic industrial inputs had to be moved from place to place.[5]

Third, the state was extending its tendrils into more and more areas of life by the movement of officials and functions and by increasing use of the mails through the auspices of the Post Office (founded in 1660).[6] Fourth, there was the magnetic pull of London. The presence of such a great metropolis provided the centre for the whole transport system in very many ways—as a focus of migration, as a node for mercantile capital and control, as a generator of fashion and news, as the pole of state power.[7] Fifth and finally, the degree of interaction produced by all this activity itself generated a demand for written and printed communication in what was a comparatively literate society and the various transport systems were the medium for the messages contained in letters, books, magazines and newspapers.[8] For example, by 1730 there were already 20 provincial newspapers in existence which were being distributed over large areas (Fig. 16.1).

The case of the roads illustrates how far transport in England and Wales had come—and how far it had to go! By 1730, the roads of England and Wales were filling up with all manner of activity. There were the ordinary people trudging from place to place or perhaps getting a ride on a waggon. There were riders on horseback (who were able to cover around 30 miles a day, although it was possible to go two or three times as far by using a string of horses).[9] More impressive still were the stage coaches, drawn by six horses at this point in time and swaying about on their leather strap springing. Such coaches were setting new standards of speed (Fig. 16.2)[10] and frequency—already by 1715 over 800 services a week were leaving London for the provincial centres. Infrequently, there were also postchaises and similar private hire vehicles and the personal carriages of the rich and titled. The roads were also crisscrossed by those moving goods.[11] There were 'diligences' (fast coaches) to carry the mail and similar items (although some preferred to send mail privately by stage coach at greater cost but also greater speed), the great waggons of the road hauliers lumbering along, sometimes pulled by oxen, the local carriers with their pack horses,

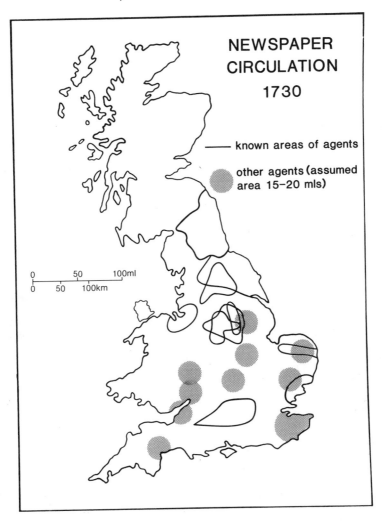

NEWSPAPER
CIRCULATION
1730

—— known areas of agents

other agents (assumed
area 15–20 mls)

0   50   100ml
0   50   100km

Fig. 16.1. Provincial newspaper circulation in 1730 (after Feather, *Provincial Book Trade*, 1985, p. 20).

the chapmen and other pedlars, even flocks of animals driven to market 'on the hoof', often over long distances.[12]

The amount and diversity of traffic was all the more remarkable because the state of the roads was hardly of the best. Many roads were described by travellers of the time as 'infernal' or 'formidable'. Some were 'mere rocky lanes'. Others reminded their travellers of nothing less than 'the world after the flood'.[13] However, the gradual diffusion of the turnpike system had done something to help the condition of some roads, countering the failure of traditional parish-based road repair systems by establishing trusts which could charge tolls and use the revenue to maintain and improve the road. The first turnpike was built in 1663 and by 1750 a basic network of

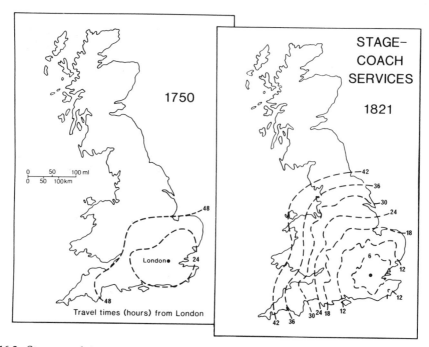

Fig. 16.2. Stage coach journey times from London in 1750 and 1821 (after Bagwell, *Transport Revolution*, 1974, p. 42 and Freeman, 'Transport', 1986, p. 82).

turnpikes radiating out from London, and some sub-regional networks, had also been formed (Fig. 16.3).[14]

Thus by 1730 the roads had already developed a social life of their own consisting of a host of activities which relied upon them: the coaching and other inns, the carriers, the farriers, the stables and so on. Each of these activities had its own specialized workforces, often with its own customs in common.[15] In turn the roads provided England and Wales with economic and social life: transporting a constant stream of people, commodities, money and information about the country and providing 'an interlinked interaction between the locality and the larger society, which both drew together provincial counties into a more densely integrated national society and at the same time introduced a new depth and complexity to their local patterns of social stratification'.[16]

But, at the same time, it is dangerous to make too much of the economic and social integration of England and Wales that the transport systems of 1730 could build. If, as Wrightson claims ' the myth of the relatively isolated, self-contained and static rural community (was) at best a half truth',[17] it *was* still half true. Many factors conspired to prevent integration becoming still greater, the structure of a space economy based on London and a few regional enclaves, the lack of a strong centralizing ambition on the part of the state,[18] the elite nature of much long-distance personal transport, even the less than perfect state of the roads.

What is clear is that 1730 cannot be depicted as a state of primal innocence in terms of transport and communication. But it would be equally foolish to suggest that over

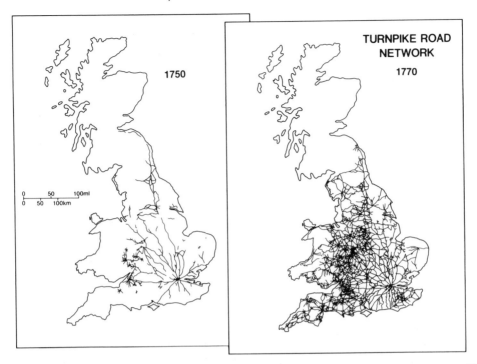

Fig. 16.3 (*left*). The turnpike road network in 1750 (after Pawson, *Transport and Economy*, 1977, p. 140).

Fig. 16.4 (*right*). The turnpike road network in 1770 (after Pawson, *Transport and Economy*, 1977, p. 151).

the next nearly two hundred years and more far-reaching changes did not occur.[19] Successive waves of transport and communication innovations made Britain anew.

The Roads

The historical geography of the roads between 1730 and 1914 consists of a mixture of innovations and refinements in the road system itself and innovations and refinements in the vehicles that were found upon it. Chief amongst these innovations and refinements were the expansion of the turnpike system, new methods of road-building, and the growth of the stage-coach network.

The designation of roads as turnpikes became a 'mania' after 1750. Between 1750 and 1772 over 500 trusts were formed, covering more than 15,000 miles of road and filling out the provincial network. By 1772 about three-quarters of the eventual 22,000 miles of road had already been turnpiked (Fig. 16.4), leaving the rest of the mileage to be completed in the booms of the early 1790s, 1809–12 and the mid-1820s.[20] At their height in the 1830s, just as the railway age began, turnpike trusts accounted for more than one-sixth of the total road mileage.

The effectiveness of the turnpike was increased by the new methods of road construction that were pioneered, especially from 1810 onwards. Through the offices of engineers like Metcalfe, Telford and Macadam many of the turnpikes came nearer to having proper foundations, good drainage, rational cambers, and 'impervious and indestructible' surfaces.[21]

The turnpikes allowed very rapid travel in certain cases but it would be unwise to see them as the motorways of their time. Some turnpikes, especially those to London and the major provincial centres, were nearly the equivalent. They were good and bore heavy traffic. But others were little more than 'formalized pack-tracks'.[22] Still, it would be churlish to deny the turnpikes' real achievement in creating something like a national network of roads. 'They made it possible for the roads to accommodate a greatly increased number of vehicles which could travel with relative safety at speeds two or even three times those of the pre-turnpike era. Even more importantly the roads now served national rather than predominantly local purposes.'[23]

The increase in the number of good quality roads, combined with a measure of economic prosperity and a rapid population increase (the English population doubled between 1780 and 1836)[24] allowed the growth of all forms of road transport. Thus, just road passenger transport increased 16-fold between 1790 and 1835.[25]

Occupying pride of place in the pantheon of road transport vehicles was the stage coach. The stage coach network developed rapidly. By the 1830s it had reached most of the significant places in England and Wales[26] although a number of towns had to wait some time to be connected up (for example, Penzance in 1820).[27] Further, in certain parts of the country served by the network, especially in Wales, the roads were sufficiently poor to keep average speeds well down.[28]

However, in general the extension of the stage coach network was matched by an increase in speeds for at least three reasons. First, the evolution of the turnpike system gave better road surfaces to operate on. Second, the rise of the mail coach after 1784 set standards of speed and punctuality which the other stage coach operations had to match.[29] Third, the use of the elliptical steel spring after 1805 reduced the centre of gravity of the coaches (and doubled passenger loads by allowing more people to be carried outside). Certainly the increase in speeds was striking.[30] By 1820 it was often quicker to travel by coach than on horseback. By 1830 movement between the major towns was as much as four or five times faster than in 1750[31](Fig. 16.2).

This increase in speed was paralleled by an increase in frequency of operation which was just as dramatic (Fig. 16.5). By the 1830s there were 700 mail coaches and 3300 stage coaches in operation in Great Britain and, on one estimate, nearly 1500 coaches were leaving London daily.[32] Many of these departures were handled by what had become large business concerns. By the early 1830s the largest, the London-based Chaplin and Co, was running 64 coaches, owned 1500 horses, and had an annual turnover of £$\frac{1}{2}$ million.[33]

But the stage coaches were only the most spectacular of the traffic on the roads and their fares were such that they tended to be confined to the growing middle classes. Above this station in life were many of the well-to-do who either 'travelled post' (using their own private carriages and hiring horses at posting houses along the way), or who hired gigs. In the more prosperous parts of the country nearly as many travelled by carriage or by gig as by stage coach. For the poor the options were more

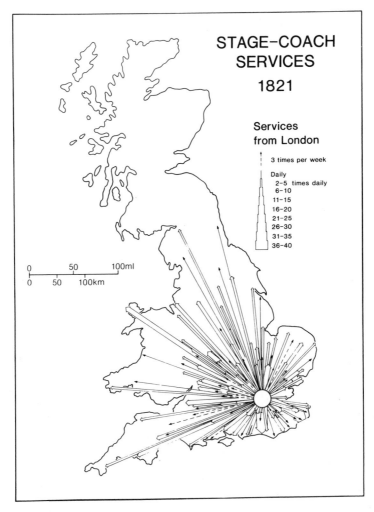

Fig. 16.5. Frequency of stage coach services from London in 1821 (after Freeman, 'Transport', 1986, p. 82).

limited, a fly van was the fastest (and most expensive) of the means of transport available. In some parts of the country could be found long coaches (or caravans). One step up from walking were the stage waggons (which often meant walking part of the way with only the luggage being carried on the waggon).[34]

The roads were also inhabited more and more by goods traffic. It is important to remember that 'Britain industrialized without the railway'[35] and the humble van, waggon and packhorse were vital instruments of this industrialization. Already by the end of the eighteenth century the carrying trade had developed a clearly defined structure with London trade and trade between the major provincial centres served mainly by larger operations like Pickfords[36] and trade between the smaller local centres served by a host of smaller (sometimes part-time) carriers. Goods tended to move in a hierarchy from national to local carriers.[37] The trade was complex and extensive. For example, in 1837, the assets of Marsh and Swann, London, Cambridge, and Norfolk carriers included 100 waggon horses, 21 waggons and vans, various carts and trucks, offices, stables, yards, granaries, blacksmiths and wheelwrights.[38] Road haulage was clearly a major undertaking and it continued to grow until competition from rail ate into its business. Even competition from the canals only diluted the trade, since road was faster and therefore more appropriate for certain kinds of goods, especially those that were high in value and low in weight or those that were perishable (for example, eggs or milk).

The Canals

Although the first deadwater canal was built in Exeter in 1564/66, the age of the canal is commonly dated from the opening of the Duke of Bridgewater's Canal between Worsley Colliery and Manchester in 1761. Until that date most transport by water had been by the rivers, sometimes improved—by 1750 Britain had some 1400 miles of navigable river. The construction of the majority of the canals was chiefly concentrated into a relatively short space of time. By 1830, 2500 miles of canal had been built with construction reaching a peak in the years between 1790 and 1810, and then subsiding—the last major barge canal was built in 1834 (Fig. 16.6).[39]

The canal network was at its best in dealing with the short-haul (often less than 20 miles) movement of bulk goods of low unit value (first and foremost coal but also goods like lime, manure, sand, gravel, stones, timber, etc.). Here, the economics were formidable. For example, '10 miles of land transport doubled the cost of coal and was in town the equivalent of 200 miles of water transport'.[40] Accordingly, it is not surprising to find that the economic advantage of canals quickly decayed with distance: the most successful of them tended to be short, were built through lowland terrain and carried bulk minerals. The advantage could be spun out by the addition of connecting tramways. These horse-worked wooden waggonways formed a substantial network in their own right.[41]

There seems little doubt that the canals played a central role in British industrialization. The roads of the time were simply not up to transport in bulk at the same value or cost. Canals reduced the price of certain bulk goods vital to industrialization (especially coal), highlighting the locational advantages of certain inland places, especially those near to coalfields, and thereby stimulated their economies' growth.[42] But it is important to qualify this picture. They did not unleash unfettered growth. Their impacts were regionally concentrated and specific.[43] It was left to the railways to play the role of Prometheus.

The Railways

Whereas the period between 1730 and 1830 is usually depicted as the age of the coach and the canal boat, the period after 1830 (when the first true railway, the Liverpool and Manchester, was opened) is often seen as the age of the railway.[44] Certainly the growth of the railway network made a major difference to the economy and to

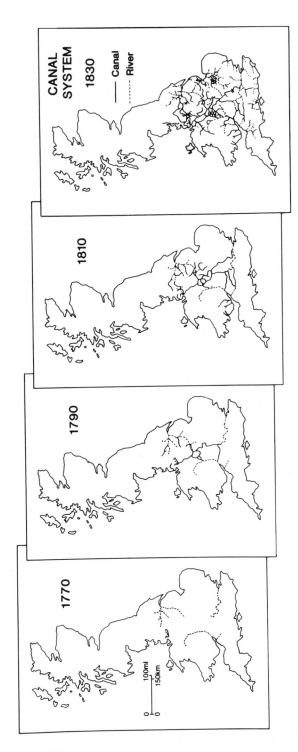

Fig. 16.6. The evolution of the canal network, 1770 to 1830 (after Turnbull, 'Canals, coal and regional growth', 1987, p. 542).

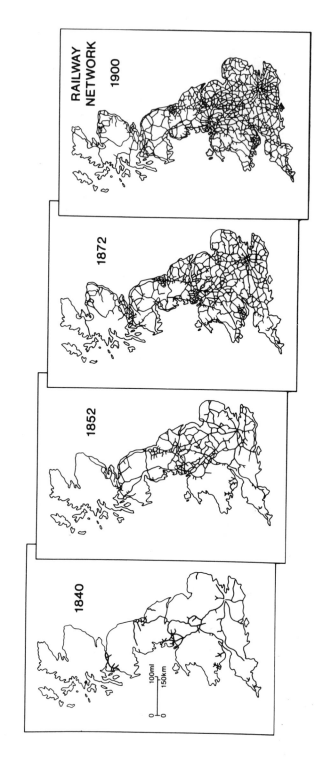

Fig. 16.7. The railway network *c.* 1840 to *c.* 1900 (after Freeman, 'Transport', 1986, p. 89).

personal communication but the speed of its growth can be exaggerated. It was not until the 1840s and especially the second 'mania' of speculative investment and construction from 1844–1847[45] that the railway network really began to expand at a rapid rate, a mania fuelled by cheap money, by a fear that railway promotion would soon be controlled by Parliament, by rising earnings and by evidence of latent demand. Most 'mania' lines have some economic or geographical justification although some lines were constructed for which little reason existed. By 1860 the basic network that exists today had already been built but construction carried on for another 50 years. By 1914, mainland Britain had a network of over 20,000 miles of track.[46] (Fig. 16.7).

The burgeoning railway network made a difference to most aspects of national life. The most spectacular difference was the speed of the trains and the consequent reduction in travel times between places which led to an enormous shrinkage in the national space (Fig. 16.8). The effects were most noticeable for the individual passenger. It is no surprise that the 'annihilation of space' by time was a favourite meditation for the Victorian writer.[47] The effects were all the more arresting because they were experienced by so many people. In 1835, at the very end of the stage coaches' history as a means of mass transport, the number of individual coach journeys made was about 10 million. This figure compares with 30 million journeys made by rail in 1845, and 336.5 million journeys made by rail in 1870.[48] This phenomenal rate of increase was boosted by the introduction of cheaper fares by the railway companies. The practice of providing third class trains spread only very gradually on trains until the passing of Gladstone's Railway Act in 1844, with its

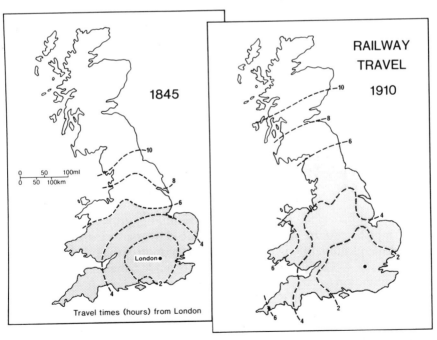

Fig. 16.8. Railway journey times from London in 1845 and 1910 (after Freeman, 'Transport', 1986, p. 90).

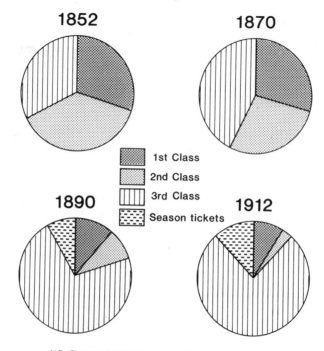

Fig. 16.9. Composition of passenger traffic receipts (total UK), 1852 to 1912 (after Bagwell, *Railway Clearing House*, 1969, p. 11).

clauses making the provision of third class accommodation on at least one train a day in each direction through a company's network obligatory. As a result of this Act and the repeal of passenger duty, between 1849 and 1870 the number of third class passengers increased by nearly six times, while first and second class travellers increased only four-fold. By 1890, the chief share of railway revenue was coming from third class passengers[49] (Fig.16.9).

The effects of reductions in travel time for freight took longer to bite. The railway companies were surprisingly slow to tap into the industrial economy. Until the late 1840s 'Road, water and waggonway transport appear to have been serving the needs of the industrialising economy without undue difficulty . . . Indeed the twelve most important canals in the country increased their tonnage from 10.5 to 14.0 million between 1838 and 1848.'[50] However, the continuing growth of the industrial economy, coupled with the spare capacity induced by many 'mania' lines, increasing inter-company competition, and the gradual solution of the problem of transhipment between the different company lines[51] persuaded the companies to devote more of their attention to carrying other than high value freight, and especially items like coal.[52] The case of London is instructive. In the 1840s London's coal came almost exclusively by sea. By 1855 roughly one-quarter came by rail, by 1870 more than one-half.[53]

The proposition that the railways had important effects on the British economy has been put beyond reasonable doubt by recent research, although the exact importance of these effects is still a matter of debate.[54] Just the reduction in transport costs that proceeded from the construction of the railways has been shown to have been a significant factor in Victorian economic growth. It should also not be forgotten that the railway companies themselves had important impacts on the British space-economy. The list is almost endless: the companies were huge business organizations by the standards of the time who mobilized capital (especially the accumulated profits of northern manufacturers and merchants) on an unprecedented scale[55] and were even responsible for the brief flowering of the provincial stock markets;[56] the companies were forced by their size to adopt important new modes of industrial organization;[57] the companies constituted important new markets for raw materials like coal, iron and steel as well as all manner of finished products from bricks to items of engineering to all manner of consumer goods to be sold to the passengers; the companies were reservoirs of professional expertise employing larger numbers of engineers, lawyers, accountants, and surveyors;[58] the companies gave work to vast armies of people directly (60,000 in 1850, 127,500 in 1860, 274,500 in 1873) and in the construction phase (257,000 construction workers in 1847, although only 36,000 by 1852);[59] finally, the companies were responsible for much of the built environment of England and Wales, from the railway station to the marshalling yard. Kellett established that in the largest cities railways consumed between 5.2 and 9.0 per cent of the 1840 built-up area by 1900, not counting much larger acreages occupied in the peripheral areas beyond.[60]

The Roads Again

In some accounts, the railways become so dominant after 1840 that until the onslaught of the motor car the history and geography of other forms of transport seem to flicker out. It is true that the railways seemed at first to have a corrosive effect on existing forms of road transport but the effect was not terminal. Thus when competition from the railways intervened, stage coach services often died away dramatically. The case of Doncaster, a major staging post, shows the impacts of railway competition. In 1839 the town had employment for seven four-horse coaches, 20 two-horse coaches, nine stage waggons and 100 post horses; in total there were 258 horses. In 1840 the railway reached the town and by 1845 it had only one four-horse coach, three stage waggons and 12 post horses, and the number of horses had fallen to 60.[61] But, ultimately, horse-drawn passenger traffic was surprisingly little affected by the railways for three reasons.[62] First, the railways actually generated traffic. By the mid-1830s it had already become axiomatic that once a railway was opened the number of persons travelling by train would at least double from the number who had previously travelled by foot, coach, or other road vehicle. This factor combined with the general increase in population to produce an enormously increased demand for travel outside the confines of the railway system. Second, not all places were served by rail. Even at the height of the railway age, only one in six places had a railway station so that there was ample opportunity for cross traffic, both between stations and from stations to other places.[63] Third, in the towns and cities, the stations prompted the use of thousands of hackney coaches and, more

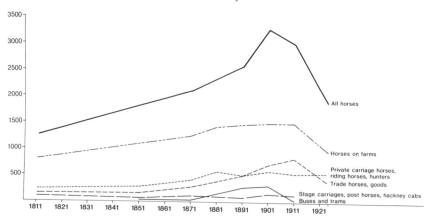

Fig. 16.10. The horse population of Great Britain, 1811–1924 (after Thompson, 'Horse sense', 1976, pp. 80–1).

importantly the two wheeler cabriolets or cabs (introduced from Paris in the 1820s) to decant passengers to their ultimate destinations. Thus, by the early 1870s, one stable keeper could declare to a House of Lords Select Committee that 'the horses have to work in connection with the railways; for every new railway you want fresh horses; fresh cab horses to begin with: I know one cab proprietor, for instance, who used to keep 60 horses and now has 120!'[64]

The same kinds of impacts of the railways could be felt for freight traffic. To begin with, the relative cheapness of inland navigation, combined with the reluctance of the railway companies to pursue freight business, insulated the canals from any precipitate decline (especially because the freight companies had considerable capital tied up in canal barges). Even when the railways began to eat into the freight business, although long distance freight carrying suffered, still there was ample short distance business for the carriers, much of it ferrying freight from the railway terminals to its final destination.[65]

It is no surprise, then, to find that the greater use of the horse was a marked feature of Victorian transport, (Fig. 16.10). The number of horses in use increased rapidly after 1850. For example, by 1901, there were 464,0000 horses engaged in commercial passenger transport, compared with 103,000 in 1851.[66] Some of this increase can be put down to the influence of the railways. But the increase was also the result of other factors, such as the increasing size of the cities and increasing wealth. Thus the ownership of private carriages (of a bewildering variety, from broughams, to open landaus and gigs) continued to grow until about 1870, when it levelled off because of new means of transport, traffic congestion, and the scarcity of mews and stable accommodation. Even in 1902, 12 out of every 1000 inhabitants of Great Britain owned some kind of private horse-drawn vehicle (compared with 14 per 1000 in 1870 and 4 per 1000 in 1840).[67]

In the cities, the growth of horse-drawn omnibus services after their introduction from Paris to London in 1829, and subsequently to other large cities like Birmingham and Manchester in the 1830s, produced yet more demand for horses.[68] The carriage and the horse-drawn omnibus (each one of which required 11 horses a day to keep running), and the growing number of suburban rail services, were essentially middle-class conveyances. The working class still went by foot—in the middle of the nineteenth century, the means of transport was still heavily class-biased. Some indication of this is given by a survey carried out in London in 1854 which found that to reach their place of work 52,000 people used their own or hired carriages, 88,000 people used horse-drawn omnibuses, 54,000 people used trains from the suburbs to the mainline terminals and 30,000 people used river steamers. But 400,000 people still walked to work.[69]

But by the late 1860s, the situation had changed. Forerunners of modern mass transport systems were being put into place, especially the horse-drawn tram (which could carry double the number of passengers of the horse-drawn omnibus). By 1875 London had an extensive network of tramways and other cities were following suit. By the 1880s even towns of 50,000 population possessed tramcars.[70] These systems transported enormous numbers of people. In London by 1896 the horse-drawn trams were carrying 280,000,000 passengers a year compared with the horse-drawn omnibus total of 300,000[71] In the face of growing competition from the railways. 'Old horsepower, better organised, was . . . performing better than the latest steam.'

In turn, the horse-drawn tram was replaced by the electric tram in the early years of the twentieth century with dramatic effects; electric tramway traffic in Britain grew from about 1,000,000 passengers per year in 1900 to 3,300,000 in 1913.[72] These tramways charged low enough fares to give general access to the working class and they combined with other innovations (for example, the opening of the first underground in London in 1863)[73] to produce, for the first time, genuine mass-transport.

The enormous growth in passenger traffic on the roads was paralleled by a growth in goods traffic, nearly all horse drawn.[74] An estimated 161,000 horses were pulling freight vehicles in Britain in 1851. By 1891 the figure was 500,000, by 1901 702,000 and by 1911 832,000.[75] The growth of this traffic was inevitable given the increase in the size of the cities, and the consequent expansion of markets, the huge trade in shop goods, and the rise of delivery rounds.[76] Most of the growth of traffic took place in the cities, but it is important to record that the carrier's waggon or cart was still a central feature of rural life. At a conservative estimate, there were at least 20,000 carriers in business in the 1880s who not only carried freight but also provided some basic services like blacksmithing as well as a rudimentary passenger service.[77]

Through the nineteenth century, three things need to be noted about road transport which have been all too often overlooked. First of all, there was the central importance throughout the period of walking, both as a mode of transport (which in rural areas very often still involved long distances) and as a way of carrying and delivering, from the porters, packmen, coster girls and street venders of urban areas to the carriers, pedlars and postmen in the countryside.[78] Second, there was the sheer diversity of experience of transport. Just as today, people did not restrict themselves to one form of transport. In just one year (1870–71) in a rural area of Wales 'Robert Kilvert used a brougham, an open carriage, a mail phaeton, a dog cart, a fly, the railway and—when the road was too icy for his horse to be employed—Shank's pony'.[79] Third, there was the gradual adoption of a form of transport which, in its flexibility and ease of use and its speed (it was four times faster than walking) foreshadowed automobile travel: the bicycle. The golden years of the bicycle followed the invention of the penny farthing (or ordinary) in 1864, and the subsequent invention of the safety bicycle in 1885 (and the pneumatic tyre in 1888). By 1885 there were already 400,000 cyclists in Britain and the 1890s saw the bicycle reach the peak of its popularity as costs fell and a second-hand market became possible. By the end of the century the Raleigh Cycle Factory was producing 12,000 cycles a year.[80] As if to mark the fact, in 1896 bicycles were issued to all police stations in the country.[81]

Communication

The improved transport services of the nineteenth century went hand in hand with improvements in communication at a distance, most especially in the form of the postal service, the national newspaper and the telegraph.

Before the railways, the Post Office was already a system for the mass conveyance of the mails. The introduction of the mail coach and the gradually improving condition of the roads saw to this; by the 1830s most mail coaches were reaching double the speed of the 1780s. In 1838 57 million letters were handled by the Post Office with a further 7 million letters passing through the privileged post used by MPs and designated public officials.[82]

However, the postal system was still geographically constricted by price bands based on distance with the result that there was considerable clandestine carriage of mail by stage coaches, carriers and other means. It was not until the introduction of the Penny Post in 1840 that the mail became a democratic instrument. It was geographically democractic in that, however distant, each customer paid a uniform rate and was also democratic in terms of cost; this was a rate that most people could afford.[84] It is no surprise, then, that while in 1839 75.9 million chargeable letters were sent, by 1840 the number had increased to 168.8 million.[84]

The establishment of the Penny Post was helped by the remarkably early involvement of the Post Office with the railways. The Post Office used the London and Manchester line within two months of its opening and through the 1830s and 1840s the circulation of mail became ever more dependent upon the railways. Travelling post offices were introduced as early as 1838 and apparatus for exchanging letter bags without the train stopping by 1831.[85] In 1846 the last London mail coach ceased to operate.

Through the nineteenth and into the twentieth century, the Post Offices carried more and more mail: 347.0 million letters in 1850, 862.6 million in 1870, 1705.8 million in 1890, 3047.5 million in 1910 and 3477.8 in 1914.[86] But it must be remembered that this progression was spatially uneven. The network of post offices expanded quite slowly, from 4028 in 1840 to 24,354 in 1913.[87] Until the 1850s posting a letter was difficult for those outside the large towns; mail had to be handed in at post offices or receiving houses. In 1858 there were only 25 Post Office letter and wall boxes in the whole of Britain. By 1875 the number had increased to 9700.[88] Delivery was also a problem and necessitated the Post Office employing over time a vast fleet of horsedrawn vans and mail carts. In 1840 there were only 356 post towns in England and Wales which had local penny posts, serving 1475 outlying villages directly and another 60–100 villages indirectly.[89] By the late 1860s deliveries were offered in most large towns but in rural areas letters were only delivered by messengers walking a few prescribed routes. Many farmers and labourers had to collect their mail still from sub post offices or receiving houses. It was not until the 1890s that bicycling postmen achieved 100 per cent house delivery throughout England and Wales.[90]

Of course, mail was not the only commodity being handled by the Post Office. Two other important items were carried. The first of these items consisted of parcels. It took some time for the Post Office to convert to the idea of carrying parcels since it believed that the mail system should not be 'encumbered'. A book post was provided in 1848 but it was not until 1883 that a full parcel post was introduced. By 1890 46.3 million parcels were being carried, a figure that climbed to 137.1 million in 1914.[91]

The second item was newspapers and periodicals. Newspaper readership had increased startlingly since 1730, encouraged by increases in population, the growth of literacy, and the reduction in 1836 and then abolition in 1855 of the stamp tax. Already in 1782, 61 newspapers were being published in Britain. By 1790 there were 114, by 1821, 216 and by 1833, 369 (London alone had 13 daily papers in 1833).[92]

These newspapers did not have large circulations by current standards. Even in 1837 *The Times'* circulation (at the height of its power) was only 11,000. But their readership was greater than their circulation might imply—by one estimate, in the 1830s each copy of a London paper was read by 30 people, and each copy of a provincial paper by between eight and 30 people.[93]

However, in the 1850s, mass circulation newspapers and periodicals began to be established, as a result of the improvements in posting methods, the impact of the railways on the course and speed of distribution, the rise of the much abhorred and much read 'penny dreadful', and slow increases in literacy. In 1863, the *Illustrated London News* was able to sell 310,000 copies of its special issue commemorating the wedding of the Prince of Wales. Finally, in the 1890s true mass circulation newspapers and periodicals with a large middle-cum-working-class readership were established, symbolized by the *Daily Mail*, founded in 1896. By 1900 it had reached a circulation not far short of a million people.[94] These developments were reflected in the numbers of newspapers (and books) carried by the Post Office. In 1860, the number of newspapers (and books) carried by the mails was 82.8 million. By 1914, the figure was 207.1 million.[95]

Of course, communication at a distance was not only by mail or parcel or newspaper. Other modes of communication came into existence through the nineteenth century, of which the most important was the telegraph.[96] The telegraph was first used in England and Wales in 1839 alongside the railway line from Paddington to West Drayton to notify the passing of trains and to send messages. By 1845 about 550 miles of telegraph line had been built.

In the following year, the Electric Telegraph Company was incorporated and between then and 1870, when the Post Office took the whole system over, the telegraph was run by a number of private companies. By 1868, 21,751 miles of line had been set up in Great Britain transmitting over 6 million messages a year, from 3381 points open to the public, often at railway stations[97] (Fig. 16.11). The service had proved its worth in all manner of situations, as an aid to police work, as a means of getting news rapidly into print and, most especially, as an essential adjunct to railway operation. The system was also gradually being used in commercial activity

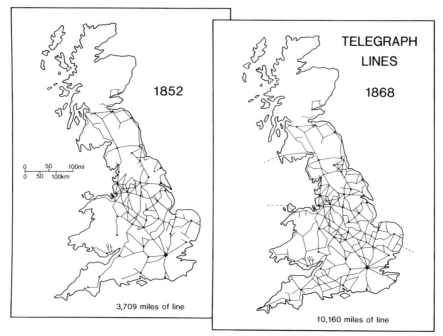

Fig. 16.11. The telegraph network of the largest telegraph company (the Electric International) in 1852 and 1868 (after Kieve, *Electric Telegraph*, 1973, p. 75).

but it was not within the pockets of ordinary people until the 1870s and even then only in emergencies. In any case, until the 1870s the telegraph system was still not accessible to a good part of the population; it was an urban-based system with 75 per cent of its revenue coming from only 15 towns and cities and 50 per cent from London alone.[98] However, after 1870 and especially after 1885 the telegraph became, by dint of more extensive lines, the opening of many new offices (especially in post offices) and a drop in the average cost of sending a telegram, an instrument of communication genuinely open to the public at large. Messages transmitted jumped from 33 million in 1885 to 66 million in 1890 to over 90 million in 1900, the peak of the system's use.[90]

1914

By 1914, transport and communication in England and Wales were on the edge of a transformation which would be as great as that introduced by the railways and the mail. This was the transformation represented by the clatter of the automobile's engine, the ringing of the telephone's bell, the scratchy echoes of the phonograph, and the flickering projections of the cinematograph.

The internal combustion engine was first applied to light vehicles in Germany in the mid-1880s but private motoring took some time to develop in England and Wales, hampered by the embryonic state of the British automobile industry and a persistent tendency to see the private car as a luxury item.[100] Demand, therefore, tended to be restricted to the wealthy and to those members of the middle class like doctors for whom an automobile was a paying proposition. By 1904, about 30,000 motor cars and motor cycles had been licensed in Britain (15 per cent of them in London). In 1914 the number licensed had increased to 250,000 (half of them motorcycles).[101]

Goods traffic was similarly relatively untouched by the internal combustion engine. The number of motorized goods vehicles in Britain grew from 4000 in 1904 to 64,000 in 1913.[102] But many of these vehicles were to be found in London even though a traffic census in 1913 found that 88 per cent of London's goods vehicles were still horse-drawn. Most goods vehicles were vans used for short haul deliveries and the like but as more reliable lorries became available so longer distances were covered. For example, Pickfords used motor lorries for transfer work from 1904.[103]

It was in the realm of passenger transport that the motorized vehicle had had its main effects by 1914. Motor cars spread quickly. Motor hackney cabs appeared in London in 1903 and by 1913 there were 8400 in the capital. Under 2000 horse-drawn hackneys and coaches were then left.[104] Motor buses also spread rapidly. Although they first appeared in 1903 in Britain, it was not until 1910 that they gained general acceptance. By 1911 London General operated no horse buses. By 1913 there were 3500 licensed buses in London, each seating 35 passengers.[105] By 1914, because of their speed, low fares, appeal to the working class and the ease with which they could be placed on new routes, they were a close competitor to the electric tramway in the capital. However, outside London, buses made less headway—by 1914 there were probably only 2000 motor buses in other cities.[106]

There was also the telephone. The first telephone to be found in England and Wales was Bell's device, exhibited in 1877. Private companies were responsible for much of the subsequent growth of a telephone system up until the point at which it was taken over by the Post Office in 1911. Compared with the United States, the telephone was slow to develop in Britain. Although exchanges had opened in most of the major cities by 1880 (beginning with London in 1879),[107] demand for telephones tended to be restricted to business and to the wealthy. Thus, in 1902, *The Times* commented that the telephone was 'a convenience for the well-to-do and a trade appliance for persons who can very well afford to pay for it.'[108] In 1890 there were only 45,000 phones in Great Britain. By 1910 there were a mere 663,000. Furthermore, the system was localized; as late as 1913, London accounted for one-third of all the telephones in the country.[109] The reasons for the lack of adoption or use of the telephone were many, but they included lack of state support, competition from the telegraph (whose long distance rates were cheaper than those of the telephone), poor service and simple cost (in 1901, an unlimited telephone service cost nearly as much in a year as a maid). Moreover, those telephones there were, were often only intermittently used. It was only after 1911 that an expansion in the use of the telephone occurred. Between 1911 and 1913 messages transmitted increased from 42,388,000 to 486,443,000.[110]

Apart from the telephone, the year 1914 also witnessed the parade of a whole series of other devices which augmented existing communication or extended its meaning. Of these devices some were concerned with sight, others with sound.

The most basic of these different instruments was the typewriter. The typewriter was increasingly prominent in the office. Although typewriters had been patented as early as 1850 it was not until the 1890s that they reached any level of general acceptance. Even then, compared with the United States, adoption of the typewriter was laggardly; many businesses were wary and there was no serious indigenous British typewriter industry. It is significant that the most popular model was the imported American Remington in its many forms.[111]

More attention was being given to the projection of images. The photograph had evolved from experiments by Daguerre in France and Fox Talbot in England. By 1854 the latter had produced fixed photographs: In the latter half of the nineteenth century photographs became commonplace. Already by the 1881 census there were 7614 professional photographers. By the census of 1901 there were 17,268.[112] But it was not until cameras became cheap enough and portable enough to allow photographs to be taken almost at will that the photograph truly entered the fabric of daily life. Kodak's portable camera, combined with the invention of celluloid film, heralded the age of the snapshot. Near to 100,000 Brownies were sold in Britain in the last year of Queen Victoria's reign. At the same time, it became possible to reproduce photographs in newspapers and the old engravings-based papers were gradually replaced.

The photograph, and the magic lantern, were in turn, forerunners of the cinema. In 1894 Edison introduced the kinetoscope and in 1896 a cinematograph had already been set up at the Empire Theatre in Leicester Square, London. By 1914, the cinema was already a major industry. There were 240 film renters who were renting out an increasing number of films (7500 were published in 1913 including *From Manger to Cross* and *Dante's Inferno*) to between 4000 and 4500 'picture houses' (Fig. 16.12). Audience numbers are still a matter of dispute but they were certainly in the millions. Film was therefore the first truly democractic art form: 'cheapness and accessibility made the film the drama of masses.'[113]

Developments did not only take place in the medium of sight. The media of sound was also being extended. The wireless was demonstrated by Marconi in 1896 and he set up the Wireless Telegraphy and Signal Company in the following year. But wireless was still the domain of maritime communication and amateur dabbling in 1914.[114] It was not controlled by entrepreneurs as the press and the cinema were, but the advent of the valve in 1913 would soon change this.

The phonograph was the other new device, allowing sound to be packaged and heard again and again. The phonograph came into its own in the 1890s and by 1914 the phonograph was a staple of middle-class life.[1115]

Thus English and Welsh society in 1914 was full to overflowing with innovations which were only just starting to realize their full potential, and which were often yet to make an impact on many parts of society. Apart from the cinema, the working class had little access to these advances, and their distribution was also heavily biased towards urban areas. The motor vehicle and the other inventions had still to 'complete that undermining of rural isolation which the stage-coach . . . and railway had begun'.[116] In this sense, the innovations of the late nineteenth century had still to fully transform daily life in 1914. To understand the use of transport and communication at that date it is necessary to look back to the age of the railway and the telegraph as well as forward to the age of the motor car, the aircraft, and the television.

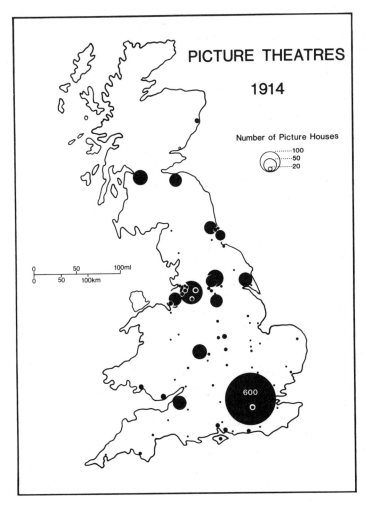

Fig. 16.12. Number of picture theatres in England and Wales, 1914 (after Low, *The History of the British Film, 1906–1947*, 1948, pp. 50–2).

Departures

In conclusion, what impacts did the changes in transport and communication described in the previous pages have on the society of England and Wales from 1730 to 1914? Three impacts seem particularly clear.

The first of these was a change in how people thought of time and space towards more recognizably modern perceptions.[117] Through the eighteenth and nineteenth centuries, ideas of time became more exact, in part because of the increasing promptitude of the system of transport and communication. As the stage coaches started to reach speeds of 8 to 10 miles per hour so a new celerity[118] could be found in human affairs. In business, for example, after 1785 a new note of exactitude could be found. This, no doubt, reflected the changing terminology of stage coach advertisements in the press. In the earlier days coaches had 'set out' 'God willing', and had recklessly promised to reach their destinations 'in about two days' or 'on the same day if the roads are good'. But in the heyday of coaching in the 1820s and 1830s they 'started' rather than 'set out' and arrived, as one irreverent wit remarked 'God willing or not!'[119] The Post Office was particularly caught up in transmitting this new sense of time. Through its need to sort and deliver more and more bundles of letters and newspapers 'on time' it provided a kind of clock for the country as a whole. So too did the mail coaches whose regular progress announced by a horn or bugle was regarded in many parts of the country as a mark of time passing.[120]

The railways' speed made further refinements a necessity. Already by 1845 a train's average speed was 20 to 30 miles per hour and the latest 'express' ran at an average speed of 46 miles per hour. Top speeds were often 60 to 70 miles per hour.[121]

The railways needed to co-ordinate exactly these fast-running trains—and passengers needed to catch them. As railway timetables flowered, greater promptitude became a norm in all manner of social conduct. The standardization of the patchwork of localities to Greenwich Mean Time in 1848 was of a symbolic as well as a practical importance in establishing a standard time to which the localities of England and Wales could run, regardless of their location.[122] Later, the bus and tram timetable, the near-ubiquity of daily newspapers and the news, the post box with its posting times, the telegraph offices and the telephone, all served to reinforce a more exact sense of time and to expand and thicken the importance of the present.[123]

The changing perception of time was linked to a changing perception of space which, again, was brought about by the new transport and communications media. This new 'spatiality' was quite different from the old. A constant topic of debate through the nineteenth century was the way that distances were shrinking as speeds of travel and communication increased (although more for passengers than for freight).

The 'annihilation of space by time' was the early-nineteenth-century characterization of this process.[124] The condensed geography of England and Wales brought with it all kinds of changes in the perception of space. First there was the experience of travel itself. As travel became more rapid and more commodified, with the traveller increasingly resembling something akin to 'bags of cotton and hardware'[125] shifted from place to place, so perceptions of the landscape do seem to have changed. A 'panoramic perception' appears, one that views landscape as it is seen from a railway carriage moving through it. This landscape is perceived as a set of fleeting impressions, a landscape from which the traveller is separated by glass, speed and attention diverted elsewhere by a newspaper or a good book.[126] Yet the old experience of landscape as 'an intense experience of the sensuous world' was not lost; the photograph became its surrogate.

Second, the new condensed geography was better known; it was no longer strange. The increasing circulation of books and newspapers, travel guides, town directories, maps and atlases underlined this fact indirectly. The increase in travel (and the increased propensity to travel) meant that people's direct knowledge of places also accumulated.

The growth of leisure travel was a particular stimulus to the accumulation of such knowledge.[127] At first, this kind of travel was restricted to the upper and upper middle classes who had the time and the money. They had their own seaside resorts (like Brighton) which were linked by stage coach and then rail to London. Increasingly, however, as the railways opened up many of the seaside resorts to lower-middle-class and then working-class excursionists and holiday makers, the upper and upper middle classes fled to the Lake District, North Wales, Cornwall and abroad, often under the auspices of Thomas Cook.[128]

Gradually, as leisure times and incomes expanded, the market for leisure travel opened up to include the 'middling class' of shopkeepers and clerks. By the late 1860s even ordinary bank clerks could afford a week's holiday and the inspector of the Bankers' Clearing House pointed out that 'they have fewer holidays than any other'.[129] Thus the main mid-Victorian growth was in this middle-class market.

It was not until after 1850 that a working-class market for leisure travel opened up. The taste for holidays was foreshadowed in the day excursion. Although there are isolated examples of day excursions dating from the 1830s and 1840s, it was the Great Exhibition of 1851 which lit the touchpaper of demand. On one estimate, more than six million people travelled to the Exhibition and it formed 'a landmark in the railway companies' pursuit of high volume/low margin traffic'.[130] The London and North Western alone brought 775,000 excursionists from the north of England. The development of working-class demand beyond the day trip was pioneered in the northern manufacturing towns, and especially the Lancashire textile district, in the 1850s and 1860s.[131] It was here that the seaside holiday was invented, with the aid of fast, cheap transport, a (relatively) good income, agreed holiday time and appropriate seaside accommodation and amenities. The working-class seaside holiday then spread to other labour forces in other areas, expanding massively in the later years of the nineteenth and early years of the twentieth centuries. The scale of demand for such travel is shown by the case of Blackpool. In 1861 the number of railway passengers handled by the town's station was 135,000, in 1879 it was a million, in 1893 two million, in 1903 three million and in 1914 four million.[132]

Third, England and Wales could be conceived of as one place not just intellectually but also emotionally. The daily newspaper, the telephone, the telegraph, all conspired to give 'a vast, shared experience of simultaneity'. Places could be linked in an instant. News of happenings in one place travelled to another place without the friction of distance.

A second major impact of changes in transport and communication on English and Welsh society was felt in the conduct of social life. Increasingly its nature changed as the relative isolation of the early eighteenth century broke down. It changed in two ways. First, as communication at a distance became easier, as people became more mobile, and as literacy increased, so communication at a distance increased in volume. This process manifested itself in various ways. There was the simple number of letters sent by each person which increased from the three letters per head per year of 1839 to the 75 per head per year of 1914.[133] More than this, there was the growth of new forms of communication sent through the mails. The Christmas card first appeared in Britain in 1843. The birthday card appeared even earlier than this, as did the valentine card. By 1870 valentines 'numbered a million and a third for London only'.[134] The postcard was first introduced in Britain in 1870.

Already by 1871, 75 million of them were used. The vogue for the postcard was boosted in 1894 when private cards (to which stamps could be affixed) were allowed for the first time. In particular, this led to the genesis of the picture postcard business which grew in parallel with the expansion of leisure travel. In 1900 419 million postcards were sent, more than half of them picture postcards. By 1914, 926 million postcards were sent.[135] The growth of the use of the telegraph and the telephone must also not be forgotten. The telegraph message had its human dimensions—as a harbinger of death, as a message read out at a wedding. The telephone was even more attuned to conveying simple human triumphs and tragedies.

Second, people's immediate social life was expanded. There seems little doubt that the range of face-to-face contacts ballooned. Obviously, there were enormous variations between classes and localities but even in a rural area like Dorset the percentage of marriages between men and women of the same parish decreased over the later nineteenth and early twentieth centuries, most especially because of the bicycle which allowed young men and women to mingle more freely over greater distances.[136] Thus, through the nineteenth century, even a known activity like romance could become more complex and, in all probability, richer in texture since new modes of travel allowed greater freedom to meet suitable partners and combined with greater need for communication at a distance through letters, postcards and valentines.

A third impact of transport and communication on English and Welsh society between 1730 and 1914 consisted of the gradual melding of the country together economically, socially and culturally. Thus, there is no doubt that the economy of England and Wales was wound more tightly together by the skeins of transport and communication. The rural economy was dramatically affected. As local markets were tied into the national market so local differences in prices were eliminated, which meant that there was greater stability of prices (making longer-term planning horizons possible). This coalescence also meant that local monopoly prices for certain products were undermined. Perishable produce and animals could be more easily marketed. Fertilizers could be brought in from farther afield. But, at the same time, the new forms of transport and communication opened up rural areas to foreign competition, sometimes with disastrous results; cheap wheat and corn from abroad produced a depression in arable farming in the late nineteenth century.[137]

More generally, the economy of England and Wales was affected by new transport and communications media in four ways. The circulation of commodities was revolutionized by new modes of transport and lower transport charges but at the cost of undermining many local centres of production which could not compete with the economies of scale offered by the large manufacturing centres.[138] The circulation of information was revolutionized as well. Business communication at a distance became easier allowing new forms of business organization to grow up. Advertising became more sophisticated with many products getting national exposure and becoming 'household names'.[139]   The circulation of capital was also revolutionized. The railways and new means of communication had a hand in the concentration of the joint-stock banks into a national banking system in the late nineteenth century and the speeding up of the circulation of notes and bills. By 1910 one financial writer declared that 'the telegraph, the telephone and the express train have carried the destruction of time and space far enough for this island to be practially one market area'.[140] Finally, the labour market was revolutionized. Labour markets became greater in extent and could be galvanized by inflows and outflows of workers now able to travel more freely over greater distances.

The new cohesion was not only economic. It was also social. The state was able to secure more cohesion through the new modes of transport and communication. Its already considerable powers of surveillance in the eighteenth century were augmented through the nineteenth and into the twentieth century by the telegraph and other methods of communication. It was able to centralize knowledge about the country within itself.[141] The new methods also gave the state more latitude in controlling public order. For example, the railways and the telegraph were vital in allowing the rapid deployment of troops by train to foil the Chartists.[142] At the same time, forces opposed to the state or to its political complexion were able to obtain greater strength from advances in transport and communications. The unstamped newspapers (which first appeared in 1830) like the *Northern Star*, the *Destructive* and the *Radical* were, even at this point in time, part of remarkably widespread informal distribution networks and 'proved to be a remarkably effective means of uniting together if not the fabric then at least some of the main threads of provincial politics'. By the mid-1830s 200,000 subscribers were being catered for.[143] Later in the century, the railways were used to circulate people trying to build regionally or nationally based unions.

A different form of social cohesion was brought about by the gradual democratization of transport and communication.[144] Nearly every new form of passenger transport in England and Wales between 1730 and 1914 started out as the province of an elite and gradually filtered down to a mass clientele.[145] Thus the railways started out as the domain of upper and middle class passengers but by 1865 about two-thirds of passengers were travelling third class while by the early twentieth century nearly 95 per cent of passengers were third class.[146] The bicycle started life as a conveyance for rich young swells but ended up known as 'the great leveller' because it made travel accessible to those who could not afford a carriage or an automobile. In time, the automobile would follow the same path. In the realm of communication a similar process occurred. The newspaper gradually became an affordable item for workers. The penny post opened the mails to literate members of the working class. The cut in the costs of the telegraph in 1885 opened its lines up to the working class. In time, the telephone would follow the same path.

But this is not to say that the various transport and communications media could not still be reserved by certain social groups.[147] Railway commuting is a case in point. Up until the 1860s, even in London with the introduction of commuting having dated from the 1820s, rail commuting was restricted to a relatively small band of first class travellers. For example, only 27,000 people at most commuted by rail into the City of London in the mid 1850s—compared with 244,000 foot and omnibus passengers.[148] After the 1860s there was a rapid expansion of commuting from the suburbs coincident with their growth but local communities tended to stay solidly middle class.[149] For most of the inhabitants of the major Victorian cities the railway journey was a rarity: the daily journey to work quite outside their experience. 'It is only the man whose position is assured' Charles Booth wrote, in the 1890s, 'who can treat railways and tram fares as a regular item of his daily budget.'[150] In London itself, at the turn of the century, there were probably no more than a quarter of a million rail commuters (in a population of nearly six and a half million).[151]

A third form of cohesion was cultural. The latest news, fashions in clothes, and songs spread more and more quickly through the towns and cities of England and Wales on the wings of the new transport and communications media. Even sport was affected. The newspaper and then the telegraph revolutionized the practice of betting on horses. Sports fixtures could be more widely publicized because of the wide availability of newspapers and more widely attended because of the railway lines. 'In the last quarter of the nineteenth century All England cricket teams used the railway to tour the county districts at the close of the season.' In Wiltshire 'a broad-shouldered cricketing farmer, from a gigantic on drive down hill, ran his partner out attempting the eleventh run! By the end of the century the spread of knowledge of MCC rules rendered such outrageously irregular practices far less likely to occur.'[152]

The economic, social and cultural cohesion fostered by the new means of transport and communication clearly had important geographical consequences. Of these, perhaps the most important was the continuing dominance of London as the centre of economic, social and cultural life. Throughout the period from 1730 to 1914 the transport and communications systems tended to reinforce rather than under-mine this dominance. Nearly every one of these systems centred on London: the turnpike roads used by the stage coaches, the 'post roads' used by the mail coaches, the railway system based by the trams, even the telegraph and telephone systems.

For some commentators, resource-based regional transport systems, based espe-cially on water transport, may have offered some respite in the early part of the nineteenth century since the network of rivers and canals was 'patchy and dis-jointed' and commercial activity tended to concentrate on regional centres.[153] The process of regional integration may have been helped by the Post Office which used tapered distance rates for mail, so exaggerating the distance between London and the provinces and maximizing commercial intercourse within them. However, with the coming of the railways and the Penny Post, London's dominance as a commer-cial centre was reasserted. For example, the London stock markets became dominant over the provincial markets. Commercial activity in London was again much greater than in any of the provincial centres.[154]

Whatever the truth of this thesis of regional invigoration it remains true that throughout the period from 1730 to 1914 London was a powerful influence on England and Wales. It was the centre of the web of government, business and upper-class social life. It was the place from which news flowed. It was the place from which the process of standardization of manners, fashion and speech emanated. It was the generator of 'London time', as Greenwich Mean Time tended to be known. Thus 'London and its institutions penetrated much more deeply into the day-to-day lives of ordinary people in the provinces.'[155]

But this does not have to mean that regional identities could not form or strengthen during the same period. Indeed, to an extent, London's commanding position may have strengthened such identities by giving them a clear yardstick of difference. This counter-process of regional integration probably functioned more in the social and cultural than the economic registers. But again, it could be helped by

advances in transport and communication: better transport encouraged the formation of local associations and clubs: local newspapers grew, as well as national
newspapers; the growth of dialect literatures encouraged introversion; travellers
wrote about regions and constituted them anew; and so on. The list could no doubt
be extended much further.[156]

The case for the importance of the impacts of the improvements in transport and
communications on the making of English and Welsh society between 1730 and 1914
seems undeniable. It was sustained by a general enthusiasm for progress[157] and by
the undoubted advantages the new modes of transport communication brought to
so many people's lives. Yet what is also striking is a constant bemoaning of the
disruptions caused to old ways of living by these new modes. A whole history of
regret for the passing of the old modes of transport and communication could be
written. The speed and danger of the new-fangled stage coaches was bemoaned in
the eighteenth century. The passing of the stage coach was bemoaned in the
nineteenth. The speed and danger of the new fangled railway was bemoaned in the
nineteenth century. The passing of the golden age of steam was bemoaned in the
twentieth. The new fangled telephone bell was considered to be a dreadful intrusion
on privacy by some in the late nineteenth century. No doubt its passing will be
bemoaned in times to come. What we see here are transport and communications as
taken-for-granted parts of ways of life, as accepted means of touching and changing
people and places.

References

1. For reasons of brevity, I have omitted any reference to shipping in this chapter, but see
   the summaries in; J. Armstrong and P. Bagwell 'Coastal shipping', in D. H. Aldcroft and
   M. J. Freeman (eds.), *Transport in the Industrial Revolution*, (Manchester, 1973), pp. 142–
   76; P. J. Bagwell, J. Armstrong 'Coastal Shipping', in M. J. Freeman and D. H. Aldcroft
   (eds.), *Transport in Victorian Britain*, (Manchester, 1988); P. S. Bagwell, *The Transport
   Revolution from 1770*, (London, 1974), Chapter 3.
2. See, for example, the comments in H. J. Dyos and D. H. Aldcroft, *British Transport. An
   Economic Survey from the Seventeenth Century to the Twentieth*, (Leicester, 1969), p. 74.
3. K. Wrightson, *English Society 1580–1680*, (London, 1982); R. W. Malcolmson, *Life and
   Labour in England 1700–1780*, (London, 1981).
4. N. McKendrick, J. Brewer and J. Plumb, *The Birth of a Consumer Society. The Commercialisation of Eighteenth-Century England*, (London, 1978). L. Weatherill, *Consumer Behaviour
   and Material Culture in Britain 1660–1760*, (London, 1988).
5. Dyos and Aldcroft, *British Transport*.
6. P. Corrigan and D. Sayer, *The Great Arch. English State Formation as a Cultural Revolution*,
   (Oxford, 1985). For the early history of the state's role in the Post Office see H. Robinson,
   The British Post Office. A History, (Princeton, New Jersey, 1948); B. Austen, *English
   Provincial Posts. 1633–1840. A Study Based on Kent Examples*, (London, 1978).
7. E. A. Wrigley, 'A simple model of London's importance in changing English society and
   economy, 1650–1750', *Past and Present*, **37**, pp. 44–70. A. L. Beier and R. Finlay (eds),
   London 1500–1700, (London, 1986).
8. M. Spufford. *Small Books and Pleasant Histories: Popular Literature and its Readership in
   Seventeenth-Century England*, (London, 1981); G. A. Cranfield, *The Development of the
   Provincial Newspaper 1700–1760*, (Oxford, 1962); G. A. Cranfield, *The Press and Society.
   From Caxton to Northcliffe*, (London, 1978); R. M. Wiles, *Freshest Advices. Early Provincial
   Newspapers in England*, (Columbus, Ohio, 1986); J. Feather, *The Provincial Book Trade in
   Eighteenth Century England*, (Cambridge, 1985).

9.   Bagwell, *Transport Revolution*; J. Thirsk, *Horses in Early Modern England: for Service, for Pleasure, for Power*, (Reading, 1978).
10. Bagwell, *Transport Revolution*; Dyos and Aldcroft, *British Transport*; Robinson, *British Post Office*, At the time, to be 'coached' meant getting used to the nausea travelling in such vehicles induced.
11. J. A. Chartres and G. L. Turnbull, 'Road transport', in D. H. Aldcroft and M. Freeman (eds.), *Transport in the Industrial Revolution*, (Manchester, 1983), p. 66. On the movement of goods see Bagwell, *Transport Revolution*; Dyos and Aldcroft, *British Transport*; J. A. Chartres, 'Road carrying in England in the seventeenth century: myth and reality', *Economic History Review*, 2nd ser. **30** (1977), pp. 73–94, G. L. Turnbull, 'Provincial road carrying in England in the eighteenth century', *Jnl. of Transport History*, new ser., **4** (1977), pp. 17–39.
12. Bagwell, *Transport Revolution*, p. 38.
13. Quotations taken from Bagwell, *Transport Revolution*, p. 35. See also the writings of D. Defoe and later, A. Young.
14. W. Albert, *The Turnpike Road System in England, 1663–1840*, (Cambridge, 1972); E. Pawson, *Transport and Economy. The Turnpike Roads of Eighteenth Century Britain* (London, 1977); W. Albert, 'The turnpike trusts', in D. H. Aldcroft and M. Freeman (eds.), *Transport in the Industrial Revolution*, (Manchester, 1983), pp. 31–63.
15. P. Clarke, *The English Ale House. A Social History 1200–1830*, (London, 1983).
16. Wrightson, *English Society*, pp. 222–3.
17. *Ibid.*, p. 41.
18. L. Colley, 'Whose nation? Class and national consciousness in Britain. 1750–1830, *Past and Present*, **113** (1986) pp. 97–117.
19. P. S. Bagwell, 'The decline of rural isolation' in G. E. Mingay (ed.), *The Victorian Countryside, Vol. 1.*, (London, 1981) pp. 30–42.
20. Albert, *The Turnpike Road System*; Pawson, *Transport and Economy*; Albert, 'The turnpike trusts'; A. Moyes, 'Transport 1730–1900', in R. A. Dodgshon and R. A. Butlin (eds.), *An Historical Geography of England and Wales*, (London, 1978), pp. 401–29.
21. Bagwell, *Transport Revolution*, Dyos and Aldcroft. *British Transport*.
22. Moyes, 'Transport 1730–1900', p. 408.
23. Bagwell, *Transport Revolution*, p. 41.
24. E. A. Wrigley and R. S. Schofield, *The Population History of England, 1541–1871; A Reconstruction*, (London, 1981).
25. Bagwell, *Transport Revolution*, p. 43.
26. Bagwell, *Transport Revolution*; Dyos and Aldcroft, *British Transport*; Robinson, *The British Post Office*; M. Freeman, 'Transport', in J. Langton and R. J. Morris (eds.), *Atlas of Industrialising Britain, 1780–1914*, (London, 1986), pp. 80–93; Chartres and Turnbull, 'Road transport'.
27. Bagwell, *Transport Revolution*, p. 45. See also M. J. Freeman, 'The stage-coach system of South Hampshire 1775–1851', *Jnl. of Historical Geography*, **1** (1975); G. C. Dickinson, 'Stage-coach services in the West Riding of Yorkshire, 1830–40; *Jnl. of Transport History*, **4** (1959). The coaches were, of course, quite strongly differentiated by price and speed.
28. Bagwell, *Transport Revolution*, p. 45.
29. See Robinson, *The British Post Office*, for an account.
30. Bagwell, *Transport Revolution*, p. 49.
31. *Ibid.*, p. 49.
32. *Ibid.*, p. 43, p. 50.
33. Dyos and Aldcroft, *British Transport*, p. 80. See also Bagwell, *Transport Revolution*, p. 50.
34. Bagwell, *Transport Revolution*, pp. 54–5.
35. Chartres and Turnbull, 'Road transport', p. 97.
36. G. L. Turnbull, *Traffic and Transport. An Economic History of Pickfords*, (London, 1979).
37. Chartres and Turnbull, 'Road transport'; M. J. Freeman, 'The carrier system of South Hampshire 1775–1851', *Jnl. of Transport History*, new ser., **4** (1977), pp. 61–85.
38. Chartres and Turnbull, 'Road transport', p. 83.

39. The chief canal 'mania' was in the 1790s. On canals, see B. F. Duckham, 'Canals and river navigations; in D. H. Aldcroft and M. Freeman (eds.), *Transport in the Industrial Revolution*, (Manchester, 1983), pp.100–41; Moyes, 'Transport 1730–1900'; P. Deane, *The First Industrial Revolution*, (2nd edn.) (Cambridge, 1979); G. Turnbull, 'Canals, coal and regional growth during the industrial revolution; *Economic History Review*, 2nd ser., **60** (1987), pp. 537–60.

40. Turnbull, 'Canals, coal and regional growth', p. 547.

41. Moyes, 'Transport 1730–1900'. It is important to remember that canals could carry passengers as well. Indeed, some of them carried large numbers of passengers, often by packet boat. Liverpool had its own suburban services, and there was a major service between Liverpool and Manchester. See Dyos and Aldcroft, *British Transport*, p. 114; Duckham, 'Canals and river navigations', pp. 133–4.

42. Towns of the north like Birmingham, Leeds, Liverpool, Manchester and Sheffield were the chief beneficiaries.

43. J. Langton, 'The industrial revolution and the regional geography of England', *Transactions, Institute of British Geographers*, new ser., **9** (1984), pp. 507–12.

44. On the history of the railways, see M. J. Freeman, 'Introduction' in M. J. Freeman and D. H. Aldcroft (eds.), *Transport in Victorian Britain*, (Manchester, 1988) pp. 1–56; T. R. Gourvish 'Railways 1830–70: the formative years', in M. J. Freeman and D. H. Aldcroft (eds.), *Transport in Victorian Britain*, (Manchester, 1988), pp. 57–91; M. J. Freeman and D. H. Aldcroft, *The Atlas of British Railway History* (Beckenham, 1985); J. Simmons, *The Railway System in England and Wales 1830–1914. Volume 1. The System and its Working*, (Leicester, 1978); J. Simmons, *The Railway in Town and Country 1830–1914*, (Newton Abbott; 1986). Also Bagwell, *Transport Revolution*'; Dyos and Aldcroft, 'British Transport'.

45. The other 'manias' were in 1837–40, and 1862–65.

46. M. J. Freeman, 'Transport', p. 88.

47. M. J. Freeman, 'Introduction'; W. Schivelsbuch, '*The Railway Journey. The Industrialisation of Time and Space in the 19th Century*, (Berkeley, 1986).

48. Bagwell, 'Transport Revolution', p. 43.

49. Bagwell, 'Transport Revolution', p. 109: See also J. Richards and J. M. Mackenzie, *The Railway Station. A Social History*, (Oxford, 1986); H. J. Dyos and D. H. Aldcroft, *British Transport*.

50. M. J. Freeman, 'Introduction', p. 19.

51. The problem of transhipment led to the setting up of the Railway Clearing House in 1842. But even by 1857 only about one-third of all goods traffic reports went through the Clearing House. See P. S. Bagwell, *The Railway Clearing House in the British Economy 1842–1922*, (London, 1968).

52. A perennial problem was that the demand was often for short journeys and small loads. See Freeman, 'Transport'.

53. Bagwell, '*Transport Revolution*', p. 114.

54. See especially B. R. Mitchell, 'The coming of the railway and United Kingdom economic growth, *Jnl. of Economic History*, **24** (1964); G. R. Hawke, *Railways and Economic Growth in England and Wales 1840–1870*, (Oxford, 1970); T. R. Gourvish, *Railways and the British Economy 1830–1914*, (London, 1980); Gourvish, 'Railways 1830–70'.

55. R. J. Irving. 'The capitalization of Britain's railways 1830–1914', *Jnl. of Transport History*, 3rd ser., **5** (1984), pp. 1–15.

56. M. C. Reed, 'Railways and the growth of the capital market', in M. C. Reed (ed.), *Railways and the Victorian Economy*, (Newton Abbott, 1969); S. Broadbridge, *Studies in Railway Expansion and the Capital Market in England 1825–1873*, (London, 1970); M. C. Reed, *Investment in Railways in Britain 1820–1844*.

57. M. J. Freeman, 'Introduction', p. 8. See T. R. Gourvish, 'Railways 1830–70' and T. R. Gourvish 'Railway enterprise', in R. A. Church (eds.), *The Dynamics of Victorian Business. Problems and Perspectives to the 1980's*, (Oxford, 1980).

58. R. A. Buchanan, 'Gentleman-engineers: the making of a profession', *Victorian Studies*, **26**

(1983); R. A. Buchanan, 'Institutional production in the British engineering profession, 1847–1914', *Economic History Review*, 2nd ser., **38** (1985), pp. 42–60; T. R. Gourvish, 'The rise of the professions', in T. R. Gourvish and A. O'Day (eds.), *Later Victorian Britain 1867–1900*, (London, 1988).

59. T. R. Gourvish, 'Railways 1830–70', pp. 70–1. See also D. Brooke, *The Railway Navvy*. (Newton Abbott, 1983); Bagwell, 'Transport revolution', pp. 102–6.

60. J. R. Kellett, *The Impact of Railways on Victorian Cities*, (London, 1969).

61. Bagwell, *Transport Revolution*, p. 139. See the moving account of the death of the stage coaches in Robinson, *The British Post Office*, pp. 241–3.

62. T. C. Barker, 'Urban transport', in M. J. Freeman and D. H. Aldcroft, *Transport in Victorian Britain*, (Manchester, 1988), pp. 134–70.

63. This was a factor helped by the railways' own large collection of delivery vans. In the 1890s one writer established that the railway companies used 6000 horses to draw these vans in London alone.

64. Bagwell, *Transport Revolution*, p. 143.

65. *Ibid.*, Barker, 'Urban transport'.

66. F. M. L. Thompson, 'Nineteenth century horse sense', *Economic History Review*, 2nd ser., **29** (1976) pp. 60–81.

67. T. C. Barker, 'Urban transport', p. 143. See also Bagwell, *Transport Revolution*, p. 144. M. J. Freeman, 'Introduction'.

68. T. C. Barker, 'Urban transport'; F. M. C. Thompson, 'Nineteenth Century horse sense'; H. J. Dyos and B. H. Aldcroft, *British Transport*; M. J. Freeman, 'Transport'; Bagwell, *Transport Revolution*.

69. Bagwell, 'Transport Revolution', p. 135.

70. T. C. Barker, 'Urban transport', p. 155.

71. *Ibid.*, p. 153.

72. *Ibid.*, p. 159.

73. Although it was the electrification of the lines from 1890 onwards that made the underground into a true mass transit system: see Bagwell *Transport Revolution*, pp. 134–87. Barker, 'Urban transport', p. 159.

74. The use of the steam carriage on the roads should be noted but the steamers were never a commercial success. See Bagwell, 'Transport Revolution', Dyos and Aldcroft, 'British Transport'.

75. Thompson, 'Nineteenth century horse sense', p. 80.

76. T. C. Barker, 'Urban transport'.

77. A. Everitt, 'Country carriers in the nineteenth century', *Jnl. of Transport History*, new ser., **3** (1976), pp. 179–202. See also A. Everitt, 'Town and country in Victorian Leicestershire: the role of the village carrier', in A. Everitt (ed.), *Perspectives in English Urban History*, (Leicester, 1973), pp. 213–40; P. S. Bagwell, 'The decline of rural isolation'. The maximum range of local carrier systems, according to Everitt, was 15 to 20 miles.

78. P. S. Bagwell, 'The decline of rural isolation', T. C. Barker 'Urban transport'.

79. P. S. Bagwell, 'The decline of rural isolation', pp. 32–3.

80. F. Alderson, *Bicycling. A History*, (Newton Abbott, 1972); J. Woodford, *The Story of the Bicycle*, (London, 1970).

81. P. J. Perry, 'Working class isolation and mobility in rural Dorset, 1837–1936: a study of marriage distances', *Transactions of the Institute of British Geographers*, **46**, p. 134.

82. D. Gregory, 'The friction of distance'.

83. See: *Ibid.*; Robinson, *The British Post Office*; M. J. Daunton, *Royal Mail. The British Post Office since 1840*, (London, 1985).

84. Daunton *Royal Mail*, p. 80.

85. *Ibid.*, p. 119–45.

86. *Ibid.*, p. 80.

87. *Ibid.*, p. 276.

88. J. Y. Farugia, *The Letter Box. A History of Post Office Pillar and Wall Boxes*, (London, 1969).

89. Gregory, 'Friction of distance', p. 147. Thus, means of letter delivery other than the Post Office continued to operate for some time to come.

90. F. M. L. Thompson, *The Rise of Respectable Society. A Social History of Victorian Britain*, (London, 1988), p. 359.
91. Daunton, *Royal Mail*, p. 80. See also pp. 55–66. Robinson, *The British Post Office*.
92. Robinson, *The British Post Office*, p. 247.
93. Cranfield, *The Press and Society*.
94. *Ibid.*, p. 220. See also S. Koss, *The Rise and Fall of the Political Press in Britain. Volume One. The Nineteenth Century*, (London, 1981); G. Boyce, J. Curran and P. Wingate (eds.), *Newspaper History*, (London, 1978).
95. M. J. Daunton, *Royal Mail*, p. 80.
96. J. L. Kieve, *The Electric Telegraph. A Social and Economic History*, (Newton Abbott, 1973); A. Briggs, *Victorian Things*, (London, 1988); P. Hall and P. Preston, *The Carrier Wave, New Information Technology and the Geography of Innovation 1846–2003*, (London, 1988).
97. J. L Kieve, *The Electric Telegraph*, p. 73.
98. In 1865, one survey found that out of 486 English and Welsh towns, 30 per cent were 'well-served', 40 per cent were 'indifferently served', 12 per cent were 'badly-served' and 18 per cent, with a population of half a million, were not served at all. These latter were mainly towns of under 2000 people. See *Ibid.*, p. 133.
99. *Ibid.*, p. 73.
100. Meanwhile in the United States the Ford Model-T was on the road in 1909.
101. Barker, 'Urban transport', p. 163. See also Bagwell, 'Transport Revolution'; Dyos and Aldcroft, *British Transport*; T. C. Barker (ed.), *The Economic and Social Effect of the Spread of Motor Vehicles*, (London, 1987); Briggs *Victorian Things*.
102. Barker, 'Urban transport, p. 164.
103. *Ibid.*, p. 163.
104. *Ibid.*, p. 163.
105. Ten more passengers than could be carried by horse-drawn omnibus.
106. *Ibid.*, p. 161. J. Hibbs, *The History of British Bus Services*, (Newton Abbott, 1968).
107. Queen Victoria first had a telephone in 1879.
108. Cited in C. R. Perry, 'The British experience 1876–1912: the impact of the telephone during the years of delay', in I. De Sola Pool (ed.), *The Social Impact of the Telephone*, (Cambridge, Mass., 1977) see also A. Briggs, 'The pleasure telephone: a chapter in the prehistory of the media', in I. de Sola Pool (ed.), *The Social Impact of the Telephone* (Cambridge, Mass., 1977); Briggs, *Victorian Things*; Hall and Preston. *The Carrier Wave*.
109. Perry, 'The British experience', p. 91.
110. Kieve, *The Electric Telegraph* p. 219.
111. Briggs, *Victorian Things*, pp. 411–14. Hall and Preston. *The Carrier Wave*. The calculator and duplicating machine soon followed. It is important to note that these inventions did not depend on electricity but were mechanical.
112. Briggs, *Victorian Things*, p. 136.
113. R. Low, *The History of the British Film 1906–1914*, (London, 1948), p. 25. See also R. Low and R. Manvell, *The History of the British Film 1896–1906*, (London, 1948); Political and Economic Planning, *The British Film Industry*, (London, 1952); G. Perry, *The Great British Picture Show*, (London, 1974); E. Betts, *The Film Business. A History of British Cinema*, (London, 1973); J. Barnes, *The Beginners of the Cinema in England* (London, 1976); J. Barnes, *The Rise of the Cinema in Great Britain.*, (London, 1983); Briggs, *Victorian Things*.
114. The British Broadcasting Company was not founded until 1922. On radio see H. G. J. Aitken, *Syntony and Spark: The Origins of Radio*, (London, 1979); A. Briggs, *The Birth of Broadcasting Volume 1*, (London, 1961); A. Briggs, *The BBC. The First Fifty Years*, (London, 1985); Hall and Preston, *The Carrier Wave*.
115. R. Gelatt, *The Fabulous Phonograph*, (London, 1977).
116. Bagwell, 'The decline of rural isolation', p. 40.
117. M. Berman, *All That is Solid Melts into Air*, (London, 1982); D. Harvey, 'Money, time, space and the City', in D. Harvey, *Consciousness and the Urban Experience*, (Oxford, 1985). pp. 1–35.
118. A phrase echoing Samuel Smiles' famous epithet on 'the new celerity of time'.

119. Bagwell, *Transport Revolution*, p. 53.
120. See the famous opening to G. Eliot, *Felix Holt. The Radical*, (Harmondsworth, 1972) first published 1866.
121. W. Schivelsbuch, *The Railway Journey*, p. 34.
122. N. J. Thrift, 'Owners' time and own time: the making of a capitalist time consciousness', 1300–1800', in A. Pred (ed.) *Space and Time in Geography: Essays dedicated to Torsten Hagerstand*, (Lund, 1981) pp. 56–84, reprinted in J. Hassard (ed.), *The Sociology of Time*, (London, 1989).
123. W. Schivelsbuch, *The Railway Journey*; S. Kern. *The Culture of Time and Space 1880–1918* (Cambridge, Mass., 1983); D. M. Lowe, *History of Bourgeois Perception*, (Chicago, 1982).
124. See the discussion in Schivelsbuch, *The Railway Journey*. Marx's use of the term, now widely noted, was simply a reflection of common usage.
125. The judgement of a coachman cited in Robinson, *The British Post Office*, p. 243.
126. Schivelsbuch, *The Railway Journey*, describes this phenomenon and also notes the spread of the habit of reading on the train, especially after 1848 when W. H. Smith got the right to sell books and papers at Euston Station. See C. H. Wilson, *First with the News. The History of W. H. Smith 1792–1975*, (London, 1985).
127. Thompson, *The Rise of Respectable Society*, pp. 260–5; G. F. A. Best, *Mid-Victorian Britain 1851–75*, (London, 1971, reprinted 1876); J. K. Walton, *The English Seaside Resort. A Social History 1750–1914*, (Leicester, 1983); S. Farrant, 'London by the sea: resort development on the south coast of England, 1880–1934', *Jnl. of Contemporary History*, **22**.
128. In 1837, the stage coaches brought about 50,000 travellers to Brighton during the whole of the year. In 1850, the railway carried 73,000 in just one week, many of them the dreaded day excursionists! Walton, *The English Seaside Resort*, p. 22.
129. *Ibid.*, p. 25. Margate is a perfect example of this kind of middle-class holiday resort.
130. Freeman, 'Introduction', p. 48. See also Bagwell, *Transport Revolution*, Briggs, *Victorian Things*.
131. See J. Simmons, 'Railways, hotels and tourism in Great Britain 1839–1914', *Jnl. of Contemporary History*, **19** (1989).
132. Walton, *The English Seaside Resort*, p. 72.
133. Daunton, *Royal Mail*, p. 81. The average number of letters per head was higher for England than for Wales. In 1863, the highest numbers of letters per head were sent from Malvern and London, followed by Leamington, Southport, Brighton, Windsor and Oxford. Then came Liverpool, Bristol, Birmingham, Bradford, Manchester, Cardiff and Sheffield. See Robinson, *The British Post Office*, p. 368.
134. Robinson, *The British Post Office*, p. 369.
135. Daunton, *Royal Mail*, p. 80. See also Robinson, *The British Post Office*.
136. Perry, 'Working class isolation'; see also D. Vincent, *Bread Knowledge and Freedom. A study of Nineteenth Century Working Class Autobiography*,
137. Bagwell, *Transport Revolution*, pp. 119–22.
138. *Ibid.*, p. 118.
139. Gregory, 'The friction of distance', W. H. Fraser. *The Coming of the Mass Market. 1850–1914*, (London, 1981), especially pp. 83–146.
140. K. Robbins, *Nineteenth Century Britain. Integration and Diversity* (Oxford, 1988), p. 125. See also P. C. Cottrell. 'Banking and finance' in J. Langton and R. J. Morris, (eds.), *Atlas of Industrialising Britain*, (London, 1986) pp. 144–55.
141. See Corrigan and Sayer, *The Great Arch*. The increase in communication meant that the state had to increase its powers of surveillance, come what may. But the degree of competence of the state should not be overstated. In 1900 the Bank of England still had not a single telephone! The state's role was not always malign. Thompson, *The Rise of Respectable Society*, p. 358, points out that 'the postman was the only representative of authority encountered in ordinary daily experience (by working people) who was, generally regarded as benign and helpful'.
142. F. C. Maher, 'The railways and the electric telegraph, and public order during the chartist period, 1837–48', *History*, **38** (1953) pp. 40–53.
143. Gregory, 'The friction of distance'; see also P. Hollis, *The Pauper Press. A Study in Working*

Class Radicalism in the 1830's, (Oxford, 1970); J. H. Wiener, *The War of the Unstamped. The Movement to Repeal the British Newspaper Tax 1830–1836*, (Ithaca, 1969); N. J. Thrift, 'flies and germs, the geography of knowledge', in D. Gregory and J. Urry (eds.), *Social Relations and Spatial Structures*, (London, 1985) pp. 366–403.

144. Kern, *The Culture of Time and Space*.
145. Sometimes the elite found itself trapped. This was especially the case when gender relations intervened. Throughout the nineteenth century, upper- and middle-class women were often quite restricted in the ways that they could travel, since they had to be carefully shut off from men and from the lower classes in general. Riding on horseback was increasingly frowned upon and light wheeled vehicles became the acceptable mode of transport. Later the railways (sometimes with 'ladies only' carriages) aided mobility. See L. Davidoff and C. Hall, *Family Fortunes. Men and Women of the English Middle Class 1780–1850*, (London, 1987) p. 286.
146. Freeman, 'Introduction', p. 47.
147. It is also not to say that certain social groups could not use transport and the media in particular ways. Thus, over the period from 1730 to 1914, the upper class were increasingly differentiated from other classes by new developments in transport and communications. Country houses spread outwards in increasing numbers from the immediate areas around London as sprung coaches and turnpike roads became more common but, at the same time, as the coaches and roads improved, so the country elites could more easily reach London with the result that the beginnings of 'the season' could be found, a combined political intrigue, social event and marriage market. By the late eighteenth century it seems likely that the country elite spent a large amount of time away from home mainly in London. However, in the latter part of the nineteenth century, there was a drift back to country living (partly because of the obsession with rural sports). The distribution of new country houses reflects this. But this country-oriented lifestyle (and especially the weekend in the country) could only be supported because the railways ensured rapid access to London. See L. Stone, *An Open Elite? England 1540–1880*, (Oxford, 1984); L. Davidoff, *The Best Circles. Society, Etiquette and the Season*, (London, 1973).
148. Kellett, *The Impact of the Railways*, p. 365.
149. There is, however, little evidence to suggest that the railways were the dominant factor in the forming of the suburbs in the nineteenth century. Other factors like rising real incomes, improved means of raising credit for house ownership, new jobs in the suburbs, the structure of the land market and immigration seem to have been as important. Further, the railway companies were often reluctant to expand suburban track or invest in the necessary rolling stock. See *Ibid.*
150. *Ibid.*, p. 95
151. *Ibid.*, p. 95. Only a few areas of cities could be found where suburban expansion and the working class could be linked together. These were mainly areas where cheap fares were offered by the rail companies, as in the case of north-east London and the Great Eastern Railway.
152. Bagwell, 'The decline of rural isolation', p. 40. On the case of cricket, see also Best, *Mid-Victorian Britain*, p. 229.
153. Langton, 'The industrial revolution', p. 162. See also Freeman, 'The Industrial revolution'; Freeman, 'Introduction', pp. 28–30 and the debate between Gregory and Langton. D. Gregory, 'The production of regions in England's industrial revolution', *Jnl. of Historical Geography*, **14** (1988), pp. 50–8; J. Langton, 'The production of regions in England's industrial revolution: a response; *Jnl. of Historical Geography*, **14** (1988), pp. 170–4. D. Gregory, 'Reply', *Jnl. of Historical Geography*, **14** (1988), pp. 174–6.
154. C. H. Lee, 'The service sector, regional specialisation and economic growth in the Victorian economy', *Jnl. of Historical Geography*, **10** (1984), pp. 139–55.
155. Gregory, 'The production of regions', p. 56. See also F. Sheppard, 'London and the nation in the nineteenth century', *Transactions of the Royal Historical Society*, **35** (1985), pp. 51–74; Freeman 'Introduction'; Stone, *An Open Elite?*, p. 35.

156. See Langton, 'The industrial revolution'; Robbins, *Nineteenth-Century Britain*; Colley, 'Whose nation?'

157. Freeman, 'Introduction', pp. 21–2; E. J. Hobsbawm, *The Age of Capital 1848–1875*, (London, 1975)

17

Landscape Design and the Idea of Improvement 1730–1900

S. Daniels and S. Seymour

From the eighteenth century the English landscape was designed on a large scale and with great attention to detail. In the countryside of Georgian England the owners of great estates displayed their power in the land by building landscape parks and refashioning estate buildings. Lesser gentry followed suit, unable or unwilling to commission nationally renowned architects and landscape gardeners, but perhaps with the help of their steward and local nurserymen and building contractors gave their estates a patrician polish. The great gentry and nobility further displayed their power, and that of the polite society they patronized, in towns and cities notably by developing their land for fashionable residential quarters. And even in urban areas where land ownership was more fragmented, various development interests combined to create coherently genteel townscapes. In Victorian England designs were made more earnestly on the living and working areas of the poor especially in cities. By the end of the nineteenth century a self-consciously democratic sense of civic pride was expressed in the building of town halls, public parks and boulevards.

The name given to these various designs, over a period of two centuries, was 'improvement'[1]. Improvement meant progressively restructuring the landscape for social and economic as well as aesthetic ends and, by extension, restructuring the conduct of those who lived in, worked in and looked upon it. The emphasis on, and relation between, the various dimensions of improvement changed in different contexts. Broadly we might say that the aesthetic dimension framed improvement in Georgian England, that the idea of improvement was closely, if sometimes tensely, connected to a painterly or theatrical idea of landscape. In Victorian England, the discourse of improvement was more explicitly inquisitive and pragmatic, concerned with the more efficient, even equitable distribution of various civilizing influences from free trade to fresh air. Moreover, the politics of improvement shifted. Originally an aristocratic term, denoting the design and management of landed estates, 'improvement' by the 1830s was part of the vocabulary of municipal and parliamentary reform and conventionally deployed *against* aristocratic power and privilege. 'Improvement' is arguably the key word in the literature culture of the eighteenth and nineteenth centuries, and certainly of that culture's designs on the landscape; in this chapter we will chart some of its complexities.

Rural Improvement

Landscape Parks

The landed gentry ruled Georgian England and their country seats were the main focus of their authority. They spent considerable sums building, extending and refashioning their mansions, gardens and parks.[2] Some of this was paid for from increasing agricultural rents but the most grandiose schemes were funded from other, still more lucrative, sources—urban ground rents, mineral leases, stocks and bonds, government sinecures, the spoils of war, overseas plantations, overseas trade. The very attention lavished on country houses and parks, both on the ground and in written and graphic representations of polite society, helped to obscure the gentry's involvement in an increasingly dynamic and diverse political economy. This is not to say that parks and gardens were designed entirely to eclipse the pragmatic or financial interests of their owners—various kinds of agricultural and even industrial enterprise were included in parkland and parkland views[3]—just that interests of whatever kind were admissible only when they conformed to the conventions of landscape. And landscape in Georgian England was not just a matter of taste; it was a highly complicated discourse in which a whole range of issues, which we might now discriminate as 'economic', 'political', 'social' and 'cultural', were encoded and negotiated.[4] The concept of improvement was integral to these negotiations.

Initially used to denote profitable operations in connection with land, notably aristocratic enclosure, by the end of the eighteenth century 'improvement' referred not just to a variety of progressive farming practices but to a broad range of activities from music to manufacturing and with a series of overlapping resonances—financial, pragmatic, moral, educational, aesthetic. A central issue of eighteenth-century polite culture, at least from a conservative point of view, was the relation between improvement in various spheres of life; the discourse of landscape provided a way both of diagnosing disharmony between these spheres and bringing them into balance. The classic conservative statement on improvement is by Edmund Burke. 'To improve', declared Burke, is 'to treat the deficient or corrupt parts of an established order with the character of the whole in mind.' The established order for Burke was presided over by the gentry, whose apparent disengagement from the day-to-day operations of society gave them the statesman's advantage of seeing society as 'whole', much as they could see their own estates as a whole—in pictures and maps as well as on the ground—and improve them accordingly. Burke's idea of improvement was not opposed to capitalism, indeed he saw capitalist exchange, 'the great wheel of circulation' he called it, as providing the momentum without which the state, or any particular estate, would stagnate. What improvement did was to integrate the imperatives of land and circulation; what landscape did was to provide a graphic model of such integration. The improved landscape brought profit within the bounds of prudence and decorum, and energized ornament with at least a semblance of pragmatism and enterprise.[5] In an early and influential statement on landscaping in *The Spectator*, Joseph Addison asked

why may not a whole Estate be thrown into a kind of Garden by frequent Plantations, that may turn as much to the profit as to the Pleasure of the Owner? A Marsh overgrown with

Willows, or a Mountain shaded with Oaks, are not only more beautiful, but more beneficial, than when they lie bare and unadorned. Fields of Corn make a pleasant prospect, and if the Walks were a little taken care of that lie between them, if the natural Embroidery of the Meadows were helped and improved by some small Additions of Art, and the several Rows of Hedges set off by Trees and Flowers, that the Soil was capable of receiving, a man might make a pretty Landskip of his own Possessions.[6]

The 'pretty Landskip' Addison commended was conventionally dignified by the rhetoric of classical antiquity. The English gentry looked to Roman literature on villa life and husbandry, notably Virgil's *Georgics*, as an exemplary model of patrician virtue. There were several translations of *The Georgics* and a strong tradition of contemporary English literature in a georgical mode. *The Georgics* prescribed a patriotic combination of beauty and use, pleasure and profit, land and commerce within a strict, but benevolent, social hierarchy. For Addison georgical poetry 'raises in our minds a pleasing variety of scenes and landskips whilst it teaches us... [it] is some part of the science of husbandry put into a pleasing dress'. The language of progressive agriculture, especially when designed to flatter the gentry, often broke into explicitly georgical mode. Notable landscape parks were glossed with georgical imagery in poems, essays and pictures. Some had it inscribed in their fabric with a programme of temples, groves, statuary and carved quotations elevating various views over the estate.[7] 'It is the delicacy as well as the practicability of the English Georgic that was responsible for its success', notes John Barrell, 'and made it well able to reflect that double image of the aristocracy, as the leisured consumers of Britain's wealth, and as the interested patrons of her agricultural and mercantile expansion'.[8] This double image is discernible in the design and management of the main ingredients of English parkland: trees, game and livestock.

Most authorities on landscaping regarded woodland design and management as a controlling principle of improvement, with implications for almost every other parkland use. Planting accentuated the impression of power in the land. Avenues, ridings, belts, clumps and screens were arranged to emphasize the apparent as well as the actual size and coherence of an estate. Formal styles of parkland planting, with long vistas radiating from the country house, expressed a military sense of command (Fig. 17.1). Informal styles were more artful but no less domineering. The siting, size and tonality of Capability Brown's clumps enhanced the extent of a park and the pleasure of running one's eyes possessively over its contours. In his influential *Observations on Modern Gardening* (1770), Thomas Whately, an advocate for Brown, recommended ridings around a park 'to extend the idea of a seat and appropriate a whole country to a mansion'. Such ridings were to be 'distinguished' from 'common roads' by their 'design', such as 'plantations of firs, whether placed in the sides of the way, or in clumps or woods in the view'. More picturesque landscaping distinguished the park less explicitly from the country beyond, a quality its advocates found less oppressive. In *The English Garden*, (1772–81) William Mason advised landscapers to reject exotic species of conifer for native hardwoods, to take account of features of the working countryside and to incorporate in the 'sylvan scene' signs of rustic happiness—'the scattered village', 'holy spire' and 'azure curl of smoke' from a cottage 'beneath the sheltering coppice'. Picturesque landscaping was discreet, sometimes merely a matter of planting a few trees in a distant hedgerow or lopping some branches of a parkland tree to disclose a view. This both softened the

Fig. 17.1. John Harris, *Dunham Massey, c. 1750.*

impression of property and, by composing the entire countryside as a picture, strengthened it. Humphry Repton's alterations to estates were more modest and superficial than those by Brown but their basis was still 'appropriation . . . that charm which only belongs to ownership, the *exclusive right* of enjoyment, with the power of refusing that others should share our pleasure'. This charm was protected in law, and by the spectre of the gallows. The 'Black Act' (9 Geo. I. c. 22) of 1722 made it a capital offence to 'cut down or otherwise destroy any trees planted in any avenue, or growing in any garden, orchard or plantation, for ornament, shelter or profit'.[9]

Parkland trees were valuable material resources, and became more so as the eighteenth century progressed. When choosing sites for planting their yield was carefully assessed against that from alternative land uses. As well as providing fuel and timber for the estate they provided a range of marketable products. Parkland plantations and coppices in the 'Dukeries' estates of Nottinghamshire yielded income from the sale of wood for timber, pit props, hop poles, bark and charcoal, fuelling a variety of local and regional enterprises.[10] The most trumpeted commercial use of parkland plantations, because it best expressed the patriotism of the gentry, was in providing timber for shipbuilding. The ascendancy of Britain as a maritime nation cemented the patriotic association of planting timber trees, especially oaks. Readers of modern editions of John Evelyn's *Silva*, still the seminal treatise on planting, were exhorted to nourish 'Those sapling oaks, which at Britannia's call/ May heavy their trunks into the main/And float the bulwarks of her liberty'. The more picturesque the oak, the more valuable it often was. Single, unrestricted oaks, growing open crowns of curved and bent branches, provided the compass timber for ship's hulls that was in such short supply. Writing in the wake of the Battle of Trafalgar, the planter William Pontey declared 'The splendid victory lately achieved, has proved Wooden Walls to be an essential part of the Title, by which not only *Estates*, but every species of property is held.' New plantations were named after victorious admirals; some had triumphal columns erected among the trees.[11]

Oak trees provided a potent symbol of landed authority. Like the ideal landed family, oaks were considered venerable, patriarchal, stately, guardian and quintessentially English. The analogy of great trees to great families was firmly established before Burke described the English aristocracy as 'the great oaks which shade a country'. Old oaks not planted by landed families were readily appropriated by them, incorporated in parkland views or used in family portraits to amplify their pedigree. The ancient Greendale Oak was a main feature of the Duke of Portland's park at Welbeck in Nottinghamshire and Portland dispensed its acorns to his most favoured guests. Although most landowners, including Portland, eagerly planted conifers, especially on thin soils, for many conservative spokesmen the precocity of conifers was all too reminiscent of the greed and calculation they ascribed not to established gentry but to *parvenus*. Having once enjoyed Portland's patronage, Humphry Repton was dismayed to take on such pretenders as clients. Of one he remarked, 'How could I hope to suggest an idea to this man who shewed me what he called "the LARGEST ACORN he had ever seen" at the same time producing the CONE of a STONE PINE that grew near an oak and had fallen among the acorns (fit emblem of him I thought who had fallen among Gentlemen but could NOT be mistaken for one).'[12]

No matter how languidly parkland animals seemed to roam across the landscape, they were no less carefully managed than trees. Many landscape parks were re-fashioned and re-stocked deer parks, and hunting remained an obsession with the gentry, if anything became more so. The gentry reserved for themselves the right to kill game and were proud to have themselves portrayed in their parks with their guns, dogs and the spoils of the hunt. Styles of landscaping changed to accommo-date changing styles of hunting. While straight rides through plantations provided for stag shooting, large expanses of turf interspersed with clumps of trees made better provision for foxhunting with hounds. Many parks groaned with game and the scale of slaughter could be formidable. The park acted as a larder for the house, but bloodsports had a more public function for the exercise of patronage, in the ritual of the hunt and in the disposal of its spoils. Venison was an important gift currency, exchanged among peers and bestowed upon social inferiors, especially at election times. Although venison was prohibited from open sale, deer proved a valuable economic crop. Mature hinds and young bucks culled annually from the herd realized high prices.[13] So central was hunting, especially deer hunting, to the definition of the gentry's authority, that their killing fields were zealously guarded, patrolled by armed keepers, ringed by high walls and fences and set with booby traps to maim poachers. Riding through Kent in 1823, William Cobbett saw the dual image of English parkland on a warning notice 'PARADICE PLACE. Spring guns and steel traps set here'[14]. In some areas, especially where private hunting grounds had been appropriated from the forest, there was effectively a state of siege. Poachers caught in the act could expect little mercy. In 1748 two young men from Salcey Forest were caught raiding Lord Cobham's deer park at Stowe.

> The wives of the men sought an interview at Stowe and begged for their husbands' lives. It seemed that old Cobham, now in his eightieth year, was moved by their tears. He promised that their husbands would be returned to them by a certain day—and so they were, for on that day their corpses were brought to their cottage doors on a cart. Cobham celebrated the occasion by striking statues of the dead men in his park, a deer across their shoulders.[15]

Deer never lost their status as a 'superb and graceful emblematization of the status of their owner' but by the later eighteenth century when the aristocracy were proclaiming their patronage of progressive farming, sheep and cattle became increasingly popular park animals. Unlike deer, sheep did not damage trees, nor were they as liable to escape and damage crops on neighbouring fields. They also played a key role in convertible husbandry. Folded on turnips, their manuring and trampling helped prepare fields for sowing. Park flocks yielded mutton and wool, but perhaps their most conspicuous use was as breeding stock. Choice specimens might be hired, sold and also presented as gifts. Such transactions helped define the network of progressive gentry. On their estates the boundary between park and farm became more permeable. As the park became more pragmatic, so the Home Farm became more stylish. Their most important rituals were the so-called 'sheep shearings', agricultural shows like the Duke of Bedford's at Woburn or Thomas Coke's at Holkham, where improved livestock and carcasses were displayed and discussed by connoisseurs of progressive farming. Sheep were not the only subject of such rituals but they were the central emblem. Unlike the turnip they were dignified by a long tradition of pastoral literature and art and featured in panegyrics to Britain's woollen industry and trade.[16]

Parkland was regularly sown with crops, serving as forage for game and livestock, usually to prepare the ground for planting trees, but also periodically with arable crops sometimes within sight of the house. Arguably, planting arable crops amounted, by definition, to disparking. A hallmark of Capability Brown's style was taking land out of tillage, and concealing neighbouring arable fields with a belt of trees. By at least feigning indifference to tillage, and its associations of work and income, Brown's aristocratic clients stamped their superiority over the lesser gentry as well as emphasizing their distance from tenants and labourers. Such a posture, in whatever style, was continually censured in conservative tracts on improvement for disrupting the fine balance of rural society. In times of social tension, too great a show of leisurely consumption was felt to invite disaffection. By the turn of the century writers on picturesque improvement were attempting to find a place for tillage in parkland aesthetics, if only because wheat prices were soaring and landlords were eagerly ploughing pastureland and even grubbing up oaks for arable fields. Moreover, in wartime, especially during Napoleon's blockade, this had the patriotic aura of a Dig-for-Victory campaign.[17] Having once declared cornfields 'totally at variance with all ideas of picturesque beauty', and unworthy of a gentleman's purview, in a Norfolk commission of 1812 Humphry Repton proposed making a cornfield a feature of the main view from the house, if foregrounded by pasture grazed by cattle and sheep and bounded by a belt of trees.[18]

The *ferme ornée*, a mixture of woodland, pasture and tillage, classically expresses a georgical view of estate improvement. Its incidence varied regionally as well as chronologically, being particularly marked in Herefordshire and in the border area between Suffolk and Essex, regions dominated by lesser gentry and gentlemen-farmers. The permutation of trees, pasture and tillage in the field of vision could vary, as two estate paintings of the Suffolk–Essex borderlands show. Gainsborough's *Mr and Mrs Andrews* (1748) (Fig. 17.2) shows the newly wedded couple posed under an oak, Mr Andrews in his shooting jacket with his flintlock and pointer, his wife with a cap under her straw hat rolled in imitation of a milkmaid's, to their right a drilled field of wheat stacked with sheaves, beyond a paddock of sheep selected for feeding on turnips and artificial grasses, and in the distance a belt of trees.[19] When Constable was commissioned in 1814 to paint a view of the local squire's estate in East Bergholt as a wedding present for the daughter, the chosen viewpoint was from the park palings looking over a cornfield to the meadows and woods of the Stour valley, not at harvest but in early spring in preparation for sowing, pride of place in the picture being given to a large dunghill and men digging out, carting and ploughing in the muck.[20]

Estate improvements of all kinds were closely implicated with transportation improvements, the most visible embodiment of Burke's 'great wheel of circulation'. The *General View of the Agriculture of Sussex* (1808) observed the 'general impetus' given by 'good roads' 'to circulation, and fresh activity to every branch of industry'. Especially when there was 'a free communication between the capital and the provinces', 'animation, vigour, life, and energy of luxury, consumption and industry...flow with a full tide through this kingdom'.[21] Such roads helped mobilize the agricultural potential of a park and the social potential of a country house.

The development of well-sprung carriages and a network of turnpike roads made country houses less remote, and their owners less reluctant to leave the gaiety of the

Fig. 17.2. Thomas Gainsborough, *Mr and Mrs Andrews, c.* 1748. Reproduced by courtesy of the Trustees, The National Gallery, London.

metropolis to take a closer and more personal interest in their estates. As estates became more profitable so country house life grew more sophisticated. Urban entertainments were introduced into the country and houses and grounds were designed to accommodate them. For assemblies, spaces were co-ordinated in terms of a variety of pastimes: within the house dancing, drinking, cardplaying, listening to music, reading, looking at paintings and prints, and outside bowling, fishing, looking at statuary and taking in various views of the park and estates. Circuits outside might be taken on foot or in a carriage. Half the pleasure of a Capability Brown style park was being driven at speed in a lightly sprung chaise over acres of smooth turf. Whole regions were reconstructed as a circuit for polite society, the company moving from this to that country house party, to race meetings, beauty spots, country towns, spa towns. Good roads made the metropolis increasingly accessible. By the end of the eighteenth century 'an energetic young man driving himself in a racing phaeton [the sports car of the time] could make weekend visits within a hundred-mile radius of London'.[22]

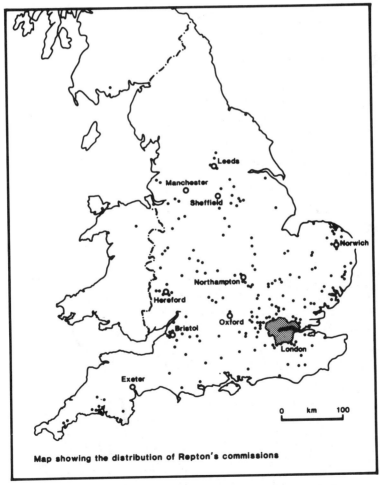

Map showing the distribution of Repton's commissions

Fig. 17.3. Distribution of Humphry Repton's commissions.

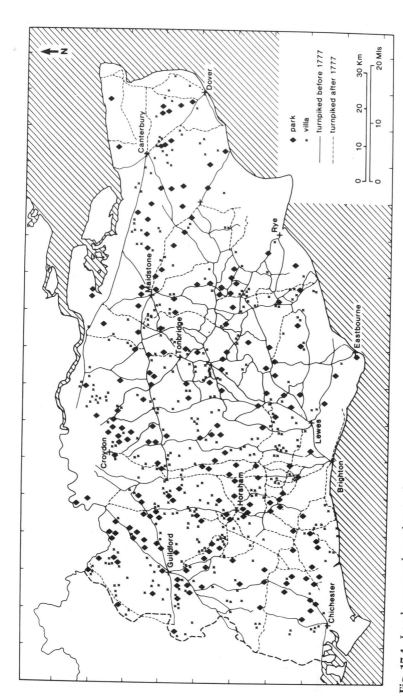

Fig. 17.4. Landscape parks and turnpike roads in the south-east. From Peter Brandon and Brian Short, *The South East from AD 1000* (Longmans, 1990).

Travelling these roads too were that highly mobile group of professional land-scape artists and landscape gardeners who helped define the nation as a patrician landscape.[23] Between 1789 and 1816 Humphry Repton claimed to have done over 400 commissions, most them over a twenty year period (Fig. 17.3). This works out at about two a month, the work for which would include a visit to survey the site and the preparation of a book of designs with text and watercolour. When demand was good Repton rationalized his work by securing local clusters of commissions and by setting aside winter months for preparing designs. In hard times he would travel far for a single commission, carefully computing his travel expenses for the account. With his business card, and work on the road—scribbling ideas in coaching inns and sometimes on the coaches themselves—Repton was something of a commercial traveller. As someone convinced of the higher calling of his art, Repton was uncomfortably conscious of this, especially in his later, insolvent years, when he would travel all day to give a few hours' advice to a *parvenu* on embellishing a few acres, remembering how once he had enjoyed the more relaxed ways of the nobility. 'I can picture their calculators thus talking of me—Landscape gardening is a good line, no risk of capital, all profit, no loss!—a very pretty mornings work!'[24] These new clients were the merchants and financiers who were lining the improved roads from London with their parks and gardens, notably in the Chilterns and the Weald (Fig. 17.4). They needed little long-term advice or activity to create their new badges of status. On cheap, thickly wooded sites they could 'enjoy the maturity and respect-ability of a park after a mere season's land clearance'.[25]

Improvement in Question

As the carriages of the new gentry flashed along improved roads, so those dis-affected with their mobility, both upward and outward, drew attention to the slower rhythmed, vernacular countryside surviving along rutted hollow ways. A day's journey across such countryside in Surrey led William Cobbett to claim that 'Those who travel on turnpike roads know nothing of England—From Hanscombe to Thursley almost the whole way is across fields or commons, or along narrow lanes. Here we see people without disguize or affectation. Against a *great road* things are made for *show*.'[26] If this discovery, or perhaps construction, of an earthier, more authentic England was part of Cobbett's radical rejection of the patrician landscape of houses and parks as a '*Picture of England*', others, more conservatively, attempted to incorporate it in a morally reformed patrician landscape, one which emphasized the less pretentious lifestyle of provincial squires. Thus in 1794 Uvedale Price upheld overgrown 'hollow lanes and bye roads', of the kind he had on his Herefordshire estate, as a paradigm of picturesque improvement because they were the product of long-term, piecemeal changes and bore the tread of local labourers and livestock. Such densely layered signs of locality, community and tradition were, Price noted, erased by the recent 'smoothing and levelling' he had seen inflicted on two lanes bordering pleasure grounds 'within thirty miles of London and in a district full of expensive embellishments'.[27]

Humphry Repton was dismayed to discover that slick city ways were penetrating the depths of 'a distant county'. In an essay published in 1816, he described how the scenery of a country road passing through the estate of an old aristocratic family had been ruthlessly transformed upon its sale to an upstart (Fig. 17.5). On one side of the road the common had been enclosed and ploughed. On the other the old deciduous trees in the park had been cut down, sold off and replaced with conifers. The 'old mossy and ivy covered pale' lining the park had been replaced with a high fence and the stile that had invited villagers to pass through the park had been replaced by 'a caution about man traps and spring guns'. While the old embowered lane had led the traveller gently into an arena of landed benevolence, the new, straightened road

Fig. 17.5. Humphry Repton, 'Improvements'.

drove him directly through an expressly financial landscape, ruthlessly mobilized for money. Repton entitled his essay 'Improvement', showing how on this estate, and by implication in the nation as a whole, the term had been reduced to a narrowly financial one, destroying that delicate blend of patrician interests Repton's own improvements were designed to enhance. During the Napoleonic Wars the 'great wheel of circulation' had been lubricated by a large and unregulated increase in paper money. Repton saw this as providing, in contrast to land, a baseless, unstable source of wealth and power. Like Burke he feared 'a paper circulation and stock-jobbing constitution', and the end of his stately art.[28]

Sheringham

Repton found one client who endorsed his conservative idea of improvement. At Sheringham in Norfolk (Fig. 17.6) in the summer of 1812, and against a background of acute social distress and tension sharpened by the threat of invasion, Repton took the opportunity to design a stable, benevolent landscape for a pious Norfolk squire, Abbot Upcher. Repton proposed creating a village green with a Maypole ('that

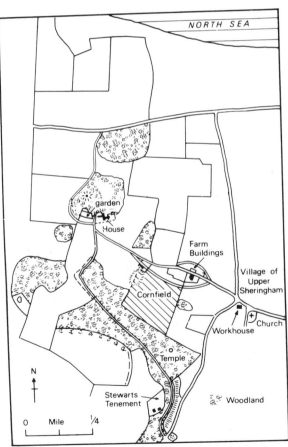

Fig. 17.6. Sheringham, after the map in Humphry Repton's *Plans for Sheringham* (1812).

almost forgotten emblem of rural happiness'), making the workhouse look less like a prison and more like an old almshouse, relieving beggars at the mansion with leftovers, letting villagers gather firewood in the park 'once a month, under the eye of the keeper', planting oaks 'Emblem of strength, increas'd by unity', organizing communal coursing matches on the beach at low tide (to promote 'a mutual intercourse betwixt the Landlord, the Tenant and the Labourer') and disclosing a cornfield beyond the park. The cornfield was not just as a sign of patriotic endeavour but intended to show the labourers working, for unlike industrial workers (then smashing machinery in textile factories and workshops which Repton said Sheringham was mercifully spared) local farm workers, like fishermen, were too exhausted by their labours to do anything but sit at home quietly with their families. The regime Repton recommended did not imply any casual intimacy between the landlord and his labourers, indeed quite the opposite. The highly controlled and stage managed landscape Repton envisaged pivoted on a new mansion that was positioned in a new park well away from the village.

While Repton proposed to improve the value of the Sheringham estate, this was not improvement in the eyes of those 'who know no standard of value but Gold and its flimsy representatives'. Perhaps Repton did protest too much. If the tone of the text to his client is sober and highminded, that of the letters to his son, a lawyer who oversaw the Enclosure Award that preceded the sale of the estate, is less so. Having purchased Sheringham at the top of the market, Upcher, in a fit of depression, concluded he could not afford it. Repton negotiated with his physician to suggest another purchaser, the government, who had £90,000 to spend for a country seat for the new Nelson peerage settled on the family after the Battle of Trafalgar. Money and favour would surely flow Repton's way. With all the speculative relish he publicly censured in others, Repton put his son forward as agent for the sale, suggesting he 'set the woods and Game & improvement from Inclosure pretty high then add so much for situation and beauty... Your advice added 2500 Slap & the odd 500 should be yours—ha! Slap.'[29]

Everything about this episode indicates how studied and self-conscious patrician performance in late Georgian England had become and how fragile was its credibility. In the various sites of their power, from assize courts to ox roasts, the style of the gentry had always been theatrical, and landscape parks were perhaps the most theatrical sites of all.[30] But it is as if the relation between the illusory and the real in landscape improvement was now breaking apart. Certainly some writers were forcing it apart. In *Mansfield Park* (1811–13) Jane Austen puts the word 'improvement' into the mouths of moral delinquents who wish to wantonly alter estates, to erase their long evolved and finely detailed social and aesthetic topography. Seeing the countryside in terms of large scenic prospects and broad vistas is censured in the novel as careless and vacuous. The glamorous Mary Crawford with her flashy London ways rides impatiently about the Mansfield Park estate, turning from this scene to that, with little knowledge and less interest in what is before her; she sees 'with little observation'. In contrast, the modest heroine Fanny Price, as much a stranger to the estate as Miss Crawford, seems almost immobile and myopic, confined to the smaller, more finely detailed parts of the estate such as the flower garden, an observer not a spectator, seeing everything 'within her grasp'. On one of her rare carriage rides she is soon 'beyond her knowledge' but extends her vigilant ways by 'observing the appearance of the country, the bearings of the roads, the differences of soil, the state of harvest, the cottages, the cattle, the children'. If for Mary Crawford, the countryside is a scenic spectacle, of the kind she would enjoy in a London theatre, for Fanny Price it is an improving text, of the kind she often reads in her room. The text offers truth, the theatre a pernicious illusion.[31]

From Landscape to Garden

Fanny Price's favourite reading, and Jane Austen's too, was the poetical works of William Cowper. It is hard to overestimate the influence of Cowper on the moral reform of polite views of the countryside and of rural improvement, a reform which became fully realized in Victorian styles of garden design. Cowper's long poem *The Task* (1785) was a favourite for reading aloud in the homes of the lesser gentry and of the commercial and professional classes in towns, suburbs, villages or farms.[32] Extracts from the poem were published throughout 1786 in *The Ipswich Journal*, a newspaper aimed firmly at these classes, and distributed throughout Suffolk.[33] 'God made the country, man made the town' declares *The Task*; but the poem is directed not just at urban dissolution but at the corruption of God's countryside too, in particular by wealthy landowners who adopted what Cowper saw as the disruptive and extravagant landscape improvements of Capability Brown. 'Improvement' was 'the idol of the age', Cowper complains 'fed with many a victim'; 'Estates are landscapes', he continues 'gaz'd upon awhile, then advertiz'd and auctioneered away'. *The Task* and the rest of Cowper's works dignify the steady rhythms of husbandry and 'the calm minutiae of everyday life in the home, the garden, the fields and woods'.[34] If parks, or at least certain parkland designs, were morally suspect, gardens offered an alternative arena for virtue, the earnest, pious, domestic code for conduct associated with the middle classes of late Georgian England which was to diffuse throughout polite society.

It is probable that many of the rural professions—for example parsons, tenant farmers, millers—did not follow the aristocratic fashion of sweeping away their gardens, even if their grounds were sufficiently sizable to make a passable imitation of the Brown style.[35] For example, the foregrounds of Constable's paintings (1815) of his father's 37 acre estate in East Bergholt, that of a corn miller and grain merchant, are dominated by formal flower and kitchen gardens which set the tone for the manicured agricultural landscape beyond.[36] Smaller squires, especially those in areas bypassed by fashion, may have retained their gardens too, although Uvedale Price expressed his remorse for uprooting his in Herefordshire in his youthful enthusiasm for Brown[37] (suggesting that he and his locality were not so unsophisticated as he pretended). Humphry Repton, upholding his own roadside villa in Essex as an example, recommended the creation of small, finely detailed gardens of flowers, shrubs and trellised walks and hedged borders, for all the houses of polite society, from suburban villas to aristocratic mansions, if species and arrangements were to be carefully adjusted for houses of different rank and character.[38]

Repton's emphasis on gardening rather than landscaping towards the end of his career, made, he acknowledged, a virtue out of the fact that large landowners were unable or unwilling to spend money on large-scale improvements, either because of taxes during the war or depressed agricultural conditions after it.[39] When Repton's successor John Claudius Loudon reported his several tours of the notable parks in the 1820s and 1830s for his *Gardeners Magazine* he noted everywhere signs of decay. At Blenheim 'the noblest place in Britain, perhaps in Europe', trees grew out of the stonework of the gate piers, the cascade dam leaked, and 'half the lake turned into a morass covered with rushes'. Even Repton's recent garden at Southgate lodge was ruinous.

Loudon put his faith in the suburban middle classes, the target audience for his voluminous writings, to restore the integrity of house and garden design (Fig. 17.7). Indeed he argued that this could only flourish in a political system which granted

Fig. 17.7. Vignette of Mrs Lawrence's garden at Drayton Green, Middlesex. From J. C. Loudon, *The Suburban Gardener and Villa Companion* (1838).

them power. Many suburban houses were rented, not owned, and the fluctuations of family fortunes prompted Loudon to provide 'a flexible template for domestic life'. His designs could be adjusted to grounds of varying dimensions and were calculated to be realized in months rather than years. It was much less the patrician ideology of property and contemplation, than the bourgeous ideology of supervision and industriousness which underlay Loudon's style. His gardens were less landscapes than workshops or laboratories. Loudon coined the term 'gardenesque' to describe his style. The term was gradually refined in Loudon's writings to denote the isolation of plants as individual specimens collected within an overall pictorial design.[40] The impulse to collect and specify was expressed throughout the house and garden, in conservatories where the more exotic plants, some from the furthest reaches of the Empire, were carefully labelled, in various containers for ferns, fishes, insects and fossils. Loudon's own writings are exercises in specification, detailing every aspect of home life 'from the planting of garden seeds, to the appropriate authors to display on a dining room bookshelf'.[41]

The obsessive interest in factual detail characterized a variety of popular discourses in Victorian England—etiquette, educational theory, natural science, natural theology, social science and ethnology (the science of reading moral character from the minutest details of clothing or physiognomy). In gardening it found expression in the so-called 'language of flowers', a reconstruction of Tudor floral iconography filtered through a sentimental model of Tudor courtliness.[42] The language of flowers was the preserve of women. Indeed, women became increasingly identified with flowers and floral gardening. Jane Webb Loudon matched her husband's industriousness as a garden writer, writing nineteen books, her *Ladies Companion to the Flower Garden* (1841) going through nine editions. She also helped him edit and produce his own work. The model of domestic virtue first popularized in poetry by Cowper and expressed in practical design and management by the Loudons reformulated gender roles. It offered a new model of manliness—bookish, kindly, sober, pious, conversant with women—a model that must have seemed contemptibly effeminate to those Regency bucks to whose conduct it was strategically opposed. The new domesticity, as Davidoff and Hall observe, both elevated the status of women and contained it 'like the plant in the pot, limited and domesticated, sexually controlled, not spilling into spheres to which she did not belong, not being overpowered by "weeds" of social disorder'. This model was deployed against the eighteenth-century reputation of women as licentious and sexually voracious, one institutionalized in the spectacle of high-class prostitutes flaunting their wares in the urban pleasure gardens of the West End of London or from their carriages in Hyde Park.[43]

In Victorian eyes, the eighteenth century was morally contaminated and Victorian garden designs looked back beyond it to periods whose styles seemed to symbolize a more virtuous code of conduct. Victorian architecture did so too. The Gothic in particular was felt to project piety and hospitality. The leader of the style George Gilbert Scott contrasted country houses in a gothic style to those great eighteenth-century classical mansions like Stowe whose 'cold and proud Palladianism seems to forbid approach—the only rural thoughts they suggest are of game-keepers and park rangers'. In fact, it was more difficult to approach country houses in Victorian times. 'The Victorian Country house was not for public viewing as the eighteenth century one had been', notes Jill Franklin. 'Privacy was now much more important than grand initial display, and in order to keep the park and the garden front of the house secluded the Victorians made the carriage drive wind around the edge of the park, so that the visitor caught his first sight of the gardens, lake and main prospect only after passing through the house. Many older houses ... had their main entrance moved round to what once had been the back.'[44]

If country houses were refashioned, enlarged and in often extravagant styles, and new formal gardens laid out next to them, parks were mostly left to mature within their Georgian designs. Loudon coined the term 'landscape husbandry' to denote the laying out of estates with due care and attention to their social fabric, in essence (as he acknowledged) a picturesque style derived from Uvedale Price.[45] But, unlike 'gardenesque', the term never caught on, a symptom perhaps of how the landed estate lost its hold on the social imagination. The structure of rural society remained as it had been in Georgian times, country-house building went on apace and parkland acreage seems to have increased, but the countryside no longer seemed full of social energies or tensions that needed to be resolved in patrician landscape terms. By the 1840s the focus on the condition of England shifted to the burgeoning industrial cities.[46] By the 1870s land had not only lost its political power and some of its social prestige but was no longer a secure investment. Estates which did not enjoy transfusions of income from urban property or stocks and shares were broken up for sale; some remained unsold. It was not the aristocracy but the lesser gentry, those who had acted as moral exemplars for Victorian England, who most felt the pinch. By the turn of the century 'the mystique of land had been exploded', writes Mark Girouard, 'but the mystique of the country house remained as strong as ever'. Professional men, the kind who subscribed to the magazine *Country Life* (which first appeared in 1899), wanted a house and grounds without the burden of an estate, 'a house in the country rather than a country house'.[47]

The nineteenth-century garden might be seen as a haven from the dynamism of an increasingly industrial world, a place where by concentrating on the little things of nature one could avoid larger, more intractable social issues. But contemporaries also saw the garden, and the habits of observation and cultivation it fostered, more extrovertly as a way of progressively framing that industrial world. The most visionary building of the age, Joseph Paxton's Crystal Palace which housed the Great Exhibition of 1851 in Hyde Park, was based on Paxton's plans for a glasshouse he had built at Chatsworth to house the Duke of Devonshire's giant waterlily *Victoria amazonica*. Built to advanced methods of industrial production, the Crystal Palace was the Exhibitions' main showpiece. 'Quite in keeping is the building with the age', declared one enthusiast, 'It is the aesthetic bloom of its practical character, and of the practical tendency of the English nation.'[48]

Urban Improvement

Spectacle

The theatrical style of Georgian society was expressed in urban design. Cities and towns were rebuilt and refashioned with elegant assembly rooms, town halls, residential squares, parades and public gardens, settings for the rituals which helped shaped a variety of interests—landed, commercial, financial, professional—into the cultural consensus of 'polite society'.[49] The conduct of these rituals was highly regulated. In the larger resort towns the company followed a strict and often supervised circuit of activities. At Bath, the master of ceremonies Beau Nash, a man of unpretentious middle-class origins, sought to establish a 'general society among people of rank or fortune'. In the process he had to reduce the nobility's tincture of haughtiness, as when the Duchess of Queensbury turned up one evening at the Assembly Rooms wearing a white apron—that is to say not bothering to take off her day-time clothes. 'Nash stripped the apron off her and threw it to her attendant ladies. The duchess swallowed the rebuke, and did not appear in an apron again.'[50]

Classical styling with the use of stone or brick and stucco established a common, nation-wide code for polite townscape as did various other improvements to its fabric such as paving, street lighting, street cleaning, and the provision of piped water supply and sewage disposal. Noxious or dangerous trades were expelled to the districts of the poor. Other areas of poor resort, notably town commons, were liable to be enclosed for the building of genteel precincts. Access to and traffic through such precincts were subject to tight controls. No less than the building of landscape parks, the building of genteel townscape articulated a growing disengagement between polite and impolite culture. This disengagement was never complete. Contemporary engravings of new residential squares and parades often show the occasional cow and keeper, perhaps a beggar, and, of course, these precincts had to accommodate a population of servants and grooms. But such signs of plebian life could be discreetly managed. Of greater moment was the threat of the crowd. Larger cities could not be securely managed as a set of enclosed spheres, and especially at elections or during civic events and celebrations they took on the older theatrical aspect of towns as 'as an open stage for the enactment of civic mystery and dispute'. 'The self-confident solidity of Georgian Squares became shaky when repeatedly occupied by shabby but sober political aspirants', notes Mark Harrison, 'And repeated activity at crucial crowd venues could create a symbolic significance the architect would never have intended.'[51]

The structure of some polite landscapes was no less patrician than their style. In London leading aristocrats, notably the Dukes of Bedford, Portland and Southampton, vied with each other to develop their estates. Long-term leases with strict conditions on the use and fashioning of houses were designed to maintain the social tone of these estates and realize a long-term financial return. Houses were cropped as oaks rather than wheat. The ducal mansion set the tone of such developments and the sides of some residential squares were run together in large palatial facades.[52] The sixth Duke of Bedford commissioned Humphry Repton (then busy on Bedford's rural estates) to landscape Russell Square and Bloomsbury Square, in the former to design an avenue of lime trees leading to a statue of the Duke.[53]

The fragmented freehold pattern of many towns compromised and sometimes defeated grandiose schemes. Nevertheless, in such towns a series of apparently *ad hoc* transactions between corporations, landowners, property developers, building contractors and architects could, even over a sometimes volatile economic era, produce a harmoniously polite townscape. Bath (Fig. 17.8), the most complete and compact example of Georgian townscape, emerged thus, its coherence decisively

Fig. 17.8. Thomas Malton, *View of North Parade, Bath c. 1777*. Reproduced by courtesy of the Board of Trustees of the V & A.

shaped by three entrepreneurs. A city councillor, Ralph Allen, exploited his quarries of oolitic limestone for building stone; Beau Nash formalized the conduct of a once licentious gambling town; the architects and contractors John Wood the Elder and Younger designed the main residential quarters. R. S. Neale maintains that despite Wood the Elder's own speculative dealings he designed residential squares and parades according to an antique model of civic virtue intended in theory to circumscribe the acquisitive instincts of Bath society. Wood's designs 'may be seen as both a protest against that society as well as a way of adjusting to it'.[54]

It was precisely the contingencies of landholding and development which helped make Bath a sociable townscape for polite society as well as a picturesque one. There were no great vistas leading to a central feature, 'instead there were a series of focal points—the different baths, the assembly rooms, the pump room and the abbey—surrounded and linked by terraces and crescents. People strolled from one to the other meeting friends on the way.'[55]

Late Georgian improvements to the West End of London made the capital more of a spectacle. Under the patronage of George IV, first as Regent, then as King, John Nash designed or refashioned parks, palaces, squares and streets into a brilliant sequence stretching from Regents Park in the north, down Regents Street to St James Park and Buckingham Palace and Gardens in the south (Fig. 17.9). When the last grazing lease on the Crown's 554 acre Marylebone Park ran out in 1811 Nash secured the commission to transform it into a landscaped park named after the Regent, with a royal residence, fifty villas for high-class office-holders scattered through the park (each screened from its neighbours but appearing to possess the park as a whole), and terraces on the perimeter. As it turned out the royal residence was not built, and only a fraction of the villas were completed, but Regents Park was realized as a garden suburb, its landscaping owing much to Nash's former partner Humphry Repton.

Nash's scheme for the Regent had a solidly practical aspect, including a canal, a new waterworks and network of drains and sewers, but it was its dazzling superstructure that caught the imagination. Flimsy as architecture but superb as scenery, the terraces around Regents Park set the style of the rest of Nash's scheme. Regents Street was planned as a scenic avenue. Its lining of stuccoed facades and colonnades was only loosely related to the building behind and did not bear close inspection, and nor was it meant to, being designed to be seen briefly and kinetically from a carriage speeding towards Westminster and Whitehall. There was money to be made from it too, not only for the Crown estate but for a number of other property developers and speculative builders, including Nash himself who put up the money for the biggest single unit, and the most theatrical, the Quadrant at the south end. This was a colonnade of Doric columns, designed to provide a covered walk for the rituals of high-class shopping, sweeping round in a great arc to Piccadilly Circus. There proved to be many obstructions to Nash's original plan for the street but his urban picturesque style could take advantage of the contingencies. He did achieve one of his main aims, to stake out a frontier between polite and impolite society, in his words to make a 'boundary and complete separation between the Streets and Squares occupied by the Nobility and Gentry, and the narrow Streets and Houses occupied by the mechanics and trading part of the community'. Regents Street

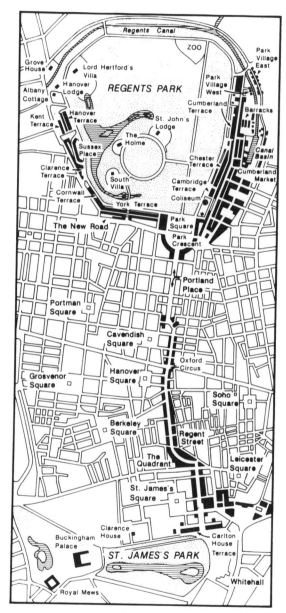

Fig. 17.9. Streets, squares and paths laid out by John Nash, 1811–35. After Fig. 25 of John Summerson, *Georgian London* (1945).

opened to the entrances of the noble streets on the west and sealed off the main streets on the east.[56]

Other improvements to the West End, notably the building of Trafalgar Square and its monuments, the erection of the triumphal arch and screen at Hyde Park Corner, the reconstruction of the Strand, the building of museums and theatres for plays and for viewing panoramas and dioramas enhanced the spectacle of metropolis. The Colosseum, built next to the grand terrace of Regent's Park, housed a panorama of London as seen from the top of St Pauls, an orderly 'absolutely ideal London', without smoke, dirt, poverty or confusion. This, the most celebrated entertainment of its day, 'helped to blur the distinction between representation and reality for the viewer' as he or she emerged into daylight to be presented with a panoramic view from the top of the Colosseum, making 'the city and its entertainments seem as one'. This may, as Nord suggests, be taken as a model of the hypertheatrical sensibility of polite society during the Regency, one that swiftly mutated in the city, as in the country, into a soberly verisimilar sensibility. 'The urban spectators of the 1820s were the precursors of more engaged Victorian urban investigators', Nord declares; 'What Regency spectators merely glimpsed and turned away from', especially the presence of the poor, 'inspired Victorian observers to invent new strategies'—in fiction, social science and environmental design—to describe, explain and transform.[57]

Surveillance

Such observational strategies were not new to the Victorian age. Their paradigm is perhaps the Panopticon, the building invented by Jeremy Bentham for surveying prisoners from a central tower, a kind of panorama for inspecting individuals in isolation, of transforming them from subjects of a spectacle into objects of information.[58] Surveillance is no less performative a strategy than spectating and historically it may be misleading to say that the new epistemology was less 'theatrical' if only because London theatres were themselves becoming more observational arenas. In Georgian London audiences openly communicated with actors and themselves, interrupting in mid-scene to approve or deride, to the point where it was difficult to draw a distinction between actor and audience. In Victorian London house lights were dimmed, to reinforce a new code of audience silence and focus on the stage, and upon actors who were expected to dress accurately for the part and to keep to the text. And so in the theatre of the city, social reformers frowned on spectacular public display. Except for high-class shopping, London became (in contrast to Paris and Vienna) a city of 'hidden pleasures'. Meanwhile the full blaze of publicity was turned on the poor and the *facts* of urban life.[59]

And dismal facts they often were. London, and city life generally, became an object of concern. While the Best Circles of Georgian England were somewhat insouciant about the lives and living conditions of the poor, as long as they were mostly kept off stage, the spectre of contagious disease spreading rampantly throughout the city, and with it a variety of social pathologies, prompted their Victorian successors into more vigorous strategies of social and environmental control. If James Elmes and Thomas Shepherd's *Metropolitan Improvements, or London in the Nineteenth Century* (1827–31) had happily celebrated the flamboyant refashioning of the West End, 'after 1830', notes Donald Olsen, 'Metropolitan improvements ceased to mean schemes for beautifying London, but came to be limited to ones that dealt with specific evils—traffic congestion, insanitary dwellings, inefficient sewage disposal—in which aesthetic considerations would be secondary, if indeed they entered at all'.[60] This more utilitarian definition of improvement might be linked to increasing middle-class control over the operation and expenditure of national and local government. The aesthetic was not neglected in metropolitan improvements, at least in new public buildings, but what emerged was a reformed aesthetic, turning away from what was seen as the dishonesty and frivolity of Regency architecture to the gravity of the Gothic and a ponderous kind of Renaissance classicism. In 1848, in a highly symbolic gesture, Nash's colonnade in the Quadrant in Regent's Street was demolished, condemned as 'a haunt of vice and immorality'.[61] But changes in cultural values and political organization little modified the residential development of high society, for the matrix of land ownership, estate management and house building established in the eighteenth century proved highly resilient.[62]

Discipline

There were a number of schemes, both privately and publicly funded, to improve the physical fabric of poorer urban districts, and by extension (it was presumed) their social and moral condition. The building of wide streets, model housing estates and public parks was informed by the belief that slums nourished, if not caused, a variety of pathologies, not just physical disease, but improvidence, crime, laziness, irreligion and insurrection. The concept of the slum itself was compounded from the variety of conditions reformers wished to erase, including dilapidation, poor drainage, stale air, high population density, multiple use, labyrinthine layout. Wide streets were valued not only for ventilating the districts they passed through (a strategy based on the theory that stagnant air was a cause of disease) but for allowing the economically invigorating circulation of trade and for exposing slum dwellers to the presence of social superiors and the police. What made such schemes improved—and improving—was not so much their appearance, or the quality of their materials, as their principles of social discipline.[63]

If the environmental discipline of the poor was not a Victorian invention, Victorians were preoccupied with extending it beyond the walls of prisons, workhouses and factories. Those places where the factory system had not been instituted were felt to be the most disorderly. The difference between Leeds and Sheffield, a Dr Holland pronounced in 1839, was that in Sheffield 'men are masters of their own time and free from the ordinary restriction of well regulated factories. They are not taught daily the value of time, or the effects of its misapplication.' Even in cities where factories were established, there seemed a blur of disorder beyond the factory gates. In 1844 the German geographer J.G. Kohl was alarmed at Manchester mill workers going home to 'those recesses of private houses which no legislative restrictions can reach, and where the searching eye of public opinion never penetrates'. Manchester of the 1840s provided a rich field for urban investigators seeking out disorder, indeed the city was the laboratory for debates on 'the condition of England'. After a visit to Manchester the factory colonies of rural Lancashire seemed exemplary models of class relations. For one enthusiast they 'afforded employers opportunities of coming frequently into personal communication with their workpeople and exercising a healthy control over their domestic habits and private morals'.[64] Many such mill colonies were not planned with much other in mind than making a secure profit but in reformist literature emphasis was placed on those that were consciously and comprehensively designed to be models of social order. The most famous was Saltaire.

Saltaire

A manufacturer of alpaca and mohair, Titus Salt decided to move his business three miles out of the dirt and confusion of central Bradford to a tranquil and scenic stretch of the Aire Valley. This was for good business reasons—he needed a new site to expand that was well served by canal and rail—but for long in his capacity as a magistrate and as Mayor of Bradford Salt had campaigned for the reform of living and working conditions in the city and expressed his disappointment with the meagre fruit of his efforts. Saltaire was to teach Bradford a lesson by combining, in its founder's words, 'every improvement that modern art and science has brought to light'. The new mill at Saltaire was opened in 1853 and around it, over the next twenty years, Saltaire developed into a town of four and a half thousand people with a range of improving institutions (Fig. 17.10) Some of the public buildings had a decorative and patrician flourish—the mill with its chimney encased in a Venetian style campanile, the large domed and columned Congregational Church opposite the mill gates, the highly wrought gothic almshouses emblazoned with Salt's family crest—but most of the houses were austere. The plan of Saltaire mattered more than its appearance. A street pattern of parallelograms co-ordinated a system of strict functional zoning. There was nothing like a village green, nor any place where people could gather for a gossip, a grumble or just some impromptu fun. An Educational Institute was built in place of a pub and the park was a highly regulated space for leisure, from which occasional offenders were evicted and persistent offenders exiled. The house at the centre of the village, designed for a mill overseer and on census night in 1871 occupied by the works' security officer, had a glass windowed tower, probably less a functional than a symbolic sign of surveillance. The overseers and mill managers who were first housed in Saltaire largely controlled the life of the settlement, occupying positions of power in the institutions and controlling the allocation of tenancies. Saltaire represented an extreme extension of the principles of factory design and management into the sphere of leisure. While contemporary illustrations of Saltaire usually show the settlement in a bucolic setting, surrounded by fields and scenes of harvest, from within it made no concession to the countryside. It shut out the picturesque scenery around it and its street pattern entirely obliterated the former intricate pattern of lanes, pathways and field boundaries. Saltaire was as much opposed to the muddle of the country as of the city. Indeed local reformers complained that urbanizing areas became slums precisely because they adhered so closely to the irregular pattern of rural land use which Saltaire had so happily erased. In spite of its setting, Saltaire was meant to produce an industrial army, not a rustic community.

Saltaire was a select place. Only the better paid mill workers, in general the more skilled and the more responsible, could afford the rents. Many of the lower paid lived

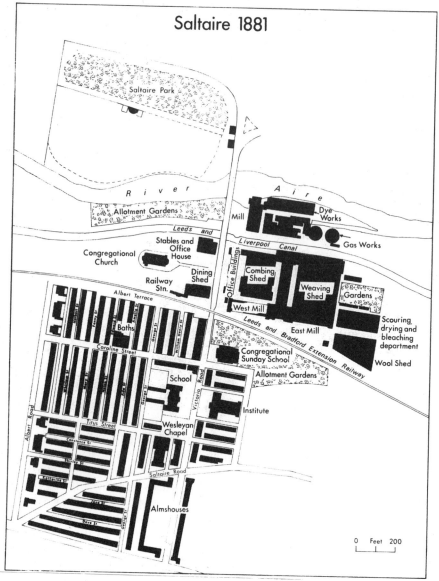

Fig. 17.10. Saltaire, 1881.

outside Saltaire in the more diverse industrial suburb of Shipley as did those who did
not care to submit to its strictures or were not thought capable of doing so. In contrast
to Shipley and to central Bradford there were in Saltaire only a handful of Irish
households. The settlement represented the most comprehensive attempt to insu-
late the respectable working class from the mass of labouring poor and the rougher
and more convivial aspects of lower-class life. Elsewhere improving institutions
such as educational institutes, savings banks, model dwellings and public parks
formed an archipelago of respectability. Whilst most such institutions were created

or sponsored by middle-class interests they represented as much an incorporation of working-class values as an imposition of middle-class ones. Sobriety, thrift and improvement were cardinal principles of independently organized working-class culture, especially by the 1850s when employment in industrial districts had risen, class tensions had eased and most working-class radicals had accepted the world of the factory as the terrain of their politics. Factory masters compromised too. A radical in politics and Dissenter in religion, Salt was a pioneer of the genial and socially responsible liberalism of mid-Victorian industrial towns. And he was applauded as such by working-class radicals (or at least by the many who had mellowed) who saw Saltaire less as a prison of middle-class control than as an outlet for (now reduced) working-class aspirations.[65]

The common ground between middle-class and working-class versions of improvement was eagerly cultivated by middle-class reformers, transplanting and grafting their varieties of fellowship, independence, rationality and respectability. Perhaps the most subtle arena of the new consensus was the public park.

The People's Parks

As towns and cities expanded and infilled, so early Victorian social reformers voiced their alarm about the disappearance of open space for public recreation. There were calls to unlock gardens in polite Georgian squares, to allow the general public on occasion into private parks on the edges of towns or into middle-class subscription gardens. There was actually not so much of a crisis in leisure-space as reformers claimed. Open country was just a walk away from most industrial towns and cities and streets in working-class districts were arenas for various games and pastimes. At issue was the use to which open space was put. The moors surrounding West Yorkshire textile towns were used for dog racing, dog fighting, prize fighting and political rallies, precisely the kinds of pursuits reformers wished to see abolished. They promoted 'rational recreation', constructive kinds of leisure, including family promenading, team sports and botanical walks. Owners of parks and gardens needed convincing that their preserves would not be vandalized or otherwise used in inappropriate ways and, even if not, of the good that was expected to be gained from admitting the public at large. In his influential *Report on the Sanitary Condition of the Labouring Population of Great Britain* (1842) Edwin Chadwick gave an example of opening gardens as a counter-insurgency strategy. He told of the occasion when Manchester's Commissioner of Police had the Botanical and Zoological Gardens of the town thrown open as a counter-attraction to a Chartist demonstration, with the effect 'that not more than 200 or 300 people attended the political meeting, which entirely failed and scarcely 5s worth of damage was done in the gardens'; moreover 'the charges before the police of drunkenness and riot were on that day less than the average on ordinary days'. Such cynical views of working-class culture were commonplace. In Manchester, and most industrial cities, there was an established working-class tradition of family excursions into the countryside, sometimes in pursuit of natural history, which new public parks and gardens reconstituted.[66]

The first purpose-built public park, the Arboretum in Derby, was opened in 1839. It was designed by a leading advocate of such institutions, J. C. Loudon, and funded by a local cotton spinner, Joseph Strutt, the first mayor of the newly-elected town

Fig. 17.11. The People's Park, Halifax. From *Illustrated London News*, August 22, 1857.

council of 1835. Planted with five thousand species of plants, each labelled with botanical details, along six thousand feet of winding paths, within a space of eleven acres, the Arboretum was intended to 'unite information with amusement'. The first municipal park, the more extensive Birkenhead Park, was designed by Joseph Paxton in 1843 to a gardenesque style. It quickly became known as 'the people's park'. 'The baker of Birkenhead has the pride of an OWNER in it', declared the American park designer F. L. Olmstead (an indication that the idea of the people here was still an exclusive one).[67] Also enjoying the pride of ownership were the residents of elegant villas built around the perimeter. From the 1850s new public walks and parks were built in most industrial towns and cities, frequently on the periphery, sometimes by enclosing commonland. Some were initially paid for by large employers and later handed over to municipal corporations. Others were from the beginning municipal ventures. New cemeteries on the edge of cities were designed for rational recreation. Undercliffe Cemetery, high above Bradford, was run as a profit-making venture by a partnership of local businessmen. Families promenaded beside the extravagant tombs of the city's leading industrial families and took in the smoky panorama of their enterprise.[68]

Some of the complexity of public park creation and design, and its implications for other adjacent townscape, will be evident by considering an example. People's Park, Halifax was opened in 1857 (Fig. 17.11). The twelve and a half acre site, made up of six separate freeholds, was purchased by the town's main employer, and MP, the carpet manufacturer Francis Crossley. It was situated in front of Crossley's villa, Belle Vue (then undergoing extensive enlargement and refashioning) on the outskirts of the town, looking over the mill-choked valley to the Pennines. At the opening of the park, Crossley gave two reasons why he had financed its building.

First, during a visit to the White Mountains of New Hampshire he had nothing short of a religious experience in gazing at the scenery, tempered only by the thought that his townspeople seemed to show even less enthusiasm for scenery than they did for religion. So he made up his mind to create a park with uplifting views 'within the walk of every working man in Halifax; that he shall go, take his stroll there after he has done his hard day's toil, and be able to get home again without being tired'. At the opening a local poet (who was given the job of park-keeper) read out some verses of dedication, beginning 'Here let me stand and gaze enraptured round/ On lovely scenes with matchless beauty crowned'.

Secondly, Crossley recalled the example of his mother who, when her sons moved into suburban villas, refused to move from the old house adjoining the mill. 'One of the greatest treats she had in her old age was to fix a mirror in her room, so that while laying in bed she could see the happy countenances of those who were coming to work and back again.' In a letter to the mayor on the tenth anniversary of the park's opening, Crossley explained how 'it has often been a great source of pleasure to me to see from the windows of Belle Vue so many thousands of my fellow townsmen enjoying themselves in the People's Park'.

The language of fellowship here may be seen as a projection of managerial surveillance but it represented for Crossley a commitment to the town, a Dissenter's stand against the blandishments of an aristocratic lifestyle (in his villa hung a painting of *Cromwell Refusing the Crown of England*). Despite his enormous wealth, Crossley had earned the confidence of one of the most radical mill towns. Indeed Crossley was himself a religious and political radical, supporting the Chartist candidate in the election of 1847 and taking on workers dismissed from their mills for Chartist activity. In the election of 1852 he himself stood as a Radical, this time against the Chartist, but in a more cordial climate of class relations, a climate which schemes like People's Park were intended to foster. At the opening Crossley was presented with a 'People's Address' of 8273 signatures 'chiefly those of working men' collected in a week. Before it a procession wound to the park from the old Chartist gathering place on Skircoat Moor, headed by a banner made of Crossley carpeting and including representatives from most of the town's improving clubs and institutions. The opening ceremony concluded with the singing of 'The Old Hundredth', sung by the crowds in 1842 when they marched through Halifax to pull the plugs of local mills (but not Crossley's) and sung again now as a hymn to class co-operation.

Under the direction of Joseph Paxton, People's Park was laid out with sinuous paths converging on a central fountain, and above them a raised terrace walk lined by statues of Roman gods with an arcaded pavilion at its centre (into which the Corporation later placed a statue of Crossley). The park had the usual battery of regulations. Patrons were requested to keep to the paths and the keeper was empowered to exclude 'improper characters'. While it was intended to be 'within the walk of every working man', People's Park was actually much more convenient for the families of the doctors, attorneys and merchants who lived nearby. Indeed Crossley used the park to stimulate respectable suburban development. Developing a road of villas on one side of the park he promised prospective residents 'the advantages of a pleasant prospect in an airy situation' and 'all the advantages of handsome pleasure grounds'. Like Birkenhead Park, and indeed many public parks, People's Park became an integral part of suburbanization. Whatever the revenue Crossley might have derived from his villas (and it seems to have been no more than 10 per cent of his initial outlay), it fell within the moral brief of the park as an arena of class contact, if this was on middle-class terms. On the pavilion was inscribed the motto 'The Rich and Poor meet together, the Lord is Maker of them all.'[69]

Civic Pride

From the reform of municipal corporations in 1835 environmental improvement was entwined with middle-class radicalism and attacks on what one Plymouth writer called 'a shabby mongrel aristocracy'. One of the first actions of the new elected Leicester Corporation was 'to sell the plate, crockery, glass-ware and mace, the symbols of older civic pride' and get to work on creating the new. 'Few towns have been more extended and improved than Leicester in the last ten years, . . . by the formation of new streets and the erection of elegant public edifices' announced a local gazeteer in 1846, adding 'the old street architecture of Leicester is rapidly vanishing . . . the greater part of the half-timbered lath-and-plaster houses, remarkable for their grotesque gables and picturesque appearance, have given place to plainer but more convenient dwellings'. But even within this one corporation there were bitter disputes between radical factions, between the 'Economists' who associated 'improvement' with the basics of sewerage, drainage and water supply and the 'Improvers' who were deploying the term in a grander manner to include the building of a new civic townscape of broad open spaces and magnificent public buildings. With the revival of urban fortunes from the 1850s it was improvement in the grand manner which captured the corporate imagination, and which in places lost its radical edge and assumed a patrician, even royal lustre.[70]

Provincial towns and cities tried to outdo each other in the architecture, setting and opening ceremonial of town halls. What is striking about the story of the most magnificent and commanding, Leeds town hall, opened in 1858, is its national, indeed imperial pretension. It was opened by Queen Victoria in a highly elaborate ceremony for which the city was transformed into a stage set, with elaborate wooden arches, colonnades, flowers and streamers embellishing the less attractive parts of the royal route. A giant imitation stone classical arch hid the hall from view until the Queen was almost upon it, 'so that the full effect of the noble structure might be realized by her majesty at once'. Around the magnificent vestibule of the town hall were the words 'Europe—Asia—Africa—America', reminding citizens 'that her majesty's dominion extends to all quarters of the globe'. 'For a portion of two days, through the condescension of Her Majesty', the *Leeds Mercury* reported, 'this old and busy seat of industry becomes in a sense the seat of the Empire.'[71]

Imperial London

Leeds had achieved what London could not. For much of Victoria's reign there were complaints that London was the least impressive of royal or imperial capitals, its setting for ceremony as slovenly as many of the ceremonies themselves. As David Cannadine shows, the monarchy took a long time to recover the esteem it had lost with the conduct of George IV and his circle. The symbolic power of the monarchy increased as its political power weakened. Freed from the factionalism of politics 'the way was open for it to become the centre of grand ceremonial once more'. From the closing decades of the nineteenth century action was taken to convert 'the fog-bound city of Dickens into an imperial capital'; 'The most significant, coherent piece of rebuilding was the widening of the Mall, the building of Admiralty Arch, the re-fronting of Buckingham Palace and the construction of the Victoria Monument in front . . . a grand, monumental, imperial ensemble, which gave London its only triumphal ceremonial way.' Royal pageantry was elaborated with a shrewd combination of preservation revival and outright invention.[72] With the onset of mass society and mass consumption the monarchy became a spectacular, highly public symbol of consensus and continuity, in the new popular press and in advertising campaigns as well as on the streets, in city squares and public gardens.

Power in the Land

By organizing our discussion in terms of the idea of improvement we have emphasized that landscape design is integral to historical–geographical development, not a superficial embellishment of it. Any adequate historical geography must take account of the ways people at the time conceived of their world and for this period landscape design provides us with particularly graphic evidence. We do not pretend that everyone's mentality can be discovered in landscape design. Design at the scale of landscape has always been the prerogative of those in power, and it is the genealogy and distribution of power which has been the focus to our inquiry.

References

1. The following discussions of the concept of improvement provided a basis for our own: Raymond Williams *Key words: A Vocabulary of Culture and Society*, (London, 1976), pp. 132–3; Raymond Williams, *The Country and the City*, (London, 1973), pp, 108–19; Alistair Duckworth, *The Improvement of the Estate: A Study of Jane Austen's Novels*, (Baltimore, 1971); Asa Briggs, *The Age of Improvement 1783–1867*, (London, 1963), pp. 1–3, 222–3, 435–45; Susanne Seymour, 'Eighteenth century parkland "improvement" on the Dukeries' Estates of North Nottinghamshire', unpublished Ph.D. (University of Nottingham, 1988). pp. 8–128.
2. The best recent general accounts of country house and park building are Tom Williamson and Liz Bellamy, *Property and Landscape: A Social History of Land Ownership and the English Countryside*, (London, 1987), pp. 116–56; David Jacques, *Georgian Gardens: The Reign of Nature*, (London, 1983); Mark Girouard, *Life in the English Country House*, (New Haven, 1978), pp. 181–244. Still essential is Hugh Prince, *Parks in England*, (Shalfleet Manor, 1967).
3. Stephen Daniels, 'Landscaping for a manufacturer: Humphry Repton's commission for Benjamin Gott at Armley in 1809–10', *Jnl. of Historical Geography*, 7 (1981), pp. 379–96.
4. This has been the subject of a growing literature in the last fifteen years, pioneered by John Barrell's *The Idea of Landscape and the Sense of Place 1730–1840: An Approach to the Poetry of John Clare*, (Cambridge, 1972), and *The Dark Side of the Landscape: The Rural Poor in English Painting 1730–1840*, (Cambridge, 1980). See also David Solkin, *Richard Wilson: The Landscape of Reaction*, (London, 1982), Ann Bermingham, *Landscape and Ideology: The English Rustic Tradition, 1740–1860*, (Berkeley, 1986), and Denis Cosgrove and Stephen Daniels (eds.), *The Iconography of Landscape*, (Cambridge, 1988) especially Chapters 3–6.
5. Seymour, 'Eighteenth-century parkland 'improvement', pp. 12–17, quotation on p.12. See also James T. Boulton, *The Language of Politics in the Age of Wilkes and Burke*, (London, 1983); C.V. Macpherson, *Burke* (Oxford, 1980); Nigel Everett, *Country Justice: the Literature of Landscape and English Conservatism*, unpublished Ph.D. (University of Cambridge, 1977); John Barrell, *English Literature and History 1780–1880: an Equal Wide Survey*, (London, 1983), pp. 51–109.
6. *The Spectator* No. 414 (*c.* 1712), quoted in Jacques *Georgian Gardens*, p. 21.
7. Seymour, 'Eighteenth-century parkland "improvement", pp. 63–127.
8. Barrell, *Dark Side*, p. 12.
9. This paragraph is condensed from pp. 43–5 of Stephen Daniels, 'The political iconography of woodland in later Georgian England', in Cosgrove and Daniels (eds.), *The Iconography of Landscape*.
10. Seymour, 'Eighteenth-century parkland "improvement", pp. 242–329.
11. Daniels, 'Political iconography of woodland', pp. 47–8.
12. *Ibid.*, pp. 48–52, 69.
13. Seymour, 'Eighteenth century parkland 'improvement', pp. 410–15.
14. William Cobbett, *Rural Rides*, (Harmondsworth, 1985), p. 207.
15. E. P. Thompson, *Whigs and Hunters*, (Harmondsworth, 1977), pp. 223.
16. Seymour, 'Eighteenth-century parkland "improvement", pp. 410–15.
17. Daniels, 'Political iconography of woodland', pp. 57–62.
18. Stephen Daniels, 'Humphry Repton and the morality of landscape', in J. R. Gold and Jacqueline Burgess (eds.), *Valued Environments*, (London, 1982), pp. 134–6.
19. Hugh Prince, 'Art and agrarian change, 1710–1815', in Cosgrove and Daniels (eds.), *The Iconography of Landscape*, pp. 28–33; Bermingham, *Landscape and Ideology*, pp. 28–33.
20. Michael Rosenthal, *Constable: A Painter and His Landscape*, (New Haven and London, 1983), pp. 84–7.
21. Quoted in Barrell, *The Idea of Landscape*, p. 88.

22. Girouard, *Life in the English Country House*, pp. 181–238.
23. On the importance of the road network to parkland development see P. F. Brandon, 'The diffusion of designed landscapes in south-east England', in H. S. A. Fox and R. A. Butlin (eds.), *Change in the Countryside*, IBG Special Publication No. 10 (1979), pp. 165–85.
24. Quoted in S. Daniels, 'The political landscape', in G. Carter, P. Goode and K. Laurie (eds), *Humphrey Repton, Landscape Gardener*, (Norwich, 1982), p. 115.
25. Brandon, 'Designed Landscapes', pp. 172–4.
26. Quoted, *Ibid.*, p. 174.
27. Daniels, 'The political iconography of woodland', pp. 47, 61–2.
28. *Ibid.*, pp. 70–2.
29. This account is abstracted from Daniels, 'Humphry Repton and the morality of landscape' and Stephen Daniels, 'Cankerous blossom: troubles in the later career of Humphry Repton documented in the Repton correspondence in the Huntington Library', *Jnl. of Garden History*, 6 (1986), pp. 148–61.
30. E. P. Thompson, 'Patrician society, plebeian culture', *Jnl. of Social History*, 7 (1974) pp. 382–405; Joan Bassin, 'The English garden in the eighteenth century: the cultural importance of an English institution', *Albion*, 11 (1979), pp. 15–32.
31. Duckworth, *The Improvement of the Estate*, pp. 34–79; Jane Austen, *Mansfield Park*, Vol. 1, Chapters VI–XI; John Murdoch, 'Foregrounds and focus: changes in the perception of landscape c. 1800', in Victoria and Albert Museum, *The Lake District*, (London, 1984), pp. 43–60.
32. Leonore Davidoff and Catherine Hall, *Family Fortunes: Men and Women of the English Middle Class 1780–1850*, (London, 1987), pp. 157–9, 162–7.
33. Rosenthal, *Constable*, p. 51.
34. Davidoff and Hall, *Family Fortunes*, p. 157.
35. John Harris, 'The flower garden 1730–1830', in John Harris (ed.), *The Garden*, (London, 1979), pp. 40–6.
36. Rosenthal, *Constable*, pp. 97–100.
37. Uvedale Price, *Essays on the Picturesque*, (London, 1810) Vol. II, pp. 118–21.
38. Carter *et al.*, *Humphry Repton*, pp. 22–31.
39. Daniels, 'The political landscape'; 'Cankerous Blossom'.
40. Brent Elliott, *Victoria Gardens* (London, 1988), pp. 21, 33–4.
41. Davidoff and Hall, *Family Fortunes*, p. 189.
42. Bermingham, *Landscape and Ideology*, pp. 174–83; Peter Fuller, 'The geography of mother nature', in Cosgrove and Daniels (eds.), *The Iconography of Landscape*, pp. 11–31; Peter Conrad, *The Victorian Treasure House*, (London, 1973) Chapter 4; Nicolette Scourse, *Victorians and their Flowers*, (London, 1981).
43. Davidoff and Hall, *Family Fortunes*, pp. 191–2.
44. Quotation from Girouard, *Life in the English Country House*, p. 242; Jill Franklin, 'The Victorian Country House', in G. E. Mingay (ed.), *The Victorian Countryside*, Vol. 2, pp. 319–413.
45. J. C. Loudon, *A Treatise on Farming, Improving and Managing Country Residences* (London, 1806), Vol. III, p. 355.
46. Daniels, 'The political iconography of woodland', p. 73.
47. Girouard, *Life in the English Country House*, pp. 300–18.
48. Quoted in Asa Briggs, *Victorian People*, (Harmondsworth, 1965), p. 45.
49. Peter Borsay, 'The English urban renaissance: the development of provincial urban culture c. 1680–1760', *Social History*, 5 (1977), pp. 581–603; 'All the town's a stage: urban ritual and ceremony 1660–1800', in Peter Clark (ed.), *The Transformation of English Provincial Towns*, (London, 1984), pp. 228–58.
50. Girouard, *Life in the English Country House*, p. 183.
51. Mark Harrison, 'Symbolism, 'ritualism' and the location of crowds in early nineteenth century English towns', in Cosgrove and Daniels (eds.), *The Iconography of Landscape*, pp. 194–213, quotation on p. 210.
52. John Summerson, *Georgian London*, (London, 1970), pp. 163–211; Donald J. Olsen, *Town*

Planning in London: The Eighteenth and Nineteenth Centuries, (New Haven and London, 1982).

53. Carter *et al.*, *Humphry Repton*, p. 153.
54. R. S. Neale, *Bath 1680–1850: A Social History*, (London, 1983).
55. Girouard, *Life in the English Country House*, p. 183.
56. John Summerson, *John Nash: Architect to King George IV*, (London, 1949).
57. Dorothy Epstein Nord, 'The city as theater: from Georgian to early Victorian London', *Victorian Studies*, **31** (1988), pp. 159–87.
58. Michel Foucault, *Discipline and Punish: the Birth of the Prison*, (London, 1977), pp. 195–228.
59. Richard Sennett, *The Fall of Public Man*, (Cambridge, 1974), pp. 107–20, 195–218; Donald J. Olsen, *The City as a Work of Art*, (New Haven and London, 1988).
60. Donald J. Olsen, *The Growth of Victorian London*, (London, 1976), p. 50.
61. Peter Jackson, *George Sharf's London*, (London, 1987), p. 129.
62. Olsen, *Victorian London*, pp. 127–86.
63. Stephen Daniels, 'Moral order and the industrial environment in the woollen textile districts of West Yorkshire', unpublished Ph.D. thesis, (University of London, 1980), pp. 118–41; Felix Driver, 'Moral geographies: social science and the urban environment in mid-nineteenth century England', *Transactions, Institute of British Geographers*, **new ser.**, **13** (1988), pp. 275–87; David Ward, 'The Victorian Slum: an enduring myth?', *Annals, Association of American Geographers*, **66** (1976), pp. 323–36.
64. Daniels, 'Moral order', pp. 130, 132, 124; Asa Briggs, *Victorian Cities*, (Harmondsworth, 1978), pp. 59–87, 88–138; Richard Dennis, *English Industrial Cities of the Nineteenth Century: A Social Geography*, (Cambridge, 1984), pp. 15–24.
65. Daniels, 'Moral order', pp. 234–90; Jack Reynolds, *The Great Paternalist: Titus Salt and the Growth of Nineteenth Century Bradford*, (London, 1983), pp. 256–325.
66. Daniels, 'Moral order', pp. 132–4; Robert Storch, 'The problem of working class leisure: some roots of middle class reform in the industrial north, 1825–1850', in A. P. Donajgrodski (ed.), *Social Control in Nineteenth Century Britain*, (London, 1977), pp. 139–82; Peter Bailey, 'A mingled mass of perfectly legitimate pleasures: the Victorian middle class and the problem of leisure', *Victorian Studies* **21**, (1977), pp. 7–28; Trygve Tholfsen, *Working Class Radicalism in Mid-Victorian England*, (London, 1976).
67. Elliott, *Victorian Gardens*, pp. 52–3; George F. Chadwick, *The Park and the Town*, (London, 1966); *The Works of Joseph Paxton*, (London, 1961).
68. Stuart Rawnsley and Jack Reynolds, 'Undercliffe Cemetery, Bradford', *History Workshop* **4** (1977), pp. 215–21.
69. Daniels, 'Moral order', pp. 202–9; Walter Creese, *The Search for Environment*, (New Haven, 1966).
70. Briggs, *Victorian Cities*, pp. 370–3.
71. *Ibid.*, pp. 166–83.
72. David Cannadine, 'The context, performance and meaning of ritual: the British monarchy and the 'invention of tradition' c. 1820–1977', in Eric Hobsbawm and Terence Ranger (eds.), *The Invention of Tradition* (Cambridge, 1983), pp. 101–64.

18

British Expansion Overseas
c. 1730–1914

Eric Pawson

At the southern end of the Canterbury Plains, in New Zealand's South Island, is the small settlement of Cave. Alone above the township stands its war memorial, a large rough boulder with one polished face. 'Through this low pass in the hills', reads the inscription, 'men from [this] district rode and walked on their way to the Great European War . . . Some of them have not returned but have left their mortal remains in foreign lands . . . that our British way of living may continue.' Those men were from families that had laboured hard to produce the neat and regular landscape that stretches away into the distance. Then as now it is a landscape of farms producing fat lambs for consumption in the British home market.

The reasons why, and the ways in which, metropolitan influence penetrated to such remote edges of the global periphery as this, form the focus of the present chapter. It is a focus of some interest to a geographer who has chosen to join those reproducing the 'British way of living' in the lands beyond Europe, no matter how changed through time, distance and local circumstance that way of living may now be. It is also a focus that may explain something to Britons themselves: about the expansion of British capitalism during the rise and relative decline of Britain as a European power, about the cultural attitudes and customs that crystallized from contact with faraway lands and peoples, and about the legacies of British economic and cultural hegemony in regions where these are still imprinted, albeit if forgotten at home.

These three themes are explored in the first three parts of this chapter, in ways which demonstrate that recounting the past is necessarily an individual and collective act of the present. Individual, inasmuch as any account is a product of its writer's experience, collective because that experience is stimulated and constrained by an existing literature. In this instance, that literature is vast, but it is one to which British geographers have contributed relatively little since the First World War. The role of geographers in imperial expansion, and their subsequent disengagement from it, is considered in the final section. But in wishing now to revive an imperial theme in British historical geography, one can only agree with Kipling's often quoted words:

Winds of the world, give answer! They are whimpering to and fro—And what should they know of England, who only England know?[1]

The Political Economy of Expansion

The expansion of European influence overseas was driven by economic imperatives, the expression of the inherent requirement of capital for widening arenas in the pursuit of further accumulation. Indeed early Marxist writers sought to explain the 'high imperialism' of late-nineteenth-century European states as the ultimate stage of capitalism, although this perspective has not survived subsequent analysis. Imperial historians, for instance, have demonstrated that the extent of European territorial empires was by no means coincident with that of trade and investment, and that the British, the greatest of the empire builders, acquired as much of it in the first half century after 1815 as they did in the second.[2]

A useful perspective for understanding these developments is that of the writers of the world systems school, who focus on the emergence of a world economy centred on Europe.[3] The competition, both military and economic, between cities and states for hegemony within Europe was also expressed in their struggles for economic and political domination in different parts of the global periphery. In this view, Britain before 1815 is an ascendant state, adopting protectionist policies to defend its then limited overseas interests against the commercial power of the Dutch and the military power of the French. Thereafter, having emerged as the 'first industrial nation', Britain became committed to the free trade and free movement of resources from which it stood to benefit the most. In the nineteenth century, British capital thus led the way in the formulation of an international division of labour between an industrializing core and a raw material and food-producing periphery. Although neoclassical revisionist economists challenge the importance of the incorporation of the periphery and the expansion of overseas trade as driving forces of British economic growth (stressing instead the domestic strengths of capital),[4] it nonetheless was so that by 1914 few parts of the globe remained untouched by European, and indeed British, influence.

Trade and Capital Flows

Taking a long-term view, however, Britain was a relatively late entrant in this process of expansion. Venice, Antwerp, Genoa and Amsterdam all preceded London as successive fulcrums of European mercantile power. The effective English conquest of Ireland had taken place in the 1580s and 1590s in response to fears of European invasion. And the eviction of the Hanse—the last group of foreign merchants to have territorial rights in England—in 1598, and the foundation of the English East India Company in 1600, signalled moves from a marginal to a more central role for British enterprise in the European economy. Nevertheless in 1730, trade was still overwhelmingly with Europe, not the world beyond, despite the planting in the seventeenth century of a string of colonies in the Americas, and the founding of further long-distance trading companies.[5]

After 1730, the rapid growth of commerce with the West Indies plantations and North American settlements was the key feature of British expansion. By the 1790s, these colonies bought half of its exports (mainly manufactures) and supplied a third of its imports (predominantly tropical goods and raw materials). The Navigation Acts of the 1650s and 1660s, implemented at the height of Dutch supremacy, were designed to ensure that this pattern of exchange developed within a protective envelope, by restricting colonial trade to British ships and British ports. At the same time these policies, subsequently labelled 'mercantilist' by historians, enabled the build-up of a national marine force in the absence of a large professional navy.[6]

Consequently, trade with Europe fell in relative importance, a decline hastened by the imposition of tariffs on both sides. Only the re-export to Europe of lucrative colonial goods, such tobacco and spices from the Americas and the East, was maintained at the same level of pre-eminence as earlier in the eighteenth century. Londoners dominated this re-exporting business and, by legal monopoly, held sway in the East Indies trade. Thus despite the growth of the outposts engaged in Atlantic commerce—Bristol, Glasgow, Whitehaven and Liverpool—London retained its position as the trading and financial centre of Britain, and indeed by the 1790s was beginning to oust Amsterdam from its European pinnacle.[7]

Yet the expansion of overseas trade was not achieved without more or less continual warfare with European rivals. Except for the American War of Independence, when Britain was frustrated by a French blockade in the Atlantic, war considerably abetted in the acquisition of colonies. The price of war was a ballooning national debt and an incidence of taxation greater than in France and probably most other European powers. That this was not revolutionary in effect is considered to be due to the brunt of extra taxation falling on domestic goods and services used by the wealthy. The Napoleonic Wars, 'the war for the defence of property', were substantially financed by those with property. Even so, tariffs rose considerably during this conflict, and by 1815, a victorious Britain was still a protectionist power.[8]

The move to free trade in the early Victorian years reflected, however, a growing realization that the future lay with industrial capital not land, and a desire to strengthen emerging British industrial capacity against competitors. An ideological basis for free trade had been laid by Adam Smtih in 1776, when he attacked the mercantilist empire as a hindrance to commercial success. But the 'pacifistic cosmopolitanism' of free trade radicals such as Cobden that derived from Smith— the belief that the expansion of capital would generate universal benefits and so end war amongst nations—was less effective in the eventual adoption of the policy than the sectional demands of industrial producers. Joseph Hume, the most persistent parliamentary advocate of free trade, argued that the Corn Laws raised the price of industrial labour, thereby stimulating foreign competition. They were held to block the exports of agricultural countries, so hindering their purchase of British goods. 'Take our corn and we will take your manufactures', said Metternich in 1837, shortly before reports of a zollverein of German states behind whose walls, it was feared, 'a great industrial machine is being constructed'. Limited moves to dismantle protection in the 1820 and 1830s accompanied the mounting export successes of Lancashire cotton interests after the abolition in 1813, when war threatened markets, of the East India Company's monopoly. Thus Hume was 'perfectly confident, that in the end our capital must triumph'.[9]

Tariff reform and the abolition of the Corn Laws came in the 1840s with the additional stimulus that industrial expansion of free trade might resolve domestic unemployment. The Navigation Acts were repealed in 1849, not only then irrelevant as colonial trade was no longer treated preferentially, but also unnecessary with the development of a strong, professional navy.[10] Hume's confidence was amply repaid by the immense expansion of British overseas commerce that ensued. By 1876–85, Britain accounted for 38 per cent of world trade in manufactures, with cotton goods alone making up quarter of its exports.

Nonetheless, in every year after 1822, commodity imports exceeded commodity exports in value. A trade surplus was generated by the sale of shipping and commercial services, and from the earnings of overseas assets. [11] This surplus financed increasing levels of capital export, a process that two great theorists of British capitalism—Wakefield and Marx—saw as a response to crises within the domestic economy. Marx drew a connexion with the penetration of Indian and Chinese markets; Wakefield propounded schemes of 'systematic colonization' to absorb surplus labour and capital, schemes initiated in a limited way in Australia and New Zealand. [12] In fact by 1914, Britain was the world's largest creditor nation, with two-thirds of the capital exported since 1865 having gone to temperate regions of recent European settlement. These were areas with a disproportionate demand for social overhead capital. Railway investment alone took two-fifths of the aggregate, financing networks in the Americas, Australasia and India. A fleet of steel steam-ships, whose tonnage by 1890 exceeded that of the rest of the world combined, took a further proportion. [13] British capital thus opened up vast regions of the global periphery for production of cheap foodstuffs and raw materials (Fig. 18.1).

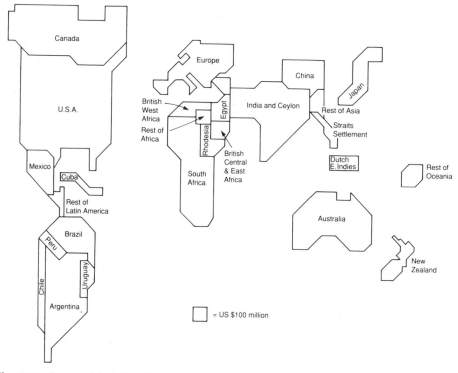

Fig. 18.1. Geographical distribution of British overseas investment, 1914 (in US dollars to nearest 50 million). *Source*: based on data assembled in W. Woodruff, *Impact of Western Man, A Study of Europe's Role in the World Economy 1750–1960* (New York, 1966), pp. 154–5.

Emigrations and Empire

The free flow of capital after the Napoleonic Wars was matched by the free emigration of labour with roughly one-fifth of the Europeans who moved overseas between 1815 and 1914, some ten million people, being British. Except for Latin America, they were numerically the most important colonists in all the regions of recent European settlement.[14] But the sheer dimensions of this transfer can detract attention from earlier, often unfree, movements of people within the European world economy.

The largest of these was the brutalizing trade in slaves between West Africa and tropical America. Probably ten million blacks were taken to the New World by Europeans, with the British share before 1700 being directed largely to the plantations of the West Indies. Between 1700 and 1776, however, the mainland American colonies took some 20 per cent. Bought by the sale of Lancashire textiles and Birmingham guns to African rulers and raiders, slave labour was transplanted to environments inherently healthier for its European owners than the 'White Man's Grave' of the African coast. Unlike many of the indigenous Indians that they supplanted across the Atlantic, these Africans had a heritage of farming and handicraft skills which were exploited to produce goods such as sugar and tobacco for British consumers and re-export to Europe.[15]

In the eighteenth century, an increasing proportion of both British and Irish emigrants sailed for the mainland American colonies, many as indentured servants. They constituted a migration flow that has been described as but an outwards extension of the endemic mobility of pre-industrial Britain.[16] The American colonies, originally private creations, enjoyed both political freedom and autonomy from each other, but were subject to the Navigation Acts — 'a state of commercial servitude and civil liberty' in Edmund Burke's words. Before the Seven Years War, during which Britain took Canada, Florida and the interior plains east of the Mississippi from France and Spain, the colonies had been but a fringe of British influence in North America. But after 1763, the posting of a metropolitan army to deter the French and contain Indian hostility led to demands from London for colonial co-operation and taxation: the beginnings of perceptions of divergent interests between Americans and Britain that culminated in the Revolution.[17]

The established pattern of economic complementarity ensured that British trade with America continued to flourish. But the political loss of the colonies stimulated a surge of commercial exploration in the southern oceans,[18] intensified concern for the eastern trades and a search for a new site to which to despatch the 'criminal classes'. So defined by the multitude of Georgian statutes that defended property, about 40,000 people had been transported across the Atlantic between 1717 and 1776. After the rejection of Africa as an alternative, the most remote solution of all was adopted. Australia was thus taken, to defend British property 'from the marauder within'. Between 1788 and 1868, over 160,000 male, female and child convicts were sent there: a forced emigration that long outlasted the British slave trade.[17] The moral fervour that won the abolition of the slave trade in 1807 (admittedly in the context of the then declining importance of West Indies plantation commerce) was not extended to those who offended against capital.[20]

After Britain's emergence as the hegemonic European power in the Napoleonic Wars, it was, however, India and the Far East that became the official focus of expansion. The English East India Company had established trading bases at Madras, Calcutta and Bombay, but the dramatic transition to territorial empire began in the eighteenth century as the Company, backed by British soldiers, moved to fill the vacuum created by the waning of Mogul power, through negotiation of alliances with, or seizing the domains of, native Indian rulers. Any competition from France was broken in 1763. Thus Britain became overlord of millions of aliens, but British India always remained a mosaic of regions of direct rule and compliant princely states. And not until the crisis of 1857–8 was the Company finally replaced by a civilian administration.[21]

India was indeed 'the jewel' of Victorian capitalist enterprise. After 1815, increasingly cost competitive Lancashire cottons wrenched the huge market of the subcontinent from indigenous producers. It yielded raw cotton and opium that were used to settle the accounts of the treasured trade in Chinese tea with Britain. The reluctance of the Chinese to continue purchase of opium, and then to grant direct access to Lancashire goods, was counteracted by force in trade wars of 1839–42 and 1856–60. India was thus a vital link to China. Under British rule, it also provided a guaranteed return on capital investment. And its tax base paid for an army of 150,000 sepoys that fought for British interests.[22]

This army, costing Britain nothing, made it a great continental power east of Suez. It was used on India's frontiers as a counter to fears of Russian expansion, and Burmese threats against Bengal. Subsequently Indians fought with British troops in south and eastern Africa. But the crux of British imperial strategy in the nineteenth century was the defence of the sea routes to India, China and the Malay peninsula. Hence the Cape, taken from the Dutch in 1806, was a cornerstone of Empire (and growing in importance with the discovery of southern Africa's mineral wealth in the 1870s). Likewise Egypt was occupied in 1882 to secure the new Suez Canal in the face of nationalist instability generated by the incursions of British and French capital.[23]

The 'high imperialism' of the 1880s and 1890s is popularized as the carve-up of Africa between European powers. If the process was less deliberate and more prolonged than this image suggests, it was nonetheless a product of renewed power rivalries at the centre of the world economy, projected into those regions of the periphery not yet under formal European control, but in which national interests were seen to be at stake. British action to forestall Germany and France in different parts of Africa led to acquisition of territories where the direct stake of capital might be low, but as in Uganda and Sudan could be of strategic importance, in these cases, for the control of Egypt's lifeline, the Nile.[24] But the picture of Empire from these years must not obscure earlier, equally expansive assumptions of territorial control by Britain and its settlers, and into regions where the stake did become much higher—across Canada, around Australia, into New Zealand, and of course in southern Africa and India.[25]

That the frontiers of capital did not replicate those of formal Empire is best illustrated by the Americas. In 1914, British investments in Latin America exceeded those throughout Asia, with British firms having a century long involvement in building and controlling infrastructure and commercial facilities for the export of minerals and food.[26] But it was the United States that was the single largest recipient of British capital and labour, with the intimacy of relations between the two countries reflected in the responsiveness of investment and emigration to American conditions. Forty per cent of British emigrants from 1853 to 1930 went to the United States mostly urban workers who contributed a key element of technical skill to American industrialization. Nonetheless, 40 per cent of all British emigrants between those two dates also returned home: apparently having taken intentionally temporary advantage of overseas opportunities and so enabled by the effectiveness of travel and information links on a world economy that for Britons was by then one of almost free transfer of resources.[27]

Britain's position in the early twentieth century as the international creditor and shipping agent, as well as imperial overlord of a quarter of the world's territory and peoples, did not mask growing anxieties over gradual loss of supremacy. Its exports were still dominated by the staple industries of textiles, shipbuilding and heavy engineering. Growing trade deficits with the rising industrial powers of Europe and America were settled by a complex pattern of multilateral settlements based on surpluses with India, the Far East and Australia.[28] After 1875, exports to the Empire were rising faster than to other markets and by 1900, protectionist and preferential trade policies were again being promoted.[29] One champion of imperial preference was the geographer politician Halford Mackinder. Whether late Victorian capitalism was failing, as traditional historiography assumes, or whether Britain was simply exploiting comparative advantage in its patterns of international trade and investment, as revisionists argue, is open to debate.[30] Contemporaries were in no doubt about the relative decline of British power and the confident Anglocentrism that had accompanied its ascendance was under seige.

The Culture of Imperialism

A necessary component of the expansion of capital and acquisition of empire by Britons was an ideology of imperialism: a cultural perspective based on self-identification that served to legitimate the subjugation of peoples and lands beyond Europe. This ideology was built upon the professed superiority of 'the British race' and thereby the inferiority of these other cultures over whom it came to assert control. It evolved within a wider Eurocentric conception of the world, in which any differences in civilized standards amongst European countries, particularly between their ruling classes, were held to be small compared with the gulf that separated Europeans from the 'other', that is the uncivilized peoples of the global periphery.

Race and Culture

In early modern Europe, that gulf was most readily discernible in religious terms, as Christianity was the one shared cultural identity of Europeans. The others were thus heathens and infidels, those who did not serve allegiance to the one true God. Yet the other need not be less powerful or technically proficient. Seventeenth-century traders could recongize the craft skills of West Africans and Indians, and respect the military power of the Moguls and Turks. Not until the nineteenth century could Europeans dictate terms of trade to the Chinese and Japanese. But it was the shifting balance of global power brought about by the expansion of the European world economy that intensified feelings of European superiority, as their growing wealth, might and technical prowess equalled and exceeded that of the cultures with whom they made contact.[31] That this happened first in the Americas is one reason why Britain and other European powers established their earliest territorial empires there.

By the end of the eighteenth century, such material achievements at the expense of others were rationalized by recourse to evolving theories of race.[32] Ultimately these derived from beliefs about the relations between people and nature drawn from Christian and scientific models. In a projection of European class hierarchies on to the natural world, it was assumed that a Great Chain of Being reached down from God to his lowliest creatures. But Christian and Cartesian thinkers alike recognized a clear break in this chain between European man and beast, a divide separating culture from nature (and reinforced in England until 1861 by the designation of bestiality as a capital offence). Women, children, the socially marginalized—even the Irish—fell closer to nature, some or all of their characteristics being held to reflect animal qualities. Likewise other cultures, particularly those without accumulated wealth or skills respected by Europeans, were assigned their place: 'the human brute, without arts or laws . . . is poorly distinguished from the rest of creation' said Gibbon. And Edward Long, in his *History of Jamaica* (1774), declared blacks to be closer to the orang-utan than to whites.[33]

It was then a short step to the quasi-scientific classifications of races in the nineteenth century, according to assigned levels of culture, in which the civilized had risen above the 'barbarian', who in turn bettered the 'savage'. Cultural difference was ascribed to racial characteristics so that David Hume expressed a common view when suspecting 'the Negroes to be naturally inferior to the white'. Thus racism, drawn from an hierarchical conception of the natural world, became 'a cultural pillar of historical capitalism', an hierarchical process of exploitation based on the superiority of class and culture.[34]

Nonetheless, the issue of race in British settled and ruled lands was not simple. Racial attitudes were tempered in situations where the British were greatly outnumbered and where they were confronted by organized religious traditions with histories as long as their own. In parliamentary debates on India in the late eighteenth century, Edmund Burke urged respect for Indian culture and a policy of gradualism sensitive to history. Significantly, Christian missionaries were banned from India till 1813, and discouraged from Islamic regions of Africa, such as northern Nigeria, where Lugard worked out the policy of indirect rule—in which the British collaborated with native elites—after 1900.[35]

This position was, however, opposed by the Evangelical movement of the early nineteenth century which, despite its view of the 'benighted' races, believed that the moral superiority of the British was compromised by the trade in slaves. Hence Evangelicals successfully campaigned for abolition in 1807, and in their efforts to treat humanely with aboriginal races, influenced the Colonial Office to negotiate a treaty ostensibly to protect the interests of the Maori when New Zealand was annexed in 1840 (a privilege not accorded earlier to the Australian Aborigines). Antagonistic to the Evangelicals and opposed to Burke were the Utilitarians, whose belief in reform based on universally applicable laws, without reverence for the past, was put to practical effect in India in the 1830s, with the institution of a penal code identical for British and Indian alike, and promotion of education to impose British standards on Indian elites.[36] In practice missionaries, including Livingstone in Africa, accepted the civilizing influence of trade, and were not so far from John Stuart Mill's view that people 'hitherto in a quiescent, indolent, uncultivated state' and 'satisfied with scant comforts and little work' might be induced by commerce 'to work harder . . . and even to save and accumulate capital'.[37] In this Mill revealed one of the lasting prejudices of European capitalism: the myth of the lazy native.[38]

Another persistent myth, that both fascinated and appalled the British overseas, was that of the sexual proclivities of other races. In his poem 'The White Man's Burden', Kipling[39] referred to them as 'half devil and half child': inferior peoples who might be taught civilized standards by allegiance to that powerful imperial metaphor, the Mother Country, but whose animal sexuality was always seen as a threat to European women, albeit a source of satisfaction to European men. Feminist research has revealed how British women, as the inferior sex within the superior race, were forbidden by strict convention from intercourse with native men. As their numbers increased in the Asian and African colonies towards 1900, the unstated role of white women became that of maintaining social distance and standards of racial superiority, by discouraging white men from taking native mistresses.[40] But belief in the rapacity of the native male persisted, particularly in Africa, with strict laws outlawing sexual contact between blacks and white women being passed in South Africa after 1900. This was despite the best efforts of missionary schools to eliminate sensuous elements of African cultures and a remarkable lack of evidence that Africans (or indeed Asians or Amerindians) found white women attractive.[41] Yet even in 1950 Doris Lessing could outrage white Rhodesians with the portrayal—in *The Grass is Singing*, her first novel—of the social decline of a European farming couple and an implied affair between the white mistress and her black manservant.[42]

Separation and Superiority

The maintenance of social distance by the British in their colonies served to reinforce both the self-identity and dominance of the ruling race. This was particularly important in lands where they were much in the minority. As late as the 1930s, for instance, there were only 165,000 Britons amongst 400 million Indians and in Southern Rhodesia in 1911, just 23,606 to 752,000 Africans.[43] In these circumstances, social distance was reproduced not only by social conventions, but also by spatial detachment. For instance, the European towns of Salisbury and Bulawayo were generally planned on a grid-street pattern, with black servants' quarters in each house backing onto lanes provided for the collection of sewage. Hidden from the public face of white society, these lanes served as the corridors of urban African social life. In South Africa, an emergent indigenous urban proletariat, mobilized to serve the needs of mining capital, was housed in African townships situated according to the 'sanitation syndrome': removed from European areas because of perceived threats to white health and security.[44]

In India, spatial detachment was also distinct. Calcutta, Bombay and Madras were planned as European settlements in neoclassical style, an architectural form symbolizing the triumph of reason over barbarism. Crowded native towns developed beyond their confines. Outside existing Indian cities, the British built separate civil stations for themselves, spacious, orderly bungalow enclaves again so located for 'sanitary' reasons. British soldiers were accommodated in detached self-contained forts, or cantonments.[45] Because, as members of the lower classes, soldiers were felt unable to repress their animal urges ('lacking the high moral capacity arising from culture', as the Surgeon General of Bombay said in 1886), the cantonments were provided with official brothels. This open double standard in colonial social relations reflected the importance of maintaining order amongst the enforcers of order. The virility of the fighting man had to be maintained, and the threats of venereal disease and homosexuality kept at bay.[46]

British colonial elites, however, reinforced social distance between themselves and the ruled by conventions of appearance and behaviour. These were epitomized in the Club, all but the least pretentious of which in India excluded Indians until the Second World War. In East Africa, the country club served the same purpose as a focus of cultural identity for scattered white farming families. But perhaps the most bizarre 'emblem of imperialism' was the white pith topi, or cork helmet, used by British officials and soldiers throughout the tropics. George Orwell, obliged to wear one as a member of the Burmese police in the 1920s, explained that it was fear of sunstroke that led to its general adoption. A morally superior race, with larger brains and thinner skulls, hence required protection which indigenous peoples with thicker skulls did not need.[47] This mythology underscores the confusion inherent in contemporary theories of climate as well as of race. Although it was disease rather than sunstroke that claimed European lives in the tropics,[48] widespread belief in the debilitating effects of climate *per se* produced the convention of an afternoon rest for British women and children, and a complete summer retreat to the hills for officials and their families. In India, the British built some 80 hill stations, including Simla, which from 1865 to 1939 served as the 'Imperial Summer Capital' of the Viceroy.[49]

The maintenance of social distance and assumption of racial superiority militated against British culture absorbing much from those others with which it came into contact. Rather as British economic hegemony came under increasing challenge in the late nineteenth century, and with rising nationalist feeling, particularly in India, the consciousness of British difference increased. The impact of this trend at home was marked, although it is poorly documented.[50] It was reflected in the growing emphasis on British racial uniqueness in politics and education, in attempts— common throughout the Anglo-Saxon world—to maintain racial strength by programmes of 'scientific' child rearing,[51] and in the introduction of ideological forms of youth recreation. Best known amongst the latter was the foundation in 1907 of the Scout Movement by Baden-Powell, one of the heroes of colonial warfare, who sought to inculcate a popular awareness of the imperial virtues of patriotism, duty and leadership. The best researched aspect of this growing imperial perception is that of the public school and Oxbridge educations of future imperial managers.[52] The public schools extolled the virtues of field sports. 'Englishmen are not superior to Frenchmen or Germans in brains or industry' said the Headmaster of Harrow, 'but they are superior in the health and temper which games impart. In the history of the British Empire it is written that England has owed her sovereignty to her sports.'[53] Britain exported her sports across the world as part of the civilizing mission to lesser races. The recruitment policy of the Sudanese Public Service, for instance, produced the sobriquet of 'the Land of Blacks ruled by Blues'.[54]

In the Empire itself, the most extraordinary statement of this race consciousness was the building of New Delhi. In 1911, the Indian government decided to move from its long-established seat in Calcutta and built, over 20 years, a vast new capital closer to the mainstream of Indian history, as legitimation of the 'natural right' of Britons to rule the subcontinent. New Delhi was uncharacteristic of an empire of trade and investment largely unmarked by grand edifices. It represents a late defensive effusion of a ruling race under threat. Kingsway, its two-mile central axis, was built twice as wide as the Champs Elysées, leading to the Viceroy's House, bigger even than Versailles. In the 1930s, 65,000 whites and their servants lived in the 33 square miles of the new capital, detached from the 350,000 Indian inhabitants of the smaller old town[55] (Fig. 18.2).

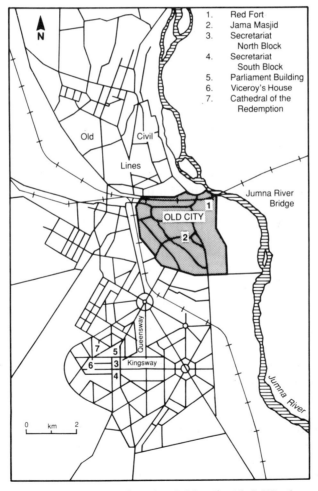

Fig. 18.2. New and Old Delhi. *Source*: based on J. Morris with S. Winchester, *Stones of Empire, The Buildings of the Raj* (Oxford, 1988), p. 218.

Progress and Assimilation

The assumption of cultural superiority persists in the historiography of British expansion, particularly that concerning the settlement colonies of the 'New World'. Few British colonists would have argued with the conclusion of a geographer in 1988 that 'over large parts of the world the British established the first effective occupation'.[56] This is simply a more explicit version of conventional descriptions of the 'regions of recent settlement'[57] that European farmers turned from 'wilderness' into productive landscapes. Forty years ago, Leacock could preface his history of Canada with a chapter on 'The empty continent', drawing a picture of a vacant land. 'Such, and no more', he said '. . . is the meaning and extent of the Indian ownership of North America.'[58] But assertions such as these merely reveal a widespread tendency to discount pre-contact indigenous population levels and to diminish the intrinsic validity of other cultures. 'It is, of course, a fact', claimed a geographer in 1979, 'that most of the Indians in what is now the United States remained quite undeveloped until the white man arrived.'[59]

It is not, of course, a fact. Rather, these are attitudes reproducing the culture of imperialism, married with unconscious use of a central Eurocentric myth, that of progress.[60] French rationalist thinkers of the eighteenth century were to the fore in developing this myth, as they strived to replace the fatalistic assumptions of reliance on divine providence with the power of reason to improve the human condition. In England, it received corroboration from those such as Adam Smith, the originator of the concept of progressive economic growth, and Malthus who (like Darwin, 50 years later) saw civilization as the outcome of a struggle for existence, as people rose above their 'natural state' of sloth (and by implication, weakness) in 'the spirit of enterprise'.[61] Progress was thus the mechanism used to explain the development of hierarchies of peoples described by nineteenth-century theories of race. Darwin lent it scientific credibility and Spencer drove home the message of human societal evolution. Both men were at work when the Great Exhibition in London in 1851 gave 'public recognition [to] the material progress of the age and the growing power of [European] man in the physical world', and over alien peoples and lands. In the nineteenth century, progress became 'the animating and controlling idea of western civilization'.[62]

'Ecological Imperialism'

To the French geographer Demangeon, writing in 1923, the 'weapons of British colonization' were typically progressive: transport systems, irrigation works, capital and scientific research.[63] Whilst the importance of such material tools of expansion is undoubted, the key weapon of British settler colonization was shared with other Europeans. It was disease. The transmission of deadly infections to the New World has recently been described as a component of 'ecological imperialism',[64] an attractive phrase which nonetheless masks an essentially biological process with a spurious mantle of intentionality. In the nineteenth century, however, its impact was increasingly interpreted as an inevitability of capitalist progress.

The peoples of the Old World had a long history of settlement habitation in close proximity to animals. The mutual exchange of viruses produced diseases such as cowpox, smallpox and measles, whilst the concentrations of population and filth in the settlements of Europe and the Middle East encouraged vermin and parasites that spread plague, typhus and malaria. Regular epidemics enabled those surviving such traumas in childhood to build up immunities denied the peoples of the Americas, Australasia and the Pacific, where such infections were unknown. In these regions of European resettlement, disease was thus the battering ram of colonization.[65]

Smallpox, taken by the Spanish to the Americas, decimated precontact populations that may have been as high as 100 million. Disease raced ahead of military and exploratory expeditions, reducing and demoralizing sophisticated, hierarchical cultures throughout the Andes, Central America and the lands east of the Mississippi.[66] North American Indian numbers remained highest in the ecologically-rich regions of the Seaboard, where village settlements of 100 to 1000 people were common. Even so, populations were insufficiently large for epidemic introductions to become endemic, leaving them vulnerable to periodic reinfection by British settlers. The natives of New England had been reduced by 80 per cent by the mid eighteenth century. The Governor of the Massachusetts Bay colony had said in 1634, 'For the natives, they are neere all dead of Small Poxe, so as the Lord hath cleared our title to what we possess.'[67] As science replaced religion as the dominant organizing metaphor in the European mind, the decline of native peoples was seen as the necessary victory of stronger over weaker races. 'When civilized nations come into contact with barbarians, the struggle is short', wrote Darwin in *The Descent of Man*, using demographic examples from Hawaii, Tasmania and New Zealand.[68] Smallpox epidemics swept through Australia from 1789, killing perhaps one-third of the Aborigines over the next half century. Between 1840 and 1858, the Maori declined in numbers from about 120,000 to 56,000. About one-fifth of Fiji's indigenous population perished in a measles epidemic in 1875, introduced by chiefs returning from discussion in Sydney on the treaty of cession to the Crown.[69] By the end of the nineteenth century, perceived white racial strength was seen to have conquered the 'dying races' in those lands that Britons had appropriated for their own resettlement programmes. Ascribing this solely to a moral weakness for alcohol, Greville in 1891 considered the future of the Aborigine 'both gloomy and discouraging . . . contact with a superior race has been fatal, and he will soon become only a name.'[70]

Analogous evolutionary reasoning was adopted to explain the apparent retreat of indigenous flora and fauna in the New World lands. The 'victory over environment' that settlers saw themselves procuring depended on human support systems that enabled introduced weeds, crops and animals to flourish. Cultivation produced disturbed ground for adventitious species such as clover, thistles and blackberry. The native plants of the American Seaboard and Australasia were unused to cloven hooves and trampling by sheep, cattle and pigs. The renowned Victorian botanist, Joseph Hooker, felt that 'many of the small local genera of Australia, New Zealand and South Africa, will ultimately disappear', whilst his New Zealand correspondent, W. T. L. Travers considered 'their defeat is almost certain' by 'superior' introductions from Europe.[71] In South Australia, 900 alien plant species became established, and in New Zealand innumerable exotic mammals, birds and weeds flourish.[72]

Taming the Wilderness

If the emptying of these new lands, albeit misunderstood, seemed providential to white settlers, in another sense emptiness was seen to be immoral. The British government was concerned, within limits, to protect the land rights of native peoples. In 1763 a Royal Proclamation, concerning the territories of Quebec, Florida and those west of the Appalachians taken by war from France and Spain, outlawed private purchase of Indian lands and laid down provisions to protect them from encroachment. So too did the Treaty of Waitangi in New Zealand in 1840. In southern Africa, the Crown attempted to restrict white frontier expansion by establishing a permanent line between the Cape Colony and indigenous African peoples.[73]

But the perspective of settlers, struggling to create a home and enhance capital in alien environments, was more predatory. The American Proclamation Line fuelled revolutionary feeling amongst colonists, the southern African policy was circumvented by the Cape Dutch, who trekked inland in the late 1830s to establish independent republics in Transvaal, Natal and the Orange Free State, and the New Zealand treaty was declared 'a simple nullity' by a colonial court in 1877. The reliance of indigenous peoples on extensive hunting ranges was offensive to those seeking land for commodity production. 'All the chaffer about the rights of natives to land, which they had let lie idle and unused for so many centuries, cannot do away with the fact that, according to . . . God's law, they have established their right to a very small portion of these islands', fumed a New Zealand newspaper in 1843.[74] God's law was the law of capital, as spelt out by Adam Smith in his discussion of cultivation rendering productive the valueless lands of the New World.[75] It also reflected the views of Emer de Vattel, perhaps the most widely read international jurist of the eighteenth century, who articulated the ancient Christian obligation to reclaim the earth, and hence denied the rights of native peoples to anything but their gardens.[76]

The standard progressive accounts of pioneer conquest of the wilderness, however, downplay the contribution that native-grown foodstuffs made to ensuring the initial survival of colonial communities on the American Seaboard and in New Zealand, and ignore the valuable botanical species and husbanding information acquired from indigenous peoples. The Americans yielded important food crops, in particular maize and potatoes, which were far more productive of calories per acre than any Old World variety except rice. The reliance on potatoes in sustaining European population growth was graphically demonstrated by the Irish diaspora after 1845, when a potato fungus from Peru took hold. American crops such as tomatoes, peppers and peanuts were nutritiously superior to European foods, whilst sugar cane and tobacco formed the basis of West Indian and American plantation economies.[77] The importance of colonial transfer of productive crops in the accumulation of capital throughout the global periphery was vital. In the nineteenth century, newly acquired plant species were exchanged via an imperial network of botanical gardens, centred on Kew in London. Kew facilitated the introduction of countless ornamental varieties into Britain. It was to Kew that Amazonian rubber seeds were smuggled in 1876, there to be acclimatized and selected for planting in Malaya, where rubber plantations grew in extent from 5000 to 1,250,000 acres between 1900 and 1913. It was Kew that sponsored the transfer of cinchona tree seedlings from the Andes to India and Ceylon in the 1860s, in order to provide an imperial supply of quinine.[78] This drug was by far the most effective container of malaria, and its widespread use by British soldiers and settlers in the tropics strengthened their hold in India and encouraged the influx of white women. Its use was also responsible for underwriting imperial penetration of Africa, enabling Europeans to modify their image of the 'White Man's Grave'.[79]

The traditional historiography of New World colonization, however, focuses less on indigenous contributions to European well-being and more on taming of the wilderness. Simplified, commodified landscapes were produced on territories acquired from their native guardians. 'Civilization . . . has advanced geometrically across the country . . . the conquest of nature by an intelligence that does not love it', wrote Northrop Frye of Canada[80] in a description equally applicable to much of New Zealand and the European farmed districts of Australia and Africa. Regular survey systems were usually laid out in advance of resettlement, with the Canadian government adopting a homesteading policy for the prairies in 1872 based on the American Homestead Act of ten years before. In Australasia, pastoralism was often initially substituted for a British yeoman ideal, persisting in regions unsuited to cultivation. 'Official' and 'popular' appraisals of agricultural land frequently diverged, with survey grids and farm sizes being modified according to water availability.[81] Even so the consequences of climatic marginality, poorly understood, were unstable frontiers of agricultural expansion in areas such as South Australia.[82]

Lack of environmental awareness and the imperatives of production led to widespread ecological destruction. The warnings of George Perkins Marsh went largely unheeded. Attempts at forest conservation in Australasia conflicted with the prevalent ethos of timber clearance for settlement and were notably less successful than in British India.[83] It was not until much later that problems of soil degradation received urgent attention.[84] Also missing in the white settler colonies was a coherent articulation of the wilderness ethic prominent in late-nineteenth-century American cultural nationalism.[85] Canada, Australia and New Zealand did establish national parks before 1900, but their natural characteristics were subordinated to the needs of wealthy visitors for recreational facilities and exotic game. Wilderness reserved was rarely at the expense of production foregone: New Zealand's parks were long to be restricted to alpine areas, and at Banff, Canada's first park, coal mining was promoted as an attraction.[86]

It would be a mistake, however, to assume that the indigenous inhabitants of these resettled lands did not violently contest loss of territory. Just as the Amerindians resisted westward expansion of the white frontier, there was continual conflict with Aboriginals in Australia.[87] The Maori fought to maintain the integrity of tribal lands and culture throughout the New Zealand Wars of the 1860s, winning countless victories over imperial and colonial troops, victories nonetheless never conceded in the official record.[88] In Africa, settler and native contested the best available land, the resolution being the creation of separate reserves. Although reserve policies varied markedly between different colonies, a common result was displacement of large numbers of Africans from their land or retention of land of insufficient quality to sustain independent forms of subsistence.[89] Similar fates were inflicted upon Maori and Amerindian, much reduced too, as the African generally was not, by disease.

Yet ultimately the evolutionary assumptions of imperialism have not been borne out. Despite death, dispossession and persistent programmes of social assimilation, indigenous cultures have survived to flourish in North America and Australasia. Today they challenge progressive models of development and vigorously promote their own conceptions of knowledge. They find allies in 'new wave' historiographies that seek to rewrite history from the other side of the frontier, and to expose progress for what it is: an ideological myth for promoting the expansion of capital.[90]

Geographers and Empire

The emergence of modern geography in late-nineteenth-century Britain has been portrayed in recent years as a product of growing imperial concern.[91] There is much to commend this view, although it should be tempered by an awareness that many of those who sought to advance the subject between the 1870s and the First World War were less interested in forging a new academic discipline than in promoting both an ideology of Empire and the acquisition of certain skills (e.g. exploration, mapping and surveying) of use in incorporating new territories. Certainly these concerns reflected a desire to secure British interests in the face of European competition. As a consequence, geography so defined perhaps had a higher profile amongst people of influence than at any time since. Its academic fortunes, however, were very much more limited.

Institutionalization

The promotion of geography was largely in the hands of the Royal Geographical Society (RGS), a social network of scientists, explorers and military men that had been founded in 1830. Not until the 1870s did it begin to seek a firm academic basis for a subject then not taught as an independent discipline at any British university. In that decade it made two unsuccessful approaches to both Oxford and Cambridge, claiming in 1874 that 'there is no country that can less afford to dispense with geographical knowledge than England'.[92] However, the Keltie Report, compiled by the Secretary of the RGS in 1885, drew invidious comparisons between the status of geography in Britain and in Europe, where university departments flourished in France, Switzerland and Germany. It also highlighted the lamentable state of geography teaching in British schools, few of whose headmasters would have agreed with their colleague from Liverpool College that the subject should give 'a comprehensive view of the greatness of the British Empire and of the under-developed capabilities of the accessible world'.[93]

After publication of the Report, Oxford and Cambridge were persuaded to accept RGS funds to establish Readerships in Geography. Publicly, the subject received notable endorsements. Sir George Robertson, addressing the RGS in 1900, declared it to be 'the science of the merchant, the statesman and the strategist'. Viscount Milner, latterly High Commissioner in South Africa, lectured to the Scottish Geographical Society in 1907 on 'Geography and Statecraft', underlining the potential for geographers to produce reliable maps and means of delimiting colonial frontiers. The same theme occupied Lord Curzon, President of the RGS and former Viceroy to India, in his Romanes Lecture in Oxford in the same year.[94] Yet an academic profile was more elusive. Oxford did not establish a separate geography department till 1899, or an Honours School with a permanent chair until 1932. This was despite its first Reader being Halford Mackinder, a charismatic teacher and profile author, who had won the appointment on the strength of a notable paper delivered before the RGS in 1886 which outlined an intellectual basis for university geography.[95] By 1918 there were barely 30 teachers of geography in half as many universities and colleges.[96]

The lowly position of academic geography reflected both the reluctance of British educationalists to promote technical and scientific subjects (in direct contrast to those in Europe), and a corresponding belief in the pedagogic importance of classics and history. Mackinder's greatest success in Oxford was in the provision of service courses for historians. The classics, however, were seen to promote the Platonic virtues of loyalty, courage, responsibility and truthfulness, so being the ideal preparation for imperial service.[97] Lord Lugard's practical expression of this was that 'as Roman imperialism laid the foundations of modern imperialism, and led the wild barbarians of these [British] islands along the path of progress, so in Africa today we are repaying the debt'. Between 1899 and 1952, of the 277 degree holders who had served in the Sudanese Public Service, 53 per cent were classicists and historians, only 4 per cent geographers.[98] Geography had little opportunity to be the hand-maiden of imperialism.

Legacies

Some academic geographers were, however, particularly concerned with empire, especially those in Oxford, the university which contributed most to imperial philosophy and sentiment.[99] Amongst Mackinder's voluminous writings, his contributions to geopolitics are best known, and these were based on a belief in the necessity of developing awareness of potential threats to the British Empire that might stem from the power of the 'heartland', that great land-locked region occupied by Britain's rival, Russia, and potentially accessible to Germany.[100] A practical expression of imperial concern came from A.J. Herbertson, Mackinder's successor at Oxford, who urged the establishment of an Imperial Intelligence Department, staffed by geographer-statisticians. 'Thinking in continents . . . might then become part of the necessary equipment of a statesman', he claimed. 'The country which first gives this training to its statesmen will have an immeasurable advantage in the struggle for existence'.[101] Herbertson's dream of an Institute of Imperial History and Geography in Oxford was never fulfilled, but before his death in 1915 he did edit, with O. J. R. Howarth, the six-volume *Oxford Survey of the British Empire*. Of more immediate import was the work of trained geographers in the First World War. H. N. Dickson of Oxford edited a series of handbooks on various parts of the world from a new Geographical Section in the Naval Intelligence Division of the Admiralty.[102] Vaughan Cornish, a well-known freelance geographer, lectured to over 10,000 military officers between 1914 and 1916 on the naval defence and strategic geography of the empire, and subsequently made a plea for the latter as a 'citizen's subject'.[103] In 1918, it was said in Cambridge that 'there is no doubt that in the present war geography has come into its own'.[104]

The post-war generation of academic geographers did not, however, carry through the imperial interests of their predecessors. In 1947, S. W. Wooldridge thought it threw 'a strong light on the position of Geography in this country that we are so calamitously and shamefully ignorant of our Colonial Empire'. Yet he had also proclaimed that 'the eyes of the fool are on the ends of the earth' and had urged the study of the human geography of Somerset rather than Somaliland.[105] In the 1930s and 1940s, geographers still struggling to establish respectability saw their fortunes lying primarily in analysis of domestic issues of the depression and post-war reconstruction. This was particularly so in the Institute of British Geographers, set up in 1933 to counter the lack of interest shown in domestic and human geography within the RGS.

Nevertheless, there persisted in the geographical literature a strong element of attitudes deriving from the imperial era. Recent work has exposed the ethnocentric basis to theories of environmental determinism popular in the inter-war years, and in more recent development and diffusionist models.[106] The general use of spatial concepts derived from Anglo-Americans experience in the 1960s and 1970s was but a subtle restatement that cultures that did not conform were in some way deviant from the expected norm. As Harvey put it in 1974, 'attitudes gleaned for many years devoted to the technics and management of Empire have yet to be expunged from our school texts'.[107] The same can still be said of some used in universities.

Conclusion

This chapter has sought to portray British activity overseas between the early eighteenth century and the First World War as a systematic process of capitalist expansion. The Empire, which in spatial terms was the visible tip of this influence, was not acquired in a fit of absence of mind. The extent of British global hegemony was a product of its increasing dominance within Europe, as it assumed the leading role in articulating an international division of labour based on industrial and commercial specialization by Europeans, and their development and control of raw material and food production in the periphery. But the periphery to Europeans was the centre of the world for diverse other cultures. Their incorporation into the arena of capital required an ideology of imperialism, theories of race and of progress, abetted in the regions of resettlement by the providential impact of disease and aided in the tropical colonies of rule by its control. However, the peoples of the periphery, denied their own histories for so long by evolutionary interpretations of British and European achievements, were not passively invalidated by the expansion of capital. In Asia, Africa and the Pacific, their growing resistance hastened the rapid collapse of imperial power after the Second World War, whilst the sharpened political consciousness of these liberated peoples has been a factor in the revival of indigenous cultures in North America and Australasia.

The two world wars of the twentieth century were once again the product of explosive power rivalries in Europe. This time the chief beneficiary was the United States, as the focus of the world economy shifted across the Atlantic. Yet the British Empire in fact reached its maximum extent in the 1920s, with the addition of mandated territories taken from the defeated powers and reallocated by the new League of Nations.[108] But in 1941, America clarified its opposition to political imperialism in the Atlantic Charter with which it entered the Second World War. Weakened by the crisis of the preceding decade, British influence in the east crumbled soon after. The massive seabase at Singapore fell to Japanese land forces in 1942, and in 1947, India was abandoned to partition and bloodshed. That Suez was still the jugular vein of Empire to Eden in 1956 merely underlines the illusions of British decline left behind in New Delhi. Nonetheless, imperialism was not to be the highest stage of capitalism as Lenin had proposed,[109] as the global political map left in its wake has proved more than satisfactory for the continued interests of British and multinational capital.

The development of this latter theme is but one of many reluctantly omitted by the dictates of space. Those included have been selected according to simple criteria. They are those that explain to the author something of the persistent but often hidden legacies of imperial endeavour and ideology that he absorbed whilst growing up and being schooled in post-imperial Britain. They are themes both exposed and clarified by a decade of working in a former colony, a country that in the 1980s has been struggling to come to terms with its implanted and indigenous heritage, as well as an economic future tied not to Britain but to the growing potential of the Pacific Basin.[110]

From this antipodean perspective, if one symbolic event is to be chosen to represent the decline of British hegemony, it is Gallipoli. In the Dardanelles campaign of 1915, Anzac troops fought alongside ill-prepared British troops, under a British command that had selected an indefensible position from which to attack the Turkish allies of Germany. Gallipoli undermined the invincibility and superiority of the British in colonial eyes.[111] It was etched into the growing national consciousness of Australians and New Zealanders, a futile but heroic deed, the price of which is permanently displayed on war memorials in every large and small settlement throughout Australasia. Like that remote example on a low hill at Cave, on the edge of the Canterbury Plains, where this recounting of British expansion overseas began.

Acknowledgements

I am grateful to Professors R. A. Butlin and R. J. Johnson, and Dr R. Le Heron for helpful comments on a draft of this chapter, to Professors A. S. Goudie and P. G. Holland for some references, and to Mr G. Banks for some assistance with research.

References

1. The English Flag, in *Rudyard Kipling's Verse, Definitive Edition*, (London, 1960), p. 221. Except in specific instances such as this, the term 'Britain' is used in this chapter to include England, Wales and Scotland (but not Ireland).
2. D. K. Fieldhouse, *Economics and Empire 1830–1914*, (London, 1973).
3. I. Wallerstein, *The Modern World-System I—Capitalist Agriculture and the Origins of the European World-economy in the Sixteenth Century*, (New York, 1974); 'The rise and future demise of the World Capitalist System: concepts for comparative analysis', *Comparative Studies in Society and History* **16**, (1974), pp. 387–415; F. Braudel, *The Perspective of the World* (London, 1984). This is not to endorse the specific methodology and empirical approach of Wallerstein, whose work is controversial: see G. Kearns, 'History, geog-

raphy and world-systems theory', *Jnl. of Historical Geography*, **14**, 3, (1988), pp. 281–92. For a review of the wide range of approaches by historical writers to the subject of imperial expansion, see P. J. Cain and A. G. Hopkins, 'The political economy of British expansion overseas, 1750–1914', *Economic History Review*, **XXXIII**, (1980), pp. 463–90.

4. See for example, R. C. Floud and D. N. McCloskey, *The Economic History of Britain since 1700*, (Cambridge, 1981); P. K. O'Brien, 'European economic development: the contribution of the periphery', *Economic History Review*, **XXXV**, (1982), pp. 1–18.

5. W. E. Minchinton, *The Growth of English Overseas Trade in the 17th and 18th Centuries*, (London, 1969), pp. 147–53. On Ireland, see L. M. Cullen, *The Emergence of Modern Ireland 1600–1900*, (London, 1981) and R. D. Edwards, *An Atlas of Irish History*, (2nd ed.) (London, 1981).

6. Minchinton, *Growth of English Overseas Trade*; P. J. Cain, *Economic Foundations of British Overseas Expansion 1815–1914*, (London, 1980), p. 11.

7. Minchinton, *Growth of English Overseas Trade*; R. P. Thomas and D. N. McCloskey, 'Overseas trade and empire 1700–1860', in Floud and McCloskey, *Economic History of Britain*, Vol. I, pp. 87–102. Any such standard sources contain detailed British trade estimates for this period.

8. P. K. O'Brien, 'The political economy of British taxation, 1660–1815', *Economic History Review*, **XLI** (1988), pp. 1–32.

9. B. Semmell, *The Rise of Free Trade Imperialism*, (Cambridge, 1970), pp. 146–50; P. Mathias, *The First Industrial Nation*, (London, 1983), pp. 261–77.

10. Cain, *Economic Foundations*, pp. 17–21.

11. C. K. Harley and D. N. McCloskey, 'Foreign trade: competition and the expanding international economy', in Floud and McCloskey, *Economic History of Britain*, Vol.2, pp. 50–69.

12. On Wakefield's legacy in Australia, see J. M. Powell, 'The patrimony of the people: the role of government in land settlement' in R. L. Heathcote (ed.), *The Australian Experience: Essays in Australian Land Settlement and Resource Management*, (Melbourne, 1988).

13. Cain, *Economic Foundations*, pp. 15–16; P. L. Cottrell, *British Overseas Investment in the Nineteenth Century*, (London, 1975); M. Edelstein, 'Foreign investment and empire, 1860–1914', in Floud and McCloskey, *Economic History of Britain*, Vol. 2, pp. 70–98.

14. D. Baines, *Migration in a Mature Economy, Emigration and Internal Migration in England and Wales, 1861–1900*, (Cambridge, 1985), pp. 1–2, 45–7.

15. P. D. Curtin, 'Epidemiology and the Slave Trade', *Political Science Quarterly*, **LXXXIII**, 2, (1968), pp. 190–216.

16. B. Bailyn, *The Peopling of British North American, an Introduction*, (New York, 1986), pp. 25–43; Baines, *Migration in a Mature Economy*, pp. 56–8.

17. D. K. Fieldhouse, *The Colonial Empires, A Comparative Survey from the Eighteenth Century*, (London, 1966), pp. 55–70.

18. D. Mackay, *In the Wake of Cook, Exploration, Science and Empire, 1780–1801*, (Wellington, 1985).

19. R. Hughes, *The Fatal Shore, A History of the Transportation of Convicts to Australia 1787–1868*, (London, 1988). The figures include Irish transportees.

20. R. T. Anstey, '"Capitalism and slavery": a critique', *Economic History Review*, **XXI**, (1968), pp. 307–20.

21. Fieldhouse, *The Colonial Empires*, pp. 138–73; M. E. Chamberlain, *Britain and India, the Interaction of Two Peoples*, (Newton Abbott 1974); B. Porter, *The Lion's Share*, (London, 1984), pp. 28–47.

22. Fieldhouse 1973, *Economics and Empire*, pp. 150–7, 210–23; J. Gallagher, *The Decline, Revival and Fall of the British Empire*, (Cambridge, 1982).

23. Fieldhouse, *The Colonial Empires*, pp. 183–4, 216; *Economics and Empire*, pp. 260–8; W. M. Louis, *Imperialism: The Robinson and Gallagher Controvery*, (New York, 1976), pp. 1–14.

24. Fieldhouse 1973, *op. cit.*

25. J. Gallagher and R. Robinson, 'The Imperialism of Free Trade', *Economic History Review*, **VI**, (1953), pp. 1–15.

26. Cottrell, *British Overseas Investment*; Edelstein, 'Foreign investment and empire'.

27. Baines, *Migration in a Mature Economy*,; F. Thistlewaite, 'Migration from Europe Overseas in the 19th and 20th Centuries, in H. Moller, (ed.), *Population Movements in Modern European History*, (New York 1964), pp. 73–92; 'The Atlantic migration of the pottery industry', *Economic History Review*, **XI**, (1958), pp. 264–78.

28. Harley and McCloskey, 'Foreign trade', p. 66; S. B. Saul, *Studies in British Overseas Trade, 1870–1914*, (Liverpool, 1960).

29. Edelstein, 'Foreign investment and empire'.

30. Mathias, *The First Industrial Nation*, pp. 369–93; R. C. Floud, 'Britain 1860–1914: a survey', in Floud and McCloskey, *Economic History of Britain*, Vol. 2, pp. 1–26; Harley and McCloskey, 'Foreign trade'.

31. P. D. Curtin (ed.), *Imperialism, Selected Documents*, (London, 1972), pp. xiii–xv.

32. R. Hallett, 'Changing European Attitudes to Africa', in J. E. Flint (ed.), *The Cambridge History of Africa, Vol. 5, c1790– c1870*, (Cambridge, 1976), pp. 458–96; R. A. Huttenback, *Racism and Empire, White Settlers and Coloured Immigrants in the British Self Governing Colonies 1830–1910*, (Ithaca, 1976), pp. 13–21.

33. K. Thomas, *Man and the Natural World, Changing Attitudes in England 1500–1800*, (Harmondsworth, 1984), pp. 39–50, 135–6.

34. Curtin, *Imperialism*, pp. 1–22; B. Davidson, *The Story of Africa*, (London, 1984), p. 16; I. Wallerstein, *Historical Capitalism*, (London, 1983), p. 80.

35. Chamberlain, *Britain and India*, pp. 65–79; A.A. Mazrui, *The African Condition, The Reith Lectures*, (London, 1980), pp. 97–100.

36. Chamberlain, *Britain and India*.

37. T. Jeal, *Livingstone*, (London 1973); Hallett, 'Changing European attitudes', pp. 490–1.

38. S. H. Alatas, *The Myth of the Lazy Native*, (London, 1977).

39. *A Choice of Kipling's Verse*, made by T.S. Eliot, (London, 1941), p. 136.

40. M. Strobel, 'Gender and Race in the 19th and 20th Century British Empire', in R. Bridenthal *et al.*, (eds.), *Becoming Visible: Women in European History*, (Boston 1987), pp. 375–94; H. Callan and S. Ardener, *The Incorporated Wife*, (Oxford, 1984).

41. Mazrui, *The African Condition*, p. 57; J. N. Brownfoot, 'Memsahibs in Colonial Malaya, A Study of European Wives in a British Colony and Protectorate 1900–1940', and D. Kirkwood, 'Settler Wives in Southern Rhodesia, A Case Study', in Callan and Ardener, (eds.), *The Incorporated Wife*, pp. 186–210, 143–64; J. Axtell, *The European and the Indian, Essays in the Ethnohistory of Colonial North America*, (New York, 1981), pp. 152–5.

42. D. Lessing, *The Grass is Singing*, (London, 1950).

43. J. Morris and S. Winchester, *Stones of Empire,the Buildings of the Raj*, (Oxford, 1986), p. 5; Kirkwood, 'Settler wives in Southern Rhodesia', p. 146.

44. Kirkwood, 'Settler wives in Southern Rhodesia', p. 148, J. Crush and C. Rogerson, 'New wave African historiography and African historical geography', *Progress in Human Geography*, 7, 2 (1983), pp. 203–31.

45. Morris with Winchester, *Stones of Empire*; A. D. King, *Colonial Urban Development, Culture, Social Power and Environment*, (London, 1976).

46. K. Ballhatchet, *Race, Sex and Class under the Raj*, (London, 1980).

47. *The Collected Essays, Journalism and Letters of George Orwell*, Vol. 2, (London, 1968), pp. 261–2.

48. P. D. Curtin, '"The White Man's Grave": Image and Reality, 1780–1850', *Jnl. of British Studies*, **1** (1961), pp. 94–110.

49. Morris with Winchester, *Stones of Empire*, pp. 198–202.

50. P. Burroughs, 'Imperial Defence and the Victorian Army', *Jnl. of Imperial and Commonwealth History*, **XV** (1986), pp. 62– 3; Huttenback, *Racism and Empire*.

51. E. Ollsen, 'Truby King and the Plunket Society. An analysis of a prescriptive ideology', *New Zealand Jnl. of History*, **15** (1981), pp. 3–23.

52. J. A. Mangan, *The Games Ethic and Imperialism, Aspects of the Diffusion of an Ideal*, (Harmondsworth, 1986); R. Symonds, *Oxford and Empire, The Last Lost Cause?*, (New York, 1986).

53. J. E. C. Welldon, 'The imperial aspects of education', *Proceedings of the Royal Colonial Institute*, **XXVI**, (1894–5), pp. 322–46.

54. C. Tennyson, 'They taught the world to play', *Victorian Studies*, **II** (1959), pp. 211–22; Mangan, *The Games of Ethic and Imperialism*, p. 74.
55. Morris and Winchester, *Stones of Empire*, pp. 216–22.
56. A. J. Christopher, *The British Empire at its Zenith*, (London, 1988), p. 217.
57. e.g. Cottrell, *British Overseas Investment*, p. 27.
58. In J. W. Watson, *Social Geography of the United States*, (London, 1979), p. 22.
59. *Ibid.*, p. 23.
60. J. Highwater, *The Primal Mind, Vision and Reality in Indian America*, (New York, 1981), pp. 18–23; Wallerstein, *Historical Capitalism*, pp. 97–110.
61. R. M. Young, 'Darwinism is social', in D. Kohn, (ed.), *The Darwinian Heritage*, (Princeton, 1985), pp. 609–38.
62. J. B. Bury, *The Idea of Progress, An Inquiry into its Growth and Origin*, (London, 1920), vii, p. 329.
63. A. Demangeon, *The British Empire, A Study in Colonial Geography*, (London, 1925), pp. 105–22, English translation.
64. A. W. Crosby, *Ecological Imperialism, The Biological Expansion of Europe. 900–1900*, (Cambridge, 1986).
65. W. H. McNeill, *Plagues and Peoples*, (New York, 1976).
66. *Ibid.*; Crosby, *Ecological Imperialism*.
67. J. Axtell, *The European and the Indian Essays in the Ethnohistory of Colonial North America*, (New York, 1981), p. 248; Crosby, *Ecological Imperialism*, p. 208.
68. C. Darwin, *The Descent of Man*, (London, 1901), pp. 283–90.
69. Crosby, *Ecological Imperialism*, p. 256; A. D. Cliff and P. Haggett, *The Spread of Measles in Fiji and the Pacific: Spatial Components in the Transmission of Epidemic Waves through Island Communities* (Canberra, 1985).
70. E. Greville, 'The Aborigines of Australia', *Proceedings of the Royal Colonial Institute*, **XXII**, 1890–91, p. 35.
71. Crosby, 1986, *Ecological Imperialism*, p. 165; W. T. L. Travers, 'On the changes effected in the natural features of a new country by the introduction of civilised races', *Transactions of the New Zealand Institute*, 1869, pp. 299–30.
72. T. Griffin and M. McCaskill. (eds.) *Atlas of South Australia*, (Adelaide, 1986), p. 56; A. H. Clark, *The Invasion of New Zealand by People, Plants and Animals, The South Island*, (New Brunswick, 1949).
73. B. Slattery, *Ancestral Lands, Alien Lands: Judicial Perspectives on Aboriginal Title*, (Saskatchewn, 1983), pp. 6–7; A.J. Christopher, *Colonial Africa* (London, 1984), pp. 125–8.
74. P. Burns, *Te Rauparaha, A New Perspective*, (Auckland, 1983), p. 240.
75. A. Smith, *The Wealth of Nations*, (Harmondsworth, 1970), pp. 194–5.
76. Curtin, *Imperialism*, pp. 41–5.
77. McNeill, *Plagues and Peoples*; A. W. Crosby, *The Columbian Exchange, Biological Consequences of 1492*, (Westport, Conn., 1973).
78. L. H. Brockway, *Science and Colonial Expansion, The Role of the British Royal Botanical Gardens*, (New York, 1979); E. R. Wolfe, *Europe and the People Without History*, (Berkeley, 1982).
79. Curtin, 'The White Man's Grave'.
80. N. Frye, *The Bush Garden, Essays on the Canadian Imagination'*, (Toronto, 1971), p. 224.
81. Christopher, *The British Empire at its Zenith*, pp. 190–212; J.M. Powell, *The Public Lands of Australia Felix, Settlement and Land Appraisal in Victoria 1834–91*, (Melbourne, 1970); Powell, 1988, 'The patrimony of the people'.
82. D. W. Meinig, *On the Margins of the Good Earth: the South Australia Wheat Frontier, 1869–1884*, (Chicago, 1962).
83. G. P. Marsh, *Man and Nature, or Physical Geography as Modified by Human Action*, (New York, 1864); P. Blaikie and H. Brookfield, *Land Degradation and Society*, (London, 1987), pp. 100–21; M. M. Roche, *Forest Policy in New Zealand, An Historical Geography 1840–1919*, (Palmerston North, 1987).
84. K. B. Cumberland, *Soil Erosion in New Zealand: a Geographic Reconnaissance*, (Wellington,

1944); A. and J. Conacher, 'The exploitation of the soils', in R. L. Heathcote, *The Australian Experience*, pp. 127–38.

85. R. Nash, *Wilderness and the American Mind*, (New Haven, 1967).

86. R. C. Brown, 'The doctrine of usefulness: natural resource and national park policy in Canada, 1887–1914', in J. G. Neilson and R. C. Scace (eds.), *The Canadian National Parks: Today and Tomorrow*, (Calgary, 1968), pp. 94–110.

87. D. Brown, *Bury My Heart at Wounded Knee, An Indian History of The American West*, (London, 1972); R. Broome, 'The struggle for Australia: Aboriginal-European warfare, 1770–1930', in M. McKernan and M. Browne (ed.), *Australia: Two Centuries of War and Peace*, (Canberra, 1988), pp. 92–120.

88. J. Belich, *The New Zealand Wars and the Victorian Interpretation of Racial Conflict*, (Auckland, 1986).

89. A. J. Christoper, *Colonial Africa*, pp. 57–60; J. Crush, 'The southern African regional formation: a geographical perspective, *Tijdschrift voor Econ. en Soc. Geografie*, **73** (1982), pp. 200–12; J. Overton, 'The colonial state and spatial differentiation: Kenya, 1895–1920', *Jnl. of Historical Geography*, **13**, (1987), pp. 267–82. On the impact of colonial capital on indigenous producer systems in the African colonies of rule, rather than those of European settlement, see M. Watts, *Silent Violence: Food, Famine and Peasantry in Northern Nigeria*, (Berkeley, 1983).

90. J. Crush and C. Rogerson, 'New wave African historiography'; H. Brody, *Maps and Dreams, Indians and the British Columbia Frontier*, (Harmondsworth, 1983); Wallerstein, 1983, *Historical Capitalism*.

91. D. K. Forbes, *The Geography of Underdevelopment*, (London, 1984), pp. 23–41; B. Hudson, 'The New Geography and the New Imperialism: 1870–1918', *Antipode*, **9** (1977), pp. 12–19.

92. T. W. Freeman, 'The Royal Geographical Society and the Development of Geography', in E. H. Brown, (ed.), *Geography, Yesterday and Tomorrow*, (Oxford 1980), pp. 1–99; D. R. Stoddart, *On Geography*, (Oxford, 1986), pp. 59–77, 83–5.

93. J. S. Keltie, 'Geographical Education', *Scottish Geographical Magazine*, **I** (1885), pp. 497–505; T. W. Freeman, *A History of Modern British Geography*, (London, 1980), p. 35.

94. G. S. Roberston, 'Political geography and the Empire', *Geographical Jnl.*, **16** (1900), p. 457; Milner, 'Geography and Statecraft;, *Scottish Geographical Magazine*, **XXIII**, (1907), pp. 617–27; G. N. Curzon, *Frontiers*, (Oxford, 1907); A. S. Goudie, 'George Nathaniel Curzon—superior geographer', *Geographical Jnl.*, **146** (1980), pp. 203–9.

95. R. Symonds, *Oxford and Empire*, pp. 140–7; H.J. Mackinder, 'On the scope and methods of geography', *Proceedings of the Royal Geographical Society*, new ser., **9**, 1887, pp. 141–60.

96. H. C. Darby, 'Academic geography in Britain, 1918–1946', *Transactions, Institute of British Geographers*, **8**, 1983, pp. 14–26.

97. Symonds, *Oxford and Empire*, p. 32.

98. Mangan, *The Games Ethic and Imperialism*, pp. 86, 102.

99. Symonds, *Oxford and Empire*.

100. H. J. Mackinder, 'The geographical pivot of history', *Geographical Jnl.*, **23** (1904), pp. 421–37; *Democractic Ideals and Reality: A Study of the Politics of Reconstruction*, (London, 1919); W. H. Parker, *Mackinder, Geography as an Aid to Statecraft*, (Oxford, 1982).

101. A. J. Herbertson, 'Geography and some of its present needs', *Scottish Geographical Magazine*, **XXVI** (1910), p. 543.

102. Darby, *Academic Geography in Britain*, p. 14; The task was repeated in the Second World War by H. C. Darby of Cambridge and K. Mason of Oxford: W. G. V. Balchin, 'United Kingdom geographers in the Second World War', *Geographical Jnl.* **153** (1987), pp. 170–1.

103. V. Cornish, *Naval and Military Geography of the British Empire*, (London, 1916), 'The strategic geography of the British Empire', *United Empire*, **VII**, (1916), pp. 142–60; A. Goudie, 'Vaughan Cornish: Geographer, with a bibliography of his published works;, *Transactions, Institute of British Geographers*, **55**, (1972), pp. 1–16.

104. Darby, 'Academic geography in Britain', p. 15.

105. S. W. Wooldridge, 'Geographical science in education', *Geographical Jnl.*, **CIX** (1947), p.

E. Pawson

202; 'Reflections on regional geography in teaching and research', in *The Geographer as Scientist, Essays on the Scope and Nature of Geography*, (London, 1956).

106. R. Peet, 'The social origins of environmental determinism', *Annals of the Association of American Geographers*, **75** (1985), pp. 309–33; J.M. Blaut, 'Diffusionism: a uniformitarian critique', *Annals of the Association of American Geographers*, **77** (1987) pp. 30–47.

107. D. Harvey, 'What kind of geography for what kind of public policy?', *Transactions, Institute of British Geographers*, **63** (1974), p. 22.

108. Gallagher, 1982, *The Decline, Revival and Fall of the British Empire.*

109. D. K. Fieldhouse, *The Theory of Capitalist Imperialism*, (London, 1967); Fieldhouse, *Economics and Empire.*

110. E. Pawson, 'Order and freedom: a cultural geography of New Zealand', in P. G. Holland and W. B. Johnston (eds.), *Southern Approaches, Geography in New Zealand*, (Christchurch, 1987), pp. 305–29.

111. K. Sinclair, *A Destiny Apart, New Zealand's Search for National Identity*, (Wellington, 1986), pp. 157–73.

19

The Years Between

B. T. Robson

If any period is a fulcrum, 1918–39—'the years between the wars'—must be seen as such. They were more a period when the post Second World War period was born than a dying spasm of the nineteenth century. They saw the creation of a new geography of production and consumption or, rather, the re-creation of an older one echoing the earlier pre-industrial pattern of the country; they saw the rise of state involvement and the laying of firm foundations for a welfare state; the development of a new relationship between housing and demography with the fission of households; they stamped a firmly suburban pattern on the settlement form of the country; and they set the stage for the growth of lifestyles moulded by greater affluence, leisure and recreation. In the onward march of time theirs is a tiny flicker, but their well-remembered events loom large. They fall within the compass of living memory, ageing and thinning though that memory may be, and more importantly, being so near and yet so undoubtedly far, they entice and tease. Fact and fiction blur uncertainly through the loving but often false depictions of artists, writers and the media. The sardonic and the sentimental jostle each other on those precious but often unreliable tapes beloved by the oral historian. Photographs amuse and amaze; family faces smile or stare and solemnly confront us; landscapes puzzle—the lineaments of whole towns have altered beyond recognition, country views have changed completely. Yet the frame of the picture holds steady, for this past is not that popular myth, another country, it is recognizably still our odd-shaped islands, lying athwart the Continental land-mass. Perhaps modern academic sophistication may sneer at Mackinder's proposition that 'great consequences lie in the simple statements that Britain is an island group set in the ocean, but off the shores of a great continent',[1] yet the consequences of that geography have marked each stage of our past as well as informing our present. Within the British Isles much of the topography remains unchanged: new roads, new towns, new man-made or man-influenced features alter the detail, but not the outline and not the relative locations. Furthermore the actors and the actions of those years remind us of ourselves, of the lessons unlearnt, of the problems still to be overcome. The phrases of nostalgia, of evocation, of example, of approval, of despair, of distaste and even fear mingle in the distorting mirrors of memory and knowledge.

Out of these emerge the conflicting views which bedevil current perception of those years. On the one hand, it was a time of peace and of increasing prosperity; not perhaps bathed in that everlasting sunlight which is deemed to brighten the pre-

1914 era, but nevertheless a period of promise. On the other, they were years of depression and unemployment, of the gathering clouds of another war, of widespread misery and misfortune; indeed the 1930s have been called the 'Devils' Decade'. It is not uncommon to find the media pundit or politician who lives by turning the popular phrase managing to marry these two views. Thus it may be said that there was indeed great distress caused through unemployment and low wages, but how well everyone behaved. Popular texts dealing with the General Strike of 1926 repeatedly remind their readers that police and strikers played football together. It is so far a cry from the bitter battle of Orgreave during the Miners' Strike of 1984-5 that it enhances the sanguine view of those years. At the same time those who concentrate on the evils of the capitalist world and the dire after-effects of the Great Crash of 1929 have their own lyrical picture of oppressed working people living together in a roseate glow of mutual understanding, forever ready to lend each other a helping hand and to fight the bosses; a view epitomized by those serious minded films of the 1930s and 1940s in which Welsh miners continuously move diagonally across the screen singing in a harmony which supposedly reflected their lives. That camaraderie is contrasted with the selfish acquisitiveness of the present day. Such manipulation of the past is a game that all can and do play. At its simplest level we all find comfort in the notion that 'time was when', and we paint in the gaps according to our present circumstances. For those who enjoy a prosperous life it enhances that enjoyment and accentuates the sense of achievement to remember that the past was hard; for those who face difficulties and distress it is consolation to be able to recall the good days.

That truism masks an unpleasant truth: the implied symmetry of checks and balances—between past and present, or fair shares in happiness and misery, prosperity and poverty—does not exist. Some people and some places have more than their share of bad fortune whilst others continuously thrive. How familiar Marwick's comment about the years 1918–39 seems today: 'now a new pattern established itself: a prosperous bustling South producing a tremendous range of new consumer goods; and a decaying North'.[2] Yet in writing that twenty years ago, he also suggested a form of geographical retribution: 'before the (1914–18) war it was London with its sweated trades which housed the most downtrodden, poverty stricken elements in the community while the miners and the skilled workers in the heavy industries had been the most prosperous members of the working class.'[3] A modern gloss might murmur that a capital city is always likely to be the place of extremes, whether of misery or of magnificence. Yet the historical geographer knows that the uplands of Britain—lying to the north and west of the line from the Wash to the Severn—have had more than their fair share of the ill-winds of misfortune. Ever the seed-bed of challenge to the power of royal or central government—whether in 1069, 1215 or 1536 or 1987—and so ever the recipient of harsh punishment, those regions were also caught by the accident of geography as being less accessible, less fertile, and far too frequently less warm and less dry than the 'lowlands'. For a brief spell upland Britain appeared triumphant; the inventors and entrepreneurs who made the First Industrial Revolution needed the resources which lurked in those historically less-favoured areas. Mineral wealth, especially coal, was to be found a-plenty in them. The great industrial cities, the small bustling factory towns, the hard-working, hard-living pit villages filled out the frame of upland Britain in a new way; with solid splendour in public and private buildings, with prison-like places of work, with palls of black smoke and dirty air, with all manner of houses from the dingy to the grand, with the wealth to redraw the lineaments of power in Britain—and with people. The challenge offered by Britain's industrial heartland was bold but doomed. Its nemesis lay not only in its reliance on declining industries, but also in the very factors it had sought so successfully to challenge; that where there was expansion and growing prosperity, development would follow. Their grip on that reality had already loosened long before the First World War, but the world-wide after-effects of that struggle broke even that slack hold.

The Financial Legacy

The industrial regions of Britain, based in the unlikely upland areas of hill and moor, relied for their continued wealth on both domestic and foreign needs for their coal, their iron and steel, their machinery, their shipbuilding and their textiles. Before 1914 this need appeared to be never-ending, but the downturn in trade of the Great Depression, beginning in 1873 and lasting almost to the end of the century, served notice that other countries were fit and ready to meet those demands as production of coal and iron and steel rose ever more vigorously in Germany and the United States. Recovery by Britain over the years 1896 to 1914 helped merely to gloss over the basic slowing down of output, the lack of internal investment, and the rising relative costs of these industries. Nor was it fully appreciated, since detailed trade statistics were not available before 1903, that since the mid-19th-century Britain's trade in visible earnings had consisted of a slowly rising deficit from about £25 million in 1850 to £160 million in 1900.[4] Only after 1918 when the record invisible earnings that covered this gap came under threat was the full extent of the problem revealed. The price of war can be measured in repudiated debts and Britain's own extensive obligation to the United States. The liquidation of overseas investments was undertaken by government order and accounted for about 15 per cent of total investment. This was in fact recovered by the end of the 1920s, but the more fraught question of international debt was not so easily overcome. Britain had in fact lent more than she had borrowed, but her political ineptitude in agreeing to worse terms of repayment to the United States than other debtors and in being unpaid herself by countries such as Russia meant a diminishing safety net for a growing imbalance in her visible imports and exports. In fact the balance of payments from invisible earnings in Britain's favour was maintained, but the fears engendered by the changed circumstances helped to underwrite the continued enthusiasm for 'sound money' which reached its peak in the return to the Gold Standard in April 1925. As early as August 1918 the Cunliffe Committee on Currency and Foreign Exchanges had recommended such a move, claiming that 'nothing can contribute more to the speedy recovery from the effects of war and the rehabilitation of foreign exchanges than the establishment of the currency on a sound basis'.[5] This view was endorsed by the British Government in April 1920 when it embarked on a severe deflationary policy. The consequences of that policy were satisfactory for the City, but not for British industry; and for the oldest sections of industry it was disastrous. 'It was unlikely that a government less responsive to the demands of the City would have taken such appalling risks with British industry.'[6] The blindness of government, bankers and even economists—Keynes being as yet a voice crying in the wilderness—allied to the increasing inherent weaknesses of ageing industries was to change the industrial map of Britain.[7] That change was structural—a point explored at the end of the period by the Barlow Report—and it was the geographical location of the declining old staple industries which gave so pronounced a spatial pattern to the outworkings of the structural shifts, creating two apparently contradictory nations of misery and of ebullience. Each of the old staples—with their locational roots so firmly in the northern uplands—was to start that long spluttering decline which brought them to current extinction after their further false kindling in the 1950s and 1960s.

The Old Staples

Coal

Coal, once the life-blood of industry and a prime overseas earner, had been faltering for some years. Old mines, worn-out seams, a lack of mechanization and modernization, a multiplicity of owners and operators—mostly greedy, selfish and incompetent—a courageous and understandably rebellious workforce and with both owners and workers characterized by obstinacy and obscurantism; these were hardly the ingredients either for keeping old customers or seeking out new. The record output in 1913 of 287 million tons with an export figure of over 90 million tons was not only never subsequently matched again, but also any optimism which it might have engendered ignored the fact that production was increasing more rapidly in America and Germany as was their share of the export market. The weaknesses in the coal-mining industry had shown up clearly at the start of the First World War when declining production and loss of miners augured ill for the war effort. Starting with control of prices and export licensing in 1915 and moving through control of the South Wales mines in December 1916 to virtual nationalization by 1918, the government showed its awareness of the need to interfere. Nevertheless it safeguarded the owners' profits and it has been suggested that the whole process was less a desire to maintain a basic industry than a need to keep consumer prices down whilst at the time trying to buy off recalcitrant workers with better wages.[8] No real attempt was made to analyse and reform the industry; only a concerted effort to exploit the richest seams. At the end of the war the government seized upon a scarcity of coal in war-ruined Europe to make a great deal of money out of exports and keep down home prices. At the same time it appeared to be willing to examine the industry more closely. In January, 1919, the Coal Industry Commission was created by Act of Parliament. Better known by the name of its chairman, Sir John Sankey, the Commission set to work to examine the state of the coal mines. Owners and miners and their supporters were almost equally divided in number, but 'they successfully kept private enterprise on trial before the commission and compelled the mine-owners to remain throughout on the defensive'.[9] That was not enough. Despite recommendations by the majority in favour of nationalization, the government failed to act. Instead in 1921, as the demand for coal began to plummet, the 3000 pits were hastily handed back to their 1500 owners, most of whom were singularly Bourbon-like, having learnt nothing and forgotten nothing. During the brief boom of coal exports at the end of the war, the export price had been almost four times that of domestic coal and the surplus had been placed in a profits pool which helped to maintain uneconomic pits. The private owners, faced with their own individual costs and, bereft of any subsidy, posted notices of new reduced wage levels and, ignoring the miners, long fought-for and recently achieved national standard, reverted to district levels. The largest reductions reflected the return of an almost forgotten geographical pattern in which upland Britain suffered more than lowland; Durham and Northumberland, South Wales and Lancashire suffered drops in employment proportionately more severe than in the 'newer' fields in Yorkshire and the East Midlands (Fig. 19.1). From almost 50 per cent wage reductions in South Wales through Cumberland, the North-East, North Wales and the

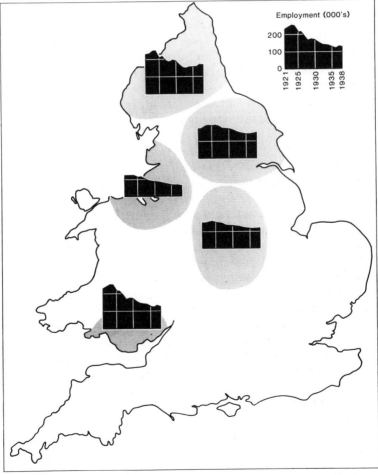

Fig. 19.1. Changes in employment in the principal coalfield areas, 1921–38. *Source*: Mitchell and Deane, *Abstract of British Historical Statistics*, 1962.

Forest of Dean, to 10 to 25 per cent in Yorkshire and the East Midlands, the lineaments of an old affliction—'the harrying of the North'—were surfacing. The decline of the coal industry, with its attendant toll in human misery, was one of the factors which helped to redraw the social and economic map of Britain.

Hindsight has prompted many arguments about the causes of decline, most of them concentrating either on sociological explanations which plump for the would-be gentleman-owner syndrome, or on economic interpretations which run the gamut from unreconstructed Marxism through all the deviations from and variations on the master.[10] Even the nowt-so-queer-as-folk approach has been adumbrated, forever encapsulated by the acid comments of Lord Birkenhead; 'it would be possible to say without exaggeration that the miners' leaders were the stupidest men in England if we had not had frequent occasion to meet the owners'. Underlying all the explanations, the differential decline in different fields owed much to the basic geological and geographical facts about the state of seams in different British coalfields—faulty in South Wales, Scotland and the North-East, thin especially in Northumberland and Scotland, abundant and accessible in the East Midlands.[11] Nor, as the years from 1921 onwards showed, was British output the most favoured by those places which needed to buy coal: Germany, Poland and America offered coal at competitive prices so that Britain's export of coal almost halved. 'Fall in the volume of exports has had profound geographical repercussions within Britain, for some British fields owing to their geographical position have specialized on the export market, and these which had an expanding output prior to 1914 have had a contracting output during the last two decades.'[12]

Iron and Steel

As other basic industries faltered so too did their need for coal, thus further depriving the coal industry of its large domestic market. Iron and steel, although much smaller even in its heyday than the coal industry, was another staple. Like coal it appeared to be thriving in the years before 1914, but that appearance was similarly deceptive. Growth was slower in the British industry than in rivals such as Germany and America. It clung to old expensive means of production; it failed to make good use of innovative ideas in the making of steel, often allowing the British-based ones such as the Gilchrist Thomas process to be snapped up by its competitors. The failure to invest in such new processes was perhaps understandable in that there had already been heavy investment in such earlier developments as the Bessemer converter, but the problem of the industry is tersely summed up by Hobsbawm: 'Obsolete plant and obsolete industrial areas anchored the British industry to an obsolete technology.'[13]

The 1914–18 war made great demands on the industry and the government paid for new plant and granted loans on easy terms to manufacturers. This encouraged new processes as well as increasing production. The switchback of output showed the precarious state of the industry and the faltering demands of the overseas and home markets (Fig. 19.2). The post-war boom which so falsely inspired the coal industry had equally disastrous effects on iron and steel. Over-production was followed by over-capitalization and, for the decade following the end of the war, production slipped back and the British share of the world market decreased. The

Fig. 19.2. Changes in output in the principal iron and steel areas, 1921–38. *Source*: Mitchell and Deane, *Abstract of British Historical Statistics*, 1962.

British iron and steel industry was 'inferior by the nature of labour supply, character of home market, lack of sufficient training, oldness of plant, changing conditions of ore supply, dearness of transport, unsuitable sites of older works, inflexibility in the face of new circumstances'.[14] By 1925 it was calculated that Britain was using only 45 per cent of its pig-iron making capacity and 58 per cent of steel making.[15] The dire effects were not only loss of markets and trade, but also heavy unemployment, both of which lasted until the early 1930s. The granting of a tariff on iron and steel in 1932 was on the understanding that the industry would re-organize itself. Even that met with some resistance from within the trade since a certain amount of semi-finished Bessemer steel was imported from Belgium and Germany. Indeed one of the side effects of the 1914—18 war had been the greater use of the open-hearth process and the gradual phasing out of the once much-used Bessemer in Britain. By 1934, however, the lure of both protection and government blessing for a cartel saw the formation of the British Iron and Steel Federation (BISF), an organization which proceeded to play a skilful game of *quid pro quo* with foreign cartels whereby British import duties were lowered on quotas from the favoured cartels and exports from Britain were to be treated similarly. But the fact that the BISF had been called into being by government, and was backed by a consortium led by the Bank of England, meant that the industry did not necessarily develop to its own best advantage. A giant new iron and steel works, which included blast furnaces, coke ovens, steel furnaces, rolling and cogging mills, cold reduction mills and a wide-strip mill, was opened in Ebbw Vale, South Wales in 1938 by Richard Thomas and Co. They had wanted to develop in Redbourn, Lincolnshire near similar thriving and growing concerns, but instead were forced into the less suitable site by government pressure and public concern over the plight of South Wales; a concern made greater by the previous obstruction offered by the BISF to the proposal for an integrated steelworks to be built in the distressed town of Jarrow. The old geography of iron making, dependent on proximity to both iron ore and coal, had grown more complicated as the industry expanded into the production of steel. One economic geographer, Wilfred Smith, could blithely outline diverse sitings of the industry during the period and make them appear rational within terms of their orefield-based or coalfield-based locations; another, however, could tartly comment that 'if there was no clear move to better sites, there was little progress made towards regional self-sufficiency either, and millions of tons of ore, coke and coal had regularly to be transported over long distances'.[16] Nevertheless by 1939 the industry showed marked signs of recovery both in terms of trade and in the numbers employed. That such recovery would provide new hostages to fortune was not then apparent; nor indeed was an Ebbw Vale or a Shotton or a Clydebridge or a Workington enough to halt the changing map of industrial Britain.

Shipbuilding

Other old-established staples like shipbuilding, engineering and textiles faced their own individual Gethsemanes. British shipbuilding, in 1914 the proud possessor of 60 per cent of the world's output, was to slip down the scale to 34 per cent by 1937.[17] The overcapacity of world shipbuilders produced by the war, coupled with the decline in demand, brought blight to north-eastern England, Clydeside and Merseyside. Unemployment varied from 36 per cent of insured workers in 1921 to over 60 per cent in 1933. Efforts to reduce capacity were made by the National Shipbuilders' Security Ltd (NSS) which was established in 1930. It represented most of the industry and was supported by the Bankers' Industrial Development Corporation, an organization which emerged in the same year. Originally the Securities Management Trust, NSS had initially been established to deal with companies taken over by the banks, but in 1930 it was launched in its new guise with a capital of £6 million. The Bank of England provided one-quarter and the major clearing banks the rest. Its brief was to help finance reconstruction in ailing staple industries and to destroy surplus capacity. NSS raised funds by taking a levy of 1 per cent on the sale of all those ships which were actually built and sold. Backed by this money it aimed to buy up shipyards and 'sterilize' them for forty years. By 1937, 28 firms with a capacity of over 1 million tons, out of a total capacity in Britain of about 3·5 million, had been bought up and destroyed. Those yards fortunate enough to escape would be in a position to compete for such trade as was available. Where there was no other industry available the effect was dire. An elderly worker vividly recalled it for the BBC programme *All Our Working Lives*:

I remember NSS came up and we discussed it. 'Oh,' I said, 'that's very good and what percentage do the men get that have been thrown on the scrapheap?' Only the employers were getting the benefit you see. The workers were getting nothing.[18]

The actions of NSS, coupled with government assistance by the British Shipping Act 1935 for the building of new ships, did help to reduce the proportion of unemployed to 24 per cent by 1937, but it also presented then and now the clearest and saddest image of the harm being done to Britain's industrial heartland. Jarrow, 'the town that was murdered', lost its shipyards to NSS in 1934; by 1935 it had almost 75 per cent unemployment: the failure to get a projected steel plant led to the Jarrow March of 1936. Two hundred men carrying a chest with a petition of 12,000 signatures asking for help to get work in the town, marched to London. Theirs was not the only long-distance march of those years, but its effect was heightened by the fact that so much of the country through which it passed was enjoying growth and increasing prosperity. Indeed the county of Surrey 'adopted' Jarrow and helped to start a relief scheme which led to the setting up of Jarrow Metal Industries Ltd,[19] but only the imminence of war eventually made any real indentation into the numbers of unemployed in the area.

Closely linked with shipbuilding was the failure in certain sections of engineering, since British shipbuilders persisted in clinging to steam when most of the world wanted oil engines so that there was a marked downturn in marine engineering. Other engineering fared better, but the most successful like the car industry and electrical engineering did not need to locate in the traditional areas of the north. They made greater use of machine tools and therefore only needed semi-skilled or even unskilled workers and were able to locate away from the coalfields.[20] It was ironic that those parts of the old staples that managed to survive and flourish did so mostly south of the Wash/Severn line or at the very least established themselves in the 'border' zone of the Midlands.

Textiles

The last of the grand old staples was textiles: of these, cotton had indeed been king: as late as 1912–13, 8000 million yards of cotton were produced of which about 75 per cent was exported.[21] And, despite the even-then growing challenge of cheap cotton from countries like India, cotton also represented 31 per cent of all manufactured exports.[22] The war of 1914–18 saw a reduction in the output of cotton goods both because of the unchecked loss of manpower and the difficulty in obtaining raw cotton—a reduction which further encouraged the development of cotton factories in India and Japan. The boom of 1919 inspired a reckless burst of buying-up of Lancashire cotton mills since about 238 mills, some 42 per cent of the total industry, changed hands. It has been calculated that over £71 million was paid for firms whose capital totalled just under £11 million.[23] When the boom collapsed the cotton industry faced the consequences both of this financial albatross and of its rapidly declining overseas markets. Prices halved almost overnight and the cotton towns of Lancashire had to face the unpalatable fact that other countries had moved into the market with more attractively priced goods of equal quality—or, more accurately, lack of quality since it was the cheaper end of the market which was most adversely affected. The grey unbleached cotton piece goods which had formed over 33 per cent of the export trade in 1913 shrank to 25 per cent in 1929 and to 16 per cent in 1935.[24] This in itself had a skewed effect on the cotton towns of Lancashire since Oldham and Blackburn–Accrington–Darwen specialized in coarser spinning and weaving whilst Bolton–Leigh and Burnley–Colne–Nelson concentrated on the finer end of the market.[25] To make matters worse there was little realization that what was taking place was a permanent change in the trade. One head of a large spinning firm said in 1924:

> Too often, alarmist and ill-informed reports get abroad to the effect that this country or that country is doing wonders in the way of cotton cloth production and is sweeping all before it in foreign markets. . . . It is an astonishing thing what credence is given to these things in Lancashire where people ought to know better.[26]

This short-sightedness failed not only to appreciate that Japan in particular had used both the traditional British textile machinery, but also had introduced electricity and faster, more automated machines. The low pay of the Japanese workers and their double shift system meant much cheaper cloth whilst the insularity of British mill owners and managers ensured that in an effort to keep workforces together ready for the expected upturn in trade, short-term working was widely used. This added greatly to costs and also militated against mobility. Furthermore, as the report of the Committee of the Economic Advisory Council on the Cotton Industry pointed out in 1930, there was an urgent need to modernize and re-organize. Britain still clung to mule spinning and specialized mills whilst other countries, including America as well as Japan, used the cheaper 'ring spinning' and produced standard cloth in large integrated factories. J. R. Clynes who chaired this committee wrote; 'Lancashire must choose between losing her trade or changing her methods.' The irony of his injunction was that it was made against a background of the onset of Depression: mill owners imposed wage cuts as they struggled to modernize or even stay in business. Wage levels for cotton workers were relentlessly forced down even when there was work and the mill was not foreclosed through bankruptcy. The introduction of limited protection in 1932 helped to safeguard the home-market for cotton and the Ottawa agreement of the same year ensured that the Dominions and the Crown Colonies took their share of cotton exports.[27]

At the end of the decade a cartel, the Lancashire Cotton Corporation (LCC), was established to try to do for cotton what NSS did for shipbuilding and BISF for iron and steel. Backed by the Bankers' Industrial Development Corporation, LCC tried to cut down on capacity. Aided by legislation in 1936 which gave it power to raise a levy from millowners in order to acquire and scrap surplus mills, it managed almost to halve the capacity of the industry.[28] Again, the parallels with the post-war years are instructive. Government was clearly beginning to play an active role in the process of production. Post-war bodies such as the Industrial Reorganization Corporation, in its restructuring of the engineering industry,[29] showed a more overt involvement of the government and the state; the principles underlying LCC, BISF and NSS were nevertheless similar and reflected the growth of state involvement of a different order of magnitude from anything that had gone before.[30]

Agriculture

A further sector of change and depression was agriculture. English agriculture, once in the vanguard of progress, had long since succumbed to the cheap food policy which brought cheap produce from all over the world to the tables of the urban island-dwellers. By 1914 only one-fifth of the wheat consumed was home-grown whereas pastoral farming fared somewhat better since there was more demand for home-grown meat. Market gardening was beginning to make some progress on the eve of war and the war itself finally brought belated government interference which ensured the ploughing up of more land for grain-growing. However, this support was not maintained subsequently and the newly converted arable farmer found himself facing the cold wind of a world downturn in prices in the early 1920s. Once more those farmers who could afford to ride out the crisis turned to livestock, dairy produce, fruit and vegetables. Cheaper imports challenged these too and by the end of the decade agriculture was both declining and depressed. Only after 1932 when the government offered it protection did it begin to revive. The protection took the form of guaranteed prices so that subsidies went directly to the farmer, keeping the price down for the consumer.[31] Such support helped to raise output but did little for the general rural economy or the low-paid agricultural worker. No doubt it sustained the rents of landlords, including such grand institutions as the colleges of Oxford and Cambridge, but it failed to stop an exodus fron the land and it did hardly anything to arrest the air of decay which was the hallmark of so much of the countryside during these years. 'Less arable land was to be seen in the landscape; the number of derelict fields, rank with coarse matted grass, thistle, weeds and brambles, multiplied; ditches became choked and no longer served as effective drains; hedges became overgrown and straggled over the edges of other fields; gates and fences fell into disrepair; farm roads were left unmade. Signs of decay were to be seen also in many of the buildings . . . the landscape of 1938 had, in many districts, assumed a neglected and unkept appearance.'[32] That mythic rural England— peaceful, prosperous, dreamy, friendly—beloved of the property speculators then and now, and of the prosperous urbanite, never really existed. What did exist were pockets of good living for those who had other resources to back their farming ventures and a great deal of poverty and hard work set in a stultified framework of class and status for farm-workers and others. One of the most dramatic changes of the post-war years has been the impact of new investment in rural areas and in the small towns and hamlets which used to serve rural populations; it was not always thus. The poverty, both material and spiritual, of the lives of rural dwellers in the interwar years has been graphically painted by Blythe's biographical sketches in *Akenfield*.[33] 'Many of the children in country schools are pale-faced, anaemic-looking, with eyes lacking lustre, undersized, under-fed and sad-faced.'[34] No wonder that people left the land. Agricultural employment fell by a quarter of a million between 1920 and 1938.[35] As in the depressed industrial areas, it was mainly the fitter and younger who left, thereby depriving rural communities of their next generation. It was an exodus which had happened before. This time, however, it was not to the old staples in the north and Scotland and Wales like cotton, coal, iron, and shipbuilding to which the emigrants were beckoned, but to the car industry in the West Midlands and Oxford or to light industry in the London area.

Structural Shifts and Regional Disparities

So the chill winds of economic depression and industrial decline returned the 'uplands' of Britain to a role they well knew: peripheral, ignored, neglected. That had long been their political and cultural status during the steady growth of the national state, focused as it was on London and the South-East. The overwhelming impression of physical decay which affected these parts of Britain are caught in the much-quoted lines from Auden (1930):

> Get there if you can and see the land you once were proud to own.
> Though the roads have almost vanished the expresses never run;
> Smokeless chimneys, damaged bridges, rotting wharves and choked canals,
> Tramlines buckled, smashed trucks lying on their side across the rails;
> Power-stations locked, deserted, since they drew the boiler fires;
> Pylons fallen or subsiding, trailing dead high-tension wires;
> Head-gears gaunt on grass-grown pit-banks, seams abandoned years ago;
> Drop a stone and listen for its splash in flooded dark below.

Such descriptive accounts bear uncanny resemblance to the deindustrialized landscapes of the northern wastelands of the 1980s. The processes through which they were created—through recession, lack of competitiveness, and the restructuring of production and of labour markets—are equally spectral echoes of our current decade.

Auden's impressionistic account can be seen as a typical offering from a member of the comfortable classes in the fashionable flush of youthful or even middle-aged enthusiasm for the 'workers'. A more moving threnody for the plight of those caught in the vicious turn of the historic wheel came from the contemporary and equally middle-class writer J. B. Priestley. His *English Journey*, first published in 1934, is required reading for those who would seek an evocative and vivid pen picture of a mixed and muddled country. His view of what had happened added a human dimension lacking in the dry bones of official figures:

> Since when did Lancashire cease to be a part of England? . . . we have marched so far, not unassisted in the past by Lancashire's money and muck, and we have a long way to go yet, perhaps carrying Lancashire on our backs for a spell. . . . No man can walk about these towns, the Cinderellas in the baronial household of Victorian England, towns meant to work in and not to live in and now even robbed of their work, without feeling that there is a terrible lack of direction and leadership in our affairs . . .'(p.286). 'For generations, this blackened North toiled and moiled so that England should be rich and the City of London be a great power in the world. But now this North is half derelict, and its people living on in the queer ugly places, are shabby, bewildered, unhappy' (p. 410). 'Was Jarrow still in England or not? Had we exiled Lancashire and the North East coast? Were we no longer on speaking terms with cotton weavers and miners and platers and riveters? Why had nothing been done about these decaying towns and workless people?[36]

Yet as Priestley himself admitted there were areas less blighted, indeed prospering, even though they did not accord with his personal dream of an ideal Britain. He found that:

> Coventry seems to have acquired the trick of keeping up with the times, a trick that many of our industrial cities find hard to learn. It made bicycles when everybody was cycling, cars when everybody wanted a motor, and now it is also busy with aeroplanes, wireless sets and various electrical contrivances, including the apparatus used by the talkies.[37]

Earlier in his journey he travelled out of London by the Great West Road where he saw abundant evidence of that other, developing England:

> These decorative little buildings, all glass and concrete and chromium plate, seem to my barbaric mind to be merely playing at being factories. You could go up to any one of the charming little fellows, I feel, and safely order an ice-cream or select a few picture postcards. . . . Actually, I know, they are tangible evidence most cunningly arranged to take the eye, to prove that the new industries have moved south. They also prove that *there are new enterprises to move south* [emphasis added][38]

The fall in Britain's export trade of the old staples was partly recompensed by the new industries like electricals, cars, bicycles, aircraft, rayon, hosiery, plastics, chemicals, stainless steel and scientific instruments. The varying percentages of growth in sectors of the economy between 1924 and 1937 (Fig. 19.3) show the clear structural shift in the economy. It was a shift which brought with it a simultaneous increase in overall employment and yet a continuation of high levels of unemployment. The apparent discrepancy was the result of demographic change which, in the face of only slow overall population growth, produced absolute and relative expansion of those of working age. Combined with internal migration which sucked large numbers from upland Britain to the South-East, the result spelled out a growing geographical schism within the country (Fig. 19.4). Between 1923 and 1937, every region of England and Wales saw an overall growth in employment, but in relative terms the divide between the South-East, the South-West and the Midlands on one hand, and the North, North-West, Yorkshire and Wales on the other was strikingly consistent. And such differences were even more marked in terms of unemployment at the end of the 1930s; the peripheral areas of the North and Wales having average figures of over 20 per cent and the North-West, Yorkshire/ Humberside and the South-West having figures of over 10 per cent, as against the Midlands and South-East with figures of below 10 per cent (Fig. 19.4).

The structural shift and the growth of 'new' industries may have spelled prosperity for the south, but was far from economic panacea for the country as a whole. From a low base of 7·4 per cent of exports in 1907, they pushed their way up to 14·6 per cent in 1930. In international terms, however, their growth was slower than in many other countries; and as the home market became more buoyant the new industries had less incentive to try to boost their performance in the overseas markets.[39] Whereas in 1872 Britain had been responsible for two-thirds of the world export of finished manufactures, its share fell to one-third in 1913 and one-fifth in 1937.[40] An economist writing in 1930 observed sadly; 'Today what is really important and significant in England is not the depression of the depressed industries, but the relatively small progress made by the relatively prosperous.'[41] Statistics indicate rather more progress than so gloomy a view suggests, but unfortunately 'Britain had reached a point at which the maintenance of a high level of prosperity depended on exceptionally drastic shifts in the use of productive resources and greater ingenuity in the

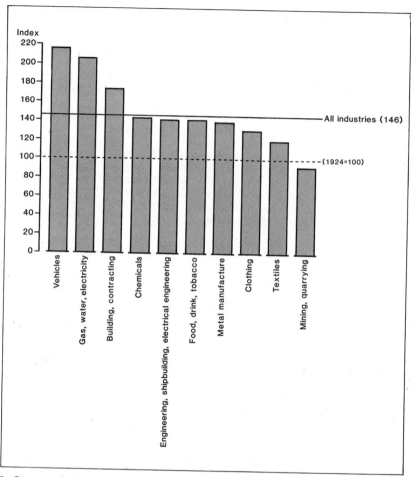

Fig. 19.3. Structural change in the economy, 1924–38. Indices of output by manufacturing sector. *Source*: Calculated from Mitchell and Deane, *Abstract of British Historical Statistics*, 1962.

development of finished products'.[42] That need was not fulfilled since the growth industries did not expand enough to absorb all the displaced labour from the declining sector. Even where steel and chemicals sited themselves in the very heartlands of old industrial regions they did not offer sufficient employment to counteract the effects of decay. For the most part, however, it was the Midlands and the South-East and more especially the Greater London area which attracted and kept the new industries. The Greater London area in particular gained in both factories and employment since, between 1932 and 1937, it accounted for five-sixths of the net increase in the number of factories and two-fifths of employment in all new factories.[43] The great bulk of such growth was prompted by the ebullience of the home market in consumer goods rather than of exports. 'It has been shown' writes Smith 'that the growth of Greater London has been due not so much to any inherent genius of the place as to the large part played in its industrial structure by those industries supplying the home market'.[44] Even some of the largest cities in the

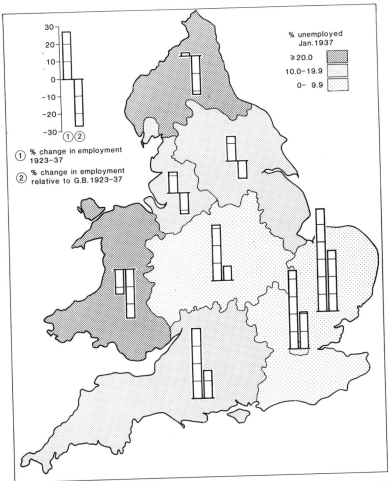

Fig. 19.4. Employment and unemployment. Bars show employment change 1923–37; shading shows levels of unemployment in January 1937. *Sources*: Mitchell and Deane, *Abstract of British Historical Statistics*, 1962; and Ministry of Labour Gazette, 1938.

depressed areas benefited to some extent from the search for domestic markets so that when finally the government turned to designating 'Special Areas', cities like Manchester, Liverpool, Cardiff, Newcastle and Glasgow were excluded.

It was this geographical shift of industry and of population which not so much refashioned England in some new and incomprehensible way as restored an old order. The ethos of government and of leading financial and cultural institutions was such that it appeared right and proper that those industries which were growing and developing should, for the most part, be drawn towards London. Mackinder writing in 1902 of the 'Great City' with its continued power and growth notes; 'Within the last hundred years for the first time in her long history London has had rivals in Britain . . . three other cities, Glasgow, Manchester and Liverpool.'[45] Yet even at the turn of the century he was quite clear where real supremacy lay: 'in a manner all south-eastern England is a single urban community. . . . The metropolis in its largest meaning includes all the counties for whose inhabitants London is 'Town', whose men do habitual business there, whose women buy and spend there, whose morning paper is printed there, *whose standard of thought is determined there*' [emphasis added].[46] His view that 'the British Isles have been built from a north-western foundation, but the British people and realm have grown in the main from south-eastern roots'[47] epitomized an attitude prevailing then—and now. The structural shift in the economy in the inter-war years merely re-asserted that long-established geographical tendency. To some extent the new locational imperatives of industry arose from the fact that the new or expanding industries did not need to be located on or near coalfields or other raw materials; equally important was access to a large mass of potential consumers since developing industries like those in electrical engineering and electrical goods relied for the most part on domestic markets. This in itself gave rise to a classic chicken-and-egg situation in that new industry located near consumers, the industry attracted labour which in turn provided more consumers and the original forgers and makers of Britain's industrial wealth watched helplessly.

Suburban England

Out of this relocation of industry came a movement of population: once more those who were able and willing packed their bags and sought the greener pastures whether it was in one of Priestley's 'charming little fellows' making insubstantial items like 'potato crisps, scent, tooth pastes, bathing costumes, fire extinguishers' or in his 'young town of long brick sheds' which housed car building in the Midlands.[48] The population drained away from upland regions like Northumberland, Durham and South Wales[49] leaving them to revert to a grim mockery of the empty places they had originally been. Their beautiful wild landscapes were now scarred by the depredations of man; their people marked by others' inhumanity. Some depressed areas like the cotton towns of Lancashire managed to hold their own partly because of short-time working and partly because some engineering survived and even developed in the region. The nimble fingers which had once made cotton became involved in making parts for radios and other electrical equipment. Greater London made a dramatic gain: from 1901 to 1938 it grew by 1,600,000.[50] By the 1930s the Greater London area accounted for one-fifth of the total population of England and Wales, one-quarter of the urban population. This spectacular growth rate (9.7 per cent between 1921 and 1931) hid the intriguing statistic that *inner* London like inner cities everywhere was losing population. Urban England was becoming suburban England, as testified by the substantial growth of the counties to the north and west of London (Fig. 19.5) as the population pendulum swung growth back to a south-eastern base.

Suburban England undoubtedly contributed to an interesting aspect of demography during these years, the falling birth rate. Whether it was indeed true that young married couples preferred a 'Baby Austin in the garage to a baby in the pram', the decline in the birth rate first noticed at the end of the nineteenth century was

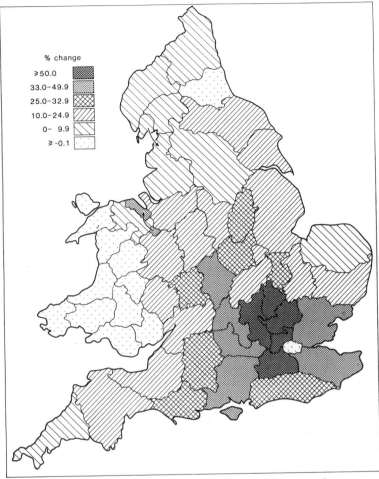

Fig. 19.5. Population change by county, 1921–51. *Source*: Census.

accentuated during the 1920s and 1930s. In 1903, 948,000 babies were born in England and Wales, by 1925 it was 711,000 and in 1931, 632,000. It dropped to 580,000 in 1933 and rallied slightly to 621,000 in 1938.[51] This continued downturn in births unbalanced the expected gains in population which should have resulted from a concurrent fall in the death rate and especially a decline in infant mortality. The cheering mortality figures suggest that even during the 'Depression' years improvements in public health and standards of living were taking place. A closer analysis shows how morbidly the geography of decline affected even the good news: the overall infant mortality rate for England and Wales went down from 153 per 1000 births during 1871–75 to a then all-time low of 57 in 1935, rising to 58 in 1937. Even here—and not unexpectedly—the starkness of the regional contrasts was apparent: in Liverpool the best that could be achieved was a drop to 82 by 1937; Sunderland was 92; Jarrow, 114.[52] Equally gloomy was the differential between classes; by the

1930s a baby born into a labourer's family was half as likely to survive as one born into the middle or upper classes.[53] The decrease in the traditional emigration figures especially during the 1930s helped to offset the falling birth rate, but it was not enough to prevent a widespread alarm—especially amongst academics at the London School of Economics—about the future of the population, an alarm which gave rise to a Commission on the subject and to its drawing what with hindsight can be seen as the misguided implication that 'a community like ours . . . can only prosper or, in the long run, survive, if its members think it worth while to have families large enough to replace themselves'.[54] This was to misinterpret the relationship between fertility and affluence.

The statistics which so alarmed scholars like Dr Enid Charles and R. M. Titmuss made a framework for the new England which Priestley noted with such grudging enthusiasm. This was:

> a large-scale, mass-production job with cut prices . . . it is an England, at last, without privileges . . . years and years ago the democratic and enterprising Blackpool, by declaring that you were all as good as one another so long as you had the necessary sixpence began all this. Modern England is rapidly Blackpooling itself. . . . Unfortunately, it is a bit too cheap. . . . Too much of it is simply a trumpery imitation of something that was not very good in its original.[55]

It was this England, the England of the suburbs, of ribbon development—of what contemporaries disparaged as 'sprawl'—of the medium-sized towns, all mainly in the South-East and the Midlands, which constituted the geography of residential change. Behind the facades of new semi-detached houses, of mock Tudor, of bungalows and even of council housing, lurked the newest heirs and heiresses to the ups of economic fortune. The expansion of London was helped by the extension of the underground system, northwards to Hendon in 1923, southwards to Morden in 1926. Each extension meant more speculative builders building more houses and enticing would-be inhabitants with much the same false rural imagery as in the 1980s. As the Metropolitan Railway pushed its way out of London, it called in 1932 on house-buyers to explore the delights of 'Metro-land'; apparent Islands of the Blest being built by their own housing company in a:

> country with elastic borders which each visitor can draw for himself, as Stevenson drew his map of Treasure Island. It lies mostly in Bucks, but choice fragments of Middlesex and Hertfordshire may be annexed with pleasure.

The promises of country delight in a sylvan setting all for £750 for a substantial detached house and far less for a semi-detached were all part of the rising expectations of the potential house-owner. The activities of speculators and estate developers and the lubricating role of the new electric railways played critical roles in ensuring the momentum of the outward growth, above all in the 'speculative suburbia' of outer London[56] and it was in outer London where the most dramatic expansion took place.[57] Suburbs—or 'dormitories' to their contemporaries—provoked polarized passions. The affectionate literary reminiscences of a Betjeman represent the voice of one of their unashamed beneficiaries. At the other extreme, A. J. P. Taylor writing the standard Oxford History of these years sneers at the suburban house as being;

> a baronial mansion on a tiny scale. It still had a hall and a drawing room (now called the lounge). There was still a separate kitchen for the non-existent domestic servant and the

family spent most of their time in it during the week. . . . Windows and doors did not fit. Draughts were everywhere. Chilblains remained a unique English malady. One room was heated by an open coal fire. The rest of the house was unheated.[58]

Even historians are not immune from indulging their prejudice. The houses may have lacked the comforts taken for granted by later generations; they may not have matched the standards of aesthetic design set by the fashionable either then or in the future, but they were the equivalent of 'open sesame' to their owners. Within them a family could establish itself, cultivate a garden, visit the nearby shops, spend Saturday night at the new Superpub or the new Supercinema, secure in the knowledge of steady work and steady pay. The growing number of white-collar salariat working in the administration of industry, in the service industries, in entertainment and in such public administration as teaching and local government were less likely to face sudden unemployment than were manual workers so that they could cope with the prospect of paying out a monthly sum of about £3–£5 for twenty years.

The families may not all have had 2·2 children (the average family size of couples married between 1927 and 1938), but they shared certain other characteristics which help to account for the massive surge in housing which so changed the face of Britain. The combination of demographic change, improvements in transport and a falling cost of living ensured that the tide of suburban expansion rose throughout the 1930s. The rising standard of living was the most important, and the most divisive, in a land where unemployment was a permanent fact of life, never dropping below a million and rising to three million in 1931. The once busy heartlands of the Industrial Revolution bore the full brunt of this, but even in those hard-hit regions those who did have work shared in the general improvement. Apart from the distorting effects of the short-lived post-war boom and the Depression of 1929–31, national income and wages remained remarkably steady whilst prices fell progressively until 1932 and then rose only slightly. With the falling cost of living, those in work enjoyed substantial rises in real wages (Fig. 19.6). The experiences of the declining industries such as coal and cotton contrasted markedly with the expanding industries such as engineering whose ebullience explains the rapid growth of prosperous dormitories in the South-East, but even so the 1930s represented for all workers a period of prosperity. The uncomfortable distinction was between those in and those out of work.[59] The expansion of the growing sectors of services and industry and of salaried employment meant that the total labour force showed striking growth even in the face of widespread unemployment. By 1938 there were 1·5 million more people in work then there had been in 1920. For those in work, the demographic changes meant a proportional growth in people of working age and this was combined with an increasing marriage rate and an increase in headship rates, all of which increased the potential demand for housing. The importance of transport improvements was that they opened up large areas of land outside the cities which could now be colonized by workers from the towns. Given the lax planning restrictions of the time, this availability of building land meant that house prices did not rise even during the astounding expansion of output in the 1930s. Such conditions of stable prices, rising real wealth for those in work and a rising number of families inevitably led to a housing boom (Fig. 19.7). The output of housing between 1934 and 1938 was never exceeded until the mid-1960s and, for private housing, has

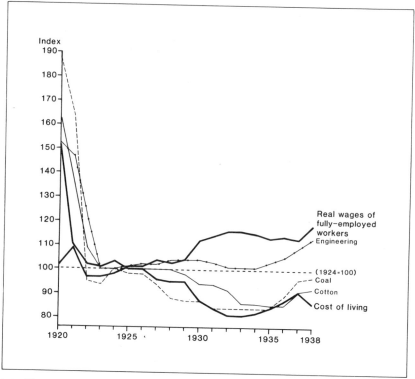

Fig. 19.6. Changes in real standards of living of those in employment. Curves show both the index of the cost of living and indices of wages of those in employment in selected industries. *Source*: Compiled from Mitchell and Deane, *Abstract of British Historical Statistics*, 1962.

never subsequently been matched. In this astonishing surge, a key institutional role was played by the expansion of the building societies. They enjoyed a high rate of return on investments compared to stocks and shares and this helped their total assets to quadruple between 1920 and 1930 and to further double to the end of the 1930s.[60]

For many wage earners, however—even in the prospering industries—buying a house was seen as too big a step and for those left festering in the black spots on the map it was out of the question. There was undoubted pressure for more cheap housing, not least as measured by the extent of sharing and of 'concealed' house-holds. Between 1911 and 1921, households had risen by 1,100,000 but housing had increased only by 300,000. Estimates of households sharing suggest an increase from 220,000 to 550,000 between 1911 and 1921 and, of 'potential' households, an increase from 8000 to over 9000.[61] For those who cared to remember there was the bitter memory of the Election Manifesto of 1918: 'One of the first tasks of the government will be to deal on broad and comprehensive lines with the housing of the people which, during the war, has fallen so badly into arrears and upon which the well-being of the nation so largely depends.' The 'homes fit for heroes' slogan which caught the imagination of a war-weary country was first to be implemented by the

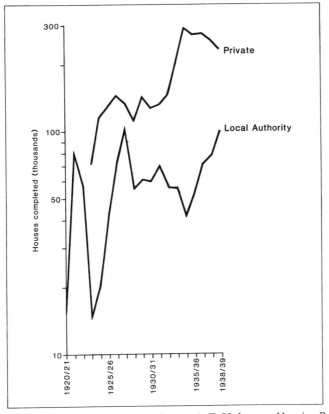

Fig. 19.7. Output of new housing, 1922–38. *Source*: A. E. Holmans, *Housing Policy in Britain: A History* (London, 1987).

Addison Act of 1919. During 1917–18, a committee of the Ministry of Reconstruction had outlined the need for more and better housing for working-class people after the war. Yet rent control and the high cost of materials and labour meant that a government subsidy would be needed to effect this. The Addison Act offered a subsidy but it was to be used through the agency of local authorities. Unfortunately like so much legislation before and since it was hastily cobbled together. The Act provided very generous open-ended financial backing for the loss incurred by local authorities beyond the product of a penny rate when they built houses. This subsidy was extended to Housing Associations and non-profit-making trusts. The private sector was supposed to be excluded, but by the end of 1919 any house built within certain dimensions qualified for a subsidy of £260. By 1921 government subsidized houses were costing £910 to build which was about three times the actual cost. Not even the most committed of socially-minded politicians could pursue such open-endedness and Lloyd George quickly intervened. The number of grants was limited, Addison left the ministry and by the end of 1922 the system was stopped and no similar progressive form of subsidy was ever to be introduced again. Most of the authorities which benefited were middle-sized towns; the very large conurbations, in which the housing problems were most severe, were still mostly in the process of surveying their horrendous housing needs when Addison subsidies were withdrawn.[62] Nevertheless 213,800 houses had been built.

The Addison Act represented an important break with the past. It ushered in large-scale, publicly rented housing, and an important principle for the future was established: that local government should act on behalf of central government as a provider of housing, using money for which it had little responsibility. Local authorities played a key role in each of what Bowley called 'the three experiments' of the inter-war years; the open-ended Addison provisions between 1919 and 1923, sound conservative financial incentives between 1923 and the early 1930s and a return to sanitary policy concerned with slum clearance between 1934 and 1939.[63] Alterations to the amount of subsidy and to the way it was given were attempted by both the Conservative Government of 1923 and the minority Labour Government of 1924. The former gave rather more help to those who least needed it since the 'Chamberlain' subsidies failed to place any strings (except for house size) on the subsidy of £6 per house, but the latter through the 'Wheatley' Act raised the subsidy to £9 per house per year provided that the house was built for letting, that it was built by workers on fair wages and that the rent did not exceed an 'appropriate normal rent' unless the loss, falling on the local rates were to become £4/10s (old money) or more per year. Both schemes ran together until the first was abolished in 1929 and the latter in 1933. Between them they built almost a million houses and coupled with non-subsidized building it was thought that the shortfall in housing identified in 1917 was being met. Only after 1930 with the advent of a second minority Labour Government was any real attention paid to the question of re-housing those at the bottom of the pile. Subsidies were directed to local authorities for the purpose of slum clearance and the easing of over-crowding. The overall figures for house building are impressive[64] but they failed to touch a sad core of need: only the wholesale evacuation of children at the start of the Second World War would show the extent of the real desperation of grinding poverty and its inevitable companion, poor housing.

Much of what was built whether it was public or private was satisfactory according to contemporary standards: just as the suburban semi offered the pride of ownership and some degree of privacy to the white-collar worker, so the early council estates presented a great escape route to other workers—as long as they had work. The standards established by the Tudor Walters Committee (Ministry of Reconstruction 1917–18) allowed for two- or three-bedroomed houses with parlour, kitchen and bath plus electric lighting and either gas or electricity for cooking; a density of not more than twelve to the acre was recommended. There is no wonder that in our age of right-to-buy, large numbers of these inter-war houses have been snapped up by their sitting tenants as real bargains. In cities like Manchester the inner-war estates boast larger gardens and more room than privately owned 'semis' built at the same time. Equally enduring are the large blocks of council-built city flats, mostly built under the slum clearance legislation of the 1930s, which have passed into the hands of private companies and housing associations. Less understandable is the unfortunate fate of some such blocks, once admired and enjoyed by their tenants, but now regarded as 'problems' or even demolished. As recently as 1956, Mowat could write; 'Leeds had 72,000 back-to-back houses, of which 33,000 were deplorably bad. The first 8000 were to be replaced by 1935, partly by houses on estates, partly by *a magnificent group of flats* built at Quarry Hill in the heart of the city and containing 938 dwellings'[65] [emphasis added]. The subsequent fate and demolition of those 'magnificent flats'—with their innovations of lifts, refuse disposal, heating system and communal provisions—has been told by Ravetz.[66] What could, in the inter-war years, be treated as physical and sanitary issues concerned predominantly with construction have, in the post-war years, become ones of management.

Social Life

Leisure

The prosperity of those in work helped feed the growth of widespread holidays and leisure pastimes, both of which became a real possibility for those who were fortunate enough to be in the right place for a job. A week's holiday with pay was not made universal until 1938 but about 1½ million people had that privilege in the 1920s, about 3 million in the 1930s; in 1939 after the Holidays with Pay Act it was calculated that 11 million people benefited.[67] Most went by train to the seaside: this was the heyday of Blackpool and Bournemouth, Morecambe and Margate, Scarborough and Southend-on-Sea. The day trip on the 'charabanc' might be to the seaside or it might be to a popular beauty spot or even a 'mystery tour'. A growing number of those who could afford to buy their own houses also bought a car and thereby revolutionized many lives. Private cars and vans increased greatly in absolute numbers—from 132,000 in 1914 to nearly 2 million in 1939—but possession of a car still remained exclusive since these numbers represented only a very small proportion of the population.[68] Nevertheless, the 'spin' out into the country for the city dweller and the gradual rise of commuting to work by car began both the long process of traffic jams for the city and the omnipresent invasion of the countryside by sentimental visitors, but the growth of private transport undoubtedly added an extra dimension to everyday life.

All of such changes were reflected in the emerging land use and built form of the country, not least in coastal resorts and the semi-rural fringes of towns. Within the towns themselves, the journey to work began to attract increasing interest as the growth of suburbs pulled workplaces and homes further apart. In many firms, the great majority of workers still walked to work. Liepmann shows that in 1936 there were factories in Lancashire, Yorkshire and London in which two-thirds of workers walked to work.[69] Many of these most extreme examples, however, are for the staple industry of textiles. The 'new' industries and services placed very different demands on transport. The tobacco firm of Carreras in London's NW1 had 7 per cent walking to work, 8 per cent travelling by bus, 21 per cent by tram, 30 per cent by train and 30 per cent by various combinations of private transport. Austin Motors in Birmingham had 10 per cent walking, 13 per cent by bicycle, 8 per cent by train, 27 per cent by tram, 25 per cent by bus, 2 per cent by motorcycle and a surprisingly high 14 per cent by private car.[70] Road engineering only slowly responded to such change; roundabouts and dual carriageways made their first appearance, as did cycle tracks. For the more affluent young, the road-house offered attractions considered shocking to their parents; road-houses were really superpubs usually situated on the main roads leaving the major cities where people could both eat and drink but also dance, swim, play tennis and if need be stay overnight.

More people ventured to travel abroad: once the preserve of the wealthy and landed, foreign travel came increasingly into the purview of the rising, striving families of the new industrial revolution who took their chance in foreign climes. Many of the mores they encountered confirmed that latent insular chauvinism which has always flourished so strongly in these islands. That chauvinism was often reinforced by popular reading matter such as the daily papers and magazines like *John Bull*. The newly introduced medium of radio (the wireless) tried to foster a more educative tone under the directorship of Sir John Reith, but its popularity resided in its comedy and light music rather than its seriousness.

> I asked a friend of mine who had been with the BBC from its earliest days if he couldn't get them to improve the popular programmes. He answered cynically:'What does it matter anyway? The morons who listen to them keep their wireless going all day so that they get a little of everything.'[71]

Despite its far-reaching effect on communication, radio was not in such common usage in the late 1920s and 1930s as in the 1940s. Nevertheless, like the greater ease of transport through train, bus and car, it made a small island even smaller: even more important it emphasized the hegemony of 'south-eastern culture'. 'London calling' was both dramatic and fateful: this was the heart of things; the measured strokes of Big Ben which were used to introduce the six o'clock news tolled for a disregarded England.

Far and away the most popular form of entertainment was the cinema. The number of cinemas in Great Britan grew to an all-time peak of almost 5000 by 1939.[72] Here even the most hard-done-by could forget their misery for a while.

> Yes, once a week we go the pictures. The three children at 2d each. I have to pay 5d. That's 11d in all. It's a big slice in the week's money but for me it's the pictures or going mad. It's the only time I forget my troubles.[73]

By 1938 cinemas took in £40 million annually; they sold 20 million tickets a week which meant that about 40 per cent of the population went to the cinema at least once a week and about 25 per cent twice a week. In the dark before the flickering screen all reality could be suspended, yet 'it is impossible to measure the effect that films must have on the outlook and habits of the people'.[74] Film stars became the new trend-setters and their styles were quickly copied and mass-produced helping towards the growing sense of a classless society noted by Priestley[75] and others. 'On one point I should imagine everyone will agree, that class distinctions have been positively toppled over since the Great War. . . .' 'Both the new rich and the new poor have learnt that the social orders were not immutable. . . .'[76] Such observations came from those who were not affected by being unemployed or poor but a more realistic perception of the cinema probably lay in the appreciation of its escapism.'The amount of pleasure we got for fourpence was amazing.' It certainly acted as a soporific; 'it provided a substitute for real life and helped people to become watchers instead of doers. The unemployed man could forget for a few pence his harsh surroundings and could move into a world of palatial halls, obsequious servants, and marble baths (though no lavatories). Why should he bother with political demonstrations?'[77] It was the twentieth-century equivalent of 'drunk for 1d dead drunk for 2d—straw for nothing.'

This essentially sedentary form of entertainment was counterbalanced by a growing interest in rambling, cycling and keep fit. The League of Health and Beauty may have been quintessentially middle class but the Ramblers' Clubs with their brave backing of assaults on privilege like the Kinder Scout trespass and the Cycling Clubs appealed to young working-class people who had a little more money and a little more leisure than they had ever had.

Women

Amongst the hikers and cyclists were many of the young women who found a much better life—at least for a few years before marriage—through the employment opportunities especially in the Midlands and the South-East. This was a time when 'the most remarkable outward change' was noted 'in the looks of women in the towns. The prematurely aged wife was coming to be the exception rather than the rule. Children were fewer and healthier and gave less trouble. . . .'[78] At last there was an improvement in the status of women: their contribution to the war effort of 1914–18 had done more good than all the courageous but futile acts of the suffragettes. Asquith, once an opponent of women's suffrage, expressed a popular view in the House of Commons in 1917 when the bill which was to become the Representation of the People Act 1918 was being discussed:

> Some years ago I ventured to use the expression; 'Let the women work out their own salvation'. Well, Sir, they have worked it out during this war.

Naturally this belated recantation did not produce a dramatic change overnight: women over 30 got the vote in 1918, over 21 in 1928. The long-fought-for franchise had little apparent effect in Parliament or in political life generally until some sixty years later but the spin-off from the implication of equality coupled with the work done by women in the war was to reap its own economic and social reward. Few women were allowed to continue in their war-time jobs, but the new industries, those 'insubstantial' replacements for the old staples, needed women. They were biddable, quick to learn and deft with their hands. 'Women undoubtedly take more kindly to these monotonous tasks and grey depths of routine chiefly I suppose because they expect less from work, have no great urge to individual enterprise, have more patience with passivity and tedium, and know that they can live their real lives either outside the factory or inside their heads . . . see their factory life as a busy but dreamy interlude between childhood and marriage.'[79] It was not just the new factories which needed women, but also shops and offices, hospitals and schools.[80] Most of the women were young and single, but an increasing number of married women were employed too: the geography of economic change ensured that in 'upland Britain' it was because work for women was sometimes all that was available, whilst elsewhere women found themselves freed by labour-saving devices and smaller families to add more to the family income. The prevailing spirit of the times was still, however, that a woman should marry and be a housewife, ill though that accorded both with the sad realism of the depressed areas and cheerful materialism of the rest. Nor was there much encouragement for women to aim at professional occupations. Even if there had been, the haphazard and geographically diverse nature of the educational system had to be overcome.

professional occupations. Even if there had been, the haphazard and geographically diverse nature of the educational system had to be overcome.

Education

Indeed that obstacle faced the majority of people, men as well as women: the much vaunted 'ladder' supposedly set up by the Education Act of 1902 had a good many rungs missing. In 1918 the Fisher Act set to work to put some of them in place. Its aim was to develop a better, more comprehensive system of public education from the nursery school to the evening class. The Board of Education was empowered to give greater financial assistance to the local education authorities (up to 50 per cent) to remove all rights to exemption from elementary schooling and, although the school leaving age was not raised to 15, there were to be day continuation schools which those who had finished schooling at 14 had to attend for the equivalent of one day a week.[81] The Act fell victim to the economies enforced by the 'Geddes axe' in 1922 which the day continuation schools failed to survive. The Hadow Report in 1926 outlined the need for a break at 11 years of age and the re-organization of the post-11 year olds into either separate schools or at least separate classes. This was easier said than done since it required both money and enthusiasm on the part of both central and local government, qualities which rarely emerged at the same time, if ever.

The patchwork quality of what was on offer was compounded by the fact that only a minority, about 25 per cent, received any sort of secondary education at all since the progress made in the 're-organization' suggested by Hadow was both slow and spasmodic. The Board of Education had itself recommended in 1928 that local authorities should go for the easier and cheaper option of dividing elementary schools into junior and senior classes so that by 1939 only the keenest of councils had actually provided purpose-built secondary schools. Worst of all was the fact that fees were charged for most secondary schools even though after 1932 those in completely state-aided schools were means-tested. The complex system of secondary schools ranged from those paid for completely out of public funds, through those aided indirectly by local education authorities to those on the 'direct grant' list from the Board of Education. Rigorous testing, the so-called 'scholarship', or more correctly the Special Place examination, tried to sort out the putatively bright few from the supposedly dull many, but those whose parents could afford full fees did not necessarily have to measure up to the same stringent standard. Only about 6 per cent of pupils from these state-aided secondary schools went on to university and about 0·4 per cent from the senior classes of elementary schools. Technical education, poised for take-off before the politicians and civil servants intervened in 1902, wilted although some large cities such as London and Manchester did provide junior technical or trade schools.[82] Both these and the 'central' schools pointed their pupils at 'useful' occupations such as local apprenticeships for boys, shorthand and typing for girls. Response to this variegated and limited educational system was heavily dependent on family circumstances: in Manchester it was reckoned that one in five pupils gaining places in secondary schools did not take them up despite the 100 per cent Special Place scheme and good maintenance grants.[83] Some families could not afford to keep a potential wage-earner in school beyond the statutory school-leaving age; others could not afford the 'extras' which seemed to keep appearing; others did not want their children to 'get above themselves'; on the other hand there were families who sacrificed a great deal to keep their children in a secondary school or who shopped around anxiously to ensure their child's entry into one. Divorced from the state system and cast in its everlasting shadow, since it educated the children of most political, business and cultural leaders, was the private sector of education which remained isolated and insulated from the ordinary world. Grimly, some of the places worst affected by the changing economic fortunes fought to ensure education for their children; Wales, Scotland and many cities like Manchester tried to provide 100 per cent Special Places, but even means-tested low fees were often too much for many families and maintenance grants varied widely. Those local educational authorities who tried to redress the balance of decline and achieved the most in the way of secondary education and staying-on rates found that their reward was a loss of their ablest young people. Just as the new light industry had located near to the mass of potential consumers so the better-educated sought the same greener pastures.

The Role of the State

And green pastures there were: in the 1930s 'most English people were enjoying a richer life than any previously known in the history of the world: longer holidays, shorter hours, higher real wages'.[84] Much of this was fortuitous since it developed from a combination of low prices, increasing consumption and productivity both domestic and international. The fact that it was geographically slewed was not of universal interest although the comfortable could be stirred when face to face with human misery as the Jarrow marchers found. One of the marchers talking about the kindnesses they encountered said later: 'I think it was one of the finest things that ever happened to our townspeople going down to the South was to recognize that there were some decent people left in the country.' There were those who were not only interested but thought that they knew how to solve the problems that had arisen. Pre-eminent was the economist, Keynes, whose advocacy of public works and public investment was to find more sympathetic hearing from President Roosevelt than any English prime minister. Little remembered now, except with anathema for his later years, was the radical programme outlined by Oswald Mosley as a junior member of the futile Labour Government of 1929–31 in which he suggested increased allowances and pensions, earlier retirement, public control of industry and banking as well as tariff protection and Imperial preference. The high hopes of the immediate post-1918 period had included:

> Nationalisation of the mines, the railways and the land; workers' control of industry; a capital levy; work or maintenance; an end to class distinction; an abolition of property and riches—these were the slogans which captured a considerable portion of the working classes.[85]

Most of this vision had been diminished by the General Strike of 1926 and the Wall Street Crash of 1929. The emasculated Labour Party after 1931 and the subdued trade unions after 1926 had little to offer. Yet a new faith was growing—in planning. Some of this sprang from political enthusiasm which admired the rigidities of the Soviet system with Five Year Plans and planned economy. 'I have seen the future and it works' trilled Lincoln Steffens the American journalist. Less partisan was Political and Economic Planning (PEP) founded in 1931 by an anonymous group of worthies amongst whom were Israel Sieff, vice-chairman and managing director of Marks and Spencer, Gerald Barry, socialistic editor of the *Weekend Review* and a director of the Bank of England, and the Conservative, Sir Basil Blackett.[86] Throughout the 1930s PEP published detailed studies of social and economic planning and each fortnight it published the broadsheet *Planning*. From the politically committed like Harold Macmillan (Conservative) and Barbara Wootton (Labour) came support for planning to a lesser or greater extent. The National Government post–1931 was not averse to exercising some economic control whether through tariffs, owners' cartels like NSS an BISF, or public corporations like the BBC, BOAC or the London Passenger Transport Board established in 1933.

Each of these bodies represented the state's increasing readiness to become directly or indirectly involved with issues of production and consumption. They signified the new interventionist role that central government had assumed. And as local authorities were given new roles in housing and education in particular, so local government began to take on something of its post-war role. This growth in state involvement was reflected in the massive increases in their finances (Fig. 19.8). In 1934 the government stirred itself to intervene in regional planning in the distressed areas of the country when it introduced the Depressed Areas (Development and Improvement) Bill. Unpaid commissioners were appointed to initiate and aid measures for the economic development and social improvement of depressed areas.[87] Two million pounds was allotted to this. It was bitterly criticized as being inadequate and unfavourable comparisons were made with the New Deal in America. The House of Lords changed its name to Special Areas Act, but did not otherwise try to alter it. The commissioners picked away at their task establishing trading estates like Treforest in South Wales or Team Valley in Tyneside and trying to encourage the location of industry such as that of the new steel plant in Ebbw Vale. Their efforts reduced the unemployment figures slightly although greater effect was probably achieved by the re-armament being undertaken toward the end of the period. In 1937 a Royal Commission, that favourite tool of dilatory government, was set up under the chairmanship of Sir Montague Barlow to look specifically at the question of industry and location. Both its Majority and Minority Reports, recommending various degrees of control over the location of industry, have an air of ghostly and ghastly prescience in the light of the last quarter of the twentieth century. In the event it did not report until 1940. Its ultimate influence, however, can in retrospect be seen as considerable: for Hall, its importance 'in the history of British urban and regional planning can never be underestimated. It was directly responsible . . . for the events that led up to the creation of the whole complex planning machine during the years 1945–52.'[88] Certainly the ground work for planning intervention was well laid in the latter half of the 1930s. Affluence was both to stir the conscience and to make it appear feasible to tackle the horrendous living conditions of the urban poor which were catalogued in a growing number of surveys and reports.[89] Simon asserted in the preface to one of his studies; 'During the next fifty years the chief task of the great towns will be the clearing of their slums and the rebuilding of their old, unhealthy, and congested districts' and for this the need was 'to understand the housing and planning problems' of the cities.[90] Alongside the

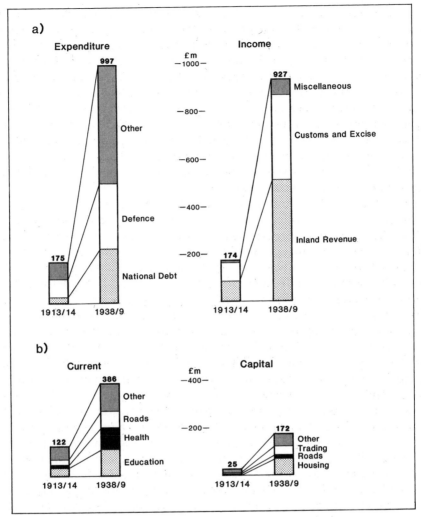

Fig. 19.8. The growth of public spending: (a) central government income and expenditure; (b) local government current and capital expenditure. *Source*: A. R. Prest, *Public Finance in Theory and Practice* (London, 1975 ed.).

Barlow Report, came the Scott Report on rural land, the Uthwatt Report on betterment and the growing influence of town planners such as Abercrombie, all of which signified that the end of the inter-war period created the context out of which emerged the post-war control of land use and urban design, the tentative control of regional investment and the nationalization of development rights in land.

Such developments in planning, however, were fashioned only at the end of the Second World War. Fear of that war shadowed much of the later part of 'the years between', yet it is open to question how widespread much of that fear was. As late as August 1938 Hore-Belisha, the War Secretary, wrote that 'he was against any threat being made that we would declare war if Germany attacked Czechoslovakia unless there was an overwhelming public demand first, and on the facts no such over-whelming public demand exists'.[91] The war itself stuttered into a beginning throughout the second half of the 1930s. A modern geographer can see all its happening through the murky glasses of anti-capitalism: 'the 1930s, that tortured prelude to a global inter-capitalist war'.[92] To suggest, however, that by 1939 there had been 'little or no revival in world trade' or that the British were 'sheltering behind Imperial Preference' and that by implication war was a capitalist necessity is overly procrustean. World trade had started to recover in 1933 'for no apparent reason than to confirm the theory of the trade cycle'.[93] The Ottawa agreement over dominion and colonial trade was made to sound more protective than it actually was since 'the result of the imperial preference system was not an increase in trade but a diversion of trade . . . even then it was not certain how far Ottawa was responsible for this diversion for it was in line with a long-term trend and with the trend of investments'.[94] Evil capitalism may be, but the factors behind mankind's wars are both more complex and less susceptible to that particular 'spatial fix' argument. The war that began in 1939 had its own version of 'spatial fix' but it was less the endless thrust of capitalism than the tension identified by Mackinder: Britain was both near the Continent yet remote from it. That century (1815–1914) of disinvolvement from Europe's affairs which coincided with Britain's period of greatest prosperity still haunted folk memory as well as setting up nostalgic longings in its leaders. On the other hand not even a dream of splendid isolation or dread of war could prevent the mingled shame and relief which swept through Britain in 1938–39. It was the classic reaction of somebody who had been caught watching a bully browbeat somebody weaker but has failed to intervene and only been interested in self-preservation. In the end Britain went to war not just to uphold a pledge to a country even more remote than Czechoslovakia, but to save her own face. Wars can never be waged if people do not want to fight them: propaganda, conscription, coercion can get armies into the field but their staying power depends in the last analysis on the will of each individual. Whether or not the Second World War was that rare thing a 'just' war is difficult to judge; more so for those of use who were born into its onset. What is clear is the effect of its totality: bombs were better than anything else at breaking up old class divisions, at uniting and healing an economically divided country, at setting in train the execution of plans for social change and welfare. War too finally provided a glass slipper for that Cinderella of Britain's industrialization, her agriculture.

Historians warn us that history never repeats itself yet we are aware of lessons to be learnt from the past as the present struggles with both its legacies and its parallels. Geographers as they fly off into the airier realms of theory may like to see space as a social construct playing, as enthusiasm or interest takes them, a greater or lesser part in a grand conceit. The story of the years between the two wars suggests that it is time to return to the earth where geography was once so firmly based. In 1988 *The Guardian* wrote an entertainingly admonitory editorial about geographers needing to know their places as purveyors and expositors of maps (8 January, 1988). Before we dismiss it, since even the editor of *The Guardian* probably realizes that 'chaps' make maps and that history and geography — space and time — are inextricably inter-woven, the matter of those maps may still have more importance than is commonly allowed. The decline of the old industries which occurred during 1918–39 owed as much to their geographical situation in areas which were the historically less favoured parts of Britain as to world economics or even the demon capitalism. The historical fact that London and the south-eastern region have been *continuously* dominant since long before the development of capitalism society is well attested.[95] That dominance owes everything to location, allied to the system of governance of the country; without that spatial factor London might have succumbed at the end of the nineteenth century to the powerful challenge from the great industrial cities. Once those regions lost their raison d'être in the form of thriving industry they were cast back into the historic shadow which was geography's gift to them. Had the industries all been sited within easy reach of London and contributing greatly to local wealth then their dereliction would have been both clear and threatening for all those who made and shaped government and opinion; there would have been public works and public investment by the million. It may well be that late in the day the message is getting home. 'Upland' or 'outland' Britain cannot be removed: its industries can wax and wane, its cities decay, its towns and villages moulder, many of its people migrate but the lineaments of its old landscape remain. 'These high moors form the western boundary of all this district: they are just the same as they always were; and there they wait, probably for the ruin of this trumpery textile trade, this flickering episode of man's activity and cunning.'[96] That concept of the immanence of nature may be overly romantic and literary, but it has as much relevance now as in the inter-war years. Indeed it is in the sense of 'I have been here before' that an academic in the 1980s looks back at the period. So many lessons, so little learnt: since 1945 the older industrial regions appeared to rally, but it was to no avail since neither then nor now is any government willing to grasp the really nasty nettles. An article in the *Manchester Evening News* on 10 Feburary 1988 began 'Move Maggie to Manchester' and outlined suggestions from the Conservative Bow Group journal *Crossbow* that all Cabinet meetings, press briefings and diplomatic receptions should be held in the North. Only concerted political action could create the incentives for foot-loose investment to overcome locational prejudices which are reinforced by the geography of localities. The case for the establishment of indepen- dent financial institutions, away from London has been cogently argued by the former Conservative minister Michael Heseltine whilst there are many voices raised in favour of regional development corporations. Last time the depressed regions needed a war to give them temporary respite; surely there is a better way to prevent the triumph of a history made by geography?

References

1. H. J. Mackinder, *Britain and the British Seas*, (London, 1902), p. 12.
2. A. Marwick, *Britain in the Century of Total War: War, Peace and Social change 1900–1967*, (London, 1968), p. 168.
3. *Ibid.*, p. 167.
4. C. L. Mowat, *Britain Between the Wars 1918–1940*, (London, 1968 edn.), p. 264.
5. Cunliffe committee, *First Interim Report of the Committee on Foreign Exchanges After the War*, Cd. 9182, Parliamentary Papers, (London, 1918).
6. S. Pollard, *The Development of the British Economy 1914– 1967*, (London, 1969), p. 219.
7. E. J. Hobsbawm, *The Pelican Economic History of Britain: Vol. 3 Industry and Empire: From 1750 to the Present Day*, (Harmondsworth, 1969), pp. 211–12.
8. Pollard, *Development of the British Economy*, p. 60.

9.   G. D. H. Cole, *Labour in the Coal Mining Industry*, (Oxford, 1923), p. 78.
10. For a full discussion of these ideas, see Hobsbawm, *Pelican Economic History of Britain*, pp. 181–93.
11. W. Smith, *An Economic Geography of Great Britain*, (London, 1949), pp. 270–315.
12. *Ibid.*, p. 274.
13. Hobsbawm, *Pelican Economic History of Britain*, p. 189.
14. H. Roepke, *Movements of the British Iron and Steel Industry 1720–1951*, (Urbana, 1956), p. 118.
15. G. C. Allen, *British Industries and their Organization*, (London, 1951 edn.), pp. 96–8.
16. Roepke, *Movements of the British Iron and Steel Industry*, pp. 115–16.
17. Smith, *An Economic Geography of Great Britain*, p. 393.
18. BBC, *All Our Working Lives*, BBC Publications, (London, 1984), p. 136.
19. Mowat, *Britain Between the Wars*, p. 443.
20. Smith, *An Economic Geography of Great Britain*, pp. 376–9.
21. G. W. Daniels and H. Campion, 'The cotton industry and trade', in Britain in Depression, Economic Science Section, *British Association for the Advancement of Science*, (London, 1935), pp. 339–40.
22. G. D. H. Cole, *British Trade and Industry: Past and Present*, (London, 1932), p. 186.
23. G. W. Daniels and J. Jewkes, 'The comparative position of the Lancashire cotton industry and trade', *Transactions of the Manchester Statistical Society*, (1927), pp. 55–101.
24. Smith, *An Economic Geography of Great Britain*, p. 480.
25. Daniels and Jewkes, 'The comparative position of the Lancashire cotton industry', pp. 55–101.
26. Quote by Sir Charles Macara in *All Our Working Lives*.
27. Smith, *An Economic Geography of Great Britain*, p. 194.
28. Pollard, *Development of the British Economy*, p. 121.
29. D. Massey and R. Meegan, 'The geography of industrial reorganization: the spatial effects of restructuring of the electrical engineering sector under the industrial reorganization corporation', *Progress in Planning*, **10** (1979), pp. 155–237.
30. W. C. Lubenow, *The Politics of Government Growth: Early Victorian attitudes Towards State Intervention, 1838–1848*, (Newton Abbot, 1971).
31. Pollard, *Development of the British Economy*, pp. 134–45.
32. Scott Report, *Report of the Committee on Land Utilization in Rural Areas*, Cmd 6378, H.M.S.O., (London, 1942), p. 15.
33. R. Blythe, *Akenfield: Portrait of an English Village*, (Harmondsworth, 1969).
34. *Liberal Land Committee*, 1925.
35. A. J. P. Taylor, *English History 1914–45*, (Oxford, 1965), p. 342.
36. J. B. Priestley, *English Journey*, (London, 1968 edn.), p. 411.
37. *Ibid.*, p. 70.
38. *Ibid.*, p. 4.
39. Mowat, *Britain Between the Wars*, p. 272.
40. A. J. Brown, *Applied Economics: Aspects of the World Economy in War and Peace*, (London, 1947).
41. A. Loveday, *Britain and World trade: Quo Vadimus and Other Economic Essays*, (London, 1931), p. 160.
42. W. Ashworth, *An Economic History of England 1870–1939*, (London, 1960), p 321.
43. Pollard, *Development of the British Economy*, p. 130.
44. Smith, *An Economic Geography of Great Britain*, p. 690.
45. Mackinder, *Britain and the British Seas*, p. 254.
46. *Ibid.*, p. 258.
47. *Ibid.*, p. 357.
48. Priestley, *English Journey*, pp. 4–5.
49. D. Freidlander and R. J. Roshier, 'A study of internal migration in England and Wales, Part 1: Geographical patterns of internal migration 1851–1951', *Population Studies*, **19** (1966), pp. 239–78; Mowat, *Britain Between the Wars*, p. 467.

50. *Report on the Location of Industry in Great Britain*, Politics and Economic Planning, (London, 1939), p. 47.
51. B. R. Mitchell and P. Deane, *Abstract of British Historical Statistics*, (Cambridge, 1962), p. 30.
52. R. M. Titmuss, *Poverty and Population: a Factual Study of Contemporary Social Waste*, (London, 1938), pp. 80–1.
53. R. M. Titmuss, *Birth, Poverty and Wealth; A Study of Infant Mortality*, (London, 1943), p. 12.
54. Report, *Royal Commission on Population*, Cmd 7695, H.M.S.O., (London, 1949), p. 232.
55. Priestley, *English Journey*, p. 402–3.
56. A. A. Jackson, *Semi–Detached London: Suburban Development, Life and Transport 1900–39*, (London, 1973), pp. 99–120.
57. J. H. Johnson, 'The suburban expansion of housing in London, 1919–1939', in J. T. Coppock and H. C. Prince (eds.), *Greater London*, (London, 1964).
58. Taylor, *English History*, p. 306.
59. *Men Without Work: A Report Made to the Pilgrim Trust*, (Cambridge, 1938).
60. H. Bellman, *The Thrifty Three-Millions: A Study of the Building Society Movement and the Story of the Abbey Road Society*, (London, 1935); E. J. Cleary, *The Building Society Movement*, (London, 1965).
61. A. E. Holmans, *Housing Policy in Britain: A History*, (London, 1987).
62. J. H. Jennings, 'The geographical implications of the municipal housing programme in England and Wales', *Urban Studies*, **8** (1971), pp. 121–38.
63. M. Bowley, *Housing and the State, 1919–1945*, (London, 1945).
64. *Ibid.*, p. 271.
65. Mowat, *Britain Between the Wars*, p. 511.
66. A. Ravetz, *Model Estate: Planned Housing at Quarry Hill, Leeds*, (London, 1974).
67. Mowat, *Britain Between the Wars*, p. 501.
68. A. H. Halsey, *Trends in British Society since 1900: A Guide to the Changing Social Structure of Britain*, (London, 1972), p. 280.
69. K. Liepmann, *The Journey to Work: Its Significance for Industrial and Community Life*, (London, 1944), pp. 164–5.
70. *Ibid.*, pp. 169 and 183.
71. P. Colson, *Those Uneasy Years*, (London, 1944).
72. Halsey, *Trends in British Society*, p. 558.
73. Quotation by Lancashire woman cited in A. Fenner Brockway, *Hungry England*, (London, 1932).
74. *New Survey of London Life and Labour*, Vol. 9, (London, 1947), p. 47.
75. Priestley, *English Journey*, p. 403.
76. F. W. Hirst, *The Consequences of the War to Britain*, (London, 1934).
77. Taylor, *English History*, pp. 315–16.
78. R. Graves and A. Hodge, *The Long Week-End: A Social History of Great Britain 1918–1939*, (London, 1940), p. 175.
79. Priestley, *English Journey*, p. 133.
80. Halsey, *Trends in British Society*, pp. 99–101 and 114–18.
81. Mowat, *Britain Between the Wars*, p. 208.
82. G. A. N. Lowndes, *The Silent Social Revolution: An Account of the Expansion of Public Education in England and Wales, 1895– 1965*, (Oxford, 1969 edn.), 147–8.
83. G. G. Leybourne and K. White, *Education and the Birth Rate: A Social Dilemma*, (London, 1940), p. 122.
84. Taylor, *English History*, p. 317.
85. A. Bullock, *The Life and Times of E. Bevan*, Vol. 1 (London, 1960), p. 99.
86. Marwick, *Britain in the Century of Total War*, p. 245.
87. Mowat, *Britain Between the Wars*, p. 465.
88. P. Hall, *Urban and Regional Planning*, (Harmondsworth, 1974), pp. 90–3.
89. e.g. B. Seebohm Rowntree, *Poverty and Progress: A Second Social Survey of York*, (London, 1941); Women's Group on Welfare, *Our Towns: A Close–Up*, (Oxford, 1943); E. D. Simon, *The Anti-Slum Campaign*, (London, 1933).

90. E. D. Simon and J. Inman, *The Rebuilding of Manchester*, (London, 1935), p. v.
91. R. J. Minney, *The Private Papers of Leslie Hore-Belisha*, (London, 1960), p. 138.
92. D. W. Harvey, 'The geopolitics of capitalism', in D. Gregory and J. Urry (eds.), *Social Relations and Spatial Structure*, (London, 1985), p. 160.
93. Mowat, *Britain Between the Wars*, p. 434.
94. Pollard, *Development of the British Economy*, pp. 197–8.
95. B. T. Robson, *Where is the North? An Essay on the North/South Divide*, North of England Regional Consortium, (Manchester, 1985).
96. Priestley, *English Journey*, p. 187.

Index